THE VICTORIA HISTORY
OF THE
COUNTIES OF ENGLAND

A HISTORY OF
STAFFORDSHIRE
VOLUME VII

Oxford University Press, Walton Street, Oxford OX2 6DP
Oxford New York
Athens Auckland Bangkok Bombay
Calcutta Cape Town Dar es Salaam Delhi
Florence Hong Kong Istanbul Karachi
Kuala Lumpur Madras Madrid Melbourne
Mexico City Nairobi Paris Singapore
Taipei Tokyo Toronto

and associated companies in
Berlin Ibadan

Oxford is a trade mark of Oxford University Press

Published in the United States
by Oxford University Press Inc., New York

© University of London 1995

British Library Cataloguing in Publication Data
A catalogue record for this book is available
from the British Library

ISBN 0 19 722786 4

Printed by H Charlesworth & Co Ltd
Huddersfield, England

THE VICTORIA HISTORY
OF THE
COUNTIES OF ENGLAND

EDITED BY C. R. J. CURRIE

THE UNIVERSITY OF LONDON
INSTITUTE OF
HISTORICAL RESEARCH

INSCRIBED TO THE

MEMORY OF HER LATE MAJESTY

QUEEN VICTORIA

WHO GRACIOUSLY GAVE THE TITLE TO

AND ACCEPTED THE DEDICATION

OF THIS HISTORY

A HISTORY OF THE COUNTY OF

STAFFORD

EDITED BY M. W. GREENSLADE

VOLUME VII

LEEK AND THE MOORLANDS

PUBLISHED FOR

THE INSTITUTE OF HISTORICAL RESEARCH

BY

OXFORD UNIVERSITY PRESS

1996

CONTENTS OF VOLUME SEVEN

LIST OF PLATES

Grateful acknowledgement is made to the following for permission to use material: the Britannia Building Society; Mrs. Christine Chester of Foxt; Miss M. F. Cleverdon of Leek; the Dean and Chapter of Lichfield Cathedral; the Leek and District Historical Society; the *Leek Post & Times*; the National Trust; Mr. G. H. Robinson of Endon; the Staffordshire Archive Service; the Staffordshire Library Service; the Staffordshire Moorlands District Council; the Trustees of the William Salt Library, Stafford; and Mr. A. R. Williamson of Endon. The illustrations numbered 4–6, 9, 21, and 48 are from photographs in the possession of the National Monuments Record of the Royal Commission on Historical Monuments (England), Crown Copyright, and those numbered 8, 27, 37, 54, and 63 are from photographs in the possession of the Staffordshire Planning and Economic Development Department; grateful acknowledgement is made to both. Photographs dated 1995 are by R. A. Meeson.

Between pages 136 and 137

LIST OF PLATES

LIST OF MAPS, PLANS, AND OTHER FIGURES

Grateful acknowledgement for permission to use material is made to the Staffordshire Archive Service, Staffordshire Library Service, the Staffordshire Planning and Economic Development Department, and the Trustees of the William Salt Library, Stafford. Figure 1 was drawn by J. A. Lawrence of the Department of Geography, Keele University, from a draft prepared by C. P. Lewis of the central Victoria County History staff and based on Ordnance Survey Map 1", index to the Tithe Survey. Figures 3–11, 14–16, 30, 32–5, 37–42, 44, and 46 were drawn by J. A. Lawrence from drafts prepared by M. W. Greenslade and N. J. Tringham, with assistance from Della Ryder and Dorothy Wilson of the Staffordshire County Planning and Economic Development Department; the drafts were based on the first edition of the relevant Ordnance Survey 6" maps.

LIST OF MAPS, PLANS, AND OTHER FIGURES

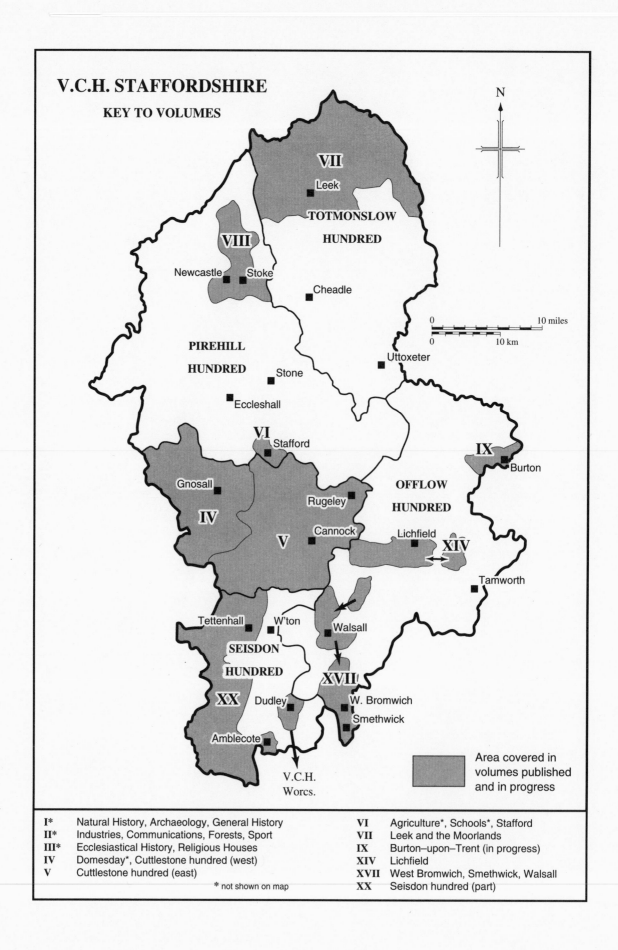

V.C.H. STAFFORDSHIRE

KEY TO VOLUMES

N

VII

Leek

TOTMONSLOW

HUNDRED

VIII

Newcastle Stoke

Cheadle

0 _____ 10 miles
0 _____ 10 km

PIREHILL

HUNDRED

Stone

Eccleshall

Uttoxeter

VI Stafford

IX

Burton

Gnosall

OFFLOW

HUNDRED

IV

Rugeley

V

Cannock

Lichfield

XIV

Tamworth

Tettenhall W'ton

Walsall

SEISDON

HUNDRED

XVII

XX Dudley

W. Bromwich

Smethwick

Amblecote

V.C.H.
Worcs.

Area covered in
volumes published
and in progress

EDITORIAL NOTE

This volume is the eleventh to appear in the Staffordshire set of the Victoria History of the Counties of England. It was begun under the supervision of the Staffordshire Victoria County History Committee, which was a partnership between the University of London, Staffordshire County Council, and the four Metropolitan Boroughs in South Staffordshire. In 1993 the boroughs found themselves unable to continue their financial contributions to the Committee, which therefore dissolved itself in July. A new partnership was then formed between the University of London, the University of Keele, which assumed responsibility for employing the staff of the Staffordshire History, and Staffordshire County Council, which agreed to continue its financial contribution. It is that partnership which has supervised the completion of this volume.

As a result of the changes in 1993 the County Editor, Mr. M. W. Greenslade, and one of the two Assistant Editors, Mr. D. A. Johnson, formally retired, and the post of the other Assistant Editor, Dr. N. J. Tringham, was transferred to the Department of History at Keele. Mr. Greenslade was thereupon re-employed as County Editor by the University of Keele and Mr Johnson as part-time Assistant Editor by the University of London. In 1995 Mr. Greenslade and Mr. Johnson retired, Dr. Tringham became County Editor, and Dr. I. J. Atherton and Dr. A. E. Tomkins were appointed Assistant Editors. The staff thenceforth combined their work for the History with lecturing in the Keele History Department.

The University of London gratefully acknowledges the past help of the Staffordshire V.C.H. Committee, the generosity of the University of Keele in taking over the local management of the History and of Staffordshire County Council in continuing its support, and also the generous help of the Britannia Building Society, which has made an annual grant towards the cost of this volume. Particular thanks are owed to Mr. A. G. Ward, C.B.E., and Mr. B. A. Price, respectively last Chairman and last Secretary of the Staffordshire Committee, and to Professor B. E. F. Fender, C.M.G., and Mr. J. H. Y. Briggs, respectively Vice-Chancellor of the University of Keele and Head of the Department of History, for their part in establishing the new partnership.

Thanks are also offered to the many people who have helped in the compilation of the volume. Most are named in the lists of plates and of figures on pp. ix–xiii and in the footnotes to the articles on which their help was given. More general help has been received from Mr. Dudley Fowkes, Staffordshire County Archivist and William Salt Librarian, and his staff, especially the late Mrs. Jane Hamparṭumian, archivist at the Lichfield Joint Record Office, and her successor, Mr. Mark Dorrington, Dr. Margaret O'Sullivan, Derbyshire County Archivist, and her staff, Dr. A. D. M. Phillips, head of the Geography Department at Keele University, and the staff at Staffordshire County Library Headquarters, Stafford, and at Leek Library. Thanks are also owed to Professor C. R. Elrington, who after his retirement as General Editor of the Victoria History in 1994 continued to help with the editing of the volume.

The structure, aims, and progress of the Victoria History as a whole are described in the *General Introduction* (1970) and its *Supplement* (1990).

LIST OF CLASSES OF DOCUMENTS
IN THE PUBLIC RECORD OFFICE

USED IN THIS VOLUME

WITH THEIR CLASS NUMBERS

Chancery

		Proceedings
C	1	Early
C	3	Series II
C	14	1842–52
C	60	Fine Rolls
C	66	Patent Rolls
		Inquisitions post mortem
C	134	Series I: Edw. II
C	142	Series II
C	145	Miscellaneous Inquisitions

Court of Common Pleas

		Feet of Fines
CP	25(1)	Series I
CP	25(2)	Series II
CP	43	Recovery Rolls

Duchy of Lancaster
DL 30   Court Rolls

Exchequer, Treasury of the Receipt
E 40   Deeds, Series A

Exchequer, King's Remembrancer
E 134   Depositions taken by Commission
E 150   Inquisitions post mortem, Series II
E 178   Special Commissions of Inquiry

Ministry of Education
ED 7   Public Elementary Schools, Preliminary Statements

Home Office
HO 45   Registered Papers
          Census Papers
HO 107   Population Returns, 1841 and 1851
HO 129   Ecclesiastical Returns

Ministry of Agriculture, Fisheries and Food
MAF 68   Agricultural Returns

Principal Probate Registry
PROB 11   Registered copies of wills proved in the Prerogative Court of Canterbury

Court of Requests
REQ 2   Proceedings

Registrar General
RG 9   Census Returns, 1861
RG 10   Census Returns, 1871
RG 11   Census Returns, 1881
RG 12   Census Returns, 1891

Special Collections
SC 2   Court Rolls
SC 5   Hundred Rolls
SC 6   Ministers' and Receivers' Accounts
          Rentals and Surveys
SC 11   Rolls
SC 12   Portfolios

Court of Star Chamber
STAC 4   Proceedings, Mary

NOTE ON ABBREVIATIONS

Among the abbreviations and short titles used, the following may require elucidation. The place of publication of printed works is London, unless otherwise stated. Local pamphlets cited are either in Leek Library or the William Salt Library, Stafford.

Alstonefield, ed. Edwards	*Alstonefield*, ed. J. Edwards (Alstonefield Local History Society, 1985)
Alstonfield Deanery Mag.	*Alstonfield Deanery Magazine* (from 1900 to 1905 *Our Parish Magazine for the Rural Deanery of Alstonfield*); incomplete set at the William Salt Library, 150/85
Alstonfield Par. Reg.	*Alstonfield Parish Register* (Staffordshire Parish Register Society, 1902)
Anderton, *Edwardian Leek*	P. Anderton, *Images of Edwardian Leek* (Keele, 1984)
B.L.	British Library, London
B.R.L.	Birmingham Central Library, Reference Library
Beresford, *Beresford of Beresford*, i	W. Beresford and S. B. Beresford, *Beresford of Beresford*, pt. i (Leek, n.d., intro. dated 1908)
Bk. of Fees	*The Book of Fees commonly called Testa de Nevill* (H.M.S.O. 1920–31)
Bowyer and Poole, *Staffs. Moorlands*	G. Bowyer and R. Poole, *The Staffordshire Moorlands, Volume 2* (Loggerheads, near Market Drayton, 1989)
C.J.	*Commons' Journals*
Cal. Chart. R.	*Calendar of the Charter Rolls preserved in the Public Record Office* (H.M.S.O. 1903–27)
Cal. Close	*Calendar of the Close Rolls preserved in the Public Record Office* (H.M.S.O. 1892–1963)
Cal. Fine R.	*Calendar of the Fine Rolls preserved in the Public Record Office* (H.M.S.O. 1911–62)
Cal. Inq. p.m.	*Calendar of Inquisitions post mortem preserved in the Public Record Office* (H.M.S.O. 1904–92)
Cal. Inq. p.m. Hen. VII	*Calendar of Inquisitions post mortem, Henry VII* (H.M.S.O. 1898–1955)
Cal. Pat.	*Calendar of the Patent Rolls preserved in the Public Record Office* (H.M.S.O. 1891–1986)
Cal. S.P. Dom.	*Calendar of State Papers, Domestic Series* (H.M.S.O. 1856–1992)
Camd. (Soc.)	Camden (Society)
Cat. Anct. D.	*Descriptive Catalogue of Ancient Deeds preserved in the Public Record Office* (H.M.S.O. 1890–1915)
Census	*Census Report(s)*
Challinor, *Lectures*	W. Challinor, *Lectures, Verses, Speeches, Reminiscences, etc.* (Leek and London, 1891)
Char. Com.	Charity Commission
Char. Dons.	*Abstract of the Returns of Charitable Donations for the Benefit of Poor Persons 1786–1788*, H.C. 511 (1816), xvi (2)
Charters of Earls of Chester	*Charters of the Anglo-Norman Earls of Chester, c. 1071–1237*, ed. G. Barraclough (Rec. Soc. Lancs. and Ches. cxxvi)
Chronicles	*Chronicles* (Journal of Leek and District Historical Society)
Close R.	*Close Rolls of the Reign of Henry III preserved in the Public Record Office* (H.M.S.O. 1902–75)
Complete Peerage	G. E. C[okayne] and others, *The Complete Peerage* (1910–59)
Cath. Rec. Soc.	*Catholic Record Society*
Cur. Reg. R.	*Curia Regis Rolls preserved in the Public Record Office* (H.M.S.O. 1922–91)
D.N.B.	*Dictionary of National Biography*
D.R.O.	Derbyshire Record Office, Matlock
Dodd, *Peakland Roads*	A. E. Dodd and E. M. Dodd, *Peakland Roads and Trackways* (second edition, Ashbourne, 1980)
Dugdale, *Mon.*	W. Dugdale, *Monasticon Anglicanum*, ed. J. Caley and others (1846)

Dyson, *Wesleyan Methodism*	J. B. Dyson, *Brief History of the Rise and Progress of Wesleyan Methodism in the Leek Circuit* (n.d., preface dated 1853)
E.H.R.	*English Historical Review*
E.P.N.S.	English Place-Name Society
Educ. Enq. Abstract	*Education Enquiry Abstract*, H.C. 62 (1835), xlii
Educ. of Poor Digest	*Digest of Returns to the Select Committee on the Education of the Poor*, H.C. 224 (1819), ix (2)
Eng. P.N. Elements	A. H. Smith, *English Place-Name Elements* (English Place-Name Society, vols. xxv–xxvi, 1956)
Erdeswick, *Staffs.*	S. Erdeswick, *A Survey of Staffordshire*, ed. T. Harwood (1844)
G.R.O.	General Register Office, Southport
G.E.C. *Baronetage*	G. E. C[okayne], *Complete Baronetage* (1900–9)
Gent. Mag.	*The Gentleman's Magazine*
H.C.	House of Commons
Heywood, *Cotton and his River*	G. G. P. Heywood, *Charles Cotton and his River* (Manchester, 1925)
Hist. MSS. Com.	Historical Manuscripts Commission
Hist. Parl., Commons	*History of Parliament, The House of Commons*
Hodgson, *Bounty of Queen Anne*	C. Hodgson, *An Account of the Augmentation of Small Livings by the Governors of the Bounty of Queen Anne* (second edition, 1845, with supplement, 1864)
inq. p.m.	inquisition post mortem
Inst. Bk.	Exchequer, First Fruits and Tenths Office, Register of Institutions to Benefices
L. & P. Hen. VIII	*Letters and Papers, Foreign and Domestic, of the Reign of Henry VIII* (H.M.S.O. 1864–1932)
L.J.	*Lords' Journals*
L.J.R.O.	Lichfield Joint Record Office
Leek Improvement Com. *Reps.* (1894)	Leek Improvement Commissioners, *Reports by Various Committees on the Origin and Progress of the Public Works belonging to the Town and the Vital Experience resulting from the Administration of the Sanitary Acts in Leek from the year 1855 to 1894* (1894)
Leek Par. Reg.	*Leek Parish Register, part 1* (Staffordshire Parish Registers Society, 1919)
Lich. Dioc. Regy.	Lichfield Diocesan Registry
Lond. Gaz.	*London Gazette*
Miller, *Leek*	M. H. Miller, *Leek: Fifty Years Ago* (Leek, 1887)
N.R.A.	National Register of Archives
N.S.J.F.S.	*North Staffordshire Journal of Field Studies*
Nat. Soc. *Inquiry, 1846–7*	*Result of the Returns to the General Inquiry made by the National Society, 1846–7* (1849)
Nicoll, *Sheen*	A. C. F. Nicoll, *St. Luke's Church and Parish, Sheen* (priv. print. 1984)
O.S.	Ordnance Survey
Olde Leeke	*Olde Leeke*, ed. M. H. Miller (2 vols., Leek, 1891, 1900)
P.R.O.	Public Record Office, London
P.R.S.	Pipe Roll Society
Pevsner, *Staffs.*	N. Pevsner, *The Buildings of England: Staffordshire* (Harmondsworth, 1974)
Pitt, *Staffs.*	W. Pitt, *A Topographical History of Staffordshire* (Newcastle-under-Lyme, 1817)
Plac. de Quo Warr. (Rec. Com.)	*Placita de Quo Warranto* (Record Commission, 1818)
Plan of Leek 1838	*Plan of Leek 1838* (Turner & Co., Edinburgh; copy in Staffordshire Record Office, D. 3359)
Plot, *Staffs.*	R. Plot, *A Natural History of Staffordshire* (Oxford, 1686)
Poole, *Leek*	R. Poole, *Yesterday's Town: Leek* (Buckingham, 1988)
13th Rep. Com. Char.	*Thirteenth Report of the Charity Commissioners for England and Wales*, H.C. 349 (1825), xi
Rep. Com. Eccl. Revenues	*Report of the Commissioners appointed to Inquire into the Ecclesiastical Revenues of England and Wales* [67], H.C. (1835), xxii

Rep. Cttee. Town Lands 1849	Report of the Committee appointed by the Freeholders of Leek and Lowe, to Inquire into the Estate and Management of the Town Lands; etc. etc. 1849
Return of Glebe Lands	Return of Glebe Lands, H.C. 307 (1887), lxiv
Rot. Chart. (Rec. Com.)	Rotuli Chartarum in Turri Londinensi asservati, ed. T. D. Hardy (Record Commission, 1837)
Rot. Litt. Claus. (Rec. Com.)	Rotuli Litterarum Clausarum in Turri Londinensi asservati, 1204–27, ed. T. D. Hardy (2 vols., Record Commission, 1833, 1844)
Rot. Litt. Pat. (Rec. Com.)	Rotuli Litterarum Patentium (Record Commission, 1835)
S.H.C.	Staffordshire Record Society (formerly William Salt Archaeological Society), *Collections for a History of Staffordshire*
S.R.O.	Staffordshire Record Office, Stafford
Sheen par. accts.	Sheen parish accounts, in the possession of the vicar of Sheen 1994
Sherlock, *Ind. Arch. Staffs.*	R. Sherlock, *The Industrial Archaeology of Staffordshire* (1976)
Sleigh, *Leek*	J. Sleigh, *A History of the Ancient Parish of Leek in Staffordshire* (second edition, dedication dated 1883)
Sleigh, *Leek* (1862)	J. Sleigh, *A History of the Ancient Parish of Leek in Staffordshire* (1862)
Staffs. Cath. Hist.	*Staffordshire Catholic History* (Journal of the Staffordshire Catholic History Society)
Staffs. Endowed Chars.	*Report on Charitable Endowments appropriated to purposes of Elementary Education in the County of Stafford* [Cd. 2129], H.C. (1906), xc
Staffs. Hist.	*Staffordshire History* (Stafford, 1984 onwards)
Staffs. Studies	*Staffordshire Studies* (University of Keele, 1988 onwards)
T.B.A.S.	Birmingham and Midland Institute: Birmingham Archaeological Society, *Transactions and Proceedings*
T.N.S.F.C.	North Staffordshire Naturalists' Field Club (from 1877 the North Staffordshire Naturalists' Field Club and Archaeological Society, and from 1897 the North Staffordshire Field Club), *Transactions* (until 1892 *Annual Report*; thereafter *Annual Report and Transactions*; *Transactions and Annual Report*; and *Transactions*)
T.S.S.A.H.S.	*Transactions of the South Staffordshire Archaeological and Historical Society*
Tax. Eccl. (Rec. Com.)	*Taxatio Ecclesiastica Angliae et Walliae* (Record Commission, 1802)
V.C.H.	*Victoria County History*
Valor Eccl. (Rec. Com.)	*Valor Ecclesiasticus* (Record Commission, 1810–34)
Wardle, *Methodist Hist.*	J. W. Wardle, *Sketches of Methodist History in Leek and the Moorlands 1753 to 1943* (n.d., preface dated 1943)
White, *Dir. Staffs.* (1834, 1851)	W. White, *History, Gazetteer, and Directory of Staffordshire* (Sheffield, 1834, 1851)
W.S.L.	William Salt Library, Stafford
W.S.L., Sleigh	William Salt Library, grangerized copies of J. Sleigh, *A History of the Ancient Parish of Leek in Staffordshire* (first and second editions, 1862 and 1883)

ANALYSIS OF SOURCES PRINTED IN
COLLECTIONS FOR A HISTORY OF STAFFORDSHIRE
(STAFFORDSHIRE RECORD SOCIETY)
AND USED IN THIS VOLUME

ANALYSIS OF *S.H.C.* SOURCES

ANALYSIS OF *S.H.C.* SOURCES

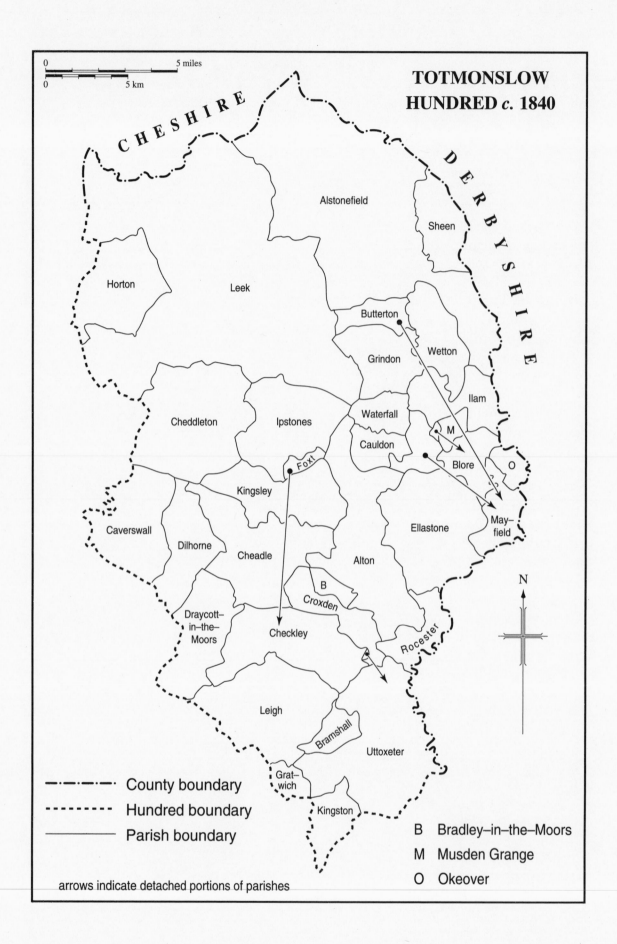

FIG. I

xxiv

TOTMONSLOW HUNDRED
(*part*)
ALSTONEFIELD

THE ancient parish of Alstonefield lay in the north-east corner of the county, the river Dane forming the boundary with Cheshire and the river Dove that with Derbyshire.[1] It consisted of the seven townships of Alstonefield, Fawfieldhead, Heathylee, Hollinsclough, Longnor, Quarnford, and Warslow and Elkstones. With an area of 23,249 a. (9,409 ha.),[2] it was the second largest ancient parish in the county after Leek. Alstonefield village, in the south-east corner of the ancient parish, is 6½ miles north-west of Ashbourne (Derb.), the nearest town. For the northern part of the ancient parish the nearest town is Buxton (Derb.), 6 miles north-west of Longnor. Leek is 10 miles from both Alstonefield and Longnor.

The underlying rock is mainly sandstone of the Millstone Grit series. A large part of Alstonefield township and part of Warslow are on limestone, and parts of Heathylee and Quarnford are on Coal Measures. Stone is the usual local building material. The land rises to over 1,000 ft. in many places. Oliver Hill in Quarnford, at 1,684 ft. (513 m.), is the highest point in Staffordshire, and Flash, on the south side of the hill at 1,526 ft. (465 m.), is the highest village in England. In Heathylee the northern end of Morridge, a long ridge of moorland, reaches 1,535 ft. (468 m.), with the river Churnet rising on its western slope and the river Manifold and a tributary, Oakenclough brook, on the eastern slope. The land is given over mainly to pasture and rough grazing, and the farming is dairy and sheep, with most of the farms under 50 ha. in size.

In the south-east part of the parish there are numerous Bronze Age barrows. There was a church at Alstonefield before the Conquest, but it was Longnor which developed as the main settlement, with a chapel apparently by the 12th century and a market and a fair by 1293. There was evidently a chapel at Warslow by the 13th century. Place-names suggest that several sites in the parish were first occupied as outlying dairy farms, using pasture beside rivers and streams for grazing. In the early 14th century there were dairy farms on the manorial demesne in Fawfieldhead and Quarnford, and several others, called stalls, were held by tenants elsewhere in the parish.[3] Much of Heathylee seems originally to have been wooded, but farms had been established by the 15th century. There was a settlement at Flash in Quarnford by the late 16th century, and a church was built there in 1744.

Before the Conquest there were estates at Alstonefield, Stanshope, and probably Warslow. By 1086 Warslow had become part of Alstonefield manor, as had Stanshope by 1307. The manor covered the whole of the parish except for Upper Elkstone, most of which belonged to Trentham priory in the Middle Ages.[4] Alstonefield manor was divided into three shares in the late 12th century, and one

[1] This introduction (written in 1994) draws together some of the topics which are treated in detail in the articles on the individual townships. Unless otherwise indicated, the sources for statements in the introduction are given in those articles. Dr. D. G. Brown of Tamworth, Betty Gouldstone of Home Farm, Hollinsclough, and Susan Gaukroger of Old School House, Hollinsclough, are thanked for their help with sources.

[2] *V.C.H. Staffs.* i. 327.

[3] *S.H.C.* N.S. xi. 257.

[4] Alstonefield manor also included the Whitle area of Sheen parish.

FIG 2. YATES'S MAP OF THE COUNTY OF STAFFORD 1775 (PART): SCALE REDUCED TO ABOUT 1 IN.
TO 1¾ MILE (APPROX. 1:110,000)

Road from Burton to Derby

D

Gimballs
Green
Summer
Hill
Old
Shaw
Tear
Hill

Witt
Shaw

Hollins
Clough
Dryenott
Tunstead

River Dove
17

E

High Lot The
Hen
Bull
Bank

Moss
Carr
LONGNOR
10

Crowdey
Cote

Pilsbury
Grange

Hollins

Booth
Low
Broadmeadow
Hall

Collshaw
Hardings Booth
Heath
House
Winch
Water
House
Kann
House
Whitle

Edge
End
Brown
Hill
Hill
end
Fawfield
Head
Hawks
Low
Sheen Gate
Mount
Spit
Kniveden
Booth
Low
Ergy
Hill

New Town
Upper Booster
School
clough
Ridge
Thelom
Ridge
End
Hill
End
Highsheen

W
Negt
Stone
Nether Booster
Bent
Broadbean
Slitt
Head
Slate
House
Sheen

Blackmore
Middle
Hill Green
Sharp
Field
Field
Head
Burnt
Hill
Brund
Harlington

er Morredge
Over Flax
Great
Fawley
Ford
Repemoor
Top
Wallbrook
Gate
New Field

Herbage
Avril
Side
Swallow Moss
Oveway
Head
Wigganstaff
Pump
Hill
Heys
Gate
Bank
Top
16
River Dove

Fairdge
High
Moor
Upper
Elkstone
Heys
Warslow
Sitch
Hulme
End
Bakes
Barriesford

A
N
Green
Lower
Elkstone
S
L
O
Copper Mine
West
Side
Wag
Side
Field
W

Acre
Gorse
Maidens
Gate
Hill
O
Narrow Dale

Mixon
Blurnt
Heys
Black
Brook
Swindle
Ecton

Butterton
10
Fields
Gateham
Steeplow
Alstonefield

Water
House
Lane Head
Butterton
Moor
Twist
Wall
Acre
Broad
Meadow
Water
House
River
Wetton Hill
at this Place the River
runs under Ground
Wetton
Hope
Heath
Hope

Road

One cote
Bull
Clough
Hulls
Dale
Mount
Pleasant
House
Thorshouse
Tor
Stanshope
Mill Dale

Highwoor
Gate
Arbor
Low Axes

Ford
Grindon
Dam
Gate
Dove Dale

Mill Braden
Brook
Deep
Dale
Old
Field

Bottom
House
Grindon
Martins
Low
Pethill
Thorn
Low
Dodge
Cistern
Arbor
Clump
Rushley

Blake Low
Long
Ditch
Black
Shaw
Waterfall
Wood
Low
Rushley

B
o
t
t
o
Waterfall
House
Winkhil
Sparry
Wood
Low

of the shares was further divided into six in the late 13th century. Farms already in existence at the time of the first division were shared out. The rents of later farms and cottages were received jointly until 1566, when they were divided by lot. The profits of the manor court were also received jointly.[5] By the end of the 16th century all but one of the shares had been secured by the Harpur family of Swarkestone (Derb.) and later of Calke (Derb.), which in 1670 bought nearly all of the remaining share. The family changed its name to Crewe in 1808, and after 1844 it used the form Harpur Crewe, changing it to Harpur-Crewe in 1961.

In the 1630s the parish was characterized by smallholdings, often under 50 a. and used mainly as pasture. There was also a large area of moorland waste, suitable for rough grazing. Alstonefield township had over three times as much farmland as waste, and Longnor twice as much; in Warslow the waste was only 100 a. in extent. In contrast, there were over 10,000 a. of waste in the other four townships and c. 6,000 a. of farmland.[6] Cottagers had been allowed to settle on the waste, which they improved at their own expense.[7] Encroachments continued, and in the later 18th century many cottagers who had extended their holdings paid only small rents or nothing at all.[8] About 1806 Sir Henry Harpur was advised not to disturb them. The policy of increasing rents as the cottagers' incomes grew had resulted in the settlement of a district 'which holds out as few natural temptations perhaps as any part of England'.[9]

In the 18th century many cottagers, especially in the area around Flash, worked as pedlars and hawkers, of whom there were c. 400 in Alstonefield parish in 1785. That year the government proposed the abolition of licensed hawkers, and a petition from those in Alstonefield helped to bring about a change of mind. John Lomas of Hollinsclough was a member of a small delegation of hawkers from the north-west of England which had an audience with the prime minister, William Pitt, and argued its case at the bar of the House of Commons. In a parliamentary debate in 1786 it was stated that hawkers in Alstonefield parish had converted 'a barren and wild spot to a rich and fertile circuit'.[10] Other cottagers around Flash in the late 18th and earlier 19th century became prosperous as button merchants, employing women and girls in the locality to make the buttons.

Coal deposits were worked in Heathylee by the early 15th century and in Quarnford by the later 16th century. Small-scale mining continued intermittently, the last mine, one at Quarnford, being closed in 1932. In the 18th and 19th centuries lead was mined at Warslow and copper at Upper Elkstone.

Until the early 19th century the Harpurs rarely visited Alstonefield, but in 1819, at the age of 24, Sir George Crewe, an Evangelical with a strong sense of social responsibility, succeeded his father.[11] He first visited his Alstonefield estate in 1819 or 1820, and he remarked later that he was probably the first head of his family who ever set foot there 'for any other purpose than shooting grouse'. He found the tenants '100 years behind the rest of the world, well disposed but ignorant and simple-minded'. Conditions were especially bad at Flash.[12] In 1830 Sir George built Warslow Hall, mainly for his agent but partly to provide occasional

5 D.R.O., D. 2375M/54/6, copy of sched. of division of messuages, 1566; D. 2375M/140/25.
6 Ibid. D. 2375M/63/53, pp. 115–84. No accompanying maps survive for the survey.
7 Ibid. D. 2375M/56/4, deed of 23 Jan. 1 Jas. I.
8 Ibid. D. 2375M/189/6, case for counsel's opinion, 1769–70.
9 Ibid. D. 2375M/110/32, observations on Sir Hen. Harpur's Alstonefield estate. For the date see D. 2375M/44/1, 17 Apr. 1831.
10 Ibid. D. 2375M/87/19, John Lomas to Sir Geo. Crewe, 11 Jan. 1820; J. Debrett, Parl. Reg. 2nd ser. xx. 24; H.-C. and L. H. Mui, Shops and Shopkeeping in Eighteenth-Century Eng. 75–6.
11 H. Colvin, Calke Abbey, Derb. 57–8; below, plate 66.
12 D.R.O., D. 2375M/44/1, 17 Aug. 1831.

accommodation for himself and his family. Writing in 1831, he praised 'the bracing effect of the mountain air' and noted that he had become deeply interested in the area and would find much to occupy him if he visited regularly.[13] He duly turned his attention to the Alstonefield estate, having already had it surveyed in the later 1820s.[14]

In 1839, under an Act of 1834 amended in 1836, the remaining waste in the manor was inclosed together with the small acreage of open fields, over 3,000 a. in all.[15] Acknowledging the 'loss of the wild and picturesque character which the country formerly bore', Sir George justified inclosure with the argument that in a time of rising population 'no land which is capable of being cultivated can be allowed to be idle for gratification to the eye'.[16] The cost of inclosure and of repairing farmhouses was heavy, and in 1839 Sir George expressed the hope of discovering 'a rich vein of ore in some of the mines here by which we may be enabled to meet the urgent necessities'.[17] He also set about improving the education of his tenants, notably in partnership with William Buckwell, incumbent of Longnor from 1830. Longnor school was moved to a better site, Warslow school was enlarged, and the schools at Alstonefield and Flash were reorganized. Chapels and schools were built at Newtown and at Reaps Moor, both in Fawfieldhead, and at Hollinsclough.

Sir George died in 1844, and his successors took a less paternal interest in Alstonefield. Game shooting was resumed, and keeper's lodges were built in the early 1850s in Fawfieldhead and near Longnor.[18] Shooting rights were reserved when in 1951 the Harpur Crewe family sold 10,753 a. (4,351 ha.) of the farmland on its Alstonefield estate to pay death duties.[19] In 1986 the family's 4,629 a. (1,873 ha.) of moorland there passed in lieu of capital transfer tax to the Peak Park joint planning board, which manages it as the Warslow Moors Estate.[20] In addition the Ministry of Defence has occupied land since 1953 as a training area, 2,707 a. (1,095 ha.) in 1994 extending from the Leek–Buxton road in Heathylee nearly to Warslow village. The ministry owns 850 a. of it and leases 886 a. from the Peak Park joint planning board; it has a licence to train over the remaining 971 a.[21]

The scenery of the parish was attracting tourists by the earlier 19th century.[22] The whole of the parish became part of the Peak National Park on its creation in 1951.[23] The area remains popular with walkers, and there are a number of holiday cottages and second homes. Longnor was included in the Peak Park joint planning board's rural development scheme of the 1980s, which encouraged tourism and also the establishment of small businesses. In 1989 the first telecottage in the United Kingdom was opened at Warslow.

THE FOREST. The townships of Fawfieldhead, Heathylee, Hollinsclough, and Quarnford lay in what was called the forest of Alstonefield in 1227.[24] The forest evidently existed by the 12th century: it was known variously as the forest of Mauban and Malbank Frith by the early 14th century,[25] from the Malbank family, lords of Alstonefield manor until 1176. The name Malbon Frith continued in use for an area which in the late 16th century consisted of 4,335 a. of waste.[26]

13 Ibid. 25 Aug. 1831.   14 S.R.O. 5322.
15 *S.H.C.* 1931, 97 (giving 3,100 a.); 1941, 15 (giving 3,500 a.); 4 & 5 Wm. IV, c. 15 (Priv. Act); 6 & 7 Wm. IV, c. 6 (Priv. Act); S.R.O., Q/RDc 24.
16 Colvin, *Calke Abbey*, 63.
17 D.R.O., D. 2375M/44/1, 27 Sept. 1839.
18 Ibid. D. 2375M/202/19, ff. 5, 7, 59, 61
19 W.S.L., S.C. E/3/26–7; *Country Life*, 1 June 1989, p. 171.

20 Inf. from the Board.
21 Inf. from Defence Land Agent (Wales & North West), Copthorne Barracks, Shrewsbury.
22 Below, Alstonefield, intro.
23 Inf. from the Peak Park joint planning board.
24 D.R.O., D. 2375M/171/1/2; *S.H.C.* iv (1), 64.
25 D.R.O., D. 2375M/53/8, deed of Ralph de Vernon to Wm. of Coton; below (next para.).
26 P.R.O., SC 6/1116/2, m. 7d.; D.R.O., D. 2375M/90/10.

Peter the forester was a tenant of the manor in 1273.[27] In 1302 Philip Draycott held the bailiwick of the forest of Mauban,[28] and by the early 15th century the Beresfords of Beresford Hall held the office of forester of Malbon Frith.[29] The foresters who made presentments at the manor court by 1399[30] were probably assistant foresters. Four presented in 1503, three in 1505, and two in 1506.[31] In 1608 Edward Beresford held two forestierships in Malbon forest.[32] By 1670 there was a tradition that there had been two officers of the Frith, a bowbearer living at Beresford Hall and a keeper living at Boosley Grange in Fawfieldhead.[33]

The lords' income from the forest in the 14th and 15th centuries included winter and summer agistment, turbary, passage tolls, and rents from tenants.[34] Such tenants were sometimes described as holding according to 'the custom of the manor of Frith'.[35] Malbon Frith was remembered in 1670 as having been stocked with deer.[36]

MANORIAL GOVERNMENT. In the mid 1270s the three lords of Alstonefield jointly claimed view of frankpledge and right of gallows.[37] A single court continued to be held for the whole manor, but jurisdiction was exercised only by the lords of the two main shares, although the perquisites were divided into three.[38] The court was held in 1530 in the name of the Blounts, lords of one of those two shares, and from 1545 in the name of Vincent Mundy, lord of both shares.[39] There was a separate court for Warslow and Longnor by the early 16th century. By 1697 the Alstonefield court was held at Hayesgate, in Fawfieldhead. It was still held there when last recorded in 1853.[40]

By the late 1390s there were five tithings in the manor, Alstonefield, Beresford, Forest, Longnor, and Warslow.[41] The Forest tithing, also known as Frith by the 1530s, covered Fawfieldhead, Heathylee, and Hollinsclough and sent two frank-pledges to the view.[42] By 1594 Fawfieldhead was a separate tithing, and Heathylee and Hollinsclough together formed another. By 1697 Heathylee and Hollinsclough too were separate tithings. Quarnford seems not to have been in the Forest tithing, probably because it formed a separate manor in the Middle Ages.

There was mention of the three-weekly small court in 1329.[43] It was held at irregular intervals in the earlier 15th century but thereafter only rarely, being last recorded in 1529.[44]

The manor formed a single constablewick by 1377,[45] with a constable appointed at the manor court by the 1450s.[46] At that time appointments seem to have been made in respect of particular tenements, a practice followed in the early 18th century.[47] By 1595 the appointment of the constable was recorded both at the Alstonefield court and at that for Warslow and Longnor.[48] In 1698, when many thefts were going unpunished because victims were unable to bear the cost of

27 P.R.O., C 134/5, m. 2.
28 S.H.C. 1911, 58–9.
29 D.R.O., D. 158M/Z3. For the Beresfords see below, Alstonefield, manors.
30 D.R.O., D. 2375M/1/6, ct. of Thurs. before feast of St. Alphege 22 Ric. II.
31 Ibid. D. 2375M/1/3, 1st ct. 19 Hen. VII, 7 Apr. 20 Hen. VII, 6 May 21 Hen. VII.
32 S.H.C. N.S. iv. 8.
33 P.R.O., E 134/21 & 22 Chas. II Hil./22, m. 5.
34 S.H.C. 1913, 22; D.R.O., D. 2375M/1/1, reeve's accts. 46–7 Edw. III sqq.; P.R.O., SC 6/988/2, m. 5; SC 6/Hen. VII/679, m. 6d.
35 e.g. D.R.O., D. 2375M/1/6, cts. of Thurs. after feast of St. Hilary 2 Hen. VI and 17 Hen. VI, ct. of Thurs. in week of Pentecost 7 Hen. VIII.
36 P.R.O., E 134/21 & 22 Chas. II Hil./22, m. 5.
37 S.H.C. v (1), 118–19.

38 S.H.C. 1913, 22; P.R.O., SC 6/988/2, m. 5; SC 6/Hen. VII/679, m. 6d.
39 D.R.O., D. 2375M/1/2; D. 2375M/1/3.
40 Ibid. D. 2375M/174/1, 22 Oct. 1697 sqq.; D. 2375M/174/2; D. 2375M/202/19, f. 44.
41 Ibid. D. 2375M/1/6, ct. of Thurs. before feast of St. Alphege 22 Ric. II.
42 Ibid. undated view following ct. of Thurs. after feast of St. Peter and St. Paul 23 Ric. II, ct. of 25 Apr. 22 Hen. VIII sqq.
43 S.H.C. 1913, 22.
44 D.R.O., D. 2375M/1/1; D. 2375M/1/3; D. 2375M/1/6.
45 S.H.C. 4th ser. vi. 8.
46 D.R.O., D. 2375M/1/1, 1st ct. 33 Hen. VI.
47 Ibid. D. 2375M/174/1, 21 Oct. 1708, 23 Oct. 1710, 26 Oct. 1721, 21 Oct. 1726.
48 Ibid. D. 2375M/57/1, cts. of 13 and 14 Oct. 37 Eliz. I.

prosecution, the constable was directed in future to prosecute thefts and to charge the cost in his accounts. At the same time it was noted that some constables had been presenting their accounts in 'dark and uncertain places' and spending large sums on such occasions. It was ordered that the constable was to present his accounts within a fortnight of leaving office at either Archford bridge or Hayesgate, those being the customary places; he was not to spend more than 20s. on the occasion.[49] A constable was still appointed in 1804.[50]

By the earlier 1370s there was a reeve for each of the two main shares of the manor. Two reeves were still appointed in 1475.[51] There was a hallswain for the manor by 1299.[52] In the earlier 1370s he received an annual stipend of 5s., reduced to 4s. by 1414. His duties included proclaiming the courts and presenting the deaths of tenants. The office still existed in 1495.[53] The court also appointed pinners and highway surveyors for the townships.

PARISH GOVERNMENT. For taxing and rating purposes the parish had been divided into three parts by 1403. One consisted of Alstonefield township and was known as the part of the parish below Archford bridge, which spanned the Manifold on the boundary between the township and Fawfieldhead. The second part, known as High Frith, covered Fawfieldhead (including the detached Beresford area), Heathylee, Hollinsclough, and Quarnford. The third part consisted of Longnor, Warslow, and Lower and Upper Elkstone.[54] High Frith had been divided by 1611 into Low Frith, covering Fawfieldhead, and High Frith, covering Heathylee, Hollinsclough, and Quarnford.[55] All four became separate townships in 1733, having decided that year to relieve their poor separately. Longnor was a separate township apparently by the later 17th century, when it seems to have maintained its own poor. Warslow and the two Elkstones also seem to have been a separate township by then.

In 1553 Alstonefield church had two churchwardens, and there were two chapelwardens at Longnor and two at Elkstone.[56] By 1569 there were four churchwardens, two for Alstonefield church and one each presumably for Longnor and for Warslow and Elkstone, the arrangement by the early 18th century.[57] A parish clerk was mentioned in 1534 when William Hall of Stanshope left 5s. towards his wages.[58] In the late 16th century it was the custom for him to receive corn from the parish.[59] That was presumably the origin of the custom recorded in the 1740s whereby he received 4d. from every farmhouse in the parish and 2d. from every cottage; the payments were still made in 1841.[60] By 1725 he was also paid a wage of 13s. 4d. a year.[61] In addition he was paid for duties relating specifically to Alstonefield church.[62]

The whole of the ancient parish except Alstonefield township was included in Leek poor-law union at its formation in 1837[63] and in Leek rural district in 1894. Alstonefield township was part of a Gilbert union until 1870 when it was added

49 Ibid. D. 2375M/174/1, 12 Oct. 1698.
50 Ibid. D. 2375M/6/1, 31 Oct. 1804.
51 Ibid. D. 2375M/1/1, reeve's accts. 46–7 Edw. III sqq.; ibid. 2nd ct. 15 Edw. IV; D. 2375M/1/6, undated view following ct. of Thurs. after St. Peter and St. Paul 23 Ric. II.
52 Ibid. D. 2375M/110/32, copy of inq. p.m. of Nic. de Audley, 1299, showing a tenant named Adam Hallesweyn.
53 Ibid. D. 2375M/1/1, reeve's accts. 46–7 Edw. III sqq.; ibid. 1st ct. 11 Hen. VII, ct. 12 Hen. VII; P.R.O., SC 6/Hen. VII/679, m. 7.

54 Alstonfield Par. Reg. 288–9.
55 D.R.O., D. 2375M/57/1, 3 Apr. 9 Jas. I; S.R.O., D. 3359/Condlyffe, Mabon Frith assessment, 1669.
56 S.H.C. 1915, 9, 11.
57 Alstonfield Par. Reg. 26, 32; S.R.O., D. 922/35, pp. 25–6.   58 L.J.R.O., B/C/11, Wm. Hall (1534).
59 D.R.O., D. 2375M/57/1, 4 Oct. 39 Eliz. I.
60 Ibid. D. 2375M/282/8/4/2; S.R.O., D. 922/20.
61 S.R.O., D. 922/20; D. 922/35–6.
62 Below, Alstonefield, local govt. (par. govt.).
63 S.R.O., D. 699/1/1/1, p. 1.

to Ashbourne union. It was in Mayfield rural district until 1934 when it was added to Leek rural district.[64] In 1974 the whole area became part of Staffordshire Moorlands district.

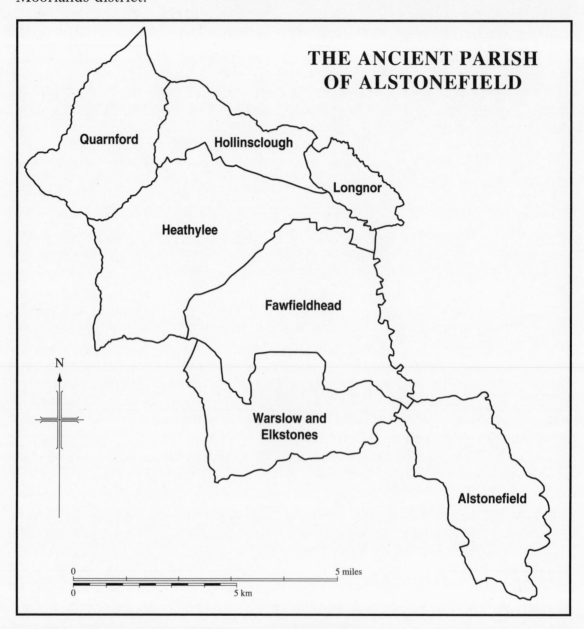

FIG. 3

ALSTONEFIELD

THE civil parish of Alstonefield is an upland rural area 3,530 a. (1,429 ha.) in extent. It was created in 1934 from the existing civil parish and former township of Alstonefield (2,938 a.) and the adjoining detached portion (592 a.) of Faw-fieldhead civil parish.[65] The river Dove forms the eastern boundary, which is also the county boundary with Derbyshire. Much of the north-

ern boundary with Sheen is formed by a tribu-tary of the Dove, and the southern boundary with Ilam follows another tributary running through Hall Dale (formerly Stanshope Dale).[66] The river Manifold forms the north-western boundary with Fawfieldhead and Wetton.

The centre of Alstonefield village stands at 914 ft. (279 m.). The land rises to the north, with

64 Staffs. Review Order, 1934, p. 63 (copy in S.R.O.).

65 Ibid. p. 63 and map 1; Census, 1931. This article was written in 1993 and 1994. Mr. and Mrs. R. Adams of Old School House, Alstonefield, and others named in footnotes are thanked for their help.

66 D.R.O., D. 2375M/56/4, deed of 23 Jan. 1624/5.

Gratton Hill reaching 1,194 ft. (364 m.) and Narrowdale Hill 1,204 ft. (367 m.). On the east the land slopes steeply to the river Dove, which runs through the gorges of Beresford Dale, Wolfscote Dale, and Mill Dale. The north side of Hall Dale rises to 1,027 ft. (313 m.). The underlying rock is mostly Carboniferous Limestone, but in the northern part of the parish it is sandstone of the Millstone Grit series, with hard sandstone on Archford moor and a softer mudstone in the area east of it. Boulder Clay overlies the rock north-east of the village and also around Gateham Grange and on Archford moor. The soil over the limestone is silty, and over the Millstone Grit it is loam and clay.[67]

Nine people in Alstonefield township were assessed for tax in 1327 and 10 in 1333.[68] In 1767 the township had 96 men and women owing suit at the manor court; there were 62 in Alstonefield village and Milldale, 8 in Hope, 10 in Stanshope, and 16 in Narrowdale, Gateham, and Westside.[69] The population of the township was 573 in 1801 and 652 in 1821. After slight fluctuation it reached 681 in 1851 but fell steadily to 471 in 1881. Having risen to 476 in 1891, it was 438 in 1901, 457 in 1911, 402 in 1921, and 367 in 1931.[70] The detached portion of Fawfieldhead had a population of 85 in 1841, which had dropped to 72 by 1851, 64 by 1861, 46 by 1871, and 43 by 1881 and had risen to 46 again by 1891.[71] The new civil parish had a population of 373 in 1951, 333 in 1961, 293 in 1971 and 1981, and 274 in 1991.[72]

The parish contains a large number of Bronze Age barrows, several at the highest points. One at Steep Low north-west of Alstonefield village contained, besides Bronze Age remains, an Anglian burial and Roman coins. Another at Stanshope contained Samian ware.[73]

The name Alstonefield is Old English, meaning Alfstan's *feld* or open ground and perhaps reflecting the situation of the village on a limestone plateau.[74] The street pattern in the centre of the village is irregular, with several small greens but no single focus. The church, a pre-Conquest foundation, stands some distance south-east of the built-up area on the road to Milldale. The road formerly ran south of the church, but in the 1830s it was realigned to pass north of it.[75] The former manor house, now called Hall Farm, stands north of the church on the edge of the village. The Rakes on the north side of the village was an inhabited area by the

later 17th century.[76] Two of the houses in the village are of the 17th century, but most appear have been built between the late 18th and the late 19th century. In 1992 six three-bedroomed houses were completed by the Peak District housing association on land on the south-west side of the village given by Henry Harpur-Crewe (d. 1991).[77]

There was an inn called the Black Lion in the village in 1815, and it may have been the building which had been taken over as a workhouse by 1817.[78] There were three inns in 1818, the Red Lion, the George, and the Harpur's Arms.[79] The Red Lion, rebuilt c. 1840, became a temperance hotel c. 1895 and was evidently closed soon after 1912. The building survived in 1994 as Fynderne House, a private residence.[80] The George was probably the 'good inn for the accommodation of tourists' mentioned in 1834.[81] It was used for the Easter vestry meeting in 1828 and for the collection of the manorial rents in the 1830s.[82] By 1896 it was advertised as 'splendidly situated' with good accommodation for travellers and tourists, stabling, and traps for hire.[83] It was the only inn in the village in 1994. The Crewe and Harpur Arms, in existence by 1850, was converted from two cottages apparently in 1848. Closed in 1957, the building survived in 1994 as a private house.[84]

There was scattered settlement outside the village by the 13th century. Stanshope in the southern part of the township was a pre-Conquest estate,[85] and it was a hamlet with its own fields by the beginning of the 13th century.[86] Hope, south-west of Alstonefield village, was an inhabited place by the 1320s.[87] Hopedale further south-west was apparently an occupied site by 1657 when there was a house of that name.[88] The New inn there existed by 1850, and from the earlier 1880s it was known as the Watts Russell's Arms (later the Watts Russell Arms).[89] The name Hope derives from the Old English *hop* meaning a valley,[90] probably the steep-sided dale which runs from Hopedale east to the hamlet of Milldale. A road between Alstonefield and Stanshope formerly ran north–south across the dale.[91] The mill from which Milldale took its name existed probably by 1282.[92] The former road between Ashbourne (Derb.) and Alstonefield crossed the Dove there by Viator's bridge, a two-arched stone structure probably of the early 16th century and probably on the site of

67 Geol. Surv. Map 1/50,000, drift, sheet 111 (1978 edn.).; Soil Surv. of Eng. and Wales, sheet 3 (1983).
68 *S.H.C.* vii (1), 218; x (1), 116.
69 D.R.O., D. 2375M/174/5/7.
70 *V.C.H. Staffs.* i. 327; *Census*, 1911–31.
71 P.R.O., HO 107/1003; HO 107/2008; ibid. RG 9/1949; RG 10/2885; RG 11/2742; RG 12/2188.
72 *Census*, 1951–91.
73 Staffs. C.C., Sites and Monuments Rec. 00090, 00102–6, 00347, 00376–8, 00383–7, 00398, 00437, 04162, 04166, 014190, 05034.
74 E. Ekwall, *Concise Oxford Dict. Eng. Place-names*; *N.S.J.F.S.* xxi. 13–14.
75 J. Phillips and W. F. Hutchings, *Map of County of Stafford* (1832); S.R.O., Q/RDc 24, map V.
76 *Alstonfield Par. Reg.* 211, 230, 272.
77 *Leek Post & Times*, 28 Oct. 1992, p. 6; *Staffs. Life*, July/Aug. 1993, 12; below, manors (Alstonefield).
78 B.L. Add. MS. 36653 (1), f. 38; below, local govt. (par. govt.).

79 Parson and Bradshaw, *Staffs. Dir.* (1818), villages, p. 1.
80 *Staffs. Advertiser*, 12 Feb. 1842, p. 1; *Kelly's Dir. Staffs.* (1892; 1896; 1912); *Alstonefield*, ed. Edwards, 40; D.R.O., D. 2375M/299/31.
81 White, *Dir. Staffs.* (1834), 715.
82 S.R.O., D. 922/36, 4 Apr. 1828; D.R.O., D. 2375M/205/11 and 13.   83 *Kelly's Dir. Staffs.* (1896).
84 P.R.O., HO 107/1003; *P.O. Dir. Staffs.* (1850); *Alstonefield*, ed. Edwards, 32.
85 Below, manors.
86 *S.H.C.* iii (1), 101; iv (1), 43; below, econ. hist. (agric.).
87 D.R.O., D. 2375M/110/32, copy of inq. p.m. of Nic. de Audley 1299.
88 Ibid. D. 231M/T712.
89 *P.O. Dir. Staffs.* (1850); *Kelly's Dir. Staffs.* (1880; 1884).
90 *Eng. P.N. Elements*, i. 259–60.
91 Dodd, *Peakland Roads*, 88–9; above, fig. 2.
92 Below, econ. hist. (mills).

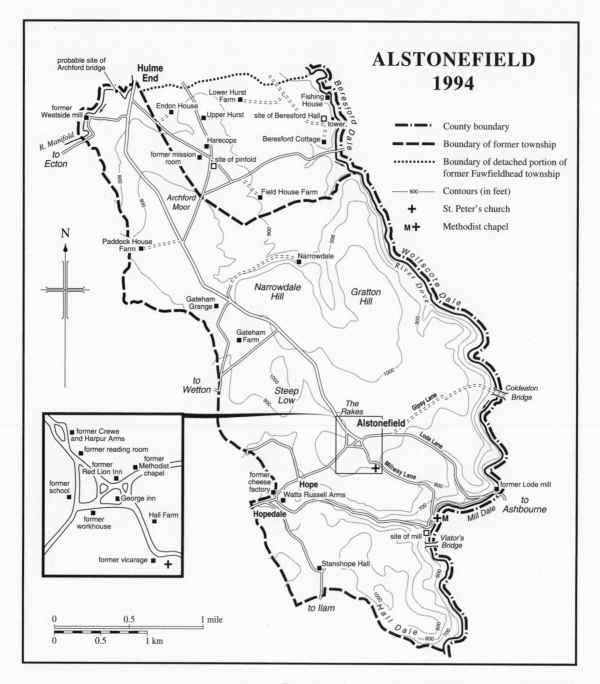

FIG. 4

the Alstonefield bridge mentioned in the late 1420s.[93] It is named from one of the characters in the section of Izaak Walton's *The Compleat Angler* contributed by his friend Charles Cotton of Beresford Hall further upstream. The road continued to Alstonefield up Millway Lane. The route is described in *The Compleat Angler*[94] and was probably that taken by John Byng, later Viscount Torrington, in 1789 when he travelled from Ashbourne via Alstonefield village to visit the copper mines at Ecton, in Wetton.[95] It was

the route followed by Henry (later Sir Henry) Ellis of the British Museum when he went from Ashbourne to Beresford Hall in 1815,[96] but on a visit the previous year Ellis evidently crossed the river further upstream at Lode mill and presumably continued to Alstonefield up Lode Lane.[97] That crossing was still a ford in 1658 when a woman was drowned there;[98] the present stone bridge is a 19th-century structure of one arch. It was the only road crossing in the later 19th century when the road on the Derbyshire

93 D.R.O., D. 2375M/1/1, 1st ct. 7 Hen. VI; below, plate 65.

94 Heywood, *Cotton and his River*, 28–30 and pl. between pp. 164 and 165; below, manors.

95 *Torrington Diaries*, ed. C. B. Andrews, ii. 57–8;

Burdett's Map of Derb. 1791 (Derb. Arch. Soc. 1975), sheet 9.

96 B.L. Add. MS. 36653 (1), f. 38.

97 Ibid. f. 21.

98 *Alstonfield Par. Reg.* 176.

side of Viator's bridge had gone out of use and the bridge was a footbridge.[99] The ford was described as at the Lode End in 1658, and Lode was a settlement by the 1670s.[1] The name derives from the Old English *lad*, meaning a watercourse or a crossing of a watercourse.[2] Gipsy Lane branching north-east from Lode Lane was formerly a road which crossed the Dove by Coldeaton bridge.[3]

Beresford, a crossing of the Dove in the north-east part of the detached portion of Fawfieldhead, gave its name to the Beresford family, who lived there by the 13th century.[4] The early spelling of the name was normally Beveresford or a variant.[5] It has been suggested that the name derives from a ford associated with beavers, but the later spelling led the family to adopt arms showing bears.[6] The stretch of the Dove through Beresford Dale was made famous for its trout and grayling by *The Compleat Angler*.[7] A lane ran south from Beresford Hall to Narrowdale, which was a settlement by the later 13th century.[8] It lies between Narrowdale Hill and Gratton Hill, and Robert Plot noted that for a quarter of the year the inhabitants never saw the sun; at other times they did not see it before *c*. 1 p.m., a time known locally as the Narrowdale noon.[9] In 1994 the settlement consisted of two 19th-century farmhouses. Gateham to the south-west was owned in the 13th century by Combermere abbey (Ches.), which established a grange there.[10] There was a house on the site of Gateham Farm south of Gateham Grange by 1775,[11] but the present house is of the 19th century.

At Westside in the north-west corner of the township there was encroachment on Archford moor by 1507, John Beresford having built a house at Westside Head.[12] There was a mill on the Manifold there by 1584.[13] There was evidently further encroachment on the moor by the late 1760s.[14] By 1775 there may have been a house on the west side of the moor on the site of Paddock House Farm, which is dated 1828. There was settlement by 1775 along Beresford Lane on the east side of the moor, and Field House Farm south of the lane existed by then.[15] New Hurst, mentioned in 1779,[16] was probably the present Lower Hurst Farm north of Beresford Lane. It consists of a stone house to

which an addition was made probably in the late 18th century with further additions in the 19th century. Upper Hurst, Harecops, and Endon House in the same area existed by 1839 and probably by 1820,[17] although Upper Hurst has been rebuilt.

The road running north from Alstonefield village across Archford moor formerly forked south of the Sheen boundary. One branch continued north to Hulme End, in Sheen, and the other ran north-west to Longnor, crossing the Manifold into Fawfieldhead at Archford bridge. The bridge was in existence by 1403.[18] In 1553 bequests of 3*s*. 4*d*. and of a sheep were made for its maintenance.[19] Both branches of the Alstonefield road formed part of the road from Warslow to Hartington (Derb.) until it was turnpiked in 1770 and realigned to cross the river *c*. 300 yd. upstream at Hulme End.[20] Archford bridge was still used as an address in 1796, but the road over it had evidently ceased to be used by 1820.[21]

Mention was made of the new well in Alstonefield village in 1596 when the manor court ordered that water was not to be taken from it for washing clothes. An order was also made for the repair of the wash pool, with another order in 1617 for its annual cleaning.[22] There was a well on the south side of the village in 1715.[23] A parish pump in Alstonefield was mentioned in 1866. A pump was erected on the north side of the village in 1896 and replaced in 1928 by another on the same site, still standing in 1994. A piped water supply became available in 1955, though not to every house.[24] A ban was placed on washing clothes and watering cattle in the wells in Hope in 1606 and in the town well in Stanshope in 1607.[25] In the late 1870s there were seven wells around Hope and a well in Stanshope.[26] A well in the garden of the former cheese factory at Hopedale served the hamlet until the coming of a mains water supply.[27] Electricity became available in Alstonefield village in 1939.[28]

There was an Alstonefield dispensary in the mid 1830s supported by annual subscription.[29] By 1912 the Alstonefield and Wetton nursing association was providing a nurse for home visits; subscriptions ranged from 2*s*. 6*d*. a year for widows and single people to £1 for the 'upper

99 O.S. Map 6", Staffs. IX. SE. (1884 edn.).
1 *Alstonfield Par. Reg.* 176, 217–18.
2 *Eng. P.N. Elements*, ii. 8–9.
3 Dodd, *Peakland Roads*, 88–9; above, fig. 2.
4 Below, manors.
5 *S.H.C.* vi (1), 256; *S.H.C.* N.S. vii. 141, 147; *S.H.C.* 1911, 168.
6 H. de la P. Beresford, *Book of the Beresfords* (Chichester, 1977), 10 and pl. facing p. 11.
7 Below, manors (Beresford).
8 D.R.O., D. 2375M/55/3; *S.H.C.* v (i), 120; *S.H.C.* 1911, 168.
9 Plot, *Staffs.* 110.
10 Below, manor (Gateham Grange).
11 Above, fig. 2.
12 D.R.O., D. 2375M/1/3, 11 Oct. 23 Hen. VII; above, fig. 2.
13 Below, econ. hist. (mills).
14 *Alstonfield Par. Reg.* 409, 413.
15 Above, fig. 2.
16 *Alstonfield Par. Reg.* 446, 482.
17 C. and J. Greenwood, *Map of County of Stafford*

(1820); J. Phillips and W. F. Hutchings, *Map of County of Stafford* (1832); S.R.O., Q/RDc 24, map V.
18 *Alstonfield Par. Reg.* 288–9.
19 L.J.R.O., B/C/11, Joan Belfeld (1553), John Grene (1554).
20 Below, Fawfieldhead, intro.
21 *Alstonfield Par. Reg.* 472; Greenwood, *Map of County of Stafford* (1820); D.R.O., D. 2375M/282/1, mins. of evidence re disputed boundary, 23 Aug. 1837, p. [4].
22 D.R.O., D. 2375M/57/1, 26 Apr. 38 Eliz. I, 10 Oct. 15 Jas. I.
23 Ibid. D. 2375M/174/1, 21 Oct. 1715.
24 Ibid. D. 2375M/202/19, p. 253; *Alstonfield*, ed. Edwards, 45–6.
25 D.R.O., D. 2375M/57/1, 29 Apr. 4 Jas. I, 21 Apr. 5 Jas. I.
26 O.S. Map 6", Staffs. IX. SE. (1884 edn.).
27 Inf. from Mr. C. Beloe, Old Cheese Factory; below, econ. hist. (trade and ind.).
28 *Alstonfield Deanery Mag.* xlii (12); xliii (1); *Kelly's Dir. Staffs.* (1940).
29 D.R.O., D. 2375M/205/11.

classes'. It still existed in 1925 when a public meeting decided to wind it up because of inadequate financial support; it was saved that year by help from the county nursing association.[30] Harvest festival collections in the mid 1920s enabled Alstonefield ecclesiastical parish to subscribe 7 guineas to the Derby Infirmary, entitling it to recommend 3 in-patients or 14 out-patients.[31]

There was a post office in the village by 1850. It was run by James Hambleton, who combined it with a grocery and drapery business.[32]

By the 1830s a wake was held on the Sunday after 29 June, the feast of St. Peter and St. Paul, the church being dedicated to St. Peter.[33] The Tuesday following the Sunday was also a festival by 1901.[34] In the earlier 1990s Wakes Sunday was marked by a procession through the village to the church, where a service was held, normally in the open air.[35] Henry Ellis, visiting Alstonefield and Ilam on 14 September 1815, noted the paper garlands hanging in the churches 'in memory of young females', although he was told that the custom was dying out.[36]

There were three friendly societies in the village in 1876, founded respectively in 1794, 1803, and 1811. The last had 115 members in 1876 and, like that of 1794, met at the George.[37] A Women's Institute was formed in 1920 as part of the Staffordshire Federation of Women's Institutes. It was closed in 1935 and in 1953 it was re-established as part of the Derbyshire Federation.[38]

Cottage House on the north side of the village was converted into a reading room, evidently in 1865.[39] In the late 1920s it became a social centre with activities including billiard matches.[40] The building was used as an A.R.P. post during the Second World War and later by the scouts and other organizations, and in 1953 it was converted into a kitchen and dining room for the school.[41] In 1994 it was a private house called the Old Reading Room. At the beginning of the 20th century there was a free lending library at the school for adults as well as children; it was open on Mondays after afternoon school.[42] A village institute was opened in 1921.[43] It was replaced in the earlier 1980s when the school, closed in 1982, was bought by the village from the Harpur-Crewe trustees and converted into Alstonefield Memorial Hall and Community Centre.[44] Alstonefield Local History Society

grew out of courses on the history of the village organized by the Workers Educational Association from 1975 to 1978, and the society was still active in 1994.[45]

There was an Alstonefield band by 1867, presumably the brass band whose revival was attempted in 1901.[46] A village band was formed in 1914, its instruments paid for by public subscription, and it still existed in 1920.[47] There was an Alstonefield choral society in 1919.[48]

The village had a cricket club and a football club by 1905.[49] Both had lapsed by 1919 when two new clubs were started.[50] A tennis club appears to have been formed in 1926.[51]

An annual flower show held in August or September was started in 1894. By 1904 it was a horticultural and poultry show and by 1912 an agricultural and horticultural show. Exhibits in 1913 included flowers, butter, sheep, and cattle. It was still held in 1923.[52]

In 1789 John Byng described Alstonefield village as set 'amidst mountains of height and beauty'.[53] William Alexander, who accompanied Henry Ellis on his visit to Beresford Hall in 1815, found the spot highly interesting both for its romantic scenery reminiscent of the paintings of Salvator Rosa and for its associations with Charles Cotton.[54] By 1834 tourists were coming to Alstonefield 'to view the wild and romantic scenery of the neighbourhood'.[55] The George inn made provision for them by the 1890s and probably by the 1830s, and the temperance hotel in the village by the mid 1890s presumably catered for tourists.[56] A refreshment room had been opened at Milldale by 1908 and another in the village by 1928.[57] The Leek & Manifold Valley light railway, opened from Waterhouses to the Fawfieldhead part of Hulme End in 1904 and closed in 1934, brought visitors to Beresford Dale.[58] In 1933 and 1936 the National Trust acquired land on both sides of the Dove below the southern end of Wolfscote Dale.[59] The area continues to attract walkers, and there are several holiday cottages and second homes in Alstonefield and Milldale, some of them converted barns.[60]

MANORS AND OTHER ESTATES. Before the Conquest *ALSTONEFIELD* was held by Godwin.[61] It has been suggested that William I gave it to his half-sister's son Hugh d'Avranches,

30 *Alstonfield Deanery Mag.* xvii (6); xxii (7); xxviii (12).
31 Ibid. xxviii (11).
32 *P.O. Dir. Staffs.* (1850); *Alstonefield,* ed. Edwards, 25–6.
33 White, *Dir. Staffs.* (1834), 717.
34 *Alstonfield Par. Mag.* Aug. 1901; July 1902; S.R.O., D. 3805/1/2, p. 23.
35 Inf. from Mr. and Mrs. Adams.
36 B.L. Add. MS. 36653 (1), ff. 42v.–43.
37 *Rep. Chief Registrar of Friendly Socs. 1876, App. P,* H.C. 429-I, p. 392 (1877), lxxvii.
38 Inf. from Derb. Federation of Women's Institutes.
39 D.R.O., D. 2375M/202/19, p. 237.
40 *Alstonfield Deanery Mag.* xxxii (6).
41 Inf. from Mr. A. J. Mundy, Old Reading Room; below, educ.
42 *Alstonfield Par. Mag.* Nov. 1901; Jan. 1902.
43 *Alstonfield Deanery Mag.* xxv (12).
44 *Alstonefield,* ed. Edwards, 34.
45 Inf. from Mr. and Mrs. Adams and Workers Educ.

Assoc., Hanley.
46 *Staffs. Advertiser,* 26 Oct. 1867, p. 7; *Alstonfield Deanery Mag.* Dec. 1906; D.R.O., D. 2375M/202/19, p. 278.
47 *Alstonfield Deanery Mag.* xviii (3); xxiv (1).
48 Ibid. xxiii (11).
49 Ibid. Oct. 1905.
50 Ibid. xxiii (7; 12).   51 Ibid. xxix (10).
52 Ibid. Aug. 1906; xvii (9), p. 7; (11), pp. 10–11; S.R.O., D. 3522/1, pp. 176–8; D. 3805/1/1, pp. 327 sqq.; D. 3805/1/2, pp. 5 sqq.
53 *Torrington Diaries,* ed. Andrews, ii. 58.
54 W. Alexander, *Journey to Beresford Hall* (1841).
55 White, *Dir. Staffs.* (1834), 715–17.
56 Above, this section [Alstonefield village].
57 *Kelly's Dir. Staffs.* (1908; 1928).
58 Beresford, *Beresford of Beresford,* i. 38 n.–39 n.; below, Leek: Leek and Lowe, communications.
59 *T.N.S.F.C.* lxxi. 29–30 and pl. facing p. 26; D.R.O., D. 2375M/131/53.   60 Inf. from Mr. and Mrs. Adams.
61 *V.C.H. Staffs.* iv. 47.

who was created earl of Chester in 1071.[62] By 1086, however, Roger, earl of Shrewsbury, held the manor, then assessed at 3 virgates.[63] In 1102 his son and successor Robert de Bellême forfeited his possessions.[64] Alstonefield seems then to have remained with the Crown until 1215 when John granted the overlordship of 1 knight's fee there to Ranulph, earl of Chester.[65] In 1283 the king held the overlordship as part of the honor of Chester,[66] but Edmund, earl of Lancaster, was overlord at his death in 1296.[67] The overlordship continued with the earldom, later the duchy, of Lancaster, which still held it in 1577 and apparently in 1596.[68]

In 1086 Alstonefield was held of the earl of Shrewsbury by William Malbank, who may have been enfeoffed by the earl of Chester.[69] He was one of that earl's principal tenants in Cheshire in 1086 and held the barony of Wich Malbank (later Nantwich). He was still living in 1093, but by 1119 he had been succeded by his son Hugh.[70] When Hugh founded Combermere abbey (Ches.) in 1133, he included half the vill of Alstonefield among its endowments, perhaps the estate which became Gateham grange.[71] He died in 1135 and was succeeded by his son William, on whose death in 1176 Alstonefield passed into the king's hands for three years.[72] William left three daughters and coheirs, Philippa, Aenora, and Alda. The three shares of the manor, one of them subdivided into six parts, were reunited in the 16th and 17th centuries.

PHILIPPA MALBANK'S SHARE. Philippa married Thomas Basset of Headington (Oxon.), who was also granted Aenora's share in 1204, evidently retaining it until c. 1218. He was dead by 1220 with three daughters as his heirs, but Philippa still held a third share of the manor in 1227.[73] The share was probably held by Sir Hugh le Despenser (d. 1265) and possibly by his father Sir Hugh (d. 1238); the younger Sir Hugh's son Hugh held it in 1274–5.[74] Created earl of Winchester in 1322, he was executed in 1326, and in 1327 the king granted his share of Alstonefield to Sir Roger Swynnerton.[75] In 1338 Sir Roger was succeeded by his son Robert, rector of Barrow (Ches.), who died in 1349 or 1350 with

his brother Sir Thomas as his heir.[76] Sir Thomas was succeeded in 1361 by his son Robert, who died probably in 1385 or 1386, leaving the manor to his daughter Maud.[77] Her first husband, Humphrey Peshall, was dead by 1388, and her second, Sir William Ipstones, died in 1399.[78] By 1401 she had married Sir John Savage.[79] In 1424 her son Richard Peshall successfully sued Sir John for his mother's share of Alstonefield,[80] and between 1454 and 1458 he was succeeded by his son Humphrey.[81]

Humphrey Peshall died in 1498, having devised his third share to his posthumous son Richard.[82] Humphrey's name was still used in a surrender made in the manor court in 1506,[83] but possibly by that year and certainly by 1530 the share had passed to Catherine, daughter of Humphrey's eldest son Hugh (d. 1490) and wife of Sir John Blount of Kinlet (Salop.).[84] John died in 1531, and their son George came of age in 1534.[85] In 1542 George sold his third share of Alstonefield to Vincent Mundy, who already held Aenora Malbank's share.[86] In 1564 Vincent granted his two-thirds share of the manor for 12 years to his son Edward,[87] with whom he conveyed it in 1569 to Richard Harpur, of Swarkestone (Derb.), justice of Common Pleas. Richard was succeeded in 1577 by his son John.[88]

AENORA MALBANK'S SHARE. Aenora married Robert Bardolf, who transferred his allegiance to the king of France in 1204 but sent his wife to England.[89] King John thereupon granted Aenora's share of Alstonefield to Thomas Basset, the husband of her sister Philippa.[90] Aenora, a widow by 1210,[91] seems to have secured its return c. 1218 and to have granted it to Henry de Audley; the grant, however, was described as made by Ranulph, earl of Chester, in a royal confirmation to Audley in 1227.[92] That third of the manor then descended in the Audley family.[93] By 1391 Nicholas, Lord Audley, had granted it for life to Sir Nicholas Stafford (d. 1394), of Throwley, in Ilam, at a rent of £12 a year.[94] On the death of Lord Audley in 1391 the third part was divided between two of his heirs, John Tuchet and Margaret Hillary.[95] It descended with their successors until 1516 when John, Lord

62 S.H.C. i. 231; Complete Peerage, iii. 164–5.
63 V.C.H. Staffs. iv. 47.
64 Complete Peerage, xi. 693.
65 S.H.C. i. 91; Rot. Litt. Pat. (Rec. Com.), 154.
66 Cal. Inq. p.m. ii, p. 287.
67 Ibid. iii, pp. 300–1, 314.
68 P.R.O., C. 142/176/28; S.H.C. 1932, 179–80.
69 V.C.H. Staffs. iv. 47; S.H.C. i. 231.
70 V.C.H. Ches. i. 309; iii. 133; Charters of Earls of Chester, p. 4.
71 Dugdale, Mon. v. 324; V.C.H. Ches. iii. 150.
72 Charters of Earls of Chester, p. 169; S.H.C. i. 91.
73 W. Farrer, Honors and Knights' Fees, ii. 264; S.H.C. iv (1), 64.
74 S.H.C. iv (1), 64; v. 118–19; Complete Peerage, iv. 259, 261–2.
75 S.H.C. 1913, 21–2; Cal. Pat. 1327–30, 33; Complete Peerage, iv. 265–6.
76 S.H.C. vii (2), 33, 36, 38.
77 Ibid. 40, 42, 44.
78 Ibid. 44–6; xv. 122.
79 Ibid. vii (2), 50; D.R.O., D. 2375M/1/1, 2nd ct. 2 Hen. IV.
80 S.H.C. xvii. 96; D.R.O., D. 2375M/53/8, copy deed of Mon. after Pentecost 24 Hen. VI.
81 S.H.C. N.S. iv. 105, 109; S.H.C. 1917–18, 269 n.–270 n.; D.R.O., D. 2375M/1/1, 1st ct. 33 Hen. VI.

82 Cal. Inq. p.m. Hen. VII, ii, pp. 369–70.
83 D.R.O., D. 2375M/1/3, 5 May 21 Hen. VII.
84 S.H.C. iv (2), 77; V.C.H. Staffs. iv. 95; D.R.O., D. 2375M/1/3, ct. of Sat. before Exaltation of the Cross 22 Hen. VIII. A ref. to a court of John Blount held in 1522 has been crossed out in the MS.: ibid. 7 Aug. 14 Hen. VIII.
85 S.H.C. iv (2), 78; Trans. Salop. Arch. Soc. 3rd ser. viii. 124; D.R.O., D. 2375M/1/3, 21 Oct. 25 Hen. VIII, 27 Sept. 28 Hen. VIII.
86 D.R.O., D. 2375M/82/23, deed of 12 Feb. 1541/2; Hist. Parl., Commons, 1509–1558, ii. 644–5; below (next para.).
87 D.R.O., D. 2375M/55/1, deed of 10 Feb. 1563/4.
88 S.H.C. xiii. 276; H. Colvin, Calke Abbey, Derb. 21, 24–5, 28.
89 Cur. Reg. R. vi. 81–2.
90 Rot. Litt. Claus. (Rec. Com.), i. 3.
91 Cur. Reg. R. vi. 82.
92 Pipe R. 1218 (P. R. S. N.S. xxxix), 3; Charters of Earls of Chester, pp. 393–4. For Aenora's grants to Audley of property in Ches. and elsewhere in Staffs. see ibid. pp. 392–3; S.H.C. N.S. xii. 45.
93 Below, Horton, manor.
94 Cal. Inq. p.m. xvi, p. 436; xviii, p. 155; S.H.C. 1917–18, 118.
95 Cal. Inq. p.m. xvi, p. 441; xviii, p. 155; xix, p. 213.

Audley, sold what were called the manors of Alstonefield and Warslow to John Mundy, a London goldsmith. John, who was knighted in 1523, died in 1537, having settled his share of Alstonefield on his younger son Vincent,[96] who in 1542 acquired Philippa Malbank's share also.[97]

ALDA MALBANK'S SHARE. Alda married Warin de Vernon, and their grandson, another Warin de Vernon, held a third of Alstonefield in 1274–5.[98] In 1293 six coparceners held that share.[99] Three of them had inherited their purparties from the sisters of the younger Warin, Maud (or Margery), Rose, and Alda:[1] Richard of Winnington, a minor, was Maud's grandson,[2] Roger of Littlebury was Rose's heir,[3] and Sir William de Stafford was Alda's son.[4] The other three were Robert Grosvenor, whose wife Margery was evidently the younger Warin's aunt,[5] David of Heswall, husband of Eustachia de Vernon, evidently Warin's cousin,[6] and Margaret of Hogelegh. Ralph de Vernon, Warin's uncle, claimed all or part of the third share but was assigned instead the family's manor of Shipbrook, in Davenham (Ches.).[7]

Richard of Winnington's share passed with his share of the manor of Leftwich, in Davenham (Ches.), to his son Richard of Leftwich.[8] Richard seems to have conveyed his share of Alstonefield in the early 1340s to the Vernons, who held part of the manor in 1427. The Vernon share was held in 1444 by John Cotton of Hamstall Ridware.[9] It passed to his son Richard and to Richard's son Richard, who was killed at the battle of St. Albans in 1461, leaving an infant son Richard as his heir. It was held by the heir's uncle, John Cotton, in 1467 and 1476.[10] Richard held it at his death in 1502, when his son Thomas succeeded.[11] Thomas died in 1506 with an infant daughter Elizabeth as his heir.[12] She died soon afterwards, and her share of Alstonefield passed to Isabella, Thomas's youngest sister, who married as her first husband John Bradbourne (d. 1523) of Bradbourne (Derb.). Their son Humphrey, a minor in 1523, held the share of Alstonefield by

1543; he was knighted in 1544 and died in 1581.[13] His eldest son William evidently sold the share to Humphrey Ferrers, husband of William's sister Anne, and in 1585 Humphrey and Anne made a settlement of part of Alstonefield manor.[14] It evidently passed to John Harpur, to whom William Bradbourne renounced all claim in 1596.[15]

Roger of Littlebury granted his share to William Wyther, whose son Sir Thomas Wyther granted it to Adam of Narrowdale in 1324.[16] Adam, perhaps alive in 1348, had been succeeded by his son John by 1354.[17] John was dead by 1369, and his heir was his daughter Agnes, wife of Richard Walker by 1382.[18] William Walker held the share in 1405–6 and Humphrey Walker by the mid 1420s. He or another Humphrey held it in 1457.[19] A Humphrey Walker held it in 1515 and 1532[20] and a George Walker in 1538.[21] In 1565 Henry Walker conveyed it to John Draycott of Paynsley, in Draycott-in-the-Moors, who in 1574 conveyed it to Richard Harpur.[22]

Sir William de Stafford's share descended with his manor of Amblecote until 1485, when it passed to Sir Robert Willoughby, by 1491 Lord Willoughby de Broke.[23] It descended with the barony until 1575, when Sir Fulke Greville, Lord Willoughby de Broke, conveyed it to Nicholas Longford of Longford (Derb.). In 1577 Longford conveyed it to Sampson Beresford and his son Edward.[24] It later passed to the Harpur family.[25]

Robert Grosvenor's share passed to his son Robert, who held it in 1343 and 1344.[26] It descended in the Grosvenor family of Hulme in Allostock, in Great Budworth parish (Ches.), until the death of Robert Grosvenor in 1465 and the division of his estates among his four daughters. The share of Alstonefield passed to the youngest, Margaret, wife of Thomas Leycester of Nether Tabley, also in Great Budworth.[27] Thomas was succeeded in 1526–7 by their son John, who was followed in 1545 by his son Peter. In 1577 Peter was succeeded by his son, also Peter, who conveyed the share of Alstonefield to John Harpur in 1580.[28]

96 P.R.O., E 150/1044/1; D.R.O., D. 2375M/189/6, deeds of 1 July 1516, 20 Sept. 1529; A. B. Beavan, *Aldermen of London*, ii. 23; below, Horton, manor.

97 Above (previous para.).

98 G. Ormerod, *Hist. of County Palatine and City of Chester* (1882), iii. 245–6, 252; *S.H.C.* v (1), 118–19.

99 *Plac. de Quo Warr.* (Rec. Com.), 713.

1 Ormerod. *Hist. Ches.* iii. 425.

2 Ibid. 273.

3 Ibid. 425.

4 *S.H.C.* 1917–18, 9–10.

5 Ormerod, *Hist. Ches.* iii. 146; *S.H.C.* xii (1), 27, 35; D.R.O., D. 2375M/55/3, grant by Ralph de Vernon to his sister Margery.

6 Ormerod, *Hist. Ches.* iii. 252, 899.

7 Ibid. 246; *S.H.C.* xii (1), 35; *Cal. Inq. p.m.* iii, p. 314; D.R.O., D. 2375M/55/3, grant by Vernon to sister. He was probably brother of Margery Grosvenor and father of Eustachia Heswall.

8 Ormerod, *Hist. Ches.* iii. 270, 273.

9 *Cat. Anct. D.* vi, C 5753; D.R.O., D. 2375M/1/1, cts. of Thurs. after feast of St. Martin and Thurs. before feast of Purification 22 Ric. II; ibid. 3rd ct. 5 Hen. VI, 3rd ct. 22 Hen. VI; ibid. lists of lords of the manor at end of vol.

10 Ormerod, *Hist. Ches.* ii. 786; iii. 902; D.R.O., D. 2375M/1/1, 1st ct. 7 Edw. IV, 2nd ct. 16 Edw. IV.

11 *Cal. Inq. p.m. Hen. VII*, ii, p. 600.

12 Ibid. iii, p. 193.

13 Ormerod, *Hist. Ches.* ii. 786; *Hist. Parl., Commons,* 1509–1558, i. 480; Folger Shakespeare Libr., Washington

D.C., Ferrers of Tamworth Castle MSS., rental 1543. Mrs. Laetitia Yeandle of the Folger Shakespeare Libr. is thanked for her help.

14 *Jnl. Derb. Arch. Soc.* lvii. 119–20; *Archives*, xix. 361; *S.H.C.* xv. 162–3.

15 D.R.O., D. 2375M/189/6, sched. of deeds 1768; D. 2375M/190/1, 20 Apr. 1596.

16 *S.H.C.* xiii. 126; D.R.O., D. 2375M/55/3, deed of 25 June 1324.

17 *S.H.C.* xii (1), 91; D.R.O., D. 2375M/55/3, deed of 19 Oct. 1354.

18 *S.H.C.* xiii. 74, 126, 172–3.

19 D.R.O., D. 2375M/1/1, 2nd ct. 3 Hen. VI, 1st ct. 7 Hen. VI, 1st ct. 8 Hen. VI, 1st ct. 26 Hen. VI.

20 Ibid. D. 2375M/1/6, cts. of Thurs. in week of Pentecost 7 Hen. VIII, 16 Sept. 24 Hen. VIII.

21 Ibid. D. 2375M/1/3, 8 June 38 Hen. VIII.

22 Ibid. D. 2375M/1/1, loose sheet relating to Draycott's lordship; *S.H.C.* xiii. 239–40; xiv (1), 169 (wrongly giving the share conveyed as 3/6 of the manor instead of 1/6 of 1/3: P.R.O., CP 25 (2)/212/16 Eliz. I East. no. [16]); *S.H.C.* 1925, 135–6.

23 *V.C.H. Worcs.* iii. 217–18 (with a correction in *V.C.H. Staffs.* xx. 54 n.); *Complete Peerage*, xii (2), 684; *S.H.C.* xi. 252.

24 W.S.L., S.MS. 47; *Complete Peerage*, xii (2), 683–90.

25 D.R.O., D. 2375M/189/6, case for counsel's opinion 1769–70.   26 *S.H.C.* xii (1), 22, 27, 35.

27 Ormerod, *Hist. Ches.* i. 620; iii. 152.

28 Ibid. i. 621; *S.H.C.* xiv (1), 212.

One of the remaining shares was evidently held by the Bedull family by the later 15th century. In 1523 it was conveyed by William Basset of Blore to Sir Anthony Fitzherbert of Norbury (Derb.), justice of Common Pleas.[29] He was succeeded in 1538 by his son Thomas (Sir Thomas from 1547), who conveyed the share to John Harpur in 1582.[30]

The other remaining share had passed to Henry, son of Richard de la Pole, by 1334, when he granted it to Richard de la Pole of Hartington (Derb.) with remainder to Richard's son John.[31] Richard was still alive in 1342.[32] By 1357 the share was evidently held by John's son John, who was dead by 1397. His heir was his son John, a minor, who was of age by 1406.[33] The share had passed to the Sacheverell family by 1516 and was held c. 1557 by Humphrey Sacheverell.[34] In 1566 Henry Sacheverell granted it to William Jackson.[35] It descended with the Jacksons' Stanshope estate until 1670 when Philip Jackson sold most of the share to Sir John Harpur.[36] By 1769 the residue had passed to two separate owners, whose rights were thought to be limited to the commons and wastes.[37]

John Harpur (Sir John from 1603) was succeeded in 1622 by his son John, a minor. Knighted in 1630, the younger John was succeeded in 1679 by his cousin, Sir Henry Harpur, Bt., of Calke (Derb.). Alstonefield then descended with the baronetcy. Sir Henry Harpur, the 7th baronet, changed the family name to Crewe in 1808 in the hope of securing the revival of the barony of Crew. His son George, who succeeded in 1819, used the name Crewe, and his son John, who succeeded in 1844, adopted the form Harpur Crewe. The baronetcy became extinct on the death of Sir Vauncey Harpur Crewe in 1924, and his estates passed to his daughter Hilda, wife of Col. Godfrey Mosley. She was succeeded in 1949 by her nephew Charles Jenney, who in accordance with her will changed his name to Harpur-Crewe in 1961. He was succeeded by his brother Henry Harpur-Crewe in 1981 and Henry by his sister Airmyne Harpur-Crewe in 1991; both had changed their name from Jenney to

Harpur-Crewe in 1981.[38] Meanwhile the family sold most of the farmland on its Alstonefield estate in 1951 to pay death duties, and in 1986 the moorland passed to the Peak Park joint planning board in lieu of capital transfer tax.[39]

In the later 13th century the Audleys' share of the manor included a manor house, but it was no longer standing in 1325.[40] In 1329 a house formed part of the demesne of the share formerly held by the Despensers, but there was no house there in 1338.[41] A house called the Hall Place was repaired by Lord Audley in 1435–6, evidently after the death of the tenant and before a new lease was granted.[42] A house 'called the Hall House or house of the demesnes', formerly part of Lord Audley's share, was leased in 1530, c. 1548, and 1557.[43] In 1600 the manor court ordered that six tenants nominated by the bailiff should each bring a load of peat annually to John Harpur's manor house at Alstonefield for fuel.[44] The house is a stone building north of the church, now called Hall Farm. The south-facing main range was built by John Harpur in 1587, and there is a rear wing at the east end.[45] Four rooms collapsed in 1711 and were promptly rebuilt.[46] The house and the farm belonging to it, having been put up for sale in 1951, were bought by Mrs. M. G. Davidson, whose son, Mr. J. S. Davidson, owned them in 1994.[47]

BERESFORD was the home of the Beresford family by the 13th century. John of Beresford held an estate there in 1232, paying 8s. a year for it to John Fitzherbert who that year granted the rent to William Fitzherbert.[48] Hugh of Beresford witnessed charters in the mid 13th century and probably earlier, and he was still alive in 1274.[49] John of Beresford was active in 1277,[50] and William of Beresford, alive in 1293, was described as lord of Beresford.[51] Adam of Beresford, active by 1292, was probably the Adam of Beresford who in 1308 held what was described as the hamlet of Beresford of the Audley family as lords of Aenora Malbank's share of Alstonefield manor by the rent of a quiver of 12 feathered and 2 bolted arrows worth 8½d.[52] He was still alive in 1336.[53] His son John had succeeded by 1342, and probably by 1338,

29 D.R.O., D. 2375M/1/1, rental of 7 Hen. VIII at end of vol.; D. 2375M/46, deed of 11 Nov. 1463; D. 2375M/54/3/9, copy of evidence delivered to John Harpur.
30 S.H.C. xv. 140; S.H.C. 1917–18, 314.
31 S.H.C. xi. 184.
32 Ibid. 152.   33 Ibid. xiii. 39; xv. 83; xvi. 56.
34 D.R.O., D. 2375M/1/1, list of lords of the manor at end of vol.; D. 2375M/161/5/6.
35 S.H.C. xiii. 260; D.R.O., D. 2375M/140/28. In 1571, however, it was said to be held by John Jackson (d. 1579): S.H.C. 1931, 124; Alstonfield Par. Reg. 37.
36 D.R.O., D. 2375M/56/4, deeds of 24 and 25 Jan. 1669/70; below, this section (Stanshope).
37 D.R.O., D. 2375M/189/6, case for counsel's opinion 1769–70.
38 H. Colvin, Calke Abbey, Derb. 31 sqq.; G.E.C. Baronetage, ii. 2; Leek Post & Times, 4 Dec. 1991, p. 17; inf. from Mr. A. R. Pegg of Ticknall (Derb.), personal representative of the late Henry Harpur-Crewe.
39 Above, Alstonefield, par. intro.
40 S.H.C. N.S. xi. 242, 247; S.H.C. 1911, 366.
41 S.H.C. vii (2), 33; S.H.C. 1913, 21.
42 D.R.O., D. 2375M/1/1, 3rd ct. 14 Hen. VI, 1st and 3rd cts. 15 Hen. VI.

43 Ibid. D. 2375M/1/3, 10 Oct. 22 Hen. VIII and loose sheet; D. 2375M/189/2, deed of 10 Oct. 1557.
44 Ibid. D. 2375M/57/1, 4 Apr. 42 Eliz. I.
45 Date stone of 1587 on main range with initials IH. It has not been possible to gain admission to the house in order to make a detailed survey.
46 D.R.O., D. 2375M/103/11/5; D. 2375M/110/32, disbursements 1711–12.
47 W.S.L., S.C. E/3/27, lot 17; inf. from Mrs. M. G. Davidson.
48 P.R.O., CP 25(1)/283/9, no. 95. A questionable descent has been claimed from a John of Beresford, allegedly lord of Beresford in 1087, through three generations (Hugh, Adam, and John) to Hugh (fl. mid and later 13th cent.), based on a list of deeds made apparently by a herald in 1621: Beresford, Beresford of Beresford, i. 7–8, 13–14, and pedigree facing p. 13.
49 S.H.C. xvi. 275; S.H.C. N.S. vii. 141, 147; Ormerod, Hist. Ches. iii. 495.   50 S.H.C. 1911, 168.
51 S.H.C. vi (1), 256; D.R.O., D. 2375M/55/3.
52 S.H.C. vii (1), 96, 172; S.H.C. N.S. xi. 257; S.H.C. 1911, 436.
53 S.H.C. vii (1), 218; ix (1), 94; x (1), 50–1, 73, 116; D.R.O., D. 2375M/55/3, deed of 23 June 1336.

and was still living in 1346.[54] John's son Adam had evidently succeeded by 1350 and was described as lord of Beresford in 1354.[55] He was dead by 1360 with his son and heir John still a minor. John's wardship was claimed by Sir Thomas Swynnerton, lord of Philippa Malbank's third of Alstonefield manor, who sued Adam's widow Agnes and others for abducting John from Beresford.[56] In 1412 John conveyed the Beresford estate to his son Adam.[57] Adam's heir was his son John, who evidently had a son and grandson each named John.[58] The last John died in 1523, and what was then called the manor of Beresford, held of John Mundy as lord of Aenora Malbank's share of Alstonefield manor, passed to his son Robert.[59] Robert was followed in 1542 by his son Sampson,[60] who was succeeded in 1593 by his son Edward.[61]

Edward Beresford was succeeded in 1623 by his granddaughter Olive Stanhope, later the wife of Charles Cotton.[62] She predeceased her husband, who died in 1658, and the heir was their son Charles, poet and author of the second part of the 1676 edition of Izaak Walton's *The Compleat Angler*.[63] In 1680 he sold the manor or reputed manor of Beresford to Joseph Woodhouse of Wolfscote, in Hartington (Derb.), who sold it in 1681 to John Beresford of Newton Grange, in Ashbourne (Derb.).[64] In 1723 John Beresford sold the manor to George Osborne, who was living there by 1739.[65] Osborne and his son Marcellus sold it in 1746 to Walter, Lord Aston, on condition that Lord Aston would lease part of it to them for 99 years. Disputes arose, continuing after the death of Lord Aston in 1748 and that of his son and heir James in 1751. An agreement was made in 1761 between the Osbornes and the guardian of James's daughters and coheirs Mary and Barbara. The estate was divided, Beresford Hall and the manorial rights being assigned to the Osbornes.[66] Marcellus had succeeded his father by 1766 and was then living at Beresford.[67] The house and some 80 a. were later bought by a Mr. Jebb, apparently of Chesterfield (Derb.), whose son owned the property in 1815.[68]

The manor and nearly 90 a. were bought in 1825 by William, Viscount Beresford, who had been buying portions of the estate since 1823.[69] The estate extended into Sheen parish, where Viscount Beresford owned 94 a. in 1845.[70] In 1832 he married his cousin Louisa, widow of Thomas Hope, and on his death in 1854 the Beresford estate passed to Louisa's youngest son, Alexander James Beresford Hope, who then changed his surname to Beresford-Hope.[71] In 1887 he was succeeded by his son Philip, who sold the 500-a. estate in 1901 to F. W. Green of York.[72] At first Green periodically lived at Bank Top House (later Beresford Manor) in Sheen, but having enlarged Beresford Cottage south of the site of Beresford Hall, he moved there.[73] In 1924 he sold the estate to F. S. Brice, a Leicester hosiery manufacturer, who used it as a country home and fishing ground and whose executors put it up for sale in 1932.[74] The Beresford Cottage estate was bought from the Robinson family c. 1960 by Rodney Felton, who sold the house to John Downes in the late 1980s.[75]

Beresford Hall as it survived in the 19th century was a stone building which consisted of a south entrance front of perhaps the mid 17th century at a right angle to a wing on its west end of perhaps the later 16th century.[76] In 1666 the hall was assessed for tax on nine hearths.[77] It was occupied as a farmhouse by 1815 and was in a dilapidated state.[78] In 1836 it was noted that some of the roofs had fallen in, but it was stated in 1838 that the south front was 'in tolerable order'. In the earlier 1840s the part not used as a farmhouse was roofless so that 'the wind whistles through its deserted halls, the windows being without casements'.[79] Even before succeeding to the estate A. J. B. Hope had plans for rebuilding the hall with William Butterfield as architect, and in 1858 much of it was pulled down.[80] A carriage road to the site was made from the Hartington road in Sheen in 1859 and planted with trees.[81] The plans for rebuilding were abandoned, but ruins remained on the site of the hall into the 20th century; most of the trees forming the avenue were cut down early in the century.[82] In 1905 F. W. Green rebuilt a tower on the hilltop east of the site of the hall, retaining the existing basement and probably using stone from the remains of the hall.[83] He

54 *S.H.C.* xi. 86; xii (1), 12, 17–18; xiv (1), 57; Beresford, *Beresford of Beresford*, i. 42.
55 *S.H.C.* xiv (1), 57; xvi. 9; D.R.O., D. 2375M/55/3, deed of 19 Oct. 1354.
56 *S.H.C.* xiii. 12. 57 D.R.O., D. 158M/Z3.
58 Beresford, *Beresford of Beresford*, i. 59–65 (with some of the refs. to *S.H.C.* N.S. iii incorrectly dated), 68, and pedigree facing p. 13; *Cal. Fine R.* 1413–22, 221; 1445–52, 38; *Cal. Pat.* 1452–61, 622; P.R.O., C 3/205/2.
59 P.R.O., C 142/40/130. 60 Ibid. C 142/71/80.
61 Beresford, *Beresford of Beresford*, i. 75.
62 Ibid. 80–1, 84–6. 63 Ibid. 88–90; *D.N.B.*
64 S.R.O., D. 538/C/13/8; W.S.L., M. 67.
65 S.R.O., D. 554/155, will of Hall Walton 1743; D. 583/3. 66 Ibid. D. 583/3; *Complete Peerage*, i. 287.
67 S.R.O., D. 538/A/5/45; D. 554/47/23, p. 1.
68 B.L. Add. MS. 36653 (1), ff. 39, 43; W.S.L., M. 47.
69 *Staffs. Advertiser*, 2 July 1825; H. W. and I. Law, *Bk. of the Beresford Hopes*, 80 n. 70 L.J.R.O., B/A/15/Sheen.
71 Law, *Beresford Hopes*, 73, 106; *Complete Peerage*, ii. 118; *D.N.B.* s.v. Hope.
72 Law, *Beresford Hopes*, 238, 242; H. de la P. Beresford, *Bk. of the Beresfords* (Chichester, 1977), 97.
73 Nicoll, *Sheen*, 78; Beresford, *Bk. of Beresfords*, 97;

Kelly's Dir. Staffs. s.v. Sheen (1904; 1908); ibid. s.v. Fawfieldhead (1912; 1916; 1924).
74 Beresford, *Bk. of Beresfords*, 97; *Kelly's Dir. Staffs.* s.v. Fawfieldhead (1928); Beresford estate sale cats. 1924, 1932 (copies in possession of Mr. A. Shipley of Raikes Farm, Sheen). Mr. and Mrs. Shipley are thanked for their help.
75 Inf. from Mr. Felton's son, who is thanked for his help.
76 Heywood, *Cotton and his River*, pp. viii, 45–6, 58, and pls. facing pp. 1, 45; B.L. Add. MS. 36653 (1), f. 38v.; below, plate 22. 77 *S.H.C.* 1925, 233.
78 B.L. Add. MS. 36653 (1), f. 43.
79 Heywood, *Cotton and his River*, 54–5.
80 Law, *Beresford Hopes*, 186–7; F. Manning, *Series of Views intended to illustrate Charles Cotton's Work* (n.d., intro. dated 1866), intro.
81 Copy of letter from Edm. Woodisse of Raikes 4 June 1859 in possession of Mr. Shipley; O.S. Map 6", Staffs. IX. NE. (1884 edn.).
82 Law, *Beresford Hopes*, 187; Heywood, *Cotton and his River*, 46; O.S. Map 6", Staffs. IX. NE. (1884, 1900, 1924 edns.). Piles of worked stone remained on the site in 1994.
83 Heywood, *Cotton and his River*, 47, 58; date stone inscribed F/WG 1905 on tower.

also laid out a yew walk with statuary along the slope west of the tower and made a terrace garden overlooking the Dove;[84] though overgrown, both survived in 1994.

In 1674 Charles Cotton built what he described as 'my poor fishing house, my seat's best grace', in a bend of the Dove north of the hall. It is a square stone building with a pyramidal roof surmounted by a sundial and ball. The keystone over the door bears the intertwined initials of Walton and Cotton, and above it is the inscription 'Piscatoribus Sacrum' with the date. The interior consists of a single room, described in *The Compleat Angler* as 'finely wainscoted, and all exceeding neat, with a marble table and all in the middle'. A description of 1784 stated that it was paved with black and white marble and that on the larger panels of the wainscoting there were paintings of nearby scenery with people fishing and on the smaller panels paintings of fishing tackle. There was also a buffet with portraits on its folding doors of Cotton with a boy servant and of Walton; on the door of the cupboard underneath were pictures of a trout and a grayling, the fish which formed the subject of Cotton's contribution to *The Compleat Angler*. By 1784 the building was decaying, inside and out, and by 1811 the floor and wainscoting had been removed and the table was in pieces.[85] The structure is now in good repair. There is a 17th-century stone bench standing to the south.

The estate known as *GATEHAM GRANGE* may have originated in the half of Alstonefield given to Combermere abbey by Hugh Malbank in 1133 as part of its endowment.[86] When the king confirmed the abbey's estates in 1253 its only property in Alstonefield apart from the church was land called Gateham which William the priest had formerly held, 1 bovate of land, common pasture, and pasture in the forest for the abbey's mares.[87] The abbey held 1 carucate at Gateham in 1291.[88] In 1532 it leased a grange at Gateham and tithes in the neighbourhood to Ralph Beresford for 80 years. At the dissolution of the abbey in 1538 the grange passed to the Crown, which in 1587 granted a 50-year lease of the grange and tithes to Sir Robert Constable, to take effect on the expiry of the earlier lease.[89] Matthew Beresford, tenant by 1594, was still the tenant at his death in 1616,[90] and Widow Beresford was in occupation in the earlier 1630s.[91]

Meanwhile in 1599 the Crown sold the grange and its tithes to John Harpur.[92] Gateham Grange then descended with Alstonefield manor and was sold as part of the Harpur Crewe estate in 1951 to P. I. Robinson. In 1952 he sold it to the tenant, Ralph Adams, who sold it in 1984 to Robert Flower.[93] The present house is of the 19th century, but the western gable and part of the back wall are of the 17th century.

Thomas of Parwich held a manor of *NARROWDALE* in 1292 or 1293 by grant of John of Narrowdale and his wife Sabina.[94] Thomas was living at Narrowdale in 1292[95] and was still alive in 1299.[96] No further mention of the manor is known, and it may have been absorbed into Beresford.[97]

Before the Conquest *STANSHOPE* was held by Wudia, but by 1086 it had passed to the king.[98] In 1227 the king granted to Henry de Audley land there which had belonged to the Stanshope family, and land in Stanshope was part of Thomas de Audley's share of Alstonefield manor at his death in 1307.[99] In the later 1550s the village of Stanshope was described as within Alstonefield lordship.[1]

A house in Stanshope held in 1515 or 1516 by William Jackson[2] may have been the house which formed part of the estate in Stanshope held by Robert Jackson at his death in 1556. He left the estate to his wife Alice and his son William jointly, with reversion of the whole to William.[3] William, who secured Henry Sacheverell's share of Alstonefield manor in 1566 and lived at Stanshope, died in 1613.[4] He was succeeded by his son Henry, whose son and heir Philip was associated with him in conveyances of property elsewhere in Alstonefield in 1616.[5] Philip compounded in 1631 for failure to receive knighthood at Charles I's coronation in 1626.[6] He was an active parliamentarian during the Civil War. Appointed captain of foot in 1642, he rose to the rank of colonel. He appears to have played a prominent part in the Moorlanders' attack on the royalist garrison at Stafford in 1643, and later the same year he was nominated to the parliamentary committee at Stafford.[7] In 1664 he was disclaimed at a heraldic visitation.[8] He was succeeded in 1675 by his son William, who died in 1679.[9] William's heir was his brother Henry, a parliamentarian captain in the Civil War and considered by Charles Cotton 'an admirable fly

84 Inscribed stone beside the walk; O.S. Map 6", Staffs. IX. NE. (1924 edn.).

85 Heywood, *Cotton and his River*, 49–52, 55, 65; below, plate 63. Mr. Michael Collins, the owner of the fishing house, is thanked for his help.

86 Above, this section (Alstonefield manor).

87 *Cal. Chart. R.* 1226–57, 428. A further confirmation in 1331 mentioned 2 bovates: ibid. 1327–41, 204.

88 *Tax. Eccl.* (Rec. Com.), 252.

89 *V.C.H. Ches.* iii. 155; P.R.O., C 66/1295, mm. 27–9.

90 D.R.O., D. 2375M/57/1, 8 May 15 Jas. I; D. 2375M/90/8/2; *Alstonfield Par. Reg.* 120.

91 D.R.O., D. 2375M/63/53, p. 133.

92 P.R.O., C 66/1498, mm. 25–30.

93 Inf. from Mr. Adams. Mr. Flower is thanked for his help.

94 D.R.O., D. 2375M/55/3, deed of 20 Sept. 1292; *S.H.C.* 1911, 46–7.   95 *S.H.C.* vi (1), 205.

96 Ibid. vii (1), 35, 46–7, 63.

97 D.R.O., D. 158M/Z2; above, Alstonefield, par. intro.

(manorial govt.).

98 *V.C.H. Staffs.* iv. 41 (giving Wudia as Wodie).

99 *Cal. Chart. R.* 1226–37, 37; *S.H.C.* N.S. xi. 257 (where Stanscip should read Stansop: *Cal. Inq. p.m.* v, p. 28).

1 D.R.O., D. 2375M/7/2, exemplification 1582 of interrogatory under writ of 1555.

2 Ibid. D. 2375M/171/1/2.

3 L.J.R.O., B/C/11, Rob. Jackson (1556).

4 *S.H.C.* xiii. 294; *S.H.C.* 1929, 56; 1930, 71; 1935, 13; 1940, 196; *Alstonfield Par. Reg.* 117; D.R.O., D. 2375M/56/4, deed of 25 Jan. 1669/70; above, this section (Alstonefield manor).

5 D.R.O., D. 2375M/56/4, deed of 25 Jan. 1669/70; *Alstonfield Par. Reg.* 88, 99; *S.H.C.* vi (1), 18–19.

6 *S.H.C.* ii (2), 17.

7 *S.H.C.* 4th ser. i. 352; ii. 19–20, 46; *Chronicles* (autumn 1994), 9.   8 *S.H.C.* v (2), 187, 345.

9 *Alstonfield Par. Reg.* 75, 217, 225; D.R.O., D. 2375M/56/4, deed of 25 Jan. 1669/70; L.J.R.O., B/C/11, Wm. Jackson (1681).

angler'.[10] He sold the Stanshope estate to John Jackson, a London merchant, in 1699 but continued to live there until his death in 1702.[11]

By 1704 John Jackson had been succeeded by his niece Mary, wife of Sir Raphe Assheton. By her will of 1720 Dame Mary, then a widow, left the estate to Strelley Pegge, great-grandson of Philip Jackson's sister Ann. Strelley secured possession in 1724 and was living at Stanshope in 1735, although by 1758 he was living at Beauchief (Derb.). In 1767 he conveyed the Stanshope estate to William Manley.[12] By the 1790s Manley was trying to sell it. He was declared bankrupt in 1799, and in 1800 the estate, consisting of two farmhouses and c. 300 a., was bought by a Mr. Harrop.[13] In 1825 the owner was John Harrop, a Lancashire cotton manufacturer.[14] George Beardmore was farming at Stanshope in 1834, and by 1851 the estate was owned by Ralph Beardmore.[15] He died in 1880, and his son Ralph continued at Stanshope until his death in 1910, leaving a son Ralph as his heir.[16] In 1912 the hall and 60 a. were offered for sale.[17] By 1918 the hall and 53 a. were let separately from the rest of the 129-a. estate, the whole of which was bought that year by J. B. Smith. He was still farming there in 1940.[18] He later sold the house to Ian Hall. In 1972 it was bought by Andrew Brownsfoot, who sold it in 1986 to Naomi Chambers and Nicholas Lourie, the owners in 1994.[19]

Stanshope Hall forms an H-plan. The west wing seems originally to have been a two-roomed house of c. 1600 with a gable chimney. The central range was added early in the 17th century and the east wing late in the same century. In 1666 the house was assessed for tax on nine hearths.[20] The south front was remodelled in the late 18th century, when the west gable was rebuilt with windows in place of the original stack. The east front was refaced probably at the same time; it is in red brick with a rusticated door surround and quoins. In the 19th century a bay window was added to the south front and service additions were made at the rear.[21]

The *RECTORY* of Alstonefield was held by Combermere abbey as part of its endowment by Hugh Malbank in 1133.[22] On the dissolution of the abbey in 1538 it passed to the Crown, which sold it in 1599 to John Harpur. From 1505, however, it was held by members of the Beres-

ford family under a series of leases, the last of which was due to expire in 1637.[23] The rectory, which in 1604 was said to be worth £200,[24] then descended with Alstonefield manor. By the late 16th century it had long been customary for the freeholders of Malbon Frith to pay cash in lieu of rectorial tithes.[25] By then too the owners or occupiers of a farm at Hardings Booth, in Heathylee, paid 2s. 7d. in lieu of rectorial tithes, but in the late 1630s Sir John Harpur tried to secure payment in kind.[26] Under the inclosure award of 1839 covering much of the parish, Sir George Crewe as impropriator was allotted lands worth £400 in lieu of great tithes.[27] In 1848 his son Sir John was granted a rent charge of £40 in lieu of great tithes in Longnor and in 1850 a rent charge of £15 10s. 6d. in lieu of great tithes in Upper Elkstone.[28]

In 1535 the subtenant of part of the tithes held a tithe barn.[29] Sir John Harpur's tithe barn at Alstonefield was repaired three times between 1702 and 1713.[30] There was a tithe barn at Warslow in the mid 17th century and probably in the later 1670s.[31]

Tutbury priory had land at Westside in the earlier 1420s.[32]

ECONOMIC HISTORY. AGRICULTURE. In 1086 Alstonefield had land for 3 ploughteams. There was 1 team in demesne, and a *villanus* had another. There were 8 a. of meadow, and woodland was 1 league in length and ½ league in breadth. The manor, including Warslow, was worth 40s.[33] Stanshope had land for 1 or 2 ploughteams.[34]

In the earlier 1630s Sir John Harpur's tenants held 1,347 a. in Alstonefield township, consisting of 475 a. of arable, 855 a. of pasture, and 17 a. of meadow. Freeholders held a further 1,398 a. There were then at least 11 open fields.[35] They included Crosslake field south of Alstonefield village, still an open field in 1709,[36] and Hall field west of the village. The hayward appointed for the township in 1728 was described as serving for Hall field and the common pastures, and Hall field was mentioned as a common field in 1730.[37] Another of the fields of the earlier 1630s, Warrilow field north-west of Stanshope, evidently belonged to that hamlet only, and it seems to have remained partially uninclosed in the late 18th century.[38] By the mid 16th century an open

10 *Alstonfield Par. Reg.* 76, 267; *S.H.C.* 4th ser. ii. 46; Plot, *Staffs.* 193; Heywood, *Cotton and his River*, 32; D.R.O., D. 161, box 5/69; D. 2375M/56/4, deed of 25 Jan. 1669/70.
11 S.R.O., D. (W.) 1747/24/2, pp. 1–2; *Alstonfield Par. Reg.* 267.
12 S.R.O., D. (W.) 1747/24/2; J. Hunter, *Hallamshire* (1819), 199.   13 S.R.O., D. (W.) 1747/24/4.
14 Ibid. D. (W.) 1702/7/4, sched. of Stanshope title deeds.
15 White, *Dir. Staffs.* (1834), 720; (1851), 745.
16 Memorial tablet in Alstonefield church.
17 D.R.O., D. 247B/ES391.
18 Ibid. D. 216B/ES1/5 (60); *Kelly's Dir. Staffs.* (1924; 1940).   19 Inf. from Naomi Chambers.
20 *S.H.C.* 1925, 239.
21 Below, plates 29, 30. The date stone of the 1780s on the gable probably refers to the work.
22 Below, church.
23 P.R.O., C 66/1498, mm. 25–30.
24 *E.H.R.* xxvi. 341.

25 D.R.O., D. 2375M/54/4, deed of 6 July 1581; P.R.O., E 134/21 & 22 Chas. II Hil./22.
26 L.J.R.O., B/C/5/Alstonefield, 1639 (tithe).
27 S.R.O., Q/RDc 24.
28 L.J.R.O., B/A/15/Longnor; ibid. Upper Elkstone.
29 *S.H.C.* 1912, 79.
30 D.R.O., D. 2375M/103/11, disbursements 1701–2; D. 2375M/103/11/5 and 9.
31 Ibid. D. 2375M/139/24; D. 2375/190/3, deed of 30 Sept. 1654.
32 Ibid. D. 2375M/1/1, ct. of 2 Hen. VI.
33 *V.C.H. Staffs.* iv. 47.   34 Ibid. 41.
35 D.R.O., D. 2375M/63/53, pp. 115–36; there is no breakdown of arable, pasture, and meadow for the freeholders. Mr. F. J. Johnson of Checkley is thanked for his help.
36 D.R.O., D. 2375M/174/1, 21 Oct. 1709.
37 Ibid. 14 Oct. 1728, 24 Apr. 1730.
38 Ibid. D. 2375M/63/53, p. 115; S.R.O., D. (W.) 1747/24/5. For the separate pinfold at Stanshope see below, local govt. (manorial govt.).

field known variously as Stanshope field and Ilam field had been created out of part of Ilam moor, and although in Ilam parish, it was treated as part of Alstonefield manor. In winter, however, the inhabitants of Ilam were allowed to pasture their beasts there along with those of Stanshope.[39]

The main areas of common pasture in the earlier 1630s were Gratton hill, with stints varying between ¼ and 2¾ gates, Hope heath (40 a.), Hope dale (100 a.), Hope marsh (146 a.), Narrowdale and Gateham Grange hills (106 a.), and Westside moor (302 a.).[40] Two of the three farms in Stanshope held by Sir John Harpur's tenants had pasture of respectively 12¾ gates and 8½ gates, evidently in the Stanshope area.[41] In 1818 a group of 32 inhabitants of Alstonefield township appointed five of their number as a committee empowered to take proceedings against outsiders who were trespassing on the commons with their livestock and inhabitants who were exceeding their pasture rights.[42] In 1839, under an Act of 1834 amended in 1836, an extensive area of common pasture was inclosed, consisting of Stanshope pasture (152 a.), Hope and Hopedale commons (14 a.), Alstonefield common and Upper marsh north of the village (73 a.), Narrowdale hill (91 a.), and Archford moor (168 a.).[43]

Sheep were evidently being grazed by 1327 when there was mention of the Sheephouse yard in Alstonefield.[44] A presentment was made in 1401 for overburdening the common pasture with 20 sheep.[45] Sheep were grazed on Gateham hill in the mid 1490s and the mid 1540s.[46] Robert Jackson of Stanshope possessed 160 old sheep and 39 lambs at his death in 1556, and John Jackson of Stanshope had 80 old sheep when he died in 1579. Philip Jackson of Stanshope (d. 1675) had 48 sheep and his son William (d. 1679) 63. William's brother Henry (d. 1702) had 236 sheep and their young, and his house contained wool worth £22.[47] In 1736 a fine of 5s. 10d. was imposed for putting sheep on Alstonefield marsh, Hope marsh, Hope green, and Greenhill; it was raised to 10s. in 1738, 'they being places subject to rot sheep, which is a disreputation to the rest of the sheep in the neighbourhood'.[48]

In the mid 20th century dairy farming predominated. All nine of the larger farms on the Harpur Crewe estate in Alstonefield civil parish which were offered for sale in 1951 were dairy farms.[49] The later part of the century saw a decline in dairying in favour of cattle rearing and sheep farming. Returns in 1988 listed 2,191 head of cattle, including calves, and 5,387 sheep. Of the 1,345.2 ha. of farmland returned, grassland covered 1,220.1 ha. and rough grazing 115.2 ha. All but one of the 41 farms returned were under 100 ha. in size, 33 of them being under 50 ha.; the remaining one was under 200 ha.[50]

Annual cattle sales, apparently in the yard of the George inn, were recorded in the 1880s and later 1890s.[51] Autumn sheep sales, begun in 1963, were still held in 1994 in a field on the Alstonefield side of the boundary with Sheen at Hulme End. Similar sales were begun on a playing field in Alstonefield village in 1981; by 1994 they were held on land called the Clays.[52]

MILLS. There was a mill in Astonefield manor by 1282.[53] It was probably in Alstonefield township, where a mill can be traced from 1348.[54] That mill was presumably on the Dove in Mill Dale, so named by the late 16th century; a mill there was mentioned in 1658.[55] It probably stood in Milldale hamlet, where there was a mill to the north of Viator's bridge by 1775.[56] A mill on that site ceased to operate in the late 1870s, although the derelict building still stood in the mid 1920s.[57]

Lode mill further upstream at the foot of Lode Lane was evidently newly built in 1814.[58] It continued in operation until c. 1930,[59] and the 19th-century mill building still stands.

Westside mill on the Manifold in the northwest corner of the township existed by 1584.[60] A mill there was worked in the late 1880s by J. W. Bassett of Hulme End, who was also a builder and contractor. He continued there in the early 20th century, but by 1924 the mill had passed to John Wilshaw Bassett & Sons, who worked it until c. 1930.[61]

There is said to have been a mill in Beresford Dale in 1658.[62]

TRADE AND INDUSTRY. In the 1680s Robert Plot recorded that limestone was dug 'in great plenty' along the banks of the Dove from Beresford downstream.[63] In the late 1870s there were two quarries near the parish boundary west of Steep Low, each with an old limekiln nearby, and there were also two quarries at Narrowdale. In 1898

39 D.R.O., D. 2375M/7/2, exemplification 1582 of interrogatory under writ of 1555.
40 Ibid. D. 2375M/63/53, pp. 119–25, 136.
41 Ibid. pp. 115–16.   42 S.R.O., D. 3920/2/1.
43 4 & 5 Wm. IV, c. 15 (Priv. Act); 6 & 7 Wm. IV, c. 6 (Priv. Act); S.R.O., Q/RDc 24, maps V, VI; D.R.O., D. 2375M/282/8/1.
44 D.R.O., D. 2375M/55/3, deed of 25 Oct. 1327.
45 Ibid. D. 2375M/1/6, ct. of Fri. before feast of Ascension 2 Hen. IV.
46 Ibid. D. 2375M/1/1, 2nd ct. 11 Hen. VII; D. 2375M/57/1, 16 Apr. 3 Jas. I.
47 L.J.R.O., B/C/11, Rob. Jackson (1556), John Jackson (1578/9), Phil. Jackson (1677), Wm. Jackson (1681), Hen. Jackson (1702).
48 D.R.O., D. 2375M/174/1, 23 Oct. 1736, 5 Oct. 1738.
49 W.S.L., S.C. E/3/27.
50 P.R.O., MAF 68/6128/52; inf. from Mr. Adams.
51 S.R.O., D. 3805/1/1, pp. 132, 143, 186–7, 200, 209, 376, 409; Alstonefield, ed. Edwards, 21–2.
52 Inf. from Mr. and Mrs. Adams.
53 S.H.C. N.S. xi. 247.
54 S.H.C. xii (1), 93.
55 D.R.O., D. 2375M/57/1, 6 Apr. 36 Eliz. I; Alstonfield Par. Reg. 176.
56 Above, fig. 2; below, plate 65.
57 P.O. Dir. Staffs. (1876); Kelly's Dir. Staffs. (1880); O.S. Map 6", Staffs. IX. SE. (1884 edn.); for the ruin see Heywood, Cotton and his River, 29.
58 B.L. Add. MS. 36653 (1), f. 20v.; B.L. Maps, O.S.D. 348; J. Phillips and W. F. Hutchings, Map of County of Stafford (1832).
59 Kelly's Dir. Staffs. (1928); D.R.O., D. 2375M/131/20, letters of May 1932.
60 D.R.O., D. 2375M/103/85/8.
61 Kelly's Dir. Staffs. (1888 and later edns. to 1928; s.v. Sheen); Nicoll, Sheen, 79; P.R.O., RG 12/2754; O.S. Map 6", Staffs. IX. NW. (1887, 1919 edns.).
62 Beresford, Beresford of Beresford, i. 87 n., 88.
63 Plot, Staffs. 152–3, 174.

there was a quarry on the road between Hopedale and Milldale and in 1919 a disused quarry on Archford moor.[64] In the later 19th century several stonemasons were recorded, notably at Milldale.[65]

Plot mentioned that there was copper ore around Beresford, though it had never been thought worth digging.[66] In the 1840s, however, it was stated that copper had been mined there.[67] Miners, some of them lead miners, were living in the Archford moor area in the mid and later 19th century,[68] but they were probably working elsewhere.

Samuel Mellor of Alstonefield, owner of the George inn when he was declared bankrupt in 1826, was also described as a cheese factor, dealer, and chapman. He was still a cheese factor living in Alstonefield in 1834.[69] Other Alstonefield cheese factors were Bartholomew Massey in the earlier 1850s, Anthony Massey by 1860 and until the earlier 1890s, and George Hambleton in the 1860s and early 1870s.[70] A cheese factory was opened at Hopedale in 1878 by 20 local farmers trading as Alstonfield Dairy Association. By 1916 the factory was run by Dovedale Dairy Association Ltd. and by 1924 by Derbyshire Farmers Ltd. It closed c. 1930 and was later converted into a private house.[71]

LOCAL GOVERNMENT. MANORIAL GOVERNMENT.

Alstonefield township formed a tithing in Alstonefield manor,[72] and by the late 1390s it sent four frankpledges to the twice-yearly view. Beresford, in the detached part of Fawfieldhead, formed another tithing, with one frankpledge.[73] Narrowdale was part of Beresford tithing in the earlier 1530s,[74] but it later became part of Alstonefield tithing. In 1594 the four Alstonefield frankpledges were described as for Alstonefield, Stanshope, Hope, and Narrowdale.[75] That continued to be the arrangement, with Narrowdale linked with Gateham and Westside, until 1800, when the number of what were then styled headboroughs was reduced from four to one.[76] One headborough still served in 1835.[77]

A manorial pinfold mentioned in 1493[78] may have been in Alstonefield township. By 1595 there was a pinner for Alstonefield village and

Hope and another for Stanshope; they also served as haywards. By custom the responsibility for providing the pinner and hayward for Alstonefield and Hope fell on a different pair of householders each year, rotating among all the householders in each place; they or the person serving were recompensed by the other inhabitants at the rate of a thrave of oats for every ploughland held.[79] There were still two pinners in 1609, but there appears to have been only one by 1611.[80] In 1620 two haywards were appointed for Alstonefield and one each for Hope and Stanshope.[81] One person was evidently serving as pinner and hayward for the whole township by 1698, and a pinner was still appointed in 1835.[82] There was a pinfold at Stanshope in 1713[83] and one at Alstonefield in 1852.[84] In the late 1870s there was a pinfold by the crossroads on Archford moor; the structure evidently still stood in 1901.[85]

Four surveyors of the highways were appointed for Alstonefield township by the manor court in 1601, one each for Alstonefield village, Hope, Stanshope, and Narrowdale with Gateham and Westside.[86] The four were still appointed in 1683.[87] There was a surveyor for Milldale in 1735.[88]

TOWNSHIP GOVERNMENT AND POOR RELIEF. Alstonefield township formed the division of the ancient parish known as the part below Archford bridge, and two of the parish's four churchwardens were for the township.[89] It ran its own poor relief. In 1766 its overseer collaborated with the overseers of several other parishes and townships, including Warslow and Onecote, in Leek, in the establishment of a workhouse at Ipstones.[90] In 1770 Elizabeth Mellor of Wetton conveyed a cottage in Alstonefield township to the churchwardens and overseer for use as a poorhouse.[91] By the 1820s there were several such parish houses, but they belonged to Sir George Crewe, whose agent in 1829 gave the overseer notice to quit.[92]

The township was one of several parishes and townships in Staffordshire and Derbyshire included in Alstonefield union formed, evidently in 1817 or 1818, under Gilbert's Act of 1782; no other part of Alstonefield parish was a member. A house in the village, possibly the former Black

64 O.S. Map 6", Staffs. IX. NE. (1884, 1924 edns.); SE. (1884, 1901 edns.).
65 P.R.O., HO 107/2146; ibid. RG 9/2522; RG 10/3600; RG 11/3424; RG 12/2754.
66 Plot, Staffs. 165.
67 R. Garner, Nat. Hist. of County of Stafford (1844), 226.
68 P.R.O., HO 107/1003; ibid. RG 9/2522; RG 10/3600.
69 D.R.O., D. 2375M/67/20, deeds of 24 and 25 Mar. 1826; White, Dir. Staffs. (1834), 720.
70 P.O. Dir. Staffs. (1850 and later edns.); Kelly's Dir. Staffs. (1880; 1892); White, Dir. Staffs. (1851), 745.
71 D.R.O., D. 2375M/207/62, corresp. about Hopedale cheese factory; Kelly's Dir. Staffs. (1880 and later edns. to 1928); Alstonfield, ed. Edwards, 51.
72 Above, Alstonefield, par. intro. (manorial govt.).
73 D.R.O., D. 2375M/1/6, undated view following small ct. of Thurs. after feast of St. Peter and St. Paul 23 Ric. II.
74 Ibid. 2375/M/1/6, 25 Apr. 22 Hen. VIII to 21 Oct. 25 Hen. VIII.
75 Ibid. D. 2375M/57/1, 6 Apr. 36 Eliz. I.
76 Ibid. D. 2375M/174/1. Narrowdale was first so linked

in 1611: D. 2375M/57/1, 3 Apr. 9 Jas. I.
77 Ibid. D. 2375M/282/9/7, list of inhabitants of Alstonefield 1835.
78 P.R.O., SC 6/Hen. VII/679, m. 6d.
79 D.R.O., D. 2375M/57/1, 2 May 37 Eliz. I, 24 Apr. 1628.
80 Ibid. 8 Apr. 6 Jas. I, 6 Apr. 7 Jas. I, 3 Apr. 9 Jas. I, 22 Apr. 13 Jas. I.   81 Ibid. 4 May 18 Jas. I.
82 Ibid. D. 2375M/174/1, 12 May 1698, 23 Oct. 1702, 27 Apr. 1727; D. 2375M/282/9/7, list of ihabitants of Alstonefield 1835.   83 Ibid. D. 2375M/174/1, 22 Oct. 1713.
84 Ibid. D. 2375M/202/19, f. 28.
85 O.S. Map 6", Staffs. IX. NE. (1884, 1900 edns.); Alstonfield Par. Mag. Feb. 1901.
86 D.R.O., D. 2375M/57/1, 3 Apr. 42 Eliz. I.
87 Ibid. D. 2375M/54/5, 19 Apr. 1683.
88 Ibid. D. 2375M/174/1, 23 Oct. 1735.
89 Above, Alstonefield, par. intro.
90 S.R.O., D. 925/5/25.
91 D.R.O., D. 2375M/56/20, deed of 22 Sept. 1770.
92 Ibid. D. 2375M/93/12, sheet headed 'Recovering parish houses'.

Lion inn, was leased and converted into a workhouse for the union, in use probably from 1819.[93] At the beginning of June 1823 it had 16 male inmates and 13 female; in the earlier 1830s the inmates were employed mainly in breaking stone and working marble slabs from the quarries at Wetton.[94] In 1821 there were 14 parishes and townships in Alstonefield union; there were 21 by 1823 and 43 by 1837.[95] The union resisted attempts by the poor-law commissioners from 1837 to suppress it,[96] and the workhouse continued in use, with 34 inmates in 1841, 19 in 1851, and 21 in 1861.[97] In 1869 Alstonefield union was dissolved and the township became part of Ashbourne poor-law union.[98] The workhouse was closed and in 1871 was described as three uninhabited buildings.[99] By 1985 the building was occupied as three houses.[1]

CHURCH. Although the earliest features of the present church are Norman, Anglo-Saxon carved stones survive on the site, most of them parts of standing crosses.[2] The church's dedication to St. Peter, recorded in 1533,[3] may also suggest a pre-Conquest foundation, that being the most common early Anglo-Saxon dedication.[4] The church served a large parish, with dependent chapels at Longnor, Warslow, and Elkstone in the Middle Ages. A chapel was opened at Flash in 1744. In 1902 separate parishes were created for Flash, Longnor, and what had become Warslow with Elkstone.

Alstonefield church was included in Hugh Malbank's endowment of Combermere abbey in 1133, and Richard Peche, bishop of Coventry 1161–82, licensed the monks to appropriate it.[5] A vicarage had been ordained by the late 13th century.[6] The abbey was dissolved in 1538,[7] and the advowson of the vicarage was retained by the Crown until the end of the century. In 1564 the lessees of the rectory, Laurence and Thomas Beresford, presented.[8] In 1599 the Crown sold the advowson with the rectory to John Harpur,[9] and it then descended with Alstonefield manor, Harpur being described as patron in 1604 and 1607.[10] From 1940 the benefice was held in plurality with that of Wetton.[11] In 1985 it was united with the benefices of Butterton, Warslow with Elkstone, and Wetton, although the parishes remained distinct. The patronage of the

united benefice was vested jointly in the trustees of the Harpur-Crewe estate as patrons of Alstonefield, the bishop of Lichfield as patron of Wetton, and the vicar of Mayfield as patron of Butterton. Alstonefield was made the vicar's place of residence.[12]

By 1535 the vicar received 6s. 8d. a year from glebe, £6 from the Easter roll (evidently 3d. from every house), and £1 from offerings, with 13s. 4d. from tithe of hay and 13s. 4d. from tithe of calves (and probably other small tithes).[13] In the late 1540s the tenant of Gateham Grange claimed that by custom and by the terms of his lease he paid the vicar one load of hay for all tithes; by the 1590s the load of hay was in lieu of tithe of corn and hay and the tenant also paid 4d. to the vicar and 4d. to the clerk in lieu of small tithes.[14] In 1604 the vicarage was stated to be worth £30.[15] There were 4 a. of glebe by 1612.[16] In 1646 the vicarial tithes were stated to be worth £40 a year in the best times but only £10 'in these times'. The committee for plundered ministers therefore granted the vicar £50 out of the impropriate rectory sequestrated from Sir John Harpur, changing the grant later the same year to £50 from the sequestrated rectory of Pattingham.[17] By 1698 Easter payments consisted of house dues of 3d. from every house in the parish and offerings of 2d. from everyone over 16, except for servant maids who paid 1d.; 2d. was paid for every mare and foal and 2d. for every stall of bees. The former Frith mill in Heathylee paid 4s. at Easter and Longnor mill, also in Heathylee, 1s. 8d. Some tithes, including tithe of hay, were then paid in cash, but those of geese, pigs, and calves were paid in kind; tithe of eggs was paid in kind in Alstonefield township only. Gateham Grange paid 6s. 8d. in lieu of all vicarial tithes.[18] In 1705 the annual income of the vicarage was given as c. £30.[19] A grant of £600 was made from Queen Anne's Bounty in 1816 and another of £300 in 1823 to meet a benefaction that year of £200 from the vicar, John Simpson.[20] The net income c. 1830 was £112, and there were still 4 a. of glebe, including the garden of the vicarage house.[21] Under the inclosure award of 1839 covering much of the parish the vicar was allotted land worth £300 in lieu of most of the small tithes and moduses, and in 1841 the land belonging to the vicar amounted to 366 a.[22] The vicarial tithes and moduses of

93 Ibid. Alstonefield workhouse; S.R.O., D. 5131/3/5/63; D. 5131/3/5/83–4.
94 Ibid. D. 5131/3/5/6; White, *Dir. Staffs.* (1834), 716.
95 Ibid. D. 5131/3/5/6; D. 5131/3/5/62–3.
96 D.R.O., D. 239M/O317 sqq.
97 P.R.O., HO 107/1003; HO 107/2146; ibid. RG 9/2522.
98 D.R.O., D. 520C/W1/8, p. 381.
99 P.R.O., RG 10/3600.
1 *Alstonefield*, ed. Edwards, 31. For a view of the building see below, plate 55.
2 Below, this section.
3 L.J.R.O., B/C/11, Edw. Tetyryngton (1533).
4 W. Levison, *Eng. and the Continent in the Eighth Cent.* 259–61.
5 *V.C.H. Ches.* iii. 150–1.
6 D.R.O., D. 2375M/55/3, undated deed witnessed by the son of Ralph, vicar of Alstonefield; *S.H.C.* N.S. xi. 208; *Cal. Pat.* 1317–21, 466.
7 *V.C.H. Ches.* iii. 155.
8 *Cal. Pat.* 1560–2, 416; 1563–6, p. 144; *S.H.C.* 1915,

9, 12.
9 P.R.O., C 66/1498, mm. 25–30.
10 *E.H.R.* xxvi. 341; D.R.O., D. 2375M/23/2, answers of John Croft, vicar of Alstonefield (1604–7: *S.H.C.* 1915, 9).
11 *Lich. Dioc. Dir.* (1940–1); Lich. Dioc. Regy., Bp.'s Reg. R, p. 296.
12 Lich. Dioc. Regy., Bp.'s Reg. S (Orders in Council), p. 76; *Lich. Dioc. Dir.* (1993). The patron of Warslow with Elkstone was the vicar of Alstonefield.
13 D.R.O., D. 2375M/116/13; L.J.R.O., B/C/5/1549, Alstonefield (tithe).
14 L.J.R.O., B/C/5/1549, Alstonefield (tithe); D.R.O., D. 2375M/90/8/2.
15 *S.H.C.* 1915, 12.
16 L.J.R.O., B/V/6/Alstonefield, 1612.
17 *S.H.C.* 1915, 12.
18 L.J.R.O., B/V/6/Alstonefield, 1698.
19 Ibid. 1705.
20 Hodgson, *Bounty of Queen Anne*, pp. cxcix, ccxcv.
21 *Rep. Com. Eccl. Revenues*, 459; *S.H.C.* 4th ser. x. 76.
22 S.R.O., Q/RDc 24; S.R.O., D. 922/20.

Longnor were commuted in 1848 for a rent charge of £29 with another of £1 in respect of Easter payments; the vicarial tithes and moduses of Upper Elkstone were commuted in 1850 for a rent charge of £20.[23] There were 258 a. of glebe in 1887, with an estimated rental of £310.[24] The income of the benefice in 1936 was £365, consisting of £75 from the Ecclesiastical Commissioners, £44 from Queen Anne's Bounty, £25 from stock, £217 from glebe rents, and £4 from fees. That year c. 70 a. of glebe on the Staffordshire bank of the river Dove were sold to the National Trust.[25]

A vicarage house was mentioned in 1609.[26] Peter Parr, vicar 1714–64, spent £180 'in repairing the vicarage house etc. etc.'[27] J. J. Dewe, on his appointment as vicar in 1821, found the house old and dilapidated and hoped to have a new house built immediately.[28] One was built in the late 1820s, the cost being met partly by Sir George Crewe and partly by a grant of £600 from Queen Anne's Bounty.[29] A new house was built on part of the garden in the mid 1980s.[30]

In 1413 there was a warden of the goods of the Virgin Mary at Alstonefield.[31] In 1533 a priest sang mass in the church every day in honour of Our Lady. There was a rent of 10s. 10d. given for his support, presumably from the cottage and garden in Alstonefield given for the chaplain of Our Lady's Service by one Walker of Castern, in Ilam.[32] There was also a guild of the Blessed Mary at the Reformation.[33] A service of St. Nicholas existed in 1533.[34] In his will of 1556 Robert Jackson of Stanshope left two sheep 'towards the beginning of Our Lady's service again at Alstonefield'; he also wished to be buried as near as possible to 'Our Lady's choir door'.[35] In 1576 Mary, the wife of John Jackson, was buried in Our Lady's choir, and John himself was buried in Our Lady's chapel in 1579.[36] There was a burial in St. Nicholas' choir in 1574.[37] The two choirs were presumably side chapels. John Beresford (d. 1523) made arrangements in his will for a priest at Beresford, presumably at the hall, for three years; John's son and heir Robert was to provide the priest with board, and the executors were to pay him his wage.[38]

Robert Aston, vicar 1564–1604, was also rector of Standon from 1570 and was buried there in 1604. He had no degree and at the end of his life was stated not to be licensed to preach. He was then described as 'a grievous swearer, whore-master, and drunkard, and very unlearned'.[39] Several curates lived in the parish during his incumbency, some of them serving the chapels of ease.[40] The longest serving was Francis Paddy, who arrived in 1577 and was then described as farmer of the vicarage. He was described as minister and curate at the time of his marriage in 1586. He was officiating at Alstonefield c. 1603, but he was stated to be not licensed to preach and without a degree. In 1604, when he was at Longnor, he was described as 'a mere worldling'. At his death in 1617 he was described as minister of Alstonefield.[41] John Bagshawe, who was admitted in 1604 to teach throughout the diocese, also had the duty of reading prayers in Alstonefield church.[42] Aston's successor as vicar, John Croft, was also vicar of Lockington (Leics.). He stated in 1607 that he preached at Alstonefield one Sunday in five, with a curate officiating at other times. He also stated that of the 1,200 or so communicants in the parish barely half attended the parish church rather than the chapels.[43] There was an assistant curate in the later 1760s and in the 1790s.[44] By 1830 there were two services on Sunday, with a lecture on Wednesday evening. The sacrament was celebrated four times a year, and there were 20 to 25 communicants.[45] On Census Sunday 1851 there was a congregation of 79 in the morning and 60 in the afternoon, besides Sunday school children.[46]

By 1900 there was a meeting on Sunday afternoon 'on Archford moor, generally at the Field', presumably Field House Farm.[47] A wooden mission room was built in 1901 near the crossroads on Archford moor, with a service and Sunday school on Sunday afternoon. A bell in a turret was installed in 1902.[48] The mission continued until the early 1960s,[49] and the building still stood in 1994.

A parish magazine was started in 1900.[50]

The parish clerk had duties relating specifically to Alstonefield church. By 1736 he was paid for ringing the curfew bell and by 1764 for looking after the clock. He was still paid for both in 1901. There was a dog whipper for the church by 1726. By 1828 Mary Beresford, the church cleaner, was paid for dog whipping, and the duties of her successor as cleaner were stated in 1841 to include dog whipping.[51]

The church of *ST. PETER* is built of coursed rubble and consists of a chancel, an aisled and clerestoried nave of four bays with north and

23 L.J.R.O., B/A/15/Longnor; ibid. Upper Elkstone.
24 *Return of Glebe Lands*, 62.
25 D.R.O., D. 2375M/131/53.
26 Ibid. D. 2375M/57/1, 6 Apr. 7 Jas. I.
27 *Alstonfield Par. Reg.* 286, 293, 393.
28 L.J.R.O., B/A/3/Quarnford, 1821, J. J. Dewe to bp. 23 Mar. 1821.   29 *S.H.C.* 4th ser. x. 76.
30 *Alstonefield*, ed. Edwards, 8.
31 D.R.O., D. 2375M/1/6, 10 Oct. 1413.
32 *S.H.C.* 1915, 10; *Cal. Pat.* 1550–3, 316; 1563–6, p. 66; D.R.O., D. 2375M/1/3, 21 Oct. 1533.
33 *S.H.C.* 1915, 10.
34 L.J.R.O., B/C/11, Edw. Tetyryngton (1533).
35 Ibid. Rob. Jackson (1556).
36 *Alstonfield Par. Reg.* 34, 37.
37 Ibid. 32.
38 Beresford, *Beresford of Beresford*, i. 69.
39 *S.H.C.* 1915, 12; *Jnl. Derb. Arch. Soc.* vi. 162.

40 *Alstonfield Par. Reg.* 26, 28–9, 30–2, 34, 44, 50, 289; *S.H.C.* 1915, 11. For mention of earlier curates see L.J.R.O., B/C/11, Wm. Adams (1537), Ralph Gylmen (1559).
41 *Alstonfield Par. Reg.* 35, 120, 139, 289; *Jnl. Derb. Arch. Soc.* vi. 161; *E.H.R.* xxvi. 342; L.J.R.O., B/C/11, Fra. Paddy (1618).
42 L.J.R.O., B/A/4/1, f. 8.
43 D.R.O., D. 2375M/23/2, answers of John Croft.
44 L.J.R.O., B/A/3/Alstonefield, 1796; B/A/3/Longnor, 1767, 1769; S.R.O., D. (W.) 1702/7/4, Revd. J. Whitaker's accts.   45 *S.H.C.* 4th ser. x. 76.
46 P.R.O., HO 129/447/4/13.
47 *Alstonfield Par. Mag.* May 1900.
48 Ibid. Feb., Aug., Sept., Oct. 1901; July and Oct. 1902.
49 *Alstonfield Deanery Mag.* lxiv (11).
50 There is a set running from May 1900 to Jan. 1903 (broken for 1900) in W.S.L. 150/709/85–150/739/85.
51 S.R.O., D. 922/35, pp. 31, 55, 126; D. 922/36.

south porches, and a west tower.[52] Evidence for a substantial church by the 12th century is provided by the chancel arch of three orders, the south doorway, which is probably reset, and loose stone fragments kept in the north aisle. When the chancel was rebuilt in the 13th century, it was both wide and long; the nave, which has aisles added at different dates in the 14th century, preserves the length and possibly the width of the early building. The south porch is early 14th-century and is probably contemporary with the south arcade, whereas the north arcade is later. New windows were inserted on each side of the chancel during the 14th century and in the south aisle in the 15th century. The tower was added or rebuilt in the 16th century; in 1534 3s. 4d. was left 'to the building of the steeple'.[53] The north aisle appears to have been largely rebuilt in the 16th century, perhaps at the same time as the clerestory was added; in 1542 a sheep was left for 'the edifying of Alstonefield church'.[54] The east end of the chancel was rebuilt in 1590.[55] An external feature of the north aisle and the clerestory is a chequer pattern of pink blocks and grey rubble; the two lower storeys of the tower have alternating bands of similar pink and grey. The chancel was restored in 1875, and the present east window in 14th-century style was inserted at the same time, in place of the window of 1590, as a memorial to Sir George Crewe (d. 1844).[56] There was a general restoration of the south aisle evidently in 1877.[57] The north porch was added in 1880, the north door having become the main entrance as a result of the earlier realignment of the road past the church.[58] The roofs are 19th-century except for the nave; its roof was renewed in 1984, although the two tiebeams of 1657 and 1797 and the two of 1879 were retained.[59]

Two stone bowls kept in the north aisle may be medieval font bowls; one was found in the churchyard in 1936.[60] In 1830 the font lacked a proper basin, and in 1841 the 'old font' was ordered to be placed in a convenient situation or broken up.[61] The present font was given in 1875 by W. Bradley of Farmer & Bradley of London, who designed it as a copy of the font in Ashbourne church; a native of Alstonefield, he gave it in memory of his parents.[62]

The fittings of the church include a finely carved two-decker pulpit dated 1637 and box pews dated 1637 and 1639; to the last date is added the name Edward Unsworth 'the workman'. A richly carved pew now at the east end of the north aisle bearing the arms of the Cotton family of Beresford Hall is of the same period,[63] as is the screen which is used to form a vestry at the west end of the south aisle. The communion rail is probably of the later 17th century.

In 1553 the church goods included two silver chalices with patens, two brass candlesticks, and three brass crosses; there were also numerous vestments.[64] In the mid 20th century the plate included a silver dish dated 1787 and a silver chalice dated 1789; the chalice was later stolen.[65] There were three great bells in 1553.[66] There was a peal of three by 1830, consisting of two bells cast by George Oldfield of Nottingham in 1677 and one of 1680, probably also the work of Oldfield. In 1989 a peal of six was installed, made up of the two 1677 bells and four which had earlier formed part of the peal in St. John's church, Longton; those four were cast in 1815 by T. Mears of London, although one had been recast in 1930 by John Taylor & Co. of Loughborough (Leics.). The 1680 bell was kept for the clock chime and for ringing as a single bell.[67] In 1682 an existing clock was replaced by one made by Edward Baily of Uttoxeter.[68] The £19 16s. paid to a clock maker by the Alstonefield churchwardens in 1792–3[69] was presumably for a new clock. In 1852 the vestry meeting decided to discontinue the annual payment of 15s. for cleaning the clock, which was worn out and useless. Payment was resumed after the installation of the present clock made in 1853 by the firm of Elleby of Ashbourne.[70]

There was a group of psalm singers by 1797, and they were still being paid in 1826–7.[71] There was an organ by 1822, described in 1830 as in a small west gallery.[72] It was moved to the north side of the chancel probably in the course of the restoration of 1875.[73]

The registers date from 1538.[74]

By 1698 most of the churchyard wall was maintained by the parish.[75] The churchyard was planted with trees in 1724 at the expense of the vicar, Peter Parr, who added two yews on the north side in 1738.[76] It was extended in 1909 and 1961 by the addition respectively of 2,100 and 1,845 square yd. of the glebe.[77]

Alstonefield has the largest number of pre-Conquest carved stones in Staffordshire, most of them parts of standing crosses.[78] The majority

52 Below, plate 13.
53 L.J.R.O., B/C/11, John Stones (1534).
54 Ibid. John Chadwycke (1542); the reference has been supplied by Mr. J. Titterton of Reading.
55 Stones on the east wall bearing the initials LB (Laurence Beresford, one of the farmers of the rectory) and the date.
56 Staffs. Advertiser, 21 Aug. 1875, p. 4.
57 Lich. Dioc. Ch. Cal. (1878), 76.
58 Date on porch; T.N.S.F.C. xxxiii. 86; above, intro.
59 Inf. from the vicar, the Revd. Prebendary D. M. Tinsley.
60 P. C. Sidebotham, 'Corpus of Anglo-Saxon Stone Sculpture and Medieval Stone Sculpture at Alstonefield, Staffs., June 1992' (Sheffield Univ. 1993), 31.
61 S.H.C. 4th ser. x. 76.
62 Staffs. Advertiser, 21 Aug. 1875, p. 4; T.N.S.F.C. xxxiii. 86.   63 Below, plate 21.
64 S.H.C. 1915, 9.   65 T.B.A.S. lxxvii. 75.
66 S.H.C. 1915, 9.

67 S.H.C. 4th ser. x. 76; C. Lynam, Ch. Bells of County of Stafford (1889), 39 and pl. 92; T. S. Jennings, Hist. of Staffs. Bells (priv. print. 1968), 68; Leek Post & Times, 29 Nov. 1989, p. 10; W.S.L., C.B./Alstonefield/14.
68 Alstonfield Par. Reg. 215.
69 S.R.O., D. 922/35, p. 199.
70 Ibid., D. 922/36, mins. 1852 and accts. 1854–5; S. Bagshaw, Dir. Derb. (1846), 352; inf. from the vicar.
71 S.R.O., D. 922/36.
72 Ibid.; S.H.C. 4th ser. x. 76.
73 T.N.S.F.C. xxxiii. 84.
74 Printed to 1812 in Alstonfield Par. Reg. All but the most recent are in S.R.O., D. 922/1; D. 3179; D. 4186; D. 5178.
75 L.J.R.O., B/V/6/Alstonefield, 1698.
76 Alstonfield Par. Reg. 311, 344.
77 Lich. Dioc. Regy., Bp.'s Reg. V, pp. 186, 203; W, p. 388; X, pp. 535–6.
78 Para. based on Sidebotham, 'Stone Sculpture at Alstonefield'.

are kept in the north aisle of the church, but two are in the churchyard, one of them re-erected in the base of what was probably a medieval cross; another piece, in the south porch in the mid 1940s,[79] has since disappeared. The carving is datable to the period between the late 9th and the mid 11th centuries, and two regional schools are represented, North Midlands and West Pennine. The unfinished state of the carving on two pieces suggests that they were being sculpted on site at Alstonefield.

NONCONFORMITY. In 1668 five Quakers and an Anabaptist were recorded in the parish.[80] One of the Quakers, Alice, wife of Henry Bowman, had been put in prison in 1664 for disturbing the administration of the sacrament on Easter Sunday.[81] In 1687 she and her son Henry conveyed a plot of land in Gypsy Lane, 16 yd. square, in trust to John Hall and John Mellor, both Quakers, specifying in 1688 that it was to be used as a burial ground. The last of the three recorded burials there was of a Henry Bowman in 1747. The trust had lapsed by 1813, when the land was sold.[82] By will proved 1740 Robert Mellor of Alstonefield left £25 to 'my poor friends at Leek meeting called Quakers'.[83]

A Baptist minister preached in Alstonefield village in 1810, causing 'a storm of accusations of conscience', but no cause was founded.[84] Soon afterwards John Benton, a Primitive Methodist missionary, preached in the houses of Daniel Stones and T. Hills in Alstonefield, and a society of 10 was established. William Clowes, a Primitive Methodist pioneer, preached in Alstonefield in 1813, and the same year Hugh Bourne, another pioneer, registered a house in Alstonefield for worship. He registered another at Milldale in 1815.[85] There were still societies at both places in the early 1820s.[86] A chapel was built at Milldale in 1835 and opened in January 1836.[87] On Census Sunday 1851 there was an afternoon congregation of 20.[88] The chapel is now Milldale Methodist church.

There was an unsuccessful attempt to establish Wesleyan Methodism at Alstonefield c. 1815, but following a revival at Wetton a class was formed at Alstonefield in 1821, meeting in the house of Mr. Hambleton. Numbers grew, and a chapel was opened in 1824 on a site given by Hambleton. It had seats for 280, but membership was only 37 in 1837.[89] On Census Sunday there was a congregation of 94 in the morning, besides Sunday school children, and 90 in the evening.[90] The chapel was rebuilt in 1879.[91] It was closed in 1981 and converted into a private house; a furniture workshop was opened in the former Sunday school building.[92] There was a Wesleyan Methodist meeting at Stanshope between 1827 and 1833.[93]

EDUCATION. Richard Hallowes (d. 1589) evidently kept a school at Alstonefield, combining it with the office of parish clerk.[94] Several schoolmasters were recorded there in the 17th and early 18th century.[95] By will proved 1727 German Pole of Alstonefield left £40 to be either lent out at interest or used to buy land; the income was to be paid to a master to teach poor children living in Alstonefield township to read. He hoped to encourage other gifts by his example.[96] There appears to have been no schoolmaster in 1732,[97] but in 1746–7 Sir Henry Harpur paid £6 for Alstonefield schools.[98] In 1748–9 the churchwardens paid for the glazing of a school window.[99] Pole's bequest was producing £1 8s. a year by the later 1780s.[1] The master was then James Brown, who continued until his death in 1796.[2]

By 1812 only c. 12 children were attending the school. To improve matters Sir Henry Crewe's steward, with the approval of the principal inhabitants, inclosed a plot of land on Archford moor and let it in 1813 for £20. That sum, with £5 5s. from Sir Henry, £2 15s. interest on a bequest from a Dorothy Green, and the £1 8s. from Pole's bequest, was assigned to the master to teach 35 poor children. About 1815 the master, Mr. Kidd, complained that a woman teaching 10–20 girls was keeping the numbers in his school low. Sir Henry's agent inclosed more land and paid her an annuity to desist. In 1816 it was stated that there were 75 children at Kidd's school.[3] When Sir George Crewe succeeded in 1819, the freeholders complained that the inclosure on Archford moor had been made without their consent, and he felt obliged to throw it open. Kidd lost the £20 rent and resigned.[4]

In 1828 Sir George re-endowed the school. He vested 29 a. on Archford moor in trust to provide an income of £17 10s. a year for a master to teach 25 poor children from Alstonefield township chosen by the trustees; the master was to be a

79 *T.N.S.F.C.* lxxxi. 21.   80 L.J.R.O., B/V/1/75.
81 S.R.O., D. 3159/1/1, f. 145v.; S.R.O., Q/SO/7, f. 103v.
82 *T.S.S.A.H.S.* xii. 39–40; xiii. 51; S.R.O., D. 3159/3/1, abstracts of deeds at end of vol., no. 1; Friends' House Libr., London, portfolio 14, no. 78. For Hall and Mellor see S.R.O., D. 3159/1/1, ff. 24v., 34v.
83 W.S.L. 340/11/40.
84 J. Leach, *Methodism in the Moorlands* (Wesley Hist. Soc., Lancs. and Ches. branch, occasional paper no. 5, 1987), 12.
85 Ibid.; *S.H.C.* 4th ser. iii. 31, 35. For Stones see *Alstonfield Deanery Mag.* xxvii (2).
86 Leach, *Methodism in the Moorlands*, 11, 13.
87 Date on building; W. H. Simcock, 'Primitive Methodism in the Leek Moorlands' (1970; TS. in Leek Libr.), 13.
88 P.R.O., HO 129/447/4/13.
89 Dyson, *Wesleyan Methodism*, 83–4; Leach, *Methodism*

in the Moorlands, 19–20.
90 P.R.O., HO 129/447/4/13.
91 *Kelly's Dir. Staffs.* (1884).
92 Bowyer and Poole, *Staffs. Moorlands,* ii. 100.
93 S.R.O., D. 3155/1.
94 D.R.O., D. 2375M/57/1, 4 Oct. 39 Eliz. I; *Alstonfield Par. Reg.* 46.
95 *Hist. of Educ.* v (2), 120, 125; L.J.R.O., B/A/4/13, 19 Apr. 1709.   96 L.J.R.O., B/C/11, German Pole (1727).
97 W.S.L., S.MS. 424, f. 68.
98 D.R.O., D. 2375M/160/13.
99 S.R.O., D. 922/35, p. 91.
1 *Char. Dons.* 1150–1.
2 D.R.O., D. 2375M/63/30; *Alstonfield Par. Reg.* 472.
3 D.R.O., D. 2375M/87/19, acct. of schs. in Alstonefield par. 1819; D. 2375M/161/90, letter of 31 May and petition of 17 June 1816.
4 *13th Rep. Com. Char.* 351.

member of the Church of England. Adjacent townships were eligible if there were not enough children from Alstonefield township. If the rent from the land exceeded the sum specified, the trustees might choose an additional child for every extra 14s.[5] For the next few years the new master received the rent, a further £5 from Sir George, and the income from German Pole's bequest, and he taught 35 children free.[6] Pole's endowment, however, was evidently never invested, and c. 1838 payments from it seem to have ceased.[7] In the mid 1830s the schoolhouse was repaired at Sir George's expense.[8] A new school was built in 1842 by subscription on a site given by Sir George. It consisted of a single room, which by 1871 was divided by sliding doors into separate schoolrooms for boys and girls.[9] As Alstonefield Church of England school it received a government grant from 1871.[10] Average attendance was then c. 35, but the number on the books reached 81 in 1892.[11] A classroom was added in 1895,[12] and a bell in a turret in 1902.[13]

By the 1850s the master's wife acted as schoolmistress, and the practice continued whenever the master was a married man. From the earlier 1880s the mistress was described as the sewing mistress.[14] By 1871 she was helped with the sewing by the vicar's wife, who was later joined by two daughters.[15] The staff was increased to three in 1893 when an assistant mistress was appointed to teach the younger children and help the master's wife with needlework.[16] The staff remained at three until 1935 when it was reduced to two because of a falling roll.[17]

Numbers dropped from 56 in 1933 to 28 in 1939 but were up to 55 by 1948.[18] They were down to 39 by 1955 and were further reduced that year when the school became a junior mixed and infants' school and 15 senior children were transferred to Leek.[19] In 1953 the village reading room was converted into the school kitchen and dining room,[20] and in 1960 alterations were made to the main building.[21] The closure of Wetton school in 1978 increased the roll at Alstonefield school from 20 to 29, but the opening of Warslow middle school in 1979 reduced it to 14.[22] The staff was reduced to one in 1981, and the school was closed in 1982, the 10 pupils then on the roll going to Warslow middle and first schools.[23]

The schoolhouse and the school building reverted to the trustees of the Harpur-Crewe estate and were sold.[24] By a Scheme of 1986 the land on Archford moor and the school garden were vested in a trust to promote the education of people aged under 25 living in Alstonefield parish or its neighbourhood and to provide instruction in the doctrines of the Church of England for children in St. Peter's parish. In 1992–3 the income consisted of £403 from investments and £678 in rents. Grants totalling £450 were made to three students, and £100 was paid to the Lichfield Diocesan Board of Education.[25] The garden has been landscaped and opened to the public.

In 1818 it was stated that at Alstonefield two or three old women taught a few girls, whose parents paid for them.[26] By 1848 John Kilvert and his wife Catherine, master and mistress of the endowed school, were also running a private school. In 1851 they advertised it as a boarding school for boys and girls, and it was still in existence in 1854.[27] Mary Partrige (or Partridge) had a boarding and day school by the later 1880s and was still running it in 1912. In 1891 her household at West View in the Rakes included a music governess.[28]

There was a Sunday school attached to the parish church by 1824, and it had c. 100 children in 1830.[29] On Census Sunday 1851 there was an attendance of 75 in the morning and 76 in the afternoon.[30] The Wesleyan Methodists started a Sunday school at Alstonefield in 1851, and there was an attendance of 29 on Census Sunday. A schoolroom was built in the same year.[31]

CHARITIES FOR THE POOR. By will proved 1702 Henry Jackson of Stanshope left £100 for the poor of Alstonefield township. It was to be used to buy land, the rent from which was to be distributed on 2 February. Land was bought in Waterfall in 1705. The rent, £4 7s. in the later 1780s, was £22 by 1824, when it was payable on Old Candlemas day (13 February). The money was distributed as soon as received in sums varying from 1s. to 10s., preference being given to those 'who are most industrious and the least burthensome to the parish'.[32] More property in Waterfall was bought in 1846 and 1849.[33]

5 Staffs. Endowed Chars. 7.
6 White, Dir. Staffs. (1834), 717; S.H.C. 4th ser. x. 76; D.R.O., D. 2375M/205/10 sqq. There was no mention of Dorothy Green's bequest after 1819: D. 2375M/161/90.
7 13th Rep. Com. Char. 351; Staffs. Endowed Chars. 6; S.R.O., D. (W.) 1702/7/4.
8 D.R.O., D. 2375M/205/11, Wm. Grindon's bill.
9 White, Dir. Staffs. (1851), 742; Staffs. Endowed Chars. 7; S.R.O., D. 4609/13, prelim. statement 13 Mar. 1871.
10 S.R.O., D. 4609/12, rep. of H.M.I. to 31 Oct. 1871; D. 4609/13, prelim. statement 13 Mar. 1871.
11 Ibid. D. 3805/1/1, p. 288; D. 4609/13, prelim. statement 13 Mar. 1871.
12 Kelly's Dir. Staffs. (1896); S.R.O., D. 4609/13, Wm. Sugden & Son to Revd. W. H. Purchas, 8 May 1895.
13 S.R.O., D. 3805/1/1, p. 474; D. 4609/13, acct. for year ending 31 Mar. 1902.
14 P.R.O., HO 107/1007; ibid. RG 9/2522; RG 12/2754; S.R.O., D. 3805/1/1, pp. 140, 152, 166, 223–4, 273.
15 e.g. S.R.O., D. 3805/1/1, pp. 1 sqq., 103, 106, 233–6.
16 S.R.O., D. 3805/1/1, pp. 310, 313.
17 Ibid. D. 3805/1/2, pp. 212, 237.
18 Ibid. pp. 237, 280.   19 Ibid. p. 293.
20 Ibid. p. 289.   21 Ibid. D. 3805/1/3, pp. 28, 34.
22 Ibid. pp. 179, 193–4.
23 Ibid. pp. 210, 218, 233.
24 S.R.O., D. 4609/5, 5 Aug. 1982; above, intro. [social and cultural activities].   25 Char. Com. file 517617.
26 Educ. of Poor Digest, 853.
27 Staffs. Advertiser, 8 July 1848, p. 1; 5 July 1851, p. 1; P.O. Dir. Staffs. (1850; 1854).
28 Kelly's Dir. Staffs. (1888; 1912), giving the principal as Ellen Partridge; P.R.O., RG 12/2754, giving her as Mary M. Partrige; Alstonefield, ed. Edwards, 37.
29 S.R.O., D. 922/36; S.H.C. 4th ser. x. 76.
30 P.R.O., HO 129/447/4/13.
31 Ibid.; Dyson, Wesleyan Methodism, 84.
32 13th Rep. Com. Char. 350; Char. Dons. 1150–1. The details of the Alstonefield charities given in the 13th Rep. were provided late in 1824: S.R.O., D. 922/45; D. (W.) 1702/7/4, R. Troward to V. Green, 31 Dec. 1824.
33 S.R.O., D. 922/43–4.

By deed of 1716 John Port of Ilam left a stock of wool to provide an annual distribution of 40s. to the poor of Alstonefield township. Payments were made by his successors in the Ilam estate until 1819. In that year Jesse Watts Russell, who had initially continued the payments after buying the estate, stopped them because he could find no documentary proof of any claim on the estate. In 1824 the charity commissioners them-

By will proved 1727 German Pole of Alstonefield left £20 for the poor of Alstonefield township. The money was to be put out at interest or used to buy land and the income distributed about Christmas time. The income was 14s. by 1786 and 20s. by 1824.[38] The capital was evidently never invested, and payment presumably lapsed like that from Pole's educational charity c. 1838.[39]

By will of 1777 William Ensor of Windley

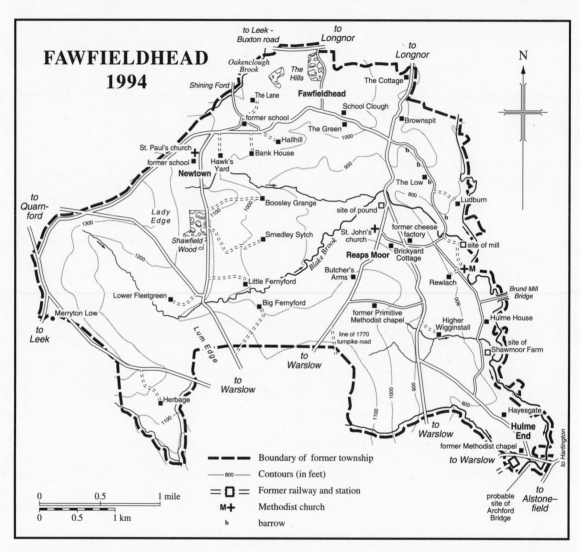

FIG. 5

selves could find no evidence to enable them to enforce payment, but the charity was subsequently revived.[34]

By will proved 1858 Constantia Bill left £93 stock, the interest to be used first for the repair of her monument, with the remainder distributed in bread to the poor.[35]

The Jackson, Port, and Bill charities were amalgamated in 1943.[36] In the early 1990s the annual income of £80 was normally distributed to people aged over 70 living in Alstonefield civil parish.[37]

(Derb.) left £300 to be invested, with half the interest used to apprentice at least one poor child from Alstonefield township annually or once every two or three years; the other half was to be used in like manner by the parish of Tissington (Derb.). Because Ensor's personal estate was insufficient to pay his debts, his son William charged the payment of the charity on part of the real estate. He was paying £6 in the later 1780s and £7 10s. by 1807. Having been advised that the legacy could not be charged on

34 *13th Rep. Com. Char.* 351–2; below, this section.
35 S.R.O., D. 922/21; S.R.O., Charities Index.
36 Ibid. Charities Index.
37 Inf. from Mr. J. Turner, Charities Officer, Staffs. Rural

Community Council.
38 *13th Rep. Com. Char.* 350–1; *Char. Dons.* 1150–1.
39 Above, educ.

the real estate, he then stopped making the payment, and the charity lapsed.[40]

At an unknown date before 1786 Richard Bowman of Old Basset in Cheddleton gave £10,

the interest to be distributed annually to the poor of Alstonefield township. In the later 1780s the income was 7s., but the charity had lapsed by 1824.[41]

FAWFIELDHEAD

FAWFIELDHEAD was formerly a township in Alstonefield parish and later a civil parish 5,383 a. (2,178 ha.) in area, including a detached portion of 592 a. to the south-east along the river Dove.[42] It is mostly pasture with scattered farms, and there are three hamlets, Fawfieldhead in the north, Newtown in the north-west, and Hulme End in the south-east. The main part of the parish lies along the river Manifold, its boundary with Sheen on the east, and extends west as far as Merryton Low on the boundary with Onecote, in Leek parish.[43] Brooks form part of the boundary on the south-east and north-west. Elsewhere the boundary runs across heathland and on the south at Lum Edge was marked by stones in 1837.[44] The detached portion was transferred to Alstonefield civil parish in 1934. At the same date 183 a. centred on a house called Herbage in the south-west of Fawfieldhead was added to Warslow and Elkstones civil parish, and there was an exchange of small acreas of land with Sheen. As a result the area of Fawfieldhead civil parish was reduced to its present 4,624 a. (1,871 ha.).[45] This article deals with the main part of the former township; the detached portion is treated in the article on Alstonefield civil parish.

The land lies at 1,588 ft. (474 m.) on the western boundary and falls gradually towards the Manifold, dropping to 699 ft. (213 m.) at Hulme End. The underlying rock is sandstone of the Millstone Grit series. There is alluvium along Blake brook and a tributary, which both flow across the parish into the Manifold, and the soil is mostly loam over clay.[46]

The number of people in Fawfieldhead owing suit at the manor court in 1769 was 143.[47] The population was 788 in 1801, 1,003 in 1811, and 1,315 in 1821. Thereafter there was a decline, to 1,017 in 1831, 923 in 1851, 750 in 1871, 570 in 1891, and 490 in 1901. The population was 471 in 1911, 474 in 1921, and 459 in 1931. After the boundary changes of 1934, it was 376 in 1951, 355 in 1961, 306 in 1971, 286 in 1981, and 300 in 1991.[48]

Four Bronze Age barrows have been identified on the east side of the township near a farmhouse

called the Low, a name derived from the Old English word (*hlaw*) commonly used for a barrow.[49]

One of the earliest medieval settlements was possibly in the north part of the township at School Clough, where a house was recorded in 1331; the name incorporates a word of Scandinavian origin.[50] In the south part of the township there was a house by 1327 beside Blake brook at Fernyford,[51] either on the site of Little Fernyford where a stone dated 1698 is set on a barn attached to the 19th-century farmhouse, or on that of Big Fernyford, which is of the 18th or early 19th century. Further upstream Lower Fleetgreen, a house partly of the 17th century, probably stands on or near the site of a house called Fleetgreen in 1514.[52] By 1439 there was a house at Herbage *c*. 1 mile south of Lower Fleetgreen.[53] The site of Smedley Sytch north of Fernyford was occupied by 1406.[54] Further north there were houses at Boosley Grange and Bank House possibly by the later 14th century, when the bounds of land belonging to Hawk's Yard, west of Bank House, included places then called Boothesley Grange and the Bank or Over Boothesley.[55] The word grange commonly indicates a monastic farm, but no abbey is known to have owned land in the township and the name probably refers to buildings used seasonally for dairying.[56] The present house at Boosley Grange retains 17th-century stonework and was probably built for the Wardle family, the occupiers in the 1640s.[57] Hallhill existed by 1406, and Bank House, west of Hallhill, existed as Audley Bothesley in the later 1430s.[58] Until the earlier 19th century Smedley Sytch, Boosley Grange, and Bank House were linked by a road which crossed Oakenclough brook at Shining Ford.[59] A hamlet at Shining Ford existed in the earlier 1630s.[60]

On the east side of the township there were houses in the Middle Ages along the road from Alstonefield village to Longnor: the Low was recorded in 1399 and Rewlach in the early 1420s.[61] South-east of the Low there was a house

40 *13th Rep. Com. Char.* 352; *Char. Dons.* 1150–1; S.R.O., D. 922/39.
41 *13th Rep. Com. Char.* 352; *Char. Dons.* 1150–1.
42 *V.C.H. Staffs.* i. 327; *Census,* 1931. This article was written in 1994.
43 For Merryton Low see below, Leek: Onecote, intro.
44 D.R.O., D. 2375M/282/1, description of Warslow-Fawfieldhead boundary.
45 *Census,* 1881, 1931; Staffs. Review Order, 1934, p. 63 and map 1 (copy in S.R.O.).
46 Geol. Surv. Map 1/50,000, drift, sheet 111 (1978 edn.); Soil Surv. of Eng. and Wales, sheet 3 (1983).
47 D.R.O., D. 2375M/174/5/9.
48 *V.C.H. Staffs.* i. 327; *Census,* 1901–91. The figures up to 1931 include the detached portion.
49 Staffs. C.C., Sites and Monuments Rec. 00118, 00119, 00333, 01398; *T.S.S.A.H.S.* xxvii. 1–26; *Eng. P.N. Elements,* i. 248–9.
50 D.R.O., D. 2375M/1/1, ct. of 1 and 2 Hen. V; *S.H.C.*

xi. 32 (as Scoldeclogh); *Eng. P.N. Elements,* ii. 123.
51 *S.H.C.* vii (1), 218.
52 D.R.O., D. 2375M/1/6, 27 Apr. 6 Hen. VIII.
53 Ibid. ct. of Thurs. after feast of Purification 17 Hen. VI (as Harebache).
54 Ibid. D. 2375M/1/1, 1st ct. 8 Hen. IV (as Snethlesych).
55 B.R.L., Keen 261A, deed of 10 July 1571, reciting deed of duke of Lancaster to Sir Edw. Mundy.
56 Below, econ. hist. (agric.).
57 D.R.O., D. 2375M/110/32, extracts of evidences re Nether Boosley Farm.
58 Ibid. D. 2375M/1/1, 1st ct. 8 Hen. IV, 2nd ct. 15 Hen. VI.
59 J. Phillips and W. F. Hutchings, *Map of County of Stafford* (1832); above, fig. 2.
60 D.R.O., D. 2375M/63/53, p. 151.
61 Ibid. D. 2375M/1/1, 1st ct. 3 Hen. IV, ct. of 9 and 10 Hen. V.

by the early 16th century at Ludburn on a road which crossed into Sheen over the Manifold.[62] There was a house at Higher Wigginstall beside a stream south of Rewlach, certainly by the early 16th century and possibly earlier as land called Wigginstall was recorded in 1396.[63] To the south pasture called Alstonefield Hayes was rented to tenants in the later 16th century, and in 1597 a cottage at Hayesgate was let to Richard Finney, licensed as an alehouse keeper in 1605.[64]

A house at Fawfieldhead in the early 15th century presumably stood in the present hamlet of that name in the north part of the township. In the earlier 1630s the hamlet was also known as Fawfieldgreen.[65] A house on the west side of the hamlet dated 1774 was extended in 1831 for Isaac Billing, a stonemason.[66] Four houses which existed by the earlier 1630s on former pasture called Fawfield Hill north of the hamlet[67] probably included the Lane, a 19th-century farmhouse which retains a date stone of 1759. East of the hamlet there was a house on the Longnor road at Brownspit by 1594.[68] The Cottage on the boundary north of Brownspit was built in Gothick style in the earlier 19th century for James Charlesworth (d. 1842), formerly of Heath House, in Heathylee.[69]

Newtown existed by 1754 as a hamlet on the edge of common waste on the west side of the township.[70] In 1836 Sir George Crewe, on a visit to the area, considered it suitable for development, and he had a church built there in 1837.[71] Despite his endeavours Newtown remained small. A settlement called Reaps Moor beyond Blake brook south-east of Newtown also existed by the later 18th century.[72] Houses there were probably the cause of the township's rapid growth in population in the early 19th century. The inhabitants may have been stone and brick workers, as later in the century.[73] A workhouse opened in 1802 was converted into a church and a school in 1842.[74] The present Butcher's Arms inn, so called by 1834, existed by the later 1820s.[75]

The hamlet of Hulme End, in Sheen, had spread into Fawfieldhead township by the early 19th century.[76] Manifold House was built c. 1900, and a pair of houses to the south called Riverside Villa and Manx Villa was built in 1907 by J. W. Bassett, a builder and miller.[77]

The road between Warslow and Hartington (Derb.) through the south-east corner of the town-ship formerly followed part of the Alstonefield–Longnor road over Archford bridge.[78] When the former was turnpiked in 1770 as a branch of the Cheadle–Buxton road,[79] it was realigned to cross the river by a new bridge c.300 yd. upstream at Hulme End. At first called Hayesgate bridge and also known as Hulme End bridge by 1778, the new bridge seems to have been completed by 1775, although work on it was still necessary in the late 1780s and in 1794–5.[80] It was rebuilt in the early 19th century. Further north there were bridges at Brund mill and Ludburn. They were the joint responsibility of Alstonefield and Sheen parishes until 1736 or 1737; the former then became Alstonefield's responsibility and the latter Sheen's.[81] The Cheadle–Buxton road turnpiked in 1770 originally ran west of Warslow village over Reaps moor. It was realigned to the east in the 1820s, rejoining the original route immediately south of Blake brook. The road was disturnpiked in 1878.[82]

The road between Leek and Longnor running over Lady Edge and on the north-west side of Fawfield Hill was mentioned in the later 14th century and was later a packhorse way.[83]

The Leek & Manifold Valley light railway, opened in 1904, ran from Waterhouses to the Fawfieldhead part of Hulme End. The line was closed in 1934, but the wooden station building remained standing in 1994.[84]

A friendly society called the Reapsmoor Club was established at the Butcher's Arms in 1835, and in 1876 it had 130 members. Its band, mentioned in 1862, played at the club's annual feast in June. The club still existed in 1940.[85] There was a lodge of Oddfellows at Reaps Moor in 1917.[86]

MANOR. Fawfieldhead was part of Alstonefield manor.

ECONOMIC HISTORY. AGRICULTURE. Faw-fieldhead is named after land called Fawfield, recorded in 1308 and meaning multi-coloured open land, presumably land bright with flow-ers.[87] The description could fit the pasture beside Blake brook and its tributary. There was a vaccary, or dairy farm, in Fawfieldhead in 1308,[88] and the names of three farms, Boosley Grange, School Clough, and Higher Wiggin-

62 Ibid. D. 2375M/171/1/2, m. 2.
63 Ibid. D.2375M/1/1, ct. of Thurs. after feast of St. John and St. Paul 20 Ric. II; D. 2375M/171/1/2, m. 2.
64 Ibid. D. 2375M/106/27, Staffs. leases, 1 Dec. 40 Eliz. I; *S.H.C.* 1940, 287; below, econ. hist. (agric.).
65 D.R.O., D. 2375M/63/53, p. 147.
66 Date stone with initials IB on extension of house; S.R.O. 5322/4, no. 90; below, econ. hist. (trade and ind.).
67 D.R.O., D. 2375M/63/53, pp. 142–3.
68 Ibid. D. 2375M/57/1, 6 Apr. 36 Eliz. I.
69 P.R.O., HO 107/1003; Charlesworth fam. tomb in Longnor churchyard.
70 S.R.O., D. 921/1, f. 133.
71 D.R.O., D. 2375M/44/1, 19 Sept. 1836; below, churches.
72 Above, fig. 2.
73 C. and J. Greenwood, *Map of County of Stafford* (1820); above, this section [pop.]; below, econ. hist. (trade and ind.).
74 Below, local govt.; churches; educ.

75 S.R.O. 5322/4, no. 931; White, *Dir. Staffs.* (1834), 720.
76 Greenwood, *Map of County of Stafford.*
77 Date stone with initials JWB; above, Alstonefield, econ. hist. (mills).   78 Above, Alstonefield, intro.
79 *S.H.C.* 4th ser. xiii. 110–11.
80 Sheen par. accts. 1720–1803, headborough's accts. 1772–3, 1778, 1786, 1790–1, 1794–5.
81 Below, Sheen, intro.
82 Below, Warslow, intro.
83 B.R.L., Keen 261A, deed of 10 July 1571; Dodd, *Peakland Roads,* 93.
84 Below, Leek: Leek and Lowe, communications; below, plate 45.
85 S.R.O., D. 121/A/PZ/2, ff. 7v., 9; *Rep. Chief Registrar of Friendly Socs. 1876, App. P.,* H.C. 429-I, p. 392 (1877), lxxvii; *Alstonfield Deanery Mag.* xliii (7).
86 *Alstonfield Deanery Mag.* xxi (7).
87 *S.H.C.* N.S. xi. 257, where 'Fanfeld' is an error for 'Faufeld': P.R.O., C 134/5, m. 1; *Eng. P.N. Elements,* i. 164, 166–7.   88 *S.H.C.* N.S. xi. 257.

stall, include words which mean a cowhouse or herdsman's shelter (*both*, *skali*) and a place where cattle were kept (*stall*).[89]

The inhabitants of Fawfieldhead enjoyed pasture rights on Fawfield Hill, a tract of 300 a. north of Fawfieldhead hamlet, until it was parcelled out among tenants by the lords of Alstonefield in the early 16th century.[90] The inhabitants of Longnor also had rights on Fawfield Hill, and in 1568 c. 100 men from Longnor pulled down fences there.[91] An award of 1575 stipulated that the part of the hill nearest Longnor was to remain open to Longnor men, as well as to the tenants of four farms in Heathylee whose land bordered the hill. The Longnor men were also to have an 80-year lease of a quarter of the inclosed part of the hill, for which each householder was to pay the lord 4*d*. and a hen each year.[92]

Pasture called Alstonefield Hayes in the south-east corner of Fawfieldhead seems to have been common in 1464.[93] Together with adjoining land called Mynnyngs field, it became the subject of a dispute over fencing between 24 tenants in Alstonefield township and 6 tenants in Fawfieldhead. The dispute was settled in 1573 by a division between the two groups, each being responsible for half the rent.[94] The pasture remained subject to manorial control. In 1594 the court ordered that no geese were to be allowed on the land between Good Friday and Michaelmas, and by 1599 two pinners were appointed to supervise the area; a single pinner was appointed between 1602 and 1620.[95] The office was discontinued in 1621 when Alstonefield Hayes and Mynnyngs field were leased for 21 years in two shares, one of 176 a. to 24 tenants in Alstonefield township and the other of 144 a. to 11 tenants in Fawfieldhead. In addition 20½ a. which had lately been inclosed were leased to two tenants, one of whom had already erected a smithy there.[96] Further inclosures had reduced 'the great pasture called the Hey' to 190½ a. by the earlier 1630s, and between 1649 and 1653 several leases were made of other newly inclosed parts.[97]

The common waste included moorland which was probably unsuitable for permanent grazing. Schal moor, mentioned in 1392, probably lay in the area of Shawmoor Farm in the south-east part of the township beside the Manifold,[98] and to the north-west lay Reaps moor, so called in 1595.[99] Heathland called Lady Edge, which extended north-west into Heathylee, was recorded in the later 14th century.[1] Only 185 a. of common waste, mostly at Lady Edge, remained in

the township in 1839, when it was inclosed under an Act of 1834 amended in 1836. All the land was allotted to Sir George Crewe, 56 a. as lord of the manor and 129 a. as the impropriator of Alstonefield rectory.[2] Shawfield Wood on the former waste south of Newtown was planted by Sir George in 1834.[3]

Of the 1,738.4 ha. of farmland returned for the civil parish in 1988, grassland covered 1,631.5 ha. and there were 53.6 ha. of rough grazing. The farming was dairy and sheep, with 2,025 head of cattle and 6,430 sheep and lambs. Of the 49 farms returned, 37 were under 50 ha. in size, 9 were between 50 and 99 ha., and 3 were between 100 and 199 ha. Woodland covered 20.3 ha.[4]

MILL. By the later 1820s John Shirley of Rewlach had a mill on Blake brook north of Rewlach.[5] Offered for sale in 1902, the mill ceased working between 1904 and 1908.[6]

TRADE AND INDUSTRY. Two stonemasons, Simon Billing and Isaac Billing, both of Fawfieldhead hamlet, were recorded respectively in 1813 and 1834.[7] Twenty-eight stonemasons or stone workers were recorded in the township in 1841, and in 1851 thirty men worked for John Lomas, a stonemason and brick and tile maker of Reaps Moor.[8]

In the early 1850s a brick and tile yard was opened at Reaps Moor by George Smith, a Tunstall brickmaker, later of Coalville (Leics.), and a noted social reformer. He worked at Reaps Moor until 1855, refusing to employ boys aged under 13 and women or girls at all and not allowing Sunday working.[9] Brickyard Cottage, east of Reaps Moor church, is a later 19th-century house partly of brick and was probably built for the manager of a brickworks at Reaps Moor offered for sale in 1877.[10] The remains of clay diggings are visible near the house.

There was a cheese factor in the township in 1840,[11] and another in 1844 and 1851.[12] In 1881 William Shirley had a cheese factory at his farm at Rewlach, and his son Samuel was the first secretary of the Manifold Valley Dairies Association Ltd., which in 1912 had a cheese factory on the Warslow–Longnor road north-west of Rewlach. The factory was closed in 1958.[13]

A furniture-making business was established in 1983 by George Fox in the former cheese factory.[14]

LOCAL GOVERNMENT. Fawfieldhead was

89 *Eng. P.N. Elements*, i. 43; ii. 123, 142.
90 D.R.O., D. 2375M/161/28, m. 2; *S.H.C.* 1931, 130.
91 *S.H.C.* 1910, 72–3.   92 D.R.O., D. 2375M/161/28.
93 Ibid. D. 2375M/1/1, 2nd ct. 4 Edw. IV.
94 Ibid. D. 2375M/139/40.
95 Ibid. D. 2375M/57/1, 6 Apr. 36 Eliz. I, 21 Apr. 41 Eliz. I sqq.
96 Ibid. D. 2375M/106/27, Staffs. leases, 1 May 19 Jas. I; D. 2375M/190/6, deed of 1 May 1621.
97 Ibid. D. 2375M/63/53, p. 138; D. 2375M/189/14.
98 Ibid. D. 2375M/1/6, extent of 1392; Greenwood, *Map of County of Stafford*.
99 D.R.O., D. 2375M/57/1, 2 May 1595.
1 B.R.L., Keen 261A, deed of 10 July 1571.
2 S.R.O., Q/RDc 24; 4 & 5 Wm. IV, c. 15 (Priv. Act); 6 & 7 Wm. IV, c. 6 (Priv. Act).

3 D.R.O., D. 2375M/205/13, bill of Thos. Edge, 1834.
4 P.R.O., MAF 68/6128/56.
5 S.R.O. 5322/4, no. 1046.
6 *Staffs. Advertiser*, 7 June 1902, p. 8; *Kelly's Dir. Staffs.* (1904; 1908).
7 S.R.O., Q/RSm; White, *Dir. Staffs.* (1834), 720.
8 P.R.O., HO 107/1003; HO 107/2008; White, *Dir. Staffs.* (1851), 746.
9 E. Hodder, *Geo. Smith* (1896), 33–6; *D.N.B.*
10 D.R.O., D. 2375M/207/12, advert. for sale of brickworks.   11 S.R.O., D. 4980/1/1, p. 150.
12 S.R.O., Q/SB, E. 1844, no. 51; White, *Dir. Staffs.* (1851), 746.
13 P.R.O., RG 11/2742; *Kelly's Dir. Staffs.* (1912); *St. Bartholomew's Ch. & Par.* [1980], 30.
14 *Leek Post & Times*, 17 Jan. 1990, p. 8.

part of the Forest tithing of Alstonefield manor by the late 1390s and remained so in the earlier 1530s.[15] By 1594 Fawfieldhead formed its own tithing, with one frankpledge.[16] The customary place for the stocks in the early 18th century was apparently Hayesgate, by then the meeting place of the manor court.[17] The 'heyes fold' mentioned in 1550 may have been a pinfold at Alstonefield Hayes, an area of pasture which had its own pinners by 1599 and until 1620.[18] What was called a new pinfold in 1575 stood on the west side of Fawfieldhead hamlet.[19] A combined pinfold and lock-up for which a plan was drawn up in 1843 probably stood at the road junction north of Reaps Moor, where there was a pinfold in the late 1870s.[20]

Two surveyors of the highways for Fawfieldhead were appointed at the manor court apparently for the first time in 1601. From 1602 there was normally only one.[21]

In the later 17th and earlier 18th century the poor of Fawfieldhead, Heathylee, Hollinsclough, and Quarnford were maintained jointly.[22] Fawfieldhead relieved its poor separately from 1733.[23] In 1802 a workhouse with an adjoining house for the governor was built on the turnpike road at Reaps Moor. The workhouse remained in use after Fawfieldhead became part of Leek poor-law union in 1837. It was converted in 1842 into a church and school.[24]

CHURCHES. By 1594 inhabitants of Fawfieldhead evidently attended Longnor church.[25] Churches dependent on Longnor were opened at Newtown in 1837 and Reaps Moor in 1842 at the expense of Sir George Crewe, prompted by the curate of Longnor, William Buckwell.[26] For serving Newtown an assistant curate was paid £50 a year by Sir George; by 1859, when serving both Newtown and Reaps Moor, he was paid £100 by Sir George's son Sir John.[27] From the early 1860s the Harpur Crewe family also provided a house, the Green, east of Fawfieldhead hamlet.[28] The churches were last served by a curate of their own in 1927.[29] In 1950 they were served by a stipendiary reader, who received £125 a year, £70 of it paid by the Harpur Crewe family. The stipend was withdrawn that year, and the stipendiary left.[30] In 1994 the vicar of Longor held services fortnightly at Newtown and monthly at Reaps Moor.

St. Paul's church at Newtown, so named in 1910,[31] is built of ashlar in a Georgian style and has a west bellcot and chimney; a south-west porch was added probably in 1891.[32] There is a Venetian east window, and formerly there were two west windows matching those on the north and south sides. In 1842 Sir George Crewe paid for a bell and a table for psalm singers.[33] On Census Sunday 1851 there was an afternoon congregation of 64, besides Sunday school children.[34] The psalm singers possibly continued to lead the services until 1861, when a harmonium was installed.[35]

St. John's church at Reaps Moor, so named in 1910,[36] occupies the upper floor of the former workhouse, an external flight of steps having been added at the south end of the building and the windows enlarged.[37] On Census Sunday 1851 there were congregations of 26 in the morning and 65 in the evening, besides Sunday school children.[38] A harmonium, mentioned in 1862, was installed probably in 1861, like that in Newtown church.[39]

In the later 19th century Higher Wigginstall, Hayesgate, and Hulme End in the south-eastern part of the township were in Warslow ecclesiastical district, but Higher Wigginstall was transferred to Longnor in 1902.[40] In 1941 St. Mark's mission was opened from Warslow using the waiting room of the railway station at Hulme End. The mission was closed in the later 1940s.[41]

NONCONFORMITY. The farmhouse at Smedley Sytch was probably the meeting place of the Methodist society formed at 'Sytch' in 1765; the society had 13 members in 1784.[42] Mary Shirley of Rewlach became a Methodist in 1785 or 1786, after hearing a Methodist preacher in Longnor market place. A Methodist class was established at her home, under the leadership of her son Joseph. In 1798 Sunday services were held there fortnightly, as well as monthly at School Clough.[43] As a Wesleyan Methodist society it had 27 members in 1837, and in 1849 a chapel was built north-east of Rewlach. On Census Sunday 1851 it had a congregation of 40 in the morning and 70 in the afternoon.[44] Occasional services were still held at the chapel in 1994.

There was a Methodist society of 12 members at Newtown in 1810, and in 1829 Sunday services

15 Above, Alstonefield, par. intro. (manorial govt.).
16 D.R.O., D. 2375M/57/1, 7 Oct. 36 Eliz. I sqq.
17 Ibid. D. 2375M/174/1, 24 Oct. 1700, 21 Oct. 1706.
18 Ibid. D. 2375M/1/2, 5 Oct. 4 Edw. VI; above, econ. hist. (agric.).
19 D.R.O., D. 2375M/161/28, m. 4.
20 Ibid. D. 2375M/93/12, plan of pinfold; O.S. Map 6", Staffs. V. SW. (1887 edn.).
21 D.R.O., D. 2375M/57/1, 21 Apr. 43 Eliz. I, 17 Apr. 44 Eliz. I sqq.
22 Ibid. D. 2375M/110/32, overseers' accts., 1689–1728; S.R.O., D. 3359/Condlyffe, Mabon Frith assessment, 1669.
23 S.R.O., Q/SO/13, f. 104v.
24 St. Bartholomew's Ch. & Par. 43; S.R.O., D. 699/1/1/1, pp. 4–5; below, churches; educ.
25 Below, Longnor, church.
26 D.R.O., D. 2375M/44/1, 26 Sept. 1839; date stones on the churches.
27 D.R.O., D. 2375M/205/15/2, 15 June 1840; D. 2375M/202/19, f. 137.

28 Ibid. D. 2375M/202/19, f. 183.
29 Lich. Dioc. Ch. Cal. (1927).
30 Alstonfield Deanery Mag. liii (3, 9, 11, 12).
31 Ibid. xiv (11).
32 D.R.O., D. 2375M/207/23/1–2; Kelly's Dir. Staffs. (1892).
33 D.R.O., D. 2375M/205/16, 28 July 1842.
34 P.R.O., HO 129/372/4/5.
35 Staffs. Advertiser, 20 Apr. 1861, p. 4.
36 Alstonfield Deanery Mag. xiv (11).
37 Below, plate 61.   38 P.R.O., HO 129/372/4/5.
39 D.R.O., D. 2375M/202/19, f. 172.
40 P.R.O., RG 10/2885; Lond. Gaz. 15 Aug. 1902, p. 5323.
41 Alstonfield Deanery Mag. xliv (1, 11); li (7).
42 Wardle, Methodist Hist. 16.
43 Dyson, Wesleyan Methodism, 40, 80; J. Leach, Methodism in the Moorlands (Wesley Hist. Soc., Lancs. and Ches. branch, occasional paper no. 5, 1987), 5.
44 S.R.O., D. 3156/1/1/2, p. 3; P.R.O., HO 129/372/4/5.

were held monthly.[45] A Wesleyan Methodist chapel was built there in 1841, and on Census Sunday 1851 it had an evening congregation of 41.[46] It was closed in 1975 and converted into a house.[47]

A Methodist society of 28 members was formed at Hulme End in 1787. Numbers increased rapidly, and in 1790 as many as 42 transferred to a society at Brownhill, in Warslow.[48] Some remaining members evidently became Primitive Methodists, and a Primitive Methodist chapel was built in the Fawfieldhead part of Hulme End in 1834. On Census Sunday 1851 it had an evening congregation of 37. Services in the chapel ceased in 1897, but the society continued to meet in houses under lay leadership until 1932.[49] The former chapel remained standing in 1994 but was derelict.

Wesleyan Methodists held Sunday services fortnightly at Hulme End in 1832, and in 1837 they had a society of 12 members. No chapel was built, and in the early 20th century they used the redundant Primitive Methodist chapel. The society was dissolved in 1932.[50]

A house at Fleetgreen, presumably near Lower Fleetgreen farmhouse, was registered for protestant worship in 1838. It may have been for Primitive Methodists, who were holding Sunday services in that area in 1874, alternately with services at Reaps Moor. In 1876 a chapel was opened at Reaps Moor south-east of the Butcher's Arms; closed in 1957, it was used as a farm outbuilding in 1994.[51]

EDUCATION. There was no school in the township in 1819.[52] In the earlier 1830s there

were three day schools with a total of 24 boys and 21 girls paying fees, and a Sunday school with 54 boys and 56 girls. One of the schools was west of Fawfieldhead hamlet.[53] In 1841 the Sunday school was held at Newtown, presumably in the church built there in 1837 by Sir George Crewe. Sir George supported the school financially, and in 1842 he paid for a teacher's stool and pupils' desks.[54] By the later 1840s it was also a National day school with 38 boys and 26 girls,[55] endowed by Sir George Crewe with £30 a year, of which the master received £25 in 1859.[56] In 1880, when managed by a committee of ratepayers, the school moved into a building south of the church.[57] The decision in 1931 that what was then Newtown Church of England school, an all-age school with 37 children on its books, should become a junior school probably took effect in the later 1940s, the senior children being transferred to Leek.[58] Newtown school was closed in 1964, and the children were transferred to Longnor primary school.[59] The school building later became a private house.

In 1842 Sir George Crewe converted the ground floor of the former workhouse at Reaps Moor into a day school. He appointed a master, who lived in the adjoining house and was paid £25 a year.[60] A National school by the later 1840s,[61] it became a council school in 1923 and had 10 children on its books in 1931.[62] It was closed in 1959, and the children were transferred to Warslow primary school.[63]

CHARITIES FOR THE POOR. None known expressly for the township.

HEATHYLEE

HEATHYLEE was formerly a township in Alstonefield parish and later a civil parish 5,535 a. (2,240 ha.) in area.[64] It is mostly pasture, with scattered farms in river valleys and with no village centre. The western boundary with Leekfrith is formed by Back brook, which flows south to join the river Churnet, and two arms of Black brook which flow north and west to join the river Dane. Most of the northern boundary with Hollinsclough runs along a ridge, and the river Manifold forms the short eastern boundary with Sheen. In 1934 the civil parish was enlarged by the addition of land from neighbouring parishes: a detached portion of Bradnop centred on

Hurdlow Farm and covering 385 a.; a detached portion of Leekfrith lying between Hurdlow and Upper Hulme and covering 10 a.; 30 a. from Onecote; and 18 a. from Longnor lying on the south side of the present course of the river Manifold east of Longnor bridge. At the same date 1 a. on the north side of the river was transferred from Heathylee to Longnor. As a result the area of Heathylee civil parish was increased to its present 5,977 a. (2,419 ha.).[65] This article deals with the former township together with the land added in 1934.

Morridge divides the township into a western part and a larger eastern part. The former is

45 S.R.O., D. 3155/1; Leek Libr., Johnson scrapbk. i (2), D/13/15 (as New-house).
46 P.R.O., HO 129/372/4/5.
47 Leach, *Methodism in the Moorlands*, 34.
48 Ibid. 5.
49 P.R.O., HO 129/372/4/5; S.R.O., D. 4087/1/15–16; W. H. Simcock, 'Primitive Methodism in the Leek Moorlands' (1970; TS. in Leek Libr.), 23–4.
50 S.R.O., D. 3156/1/1/2, p. 3; D. 3156/1/1/24; Leach, *Methodism in the Moorlands*, 15, 23.
51 *S.H.C.* 4th ser. iii. 86; S.R.O., D. 4087/1/1–2; Simcock, 'Primitive Methodism', 30, 33.
52 D.R.O., D. 2375M/87/19, acct. of schs. in Alstonefield par. 1819.
53 *Educ. Enq. Abstract*, p. 868; S.R.O. 5322/4, no. 141.
54 D.R.O., D. 2375M/206/16, 28 July 1842; D.

2375M/281/6, 20 Dec. 1841.
55 Nat. Soc. *Inquiry, 1846–7*, Staffs. 2–3.
56 D.R.O., D. 2375M/202/19, f. 134; White, *Dir. Staffs.* (1851), 743.
57 P.R.O., ED 7/108/135; *Kelly's Dir. Staffs.* (1884).
58 Staffs. C.C. *Record for 1931*, 835–6; below, Longnor, educ.   59 S.R.O., CEH/203/1, 9 Mar. 1964.
60 D.R.O., D. 2375M/205/16, receipts of 6 June and Christmas 1842.
61 Nat. Soc. *Inquiry, 1846–7*, Staffs. 2–3.
62 P.R.O., ED 7/110/371; Staffs. C.C. *Record for 1931*, 835–6.
63 Inf. from Manifold primary sch., Warslow.
64 *V.C.H. Staffs.* i. 327. This article was written in 1994.
65 *Census*, 1931; Staffs. Review Order, 1934, p. 63 and map 1 (copy in S.R.O.).

FIG. 6

drained by the Churnet and the latter by the Manifold and a tributary, Oakenclough brook. The land lies at 825 ft. (251 m.) in the south-west corner beside Back brook. To the north and east on Morridge it reaches 1,535 ft. (468 m.) near Morridge Top Farm and 1,590 ft. (487 m.) near Blake Mere. On the east side of the township the land lies at 942 ft. (287 m.) where the Leek–Longnor road crosses Oakenclough brook at Hardings Booth and 862 ft. (263 m.) where the road crosses the Manifold at Longnor bridge. The underlying rock is sandstone of the Millstone Grit series, which outcrops on the west side of the township at Ramshaw Rocks and near Newstone Farm. A shallow basin of the Coal Measures overlies the rock in the Blue Hills area along the western boundary. The best soil lies in the east where it is coarse loam. Elsewhere it is mostly clay and loam, with peat on the west side of Morridge.[66]

The number of people in Heathylee owing suit at the manor court in the late 1760s was 100.[67] The population of the township was 520 in 1801, 706 in 1811, and 788 in 1821. By 1831 it had fallen to 689, and a steady decline thereafter reduced it to 504 in 1861, 361 in 1891, 353 in 1901, 331 in 1911, 333 in 1921, and 345 in 1931. The population of the enlarged civil parish was 280 in 1951, 279 in 1961, 258 in 1971, 265 in 1981, and 244 in 1991. The population of the Hurdlow Farm area added in 1934 was 25 in 1841 and 23 in 1881.[68]

The earliest medieval settlement was probably in the south-west corner where the hamlet of Upper Hulme existed on the Leekfrith side of Back brook by the mid 13th century.[69] There was an estate called Broncott on the Heathylee side of the brook by 1299; the name is derived from words meaning broom cottage.[70] A house built north of Broncott Farm in the later 18th century almost certainly for Joseph Billing, who worked a quarry there, was an inn by the later

66 Geol. Surv. Map 1/50,000, drift, sheet 111 (1978 edn.); Soil Surv. of Eng. and Wales, sheet 3 (1983).
67 D.R.O., D. 2375M/174/5/8.
68 V.C.H. Staffs. i. 327; Census, 1901–91. The figures for the Hurdlow area are taken from P.R.O., HO 107/1005; ibid. RG 11/2740.
69 Below, Leek: Leekfrith, intro.
70 Eng. P.N. Elements, i. 52, 108; below, estates.

1820s. It was then called the New inn, and it survived as a public house, the Olde Rock, in 1994.[71] A cottage beside Back brook west of the inn has the date 1778 over a fireplace. To the north of Upper Hulme a house called Naychurch, in existence by the early 15th century,[72] retains 17th-century stonework.

There was a house on the site of Knowles Farm north-east of Upper Hulme probably by 1308, when Robert of Knolles was recorded as a tenant of Alstonefield manor, and certainly by 1476.[73] To the east, across the headstream of the Churnet, pasture on Morridge was called Swains moor by the early 14th century.[74] There was house called Strines on the edge of the moor by 1415,[75] and one to the west on the site of Little Swainsmoor Farm by the early 16th century.[76] South of Swains moor, the detached portion of Bradnop township added to Heathylee in 1934 was centred on Hurdlow Farm, which belonged to Dieulacres abbey at the end of the Middle Ages. The name Hurdlow combines Old English *hord*, treasure, and *hlaw*, a hill or possibly a barrow.[77] There was a house at Stoney Cliffe south-west of Hurdlow by 1586.[78]

On the east side of the township there was a settlement at Hardings Booth at the confluence of the Manifold and Oakenclough brook by 1327.[79] The site of Oakenclough Hall to the south-west in the valley of Oakenclough brook was inhabited by the early 15th century.[80] A 17th-century stone house there, styled a hall in 1747,[81] was replaced by the present house built on an adjacent site in the later 1890s.[82] The site of Badger's Croft further west was probably inhabited by 1308, when Robert of Bochardescroft was recorded as a tenant of Alstonefield manor. The house was known as Butcher's or Badger's Croft in the 18th century.[83]

A house called Heathylee was recorded in 1406. Its site was probably in the Manifold valley north-west of Hardings Booth, where there were two houses called Heathylee in 1571.[84] There was a house in the upper part of the valley at Thick Withins by 1406,[85] and others to the east at Fawside by *c.* 1420[86] and Ball Bank by 1444.[87] There were also houses by the earlier 15th century on the south side of the Manifold: Hole Carr was recorded in 1414,[88] Bradshaw in 1429,[89] and Marnshaw in 1444.[90] Houses at Coldshaw and Merril Grove beside the Longnor road were recorded respectively in 1429 and

1439.[91] The place-name 'shaw' means a copse, and its use suggests late-medieval settlement in a wooded landscape.[92] The site of Heath House on the Longnor road east of Hardings Booth was occupied by 1406.[93] Waterhouse Farm at the township's eastern tip beside the Manifold was so called by 1571. There were then two adjacent houses, Over Waterhouse and Stewards Place, the latter possibly once used by the steward of Alstonefield manor. There were still two houses there in the later 18th century.[94]

Blue Hills north of Upper Hulme was probably the last area of the township to be settled. So called by *c.* 1680, it apparently takes its name from the colouring of watercourses by coal deposits, which were mined by the early 15th century.[95] A house called Gylfields in 1481 stood near Gib Torr Rocks (in Quarnford), possibly on the site of the present Gib Torr Farm. There was certainly a house called Gib Torr by 1564.[96] The present house is probably of the 19th century, and a barn carries the initials of Sir George Crewe and the date 1841. There was a house at Hazel Barrow by 1719,[97] and Newstone Farm is dated 1773.

A pool called Blake Mere on the east side of Swains moor was evidently so called in the 14th century, when the name was used for a nearby house (the present Mermaid inn) in Onecote, in Leek parish.[98] A belief that the pool was bottomless and that cattle would not drink from it or birds fly over it was dismissed as fanciful by the antiquary Robert Plot, writing *c.* 1680. He accepted, however, a story about the rescue of a woman whose lover tried to drown her in the pool. The event was the subject of Robert Southey's poem 'Mary, the Maid of the Inn', written in 1796.[99]

The Leek–Buxton road through Heathylee was laid out in the later 1760s as a branch of the road from Newcastle-under-Lyme to Hassop (Derb.) via Leek and Longnor, turnpiked in 1765.[1] Two miles north of Upper Hulme the Hassop road followed the line of a road which existed by 1408, when it was apparently known as Jaggers Lane in the Hardings Booth area;[2] a jagger was a carrier or packman. At that time it probably ran across the breadth of the township, crossing into Quarnford past Gib Torr. There was an inn by 1805 where the Buxton branch left the main road. By 1833 it was called the Royal Cottage, a name taken from a belief that Prince Charles

[71] S.R.O. 5322/5, no. 12; below, econ. hist. (trade and ind.).
[72] D.R.O., D. 2375M/1/1, 1st ct. 10 Hen. VI (as Knachurche).
[73] Ibid. D. 2375M/53/8, deed of feast of Annunciation 16 Edw. IV; *S.H.C.* N.S. xi. 258.
[74] *S.H.C.* 1911, 58–9.
[75] D.R.O., D. 2375M/1/1, ct. of 2 and 3 Hen. V.
[76] Ibid. D. 2375M/171/1/2, m. 1.
[77] *Eng. P.N. Elements*, i. 248–9, 261; below, estates.
[78] W.S.L. 132/9A/47, deed of 31 July 1586.
[79] *S.H.C.* vii (1), 218.
[80] D.R.O., D. 2375M/1/1, ct. of 7 and 8 Hen V.
[81] Sheffield City Archives, NSC 130.
[82] D.R.O., D. 2375M/207/9, specification for building Oakenclough farmhouse, 1894; D. 2375M/207/19, tenders for building farmhouses, 1896.
[83] *S.H.C.* N.S. xi. 257; D.R.O., D. 2375M/105/36.
[84] D.R.O., D. 2375M/1/1, 1st ct. 8 Hen. IV; D. 2375M/54/5.

[85] Ibid. D. 2375M/1/1, 1st ct. 8 Hen. IV.
[86] Ibid. ct. of 7 and 8 Hen. V.
[87] Ibid. 2nd ct. 22 Hen. VI.
[88] Ibid. ct. of 1 and 2 Hen. V (as Holehouse). Hole Carr in 1568: ibid. D. 2375M/55/1, rental of 1568.
[89] Ibid. D. 2375M/1/1, 5th ct. 7 Hen. VI.
[90] Ibid. 2nd ct. 22 Hen. VI.
[91] Ibid. 1st ct. 8 Hen. VI, 4th ct. 17 Hen. VI.
[92] *Eng. P.N. Elements*, ii. 99.
[93] D.R.O., D. 2375M/1/1, 1st ct. 8 Hen. IV.
[94] Ibid. D. 2375M/54/5; above, fig. 2.
[95] Plot, *Staffs.* 98; below, econ. hist. (trade and ind.).
[96] D.R.O., D. 2375M/1/1, 1st ct. 21 Edw. IV; *S.H.C.* 1938, 99.
[97] S.R.O., D. 921/1, f. 47.
[98] Below, Leek: Onecote, intro.
[99] Plot, *Staffs.* 44, 291; *Poetical Works of Robert Southey* (1838), vi. 1–9.
[1] Below, Leek: Leek and Lowe, communications.
[2] D.R.O., D. 2375M/1/1, ct. of 9 Hen. IV.

Edward Stuart slept in the house in 1745. In fact he stayed in Leek, and it is not known that there was a house on the site before the turnpike road was laid out.[3] The bridge over Oakenclough brook at Hardings Booth was rebuilt in 1779 and again shortly after 1808, by which date it was a county responsibility.[4] A side road running north-west from the Royal Cottage via Gib Torr to Manor Farm, in Quarnford, was turnpiked in 1773. Another road to Manor Farm running across the Blue Hills area via Hazel Barrow was turnpiked in 1793.[5] A tollgate and house were erected at Gib Torr in 1775; the gate was removed in 1825, when another was set up further along the road in Quarnford.[6] A road from Warslow laid out in the late 1810s joined the Leek–Buxton road south of the Royal Cottage, and by the later 1820s there was a tollbar east of the junction.[7] A tollhouse was built on the main road near Ramshaw Rocks in 1842.[8] The road system was disturnpiked in 1875.[9] A new stretch of road was built in 1955 to bypass Upper Hulme on the east.[10]

A short stretch of the Cheadle–Buxton road runs through the east side of the township. Formerly it joined the Longnor road near Longnor mill, but after being turnpiked in 1770 it was realigned to run directly to Longnor village by way of a bridge at Windy Arbour.[11] By 1818 there was a tollgate at the junction of the old and new routes.[12] The road was disturnpiked in 1878.[13]

A surviving stone bridge across a stream north-west of Stoney Cliffe carried a packhorse way between Cheshire and Nottinghamshire, which crossed the south-western tip of the township before climbing Morridge to the Mermaid inn in Onecote.[14]

Heathylee was connected to a mains electricity supply in 1963.[15]

It was apparently a custom in the early 19th century for people to gather on May Day at the Bald Stone west of the Royal Cottage and to paint it white.[16] The New inn at Upper Hulme was the meeting place of the Colliers' Refuge friendly society, established in 1842 as a lodge of the Order of Foresters. The society had 162 members in 1876.[17] A brass band formed at Upper Hulme by 1850[18] was probably drawn from members of the lodge.

ESTATES. An estate centred on *BRONCOTT FARM* at Upper Hulme probably existed by 1299 when the widow of Henry of Broncott held a house of Nicholas de Audley, the lord of Aenora Malbank's share of Alstonefield manor.[19] In 1327 Ranulph of Bagnall gave his son William lands and tenements in the vill and fields of Broncott, and in 1341 Thomas of Bagnall acquired a 'great house' there with further land. In 1370 the estate was held by Thomas's son John, and in 1432 John's son William granted it to Roger Fowall, retaining a life-interest.[20] Richard Fowall held the estate in 1557, when he was succeeded by his son William,[21] and Roger Fowall held it in 1567 and 1577. The owner in 1591 was Ralph Fowall, who became the tenant in 1592 on selling the estate to John Harpur, lord of Alstonefield manor.[22] In 1633 the tenant of what was then a 52½-a. farm was Robert Brough (d. 1657).[23] He was succeeded by his son Thomas, and Thomas by his son Robert, the tenant in 1679.[24] He or another Robert was succeeded in 1712 by his son Robert (d. 1753).[25] The tenant when the Harpur Crewe family offered the farm for sale in 1951 was Colin Lownds (d. 1975), whose daughter Edith and her husband William Waters were the owners in 1994.[26] The stone-built farmhouse is dated 1833.

The detached portion of Bradnop added to Heathylee in 1934 consisted of an estate centred on *HURDLOW FARM*. The estate belonged to Dieulacres abbey at the Dissolution, and in 1546 the Crown sold it to two speculators, Hugh and Robert Thornhill.[27] By 1625 it was owned by the Hollinshead family, later of Ashenhurst Hall in Bradnop, who still held it in 1680.[28] The later descent is unknown until 1835, when a house and 189 a. were offered for sale under the will of John Bourne, possibly of Lane End in Longton.[29] The property was again offered for sale in 1845, and 177 a. were bought by the Revd. John Sneyd of Basford Hall, in Cheddleton.[30] Rebuilt in the 19th century, the house with its

3 Ibid. D. 2375M/163/15; *T.N.S.F.C.* lxxiii. 121; below, Leek: Leek and Lowe, general hist. (18th cent.). Another story named Charles I: *Reliquary*, v. 134.
4 S.R.O., D. 3359/Buxton Rd. order bk. 1765–1800, 2 July 1779; S.R.O., Q/SO/24, f. 21.
5 *S.H.C.* 4th ser. xiii. 105; S.R.O., D. 3359/Buxton Rd. order bk. 1765–1800, 16 Nov. 1792.
6 S.R.O., D. 3359/Buxton Rd. order bk. 1765–1800, 30 June 1775; below, Quarnford, intro.
7 D.R.O., D. 2375M/120/17/10; S.R.O. 5322/5, no. 312; C. and J. Greenwood, *Map of County of Stafford* (1820).
8 Buxton Rd. acct. bk. 1809–60, acct. 4 Aug. 1842 (in possession of Mr. R. Stones of Malpas, Ches., 1994).
9 S.R.O., D. 3359/Leek, Buxton, and Monyash turnpike trust acct. bk. 1861–76.
10 Leek Libr., newspaper cuttings 1954–7, p. 46.
11 *S.H.C.* 4th ser. iii. 110. The new route is not shown on a map of Longnor made in the earlier 1770s, but it had been laid out by 1775: D.R.O., D. 2375M/161/3; above, fig. 2.
12 S.R.O., D. 5131/3/8/13; Greenwood, *Map of County of Stafford*.
13 S.R.O., D. 239/M/14/63, cert. of 25 Nov. 1878.
14 *V.C.H. Staffs.* ii. 278–9 (based on W.S.L., D. 1798/617/76; D. 1798/618/15).

15 S.R.O., CEH/110/1, 17 Oct. 1960, 15 July 1963.
16 *T.N.S.F.C.* xlviii. 162.
17 *Rep. Chief Registrar of Friendly Socs. 1876, App. P,* H.C. 429-I, p. 410 (1877), lxxvii; *Staffs. Advertiser,* 18 June 1853, p. 4; below, econ. hist. (trade and ind.).
18 'Diary of John Plant of Hazelwood, 1849–53', entry for 1 Oct. 1850 (TS. in W.S.L.).
19 D.R.O., D. 2375M/110/32, copy of inq. p.m. of Nic. de Audley, 1299 (as Bromekote).
20 Ibid. D. 2375M/126/2/2–3, 6, 10–11.
21 L.J.R.O., B/C/11, Ric. Fowall (1557).
22 D.R.O., D. 2375M/25/3, bdles. 1 and 2; D. 2375M/126/2/14.
23 Ibid. D. 2375M/63/53, p. 167; *Leek Par. Reg.* 12, 122.
24 D.R.O., D. 2375M/189/14, deed of 30 June 1679.
25 L.J.R.O., B/C/11, Rob. Brough (1713), Rob. Brough (1753).
26 W.S.L., S.C. E/3/26, no. 150; *St. Paul's, Quarnford* (1994), app. p. xv.
27 W.S.L., M. 540; *L. & P. Hen. VIII*, xxi (1), p. 762.
28 B.L. Add. Ch. 46768; Add. MS. 36664, f. 35; W.S.L. 329/10/40.
29 *Staffs. Advertiser,* 18 Oct. 1834, p. 3; 13 June 1835, p. 1.
30 Ibid. 22 Nov. 1845, p. 1; W.S.L. 132/13/47.

farmland was owned by the Belfield family in 1994.

ECONOMIC HISTORY.

AGRICULTURE. Over field and Nether field recorded at Broncott in 1341 may have been open fields.[31] The common waste lay chiefly on Morridge and covered 940 a. in 1839 when it was inclosed under an Act of 1834 amended in 1836. Sir George Crewe was awarded 48 a. as lord of the manor and 276 a. as impropriator of Alstonefield rectory, and the inclosure commissioners sold him a further 332 a.[32] Sir George also acquired by exchange in 1839 the 207 a. which had been awarded in lieu of tithes to the vicar of Alstonefield.[33]

Of the 2,034.9 ha. of farmland returned for the civil parish in 1988, grassland covered 1,609.6 ha. and there were 402.6 ha. of rough grazing. The farming was dairy and sheep, with 2,065 head of cattle and 7,438 sheep and lambs. One farm specialized in fattening pigs, of which there were 2,032 in the civil parish. Of the 55 farms returned, 47 were under 50 ha. in size, 5 were between 50 and 99 ha., and 3 were between 100 and 199 ha.[34]

MILLS. What was called Frith mill by 1404[35] almost certainly stood on the Manifold in Heathylee near Longnor bridge: land called Milne Holme, with which the mill was held in the 16th century, lay in that area.[36] In 1605 Sir John Harpur replaced it with a mill on a nearby site called Longnor mill and powered by a cut from the Manifold.[37] Shortly before 1770 Longnor mill was rebuilt by a corn dealer and chapman, Richard Gould of Brownhill, in Warslow. Gould became bankrupt in 1773, and the mill may have fallen into disuse.[38] It was working again by 1831, when it was enlarged to include a bone mill.[39] The mill was used for grinding corn until c. 1870 and for grinding bone until c. 1890. By 1884, and possibly by 1880, the mill was also used as a saw mill, specializing in the manufacture of rakes.[40] It remained a saw mill until it ceased working in the mid 1980s.

TRADE AND INDUSTRY. In 1401 Richard Strongarme took a year's lease of two coal mines and a forge at Back brook and Thomas Smyth a year's lease of a vein of coal at Black brook. In 1404 a smith named John Toples took a lease for life of 140 ft. of coal at Black brook. He seems to have worked the mine only until 1407. About 1415 a mine was let for 12 years to Robert of Hulme.[41] A mine in the Blue Hills area was being worked c. 1680.[42] In 1764 Sir Henry Harpur let a mine at Blue Hills for 21 years to James and Tobias Mallors, stipulating ⅒ of the coal as rent.[43] What was called the Bluehills Colliery in 1796 was then owned by the earl of Macclesfield. It still existed in 1869, when it was offered for lease.[44] Four miners lived in the Blue Hills area in 1871, but only one in 1881.[45]

The house north of Broncott Farm which became the New inn was occupied in 1786 by Joseph Billing, a stone cutter who presumably worked the quarry still open there in the early 19th century.[46] Several small quarries were opened along the Longnor road later in the 19th century, and there were 3 stonemasons and 3 stone breakers in the township in 1861 and 2 masons in 1881.[47] In the later 1820s there was a brickyard east of Heath House.[48]

In 1601 a button maker lived at Stonieway, apparently near Hardings Booth.[49] About 1680 a stream issuing from a mine at Blue Hills was used to dye button moulds, and poor people of that area were then said to be much employed in making buttons.[50] It was common for women and girls in the township to work as button makers in the earlier 19th century, and some of them may have been involved in an attempt to establish a trade union in 1834.[51] Only 6 women button makers were recorded in the township in 1841, but there were 38 in 1851 and 42 in 1861. Only 5 were recorded in 1881.[52]

In the later 1760s Adam Billing of Boarsgrove, south-west of Oakenclough Hall, traded as a hawker, selling goods from Manchester, possibly small wares, in the summer and fish in the winter. Isaac Belfield, who lived at Barrow Moor on the Longnor road in 1772, also seems to have been a dealer in small wares.[53]

LOCAL GOVERNMENT.

Heathylee was part of the Forest tithing of Alstonefield manor by the late 1390s and remained so in the earlier 1530s.[54] By 1594 it shared a frankpledge with Hollinsclough, the joint tithing sometimes being called High Frith.[55] That was still the arrangement in 1676, but by 1697 Heathylee had its own frankpledge, by then styled a headborough.[56]

31   D.R.O., D. 2375M/126/2/3–5.
32   S.R.O., Q/RDc 24; 4 & 5 Wm. IV, c. 15 (Priv. Act); 6 & 7 Wm. IV, c. 6 (Priv. Act).
33   D.R.O., D. 2375M/282/5(1), exchange of glebe land.
34   P.R.O., MAF 68/6128/58.
35   D.R.O., D. 2375M/1/1, ct. of 5 Hen. IV.
36   Ibid. D. 2375M/63/53, p. 149; D. 2375M/161/28, p. 2; S.H.C. 1931, 204.
37   D.R.O., D. 2375M/57/1, 28 and 29 Apr. 4 Jas. I; D. 2375M/142/11.
38   Ibid. D. 2375M/54/16, deed of 30 Mar. 1772; D. 2375M/54/18, proposals re Longnor mill, 1770; D. 2375M/54/39, docs. re Ric. Gould.
39   Ibid. D. 2375M/93/12, notification of 12 Sept. 1831.
40   P.O. Dir. Staffs. (1868; s.v. Longnor); Kelly's Dir. Staffs. (1880 and later edns. to 1900; s.v. Longnor).
41   D.R.O., D. 2375M/1/1, cts. of 6 and 14 Hen. IV and ct. of 2 and 3 Hen. V; D. 2375M/1/6, ct. of Thurs. before Christmas 2 Hen. IV.   42   Plot, Staffs. 98.
43   D.R.O., D. 2375M/189/6, deed of 1 Dec. 1764.

44   Ibid. D. 2375M/110/32, Geo. Greaves to Rob. Greaves; Staffs. Advertiser, 7 Aug. 1869, p. 8.
45   P.R.O., RG 10/2885; RG 11/2742.
46   D.R.O., D. 2375M/64/9, deeds of 16 May 1786 (as Billings), 2 May 1846 (as Billing); J. Farey, Gen. View of Agric. and Minerals of Derb. (1811), i. 417.
47   P.R.O., RG 9/1949; RG 11/2742; O.S. Map 6″, Staffs. IV. NE. (1887 edn.).   48   S.R.O. 5322/5, map.
49   Alstonfield Par. Reg. 60; D.R.O., D. 2375M/161/28, p. 2.   50   Plot, Staffs. 98.
51   Below, Quarnford, econ. hist. (trade and ind.).
52   P.R.O., HO 107/1003; HO 107/2008; ibid. RG 9/1949; RG 11/2742.
53   S.R.O., D. 3359/Condlyffe, brief in case Billing v. Morris, 1766, and letter from John Harmar to Wm. Condlyffe, 27 July 1772.
54   Above, Alstonefield, par. intro. (manorial govt.).
55   D.R.O., D. 2375M/57/1, 7 Oct. 36 Eliz. I sqq.
56   Ibid. D. 2375M/57/2, 11 Oct. 1676; D. 2375M/174/1, 29 Apr. 9 Wm. III.

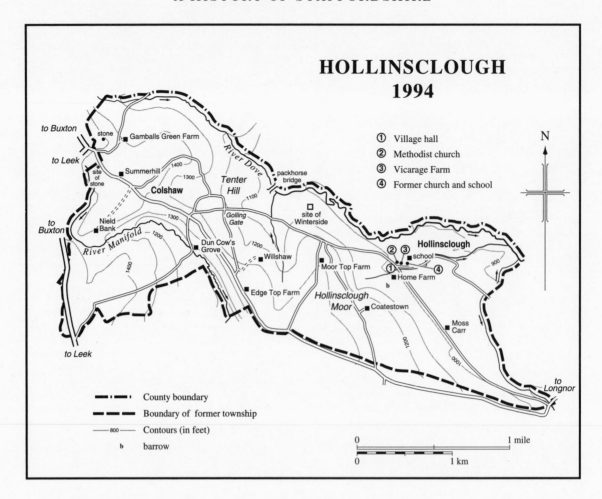

HOLLINSCLOUGH
1994

to Buxton

to Leek

stone

Gamballs Green Farm

Summerhill

1400

1300

Colshaw

River Dove

Tenter Hill

packhorse bridge

1100

① Village hall
② Methodist church
③ Vicarage Farm
④ Former church and school

N

to Buxton

Nield Bank

1300

River Manifold

1200

Golling Gate

Dun Cow's Grove

1200

site of Winterside

② ③ **Hollinsclough**

school

①

④

Willshaw

Moor Top Farm

Home Farm

b

1400

to Leek

Edge Top Farm

Hollinsclough Moor

Coatestown

900

Moss Carr

1200

1000

to Longnor

—∙∙—∙∙— County boundary

— — — Boundary of former township

—800— Contours (in feet)

b barrow

0   1 mile
0   1 km

FIG. 7

There was a pinner for the joint tithing by 1596.[57] In the later 1820s there was a pinfold on the Longnor road west of Hardings Booth.[58]

Two surveyors of the highways for Heathylee were appointed at the manor court apparently for the first time in 1601. From 1602 there was normally only one.[59]

In the later 17th and earlier 18th century the poor of Heathlyee, Fawfieldhead, Hollinsclough, and Quarnford were maintained jointly.[60] Heathylee relieved its poor separately from 1733.[61] It became part of Leek poor-law union in 1837.[62]

CHURCH. In 1559 Ralph Gylmen of Merril Grove in Heathylee bequeathed a lamb for 'God's service' at Longnor, probably an indication that he attended Longnor church; people from Heathylee certainly did so by the late 17th century.[63] From 1744 those living in the western part of the township attended the church built

that year at Flash, in Quarnford, and in 1902 that part of Heathylee was assigned to Quarnford parish.[64] By 1900 and at least until the later 1950s mission services were held in the schoolroom on the Buxton road.[65]

NONCONFORMITY. A Methodist society met at Ridge Head, the home of Isaac Billing on the Longnor road, in the late 18th and early 19th century.[66] It numbered 46 in 1803 but only 8 in 1819, members presumably having moved to other societies in the area.[67] In 1829 Wesleyan Methodist services were held fortnightly on Sundays at Hole Carr and at Upper Hulme and once a month at Ridge Head. A Sunday service was also held twice a month at Hazel Barrow and at Newstone Farm, where a meeting room or chapel had been added to the farmhouse apparently in 1816. By 1832 Sunday services were held three times a month at Newstone and once a month elsewhere in the township.[68] A

57 Ibid. D. 2375M/57/1, 26 Apr. 38 Eliz. I.
58 S.R.O. 5322/5, map.
59 D.R.O., D. 2375M/57/1, 21 Apr. 43 Eliz. I, 17 Apr. 44 Eliz. I sqq.   60 Above, Fawfieldhead, local govt.
61 S.R.O., Q/SO/13, ff. 104v.–105.
62 S.R.O., D. 699/1/1/1, p. 4.
63 L.J.R.O., B/C/11, Ralph Gylmen (1559); below, Longnor, church.

64 S.R.O., D. 1029/1/1; *Lond. Gaz.* 15 Aug. 1902, p. 5321.
65 *Lich. Dioc. Ch. Cal.* (1900), 115; (1957), 129; *Alstonfield Deanery Mag.* lxiv (10).
66 Dyson, *Wesleyan Methodism*, 71–2; D.R.O., D. 2375M/70/5, Heathylee, p. 4.   67 S.R.O., D. 3155/1.
68 Ibid. D. 3156/1/1/24; P.R.O., HO 129/372/4/1; Leek Libr., Johnson scrapbk. i (2), D/13/15.

chapel opened at Upper Hulme in 1837 had an evening congregation of 30, besides Sunday school children, on Census Sunday 1851.[69] Services were still held at the chapel in 1994. The average attendance at Newstone in 1851 was between 50 and 60 adults. Services were last held there in 1930.[70]

A Primitive Methodist chapel opened in 1853 at 'Morridge End' was replaced c. 1880 by one on the Buxton road north of Morridge Top Farm. That chapel was closed in 1972 and was used in 1994 as a farm outbuilding.[71]

EDUCATION. There was no school in the township in 1819.[72] In the earlier 1830s there were two day schools, with between 30 and 40 children who paid fees. There was also a Sunday school in which 120 children were taught free.[73] A Wesleyan Methodist Sunday school at Upper Hulme had an attendance of 28 on Census Sunday 1851.[74] There was evidently a dame school in 1841, when a schoolmistress lived in the township. A mistress was again recorded in 1851, 1861, and 1881.[75]

A school board for Heathylee was formed compulsorily in 1880, and in 1884 a school was built on the Buxton road south of the Royal Cottage. The cost was met by Sir John Harpur Crewe. It became Ramshaw council school in 1903.[76] The decision in 1930 that what was then an all-age school with 40 children on its books should become a junior school took effect in 1940, the senior children being transferred to Leek.[77] Ramshaw school was closed in 1970, and the building was later converted into a house.[78]

CHARITY FOR THE POOR. By will of 1793 John Robinson of Fawside left half the interest on £196 9s. 6d. for the poor of Heathylee and Longnor. In 1972 the charity was administered jointly with others for Longnor.[79]

HOLLINSCLOUGH

HOLLINSCLOUGH was formerly a township in Alstonefield parish and later a civil parish 1,842 a. (745 ha.) in area.[80] A village with a chapel and a school but no inn or shop lies in a secluded valley in the north-east corner. Elsewhere the land is upland pasture. The river Dove forms the northern boundary, which is also the county boundary with Derbyshire, and tributaries of the Dove and the river Manifold form the eastern boundary with Longnor. The south-western boundary with Heathylee runs along a ridge. On the west Hollinsclough broadens out, taking in the headstream of the Manifold, which forms the boundary with Quarnford.

The land lies at its highest at the west end of the ridge where a house called Summerhill stands at 1,513 ft. (461 m.). The ridge tapers to the south-east, the land dropping gradually to 883 ft. (269 m.) at the south-eastern tip of the township. The underlying rock is sandstone of the Millstone Grit series. The upland soil is coarse loam; there is loam of better quality over clay on the lower ground.[81]

The number of people in Hollinsclough owing suit at the manor court in 1769 was 115.[82] The population of the township was 562 in 1801 and 513 in 1811. By 1831 it had risen to 564 but had fallen to 457 by 1841 and 393 by 1861. An increase to 425 by 1871 was followed by a steady decline to 259 in 1901, 224 in 1911, 210 in 1921, 194 in 1931, 183 in 1951, and 170 in 1961. It was 201 in 1971 and 161 in 1981 and 1991.[83]

There is a Bronze Age barrow on the hillside south-west of the village.[84] The village takes its name from its position at the mouth of a short ravine formed by a stream which flows north into the Dove: when first recorded in the late 1390s the settlement was known as Howelsclough, the first part of the name possibly deriving from Old English hol, a hollow.[85] The form Hollinsclough, used occasionally by the later 18th century, became standard in the early 19th century.[86] The village had only 3 houses and 7 cottages in the earlier 1630s;[87] an inn was closed in 1785.[88] Home Farm and Vicarage Farm, both of the early 19th century, are the principal houses in the village. In 1974 the former Anglican church, closed in 1966, became a residential field centre for Frank Wheldon comprehensive school, Nottingham. The centre is named after Michael Hutchinson, the head teacher when the building was bought from the Harpur-Crewe estate in 1985.[89]

The village stands on a road which until the early 19th century was the route between the Leek–Buxton road, just over the Quarnford boundary, and Longnor.[90] East of Colshaw on the west side of the township the road runs

69 P.R.O., HO 129/372/4/1; date stone on building.
70 P.R.O., HO 129/372/4/1; S.R.O., D. 3457/1/5.
71 S.R.O., D. 3457/7/2; St. Paul's, Quarnford (1994), 35.
72 D.R.O., D. 2375M/87/19, acct. of schs. in Alstonefield par. 1819.
73 Educ. Enq. Abstract, 868.
74 P.R.O., HO 129/372/4/1.
75 Ibid. HO 107/1003; HO 107/2008; ibid. RG 9/1949; RG 11/2742.
76 List of Sch. Boards, 1902 [Cd. 1038], p. 637 (1902), lxxix; Kelly's Dir. Staffs. (1884); S.R.O., CEH/165/1.
77 Staffs. C.C. Record for 1930, 867; S.R.O., CEH/165/1, p. 129.
78 S.R.O., CEH/110/1.
79 Below, Longnor, charities.
80 V.C.H. Staffs. i. 327. This article was written in 1994.

81 Geol. Surv. Map 1/50,000, drift, sheet 111 (1978 edn.); Soil Surv. of Eng. and Wales, sheet 3 (1983).
82 D.R.O., D. 2375M/174/5/10.
83 V.C.H. Staffs. i. 327; Census, 1901-91.
84 Reliquary, iii. 162-3; Staffs. C.C., Sites and Monuments Rec. 00123.
85 D.R.O., D. 2375M/1/1, 4th and 5th cts. 22 Ric. II; Eng. P.N. Elements, i. 257.
86 S.R.O., D. 921/1-2.
87 D.R.O., D. 2375M/63/53, pp. 158-9.
88 Memorials of the late John Lomas of Hollinsclough, ed. J. Birchenall (Macclesfield, preface dated 1848; photocopy in W.S.L.), 5.
89 Inf. from Mr. J. P. Carrington, the centre's head; below, church.
90 Above, fig. 2.

through a deep valley past Golling Gate and crosses Hollinsclough moor before dropping into the village. It formerly continued to Longnor, leaving the village in the north-east. A more direct route to Longnor running to the south-east past Moss Carr was laid out in 1843–4.[91] By 1820 there was also a road to Longnor which avoided the drop at Golling Gate and bypassed the village by continuing along the high ground south-east of Colshaw.[92]

The earliest settlements outside the village included one to the south-east at Moss Carr, probably the site of a house called Moscure which was recorded in Alstonefield manor in the earlier 15th century. There was certainly a house at Moss Carr by the late 16th century.[93] North-west of the village there was a house called Winterside in 1400 on a site still occupied in the early 20th century.[94] Two other early settlements lay beside the Manifold on the west side of the township: a house called the Neelde in 1455 almost certainly stood on the site of Nield Bank,[95] and Dun Cow's Grove was recorded as Duncote Greave in 1600.[96] Gamballs Green Farm in the north-west corner of the township takes its name from a green called Gamon green in 1564, Gambushe green in 1600, and Gambles green in 1720.[97]

There was settlement by the earlier 18th century at Colshaw.[98] A house there called Summerhill is dated 1757 and was built for John Gaunt, a button merchant. Edge Top Farm to the south-east is dated 1787 and was built for Micah Mellor, a hawker.[99] Houses on Hollinsclough moor include Coatestown, possibly the home of Isaac Coates, a chapman, in the later 18th century, and Moor Top Farm, built in the early 19th century for John Tunnicliff.[1]

North-east of Golling Gate a packhorse bridge, surviving in 1994, crossed the Dove, and there was once another packhorse bridge downstream near Hollinsclough village.[2]

Hollinsclough was connected to a mains electricity supply in the early 1960s. It received a mains water supply in 1984 after a reservoir had been constructed north of Flash, in Quarnford.[3]

Hollinsclough Silver Band, formed by 1920,[4] still existed in 1994, drawing its members from surrounding villages and further afield. A village hall was opened in 1992.[5] Among its users is a community group called History Live, which organizes talks and exhibitions on the history of the area.[6]

MANOR. Hollinsclough was part of Alstonefield manor.

ECONOMIC HISTORY. AGRICULTURE. An open field called Town field was mentioned in 1617.[7] It presumably lay near the village, where in the earlier 1630s there were 11 a. of arable in pieces 'in the field'; a further 8½ a. then lay in what was called the corn field.[8] Town field was still open in 1725.[9]

The common waste lay on Hollinsclough moor south-west of the village and covered 386 a. in the late 18th century.[10] Most of it was presumably inclosed privately, and in 1839 only 25 a. were inclosed under an Act of 1834 amended in 1836.[11]

Of the 649.6 ha. of farmland returned for the civil parish in 1988, grassland covered 547.3 ha. and there were 101.7 ha. of rough grazing. The farming was dairy and sheep, with 815 head of cattle and 1,302 sheep and lambs. Of the 24 farms returned, 22 were under 40 ha. in size, one was between 50 and 99 ha., and one was between 100 and 199 ha.[12]

TRADE. A fulling mill stood above Hollinsclough village in 1564, probably on the Dove north-west of the village. Cloth working in that area is suggested by the name Tenter Hill, used by 1775 for the hill between the river and Golling Gate.[13]

A pedlar was recorded in Hollinsclough in 1600.[14] Isaac Coates, possibly of Coatestown on Hollinsclough moor, was a dealer and chapman from the late 1750s. At first he bought goods from travellers, but c. 1770 he started to buy directly from manufacturers in Manchester and employed two or three men to sell for him. He was declared bankrupt in 1774.[15] John Lomas, the son of a pedlar, George Lomas, who lived at Colshaw in the later 1740s, at first assisted his father; in 1764 he became a hawker on his own account and later a wholesale dealer. He moved to Hollinsclough village in 1785,[16] the year he appeared before the House of Commons to argue successfully against a proposal to abolish licensed hawkers and pedlars.[17] Micah Mellor of Edge Top Farm was described as a hawker and pedlar at his death in 1791.[18]

A button merchant, William Wood, lived in Hollinsclough probably in 1757 and certainly in 1769, and Ezekiel Wood of Colshaw was de-

91 D.R.O., D. 2375M/93/12, Mr. Johnson's estimate for Hollinsclough road, 15 Jan. 1844.
92 C. and J. Greenwood, *Map of County of Stafford* (1820).
93 D.R.O., D. 2375M/1/1, ct. of 4 Hen. V; *Alstonfield Par. Reg.* 103 (as Mosker).
94 D.R.O., D. 2375M/1/6, ct. of Thurs. after feast of St. Thos. the apostle 2 Hen. V; O.S. Map 6", Staffs. II. SW. (1924 edn.).
95 D.R.O., D. 2375M/1/1, 1st ct. 34 Hen. VI.
96 *Alstonfield Par. Reg.* 63.
97 Ibid. 62; *S.H.C.* 1938, 99; S.R.O., D. 921/1, f. 53.
98 S.R.O., D. 1029/1/1, p. 13.
99 Below, econ. hist. (trade).
1 Ibid.; White, *Dir. Staffs.* (1834), 721.
2 Dodd, *Peakland Roads*, 93–4.
3 S.R.O., CEH/110/1, 17 Oct. 1960; Leek Libr., newspaper cuttings 1984 (1), p. 13.
4 *Alstonfield Deanery Mag.* xxiv (2), Quarnford section.

5 Date stone on building.
6 Postscript in *The Farmer's Wife* (booklet for exhibition at Home Fm., Hollinsclough, 1993).
7 D.R.O., D. 2375M/57/1, 8 May 15 Jas. I.
8 Ibid. D. 2375M/63/53, pp. 158–9.
9 Ibid. D. 2375M/174/1, 21 Oct. 1725.
10 Ibid. D. 2375M/161/11.
11 S.R.O., Q/RDc 24, m. 16 and map I; 4 & 5 Wm. IV, c. 15 (Priv. Act); 6 & 7 Wm. IV, c. 6 (Priv. Act).
12 P.R.O., MAF 68/6128/60.
13 D.R.O., D. 2375M/1/1, 1564 rental, entry at foot of 4th col.; above, fig. 2.   14 *Alstonfield Par. Reg.* 104.
15 D.R.O., D. 2375M/54/39, memo. re Isaac Coates, 1774; D. 2375M/174/5/10.
16 Ibid. D. 2375M/87/19, John Lomas to Sir Geo. Crewe, 11 Aug. 1820; S.R.O., D. 1029/1/1, p. 13; *Memorials of John Lomas*, 5.
17 Above, Alstonefield, par. intro.
18 L.J.R.O., B/C/11, Micah Mellor (1791).

scribed as a button maker in 1764.[19] John Gaunt of Summerhill, recorded as a button merchant in 1764, was known locally in 1772 as 'the king of the Flash', a reference to the village of that name in Quarnford which was the centre of the area's button trade.[20] Obadiah Tunnicliff, who was living at Colshaw in 1769, was described as a button manufacturer of Flash in 1787,[21] and his son Moses probably continued in the trade: in 1820 Moses had a warehouse and factory in Macclesfield (Ches.).[22] Three Hollinsclough button manufacturers were mentioned in 1800, Micah Mellor of Edge Top, William Mellor of Willshaw Side, and Ezekiel Wood of Golling Gate,[23] and two were listed in 1834, John Weston and William Wood, the latter a silk, twist, and button manufacturer.[24] Women button makers from Hollinsclough were probably involved in an attempt to establish a trade union in 1834.[25] Three such workers were recorded in the township in 1841, 13 in 1851, and 21 in 1861. Both men and women worked as silk weavers during the same period: 4 were recorded in 1841, 37 in 1851, and 13 in 1861.[26]

LOCAL GOVERNMENT

Hollinsclough was part of the Forest tithing of Alstonefield manor by the late 1390s and remained so in the earlier 1530s.[27] By 1594 it shared a frankpledge with Heathylee, the joint tithing sometimes being called High Frith.[28] That was still the arrangement in 1676, but by 1697 Hollinsclough had its own frankpledge, by then styled a headborough.[29] There was a pinner for the joint tithing by 1596 but one for Hollinsclough alone by 1697.[30] A pinfold which stood on the east side of the village in the later 1820s was rebuilt in 1858.[31]

Two surveyors of the highways for Hollinsclough were appointed at the manor court apparently for the first time in 1601. From 1602 there was normally only one.[32]

In the later 17th and earlier 18th century the poor of Hollinsclough, Fawfieldhead, Heathylee, and Quarnford were maintained jointly.[33] Hollinsclough relieved its poor separately from 1733.[34] It became part of Leek poor-law union in 1837.[35]

CHURCH

From the late 17th century and presumably earlier people from Hollinsclough attended Longnor church.[36] From 1744 those living in the western part of the township attended the church built that year at Flash, in Quarnford, and in 1902 that part of Hollinsclough was assigned to Quarnford parish.[37]

In 1840 Sir George Crewe, prompted by the curate of Longnor, William Buckwell, rebuilt a barn in Hollinsclough village as a church and a school; he also converted a farmhouse, probably the present Vicarage Farm, into a house for a curate.[38] The church was licensed in 1841 and named St. Agnes in 1906.[39] The first curate, who was paid £50 a year by Sir George,[40] was Henry Smith, of whom Sir George remarked that 'no one but a man in every sense of the word of a missionary spirit could possibly live there'; he had left by 1846.[41] From 1850 the church was served by the curate of Quarnford, who lived in the Hollinsclough house.[42] On Census Sunday 1851 he took two services at Hollinsclough, with attendances of 24 in the morning, besides Sunday school children, and 56 in the evening.[43] Hollinsclough was still served by the curate of Quarnford in 1865, but by 1871 it was served from Longnor.[44] Regular services were last held apparently in 1956, and the church was closed in 1966, later becoming a residential field centre.[45] Of coursed rubble with ashlar dressings, the former church was a rectangular building with a short east chancel and a south porch. There was a west gallery, and a bell turret was added in 1924.[46]

NONCONFORMITY

The hawker John Lomas became a Methodist in 1783. He moved from Colshaw to Hollinsclough village in 1785 and formed a Methodist society which had 11 members in 1786.[47] A chapel built by Lomas in the village was registered in 1797, with Lomas as minister.[48] Sunday services were held there fortnightly in 1798, alternating with services at Longnor.[49] Lomas rebuilt the chapel in 1801, and by 1802 there was a weekly Sunday service.[50] The society had 23 members in 1803.[51] Lomas died in 1823, leaving instructions that a manuscript entitled 'The Last Legacy of John Lomas

19 D.R.O., D. 2375M/174/2, 11 Oct. 1757; D. 2375M/174/5/10; S.R.O., D. 921/4, no. 29.
20 S.R.O., D. 1029/1/2, pp. 16–17; D. 3359/Condlyffe, J. Whitaker to Wm. Condlyffe, 5 Aug. 1772; below, Quarnford (trade and ind.).
21 S.R.O., D. 1029/1/2, p. 44; W. Tunnicliff, Topog. Survey of Counties of Stafford, Chester, and Lancaster (Nantwich, 1787), 32.
22 S.R.O., D. 1029/1/2, p. 44; L.J.R.O., B/C/11, Moses Tunnicliff (1821).
23 D.R.O., D. 2375M/101/4, deed of 25 Mar. 1800.
24 White, Dir. Staffs. (1834), 721.
25 Below, Quarnford, econ. hist. (trade and ind.).
26 P.R.O., HO 107/1003; HO 107/2008; ibid. RG 9/1949.
27 Above, Alstonefield, par. intro. (manorial govt.).
28 D.R.O., D. 2375M/57/1, 7 Oct. 36 Eliz. I sqq.
29 Ibid. D. 2375M/57/2, 11 Oct. 1676; D. 2375M/174/1, 29 Apr. 9 Wm. III.
30 Ibid. D. 2375M/57/1, 26 Apr. 38 Eliz. I; D. 2375M/174/1, 29 Apr. 9 Wm. III.
31 Ibid. D. 2375M/202/19, f. 111; S.R.O. 5322/6, no. 662.
32 D.R.O., D. 2375M/57/1, 21 Apr. 43 Eliz. I, 17 Apr. 44 Eliz. I sqq.
33 Above, Fawfieldhead, local govt.
34 S.R.O., Q/SO/13, f. 105.
35 S.R.O., D. 699/1/1/1, p. 4.
36 Below, Longnor, church.
37 S.R.O., D. 1029/1/1; Lond. Gaz. 15 Aug. 1902, pp. 5321–3.
38 D.R.O., D. 2375M/40/14, 28 Aug. 1841; D. 2375M/44/1, 20 Aug. 1840; D. 2375M/205/15/1, Joseph Millward's bill.
39 Lich. Dioc. Regy., Bp.'s Reg. 30, pp. 182–3; Alstonfield Deanery Mag. Nov. 1906.
40 D.R.O., D. 2375M/205/16, receipts of Mr. Buckwell and Mr. Smith, 1842.
41 Ibid. D. 2375M/44/1, 20 Aug. 1840; D. 2375M/205/17, receipt of Ric. Evans, 1846.
42 Lich. Dioc. Regy., Bp.'s Reg. 31, p. 230; P.R.O., HO 107/2008.   43 P.R.O., HO 129/372/4/3.
44 D.R.O., D. 2375M/202/19, p. 235; Lich. Dioc. Ch. Cal. (1871), 156.
45 Alstonfield Deanery Mag. lix (11); lxix (6); above, intro.
46 Alstonfield Deanery Mag. xxviii (1); below, plate 60.
47 Memorials of John Lomas, 4–5; Dyson, Wesleyan Methodism, 71, 73.   48 S.H.C. 4th ser. iii. 135.
49 Dyson, Wesleyan Methodism, 40.
50 D.R.O., D. 3568/4/1/1; date stone on chapel.
51 S.R.O., D. 3155/1.

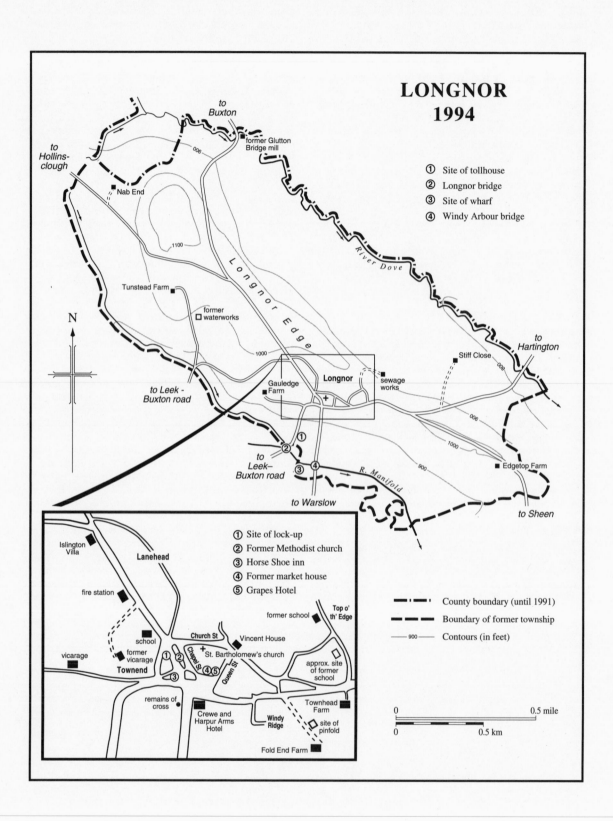

LONGNOR 1994

① Site of tollhouse
② Longnor bridge
③ Site of wharf
④ Windy Arbour bridge

to Buxton

to Hollins-clough

former Glutton Bridge mill

Nab End

River Dove

to Hartington

1100

Longnor Edge

Tunstead Farm

former waterworks

N

Stiff Close

1000

Longnor

sewage works

Gauledge Farm

to Leek - Buxton road

Edgetop Farm

①
②

to Leek–Buxton road

③ ④

R. Manifold

1000

900

to Warslow

to Sheen

① Site of lock-up
② Former Methodist church
③ Horse Shoe inn
④ Former market house
⑤ Grapes Hotel

Islington Villa

Lanehead

fire station

school

vicarage

former vicarage

Townend

① ②

③

remains of cross

Church St

Chapel St

Queen St

Vincent House

St. Bartholomew's church

④ ⑤

former school

Top o' th' Edge

approx. site of former school

Townhead Farm

Crewe and Harpur Arms Hotel

Windy Ridge

site of pinfold

Fold End Farm

—·—·— County boundary (until 1991)
— — — Boundary of former township
——900—— Contours (in feet)

0   0.5 mile
0   0.5 km

Fig. 8

40

to the People of Hollinsclough and its Vicinity' should be published and a copy given to every household in Hollinsclough and within a mile of it. Probably a religious exhortation, the text seems to have been partly incorporated into a printed version of Lomas's diary, published in 1848.[52] On Census Sunday 1851 there was an afternoon congregation of 26, besides Sunday school children.[53] The church was still open in 1994.

EDUCATION. In the 1750s Dinah Lomas (d. 1761) of Gamballs Green ran a dame school,[54] and in 1759 the inhabitants of Hollinsclough nominated John Lomas as the master of a school in the township.[55] The school may have been established by John Bourne of Newcastle-under-Lyme, the benefactor of a school built at Flash in Quarnford in 1760: he was described as 'a considerable benefactor to the schoolhouse at Colshaw'.[56] The building was probably east of Summerhill, its site in the early 19th century.[57] Nothing further is known about it.

There was a Methodist Sunday school in 1811, possibly the Sunday school with 32 boys and 38

girls recorded in the township in the earlier 1830s.[58] A free day school opened at Flash in 1834 was intended partly for children from Hollinsclough, but an endowment to support it ceased in 1835.[59]

A school occupied the west end of the church built in Hollinsclough village in 1840. A National school by the later 1840s, it was managed by a committee of ratepayers probably from 1864 and certainly by 1871, when it had 38 children on its books. In 1873 a schoolroom was built on the west side of the church.[60] The decision in 1931 that what was then Hollinsclough Church of England school, an all-age school with 33 children, should become a junior school probably took effect in the later 1940s, the senior children being transferred to Leek.[61] Hollinsclough school took controlled status in 1955.[62] A new school building was opened on an adjacent site in 1960, when there were 25 children.[63] In 1993 the school took maintained status.[64]

CHARITIES FOR THE POOR. None known expressly for the township.

LONGNOR

LONGNOR was formerly a township in Alstonefield parish and later a civil parish 813 a. (329 ha.) in area.[65] Longnor village, which has the appearance of a small market town, stands on a saddle in the ridge which dominates the area and gives the township its Old English name *langen ofer*, long slope.[66] The river Dove forms the western boundary, which is also the boundary with Derbyshire, except at the north-west end where by the later 1820s some land south of the river was in Derbyshire.[67] The old course of the river Manifold and a tributary brook formed the south-western boundary with Heathylee and Hollinsclough. The old course, still in existence in the earlier 1770s, had been replaced by a canalized stretch by 1820.[68] The new course was taken as the boundary of the civil parish in 1934, when 18 a. south of the river east of Longnor bridge were transferred to Heathylee civil parish and 1 a. north of the river was transferred from Heathylee to Longnor. As a result the area of Longnor civil parish was reduced to 796 a. (322 ha.).[69] In 1991 the 34 a. (14 ha.) on the south side of the Dove which

belonged to Hartington (Derb.) were transferred to Longnor.[70]

The land rises to 1,182 ft. (360 m.) near Nab End in the north-west corner of the township. Longnor village stands at 956 ft. (291 m.), the land to the south-east rising to 1,016 ft. (310 m.) near Edgetop Farm. The land is at its lowest, 800 ft. (244 m.), where the road east from Longnor village crosses the Dove. The underlying rock is sandstone of the Millstone Grit series. The soil is mostly clay but south of the village it is loam and clay.[71]

Twenty-five people in Longnor were assessed for hearth tax in 1666, and the number of people owing suit at the manor court in 1769 was 58.[72] The township's population in 1801 was 391, rising to 467 in 1811. It was 460 in 1821 and 429 in 1831 but had risen to 485 by 1841 and 561 by 1851. By 1861 it had fallen to 514. It was 520 in 1871 and 534 in 1881, after which it fell to 509 in 1891 and 480 in 1901. The population was 517 in 1911, 444 in 1921, 466 in 1931, 443 in 1951, 381 in 1961, 352 in 1971, 381 in 1981, and 380 in 1991.[73]

There was a church at Longnor apparently by

52 L.J.R.O., B/C/11, John Lomas (1823); *Memorials of John Lomas*, 2–5.
53 P.R.O., HO 129/372/4/3.
54 D.R.O., D. 2375M/87/19, John Lomas to Sir Geo. Crewe, 11 Aug. 1820; S.R.O., D. 1029/1/1, p. 117.
55 L.J.R.O., B/A/11B.
56 Benefaction board in Flash church, Quarnford; below, Quarnford, educ.
57 D.R.O., D. 2375M/70/5, Hollinsclough, p. 18; S.R.O. 5322/6, no. 50.
58 *Memorials of John Lomas*, 21; *Educ. Enq. Abstract*, 868.
59 Below, Quarnford, educ.
60 Nat. Soc. *Inquiry, 1846–7*, Staffs. 2–3; P.R.O., ED 7/109/167; below, plate 60.
61 Staffs. C.C. *Record for 1931*, 835–6; below, Longnor, educ.
62 *Lich. Dioc. Dir.* (1955–6), 91.
63 'Hollinsclough. Our Village' (TS. in W.S.L., n.d. but probably 1967).
64 *Leek Post & Times*, 3 Nov. 1993, p. 18.
65 *V.C.H. Staffs.* i. 327. This article was written in 1993–4. The Revd. A. C. F. Nicoll, vicar of Longnor, is thanked for his help.
66 *Eng. P.N. Elements*, ii. 15, 54; M. Gelling, *Place-Names in the Landscape*, 173–4.
67 S.R.O. 5322/7.
68 D.R.O., D. 2375M/161/3; C. and J. Greenwood, *Map of County of Stafford* (1820).
69 *Census*, 1931; Staffs. Review Order, 1934, p. 63 and map 1 (copy in S.R.O.).
70 Ches., Derb., Heref. and Worc. and Staffs. (County Boundaries) Order 1991 (S.I. 1991 no. 311), map 5; *Census*, 1981–91.
71 Geol. Surv. Map 1/50,000, drift, sheet 111 (1978 edn.); Soil Surv. of Eng. and Wales, sheet 3 (1983).
72 *S.H.C.* 1925, 234; D.R.O., D. 2375M/174/5/12.
73 *V.C.H. Staffs.* i. 327; *Census*, 1901–91.

the 12th century and certainly by the earlier 15th century. It presumably stood in the present churchyard, in the centre of what was formerly a large open space used for a market and fairs.[74] About 1600 Longnor village, the most important settlement in Alstonefield parish, was described as 'now something spoken of', and it had nine or ten licensed alehouse keepers in 1604.[75] The market place was by then already being encroached upon: the present Horse Shoe inn retains a stone dated 1609, probably from an earlier house on the site, and by the later 18th century there were houses on both the east and west sides of the market place, the west side being known by the mid 19th century as Carder Green.[76] The principal houses surviving from the 18th century are one in Chapel Street which is dated 1774 and has an ashlar front with rusticated quoins and door surround,[77] and one on the south side of the market place which has a western block of red brick with ashlar quoins. The latter is an inn called the Harpur Arms in 1781 and the Crewe and Harpur Arms by 1818. There was formerly an inn, called the White Horse by 1794, at Townend on the west side of the market place.[78]

Longnor remained important as a market centre in the 19th century, and several shops were opened in the village.[79] In addition to the Crewe and Harpur Arms, which was a coaching inn on a route between London and Buxton in 1803, and the White Horse there were a further five inns in 1818, the Bell, Red Bull, Cheshire Cheese, Horse Shoe, and Swan.[80] An inn on the north side of the market place called the Board in 1850 and the Butcher's Arms in 1860 became the Grapes c. 1866.[81] A horse post which operated between Longnor, Hartington (Derb.), and Leek three days a week in 1829[82] may have been based in Longnor. Joseph Wain of Longnor was described as a postman that year, and by 1834 letters were sent to Leek three days a week by horse post from a post office in Longnor run by Isaac Wain. By 1851 letters were sent daily to Buxton.[83] The economy, however, was insufficient to support a sub-branch of the District Bank which was opened from Leek in 1864; it was closed in 1866.[84] Longnor in the 19th century was also a centre for professional people. Two surgeons, George Fynney and Frederick Wyatt, lived in Longnor in 1813, but apparently only Wyatt in 1818.[85] Other surgeons included William Flint, who lived in Longnor at least

between 1834 and 1851,[86] and Joseph Poole, who practised in the 1870s and 1880s.[87] There were boys' and girls' boarding schools by the 1840's and a solicitor lived in the village in 1864.[88] Longnor's attraction derived partly from its situation, described in 1865 as 'quite as beautiful as that of Buxton'; its air was invigorating, and the scenery striking and romantic.[89] New houses were built especially on the east side of the village, where there is a row of four cottages dated 1837 opposite Townhead Farm. A row of six cottages in Queen Street between the market place and Church Street is dated 1897.

Several council houses were built from the 1930s. Two pairs on the east side of the village beyond the lane leading to Folds End Farm are dated 1933. A row of six called River View was built east of the Crewe and Harpur Arms in the early 1950s,[90] and three pairs called Dove Ridge were built in the late 1960s on the road to Top o' th' Edge on the north-east side of the village.[91] Three houses and four old people's bungalows were built at Lanehead on the north side of the village in the mid 1970s.[92]

One effect in Longnor of the economic decline experienced by rural communities in the later 20th century was the closure in 1978 of a branch of the National Westminster Bank, opened in 1932.[93] An attempt to arrest the decline was made in the 1980s by the Peak Park joint planning board, which included Longnor in its Integrated Rural Development project, started in 1983. Business ventures and tourism were encouraged, and in 1984 an estate of 14 houses was built at Windyridge, on the east side of the village. The project ended in 1990.[94] The main employer, Microplants, established in 1983, left Longnor in 1993.[95] In 1991 the former market house, used since 1984 as an artist's studio, was opened as a craft centre by George Fox, a furniture maker working in Fawfieldhead. It displays the work of artists and crafts people mostly living in the Peak District and also contains a café.[96]

The site of Folds End Farm on the east side of the village was occupied by 1505.[97] The earliest part of the present farmhouse is probably of the 18th century, and there is a barn dated 1829. Land called Gorlage in 1415 was probably the site of a house recorded in 1608 at Gauledge west of the village.[98] In the north-western part of the township there was a house at Tunstead by 1415[99] and one at Nab End by 1613.[1] What

74 Below, econ. hist. (market and fairs); church.
75 Erdeswick, *Staffs.* 480; *S.H.C.* 1940, 187.
76 D.R.O., D. 2375M/161/3; P.R.O., HO 107/2008.
77 Below, plate 68.
78 S.R.O., D. 3359/Buxton Rd. order bk. 1765–1800, 5 June 1781 (giving Harper Arms); Parson and Bradshaw, *Staffs. Dir.* (1818), 192; L.J.R.O., B/C/11, Moses Charlesworth (1795); D.R.O., D. 2375M/299/18/9.
79 Below, econ. hist. (market and fairs; trade and ind.).
80 Dodd, *Peakland Roads*, 175; Parson and Bradshaw, *Staffs. Dir.* (1818), 192–3.
81 *P.O. Dir. Staffs.* (1850 and later edns.).
82 Pigot, *New Com. Dir.* [1829], 712.
83 S.R.O., D. 4980/1/1, p. 85; White, *Dir. Staffs.* (1834), 721; (1851), 747.
84 T. J. Smith, *Banks and Bankers of Leek* (Leek, priv. print. 1891), 31.
85 D.R.O., D. 2375M/64/9, Wyatt's name on packet marked 'For Mrs. Mary Billing at Broncott, 9 Mar. 1813'; S.R.O., D.

4980/1/1, p. 4; Parson and Bradshaw, *Staffs. Dir.* (1818), 193.
86 White, *Dir. Staffs.* (1834), 721; P.R.O., HO 107/2008.
87 *P.O. Dir. Staffs.* (1872); *Kelly's Dir. Staffs.* (1888).
88 *P.O. Dir. Staffs.* (1864); below, educ.
89 *Reliquary*, vi. 75.
90 S.R.O., D. 4727/1/1, pp. 153, 164.
91 Ibid. p. 252; D. 4727/1/2, p. 17.
92 Ibid. D. 4727/1/2, pp. 102, 106.
93 Ibid. p. 221; *Kelly's Dir. Staffs.* (1932).
94 *Two Villages, Two Valleys* (Peak Park Joint Planning Bd. 1990), 45–67; Leek Libr., newspaper cuttings 1984 (1), pp. 30–1.   95 Below, econ. hist. (trade and ind.).
96 Craft centre publicity leaflet (1994).
97 D.R.O., D. 2375M/1/3, 8 Apr. 20 Hen. VIII.
98 Ibid. D. 2375M/53/9, deed of feast of St. Peter and St. Paul 3 Hen. V; D. 2375M/57/1, 7 Apr. 6 Jas. I.
99 Ibid. D. 2375M/53/9, deed of feast of St. Peter and St. Paul 3 Hen. V.
1 Ibid. D. 2375M/190/2, deed of 1 Mar. 10 Jas. I.

was called Edge Houses in 1600 probably stood on the site of Edgetop Farm, so called in 1785, on the Sheen road south-east of Longnor village.[2]

The road from Leek crossed the Manifold by a bridge in existence by 1401 and called Longnor bridge in 1478.[3] The present bridge was built in 1822–3 after its predecessor had been washed away by a flood in 1821.[4] East of Longnor village the route into Derbyshire over the Dove was through Crowdecote, in Hartington (Derb.), where a foot bridge was stated in 1709 to be on 'a great road'. That year the county justices gave £20 towards rebuilding it in stone as a horse bridge.[5] The present bridge was built in 1809.[6] The road was turnpiked in 1765 as part of the route from Newcastle-under-Lyme to Hassop (Derb.).[7] A tollgate was erected north of Longnor bridge, and there was a house for the keeper by 1775.[8] The road was disturnpiked in 1875.[9]

The road from Warslow which formerly met the Leek road on the Heathylee side of Longnor bridge was realigned to cross the Manifold at Windy Arbour bridge after it had been turnpiked as part of the route from Cheadle to Buxton in 1770.[10] The line of the road on the north-west side of Longnor market place was probably laid out at the same time, replacing an earlier line which ran to the east through Lanehead. Windy Arbour bridge was rebuilt in the early 19th century, as was Glutton bridge, which takes the road over the Dove. The road was disturnpiked in 1878.[11]

An association for the prosecution of felons was formed in Longnor in the 1840s.[12] There was a resident policeman in 1847 and a sergeant and a constable in 1881.[13] A beehive shaped lock-up at Carder Green was demolished apparently in 1886.[14] A police station which occupied Vincent House in Church Street apparently from 1896 and certainly by 1918 was closed in 1962, but Longnor had a resident police officer until 1968.[15]

A mains water supply was provided from a waterworks built near Tunstead Farm in 1877 or 1878.[16] It was closed in the later 1950s and an alternative mains supply connected.[17] A sewage works was built north-east of the village in the early 1960s.[18] There was a mains electricity supply by 1940.[19]

A fire brigade was formed at Longnor during the Second World War. The fire station on the Buxton road dates from the earlier 1960s.[20]

SOCIAL AND CULTURAL ACTIVITIES. In 1697 Longnor wakes were held in August,[21] probably on the feast of St. Bartholomew (24 August), the saint to whom the church is dedicated. By 1772 the wakes began on the first Sunday in September. They continued for the rest of the week and included what were probably foot races on the Monday and Tuesday.[22] In 1831 a bull was baited in the market place on the Tuesday in wakes week.[23] Horseracing was introduced at the beginning of the 20th century,[24] and trotting ponies were a feature of the sports held on the Thursday in wakes week in the early 1990s.

The town wells were dressed in 1950 in an unsuccessful attempt to revive earlier practice. Since 1983 well-dressing has taken place on wakes Sunday.[25]

There were four friendly societies in Longnor in 1803, with a total membership of 238.[26] A Freemasons' Lodge of Unity established in 1811 had 25 members in 1813, but only seven lived in Longnor itself; the rest came from neighbouring places, including Tissington (Derb.). The lodge was dissolved in 1829.[27] A later lodge was dissolved in 1866.[28] A Women's Institute was established in 1920.[29]

A clubroom attached to the White Horse inn was described in 1810 as newly erected, and the Grapes inn had an assembly room in 1867.[30] A parish library was opened in 1858, probably in the reading room mentioned in 1868.[31] That room had apparently been closed by 1872; another room was opened at Townend in 1890 and was closed in 1917.[32] In 1931 the former market house became a social hall for the parish. Known as Longnor village hall by 1940, it remained in use until the later 1970s.[33]

A brass band for Longnor and Sheen had been formed by 1867, and a band still played in Longnor in the early 20th century.[34] A choral society formed by 1920 survived until the late 1930s.[35]

MANOR AND OTHER ESTATES. Longnor was part of Alstonefield manor until the 16th

2 Alstonfield Par. Reg. 63; D.R.O., D. 2375M/174/3, 26 Oct. 1785.
3 D.R.O., D. 2375M/1/1, 1st ct. 18 Edw. IV; D. 2375M/1/6, ct. of Thurs. before Christmas 3 Hen. IV.
4 S.R.O., D. 3359/Buxton Rd. order bk. 1814–32, 13 Sept. 1821; S.R.O., Q/FAa/8, 29 Mar. 1823.
5 S.R.O., Q/SO/11, Easter 1709.
6 Ibid. Q/SO/24, f. 116v.
7 S.H.C. 4th ser. xiii. 105.
8 S.R.O., D. 706/2, p. 31; D. 3359/Buxton Rd. order bk. 1765–1800, p. 5; above, fig. 2.
9 S.R.O., D. 3359/Leek, Buxton, and Monyash turnpike trust, acct. bk. 1861–76.
10 S.H.C. 4th ser. xiii. 110.
11 S.R.O., D. 239/M/14/63, cert. of 25 Nov. 1878.
12 St. Bartholomew's Ch. & Par. [1980], 28.
13 S.R.O., D. 4980/1/1, p. 186; P.R.O., RG 11/2742.
14 St. Bartholomew's Ch. & Par. 27, and illus. facing p. 57.
15 Ibid. 27; S.R.O., D. 4727/1/1, p. 227; D. 4727/1/2, p. 11; O.S. Map 1/2,500, Staffs. V. 2 (1922 edn.).
16 S.R.O., D. 1422/5/8.
17 Inf. from the vicar.
18 S.R.O., D. 4727/1/1, pp. 203, 234.
19 Kelly's Dir. Staffs. (1940).
20 J. R. Powner, A Duty Done: Hist. of Fire-Fighting in Staffs. (Staffs. C.C. 1987), 132, 134; inf. from Staffs. Fire and Rescue Service H.Q.   21 S.R.O., Q/SR/104, f. 33.
22 S.R.O., D. 3359/Condlyffe, John Harmar to Wm. Condlyffe, 15 Aug. 1772.
23 Staffs. Advertiser, 24 Sept. 1831, p. 4.
24 Memories of the Moorland Farmer, ed. S. Gaukroger and J. Holliday (Buxton, 1994), 55.
25 Alstonfield Deanery Mag. liii (6, 8); local inf.
26 Poor Law Abstract, H.C. 98, pp. 472–3 (1803–4), xiii.
27 S.R.O., Q/RSm; F. W. Willmore, Hist. of Freemasonry in Province of Staffs. (1905), 61.
28 T.N.S.F.C. xlii. 196.
29 Alstonfield Deanery Mag. xxiv (11).
30 D.R.O., D. 2375M/299/18/4; Staffs. Advertiser, 26 Oct. 1867, p. 7.
31 St. Bartholomew's Ch. & Par. 27; P.O. Dir. Staffs. (1868).
32 P.O. Dir. Staffs. (1872); Kelly's Dir. Staffs. (1892); Alstonfield Deanery Mag. xxi (4).
33 Alstonfield Deanery Mag. xxxiv (5); xliii (6); local inf.
34 Staffs. Advertiser, 26 Oct. 1867, p. 7; local inf.
35 Alstonfield Deanery Mag. xxiv (10); local inf.

century, when it became part of the manor of Warslow and Longnor. From 1593 that manor was owned by the Harpur family, also lords of Alstonefield.[36] Longnor was styled a barony in 1592, a name still used in the late 18th century.[37]

In the earlier 1630s the lord owned under half the land in the township.[38] The rest belonged to freeholders, some possibly the successors of the owners of medieval ecclesiastical estates. Combermere abbey (Ches.) had land in Longnor in the mid 13th century, and at the Dissolution it owned at least two houses in the township.[39] Dieulacres abbey near Leek owned a house in Longnor by the 1530s.[40] A chantry at the altar of St. Oswald in Ashbourne church (Derb.) had land in Longnor before its dissolution.[41]

ECONOMIC HISTORY. AGRICULTURE. There was an open field in Longnor in 1500. Town field was mentioned in 1594, and again in 1597 together with what was called the corn field.[42] In the earlier 1630s Sir John Harpur's tenants in the township held 206 a. (of which 74 a. were arable) and the freeholders 283 a. (of which 92 a. were arable). There were 253 a. of common waste.[43] The manor court still regulated open fields in the 1770s.[44] Some consolidation of strips had taken place by then, especially on the south-east side of the township where narrow walled fields remain a feature of the landscape. The inclosure of 160 a. of open-field land, mostly on the north-west side of the township along the Dove, and 300 a. of common waste took place in 1785 under an Act of 1784.[45]

Dairy farming is suggested by meadow in Longnor called Cheseford in the mid 13th century.[46] In the early 16th century the stint on Longnor's open fields was one beast for each acre held, and besides pasture there and on the wastes in the township Longnor men had pasture on Fawfield Hill, in Fawfieldhead township.[47] Although cattle were probably the main item of stock, a tenant was presented in 1730 for overburdening the commons with sheep and horses.[48]

Of the 304 ha. of farmland returned for the civil parish in 1988, grassland covered 253 ha. and there were 50 ha. of rough grazing. The farming was dairy and sheep, with 518 head of cattle and 110 sheep and lambs. Of the 19 farms returned, 16 were under 20 ha. in size, 2 were between 30 and 49 ha., and one was between 50 and 99 ha.[49]

MILL. By the later 1820s there was a mill at Glutton bridge on the Dove. It ceased to operate in the earlier 1930s.[50]

MARKET AND FAIRS. The market and fair which the lords of Alstonefield manor claimed in 1293[51] were almost certainly held at Longnor in the large open space which formerly surrounded the church. The remains of what may have been a market cross survive beside the Warslow road where it enters the market place.[52]

In 1595 the Crown granted John Harpur a Tuesday market at Longnor.[53] In the early 1770s there was a proposal, possibly connected with the recent turnpiking of the roads through the village, to build a market house.[54] It is not certain when it was in fact built: the contractor, Richard Gould, went bankrupt in 1773, and a contemporary plan of the village shows only the 'site of the market house'.[55] There was certainly a market house by 1817, evidently on the north side of the market place. Although the market was then held only between 4 and 6 p.m., it was well attended.[56] In 1836 Sir George Crewe noted that the market house needed to be rebuilt. It seems that nothing was done, as in 1839 he contemplated replacing it with a building on the site of the White Horse inn at Townend. The market house was eventually rebuilt in 1873 by Sir John Harpur Crewe.[57] The market was small in the early 20th century, much of its potential trade being drawn to towns with better communications, and the market house probably ceased to be used for commerce some years before its conversion to a parish hall in 1931.[58]

Longnor fair was mentioned in 1478. There were four fairs by 1549, each having on average between 12 and 24 booths. In 1555 one of the fairs was held on the Tuesday before Michaelmas.[59] Held by the Crown in 1594, they were acquired by John Harpur later in the 1590s, when their dates were St. George's day (23 April), Tuesday in Whitsun week, St. James's day (25 July), and Michaelmas.[60] One of them may have been a goose fair in the late 18th century: the manor court in 1778 complained about the number of geese in the town.[61] In 1817 there were eight fairs: on Candlemas Day, Easter Tuesday, 4 and 17 May, Whit Tuesday, 6

36 Below, Warslow, manors; local govt.
37 D.R.O., D. 2375M/82/23, deed of 2 May 34 Eliz. I; D. 2375M/174/3, 24 Oct. 1780.
38 Below, next para.
39 D.R.O., D. 2375M/53/9, deed of Ric. son of John of Bentley; D. 2375M/82/23, deed of 12 Aug. 36 Eliz. I.
40 Valor Eccl. (Rec. Com.), iii. 123.
41 D.R.O., D. 2375M/53/9, deed of 3 May 33 Eliz. I.
42 Ibid. D. 2375M/1/3, 1st ct. 16 Hen. VII; D. 2375M/57/1, 6 Apr. 36 Eliz. I, 31 Mar. 39 Eliz. I.
43 Ibid. D. 2375M/63/53, p. 184.
44 Ibid. D. 2375M/174/2, 24 Oct. 1770; D. 2375M/174/3, 26 Oct. 1778.
45 Ibid. D. 2375M/161/3; S.R.O., Q/RDc 6; 24 Geo. III, c. 5 (Priv. Act).
46 D.R.O., D. 2375M/53/9, deed of Ric. son of John of Bentley.
47 Ibid. D. 2375M/57/1, 28 Apr. 4 Jas. I; above, Fawfieldhead, econ. hist. (agric.).
48 D.R.O., D. 2375M/174/3, 27 Apr. 1730.

49 P.R.O., MAF 68/6128/68.
50 S.R.O. 5322/7, no. 46; Kelly's Dir. Staffs. (1932; 1936).
51 S.H.C. vi (1), 246.
52 The cross still stood in the market place in 1933: S.R.O., D. 4727/1/1, pp. 98–101.
53 P.R.O., C 66/1426, m. 10.
54 D.R.O., D. 2375M/54/39, statement of Ric. Gould's debt.
55 Ibid. D. 2375M/161/3; above, Heathylee, econ. hist. (mills).
56 Pitt, Staffs. 244; J. Nightingale, Staffs. (Beauties of Eng. and Wales, xiii), 1169; L.J.R.O., B/A/15/Longnor, no. 231.
57 D.R.O., D. 2375M/44/1, 17 Sept. 1836, 26 Sept. 1839; P.O. Dir. Staffs. (1874); date on building; below, plate 70.
58 T.N.S.F.C. xlii. 195; above, intro. (social and cultural activities).
59 D.R.O., D. 2375M/1/1, 1st ct. 18 Edw. IV; P.R.O., STAC 4/3/27; S.H.C. 1915, 11.
60 D.R.O., D. 2375M/138/18/2, 4–6.
61 Ibid. D. 2375M/174/3, 26 Oct. 1778.

August, Tuesday before Old Michaelmas Day (10 October), and 12 November. In 1834 the Candlemas fair was stated to be held on Tuesday before 13 February (Old Candlemas Day), and there was no longer a fair in August. The November fair was then for the sale of cheese.[62] There were only four fairs in 1896, on Easter Tuesday, 4 and 17 May, and Whit Tuesday. Still held in 1928, there is no later record of the fairs.[63]

Longnor was one of the few places in Staffordshire which still had a hiring fair in the early 20th century.[64]

TRADE AND INDUSTRY. Richard Smyth of Longnor was described as a carrier and a salter in 1601.[65] Richard Charlesworth of Longnor was a carrier in 1763, as was his son Moses, a benefactor of Longnor's school and poor.[66] Carriers passed through the village in 1834, and in 1851 Joshua Knowles of New Lodge, in Quarnford, travelled to Leek and Sheffield from a base in Longnor.[67] There was a resident carrier in 1860, James Smedley, who by 1880 ran an omnibus service to Leek on Wednesdays and Buxton on Saturdays.[68]

About 1818 an anonymous correspondent complained to Sir George Crewe that his agent was ejecting old tenants in favour of people in trade.[69] In 1818 William Johnson, the landlord of the Crewe and Harpur Arms, also worked as an auctioneer, and there were two auctioneers in 1834, James Charlesworth and Thomas Needham, the latter also a shopkeeper. Besides Needham's shop there were four grocers in 1834, one also a druggist and another also a chandler. Besides bakers, butchers, shoemakers, and tailors, Longnor had at least 10 shopkeepers in 1851, including drapers and grocers.[70]

In the 19th century hawkers and itinerant workers stayed in lodging houses in and around Longnor village. Lodgers at Carder Green on Census Day 1851 included a linen weaver, a flax dresser, a clothespeg maker, and two hawkers, while a further three hawkers lodged in Church Street. On Census Day 1871 a lodging house at Carder Green included two hawkers, one selling cutlery and the other stockings; another hawker, Marcellin Macenski from Liverpool, lodged in a house at Islington on the Buxton road north of the village. The Islington house on Census Day 1881 had 12 lodgers, who included three hawkers, a cattle driver, an umbrella maker, and a pedlar.[71]

There was a limekiln 'in the lower end of the town' in 1682.[72] The wharf which Joseph Redfern had on the Manifold east of Longnor bridge in the 1770s was probably used for the transport of stone: in 1770 Redfern was one of five men who had stone quarries on Longnor Edge.[73] Stonemasons in 1851 included another Joseph Redfern and his sons George and Joseph, James Redfern, and Isaac Swindell. One or more of them presumably worked a quarry and limekiln near Edgetop Farm which were disued by the late 1870s. There were 3 stonemasons, 3 quarrymen, and a limeburner in Longnor in 1881.[74]

In 1818 there were two cheese factors in the township, Thomas Gilman and Samuel Sherwin. Peter Needham was recorded as a cheese factor in 1851, and Charles Charlesworth in 1872 and 1880.[75]

As part of the revitalization of the village in the early 1980s a firm called Microplants was established in 1983 on a site next to the fire station. It grew plants from tissue cultures by means of micropropagation, and by 1985 it employed 13 people.[76] The firm remained at Longnor until 1993.

LOCAL GOVERNMENT. Longnor formed a tithing in Alstonefield manor.[77] By the late 1390s it sent one frankpledge to the twice-yearly view.[78] In 1500 Longnor had its own six-man jury at the manor court, and by 1502 it had a 12-man jury. By April 1505 the jury met with its Warslow counterpart at a separate great court, held on the day after the Alstonefield view and possibly at Warslow.[79] At least between 1525 and 1535 there was a separate view of frankpledge for Warslow and Longnor, but only a great court once more c. 1550. From 1594 there was again a view of frankpledge for Warslow and Longnor, but Longnor had its own view from 1611. From 1675 there was once more a joint view with Warslow. In 1697, apparently for the first time, Longnor was the meeting place of the spring view and from 1775 that of the autumn view as well. The venue was specified in 1790 as the Harpur Arms. The court still met at Longnor when last recorded in 1853.[80]

Stocks were mentioned in 1601 and 1614, and a new pair was apparently made as late as 1861.[81] There was a pinfold in the township in 1546, and a pinner was mentioned in 1596.[82] In the later 1820s there was a pinfold on the east side of the village in the lane leading to Folds End Farm. It remained in use apparently until 1908.[83]

62 Pitt, *Staffs.* 244; White, *Dir. Staffs.* (1834), 718–19. The Old Michaelmas Day fair was not recorded in 1834, possibly in error, as it still existed in 1851: White, *Dir. Staffs.* (1851), 743.   63 *Kelly's Dir. Staffs.* (1896; 1928).

64 *V.C.H. Staffs.* vi. 145.

65 *Alstonfield Par. Reg.* 60, 65.

66 D.R.O., D. 2375M/299/18/1–2; L.J.R.O., B/C/11, Moses Charlesworth (1795).

67 White, *Dir. Staffs.* (1834), 722; (1851), 748.

68 *P.O. Dir. Staffs.* (1860); *Kelly's Dir. Staffs.* (1880).

69 D.R.O., D. 2375M/99/32, 'Gratia' to Sir Hen. Crewe, c. 1818.

70 Parson and Bradshaw, *Staffs. Dir.* (1818), 192; White, *Dir. Staffs.* (1834), 721–2; (1851), 747.

71 P.R.O., HO 107/2008; ibid. RG 10/2885; RG 11/2742.

72 D.R.O., D. 2375M/54/3/13, 3 May 1682.

73 Ibid. D. 2375M/161/3; D. 2375M/174/2, 24 Oct. 1770.

74 P.R.O., HO 107/2008; ibid. RG 11/2742; O.S. Map 6", Staffs. V. NW. (1884 edn.).

75 Parson and Bradshaw, *Staffs. Dir.* (1818), 192–3; White, *Dir. Staffs.* (1851), 747; *P.O. Dir. Staffs.* (1872; 1876); *Kelly's Dir. Staffs.* (1880).

76 Leek Libr., newspaper cuttings 1984 (2), p. 25; 1985 (2), p. 114.

77 Above, Alstonefield, par. intro. (manorial govt.).

78 D.R.O., D. 2375M/1/6, undated view following ct. of Thurs. after feast of St. Peter and St. Paul 23 Ric. II.

79 D.R.O., D. 2375M/1/3, 1st ct. 16 Hen. VII, 2nd ct. 17 Hen. VII, 8 Apr. 20 Hen. VII.   80 Below, Warslow, local govt.

81 D.R.O., D. 2375M/57/1, 20 Apr. 43 Eliz. I, 5 May 12 Jas. I; D. 2375M/202/19, f. 163.

82 Ibid. D. 2375M/1/2, 8 June 38 Hen. VIII; D. 2375M/57/1, 8 Oct. 38 Eliz. I sqq.

83 S.R.O. 5322/7, no. 293; S.R.O., D. 4727/1/1, pp. 46, 50.

Two surveyors of the highways for Longnor were appointed at the manor court in 1601. By 1664 only one was appointed.[84]

The poor of Longnor were apparently relieved separately from the rest of Alstonefield parish by the later 17th century.[85] There may have been a workhouse in 1826, when a workhouse governor lived in Longnor. The township certainly had its own poorhouse in 1837, the year in which Longnor became part of Leek poor-law union.[86]

CHURCH. The survival of a Norman font in the present church may indicate the existence of a church at Longnor by the 12th century. A church was first mentioned, however, in 1448.[87] It had its own wardens in 1553.[88] In 1594 the inhabitants of Fawfieldhead were reminded of their duty to help maintain Longnor graveyard, a fact which suggests that Fawfieldhead was part of a chapelry served by Longnor church. The townships of Fawfieldhead, Heathylee, Hollinsclough, and Quarnford were certainly part of Longnor chapelry by the late 17th century.[89] A separate chapelry for Quarnford was established in 1744.[90] Longnor was a perpetual curacy from 1735, the patron being the vicar of Alstonefield, and the benefice was styled a vicarage from 1868.[91] A parish of Longnor, covering Longnor, most of Fawfieldhead, and the eastern halves of Heathylee and Hollinsclough, was created in 1902.[92] In 1985 the benefice was united with those of Quarnford and Sheen, although all three parishes remained separate, and the patronage was vested jointly in the bishop of Lichfield as patron of Sheen, the trustees of the Harpur-Crewe estate as patrons of Quarnford, and the vicar of Alstonefield. Longnor was made the incumbent's place of residence.[93]

In 1549 the curate was stated to be entitled to a toll of 1d. for every covered booth and ½d. for every open stand at each of Longnor's four fairs. The value of the tolls was then 4s. a year.[94] In 1644 the parliamentary committee at Stafford awarded Anthony Gretton of Longnor, evidently the curate, a salary of £5 from the estate of Sir John Harpur, and the income survived the Restoration.[95] In 1661 Vincent Weston vested land at Sheen in trustees who were to use the income to pay a minister of their choice to preach a sermon at Longnor on the first Tuesday of every month. The land appears to have become part of the Longnor glebe by the early 19th century.[96] In 1733 the inhabitants of the chapelry agreed to make payments in order to secure the residence of Joseph Bradley, a curate recently chosen by them with the approval of the vicar of Alstonefield. The payments were for a period of seven years, or until the governors of Queen Anne's Bounty could be persuaded to make a grant.[97] Grants of £200 were made in 1737 and 1751, and by 1768 the living was worth £10 a year.[98] A further scheme to increase the curate's stipend, initiated by Bishop Egerton in 1769, involved Sir Henry Harpur's settling £10 a year, in addition to the £5 charged on his family's estate since 1644. In the event he agreed in 1775 to give £7 10s., in respect of which the Bounty governors gave another £200 in 1776. The money was evidently handed over to Sir Henry, who charged Potlock farm at Findern, in Mickleover (Derb.), with a rent of £15. The £5 annuity was also charged on the farm.[99] In 1824 the endowment consisted of £21 from glebe, which comprised 22 a. in Sheen and Fawfieldhead, the £20 charged on Potlock farm, and £6 from a farm near Barnsley (Yorks. W.R.). In 1825 Queen Anne's Bounty gave a further £1,200. Because of the curate's non-residence, the money had accumulated by 1836 to £1,600 and produced £48 a year.[1] There were 25 a. of glebe in 1887, with an estimated rental of £40 5s.[2]

In 1830 the newly appointed curate, William Buckwell, lived just outside the village, probably at Townend where in 1831 Sir George Crewe rebuilt a house for him.[3] The present vicarage was built to the west in 1986.[4]

Francis Paddy, the curate of Longnor in 1604, also officiated at Alstonefield.[5] The financial arrangements of 1733 were made to secure a resident curate, and Robert Robinson was appointed in 1735. By 1751 Robinson was also the incumbent of Sheen and lived on his estate at Waterfall. He had resigned Sheen by 1760 but continued as curate of Longnor until 1768.[6] When Luke Story became curate in 1769, he was already assistant curate at Alstonefield and also apparently served the chapels at Warslow and Elkstone. He was keen to move to Longnor, even though he considered that it lay 'in a disagreeable country'.[7] In the 1820s the cure was served for the absentee curate by James Roberts, the curate of Quarnford. He lived at Flash and was unable to visit Longnor as often as he would have liked. Pastoral care suffered, and in 1825 he complained that 'Longnor has been like a furnace of affliction to me', mainly because of

84 D.R.O., D. 2375M/57/1, 20 Apr. 43 Eliz. I; D. 2375M/57/2, 21 Apr. 1675 sqq.; D. 2375M/138/23/2.
85 Above, Alstonefield, par. intro. (par. govt.).
86 S.R.O., D. 699/1/1/1, pp. 4–5; D. 4980/1/1, p. 70.
87 D.R.O., D. 2375M/1/1, 2nd ct. 26 Hen. VI.
88 Below, this section [wardens].
89 D.R.O., D. 2375M/57/1, 8 Oct. 36 Eliz. I; S.R.O., D. 921/1.   90 Below, Quarnford, church.
91 P.R.O., Inst. Bks. Ser. C, i (1), f. 87v.; Lich. Dioc. Ch. Cal. (1869).   92 Lond. Gaz. 15 Aug. 1902, p. 5321.
93 Lich. Dioc. Regy., Bp.'s Reg. S (Orders in Council), p. 77.
94 S.H.C. 1915, 11.
95 S.H.C. 4th ser. i. 163; below (this para.).
96 D.R.O., D. 2375M/161/13; below (this para.).
97 D.R.O., D. 2375M/110/32, declaration of financial support for curate, 1733.

98 Hodgson, Bounty of Queen Anne, p. ccxcvii; L.J.R.O., B/A/3/Longnor, 1767, L. Story to bp.'s sec., 22 June 1768.
99 D.R.O., D. 2375M/113/44, papers re endowment of Longnor curacy, 1772–3; Hodgson, Bounty of Queen Anne, pp. clxii, ccxcvii (where Sir Hen.'s benefaction is entered under 1795, presumably in error for 1775).
1 L.J.R.O., B/V/6/Longnor, 1824, 1841; Hodgson, Bounty of Queen Anne, p. ccxcvii.
2 Return of Glebe Lands, 65.
3 S.H.C. 4th ser. x. 93; D.R.O., D. 2375M/44/1, 25 Aug. 1831; P.R.O., HO 107/2008.
4 Inf. from the vicar.
5 Above, Alstonefield, church.
6 P.R.O., Inst. Bks. Ser. C, i (1), f. 87v.; L.J.R.O., B/A/3/Longnor, 1767, L. Story to bp.'s sec., 22 June 1768; B/A/3/Sheen, 1760; B/V/5/Sheen, 1751.
7 L.J.R.O., B/A/3/Longnor, 1767 and 1769.

the activities of Methodists.[8] The appointment of William Buckwell as resident curate in 1830 brought a change. Described by Sir George Crewe as pious and worthy, Buckwell put the church's fabric into good order and encouraged Sir George to establish dependent chapels in Fawfieldhead and Hollinsclough.[9]

Before the Reformation there was a light in the church,[10] perhaps indicating a fraternity for its maintenance. Psalm singers at Longnor were mentioned in the later 1760s and in the 1790s.[11] They may have survived until the mid 19th century: the church did not acquire an organ until 1852, although there was apparently a barrel organ from 1832.[12] There was only one Sunday service in 1830, and Communion was celebrated four times a year.[13] On Census Sunday 1851 there were two Sunday services, with attendances of 135 in the morning and 126 in the afternoon, besides Sunday school children.[14]

Two chapelwardens for Longnor were recorded in 1553.[15] One of the four churchwardens of Alstonefield parish recorded in 1569 may have been for Longnor, the arrangement in the early 18th century.[16] He presented accounts at the Easter vestry for Alstonefield parish until 1827.[17] Longnor chapelry, however, continued to contribute to the maintenance of Alstonefield church.[18] The warden was paid a salary of £4 a year in 1842, raised to £5 in 1844.[19] Longnor township was not obliged to provide candidates for the wardenship as were the other townships in the chapelry. The system was altered in 1854, when Longnor became liable in rotation with the others.[20] Longnor had a clerk by 1767.[21] There was a dog whipper by the earlier 1720s and still in 1827,[22] and a sexton by 1842.[23]

The present church of *ST. BARTHOLOMEW*, a dedication probably in use by 1631,[24] dates from the later 1770s. Only the plan of its predecessor is known. It was apparently a long, narrow building with a nave and a chancel, and in the later 18th century the pulpit and reading desk stood against the north wall of the nave.[25] Between 1774 and 1781 the church was demolished and a new one built on a site to the north.[26] Of coursed ashlar, it is a rectangular building of five bays with a west tower; there is a Venetian

east window. An upper arcade of windows was added to light west and south galleries inserted in 1812, and it was probably then that the tower was heightened.[27] Formerly there was a door half way along the south side of the nave, but it was blocked up in 1897.[28] The west gallery is approached by an external staircase on the north side of the tower. In 1857 the pulpit and reading desk were separated, the pulpit being placed on the south side of the communion table and the desk on the north side.[29] The organ, installed in the south gallery in 1852, was moved in 1864 to the west gallery, possibly after the dismantling of the south gallery, which no longer exists.[30] The organ was later placed on the south side of the chancel. A false ceiling was inserted c. 1949, making the upper windows blind.[31]

The present Norman font was in the churchyard in 1830, when the archdeacon ordered it to be put back into the church; he had to repeat the order in 1837. In 1857 the font stood at the west end of the nave.[32] There was a single bell in 1553. A bell of 1745 was replaced by a new one in 1947.[33] The plate in 1553 comprised a silver gilt chalice with paten. There was also a wooden cross.[34] The present plate includes a silver chalice of c. 1675, a silver paten of 1715, and a flagon and plate bought in 1791–2.[35] Royal arms of the 18th century hang on the front of the west gallery. Boards of 1793 with the text of the Commandments and the Lord's Prayer hang at the west end of the nave, along with a benefaction board which dates probably from the 1790s.

The registers date from 1691.[36] In the later 19th century there was also a register dating apparently from c. 1600.[37]

Stone gateposts dated 1833 were part of a general improvement of the churchyard undertaken by the curate, William Buckwell.[38] It was closed for burials in 1888 and ½ a. north of the church was consecrated instead in 1891.[39] An extension of ⅖ a. was consecrated in 1934.[40]

NONCONFORMITY. Elihu Hall, a Longnor mercer recorded in 1685, was possibly the Elijah Hall who in 1723 registered his house in Longnor

---

8 D.R.O., D. 2375M/87/19, Jas. Roberts to Sir Geo. Crewe, 23 Dec. 1825.

9 *S.H.C.* 4th ser. x. 93; Lich. Dioc. Regy., Bp.'s Reg. 29, p. 198; D.R.O., D. 2375M/44/1, 25 Aug. 1831.

10 *Cal. Pat.* 1560–3, 259.

11 S.R.O., D. 922/35, pp. 137, 211, 217.

12 *St. Bartholomew's Ch. & Par.* [1980], 37; *Staffs. Advertiser*, 5 June 1852, p. 4.

13 *S.H.C.* 4th ser. x. 93.

14 P.R.O., HO 129/372/4/4.

15 *S.H.C.* 1915, 11.

16 Above, Alstonefield, par. intro. (par. govt.).

17 S.R.O., D. 922/35–6.

18 Ibid. D. 922/36, memo. of 1848.

19 Ibid. D. 3598/1, ff. 1, 3.

20 Ibid. ff. 11, 13v.

21 Ibid. D. 921/1, f. 185.

22 Ibid. D. 922/35, p. 26; D. 922/36, acct. 1826–7.

23 Ibid. D. 3598/1, f. 1.

24 Two parishioners were reported for working on St. Bartholomew's day in 1631: L.J.R.O., B/V/1/51, f. 183v.

25 Photocopy (at Longnor church, 1994) of part of a later 18th-cent. seating plan of unidentified church, presumably Longnor, 22 ft. wide with a 52-ft. nave and a 23-ft. chancel.

26 B.L. Church Briefs B. xiv. 7; doc. appointing arbitrators to allocate pews in new church, 1781 (at Longnor church, 1994). For site of the former church see D.R.O., D. 2375M/161/3.

27 White, *Dir. Staffs.* (1834), 719; below, plate 10.

28 Plaque on S. face of church.

29 S.R.O., D. 3598/1, f. 12v.; Lichfield Cath. Libr., Moore and Hinckes drawings, iv. 24.

30 *Staffs. Advertiser*, 5 June 1852, p. 4; *Lich. Dioc. Ch. Cal.* (1865), rec. of diocese, p. ii.   31 Inf. from the vicar.

32 *T.B.A.S.* lxviii. 16 and pl. 6B; *S.H.C.* 4th ser. x. 93; Lichfield Cath. Libr., Moore and Hinckes drawings, iv. 24.

33 *S.H.C.* 1915, 11; C. Lynam, *Ch. Bells of County of Stafford* (1889), 52; *Alstonfield Deanery Mag.* 1 (3).

34 *S.H.C.* 1915, 11.

35 *T.B.A.S.* lxxvii. 67, 69, and pl. 10B; S.R.O., D. 922/35, p. 198.

36 Those not in current use are in S.R.O., D. 921/1–5 and D. 4980/1/1–6.

37 Ibid. D. 921/1, memo. of Jas. Roberts in folder; *P.O. Dir. Staffs.* (1864).   38 *S.H.C.* 4th ser. x. 93.

39 *Lond. Gaz.* 11 May 1888, p. 2694; *Kelly's Dir. Staffs.* (1892); date on gate posts.

40 *Alstonfield Deanery Mag.* xxxiii (6); xxxvii (6).

as a meeting place for Quakers.[41] In 1736 two Quakers, Joseph Hall and his son Elihu, were baptized by the curate.[42] In 1731 a Quaker named James Plant was Longnor's headborough.[43]

In 1769 a group of Methodists met at Stiff Close, the home of a Mr. Billing.[44] In 1772 John Wesley held a private prayer meeting at Longnor attended by 17 or 18 people.[45] In 1784 there was a society with 42 members, but by 1790 it had only 32, some presumably having transferred to other societies in the area.[46] Three members of the Billing family were among the petitioners in 1777 for the registration of a newly erected building for worship by protestant dissenters, presumably Methodists.[47] A Methodist chapel which stood north-east of the village at Top o' th' Edge was replaced in 1797 by one in a road leading off the north-west side of the market place.[48] Sunday services were held there every fortnight in 1798, with services at Hollinsclough on the alternate Sundays. A weekly Sunday service was held at Longnor by 1802.[49] The attendance on Census Sunday 1851 was 30 in the afternoon, besides Sunday school children, and 70 in the evening.[50] The chapel was enlarged in 1853 for the erection of galleries and was re-fronted at the same time.[51] It was closed in 1993.

EDUCATION. In 1597 an agreement was made in Alstonefield manor court, possibly as a confirmation of existing practice, whereby a schoolmaster at Longnor was paid in corn by the inhabitants of the township.[52] Francis Paddy, the curate in 1604, was then also the schoolmaster at Longnor.[53] Masters were again recorded between 1662 and 1737.[54]

A school was built in the earlier 1750s north-east of the village in the road leading to Top o' th' Edge, and in 1799 it was moved further up the road to the former Methodist chapel.[55] The teaching of poor children was supported by charity money: half the interest on £196 9s. 6d. left by John Robinson of Fawside, in Heathylee, by will of 1793; the interest on £20 left by Moses Charlesworth of Tunstead by will of 1795; and the interest on £50 left by Ann Collier by will of 1834.[56] In the earlier 1830s the school's income was £5 18s. Six children were taught free and a further 24 paid fees. Most of the pupils were boys. There were two infant schools, at which 40 children, mostly girls, were taught at their parents' expense. There was also a

Wesleyan Methodist Sunday school which took c. 100 children.[57] On Census Sunday 1851 there was an attendance of only 18 children at the Wesleyan Sunday school, but a Church of England Sunday school, established in the late 1840s, had attendances of 91 in the morning and 86 in the afternoon.[58]

The endowed school was moved to a site on the west side of the village in 1833, and the building was extended in 1853.[59] The move probably coincided with the reorganization of the school by the curate, William Buckwell, as a National school.[60] In 1854 Buckwell proposed that the proceeds from the sale of the schoolroom at Top o' th' Edge should be used to help defray the cost of completing the new one and of extending a house which the owner, Sir John Harpur Crewe, had agreed to let rent free for the master.[61] There were c. 100 children on the books in 1871, and in 1872 the school was rebuilt, the cost being met by Sir John; a classroom was added in 1895.[62]

In 1931 it was decided that what was then Longnor Church of England school, an all-age school with 125 children on its books, should become a junior school and that a senior school should be built at Longnor for children from Longnor, Fawfieldhead, Hollinsclough, and Quarnford.[63] Most of the funds needed to provide the necessary facilities for the senior school had been raised by 1939, but the outbreak of war caused the plan to be abandoned. From the later 1940s senior children from Longnor were sent to secondary schools in Leek.[64] Longnor school had taken controlled status by 1959 and was given its present name, St. Bartholomew's Church of England (Controlled) primary school, in 1961. The building was extended in 1964.[65] The master's house was sold in 1985.[66]

By 1835 a boarding school for boys was run by Henry Field at Townend. It had 21 pupils in 1841 and 36 in 1851 but no longer existed in 1861.[67] A girls' boarding school was run by the Misses Etches in 1849 in a house on the east side of the market place.[68] There was still a girls' boarding school in 1868, when it was run by the Misses Deakeyne. Two day schools were run by women teachers in 1884; both were closed c. 1890.[69]

CHARITIES FOR THE POOR. By will of 1793 John Robinson of Fawside, in Heathylee,

41 S.H.C. 4th ser. iii. 119; S.R.O., D. (W.) 3222/347/7.
42 S.R.O., D. 921/1, f. 109v.
43 D.R.O., D. 2375M/174/3, 14 Oct. 1731.
44 Dyson, Wesleyan Methodism, 53.
45 Jnl. of John Wesley, ed. N. Curnock, v. 482.
46 Wardle, Methodist Hist. 5.
47 S.H.C. 4th ser. iii. 125.
48 Dyson, Wesleyan Methodism, 62; below, educ.
49 Dyson, Wesleyan Methodism. 40; D.R.O., D. 3568/4/1/1.
50 P.R.O., HO 129/372/4/4.
51 Dyson, Wesleyan Methodism, 63; below, plate 69.
52 D.R.O., D. 2375M/57/1, 4 Oct. 39 Eliz. I.
53 E.H.R. xxvi. 342.
54 L.J.R.O., B/A/4/3, f. 28; B/A/4/5, 22 Sept. 1668; B/A/4/7, 19 Apr. 1695; D.R.O., D. 2375M/57/2, 25 Apr. 1677; S.R.O., D. 921/1, f. 111.
55 13th Rep. Com. Char. 354; S.R.O., Q/RDc 6, description of lot 42; S.R.O. 5322/7, no. 254.
56 13th Rep. Com. Char. 354; White, Dir. Staffs. (1834), 717; below, charities.   57 Educ. Enq. Abstract, 868.
58 P.O. Dir. Staffs. (1850); P.R.O., HO 129/372/4/4.
59 P.R.O., ED 7/109/219.
60 Nat. Soc. Inquiry, 1846–7, Staffs. 2–3; P.O. Dir. Staffs. (1850).   61 S.R.O., D. 3598/1, f. 9v.
62 P.R.O., ED 7/109/219; Kelly's Dir. Staffs. (1888; 1896).   63 Staffs. C.C. Record for 1931, 835–6.
64 Alstonfield Deanery Mag. xl (8); xlii (7); xlix (11); li (10).
65 S.R.O., CEH/203/1, 13 Feb. 1959, 6 Nov. 1961, 9 Mar. 1964 (headmaster's rep.).   66 Ibid. CEH/203/3.
67 Staffs. Advertiser, 2 Jan. 1836, p. 2; 13 Jan. 1849, p. 1; L.J.R.O., B/A/15/Longnor, nos. 183–4; P.R.O., HO 107/1003; HO 107/2008; ibid. RG 9/1949.
68 Staffs. Advertiser, 13 Jan. 1849, p. 1; L.J.R.O., B/A/15/Longnor, no. 234.
69 P.O. Dir. Staffs. (1868); Kelly's Dir. Staffs. (1884; 1888; 1892).

left half the interest on £196 9s. 6d. for the poor of Longnor and Heathylee. A distribution to poor widows of sums varying between 12s. and 4s. was made in the early 19th century.[70] By will proved 1795 Moses Charlesworth of Tunstead left the interest on £20 to be distributed to four poor widows of Longnor township on Christmas day.[71] By will proved 1834 Ann Collier left the interest on £30 for clothing poor widows in Longnor township. By will proved 1926 Henry Charlesworth left the interest on £250 to the poor of Longnor parish. By 1972 all

four charities were administered jointly and £15 was distributed that year in 50p lots.[72] By will proved 1863 Robert Oliver left the interest on £100 for the distribution of bread among poor widows of Longnor township and poor members of Longnor Wesleyan Methodist church. By will proved 1870 Peter Needham left the interest on £500 for a similar distribution, but in cash. A distribution of £2.50 was made in respect of Oliver's charity in 1972, when the income from Needham's charity was being allowed to accumulate.[73]

QUARNFORD

QUARNFORD was formerly a township in Alstonefield parish and later a civil parish 3,141 a. (1,271 ha.) in area.[74] It is mostly pasture, and occupies the north-east corner of Staffordshire, marching with Cheshire and Derbyshire. The river Dane forms the boundary with Cheshire on the west and a tributary, Black brook, the southern boundary with Leekfrith. The headstreams of the rivers Dove and Manifold form short parts of the boundary on the east side, respectively with Hartington (Derb.) and Heathylee. The source of the Dove is marked with a capstone bearing the initials of the anglers Charles Cotton and Izaak Walton.[75]

The village of Flash on the east side of the township is the highest in England, its school standing at 1,526 ft. (465 m.). Oliver Hill north of Flash rises to 1,684 ft. (513 m.) and is the highest point in Staffordshire. South of Flash the land falls to 1,261 ft. (383 m.) near Flash Bottom, and Manor Farm on the western boundary stands at 870 ft. (265 m.). Goldsitch Moss, in the south part of the township, is an area of flatter ground, lying at 1,170 ft. (356 m.) at its centre. The land rises again in the west, reaching 1,310 ft. (398 m.) on Gradbach Hill. The underlying rock is sandstone of the Millstone Grit series, which outcrops in the north part of the township at Turn Edge, Wolf Edge, and Drystone Edge. There are shallow Coal Measures in the north-west corner of the township and at Goldsitch Moss. The soil is poor-quality clay and loam, and there are patches of peat.[76]

Panniers Pool or Three Shire Heads on the north-west boundary was held in 1533 to be the meeting point of Staffordshire, Cheshire, and Derbyshire.[77] By the early 17th century, however, three stones on the top of Cheeks Hill at the northern tip of the township were thought to mark the meeting point, and they still existed

in the early 19th century.[78] When the common waste of Hartington parish in Derbyshire was inclosed in 1804, Panniers Pool was confirmed as the point were the counties met.[79] The pool probably takes its name from the baskets carried by packhorses; several packhorse ways converge at the pool.[80]

In 1751 there were 218 people aged over 16 in the township.[81] The population was 737 in 1801. It was 699 in 1811 and 695 in 1821, but by 1831 it had risen to 783. Thereafter it fell to 709 in 1841, 549 in 1861, 436 in 1881, 339 in 1901, 311 in 1911, and 295 in 1921. It was 296 in 1931, 243 in 1951, 216 in 1961, 220 in 1971, 270 in 1981, and 222 in 1991.[82]

The name Quarnford, recorded in 1227, is derived from Old English cweorn, a quern or millstone.[83] The ford was probably over the Dane near Manor Farm, and the name may refer to a stopping place on a route for the carriage of millstones. Manor Farm, a mainly 19th-century farmhouse which retains a date stone of 1739, was called Quarnford House until c. 1895 and presumably stands on the site of Quarnford Farm, in existence by 1597.[84] Birchen Booth further up the Dane from Manor Farm was possibly the site of a dairy farm in the Middle Ages, and a house there was recorded in 1597.[85] Birchen Booth farmhouse was still occupied in 1940[86] but was later abandoned.

There was a house at Gradbach south-west of Manor Farm possibly by 1374, when there was mention of Henry Gratebache. There was certainly a house by the earlier 1630s on the site of Gradbach Old Hall, a mainly 19th-century house which retains 17th-century stonework.[87] The nearby Gradbach House Farm was built in the early 20th century.[88] In 1951 Gradbach Old Hall was bought by the Buxton and District Scout Association, which uses its fields as a camping ground. Since the death of the tenant

70 13th Rep. Com. Char. 354; benefaction board in church.
71 L.J.R.O., B/C/11, Moses Charlesworth (1795).
72 Char. Com. files 217901–4.   73 Ibid. 244254–5.
74 V.C.H. Staffs. i. 327. This article was written in 1994.
75 Heywood, Cotton and his River, 165.
76 Geol. Surv. Map 1/50,000, drift, sheet 111 (1978 edn.); Soil Surv. of Eng. and Wales, sheet 3 (1983).
77 Chatsworth House (Derb.), Bateman MSS. ii, Hartington. Mr. M. Pearman, librarian and archivist to the trustees of the Devonshire Settled Estates, and his assistant Mr. T. Askey are thanked for their help.
78 J. Speed, Map of Staffs. (1610); G. Ormerod, Hist. of County Palatine and City of Chester (1882), iii. 544; J.

Nightingale, Staffs. (Beauties of Eng. and Wales, xiii), 1174.
79 D.R.O., Q/RIc 32.
80 Dodd, Peakland Roads, 96.
81 S.R.O., D. 1029/1/1, reverse pages.
82 V.C.H. Staffs. i. 327; Census, 1901–91.
83 S.H.C. iv (1), 64; Eng. P.N. Elements, i. 122.
84 D.R.O., D. 2375M/56/13, copy deed of 24 Oct. 39 Eliz. I; White, Dir. Staffs. (1834), 722; Kelly's Dir. Staffs. (1892; 1896).
85 D.R.O., D. 2375M/56/13, copy deed of 24 Oct. 39 Eliz. I; below, econ. hist. (agric.).
86 Kelly's Dir. Staffs. (1940).
87 S.H.C. xiv (1), 136; D.R.O., D. 2375M/63/53, p. 155.
88 O.S. Map 6", Staffs. IV. NW. (1900, 1926 edns.)

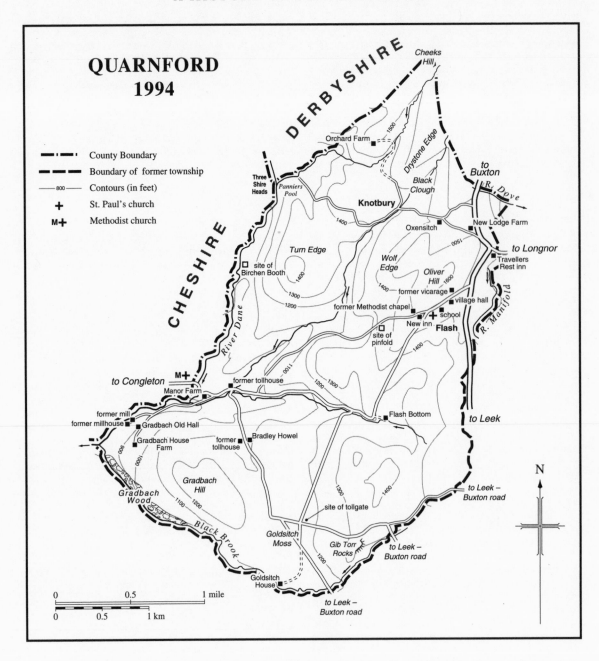

QUARNFORD
1994

‑‑‑∙‑‑∙‑‑ County Boundary
‑‑ ‑‑ ‑‑ Boundary of former township
—— 800 —— Contours (in feet)
+ St. Paul's church
M+ Methodist church

F<small>IG</small>. 9

in 1956 the house has provided accommodation for visitors and staff.[89] A cotton mill was erected beside the Dane in the late 18th century. In 1984 the mill and mill house were converted into a youth hostel.[90]

Goldsitch Moss probably takes its name from marigolds growing by Black brook.[91] A house there occupied in 1634 by a coal prospector[92] almost certainly stood on the site of Goldsitch House, which is partly of the 17th century.

Flash on the east side of the township, whose name means a swamp, had at least five houses

in 1597.[93] During the 18th century the area was settled by pedlars and hawkers, and the present village grew up around a church built in 1744.[94] It had three inns and three shops in 1817 and was the main centre in the north-west part of Alstonefield parish.[95] When Sir George Crewe first visited Quarnford in 1819 or 1820, it appeared to him as 'the very end of the civilized world', and Flash village was 'dirty, and bore marks principally of Poverty, Sloth, and Ignorance'.[96] Sir George was probably responsible for improving c. 1840 the former Leek–Buxton

89 Inf. from Mr. K. Bagshaw of Buxton, district scout commissioner.
90 Below, econ. hist. (trade and ind.).
91 *Eng. P.N. Elements*, i. 205; ii. 121–2.
92 Below, econ. hist. (trade and ind.).
93 D.R.O., D. 2375M/56/13, copy deed of 24 Oct. 39 Eliz. I; *Eng. Dialect Dict.* ed. J. Wright, ii. 385.
94 Below, econ. hist. (trade and ind.); church.
95 Pitt, *Staffs.* 245.
96 D.R.O., D. 2375M/44/1, 27 Aug. 1831.

road runnning to the village over Goldsitch Moss.[97] There was a village post office by 1904.[98]

The Leek–Buxton road formerly entered the township near Goldsitch House. It ran over Goldsitch Moss and continued north over the west side of Oliver Hill, crossing into Derbyshire beyond Oxensitch.[99] By 1749, however, it had been realigned to run north-east through Flash.[1] A new route for the Buxton road running mostly through Heathylee was laid out in the later 1760s as a branch of the road between Newcastle-under-Lyme and Hassop (Derb.) via Leek and Longnor, turnpiked in 1765. A tollgate called Flash Bar and a tollhouse were built in 1771 at the junction with a road to Longnor north-east of Flash.[2] An Act of 1773 turnpiked a side road running north-west from the Leek– Buxton road at the Royal Cottage, in Heathylee, to Manor Farm across Goldsitch Moss. Another side road to Manor Farm which entered Quarnford from the Blue Hills area of Heathylee was turnpiked under an Act of 1793.[3] In 1825 a tollgate, replacing one at Gib Torr, in Heathylee, was erected on Goldsitch Moss, and a tollhouse was built to the north-west at the home (now Bradley Howel) of John Bradley.[4] The tollhouse was replaced in 1842 by a house and gate at the road junction further north. The gate remained in use until 1852 when both it and the Goldsitch Moss gate were removed.[5] The Act of 1773 also turnpiked a side road which ran west from Flash Bar to Knotbury and then to coal pits on the Cheshire side of the Dane.[6] A tollgate erected at Oxensitch in 1829 was apparently no longer used in 1839.[7] The road system was disturnpiked in 1875.[8]

Flash association for the prosecution of felons existed in 1811.[9] A police constable recorded in Quarnford in 1896 probably lived at Flash.[10] A mains electricity supply was connected in 1962, and in 1984 the civil parish received a mains water supply, after a reservoir had been built on Oliver Hill.[11]

Quarnford Club, mentioned in 1767, was probably a burial or sick club.[12] By 1840 a sick club was based at the Travellers Rest,[13] an inn on the Buxton road north-east of Flash in exist-

ence by the later 1820s and so called by 1834.[14] The Flash Loyal Union friendly society was established in 1846. Known as the Tea Pot Club by 1906, it was dissolved in the early 1990s.[15] There was a lodge of the Order of Foresters in 1906.[16] From 1905 the post office at Flash housed a parish lending library and probably a reading room.[17] A village hall was opened north-east of the village in 1959.[18] A Women's Institute was formed in 1962.[19]

The belief that coins were counterfeited at Flash is an erroneous inference from its name, although a coining machine has been found in the neighbourhood at a farm in Sutton, in Prestbury (Ches.).[20] The alleged counterfeiting of bank notes at Flash in the early 19th century[21] was the main theme of the novel *Flash* (1928), an historical romance by Judge Alfred Ruegg.

MANOR. What was called the manor of *QUARNFORD* in 1321 was held by Hugh Despenser, created earl of Winchester in 1322.[22] It may have originated in the early 13th century, when Hugh's grandfather owned a park in Quarnford.[23] Hugh Despenser was executed in 1326, and in 1327 the Crown assigned Quarnford to Sir Roger Swynnerton, along with Despenser's share of Alstonefield manor and his manor of Rushton Spencer, in Leek.[24] At his death in 1338 Sir Roger was stated to hold what was described merely as pasture on the moors in Quarnford, for which he paid a chief rent of two arrows a year to James, Lord Audley, lord of Aenora Malbank's share of Alstonefield. By 1515 the rent was 2d. a year.[25] In the mid 15th century Quarnford and Rushton were acquired by John Savage,[26] whose descendant Sir John Savage in 1597 conveyed farms and waste ground in Quarnford to John Harpur, the lord of Alstonefield.[27]

ECONOMIC HISTORY. AGRICULTURE. Quarnford was in the forest of Alstonefield. About 1200, when Peter the clerk, a member of the earl of Chester's household, created a park there. In Peter's time the park was not fenced but was guarded by his men while the grass was growing;

97 S.R.O., D. 1029/1/5, p. 94; below, next para.
98 *Kelly's Dir. Staffs.* (1904).
99 Dodd, *Peakland Roads*, 174; *T.N.S.F.C.* N.S. iv. 37–8.
1   E. Bowen, *Improved Map of the County of Stafford* (1749).
2   *S.H.C.* 4th ser. xiii. 105; S.R.O., D. 3359/Buxton Rd. order bk. 1765–1800, 22 Mar. 1770, 12 July 1771; S.R.O., Q/RDc 24.   3 *S.H.C.* 4th ser. xiii. 105.
4   S.R.O., Q/RDc 24; S.R.O., D. 3359/Buxton Rd. order bk. 1814–32, 23 July 1825; Buxton Rd. acct. bk. 1809–60, acct. 7 Feb. 1826 (in possession of Mr. R. Stones of Malpas, Ches., 1994).
5   Buxton Rd. acct. bk. 1809–60, acct. 4 Aug. 1842; Buxton Rd. gates' acct. bk. 1844–68, acct. 1852 (in possession of Mr. Stones).
6   *S.H.C.* 4th ser. xiii. 105.
7   S.R.O., Q/RDc 24, map I; S.R.O., D. 3359/Buxton Rd. order bk. 1765–1800, 11 July 1777; 1814–32, 8 June 1829, 6 Dec. 1830.
8   Ibid. D. 3359/Leek, Buxton, and Monyash turnpike trust acct. bk. 1861–76.
9   *Macclesfield Courier*, 2 Feb. 1811, p. 1 (ref. supplied by Mr. A. W. Bednall of Macclesfield).
10 *Kelly's Dir. Staffs.* (1896).

11 *St. Paul's, Quarnford* (1994), 74; Leek Libr., newspaper cuttings 1984 (1), p. 13.
12 S.R.O., D. 1029/1/2, p. 35.
13 D.R.O., D. 2375M/205/15/2, receipt of 11 Jan. 1840.
14 S.R.O. 5322/8, no. 141; White, *Dir. Staffs.* (1834), 722.
15 *Alstonfield Deanery Mag.* July 1906; *St. Paul's, Quarnford*, 60.
16 *Alstonfield Deanery Mag.* July 1906.
17 Ibid. June and Nov. 1905.
18 *St. Paul's, Quarnford*, 72.
19 Inf. from Staffs. Federation of Women's Institutes.
20 *St. Paul's, Quarnford*, 23–5; [P. L. Brocklehurst], *Swythamley and Its Neighbourhood* (priv. print. 1874), 17 and pl. on facing page.   21 *Notes & Queries*, 5th ser. x. 521.
22 *Cal. Close*, 1318–23, 544; *Complete Peerage*, iv. 265.
23 Below, econ. hist. (agric.).
24 *S.H.C.* 1913, 22; above, Alstonefield, manors (Philippa Malbank's share).
25 *S.H.C.* 1913, 22; *Cal. Inq. p.m.* viii, p. 112; D.R.O., D. 2375M/171/1/2.
26 *S.H.C.* N.S. iii. 177; below, Leek: Rushton Spencer, manor.
27 D.R.O., D. 2375M/56/13, copy deed of 24 Oct. 39 Eliz. I.

after the grass had been cut, the park was laid open as common pasture. Peter was succeeded by Hugh le Despenser, also a member of the earl of Chester's household. Hugh erected a fence around the park, but in 1227 he agreed to take it down and to restore pasture rights.[28] The park possibly lay in the south-west corner of the township: there was land in the Gradbach area called the Park in the earlier 1630s.[29]

There was a vaccary, or dairy farm, in Quarnford in 1308.[30] It was possibly beside the Dane on the site of Birchen Booth, which derives the second part of its name from *both*, a cowhouse or herdsman's shelter.[31] In 1597 Ralph Rudyard held a lease of 300 sheep gates in Quarnford,[32] and sheep farming was evidently important in 1703 when a farmer was presented for grazing sheep in Quarnford in the summer but not in the winter, thereby evidently depriving the ground of manure.[33]

Quarnford's claim to a share of the common waste which lay north of Flash and spread into the Derbyshire manor of Hartington was disputed in the early 17th century.[34] In 1674 arbitrators awarded part of the waste to Sir John Harpur, as owner of Quarnford, and by 1737 c. 50 a. had been inclosed at Orchard Farm.[35] The remaining 134 a. of common waste in that area was inclosed in 1839 under an Act of 1834 amended in 1836, as were 136 a. south-east of Gradbach. All the inclosed land was awarded to Sir George Crewe, as impropriator of Alstonefield rectory.[36]

Gradbach wood along Black brook covered 26 a. in the early 19th century. The owner, Sir Henry Harpur, was informed in 1810 that trees were being felled illegally, and some replanting took place in 1837.[37]

Of the 1,210.1 ha. of farmland returned for the civil parish in 1988, grassland covered 725.7 ha. and there were 475.5 ha. of rough grazing. The farming was dairy and sheep, with 843 head of cattle and 6,905 sheep and lambs. Of the 41 farms returned, 37 were under 40 ha. in size, 3 were between 50 and 99 ha., and one was between 100 and 199 ha. Woodland covered 2.3 ha.[38]

MILL. There may have been a corn mill at Gradbach in 1640. That or a later mill on the site was apparently burnt down in 1785.[39]

FAIRS. In 1851 fairs were held at Flash on the Saturdays before Easter Sunday and Whit Sunday, at Michaelmas, and on the Saturday before the fair at Rugeley on the second Tuesday in December. The Michaelmas fair dated from c. 1839 and was for sheep and cattle.[40] A walled enclosure in a field north of Flash school in the late 1870s was probably used for cattle sales; such sales took place monthly in the earlier 20th century and possibly later.[41]

TRADE AND INDUSTRY. There were coal pits in the Goldsitch Moss area in 1564 and coal workings at Black Clough in the north part of the township in 1602.[42] When Sir John Harpur let a house and 37 a. at Goldsitch Moss to Peter Higson in 1634, he included all coal works in Quarnford. The lease was for 21 years, Higson paying an annual rent of £12 and 2 fat hens.[43] In 1673 coal was dug where it outcropped along streams south and east of the later Orchard Farm.[44] The mines were worked despite their expense. In his will of 1718 William Wardle of Boosley Grange, in Fawfieldhead, who in 1677 had taken a lease of coal mines in Alstonefield parish, asked Sir John Harpur to renew the lease in favour of his son, another William, in consideration of 'the vast charge' which the elder William had borne in improving tenements and in draining the mines.[45] In the earlier 18th century the younger William Wardle had to repair a road damaged by the number of coal-laden sledges from mines at Knotbury.[46] In 1765 Sir Henry Harpur let coal mines at Goldsitch and Knotbury to two Derbyshire men, George Goodwin and John Wheeldon, and to James Slack of Knotbury for 21 years at a rent of £10 15s. a year. It is probable that Goodwin and Wheeldon provided the money for the lease and that Slack worked the mines. The lease included a forge which Slack had recently set up.[47] There were 20 coal miners and colliers in the township in 1841 and 32 in 1851; the number had declined to 14 by 1881.[48] The main workings in the late 19th century were at Knotbury and near Orchard Farm, and they were closed and reopened according to local demand. The last mine, Hope Colliery near Orchard Farm, was worked between 1925 and 1932.[49]

In the 18th century Flash became a centre for pedlars and hawkers who travelled in North Staffordshire, Cheshire, and Derbyshire. The description 'a Flash man' was used for one of them in 1766.[50] The pedlars' goods consisted

28 *S.H.C.* iv (1), 64.
29 D.R.O., D. 2375M/63/53, p. 155.
30 *S.H.C.* N.S. xi. 257.
31 *Eng. P.N. Elements*, i. 43.
32 D.R.O., D. 2375M/56/13, copy deed of 24 Oct. 39 Eliz. I.
33 Ibid. D. 2375M/174/1, 25 Oct. 1703.
34 Chatsworth House (Derb.), map 2063.
35 D.R.O., D. 2375M/56/13, copy award of 1674; D. 2375M/190/4, deed of 10 June 1737.
36 S.R.O., Q/RDc 24; 4 & 5 Wm. IV, c. 15 (Priv. Act); 6 & 7 Wm. IV, c. 6 (Priv. Act).
37 D.R.O., D. 2375M/110/32, docs. re Gradbach wood; D. 2375M/205/13, receipt of 13 July 1837; S.R.O. 5322/8, no. 850.
38 P.R.O., MAF 68/6128/71.
39 Dodd, *Peakland Roads*, 96; Leek Libr., newspaper cuttings iii, p. 21.
40 White, *Dir. Staffs.* (1851), 472, 744.

41 O.S. Map 6", Staffs. I. SE. (1883 edn.); W.S.L., S.C. E/3/26, no. 66; *Memories of the Moorland Farmer*, ed. S. Gaukroger and J. Holliday (Buxton, 1994), 31.
42 *S.H.C.* 1938, 99; D.R.O., D. 2375M/57/1, 12 Oct. 44 Eliz. I. For the site of Black Clough see D.R.O., D. 2375M/71/84.   43 S.R.O., D. 424/M/19.
44 D.R.O., D. 2375M/71/84.
45 Ibid. D. 2375M/82/23, deed of 10 Apr. 1672, endorsement; L.J.R.O., Reg. of Wills C, f. 268.
46 D.R.O., D. 2375M/56/21, case re tithes and coal mines, 1744; D. 2375M/174/1, 25 Oct. 1733.
47 Ibid. D. 2375M/56/13, deed of 9 Feb. 1765; J. Farey, *Gen. View of Agric. and Minerals of Derb.* (1811), i. 396.
48 P.R.O., HO 107/1003; HO 107/2008; ibid. RG 11/2742.
49 *Leek Post & Times*, 31 Dec. 1992, p. 10; inf. from Mr. J. Leach of Buxton Mus.
50 S.R.O., D. 3359/Condlyffe, brief in case Billing v. Morris 1766.

chiefly of silk ribbons from Leek, buttons from Macclesfield, and smallwares from Manchester.[51] The benefactors of the church built at Flash in 1744 included six button men and two petty chapmen of Quarnford.[52]

Buttons were also made in the area around Flash by the late 18th century,[53] and in February 1834 the Travellers Rest was the scene of an attempt to establish a trade union for the female button makers of the locality. Five men organized a meeting at which, after prayers, oaths were taken from the women. They swore not to make buttons for less than certain piece rates and to 'turn out for wages', presumably meaning to strike, in three months' time. The women would then receive 6s. a week, having contributed 2d. a week to the union during the intervening period. The oaths were repeated in March, apparently as a defiant response to the conviction of trade unionists from Tolpuddle (Dors.). The promoters were brought to trial at Stafford in July, and the case was heard by Sir John Williams, the judge who had sentenced the Tolpuddle Martyrs to transportation. The defendants pleaded guilty, and because of their good character and the prosecution's call for leniency they were merely lectured by the judge and released on their own recognizances.[54]

Women and girls in Quarnford township continued to work as button makers. Only one was recorded in 1841, but there 34 in 1851 and 30 in 1861. Although only one was again recorded in 1881, there may have been many part-time workers: in 1884 it was stated that buttons were still made by hand in villages around Leek, principally Flash.[55]

In 1792 Thomas and James Oliver of Longnor and Thomas White of Hartington (Derb.) took a 31-year lease from Sir Henry Harpur of land by the Dane at Gradbach in order to build a mill to spin wool, cotton, or silk.[56] The mill was duly built, but in 1794 the lessees, then described as cotton spinners, dealers, and chapmen, went bankrupt. In 1798 the remainder of the lease was transferred to John and Peter Dakeyne, cotton spinners of Darley (Derb.). They converted the mill to flax spinning and erected a warehouse.[57] In 1837 the buildings included the mill and two warehouses, of two and three storeys; there was also a large house.[58] The mill provided employment for 64 people in 1838.[59] The Dakeyne family continued as lessees, and in 1850 Bowden Dakeyne worked both flax and silk at the mill. He still ran it in 1864, but it had been closed by 1868.[60] In 1978 the Youth Hostels Association

bought the land and buildings from the Harpur-Crewe estate and converted both the mill and the mill house into a hostel, opened in 1984 as Gradbach Mill youth hostel.[61]

LOCAL GOVERNMENT. Quarnford seems not to have come within the jurisdiction of Alstonefield manor court in the Middle Ages: no matters relating to the township were entered in the surviving court records.

In 1613 Alstonefield manor court appointed a surveyor of the highways for Quarnford, and in 1614 the frankpledge for Heathylee and Hollinsclough also represented Quarnford. Quarnford no longer shared that officer in 1615, although the court appointed a highway surveyor jointly for Quarnford and Hollinsclough from 1617 until 1629 or later.[62] By 1697 Quarnford formed its own tithing with a frankplege, by then styled a headborough.[63] Probably from 1745 and certainly from 1751 a separate view of frankpledge was held for Quarnford; it continued until 1756 or later, but from 1761 the headborough once more attended the view at Alstonefield. The Quarnford view was revived in 1775.[64] The court met at Manor Farm in the earlier 19th century and was still held in 1853.[65]

An order was made in 1714 for stocks to be set up on a green at 'Flashhead', presumably in the area of the later village.[66] There was a pinfold in the township in 1620. No pinner specifically for Quarnford is recorded before 1751, when one was appointed at the Quarnford view.[67] There was a pinfold south-west of Flash village in the late 1870s.[68]

In the later 17th and earlier 18th century the poor of Quarnford, Fawfieldhead, Heathylee, and Hollinsclough were maintained jointly.[69] Quarnford relieved its poor separately from 1733.[70] It became part of Leek poor-law union in 1837.[71]

CHURCH. By the late 17th century and presumably earlier people from Quarnford attended Longnor church.[72] In 1744 a church was built at Flash by the inhabitants of Quarnford township on land given by Sir Henry Harpur.[73] The perpetual curate was to receive £15, of which £10 was paid as a subscription by 32 inhabitants and landholders of Quarnford, each of whom was allotted a pew, and £5 by the trustees of the chapel.[74] The fees were to be retained by the vicar of Alstonefield and the curate of Longnor,

51 J. Aikin, *Description of Country from thirty to forty miles round Manchester* (1795), 437.
52 S.R.O., D. 1029/2/1.   53 *Reliquary*, v. 140–1.
54 *Staffs. Advertiser*, 2 Aug. 1834, p. 2.
55 P.R.O., HO 107/1003; HO 107/2008; ibid. RG 9/1949; RG 11/2742; *2nd Rep. Com. Technical Instruction, vol. III* [C. 3981-II], p. xlviii, H.C. 1884, xxxi (2).
56 D.R.O., D. 2375M/56/14, deed of 25 June 1792.
57 Ibid. D. 2375M/56/14, deed of 10 Oct. 1798 and abstract of tenancy c. 1803; D.R.O., D. 195Z/E4.
58 *Staffs. Advertiser*, 10 June 1837, p. 2.
59 *V.C.H. Staffs.* ii. 216 (locating it merely in Alstonefield parish).   60 *P.O. Dir. Staffs.* (1850; 1864; 1868).
61 Leek Libr., newspaper cuttings 1984 (1), pp. 28–9; inf. from the Northern Region Office of the Youth Hostels Assoc., Matlock (Derb.); below, plate 52.

62 D.R.O., D. 2375M/57/1, 14 Apr. 11 Jas. I sqq.
63 Ibid. D. 2375M/174/1, 29 Apr. 9 Wm. III sqq.
64 Ibid. 22 Oct. 1745; D. 2375M/174/2, 22 Oct. 1761 sqq.; D. 2375M/174/4, 25 Apr. 1751 sqq.
65 Ibid. D. 2375M/202/19, f. 45; White, *Dir. Staffs.* (1834), 719.
66 D.R.O., D. 2375M/174/1, 22 Oct. 1714.
67 Ibid. D. 2375M/57/1, 4 May 18 Jas. I; D. 2375M/174/4, 25 Apr. 1751.
68 O.S. Map 6", Staffs. I. SE. (1883 edn.).
69 Above, Fawfieldhead, local govt.
70 S.R.O., Q/SO/13, f. 105.
71 S.R.O., D. 699/1/1/1, p. 4.   72 Ibid. D. 921/1.
73 Ibid. D. 1029/2/1 and 2.
74 Ibid. D. 1029/2/1; D. 1029/2/3–5; D.R.O., D. 2375M/58/14, deed of 22 Sept. 1744.

although a small payment was made to the chapel out of parish funds until 1768 or later.[75] There was a chapelwarden by 1747.[76]

The benefice was vested in the Harpur family, and was styled a vicarage from 1868.[77] A parish of Quarnford, covering Quarnford and the western halves of Heathylee and Hollinsclough, was created in 1902.[78] The church retained its own vicar until 1963, and from 1965 it was served successively by the vicar of Meerbrook, in Leekfrith, and the vicar of Longnor as priests-in-charge.[79] In 1985 the benefice was united with those of Longnor and Sheen, although all three parishes remained separate. The vicar was to live in Longnor.[80]

In 1752, 1754, and 1800 Queen Anne's Bounty made grants of £200. By 1824 some of the money was used to buy 27 a. south of Hare House in Bradnop, in Leek parish. The Bounty made a further grant of £1,000 in 1822. In 1824 the rent from the Bradnop land was £30, and the interest on the remaining Bounty money was £44. Sir George Crewe then paid the £5 formerly paid by the trustees.[81] In 1829 Peter or William Walmesley left £50, but Sir George Crewe held the money in 1836 and it seems not to have been invested.[82] About 1830 the living was worth £85.[83] The £10 subscription established in 1744 came to be treated as a rent for the pews allocated to the original subscribers and was not always forthcoming. It was stated in 1834 that some pew-holders were too poor to pay and that some were annoyed at being expected to contribute when other worshippers paid nothing. Moreover the heirs of some of the benefactors were Methodists, and they presumably did not pay anything. As a result the curate usually received only half of what was due.[84] In 1874 the Ecclesiastical Commissioners gave an annuity of £6 13s. 4d. to meet a benefaction of £500, comprising £200 from the Poor Benefice Fund, £100 from the Lichfield Diocesan Church Extension Society, and £200 from donations by the patron and others and from collections in Alstonefield and Flash churches. The Commissioners themselves made a grant of £400 in 1885.[85] There were 29 a. of glebe in 1887, with an estimated rental of £40.[86]

The first curate, Daniel Turner, was already the curate at Meerbrook, in Leekfrith, and he later became the curate of Rushton Spencer also. He lived at Meerbrook, where he died in 1789.[87] His successor, James Whitaker, became vicar of Alstonefield in 1814 and employed stipendiaries to serve Quarnford. They included Robert Balderson, whom the chapelwarden tried to bar from the church in 1821 as 'a most depraved and drunken man'.[88] The appointment of James Roberts as perpetual curate later the same year brought an improvement. He lived in a house at Flash rented from Sir George Crewe, who had it enlarged for the purpose.[89] By 1840 the house was in a bad condition,[90] and when Roberts's successor was appointed in 1850 he chose to live in Hollinsclough village.[91] The curate of Quarnford continued to live at Hollinsclough until a vicarage house was built north-east of Flash in 1884.[92] No longer needed after 1963, it was sold and became a private house.

The chapel clerk in 1760 was described as having a good voice and understanding psalmody well, and in 1833 there was a singers' club at the church.[93] In 1830 there was one Sunday service at Flash, and Communion was celebrated four times a year.[94] The curate also served Hollinsclough until at least 1865, and on Census Sunday 1851 only an afternoon service was held at Quarnford. The attendance was 48, besides Sunday school children; the average adult attendance, however, was stated to be 80.[95]

A building on the east side of Gradbach mill was opened as a place of worship in 1833, presumably for mill workers.[96] It was known by 1870 as the Lodge, and services were still held there in 1886.[97] By 1900 and at least until the later 1950s a mission held at Ramshaw schoolroom in Heathylee was served from Quarnford.[98]

The present church of *ST. PAUL* at Flash dates from 1901. The church of 1744 was a single-cell building of brick with stone dressings, entered through a west door.[99] A west tower was added in 1750, with an external staircase probably giving access to a west gallery erected in the same year.[1] The church was extended eastwards in 1754 at the cost of John Bourne of Newcastle-under-Lyme, a noted benefactor of churches in North Staffordshire.[2] The extension had a Venetian east window.[3] By 1830 there was

[75] S.R.O., D. 922/35; D. 1029/2/6.
[76] Ibid. D. 1029/1/1, chapelwardens' accts. on reverse pages.
[77] D.R.O., D. 2375M/56/13, deed of 17 Sept. 1744; L.J.R.O., B/A/3/Quarnford; *Lich. Dioc. Ch. Cal.* (1869).
[78] *Lond. Gaz.* 15 Aug. 1902, p. 5321.
[79] *Lich. Dioc. Dir.* (1963 and later edns.).
[80] Above, Longnor, church.
[81] Hodgson, *Bounty of Queen Anne,* p. ccxcviii; L.J.R.O., B/V/6/Quarnford, 1824, 1841. For the site of the Bradnop land see W.S.L., S.C. H/2/7.
[82] S.R.O., D. 1029/1/5, memo. of Apr. 1829 at front of vol.; benefaction board in church.
[83] *Rep. Com. Eccl. Revenues,* 494–5.
[84] D.R.O., D. 2375M/87/19, notes on Quarnford church, 1834.
[85] Lich. Dioc. Regy., Bp.'s Reg. R, p. 673; S, p. 721; benefaction board in church.
[86] *Return of Glebe Lands,* 66.
[87] S.R.O., D. 1029/1/4, note at front of vol.; below, Leek: Leekfrith, church; Rushton Spencer, church.
[88] L.J.R.O., B/A/3/Alstonefield, 1814; S.R.O., D. 1029/1/5, facing p. 1; D.R.O., D. 2375M/58/14, petition for removal of curate, 1821.

[89] L.J.R.O., B/A/3/Quarnford, 1821; D.R.O., D. 2375M/87/19, Jas. Roberts to Sir Geo. Crewe, 5 Mar. 1822.
[90] D.R.O., D. 2375M/44/1, 21 Aug. 1840.
[91] Above, Hollinsclough, church.
[92] *Kelly's Dir. Staffs.* (1884); Lich. Dioc. Regy., Bp.'s Reg. S, pp. 722–3.
[93] S.R.O., D. 1029/1/1, p. 104; D.R.O., D. 2375M/205/10, Jas. Roberts to ? Sir Geo. Crewe, 18 Dec. 1833.   [94] *S.H.C.* 4th ser. x. 96.
[95] P.R.O., HO 129/372/4/2; above, Hollinsclough, church.
[96] White, *Dir. Staffs.* (1834), 719; *St. Paul's, Quarnford* (1994), 27.   [97] *Lich. Dioc. Ch. Cal.* (1871), 156; (1887), 114.
[98] Above, Heathylee, church.
[99] D.R.O., D. 2375M/58/14, deed of 28 Sept. 1744; S.R.O., D. 1029/1/1, acct. of consecration service at front of vol.; W.S.L., Staffs. Views, vii. 5.
[1] S.R.O., D. 1029/1/1, reverse pages; W.S.L., Staffs. Views, vii. 5.
[2] L.J.R.O., B/C/5/1754/72; S.R.O., D. 1029/1/2, notes at front of vol.; benefaction board in church. For Bourne see *V.C.H. Staffs.* viii. 21, 154, 233, 307.
[3] Lichfield Cath. Libr., Moore and Hinckes drawings, iv, no. 26.

a small north-east vestry and additional east and south galleries, and in 1857 the pulpit and reading desk were on the north side of the nave.[4] An organ was acquired from St. John's church in Buxton (Derb.) in 1871, and in 1873 Lady Harpur Crewe gave a font.[5]

The fabric was probably in poor condition in 1794, when there was a plan to rebuild the church. That was still the intention in 1841, but the parishioners could not afford the cost and in 1850 the church was in 'a most neglected condition'.[6] The church was rebuilt in 1901. Of coursed ashlar in a Gothic style to the design of W. R. Bryden of Buxton, it consists of a chancel with south organ chamber and north vestry, a nave, and a west tower. Fittings include a stone pulpit carved and given by a local sculptor, Edward Ash, a stone and marble reredos given by James Oliver of Meerbrook, in Leekfrith, and an oak lectern given by the Knowles family of New Lodge.[7] The glass in the east window was given in memory of Thomas and Maria Beswick of Northfield Farm in Flash village.[8]

There is an 18th-century silver chalice, presumably that given by William Trafford of Swythamley, in Heaton (d. 1762). Trafford also gave a silver paten, apparently no longer at the church in 1830. The church then had a silver-plated flagon and dish. A set of plate was given by Lady Harpur Crewe in 1901.[9]

An early 19th-century Commandments board hangs on the north wall of the chancel, and four benefaction boards on the west wall of the nave include one of 1820 relettered in the later 1850s.

The registers date from 1744.[10]

The churchyard of 1744 was extended in 1857, 1898, and 1927.[11]

NONCONFORMITY. A house in Quarnford registered for protestant dissenters by Thomas Redfern in 1772 was evidently for Methodists, estimated by the curate in 1773 as numbering c. 40.[12] The meeting place was probably at Flash, where a Methodist chapel was built in 1784. A Methodist society there had c. 60 members that year and more than 90 by 1790.[13] Sunday services were held fortnightly in 1798 and weekly in 1802.[14] As other Methodist societies were established in neighbouring villages the size of the society at Flash declined, and by 1803 it numbered 56.[15] It remained the largest in the area,

however, and the chapel was rebuilt for Wesleyan Methodists in 1821.[16] On Census Sunday 1851 the attendance was 80 in the afternoon, besides Sunday school children, and 180 in the evening.[17] Closed in 1974,[18] the chapel was later converted into a house.

Methodists held a Sunday service at Gradbach monthly in 1798 and fortnightly in 1802.[19] A Wesleyan Methodist chapel was built on the Cheshire side of the boundary beyond Manor Farm in 1848 but was apparently used only from 1849.[20] It was known as Gradbach Wesleyan chapel in 1994.

EDUCATION. John Bourne of Newcastle-under-Lyme built a school at Flash in 1760, a building which in 1994 was attached to the New inn. The chapel clerk was the schoolmaster in 1764.[21] What was probably the same school in 1819 had no endowment, and the master presumably charged fees.[22]

The school was reorganized in 1834 as a free day school, with the support of Sir George Crewe, who gave £10 a year, and Joseph Tunnicliffe of Macclesfield (Ches.), who gave £10 to pay for children from Hollinsclough. Tunnicliffe's donation ceased in 1835. The curate believed that if Sir George continued to contribute, it would be possible to teach 15 children free.[23] By the later 1840s the school was a National school, and in 1850 the master taught 36 children free.[24] The school was rebuilt in 1873 on a site north-east of the church and was enlarged in 1895.[25]

What was called Quarnford Church of England school in 1931 remained an all-age school until 1940, when the senior children were transferred to Leek. Quarnford school took controlled status in 1950, and by 1965 it was known by its present name, Flash Church of England (Controlled) primary school.[26]

A schoolmaster living at Goldsitch Moss in 1841 probably taught at Gradbach, where a National school had 10 boys and 10 girls in the later 1840s.[27] The school probably met in the mission church at Gradbach mill. Nothing further is known about it.

In 1830 the township had a Sunday school, attended by both Anglicans and Wesleyan Methodists.[28] The school received £5 a year left by Laurence Heapy (d. 1828), curate of Macclesfield (Ches.), for the religious education of

4 Ibid.; S.H.C. 4th ser. x. 96.
5 Lich. Dioc. Ch. Cal. (1872), 92; inscrip. on font.
6 B.L. Church Briefs B. xxxv. 1; S.H.C. 4th ser. x. 97; P.O. Dir. Staffs. (1850).
7 Lich. Dioc. Regy., Bp.'s Reg. U, pp. 470–3; Pevsner, Staffs. 132; Kelly's Dir. Staffs. (1904).
8 Inscrip. on glass.
9 T.B.A.S. lxxvii. 76; S.H.C. 4th ser. x. 96; Kelly's Dir. Staffs. (1904); benefaction board in church.
10 Those not in current use are in S.R.O., D. 1029/1.
11 S.R.O., D. 1029/2/7; Lich. Dioc. Regy., Bp.'s Reg. P, pp. 642–7; U, pp. 285, 287; W, pp. 282, 288–9.
12 L.J.R.O., B/V/5/Quarnford, 1772–3; S.H.C. 4th ser. iii. 124.
13 Dyson, Wesleyan Methodism, 40, 68–71; Wardle, Methodist Hist. 5.
14 Dyson, Wesleyan Methodism, 40; D.R.O., D. 3568/4/1/1.
15 S.R.O., D. 3155/1.
16 Dyson, Wesleyan Methodism, 71.
17 P.R.O., HO 129/372/4/2.   18 Local inf.
19 Dyson, Wesleyan Methodism, 40; D.R.O., D. 3568/4/1/1.
20 J. W. Wardle, Gradbach Methodism, 1849–1949 (copy in S.R.O., D. 3457/12/1); date stone on chapel.
21 S.R.O., D. 1029/1/2, p. 16; date stone on building.
22 D.R.O., D. 2375M/87/19, acct. of schs. in Alstonefield par. 1819.
23 White, Dir. Staffs. (1834), 719; D.R.O., D. 2375M/87/19, Jas. Roberts to Sir Geo. Crewe, 4 Apr. 1835.
24 Nat. Soc. Inquiry, 1846–7, Staffs. 2–3; P.O. Dir. Staffs. (1850).
25 Staffs. Advertiser, 11 Oct. 1873, p. 7; Kelly's Dir. Staffs. (1896).   26 S.R.O., CEH/167/1–2.
27 P.R.O., HO 107/1003; Nat. Soc. Inquiry, 1846–7, Staffs. 2–3.   28 S.H.C. 4th ser. x. 96.

poor children who attended the church at Flash.[29] In the earlier 1830s there were two Sunday schools, presumably one for Anglicans and the other for Methodists; the children numbered 114 boys and 105 girls.[30] On Census Sunday 1851 there was an attendance of 50 at the Church of England Sunday school, although

the average attendance was stated to be 70. The attendance at a Wesleyan Methodist Sunday school at Flash on the same day was 51.[31]

CHARITIES FOR THE POOR. None known expressly for the township.

FIG. 10

WARSLOW AND ELKSTONES

WARSLOW, Lower Elkstone, and Upper Elkstone were formerly a township in Alstonefield parish and later a civil parish called Warslow and Elkstones 3,597 a. (1,456 ha.) in area.[32] The land is mostly pasture. Warslow village on the east side of the parish is the main centre of population, with a smaller village at Upper Elkstone

nearly 2 miles to the west. North of Warslow village there is a small estate centred on Warslow Hall. The river Manifold forms the eastern boundary with Wetton and a tributary, Warslow brook, part of the southern boundary with Butterton. The river Hamps forms the western boundary with Onecote, in Leek parish. In 1934

29 Staffs. Endowed Chars. 100; J. P. Earwaker, East Ches. ii (1880), 507; benefaction board in church.
30 Educ. Enq. Abstract, 869.
31 P.R.O., HO 129/372/4/2.
32 V.C.H. Staffs. i. 327. This article was written in 1994.

183 a. centred on Herbage in Fawfieldhead were transferred to Warslow and Elkstones.[33]

Warslow village lies at 984 ft. (300 m.). To the east and south the land falls gently and lies at 662 ft. (202 m.) at the confluence of the Manifold and Warslow brook. Heathland north-west of the village rises to 1,312 ft. (400 m.) on the top of Revidge. Upper Elkstone village stands on the east side of a hill which rises to 1,376 ft. (419 m.). The underlying rock is sandstone of the Millstone Grit series as far east as Warslow village, where it becomes Carboniferous Limestone. On the sandstone the soil is clay or fine loam over clay; on the limestone it is loam.[34]

Fourteen taxpayers were recorded in Warslow in 1327 and 10 in 1332; a further 10 were recorded separately at Elkstone in 1332. Forty-three people were assessed for hearth tax in 1666 in Warslow and Lower Elkstone and 19 in Upper Elkstone.[35] The number of people owing suit at the manor court in 1769 was 77 in Warslow and 18 in Lower Elkstone.[36] A population increase noted in 1784 was chiefly the result of mining at Ecton, in Wetton,[37] and the township's population was 731 in 1801, 828 in 1811, and 854 in 1821. Mining at Ecton declined in the 1820s, and by 1831 Warslow's population had fallen to 696. Mining in Warslow itself presumably accounted for the rise to 772 by 1841. The population was 715 in 1851 and 720 in 1871. There was a decline to 574 in 1881, 494 in 1901, 464 in 1911, and 419 in 1921. The population was 444 in 1931, 368 in 1951, 357 in 1961, 341 in 1971, 326 in 1981, and 313 in 1991.[38]

There is a Bronze Age barrow on the north-eastern side of Warslow village, with two others further east, and one at Brownlow to the south-west. Three Bronze Age barrows also stand on top of the hill south-west of Upper Elkstone village.[39] The position of Warslow village on a site from which there are views down the Manifold valley as far as Thor's Cave in Wetton may explain the first part of its name, which is apparently derived from Old English *weard*, guard, and *setl*, a habitation.[40]

There was a church at Warslow possibly by the 13th century and certainly by the earlier 16th century.[41] The present Greyhound hotel was known as the Greyhound and Hare in 1789,[42] and by the later 1820s there were two other inns, the Crewe and Harpur Arms and the Red Lion, respectively west and north-east of the church.[43]

They served a village enlarged by 1784 by miners who worked the duke of Devonshire's copper mines at Ecton.[44] As mining at Ecton declined in the 1820s, some miners presumably transferred to work in mines already opened in Warslow, where mining continued until 1874.[45] By 1860 the Crewe and Harpur Arms had been reopened as the Grouse, which became a temperance hotel between 1900 and 1904; still open in 1916, it had been closed by 1924, and the Greyhound thereafter was the only village inn.[46]

The first telecottage in the United Kingdom was opened at Warslow in 1989. Housed in Manifold primary school, it provides access to computers, fax machines, and other equipment relating to information technology, the intention being to enable people to work at a distance from urban centres of employment. Community groups also use the equipment, through funding by Staffordshire county council.[47] In a further effort to arrest the decline in population, land behind the former Grouse inn was being developed in 1994 by Coventry Churches Housing Association for 16 one-bedroomed flats and bungalows.[48]

A house in existence by 1515 at Brownhill to the north-east of the village was rebuilt in 1830 as Warslow Hall.[49] The nearby Upper Brownhill Farm is partly of the 17th century. A cottage which existed by 1600 at Cowlow on the Hartington road east of Warslow Hall was rebuilt as the present farmhouse in 1860.[50] Ivy House Farm, dated 1742, stands in School Lane, which runs south from the village and formerly continued to Butterton. There was a cottage at Oils Heath west of the village by 1665.[51] Brownlow Farm south-west of the village was built in 1854.[52]

Elkstone was recorded *c.* 1215 as Elkesdon, the name presumably referring to the *dun*, or hill, south-west of Upper Elkstone village. By the earlier 1440s the name had become Elkstone.[53] The mention of Over Elkstone in 1272 suggests that there was by then also a settlement at Lower Elkstone; it existed as Nether Elkstone by 1290.[54] Upper Elkstone was in different ownership from Lower Elkstone, and it had its own church by the 1530s.[55] Strung out on the hillside, the village had an inn by 1816, called the Cock in 1834; it was closed in 1976.[56] The site of Hill House south of Upper Elkstone village was occupied probably by 1521 and certainly by 1660.[57]

33 Staffs. Review Order, 1934, p. 63 and map 1 (copy in S.R.O.).
34 Geol. Surv. Map 1/50,000, drift, sheet 111 (1978 edn.); Soil Surv. of Eng. and Wales, sheet 3 (1983).
35 *S.H.C.* vii (1), 218; x (1), 116; *S.H.C.* 1925, 235–6.
36 D.R.O., D. 2375M/174/5/13.
37 Below, this section [Warslow village].
38 *V.C.H. Staffs.* i. 327; White, *Dir. Staffs.* (1834), 719; *Census*, 1901–91.
39 Staffs. C.C., Sites and Monuments Rec. 00145, 00146, 00356, 00357, 00359, 00360, 04189.
40 *Eng. P.N. Elements*, ii. 247; M. Gelling, *Signposts to the Past* (1978), 146.
41 Below, churches.
42 *Torrington Diaries*, ed. C. B. Andrews, ii. 58.
43 S.R.O. 5322/9, nos. 294, 414.
44 D.R.O., D. 2375M/189/13, observations on Sir Hen. Harpur's Warslow estate, 1783; L.J.R.O., B/C/5/1784/ Alstonefield (faculty); J. Nightingale, *Staffs.* (Beauties of Eng. and Wales, xiii), 1016, where 'Onecote' is given in error

for Warslow.
45 White, *Dir. Staffs.* (1834), 772; below, econ. hist. (trade and ind.).
46 *P.O. Dir. Staffs.* (1860); *Kelly's Dir. Staffs.* (1900 and later edns. to 1924).
47 *The Times*, 7 Dec. 1989, p. 37; inf. from Mr. S. Brooks, Community Education Officer at Warslow telecottage.
48 *Leek Post & Times*, 25 Aug. 1993, p. 6.
49 D.R.O., D. 2375M/1/1, ct. of Pentecost week 7 Hen. VIII; below, manors.
50 *Alstonfield Par. Reg.* 64; date stone on house.
51 D.R.O., D. 2375M/82/23, deed of 10 Apr. 1665.
52 Ibid. D. 2375M/202/19, ff. 55, 61.
53 *S.H.C.* xi. 331–2; P.R.O., SC 6/1109/3.
54 *S.H.C.* iv (1), 197; vi (1), 197.
55 Below, manors; churches.
56 S.R.O., D. 4184/1/3, p. 5; White, *Dir. Staffs.* (1834), 720; *Elkstones*, ed. P. Grant (Leek, 1994), chapter 8.
57 P.R.O., SC 2/202/61, m. 1; S.R.O., D. 3359/misc. deeds, deed of 16 Mar. 1659/60.

By 1444 there was a house called Black Brook in the south-west corner of the township beside a tributary of the river Hamps.[58] Hill Farm to the east beside a tributary of Warslow brook existed by the mid 17th century,[59] and the site of Hole Farm further north was occupied probably by 1608 and certainly by 1738.[60] On the edge of the common waste north of Lower Elkstone there was a house at Averhill Side by the earlier 16th century.[61]

A road to Ecton crosses the Manifold east of Warslow village, where a bridge was recorded c. 1220.[62] The road between Cheadle and Buxton (Derb.) via Longnor was turnpiked in 1770, and by 1781 there was a tollgate where it entered the township at Brownlow. A branch to Hartington (Derb.) was also turnpiked in 1770. It ran through Warslow village and then north-east past Cowlow, and by 1781 there was a tollgate east of the village at a place called Dale.[63] The original line of the Buxton road ran some distance west of Warslow village. In the 1820s Sir George Crewe began to lay out a new line to run along the south and east sides of the village. The new line was sanctioned by an Act of 1833, as was a new line for the branch to Hartington running south of Warslow Hall and replacing the earlier line to Cowlow.[64] The road was disturnpiked in 1878.[65]

A packhorse way through Warslow village probably followed the road across Lum Edge mentioned in 1662.[66]

The Leek & Manifold Valley light railway, opened in 1904, ran through the east side of the township, with a station where it crossed Warslow brook. The line was closed in 1934.[67]

A horse post which operated between Longnor, Hartington (Derb.), and Leek three days a week in 1829 passed through Warslow, and in 1834 a carrier to Ashbourne (Derb.) also handled mail.[68] There was a village post office by 1861.[69] There was a police constable in Warslow by 1844.[70] A cottage at Seven Chimneys on the west side of the village was a police station by 1871, and it retains part of the original cell with its wooden bed.[71] A police station and two police houses were built north of the former Grouse inn in the early 1950s; one of the houses was sold in 1993.[72]

A mains electricity supply was available in Warslow by 1940, but not until 1962 in Upper and Lower Elkstone.[73]

Love ales were held at Upper Elkstone in 1521 and at Warslow in 1556.[74] In the earlier 19th century Warslow wake took place on the second Sunday in August, near the feast of St. Lawrence (10 August), the patron saint of the church.[75] Elkstone had its own wake by 1903, when it was held on the second Sunday in July. In 1947 the date was changed to the Sunday nearest the feast of St. John the Baptist (24 June), the patron saint of the church.[76] After the closure of the Cock inn in 1976 the Elkstone wake ceased. It was revived by the Elkstonian Society, a group of local people formed in 1978 to preserve Elkstone's heritage.[77]

A lodge of the Manchester Unity of Oddfellows was established at Warslow in 1842; it was dissolved in 1983.[78] A Women's Institute was formed at Warslow in 1928.[79]

There was a brass band at Warslow by 1873. It became a silver band in the early 1950s and still existed in 1994.[80] Warslow had a reading room by 1884. Still open in 1933, it was then in financial difficulties and was closed probably soon afterwards.[81] Warslow village hall, designed by the Leek architect R. T. Longden, was opened in 1935.[82]

MANORS. The separate recording of *WARSLOW* in the Domesday Book entry for Alstonefield manor may indicate that it had been a separate estate before the Conquest.[83] It was part of Alstonefield manor until 1516, when it was bought by John Mundy (d. 1537).[84]

In 1563 John's younger son Vincent granted what was then styled the manor of Warslow and Longnor to his uncle, John Browne, who was succeeded in 1570 by his son William.[85] In 1593 William's son John sold the manor to John Harpur, the lord of Alstonefield,[86] and it again descended with Alstonefield manor. By 1594 the manor of Warslow and Longnor was called a barony, a style already applied in 1592 to Longnor alone. The manor was still styled a barony in 1612, but by 1614 the name was again used only to describe Longnor.[87]

58 D.R.O., D. 2375M/1/1, 2nd ct. 22 Hen. VI.
59 W.S.L. 340/40.
60 *Alstonfield Par. Reg.* 111; docs. at St. Edward's church, Leek, deed of 20 Mar. 1737/8.
61 *S.H.C.* N.S. ix. 65.
62 *S.H.C.* 4th ser. iv. 163–4.
63 Ibid. 4th ser. xiii. 110–11; Dodd, *Peakland Roads,* 177; above, fig. 2.
64 *S.H.C.* 4th ser. xiii. 110–11; D.R.O., D. 2375M/44/1, 17 Sept. 1836; D. 2375M/71/182.
65 S.R.O., D. 239/M/14/63, cert. of 25 Nov. 1878.
66 Dodd, *Peakland Roads,* 127; D.R.O., D. 2375M/30/27, description of boundary of Warslow common, 1662.
67 Below, Leek: Leek and Lowe, communications.
68 Pigot, *New Com. Dir.* [1829]. 712; White, *Dir. Staffs.* (1834), 723.
69 P.R.O., RG 9/1949.
70 S.R.O., D. 4184/1/2, pp. 87, 91, 95, 102.
71 P.R.O., RG 9/1949; RG 10/2885; inf. from Ros Prince of the Old Nick, Seven Chimneys.
72 Staffs. C.C. deeds, C. 608.
73 *Kelly's Dir. Staffs.* (1940); *Alstonfield Deanery Mag.*

lxv (2).
74 P.R.O., SC 2/202/61, m. 1; D.R.O., D. 2375M/1/2, 8 Oct. 3 & 4 Phil. and Mary.
75 White, *Dir. Staffs.* (1834), 719.
76 *Alstonfield Deanery Mag.* Aug. 1903; ibid. l (6).
77 Leek Libr., newspaper cuttings 1985 (1), p. 16.
78 Inf. from Independent Order of Odd Fellows (M.U.) head office, Manchester.
79 Inf. from Staffs. Federation of Women's Institutes.
80 W.S.L., Sleigh scrapbk. ii, f. 97; inf. from Mr. A. Grindon of Leek, a former member.
81 *Kelly's Dir. Staffs.* (1884); *Alstonfield Deanery Mag.* xxxvi (12).
82 Programme for opening ceremony (copy in D.R.O., D. 2375M/80/36).
83 *V.C.H. Staffs.* iv. 47.
84 Above, Alstonefield, manors.
85 D.R.O., D. 2375M/47/24, deed of 14 May 5 Eliz. I; P.R.O., PROB 11/52, ff. 215–16.
86 *S.H.C.* xvi. 126.
87 D.R.O., D. 2375M/57/1, 7 Oct. 36 Eliz. I, 16 Apr. 10 Jas. I, 6 May 12 Jas. I; above, Longnor, manor.

Warslow Hall, north of Warslow village, was built by Sir George Crewe in 1830 principally for the agent of his Alstonefield estate, Richard Manclark, but also as a summer residence for himself and his family. It stands on the site of Brownhill Farm, evidently Manclark's home by 1826: his initials and that date are on the surviving outbuildings, which are extensive. The Georgian-style house is a rectangular stone block with a north wing, and the main entrance on the east has a Tuscan porch. There is a drawing room and a dining room on either side of the front hall and an office for the agent at the rear. After Manclark's death in 1850 Sir John Harpur Crewe used the house as a shooting lodge, and two service wings were added on the north side. The kitchen wing was removed in 1973; the other wing, containing the servants' hall, survives.[88] The grounds, 115 a. on either side of the Longnor road, were landscaped and planted with trees in the early 1830s, and there was a grotto by 1835.[89] Two pools on either side of the road feed a series of small cascades in the steep-sided valley south of the house.

About 1215 Geoffrey Griffin gave to Trentham priory land in Elkstone together with his body for burial.[90] In 1253 the prior was sued for what was called the manor of *ELKSTONE* by Adam of Elkstone, and in 1272 Adam's three surviving sisters and the heirs of two others sued the prior for what was called the manor of Over Elkstone. Judgement was given in the plaintiffs' favour in 1272, and the manor was divided into five parts.[91] The manor covered only part of Upper Elkstone, and in 1272 there was a separate estate of four houses with land, possibly identifiable as the estate in which Maud of Elkstone had successfully claimed dower against Geoffrey Griffin and others in 1227.[92] In 1337 Maud Basset of Nuneaton (Warws.) granted the houses to Trentham priory,[93] which later regained possession of the manor: it was holding manor courts by the late 15th century.[94] At the priory's dissolution in 1537 it had four tenants holding houses at will, probably corresponding to the houses acquired in 1337. The priory's estate evidently comprised six other houses, which were included in the Crown's grant of the priory's land at Elkstone to Sir William Herbert in 1550.[95] Sir William promptly granted his Elkstone estate to Edward North.[96] The later descent is unknown until 1605, when Henry Offley of Madeley settled the manor of Elkstone on his son John. It

was still confined to the Upper Elkstone area, Lower Elkstone then being part of Sir John Harpur's Alstonefield estate.[97] Elkstone manor descended in Offley's family, which adopted the surname Crewe in 1708.[98] In 1778 John Crewe conveyed the manor to trustees, who in 1789 granted it to the duke of Devonshire.[99] The dukes were still the lords in 1834.[1] Nothing further is known about the manor.

ECONOMIC HISTORY. AGRICULTURE. In 1086 Warslow had 4 *villani* and 2 bordars with 1 ploughteam.[2] There were probably at least two open fields in the Middle Ages: the names Smith field and Town field survived in the later 1820s for land respectively south-west and north-east of Warslow village.[3] In the late 1460s a customary payment of 3*d.* was made to a man for guarding a gate on the north side of the village, probably to prevent cattle wandering into Town field.[4] New field west of the village was created in the earlier 1550s, following the inclosure of 240 a. of common waste at the request of cottagers.[5] At least part of New field was managed as an open field and probably accounted for the 135 a. of arable held by Sir John Harpur's tenants in the Warslow part of the township in the earlier 1630s.[6] The tenants also held 386 a. of pasture. Freeholders at the same date held 190 a., but the balance between arable and pasture is unknown. There were also 118 a. of common pasture, lying mostly at Brownlow, where the township's bull was kept in 1612, and at Lord's Wood beside the Manifold south-east of the village.[7] In 1839 open-field land and common pasture totalling 78 a. were inclosed under an Act of 1834 amended in 1836.[8]

At Lower Elkstone an open field called White field was mentioned in 1595 and one called Town field in 1599.[9] No open-field land was recorded in the earlier 1630s.[10] It is not known whether Upper Elkstone had any open-field land.

Rough pasture on Revidge, Swallow Moss, and Lum Edge was inclosed in 1839 under the 1834 Act. Sir George Crewe was allotted 384 a. as impropriator of Alstonefield rectory and 8 a. as lord of the manor, and the vicar of Alstonefield was allotted the remaining 128 a.[11] At Upper Elkstone 275 a. of common waste were inclosed in 1822 under an Act of 1813. The duke of Devonshire as lord of the manor was allotted 14 a. and the curate of Upper Elkstone 9 a.[12]

88 D.R.O., D. 2375M/44/1, 17 Aug. 1831; *Country Life*, 1 June 1989, pp. 168–71; below, plate 35. Miss Airmyne Harpur-Crewe of Warslow Hall and Mr. A. R. Pegg of Ticknall (Derb.), personal representative of the late Henry Harpur-Crewe, are thanked for their help.
89 *Country Life*, 1 June 1989, pp. 170–1; D.R.O., D. 2375M/205/11, Ralph Woodisse's bill, 1834–5.
90 *S.H.C.* xi. 331–2.
91 Ibid. iv (1), 126, 197–8; ibid. vi (1), 84.
92 Ibid. iv (1), 42, 197.   93 Ibid. xi. 331.
94 Below, local govt.
95 P.R.O., SC 12/3/47; *Cal. Pat.* 1550–3, 32.
96 W.S.L., S.D. Pearson 182.
97 P.R.O., C142/363/191; D.R.O., D. 2375M/63/53, p. 178.
98 G. Ormerod, *Hist. of County Palatine and City of Chester* (1882), iii. 314; *Complete Peerage*, iii. 535.
99 Copy of conveyance of Elkstone manor, 1778 (in

possession of Mr. R. Stones of Malpas, Ches., 1994); docs. at St. Edward's church, Leek, deed of 24 June 1789.
1 White, *Dir. Staffs.* (1834), 718.
2 *V.C.H. Staffs.* iv. 47.
3 S.R.O. 5322/9, nos. 193–7, 538, 569–70.
4 P.R.O., SC 6/988/2, m. 5d.
5 D.R.O., D. 2375M/1/2, 6 July 1 Phil. and Mary; D. 2375M/161/5/1 and 4.
6 Ibid. D. 2375M/57/1, 11 Oct. 15 Jas. I, 8 Apr. 22 Jas. I; D. 2375M/63/53, p. 177.
7 Ibid. D. 2375M/57/1, 16 Apr. 10 Jas. I; D. 2375M/63/53, pp. 170–5, 177; S.R.O. 5322/9, nos. 84, 504.
8 S.R.O., Q/RDc 24; 4 & 5 Wm. IV, c. 15 (Priv. Act); 6 & 7 Wm. IV, c. 6 (Priv. Act).
9 D.R.O., D. 2375M/57/1, 3 May 37 Eliz. I, 20 Apr. 41 Eliz. I.   10 Ibid. D. 2375M/63/53, pp. 178–80.
11 S.R.O., Q/RDc 24.
12 Ibid. Q/RDc 21; 53 Geo. III, c. 61 (Priv. Act).

Of the 908 ha. of farmland returned for the civil parish in 1988, grassland covered 742.3 ha. and there were 151.4 ha. of rough grazing. The farming was dairy and sheep, with 1,244 head of cattle and 2,721 sheep and lambs. Of the 38 farms returned, 32 were under 40 ha. in size, 5 were between 40 and 49 ha., and one was between 50 and 99 ha. Woodland covered 8.3 ha.[13]

A tithe barn in Warslow township in the 17th century probably stood in Warslow village: there was a building called the tithe barn north-east of the Greyhound in the later 1820s.[14]

MILLS. There was a mill in Warslow in 1396. It probably stood on Warslow brook south-west of the village, where there was a mill in 1592.[15] A mill there was still worked in 1834 but seems to have been abandoned soon afterwards.[16]

There was a mill at Upper Elkstone apparently c. 1215 and certainly in 1272.[17] Nothing further is known about it.

TRADE AND INDUSTRY. Lead mining in Warslow, which became important in the earlier 19th century, appears to have been first attempted in 1717 when Sir John Harpur licensed three Derbyshire men to dig in Warslow and at Fleetgreen, in Fawfieldhead. The licence was for 11 years, and Sir John was to take $\frac{1}{7}$ of lead ore.[18] The search was probably soon abandoned, and in 1723 Sir John licensed four other Derbyshire men to dig for lead and copper in Alstonefield parish for 18 years, paying him $\frac{1}{9}$ of the ore.[19] On the expiry of that licence in 1741 Sir Henry Harpur made a new one on the same terms for 21 years to a partnership headed by John Wall and Thomas Fisher, stewards of the Harpur estates respectively in Staffordshire and Derbyshire; his son, also Sir Henry, renewed the lease in 1762. What was believed to be a rich seam of lead ore was discovered in Warslow in 1766.[20] Productive by 1769, the mine lay east of Warslow village beside the Ecton road and was called Dale mine by 1771.[21] In 1789 Sir Henry Harpur renewed the lease in favour of Charles Greville.[22]

In 1800 a group of 25 men, mostly local and headed by John and Peter Dakeyne of Gradbach mill in Quarnford, took a 21-year lease of mines in Warslow, Lower Elkstone, and part of Fawfieldhead. Sir Henry included himself in the partnership, which by 1801 operated as the Dale

Mine Co. and apparently still existed in 1811.[23] Dale mine and a mine at Hayesbrook Gate on the Warslow–Fawfieldhead boundary were the chief workings, and they were included in a lease made by Sir George Crewe in 1823 to a successor partnership, the Warslow Mineral Co. Work at Dale mine at least had ceased by 1832.[24] With the formation in 1836 of a public joint stock company, the North Staffordshire Lead and Copper Mining Co., the Warslow mines were exploited on a larger scale. Dale mine was reopened, and others were started at White Roods, west of Cowlow, and at Lime Pits, south-east of Warslow village. By 1842 the company employed 20 miners, the number rising to 50 by 1849.[25] In 1858 a partnership which had taken over from the company in the early 1850s was itself replaced by Dale Mining Co. Ltd., formed in the previous year.[26] Under the management of Richard Niness, also the manager of mines at Upper Elkstone, the Warslow mines prospered, and in 1863 New Dale mine was opened north of the original Dale mine. The company was replaced in 1868 by New Dale Mining Co. Ltd., which survived until 1874 when all lead mining in the area ceased.[27]

Copper ore had been discovered at Upper Elkstone by c. 1680.[28] It was worked, possibly for the first time, from 1730 when mining rights at Royledge by the river Hamps were leased. In 1736 land elsewhere in Upper Elkstone was leased to a prospector for seven years.[29] Trial digging was still taking place in the late 18th century,[30] and not until 1849 is there evidence that mines were worked commercially, and then only on a small scale. There were two mines adjacent to each other, New York and Royledge; the former was closed in 1859 and the latter in 1862.[31]

Two lime pits mentioned in 1679 possibly lay south-east of Warslow village, where there was land called Upper and Near Lime Pit in the later 1820s.[32] The Warslow Lime Kiln Co. mentioned in 1833 was possibly established to work a lime kiln built that year by Sir George Crewe.[33] Lime working in Warslow apparently continued until the earlier 1860s.[34]

LOCAL GOVERNMENT. Warslow and Lower Elkstone formed a tithing in Alstonefield manor.[35] By the late 1390s it sent two frank-

13 P.R.O., MAF 68/6128/76.
14 S.R.O. 5322/9, no. 424; above, Alstonefield, manors (rectory).
15 D.R.O., D. 2375M/47/24, Warslow rental dated eve of feast of St. Chad 19 Ric. II, and 1592 survey of John Browne's lands.
16 White, Dir. Staffs. (1834), 722. There was apparently no miller in Warslow in 1841: P.R.O., HO 107/1003.
17 S.H.C. iv (1), 197; xi. 332.
18 D.R.O., D. 2375M/190/2, deed of 14 Nov. 1717.
19 Ibid. D. 2375M/189/1, deed of 18 Mar. 1722/3.
20 Ibid. D. 2375M/54/3/2, counsel's opinion re leases of mines, 1767; D. 2375M/189/2, deed of 16 Oct. 1741; D. 2375M/189/14, deed of 28 Apr. 1762.
21 Ibid. D. 2375M/189/13, John Taylor to Mr. Greaves, 7 Oct. 1769, and section of Dale mine, 7 Mar. 1771; D. 2375M/282/11, plan of position of Dale mine.
22 Ibid. D. 2375M/189/13, draft corresp. and articles of agreement, 1787–9.
23 Ibid. D. 2375M/101/4, deed of 25 Mar. 1800; D.

2375M/268/11 and 21.
24 Bull. Peak Dist. Mines Hist. Soc. v (2), 95–6.
25 D.R.O., D. 2375M/56/11, deed of 29 Sept. 1836; D. 2375M/99/6, letter re inspection of Warslow mines, 5 Nov. 1849; D. 2375M/154/15 and 23.
26 Ibid. D. 2375M/67/27, deed of 30 Nov. 1858; Bull. Peak Dist. Mines Hist. Soc. v (2), 97; v (3), 161–2.
27 Bull. Peak Dist. Mines Hist. Soc. iv (5), 362–7; v (1), 9 (photo. of Niness); v (3), 162–5; v (5), 279–83; D.R.O., D. 2375M/254/9, papers re closure of New Dale mine.
28 Plot, Staffs. 165.
29 S.R.O., D. 3359/Cruso, draft deed of 1731 rehearsing lease of 17 July 1730; W.S.L., H.M. Chetwynd 24.
30 S.R.O., D. 3359/Cruso, deed of 6 July 1785.
31 Bull. Peak Dist. Mines Hist. Soc. v (1), 1–7.
32 D.R.O., D. 2375M/190/8, deed of 23 Oct. 1679; S.R.O. 5322/9, nos. 389–90.
33 D.R.O., D. 2375M/205/10, receipt of 5 Dec. 1833.
34 Ibid. D. 2375M/167/12, p. 11.
35 Above, Alstonefield, par. intro. (manorial govt.).

pledges to the twice-yearly view.[36] In 1499 a 12-man jury for Warslow was empanelled separately from a similar jury for the rest of Alstonefield manor, and in 1500 a separate great court was held for Warslow. It met at Alstonefield, apparently on the same day as the Alstonefield view of frankpledge. In April 1505 the Warslow court met on the day after the Alstonefield view and possibly at Warslow.[37] Two 12-man juries were empanelled at that court, one for Warslow and the other for Longnor. A separate view of frankpledge for Warslow and Longnor was held by 1525, but it apparently ceased after 1535.[38] A Warslow great court, however, met in the late 1540s and earlier 1550s.[39] In April 1594 a view of frankpledge was held for Alstonefield, Warslow, and Longnor, but from October that year a separate view for Warslow and Longnor was held either on the day after or the day before a view for the rest of Alstonefield manor. From 1611 there was a further division, a separate view being held for Longnor on the same day as one for Warslow. That remained the pattern in 1629.[40] Separate views for Warslow and Longnor were still held in October 1674, but on different days. From 1675 a joint view was held, two frankpledges (by then styled headboroughs) representing Warslow with Lower Elkstone, and one representing Longnor.[41] In 1697, apparently for the first time, the spring view was held at Longnor. From 1708 it was normal to hold only an autumn view, for which Warslow was the usual venue, although spring views were occasionally held at Longnor. From 1775 there were again spring and autumn views, and Longnor had replaced Warslow as the meeting place for both. The Harpur Arms in Longnor market place was mentioned as the venue in 1790.[42] The court still met at Longnor when last recorded in 1853.[43]

It was stated in 1674 that there had never been a pillory in Warslow, but stocks and a whipping post were mentioned in 1686.[44] An order to set up stocks was made in 1713.[45] The remains of what may be 19th-century stocks survived in 1994 at the corner of the Longnor road and School Lane. There was a pinfold in Warslow in 1532, and a pinner was mentioned in 1596.[46] A pinfold whose construction, on the site of a ruined pinfold, was ordered in 1715 probably stood in School Lane: one certainly stood there north-east of Ivy House Farm in the later 1820s.[47] In the late 1870s a pinfold stood on the

north-west side of the village near the former workhouse; it had been removed by the late 1890s.[48]

Warslow apparently had a surveyor of the highways in 1594. By 1601 two surveyors were appointed at the manor court, one of them probably for Lower Elkstone, as was the case in the later 17th century.[49]

The prior of Trentham held courts at Upper Elkstone infrequently in the late 15th century but apparently annually in the earlier 16th century.[50] A court was held by the duke of Devonshire in the earlier 1830s.[51] The manor apparently formed a constablewick in 1377, and a constable for Upper Elkstone was mentioned in 1728.[52]

The poor of Warslow, Lower Elkstone, and Upper Elkstone were maintained jointly probably by the later 17th century and certainly by 1750.[53] There was a workhouse north-west of Warslow village by the later 1820s. The township became part of Leek poor-law union in 1837.[54]

CHURCHES. There may have been a chapel at Warslow by the 13th century, on the evidence of the font in the present church, and part of the shaft and base of a late medieval cross survives in the churchyard on the south side of the church. A chapel at Warslow was mentioned in 1524, and its dedication to St. Katharine was recorded in 1533. A chapel at Elkstone, also mentioned in 1524, probably stood at Upper Elkstone, where there was a church in 1682.[55]

A grant from Queen Anne's Bounty shortly before 1766 was lost because neither Warslow nor Elkstone chapel had a nominated curate. The chapels were then served by the vicar of Alstonefield's curate, Luke Story, who visited the area frequently 'for a very small subscription', recorded in 1784 as £1 6s. 8d.[56] The two chapels were served jointly by a perpetual curate from 1785, the patron being the vicar of Alstonefield.[57] There was a separate benefice for each, and each was styled a vicarage from 1868.[58] The parish of Warslow with Elkstone was created in 1902, and the benefices were united in 1908.[59] In 1985 the benefice of Warslow with Elkstone was united with those of Alstonefield, Butterton, and Wetton, although all four parishes remained separate. Alstonefield was made the vicar's place of residence.[60]

36 D.R.O., D. 2375M/1/6, undated view following ct. of Thurs. after feast of St. Peter and St. Paul 23 Ric. II.
37 Ibid. D. 2375M/1/3, 14 July 14 Hen. VII, 1st ct. 16 Hen. VII, 8 Apr. 20 Hen. VII.
38 Ibid. memo. re Warslow views held at Alstonefield, 16–27 Hen. VIII; D. 2375M/1/6, 25 Apr. 22 Hen. VIII sqq.
39 Ibid. D. 2375M/1/2, 27 Sept. 2 Edw. VI sqq.
40 Ibid. D. 2375M/57/1, 8 Oct. 36 Eliz. I sqq.
41 Ibid. D. 2375M/57/2, 24 and 25 Oct. 1674 sqq.
42 Ibid. D. 2375M/174/3, 30 Apr. 9 Wm. III sqq.
43 Ibid. D. 2375M/202/19, f. 41.
44 Ibid. D. 2375M/57/2, 24 Oct. 1674; D. 2375M/54/3/13, 23 Apr. 1686.
45 Ibid. D. 2375M/174/3, 23 Oct. 1713.
46 Ibid. D 2375M/1/6, 16 Sept. 24 Hen. VIII; D. 2375M/57/1, 27 Apr. 38 Eliz. I sqq.
47 Ibid. D. 2375M/174/3, 22 Oct. 1715; S.R.O. 5322/9, no. 344.
48 O.S. Map 6", Staffs. IX. NW. (1887 and 1900 edns.).

49 D.R.O., D. 2375M/57/1, 6 Apr. 36 Eliz. I, 20 Apr. 43 Eliz. I sqq.; D. 2375M/57/2, 21 Apr. 1675.
50 P.R.O., SC 2/202/60–1.
51 White, Dir. Staffs. (1834), 718.
52 S.H.C. 4th ser. vi. 8; D.R.O., D. 2375M/110/32, constable's acct., 1728.
53 D.R.O., D. 2375M/53/3/12, Wm. Wardle's note on manorial govt. in Alstonefield par., 1750; above, Alstonefield, par. intro. (par. govt.).
54 S.R.O. 5322/9, no. 270; S.R.O., D. 699/1/1/1, p. 419.
55 L.J.R.O., Reg. of Wills 1, p. 84; ibid. B/C/11, Edw. Tetryngton (1533); Plot, Staffs. map.
56 L.J.R.O., B/A/3/Longnor, 1767, L. Story to bp.'s sec., 11 Sept. 1766; B/C/5/1784/Alstonefield (faculty).
57 Ibid. B/A/3/Elkstone; B/A/3/Warslow.
58 Lich. Dioc. Ch. Cal. (1869).
59 Lond. Gaz. 15 Aug. 1902, pp. 5321–3; 18 Aug. 1908, pp. 6069–70.
60 Above, Alstonefield, church.

In 1785 Warslow and Elkstone were each assigned a grant of £200 from Queen Anne's Bounty. Warslow received further grants of £200 in 1786, 1790, 1808, and 1813, and Elkstone received similar grants in 1786, 1789, and 1792 and one of £400 in 1824. The money was used in 1826 to buy 31 a. in Longnor as an endowment for both Warslow and Elkstone.[61] In 1824 Warslow was awarded £1,400 by Queen Anne's Bounty on account of its increased population. In 1825 Elkstone received another £200 grant, and in 1829 a grant of £200 was made to Warslow to meet a benefaction of £600.[62] By 1832 the endowments comprised the land in Longnor, a 40-a. farm in Ipstones, and 12 a. in Upper Elkstone. The curate's income was then £105 for Warslow and £74 for Elkstone.[63] There were 104 a. of glebe in 1887, with an estimated rental of £143 3s.[64] By will of 1897 George Sutton left Black Brook farm to augment the living; it was sold for £1,024 8s.[65]

In 1590 the curate of Warslow was the tenant of a house in Warslow churchyard.[66] A house south-west of Warslow village was built in 1829 for the newly appointed curate, Richard Pidcocke. It is a large, stone house with a central porch and Gothick windows.[67] It was sold in 1982.[68]

In 1604 Sunday services at Elkstone were taken by Richard Bullock, a reader who was not licensed to preach and who was described as 'a young scholar, going to a grammar school all the week'; his stipend was £1 a year together with 'holiday board'. Henry Smith, also an unlicensed reader, served Warslow at the same date.[69] Both chapels were still served by readers in the later 17th century.[70] It is not known whether the perpetual curate appointed in 1785 resided, and when Warslow church was rebuilt in 1820 it was being served by an assistant, William Richardson.[71] The curate appointed in 1828[72] took Sunday services alternately at Warslow and Elkstone in 1830; Communion was celebrated four times a year at each church. There were psalm singers at Warslow in 1820 and at Elkstone in 1830.[73] They possibly survived at Warslow until an organ was acquired in the mid 1860s.[74] On Census Sunday 1851 there was a morning service at Elkstone attended by 18 adults and one in the afternoon at Warslow attended by 200, besides Sunday school children.[75] High Church practices introduced at Warslow by William Hill, vicar 1908–34, were continued by his successor Albert Oliver (1934–60).[76]

Elkstone chapel had two wardens in 1553.[77] One of the four churchwardens of Alstonefield parish recorded in 1569 may have been for Warslow and Elkstone, the arrangement in the early 18th century. From the late 1780s Warslow and Elkstone each had its own churchwarden. The wardens presented at the Easter vestry for Alstonefield parish until 1827.[78] Both chapelries, however, continued to contribute to the maintenance of Alstonefield church.[79] In 1830 Warslow and Elkstone shared a clerk, who was paid £2 12s.[80] Warslow church had a dog whipper by the earlier 1720s. He was paid 5s. a year, still his salary in 1827.[81]

The present church of ST. LAWRENCE at Warslow, so called by 1850,[82] dates from 1820. Its predecessor was a narrow building, 44 ft. long and 20 ft. wide, which dated at least in part from the earlier 17th century: a stone dated 1631 is on the east wall of the present church. Permission was given in 1784 to insert a west gallery and to repew the nave; the pulpit then stood on the north side of the nave.[83] The church was rebuilt in Georgian style in 1820, 2 ft. shorter than the earlier building but 7 ft. wider. Of coursed ashlar, it consisted of an aisleless nave with a west gallery, a south door, and a west tower. The communion table stood at the east end of the nave and a combined pulpit and reading desk on its north side; there were pews for the clerk and for the churching of women at the north-east end of the nave.[84] A chancel, north vestry, and south organ chamber were added in 1908, at the expense of Sir Thomas Wardle of Leek, whose country seat was at Swainsley, in Butterton. The architect was Charles Lynam of Stoke-upon-Trent. The box pews in the nave were replaced with open benches, and a pew for the Harpur Crewe family was provided at the east end of the nave on the south side. Lady Harpur Crewe gave altar furnishings.[85] Glass by Morris & Co. was inserted in 1909 in the side windows of the chancel in memory of Thomas and Mary Lloyd of the Greyhound and their children. In 1910 the east window was filled with glass also probably by Morris & Co., in memory of Sir Thomas Wardle and his wife. Further Morris & Co. glass was inserted in the centre window on the north side of the nave as a war memorial in 1920.[86] The present pulpit is dated 1935. A south porch was added in 1970.[87]

The font dates from the 13th century. Removed from the church at an unknown date, it was reinstated in 1937.[88] There was a single bell

61 Hodgson, *Bounty of Queen Anne*, pp. ccxcvi, ccxcviii; S.R.O., D. 922/31.
62 Hodgson, *Bounty of Queen Anne*, pp. ccxcvi, ccxcviii; S.R.O., D. 922/34.
63 L.J.R.O., B/V/6/Elkstone; *Rep. Com. Eccl. Revenues*, 476–7, 504–5.   64 *Return of Glebe Lands*, 68.
65 Plaque in Warslow church.
66 D.R.O., D. 2375M/190/2, deed of 27 May 32 Eliz. I.
67 S.R.O., D. 922/30; L.J.R.O., B/A/3/Warslow, 1828; below, plate 33.
68 Inf. from the present owners, Mr. and Mrs. D. Rooke.
69 *S.H.C.* 1915, 11–13; *E.H.R.* xxvi. 342.
70 L.J.R.O., B/A/4/5, 23 Aug. 1663 (Warslow), 4 Apr. 1679 (Elkstone).
71 Ibid. B/C/5/1820/Warslow (faculty).
72 Ibid. B/A/3/Elkstone, 1828; B/A/3/Warslow, 1828.
73 Ibid. B/C/5/1820/Warslow (faculty); *S.H.C.* 4th ser.

x. 85.   74 D.R.O., D. 2375M/202/19, p. 222.
75 P.R.O., HO 129/372/4/6–7.
76 *Alstonfield Deanery Mag.* lii (8).
77 *S.H.C.* 1915, 11.
78 *Alstonfield Par. Reg.* 26; S.R.O., D. 922/35–6.
79 S.R.O., D. 922/36, memo. of 1848.
80 *S.H.C.* 4th ser. x. 85, 101.
81 S.R.O., D. 922/35, p. 35; D. 922/36, acct. 1826–7.
82 *P.O. Dir. Staffs.* (1850).
83 L.J.R.O., B/C/5/1784/Alstonefield (faculty).
84 Ibid. B/C/5/1820/Warslow (faculty); dated plaque over SW. door; below, plate 11.
85 *Staffs. Advertiser*, 10 Oct. 1908, p. 5; 9 Jan. 1909, p. 3.
86 *Alstonfield Deanery Mag.* xiv (70); xv (3); xxv (6); inscrip. on glass.   87 Inscrip. in porch.
88 *Alstonfield Deanery Mag.* xl (8); *T.B.A.S.* lxviii. 17 and pl. 6A.

in 1553, besides what was probably a hand bell.[89] The church of 1820 originally had one bell. It had three by 1850, two of which were destroyed by fire in 1887. The loss was made good in 1906 with the gift of two bells by Mary Lloyd of the Greyhound.[90]

The plate in 1553 consisted of a silver chalice and paten.[91] The present plate includes a silver paten of 1751 and a silver chalice of 1784.[92] A clock made by Francis Abbott of Manchester was installed in the tower in 1837.[93] Four boards with the text of the Commandments, the Lord's Prayer, and the Creed date from 1820.

The registers date from 1785 for baptisms and 1791 for burials.[94]

A churchyard seems to have been no longer in use in 1552.[95] The later churchyard was enlarged in 1963.[96]

The church of *ST. JOHN THE BAPTIST* at Upper Elkstone dates from the late 1780s. Built of coursed ashlar, it is a rectangular-shaped building with a south door and a west bellcot. It was built 'under the care and inspection' of William Grindon at a cost of £200, of which £140 was raised by a brief and the rest by a levy from the township.[97] The church has 18th-century fittings consisting of a pulpit with a sounding board and a clerk's desk, box pews with name plates, and a west gallery originally entered through the west gable.[98] An internal staircase and a vestry were later added in place of pews at the west end. Royal arms of George III hang over the Venetian east window, and there are boards with the Commandments, Lord's Prayer, and Creed.

No plate was mentioned at Elkstone in 1553, although there were altar furnishings. From the 19th century, and possibly earlier, the church used the same plate as Warslow.[99] There is a single bell.

The Warslow register contains entries for Elkstone from 1791 to 1812.[1] Thereafter there are separate registers for Elkstone.[2]

The churchyard was enlarged in 1905.[3]

NONCONFORMITY. In 1766 Luke Story, the stipendiary curate, reported that before he began to visit the Warslow area Methodists had made gains there and that he had been very hard on them since.[4] In 1790 there was a Methodist society with 42 members at the home of Richard

Gould of Brownhill.[5] It still existed in 1811, when a Sunday service was held fortnightly, but no longer in 1829.[6] A Wesleyan Methodist chapel was built in Warslow village in 1848, and on Census Sunday 1851 it had a morning congregation of 65.[7] Primitive Methodists registered a house in Warslow in 1814,[8] and in 1848 they built a chapel north-west of the village. On Census Sunday 1851 there were attendances of 12 in the morning and 67 in the evening.[9] The Wesleyan chapel remained in use until 1938, when the combined Wesleyan and Primitive Methodist congregations moved into the former Primitive Methodist chapel.[10] That chapel was closed in 1992.[11] In 1994 the derelict Wesleyan chapel was being converted into a house, and the Primitive Methodist chapel stood unused.

There was a Primitive Methodist society at Elkstone in 1857, and a chapel was opened north-west of Upper Elkstone village in 1872. Services continued until *c.* 1930, and the chapel was demolished in 1955.[12]

EDUCATION. A schoolmaster recorded at Warslow in 1640 was probably also responsible for reading prayers in church: he was described as the curate of Warslow at his death in 1656.[13] A master who subscribed in 1663 was licensed to read prayers.[14] Thomas Smith (d. 1730), apparently the curate of Warslow, left £200 to Warslow school, and his trustees nominated the master who subscribed in 1744.[15] By will proved 1734 Thomas Gould left £2 10s. a year for teaching six poor children, and by will proved 1804 Thomas Grindon left an annuity of £1 10s. also for teaching poor children; about 1807 *c.* 9 a. were inclosed from the waste to provide funds for the same purpose.[16] In or shortly before 1819 Jesse Watts Russell of Ilam Hall gave £20 to provide free teaching for poor children. He gave a further £20 in 1820.[17] In the earlier 1830s the master taught 15 children free in respect of £12 15s. received as rent from the inclosed waste and five children in respect of the legacies of Gould and Grindon. A further 40 children were taught at their parents' expense.[18] In 1784 the school was held at the west end of Warslow church. A building for it was erected by subscription south of the church in 1788; it was enlarged in 1834 by Sir George Crewe and in 1856 by Sir John Harpur

89 *S.H.C.* 1915, 11.
90 *S.H.C.* 4th ser. x. 100; *P.O. Dir. Staffs.* (1850); *Alstonfield Deanery Mag.* May 1906; ibid. xl (8).
91 *S.H.C.* 1915, 11.
92 *T.B.A.S.* lxxvii. 72, 75.
93 D.R.O., D. 2375M/205/13, Warslow clock acct. 1837.
94 Those not in current use are in S.R.O., D. 4184/1/1–2.
95 D.R.O., D. 2375M/1/3, 2 May 6 Edw. VI.
96 Lich. Dioc. Regy., Bp.'s Reg. X, p. 617.
97 B.L. Church Briefs B. xxv. 1; stone dated 1786 over S. door; board inside church recording the completion of the rebuilding in 1788.
98 Below, plate 18.
99 *S.H.C.* 1915, 10–11; L.J.R.O., B/V/6/Elkstone, 1845.
1 S.R.O., D. 4184/1/1 and 3.
2 A register no longer in current use is in S.R.O., D. 4184/1/3.
3 Lich. Dioc. Regy., Bp.'s Reg. V, p. 8.
4 L.J.R.O., B/A/3/Longnor, 1767, L. Story to bp.'s sec., 11 Sept. 1766.

5 Wardle, *Methodist Hist.* 5, 43; *S.H.C.* 4th ser. iii. 136.
6 D.R.O., D. 5368/4/1/2; Leek Libr., Johnson scrapbk. i (2), D/13/15.
7 P.R.O., HO 129/372/4/6.
8 *S.H.C.* 4th ser. iii. 33.
9 P.R.O., HO 129/372/4/6.
10 W. H. Simcock, 'Primitive Methodism in the Leek Moorlands' (1970; TS. in Leek Libr.), 27–8.
11 Local inf.
12 J. Leach, *Methodism in the Moorlands* (Wesley Hist. Soc., Lancs. and Ches. branch, occasional paper no. 5, 1987), 13, 29.
13 D.R.O., D. 2375M/190/8, deed of 20 Sept. 16 Chas. I; *Alstonfield Par. Reg.* 172.
14 L.J.R.O., B/A/4/5, 23 Aug. 1663.
15 Ibid. B/A/4/32, 30 Oct. 1744; *Alstonfield Par. Reg.* 324.
16 *13th Rep. Com. Char.* 353.
17 D.R.O., D. 2375M/87/17, Wm. Richardson to Sir Geo. Crewe, 11 Dec. 1820.
18 *13th Rep. Com. Char.* 353; *Educ. Enq. Abstract*, 868.

Crewe.[19] In 1871 there were 72 children on the books.[20]

The school became a board school after a board had been compulsorily formed for Warslow and Elkstones in 1875.[21] The school became Warslow council school in 1903 and was called Manifold primary school by 1969. It became Manifold first school in 1980, after the opening in 1979 of a middle school in Warslow. The schools shared premises in a building north-west of the village previously occupied by Warslow secondary school. The first school served Warslow and Elkstones, Butterton, Sheen, and from 1982 Alstonefield; the middle school served Warslow and Elkstones, Hollinsclough, Longnor, Quarnford, and Onecote, in Leek parish. The middle school was closed in 1988, and the first school became Manifold Church of England (C.) primary school.[22]

A secondary school was opened in 1959 with 210 children on its books, nearly a quarter of whom came from Derbyshire. It was closed in 1979.[23]

A board school was built at Upper Elkstone in 1880.[24] It became Upper Elkstone council school in 1903 and was called Cloughside county primary school by 1960. It was closed in 1970 and the children were transferred to Manifold primary school.[25] The building later became a house.

There was a Church of England Sunday school at Warslow by 1830, and in the earlier 1830s it had 40 boys and 50 girls. A Wesleyan Methodist Sunday school was established in 1833 with 20 boys and 20 girls.[26] On Census Sunday 1851 there was an attendance of 122 at the Church of England Sunday school; no Sunday school was recorded that day at the Wesleyan Methodist chapel.[27] A Church of England Sunday school was started at Elkstone in 1865.[28]

CHARITY FOR THE POOR. By 1786 William Mellor had left £40 for the poor, but the charity no longer existed in the earlier 1820s.[29] Also by 1786 John Greensmith had left 20s. a year for four poor widows in Warslow. A distribution was still made in 1883, but nothing further is known about the charity.[30]

[19] L.J.R.O., B/C/5/1784/Alstonefield (faculty); White, Dir. Staffs. (1834), 717; benefaction board in Warslow church.   [20] P.R.O., ED 7/110/343.
[21] List of Sch. Boards, 1902 [Cd. 1038], p. 638 (1902), lxxix.
[22] S.R.O., CEH/43/2; CEH/305/1–3; ibid. CEI/26/1; programme for opening of middle sch. (copy in D.R.O., D. 2375M/270/34).
[23] S.R.O., CEK/62/1–2.   [24] P.R.O., ED 7/110/344.
[25] S.R.O., CEH/43/1–2.
[26] S.H.C. 4th ser. x. 101; Educ. Enq. Abstract, 868.
[27] P.R.O., HO 129/372/4/6.
[28] Lich. Dioc. Ch. Cal. (1866), 84.
[29] 13th Rep. Com. Char. 353.
[30] Ibid.; S.R.O., D. 5181, section on charity disbursements; benefaction board in Warslow church.

HORTON

HORTON, 4 miles north-west of Leek, was formerly a chapelry of Leek but a separate parish probably by the 16th century.[1] The area is rural and in the north-west part includes Horton Hay, formerly a tract of woodland pasture. There is a small village around the church on the east side of the parish, with larger settlements dating mainly from the 19th century on the western boundary at Biddulph Moor and on the eastern boundary at Rudyard. The ancient parish was 4,975 a. (2,013 ha.) in area[2] and was compact and regular in shape, stretching 3 miles east–west and 3½ miles north–south. The western boundary followed the river Trent, which rises in Horton, and the northern and eastern boundaries followed Dingle brook, dammed in 1799 to create Rudyard Lake.[3] Streams also marked much of the south-eastern and southern boundaries. In 1934 975 a. in the west of the parish were transferred to Biddulph urban district and 86 a. in the south-west to Endon and Stanley civil parish. What remained of Horton was amalgamated with Rudyard civil parish, formerly a township in Leek parish, to form a civil parish of 5,349 a. (2,165 ha.).[4] The new civil parish was at first called Rudyard, presumably because Rudyard village was the main centre of population, but it was renamed Horton later the same year.[5] The civil parish was in Leek rural district until 1974, when it became part of Staffordshire Moorlands district. This article deals with the area which formed Horton ancient parish.

Sandstone of the Millstone Grit series forms two ridges, Lask Edge and Grindlestone Edge, divided by Horton brook which flows south-east across the parish. The land falls from 1,100 ft. (365 m.) on Lask Edge in the north-west part of the parish into the valley of Horton brook. Horton village stands east of the brook at 650 ft. (198 m.) on a spur of Grindlestone Edge, whose east side is an escarpment called Whorrocks Bank. Rudyard village stands at 553 ft. (169 m.). In the south part of the parish the hamlet of Gratton stands at 626 ft. (191 m.) on the west side of Horton brook. The land lies at 527 ft. (160 m.) where the brook leaves the parish near the former Endon mill. Boulder Clay covers much of the parish, and there is alluvium along Horton brook. The soil is mostly fine loam, with clay over peat on the high ground and coarse loam along the side of Rudyard Lake.[6]

Seventy-seven people were assessed for hearth tax in the parish in 1666, including 6 people at Gratton.[7] In 1801 the population was 752, rising

to 970 by 1831 and then falling to 942 by 1841. There followed a steady growth during the rest of the 19th century, and by 1901 the population was 1,295. The increase was most pronounced at Biddulph Moor.[8] The population was 1,323 in 1911, 1,504 in 1921, and 1,421 in 1931. After the 1934 boundary change it was 813 in 1951, 855 in 1961, 754 in 1971, 789 in 1981, and 713 in 1991.[9]

The oldest settlements in the parish are presumably Horton village and Gratton: both place-names incorporate the Old English word *tun*, meaning a settlement. Horton village stands on a restricted site around the medieval church, the land falling steeply on the west and east sides but less so on the south. Horton Hall, north-west of the church, is of the 17th century but replaced a house in existence by the earlier 14th century.[10] Boot Hall, north of Horton Hall, is also of the 17th century and presumably takes its name from a family called Boot, which lived in the parish in the early 18th century.[11] New House Farm and Horton Head Farm south of the church are both of the 18th century. The inn run by John Horsley of Horton in 1677 may have stood south of the church, where the present Crown inn was so called in 1834. It was known in 1818 as the Court House, presumably because the manor courts were held there.[12] Heath House and Stone House, on top of Grindlestone Edge north of the village, existed respectively by 1446[13] and probably 1599.[14] Steel House Farm south-east of Horton village on the Longsdon road was so called in 1561, but its site was probably occupied by the late 13th century, when the toponym Style was used by a tenant of Horton manor.[15]

There was a hamlet at Gratton by the earlier 12th century, and the site of Gratton Hall Farm was probably occupied by the late 12th century.[16] Hall Gate Farm to the north is of the 17th century with a matching bay added in 1991.[17] Dams Lane House, north-west of Gratton hamlet, is also of the 17th century, and there was a house at the Ashes on the rising ground further west by 1658.[18] Brook House and Bond House beside a tributary of Horton brook north of Gratton were so called by the later 16th century[19] and stand in an area known as Lee in the earlier 19th century and as Lea Lathton in 1841.[20] The modern name is Lea Laughton.

The hamlet of Blackwood Hill, south-west of Gratton, existed by the late 13th century.[21] A house there owned in the later 15th century by

[1] Below, church. This article was written mainly in 1991. [2] *V.C.H. Staffs.* i. 327.
[3] Below, this section (Rudyard Lake).
[4] *Census*, 1931; Staffs. Review Order, 1934, pp. 59, 63, 67, and map 1 (copy in S.R.O.).
[5] Staffs. C.C. *Record for 1934*, 517.
[6] Geol. Surv. Map 1", drift, sheet 110 (1968 edn.); Soil Surv. of Eng. and Wales, sheet 3 (1983).
[7] *S.H.C.* 1925, 157–9, 241–2.
[8] *V.C.H. Staffs.* i. 327; P.R.O., HO 107/1004; HO 107/2008; ibid. RG 9/1947; RG 10/2883; RG 11/2740.
[9] *Census*, 1911–91.
[10] Below, manors (Horton Hall).
[11] L.J.R.O., B/C/11, Wm. Boote (1726).

[12] S.R.O., D. 3359/misc. deeds, deed of 10 May 1677; Parson and Bradshaw, *Staffs. Dir.* (1818), villages section, p. 13; White, *Dir. Staffs.* (1834), 748.
[13] S.R.O., D. (W.) 1490/6, m. 31.
[14] Ibid. D. (W.) 1490/16, ct. of 11 Oct. 1599.
[15] Ibid. D. (W.) 1490/14/5.; *S.H.C.* N.S. xi. 254–5.
[16] *S.H.C.* vi (1), 28; below, manors (Gratton).
[17] *Chronicles* (autumn 1992), 9–13.
[18] *Leek Par. Reg.* 136.
[19] W.S.L. 52/46; N. C. Rowley, *Ford Green Story* (Leek, 1983), 88.
[20] S.R.O., D. 4069/1/5, p. 21; P.R.O., HO 107/1004.
[21] *Sel. Bills in Eyre 1292–1333* (Selden Soc. xxx), 65–6; *S.H.C.* N.S. xi. 253.

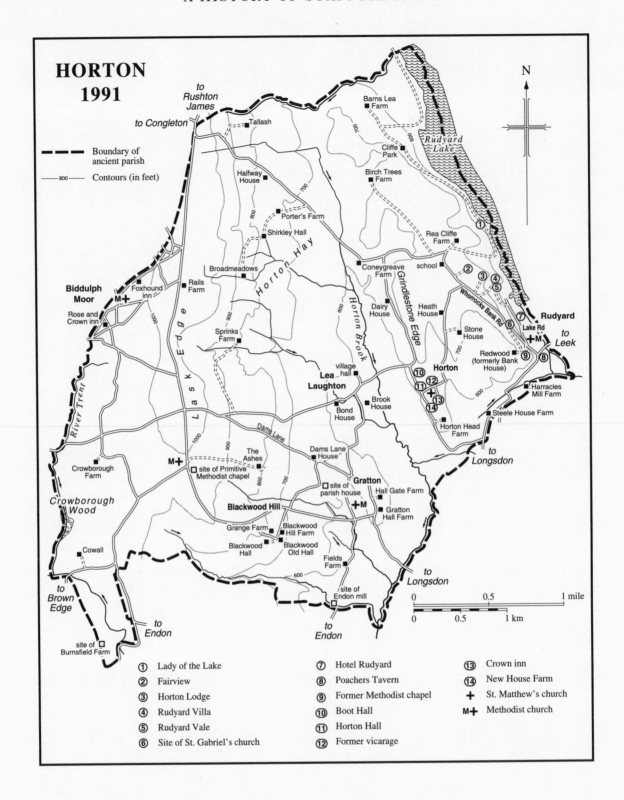

HORTON 1991

- - - Boundary of ancient parish
—800— Contours (in feet)

① Lady of the Lake
② Fairview
③ Horton Lodge
④ Rudyard Villa
⑤ Rudyard Vale
⑥ Site of St. Gabriel's church
⑦ Hotel Rudyard
⑧ Poachers Tavern
⑨ Former Methodist chapel
⑩ Boot Hall
⑪ Horton Hall
⑫ Former vicarage
⑬ Crown inn
⑭ New House Farm
✝ St. Matthew's church
M✝ Methodist church

FIG. 11

the Wedgwood family, later of Harracles in Longsdon, was incorporated in Blackwood Hall, built of brick with stone dressings in 1885 for John Challenor, probably the son of John Challenor (d. 1833) of Overton, in Biddulph.[22] The nearby Grange Farm was probably also built by Challenor, whose initials are on a barn there dated 1834. The hamlet also includes Blackwood Old Hall, which retains a date stone of 1670 from an earlier house, and Blackwood Hill Farm (formerly Old Hall Farm), which is dated 1698 but retains timber-framing possibly of the 16th century. Both houses were formerly occupied by the Reade family, which moved to Fields Farm on the Endon road south of Gratton in the early 18th century.[23] Called the Fields in 1588, Fields Farm was rebuilt in the early 18th century and a north wing of brick with stone dressings was added later in the century.[24]

Another area settled by the 13th century was Crowborough, beside the river Trent in the south-west part of the parish. The second part of the name is derived from an Old English word *bearu*, meaning a wood or grove,[25] and there may have been an early clearing in woodland. Crowborough Farm probably stands on the site of a house held in 1299 by John of Crowborough,[26] and there were houses to the south at Cowall by 1308 and at Burnsfield by 1474.[27]

The northern part of the parish is crossed by a road between Leek and Congleton (Ches.), which climbs steeply up Whorrocks Bank. The bank derives the first part of its name from a word meaning hoar (or grey) oak trees, used as a toponym in the later 13th century.[28] A house described in 1607 as at Whorrocks and then occupied by Thomas Knight[29] probably stood on the site of the later Poachers Tavern at the foot of Whorrocks Bank Road: the inn incorporates on its west side a stone with the initials TK and IK and the date 1610. By the later 18th century a hamlet there was known as Harpers Gate.[30] Bank House, on top of the southern end of Whorrocks Bank, was so called in 1613. Rebuilt in Gothick style, probably for James Challinor, who lived there in 1851, the house was renamed Redwood in the 1920s.[31] Rea Cliffe Farm at the north end of Whorrocks Bank Road existed by 1675.[32] To the west a road to Rushton James ran past Birch Trees Farm, which is probably of the later 18th century, and Barns Lee Farm, which is partly of the 17th century.

The road was stopped up after the Cliffe Park estate was created in the early 19th century.[33]

Horton Hay, covering the north-west quarter of the parish, was formerly an area of woodland pasture.[34] The chief house, Dairy House on the hay's east side, was built in the earlier 17th century.[35] Coneygreave Farm to the north-west is dated 1897 but replaced a house in existence by the later 18th century.[36] On the hay's west side a house called the Rails, from the fence that enclosed the hay in the early 15th century,[37] may have been occupied by Thomas Challinor (d. 1577). It is the most likely site for the house of his son William, who lived at Horton Hay, and was certainly the home of William's grandson William Challinor (d. 1721).[38] Other farmhouses were first occupied when the rest of the hay was converted into farmland in the later 17th century.[39]

Biddulph Moor, a settlement on Horton's western boundary in existence by the late 17th century, was populated largely by coalminers in the 19th century.[40] There are two inns, the Foxhound, known in 1840 as the King William New inn, and the Rose and Crown, so called by 1868.[41] Most of Biddulph Moor, including the Anglican church, lies on the Biddulph side of the boundary.

Following the exploitation of Rudyard Lake as a tourist resort from the mid 19th century, the hamlet at Harpers Gate expanded and was renamed Rudyard. Hotel Rudyard at the southern end of the lake was opened as an inn in 1851, and from the 1880s houses were built to the south in Lake Road.[42] By 1854 Knight's house at Harpers Gate (the present Poachers Tavern) had been converted into the Railway inn, named after the Leek–Macclesfield railway line of 1849 which ran along the east side of Rudyard Lake. By 1888 it was called the Railway hotel and by 1900 the Station hotel.[43] There was a village post office by 1898, and a police station was opened in the mid 1950s but was later closed.[44] There are council houses of the 1950s at the north end of Lake Road, and to the south near Hotel Rudyard there are privately built houses of the 1970s and 1980s.

In the later 19th century detached houses were built on the east side of Whorrocks Bank Road overlooking Rudyard Lake. The earliest is Rudyard Vale (later Rudyard Villa), designed in 1859 by the Leek architect William Sugden for

22 Sleigh, *Leek*, 155 n.; *Staffs. Advertiser*, 16 Feb. 1833, p. 3; date stone on house.
23 A. L. Reade, *Reades of Blackwood Hill* (priv. print. 1906), 4–5, and pls. II–VI.
24 S.R.O., D. (W.) 1490/15, ct. of 4 Oct. 1588; date stones on house.
25 *Eng. P.N. Elements*, i. 22.
26 *S.H.C.* N.S. xi. 253.
27 Ibid. 255 (where Conhalg should read Couhalg: P.R.O., C 134/5, m. 2); S.R.O., D. 538/2/3.
28 N.R.A. list 216 (Roger of Horhoc); *S.H.C.* N.S. xi. 255 (John of Horchok).
29 S.R.O., D. (W.) 1490/17, ct. of 23 Oct. 1607.
30 Above, fig. 2.
31 L.J.R.O., B/C/11, Thos. Higinbothome (1613); White, *Dir. Staffs.* (1851), 749; *Kelly's Dir. Staffs.* (1916; 1924), entry for Hugh Sleigh; O.S. Map 1/2,500, Staffs. VII. 8 (1925 edn.).   32 S.R.O., D. 4069/1/1, f. 11.
33 Below, manors (Cliffe Park); above, fig. 2.

34 Below, econ. hist. (agric.).
35 Below, manors (Horton Hay).
36 Above, fig. 2.
37 S.R.O., D. (W.) 1490/2, m. 28.
38 P. W. L. Adams, *Notes on some N. Staffs. Families* (Tunstall, priv. print., foreword dated 1930), 102–4; L.J.R.O., B/C/11, Wm. Challinor (1721). The 16th-cent. spelling of the surname was Chalner.
39 Below, econ. hist. (agric.).
40 S.R.O., D. 4069/1/1, f. 16v.; below, econ. hist. (trade and ind.).
41 S.R.O., D. 3539/1/28; *P.O. Dir. Staffs.* (1868; s.v. Biddulph).
42 O.S. Map 6", Staffs. VII. NE. (1900 edn.); below, this section (Rudyard Lake).
43 *P.O. Dir. Staffs.* (1854); *Kelly's Dir. Staffs.* (1888; 1900).
44 O.S. Map 6", Staffs. VII. NE. (1900 edn.); Staffs. C.C. deeds, C. 773.

Matthew Gaunt, brother of Josiah Gaunt of Horton Hall.[45] The name had been changed from Vale to Villa by 1871, presumably to distinguish the house from another Rudyard Vale, built in the mid 1860s to the south.[46] Since the 1930s the grounds of Rudyard Vale have been used as a caravan park.[47] Horton Lodge to the north-west was built in 1890 for a Manchester businessman, Stephen Chesters-Thompson. He sold the house to William Tellwright (d. 1894), the owner of a colliery at Sneyd in Burslem, who extended it and laid out gardens.[48] In 1924 the house was bought by the North Staffordshire Miners' Welfare Association, which converted it into a convalescent home in 1925. In 1948 it was let to the Workers Educational Association, which used it for week-end residential courses until 1950. The house then became a school for children with special needs.[49] Fairview, north of Horton Lodge, was built in the early 1880s for John Munro, a Hanley wine merchant. It became a home for the mentally ill in 1988 and was enlarged in 1991.[50]

A mains electricity supply was available in the parish by 1940, and a mains water supply from c. 1960.[51]

After the change of calendar in 1752 the parish wake took place on the Sunday nearest Old Michaelmas Day. It was still held in the early 20th century.[52] A stone pillar set up at the junction of Lake Road and Whorrocks Bank Road to commemorate Queen Victoria's Diamond Jubilee of 1897 also serves as a memorial to parishioners killed in the Boer War and the two world wars. Rudyard Memorial Institute in Lake Road was built in 1922 and enlarged in 1934; a porch was added in 1939 to commemorate the coronation of 1937, and the building was further enlarged in 1947.[53] The former parish school at Lea Laughton became a village hall in 1962 and was extended in 1990.[54] Rudyard Women's Institute was formed in 1932.[55]

James Heath (1757–1834), historical engraver from 1794 to George III and his successors, was born in the parish.[56] Hall Gate Farm at Gratton was the birthplace of George Heath (1844–69), the Moorland Poet.[57] There is a memorial to him in Horton churchyard. The philosopher Thomas Ernest Hulme (1883–1917) was born at Gratton Hall Farm. There is a memorial window to him in Endon church, and a bronze bust sculpted by his friend Jacob Epstein in 1916 is in private hands.[58]

RUDYARD LAKE. Rudyard Lake, two miles long and covering 163 a., was created in 1799 as a reservoir for the Caldon canal, the water reaching the canal by a feeder which enters a branch canal in Longsdon. The reservoir was fed by Dingle brook and Rad brook, the latter formerly flowing north to the river Dane but diverted south at Ryecroft Gate in Rushton James.[59] A more substantial supply was provided by a feeder constructed c. 1811 from the Dane in Heaton.[60]

The reservoir was described in 1813 as 'little inferior to some of the Cumberland lakes'.[61] Its potential as a tourist attraction was exploited by the North Staffordshire Railway Co., the owner from 1847,[62] after the Leek–Macclesfield railway line was opened in 1849. The wooded ground on the west side of the reservoir was landscaped with walks and seats by William Nunns, a Leek gardener, and on Easter Monday 1851 the company organized a fête and regatta at what was by then called Rudyard Lake. Special trains brought between 7,000 and 8,000 tourists from Manchester, Stockport, and Macclesfield as well as the Potteries and other Staffordshire towns. The festivities included boat races and trips on a steamer, and the occasion was described as 'a very pleasant combination of the cheap excursion, the village fair, and the modern fête'.[63] Another regatta was held on Whit Monday, but a third, planned for later in the summer, was stopped by an injunction secured by Fanny Bostock of Cliffe Park, who was alarmed by the number of tourists and their behaviour. Despite a judgement by the Lord Chief Justice in 1852 that a railway company could not legally organize such an event, the company again advertised a fête for Whit Monday that year. It appears not to have been held, Miss Bostock having applied for another injunction. Her argument that the company was not entitled to use the reservoir for any other purpose than its original one of supplying water to the canal was supported by Queen's Bench in 1855.[64] The lakeside, however, remained popular with visitors, who in 1863 included the future parents of the writer Rudyard Kipling, named after the lake.[65]

Hotel Rudyard, which incorporates a house originally built for the reservoir keeper, was opened in time for the Easter Monday fête in 1851 by a Congleton innkeeper, Peter Ullivero. It was first known as Rudyard Lake Hotel; its present name was adopted c. 1886.[66] About 1870

45 S.R.O., D. 3359/Gaunt, Sugden's elevations for house at Rudyard, 1859; P.R.O., RG 9/1947; Sleigh, Leek, 7.
46 P.R.O., RG 10/2883; P.O. Dir. Staffs. (1868); W.S.L., Sleigh scrapbk. i, f. 94. 47 Inf. from the warden.
48 Memorial inscription of Wm. Tellwright in east window of north aisle in Horton church; Staffs. Advertiser, 11 July 1925, p. 4; W.S.L. 498/34, cutting of 21 Jan. 1899.
49 Inf. from the head teacher, Mr. R. M. Orme; below. educ.
50 Kelly's Dir. Staffs. (1884); inf. from the owner, Mrs. P. Harris.
51 Kelly's Dir. Staffs. (1940); Leek R.D.C. Ann. Rep. of M.O.H. 1960 (copy in S.R.O., C/H/1/2/2/22).
52 White, Dir. Staffs. (1834), 747; Kelly's Dir. Staffs. (1908).
53 Date stones on building.
54 Leek Post & Times, 16 May 1990, p. 18.
55 Inf. from Staffs. Federation of Women's Institutes.
56 D.N.B.
57 Poems of George Heath, ed. J. Badnall (1870).
58 M. Roberts, T. E. Hulme (1938), 13, 38; E. Silber, Sculpture of Epstein (1986), 138–9.
59 V.C.H. Staffs. ii. 291; P. Lead, Caldon Canal and Tramroads (Headington, 1990), 51–3, 55 n.
60 S.R.O., D. 607/1, 3 June 1811; D. 3186/8/1/30/10.
61 J. Nightingale, Staffs. (Beauties of Eng. and Wales, xiii), 1169. 62 Lead, Caldon Canal and Tramroads, 33.
63 Staffs. Advertiser, 26 Apr. 1851, p. 7; W.S.L., Sleigh scrapbk. ii, f. 109v.; Guide to Rudyard Lake and Alton Towers (1851; copy in Leek Libr., Johnson scrapbk. 2 (ii), 2/1).
64 Staffs. Advertiser, 7 June 1851, p. 1; 14 Feb. 1852, p. 6; 29 May 1852, p. 3; 12 May 1855, p. 2.
65 C. Carrington, Rudyard Kipling (1978), 33, 36.
66 S.R.O., Q/RDc 69, plan II; Staffs. Advertiser, 26 Apr. 1851, p. 7; White, Dir. Staffs. (1851), 729, 749; Kelly's Dir. Staffs. (1884; 1888; s.v. Rudyard).

RUDYARD LAKE HOTEL
AND
PLEASURE GROUNDS.
HENRY PLATT PROPRIETOR.

FIG. 12

the hotel was taken over by Henry Platt, who enlarged it, notably with a ballroom in 1873. The grounds were improved with areas for archery and croquet, and a roller-skating rink was opened in 1876.[67] To attract more visitors Platt started a well-dressing festival in May 1871, the railway company laying on special trains from the Potteries and Macclesfield. The festival was still held in 1873.[68] In 1896 a later hotelier promoted the area as 'the Switzerland of England'.[69]

The railway company acquired the Cliffe Park estate in 1903 and was empowered in 1904 to hire out motor launches and rowing boats on the lake.[70] By 1905 a golf course had been laid out, and a golf club was formed in 1906, using Cliffe Park as a clubhouse. The club was closed in 1926.[71]

From the late 19th century boathouses were built along the west side of the lake, some later converted into dwellings. Among the earliest is that built in 1891 for Horton Lodge and occupied from 1970 as a house called Lower Horton Lodge.[72] To the north a boathouse built in 1893 to a design by the Leek architect Larner Sugden has a façade incorporating a ship's figurehead.[73] It too was a house in 1991, called the Lady of the Lake.

The lake remained popular in the 1990s for sailing, rowing, and fishing. Rudyard Lake sailing club was formed in 1956. It first used a lakeside bungalow as a clubhouse and from 1958 to 1963 the former lodge to Cliffe Park. A new clubhouse was built in 1963 and enlarged in 1978.[74] The North Staffordshire rowing club, established at Trentham in 1970, moved to Rudyard in 1989 and has a boathouse at the south end of the lake. The lake's owners, British Waterways, appointed a ranger in 1988, and an information centre was opened at the south end of the lake in 1989.[75]

MANORS AND OTHER ESTATES. About 1140 Robert de Stafford gave *HORTON* with Gratton to Stone priory, of which he was patron.[76] His grant was ultimately ineffective. The Staffords remained overlords, and in 1276 the Audleys held Horton of them in socage, paying a rent of 10s.[77] The overlordship descended in the Stafford family at least until 1408, when it was held by the earl of Stafford.[78]

Ralph son of Orm was the tenant in the later 12th century. He was succeeded by his daughter Emma, the wife of Adam de Audley. Their son Adam (d. by 1211) was succeeded by his brother

67   *Clemesha's Penny Guide to Rudyard*, 7 (copy in Leek Libr., Johnson scrapbk. 2 (ii), 2/2); *P.O. Dir. Staffs.* (1872); *Staffs. Advertiser*, 4 Jan. 1873, p. 1; *Macclesfield Courier & Herald*, 3 June 1876, p. 8.
68   *Staffs. Advertiser*, 20 May 1871, p. 4; 22 June 1872, p. 7; 31 May 1873, p. 1.
69   *Kelly's Dir. Staffs.* (1896), advertisements, p. 53.
70   4 Edw. VII, c. 44 (Local and Personal).
71   R. Keys, *Churnet Valley Railway* (Hartington, 1974), 12–13;

B. Jeuda, *Rudyard Lake Golf Club, 1906–1926* (Leek, 1993).
72   Inf. from the owners, Mr. and Mrs. J. W. Thatcher.
73   *The Architect*, 29 Dec. 1893, p. 407.
74   Inf. from the club secretary, Mr. H. A. Cheesewright.
75   Inf. from the ranger, Mr. M. Booth.
76   *S.H.C.* vi (1), 28; *V.C.H. Staffs.* iii. 240–1.
77   *S.H.C.* N.S. xi. 244, 247.
78   Ibid. 254–5; *Cal. Inq. p.m.* vi, p. 42; xvi, p. 72; xviii, p. 156; xix, p. 152.

Henry de Audley.[79] In 1227 Henry successfully held the manor against Hervey de Stafford. After a judicial duel Hervey acknowledged Henry's right to Horton in return for a payment of 50 marks and land in Norton-in-the-Moors.[80] Henry, sheriff of Staffordshire and Shropshire 1227–32, was succeeded in 1246 by his son James (d. 1272). Four of James's sons succeeded in turn, three of them dying childless: James (d. 1273), Henry (d. 1276), William (d. 1282), and Nicholas (d. 1299). Nicholas's son and heir Thomas was succeeded in 1307 by his brother Nicholas, from 1313 Baron Audley. Horton then descended with the barony until the death of Nicholas, Lord Audley, without issue in 1391, when the manor was divided into three parts. One share passed to his sister Margaret and her husband Sir Roger Hillary; another to John Tuchet, later Lord Audley, grandson of Nicholas's sister Joan; and the third to Fulk FitzWarin, grandson of Nicholas's half-sister, also called Margaret.[81] On Margaret Hillary's death in 1411 her share passed to James, Lord Audley, the son of John Tuchet.[82] That two-thirds share descended with the Audley barony until 1535, when John, Lord Audley, gave it with other estates to the Crown to pay off his debts.[83] The FitzWarin share remained with Fulk's descendants, earls of Bath from 1536.[84]

In 1554 the Crown's two-thirds share of Horton was sold to Thomas Egerton, later of Wall Grange, in Longsdon, and his son-in-law John Wedgwood, later of Harracles, also in Longsdon.[85] Wedgwood's share descended with Harracles.[86] In 1571 Egerton settled his share on his son Timothy (d. between 1578 and 1584), along with Wall Grange.[87] The share may at first have descended with Wall Grange, but in 1595 it was held by Timothy's cousin Thomas Egerton, a London mercer. That year he settled it on his three sons, one of whom, also Thomas, was the sole owner by 1609 when he settled it on his son Timothy.[88] In 1625 Timothy sold it to John Bellot of Great Moreton, in Astbury (Ches.),[89] who had acquired the earl of Bath's one-third share of the manor between 1619 and 1625.[90] The manor was reunited in 1711 when John Bellot's great-grandson, Sir John Bellot, Bt., sold his interest to John Wedgwood of Harracles.[91]

The reunited manor descended with Harracles until 1791, when Harracles was sold. The vendor, Sir Brooke Boothby, Bt., retained Horton until 1796 when he sold it to Thomas Harding. In 1799 Harding sold a half share to Thomas Fletcher, and in 1804 their sons, Samuel Harding and William Fletcher, sold both parts of the manor to Edmund Antrobus, a London banker.[92] Antrobus, created a baronet in 1815, died unmarried in 1826, and Horton passed to his nephew Gibbs Crawfurd Antrobus of Eaton Hall, in Astbury (Ches.). He was succeeded in 1861 by his son John (d. 1916). John's son Crawfurd sold all his freehold land in the parish in 1920 and 1921 but retained the lordship of the manor. He was succeeded in 1940 by his brother Lt.-Col. Ronald Henry Antrobus (d. 1980). In 1994 the lordship was bought from the Antrobus estate by Mr. and Mrs. E. J. D. Warrillow, two of the owners of Horton Hall.[93] The medieval manor house, whose site is unknown, was probably occupied in 1308 by a tenant named Adam de la Halle.[94]

In the early 19th century John Haworth owned 782 a. in the north-east corner of the parish, within which he created *CLIFFE PARK*, an estate of 135 a. overlooking Rudyard Lake.[95] By 1818 he had built a house,[96] around which he laid out gardens and plantations. Haworth was succeeded in 1831 by his cousin, Fanny Bostock, who died unmarried in 1875.[97] In 1885 the Revd. Edward Duncan Boothman, husband of Fanny Bostock's niece Georgina, bought the estate.[98] He sold it in 1903 to the North Staffordshire Railway Co., which had a golf course there until 1926.[99] Advertised for sale with 38 a. in 1928, the house was bought in 1933 by the Youth Hostels Association. It remained a hostel until 1969, when it was bought by Mr. Brian Dalley, the owner in 1991.[1] The house, which is of coursed stone, has a symmetrical main front with a central bow and is decorated with battlements and other Gothic ornaments.[2]

In 1199 Adam son of Ranulph (or Ralph) held a carucate at *GRATTON*.[3] In 1281 the estate was held by Adam's son Ralph,[4] and in 1308 by Hugh de Audley, youngest son of James de Audley (d. 1272). Hugh, later Baron Audley, died in 1325 or 1326, and Gratton passed to his youngest son, also Hugh, who was created earl of Gloucester in 1337. Earl Hugh was succeeded in 1347 by his daughter Margaret, wife of Ralph, earl of Stafford. Ralph held Gratton at his death in 1372.[5] What was styled the manor or hamlet of Gratton in 1387 descended in the Stafford

79 *S.H.C.* iv (1), 50; *S.H.C.* N.S. ix. 259–60.
80 *S.H.C.* iv (1), 50, 67, 226–7.
81 *Complete Peerage*, i. 337–40; *Cal. Close*, 1389–92, 468, 514; *Cal. Inq. p.m.* xvi, pp. 440, 442.
82 *Complete Peerage*, i. 337–41; *S.H.C.* xi. 209; *Cal. Close*, 1409–13, 254.
83 *Complete Peerage*, i. 341–2; S.R.O., D. (W.) 1490/2–11; Act concerning lands of John Tuchet, Lord Audley, 27 Hen. VIII, c. 31.
84 S.R.O., D. (W.) 1490/2–17; *Complete Peerage* ii. 16; v. 502–11.
85 *Cal. Pat.* 1554–5, 25–6, 229; Sleigh, *Leek*, 147; S.R.O., D. (W.) 1702/2/32.
86 Below, Leek: Longsdon, manors (Harracles).
87 Sleigh, *Leek*, 147, 155–6; below, Leek: Longsdon, manors (Wall Grange).
88 Sleigh, *Leek*, 156; S.R.O., D. (W.) 1702/2/30.
89 *S.H.C.* N.S. x (1), 69–70; S.R.O., D. (W.) 1490/20.
90 S.R.O., D. (W.) 1490/17, ct. of 25 Mar. 1619; D. (W.) 1490/20/1, ct. of 6 Oct. 1625; D. (W.) 1761/B/3/70.

91 Sleigh, *Leek*, 148, 155; S.R.O., D. (W.) 1490/36, mm. 35, 39.   92 S.R.O., D. (W.) 1761/A/4/244–9.
93 Burke, *Peerage and Baronetage* (1931), 130; sale partics. 1920 and 1921 (copies in S.R.O., D. (W.) 1909/F/9/1); inf. from Mr. Warrillow.
94 *S.H.C.* N.S. xi. 255.
95 S.R.O., D. (W.) 1909/D/4/3.
96 Letter addressed to Howarth at Cliffe Park and dated 1818 in possession of Mrs. C. Chester of Foxt, in Ipstones.
97 Sleigh, *Leek*, 159; *Staffs. Advertiser*, 3 Dec. 1831, p. 4; P.R.O., PROB 11/1793, f. 59.
98 S.R.O., D. (W.) 1909/F/4/2; W.S.L., Sleigh, iii, f. 256.
99 4 Edw. VII, c. 44 (Local and Personal), second schedule; above, intro. (Rudyard Lake).
1 Inf. from Mrs. Chester.
2 Below, plate 34.
3 *S.H.C.* iii (1), 61, 168–9.
4 Ibid. vi (1), 64, 149.
5 *S.H.C.* N.S. ix. 262–3; N.S. xi. 255; *Complete Peerage*, i. 346–8; *Cal. Inq. p.m.* xiii, p. 188.

family until 1572, when Edward, Baron Stafford, sold it to Richard Hussey of Albright Hussey (Salop.).[6] Richard was succeeded in 1574 by his son Edward, still alive in 1601.[7] In 1614 Edward's son, Sir Richard Hussey, sold the manor to William Bowyer of Knypersley, in Biddulph.[8] In 1700 it was owned by the lord of Horton manor, Sir Thomas Bellot, Bt. (d. 1709).[9] The later descent is unknown. The estate was probably centred on Gratton Hall Farm, a brick house of the mid 18th century with stone dressings, enlarged in the late 19th century.

An estate centring on what came to be called *HORTON HALL* originated in the later 1330s, when a house in Horton was acquired by Adam de Egge of Horton.[10] It remained in the Egge (later Edge) family, passing in the early 17th century to Richard Edge. Richard was succeeded in 1647 by his younger son Timothy, a parliamentarian, in preference to his elder son John, a royalist. Of Presbyterian sympathies,[11] Timothy, who was appointed a justice of the peace in 1653, died unmarried in 1683 and was succeeded by his cousin Ralph Edge (d. 1684). Ralph's heir was a distant relative, Nicholas Edge, who retained possession despite allegations that he had forged a deed of settlement. In 1720 his son Timothy sold the estate to John Alsop. John's heir was his wife's niece Elizabeth, wife of Henry Fowler, whose son John owned 458 a. in Horton c. 1820. The house was then called Horton Hall.[12]

John Fowler was succeeded in 1827 by his daughter Phoebe (d. 1854), who married FitzJames Watt in 1836.[13] In 1850 the house was occupied by Phoebe's half-brother Josiah Gaunt and after Josiah's death in 1868 by his son Frederick (d. 1875).[14] In 1881 Phoebe's son Arthur was living at the house while on leave from India, where he was a civil judge at Poona; he died in 1885.[15] Ownership of the house and 472 a. in Horton was shared by Arthur's seven children, of whom two survivors sold the estate in 1917 to Charles Cowlishaw. He broke it up, selling the house in 1918 to Robert Hall (d. 1926). In 1948 Hall's widow Margaret sold the house to Maj. George Greaves, from whom it was bought in 1951 by John Moxon (d. 1987). Until 1991 Moxon's widow Doreen lived at the house, which in 1992 was sold jointly to Philip Cooklin, his wife Christine, and Mrs. Cooklin's parents Mr. and Mrs. E. J. D. Warrillow.[16]

The 17th-century house, which is of coursed ashlar, consists of a central range with cross wings.[17] An outbuilding retains a reset doorhead possibly from the north-east side of the house and dated apparently 1640 with the initials of Richard Edge. The principal and secondary staircases survive, but the main rooms were remodelled in the mid 18th century. At that date the south front was given sash windows on the ground and first floors and the doorway was moved to the centre to create a near symmetrical elevation. The short service wing on the north-east corner was probably built at that time. Early in the 19th century canted bay windows were added to the west front. A coach house with stables was built north of the house in the later 19th century. The walled garden on the west has an entrance with a doorhead dated 1668 and the initials of Timothy Edge.

Ownership of *HORTON HAY* descended with the manor until the execution of James, Lord Audley, in 1497, when his two-thirds share of the hay passed, presumably by royal grant, to his younger son Thomas. Thomas was succeeded in 1507 by his daughter Anne, wife of George Twynyho.[18] In 1546 Anne and her second husband, Richard Inkpen, sold their interest in the hay to Richard Biddulph of Biddulph.[19] From 1538 Biddulph had been the lessee of the earl of Bath's one-third share of the hay, and his family acquired the freehold of that estate in 1617.[20] In 1673 the Biddulphs sold the hay to Thomas Kynnersley, whose great-grandson Clement Kynnersley sold it in 1791 to Edmund Antrobus, later lord of Horton manor.[21]

Dairy House, the principal house on the hay, was so named by 1645. A large house mainly of the 17th century with two cross wings, it has a date stone of 1635 on the service wing with initials which evidently stand for John, son of Francis Biddulph (d. 1636), and John's wife Mary. The Biddulphs were Roman Catholics, and a sculptured stone with initials for Jesus and the Virgin Mary survives on the front of the house. John Biddulph was among the royalists killed at the battle of Hopton Heath in 1643; his estate was sequestrated and in 1645 Dairy House was assigned to a parliamentarian, Maj. Edward Downes.[22] In 1673 the house was owned by Thomas Endon of Leek.[23] The later descent is unknown until 1909 when Richard Turnock left Dairy House farm to his brother William,[24] whose family still lived at the house in 1991.

The *TITHES* of Horton belonged in the Middle Ages to Dieulacres abbey as rector of Leek, and by 1470 the abbey had two tithe barns in the parish.[25] The rectory was acquired in 1560 by Sir Ralph Bagnall, who in 1565 sold the great

6 *Cal. Inq. p.m.* xvi, p. 170; *Complete Peerage*, xii (1), 177–85; *S.H.C.* xiii. 287.
7 P.R.O., C 142/167/175; B.R.L., Norton Colln. 1524.
8 *S.H.C.* N.S. iv. 68; *S.H.C.* 1934 (2), 31.
9 P.R.O., CP 43/470, m. 216; *S.H.C.* 1920 and 1922, 198 (correcting G.E.C. *Baronetage*, iii. 278–9).
10 Para. based on Sir Ric. Edge, 'Family of Edge' (TS. in W.S.L.), i. 195–243, 281–93; J. F. Moxon, 'Horton Hall' (TS. in W.S.L.); L.J.R.O., B/C/11, Tim. Edge (1683); Sleigh, *Leek*, 7, 158–9.
11 *Autobiog. of Henry Newcome* (Chetham Soc. [1st ser.], xxvi), 42.   12 S.R.O., D. (W.) 1909/D/4/3.
13 Sleigh, *Leek*, 7; *Staffs. Advertiser*, 10 Dec. 1836, p. 3.
14 *P.O. Dir. Staffs.* (1850; 1868); Sleigh, *Leek*, 7; P.R.O., RG 9/1947.
15 P.R.O., RG 11/2740; memorial brass in nave of Hor-
ton church.
16 Inf. from Mr. Ian Moxon of Ellis Moxon, solicitors of Hanley, and Mr. and Mrs. Cooklin.   17 Below, plate 26.
18 *Complete Peerage*, i. 342; *Cal. Inq. p.m. Hen. VII*, iii, p. 244; T. C. Banks, *Dormant and Extinct Baronage of Eng.* ii. 18.
19 *S.H.C.* xi. 292; S.R.O., D. (W.) 1761/A/4/175–6.
20 S.R.O., D. (W.) 1761/A/4/180; *S.H.C.* 1912, 135.
21 S.R.O., D. (W.) 1761/A/4/230, 232; D. (W.) 1761/B/3/132.
22 J. Ward, *Borough of Stoke-upon-Trent* (1843), 279; *S.H.C.* 4th ser. i. 246. For Downes see below, Leek: Longsdon, manors (Wall Grange).
23 S.R.O., D. 3359/misc. deeds, deed of 17 Feb. 1676/7.
24 W.S.L. 498/34, cutting of Oct. 1909.
25 P.R.O., SC 6/988/2.

tithes of Horton (except those of Horton Hay) to John Wedgwood, the joint lord of the manor, and in 1566 those of Horton Hay to Francis Biddulph, the lessee of the hay.[26]

ECONOMIC HISTORY. AGRICULTURE. In 1273 the income from the herbage and pannage of Horton Hay was nearly a third of the value of Horton manor.[27] The payment of cowscot, which the lord of Horton received from neighbouring manors, was probably a charge for pasturing cattle on the hay. The payment, variously called scout, scuth, stuth, and stuff, was recorded in 1278, when Endon and Longsdon each paid 20s. every third year and Endon additionally 2s. 6d. every second year. No payment was made by Longsdon in 1308, but the lord of Rushton James then paid a scot of 10s. every third year.[28] Scot from Endon and Rushton James was still demanded in 1607, when that from Rushton James was said to be paid by the free tenants.[29] In the early and mid 18th century Rushton James apparently paid its scot annually.[30]

Officials called *caronatores*, responsible either for inspecting carcasses or for separating old animals from a herd, were recorded in the manor in 1387, and their duties were probably associated with Horton Hay.[31] Although sheep were kept on the hay in the earlier 16th century,[32] its main use was probably as pasture for dairy cattle: the principal house was called Dairy House by 1645.[33] In the later 17th century the hay was divided into farms, on which dairying may have continued to predominate.[34] In 1805 there were eight farms, besides Dairy House: Shirkley Hall (198 a.), Broadmeadows (180 a.), Rails (164 a.), Tallash (127 a.), Porter's (110 a.), Halfway House (94 a.), Sprinks (53 a.), and a farm later incorporated into Halfway House farm (49 a.). Together those farms had cowhouses for 156 cows.[35] Some cropping took place. In 1665 the tenant at Sprinks farm, besides a rent of £10 for his 21-year lease, had to pay 40s. a year during the last four years of the lease for each acre which he ploughed over 13 a. In 1805 the tenant at the same farm ploughed his land once every eight to ten years and sowed oats.[36]

In the early 14th century arable land elsewhere in the parish was worked in small tenements.[37] Of the 495 a. of recorded farmland held by customary tenants in 1607 half was in 10 holdings of between 24 a. and 36 a. and half in some 20 smaller ones.[38] The main area of common waste lay south-west of Horton Hay on Lask Edge, so called by 1239.[39] It covered 143 a. in 1805 and was inclosed in 1815 under an Act of 1808 along with 110 a. of waste elsewhere in the parish, notably in the area of Whorrocks Bank.[40] Some 4,000 a. of farmland was recorded in the parish in 1851, of which 6 farms on Horton Hay had 877 a.; 8 other farms of 80 a. or over and 7 smallholdings shared 884 a. in the north part of the parish. Smallholdings were characteristic in the south part of the parish, where only two of the 56 farmers recorded in 1851 had over 100 a. (farms of 110 a. at Gratton Hall and 158 a. at Bond House); 18 farmers had between 100 a. and 50 a., 7 between 50 a. and 25 a., and 29 less than 25 a.[41]

Of the 2,037.9 ha. of farmland returned for the civil parish in 1988, grassland covered 1,890.2 ha. and there were 97.7 ha. of rough grazing. Dairy farming predominated, and there were 3,803 head of cattle. Sheep and lambs numbered 2,157, and there were 1,144 pigs and 1,967 hens. Of the 71 farms returned, 59 were less than 50 ha. in size and 12 were between 50 and 99 ha.[42]

WOODLAND. The lord of the manor felled a wood of 300 a. on Horton Hay in the 1230s to provide fuel for iron forges.[43] In the earlier 15th century oak and ash on the hay were felled illegally,[44] and in 1538 it was alleged that 300 trees there had been felled without licence and 200 loads of underwood carted away.[45] When timber on Horton Hay was valued in 1820, there were only 744 trees, mostly alder and sycamore with some oak.[46] A woodward recorded in Horton manor in 1387 was probably responsible for the sale that year of timber from 'Horewode', possibly in the Whorrocks Bank area on the east side of the parish.[47] A wood at Rea Cliffe was mentioned in the late 1530s.[48] In 1988 woodland covered 32.6 ha.[49] It lay chiefly along the edge of Rudyard Lake and included specimen trees planted on the Cliffe Park estate.

WARREN AND HUNTING. In 1252 James de Audley was granted free warren at Horton and Gratton.[50] Coneygreave Farm, on the north-east side of Horton Hay, may stand on the site of a rabbit warren. When Francis Biddulph let Sprinks farm on Horton Hay in 1665, he reserved the right to hawk, hunt, and course, and the tenant as part of his rent had to provide a hound, greyhound, or spaniel.[51]

The keeping of deer in the parish is suggested by land called Damsgate, mentioned in 1445 and presumably lying in the Dams Lane area north-west

[26] S.R.O., D. (W.) 1702/2/11; D. (W.) 1761/A/4/177; below, Leek: Leek and Lowe, manors (rectory).

[27] *S.H.C.* N.S. xi. 242.

[28] Ibid. 245, 255–6. The payment may have been mentioned in a charter of Earl Ranulph of Chester to Dieulacres abbey in the 1220s, where 'Cockstuth' in the surviving copies of the charter may be a misreading of 'cowstuth' (*Charters of Earls of Chester*, pp. 383–4).

[29] S.R.O., D. (W.) 1490/17, ct. of 23 Oct. 1607.

[30] Ibid. D. (W.) 1761/B/3/1 and 81.

[31] P.R.O., SC 2/202/62, m. 1.

[32] *S.H.C.* N.S. x (1), 152.

[33] Above, manors (Horton Hay).

[34] S.R.O., D. (W.) 1761/A/4/182–3, 187–94.

[35] Ibid. D. (W.) 1761/B/3/141–2.

[36] Ibid. D. (W.) 1761/A/4/183; D. (W.) 1761/B/3/141.

[37] *S.H.C.* N.S. xi. 254–5.

[38] S.R.O., D. (W.) 1490/17, ct. of 23 Oct. 1607.

[39] *Cur. Reg. R.* xvi, p. 122 (as Laxege).

[40] S.R.O., Q/RDc 69; ibid. D. (W.) 1761/B/3/141; 48 Geo. III, c. 132 (Local and Personal).

[41] P.R.O., HO 107/2008.   [42] Ibid. MAF 68/6128/79.

[43] *Cur. Reg. R.* xvi, p. 122.

[44] S.R.O., D. (W.) 1490/2, m. 27; D. (W.) 1490/6, m. 29d.

[45] *S.H.C.* N.S. x (1), 139.

[46] S.R.O., D. (W.) 1909/D/4/2.

[47] P.R.O., SC 2/202/62, m. 1.

[48] *S.H.C.* N.S. x (1), 139.

[49] P.R.O., MAF 68/6128/79.

[50] *Cal. Chart. R.* 1226–57, 409.

[51] S.R.O., D. (W.) 1761/A/4/183.

of Gratton, and by land in Crowborough called Buckstall in 1476.[52] The places may have been associated with the park in Endon owned by the lords of Horton.[53]

MILLS. Gratton mill was recorded in the early 1290s and presumably stood on Horton brook east of Gratton hamlet.[54] It ceased working probably in the late 16th century when part of its water supply, a tributary of Horton brook which rose in Longsdon, was diverted to feed a new mill called Harracles mill erected on the east side of the parish by John Wedgwood of Harracles Hall in Longsdon.[55] Rebuilt in the 19th century and later powered by steam turbines, Harracles mill ceased working probably in the 1930s[56] but the mill building and machinery survived in 1991.

Endon mill on the Horton side of the parish boundary south of Gratton was built in 1805 by John Lees of Stanley. It ceased working in 1910 and was demolished in 1936.[57]

TRADE AND INDUSTRY. Having successfully upheld his claim to Horton manor in 1227, Henry de Audley began to exploit reserves of iron ore, evidently on Horton Hay, and by 1239 he had set up forges.[58] Iron was presumably still being worked in 1308, when Adam the smith (*ferror*) was a tenant of the manor.[59] The tenants of a water-driven forge built on the hay in 1438 had the right to cut down wood there for a term of eight years.[60] A forge on the hay was held by Hulton abbey in 1528, when it was destroyed by local men.[61] Rebuilt by 1532, it was again pulled down in 1537.[62]

Coal was dug at Horton in 1317 and 1386, probably near the boundary with Biddulph.[63] Stone was dug in different parts of the parish in the earlier 17th century. Thomas Brindley and William Jolliffe, both of Leek, were presented at the manor court for taking away stone from land in the area of Whorrocks Bank in 1638, and William Brount of Leek was presented for taking away 32 cartloads of stone from the same area in 1694.[64] A man from Biddulph was presented in 1658 for digging stone, probably on Horton Hay.[65] In 1815 there was a quarry on the west side of Whorrocks Bank Road and another south of Stone House. Quarries on the east side of Whorrocks Bank Road by 1856 were still worked in 1884 but had been closed by the late 1890s.[66] There was also a quarry at Biddulph Moor on the western boundary in 1815.[67] Stone was still dug in that area in the later 1870s, five stone

masons recorded in the parish in 1881 all living at Biddulph Moor.[68]

Although Horton's 19th-century workers were chiefly involved in agriculture, several probably combined seasonal farm work with other trades. There was a nailer's shop at Whorrocks Bank *c.* 1807, and a nailmaker lived at Gratton in 1841.[69] Colliers and coalminers lived at Biddulph Moor, close to mines in Biddulph parish: 4 were recorded in 1841, 10 in 1851, over 40 in 1871, and over 30 in 1881. Other workers living there included pot sellers (17 in 1841 and 5 in 1861) and silkworkers and button makers (26 in 1851, but only 2 in 1881).[70]

LOCAL GOVERNMENT. In 1293 Nicholas de Audley claimed view of frankpledge, assize of bread and of ale, waif, and infangthief in Horton manor, and a jury stated that the same rights had been held by Hervey de Stafford before 1227.[71] By 1308 the Audleys used the court at Horton to administer adjacent manors,[72] and by 1351 the twice-yearly view was attended by a frankpledge for each of the tithings of Horton, Gratton, Rushton James, Endon, Longsdon, Stanley, and Bagnall. There was then a single panel of jurors, but by 1381 there were two, one called the great (later the king's) jury or inquisition and the other the office (later the customary or the lord's) jury. The former made presentments relating to public offences and the latter presentments relating to breaches of manorial customs. After the division of Horton manor in 1392 a single court was still held jointly by the lords, although the profits were divided and reeves were appointed for each share of the manor. By 1513, however, Lord Audley held a court for his two-thirds share of the manor, and in 1536 the earl of Bath held a court for his third share. The earl's court was last recorded in 1619, and by 1625 the lords again held a joint court. Presentments ceased to be made according to tithing from the beginning of the 18th century, although frankpledges (by then styled headboroughs) were still appointed at the end of the century. The view of frankpledge was last recorded in 1796 and the court baron in 1821.[73] A court leet, however, was still held in 1908, on the Thursday before the parish wake in September.[74] The court presumably met at the Crown inn in Horton village in the early 19th century, when the inn was known as the Court House.[75]

It appears that small courts were held at one

52 Ibid. D. (W.) 1490/6, mm. 30, 49d.
53 Below, Leek: Endon, econ. hist. (warren and park).
54 *S.H.C.* vi (1), 201.
55 S.R.O., D. (W.) 1702/2/17A and 32.
56 *Kelly's Dir. Staffs.* (1932; 1940).
57 Ibid. (1904; 1908; s.v. Endon); *Old Road to Endon*, ed. R. Speake (Keele, 1974), 95–6; date stone on house.
58 *Cur. Reg. R.* xvi, p. 122.
59 *S.H.C.* N.S. xi. 255.
60 S.R.O., D. (W.) 1490/6, m. 21d.
61 *S.H.C.* 1912, 25–6.
62 Ibid. 1910, 39–41; S.R.O., D. (W.) 1490/10A.
63 *S.H.C.* 1911, 338; *Cal. Inq. p.m.* xvi, p. 72.
64 S.R.O., D. (W.) 1490/20/19A; D. (W.) 1490/32, m. 34.
65 Ibid. D. (W.) 1490/23, m. 17.

66 Ibid. Q/RDc 69, plan II, nos. 143, 181; D. 4069/6/2/1; *Kelly's Dir. Staffs.* (1884); O.S. Map 6", Staffs. VII. NE. (1900 edn.).
67 S.R.O., Q/RDc 69, plan I, no. 39.
68 O.S. Map 6", Staffs. VII. NE. (1887 edn.), NW. (1889 edn.); P.R.O., RG 11/2740, s.v. Hot Lane.
69 S.R.O., D. (W.) 1909/D/4/1; P.R.O., HO 107/1004.
70 P.R.O., HO 107/1004; HO 107/2008; ibid. RG 9/1947; RG 10/2883; RG 11/2740.
71 *S.H.C.* vi (1), 243; vii (1), 16–17.
72 *S.H.C.* N.S. xi. 254–6.
73 S.R.O., D. (W.) 1490 (Horton manor ct. rolls, surviving from 1349).
74 Ibid. D. (W.) 1909/I/2; *Kelly's Dir. Staffs.* (1908).
75 Above, intro.

time for Gratton: a rental was drawn up at a small court held there in 1605.[76]

By 1539 a constable for Horton was chosen at the autumn view of frankpledge. In the later 17th century the constablewick covered Horton itself and the manor's other tithings. A constable was still appointed in the late 1790s.[77]

A payment to the lord of Horton called tallage in 1404 and 'yilte' in 1485 may have been a form of geld payable at some earlier date to the king and charged by the lord on his tenants.[78] The amount paid in 1470 was 38s. 5½d., the same as in 1532.[79] In 1607 it was charged on most customary tenements in Horton, Endon, and Longsdon in amounts varying from 3d. to 22½d.[80]

In 1490 the lord received a Whitsuntide payment of 2s. 9d. from the frankpledges. The payment, a form of chevage or general charge on the tithings, was called chief silver in 1532 and head or headborough silver by the later 16th century. It was still demanded in 1607.[81]

By the early 15th century the lord took a 2s. charge called farefee, apparently when a tenant surrendered his entire holding in the manor. It possibly derived from a payment taken from a neif when he wished to leave the manor.[82] Farefee was still recorded in 1616.[83]

Orders to repair the stocks in Horton were made in 1654 and 1747.[84] There was a pinfold near the forge on Horton Hay in 1534 and one, possibly elsewhere in the parish, in 1626. A pinfold was mentioned as out of repair in 1706.[85] A stone enclosure which stood east of Horton church in 1991 was probably once used as a pinfold.

A surveyor of highways was recorded for Gratton in 1699, one for Horton in 1701, and one for Crowborough in 1751. They were responsible to Horton manor court.[86]

There were two churchwardens in 1553.[87] The parish clerk was salaried by 1714, receiving £1 a year.[88]

Horton had at least two overseers of the poor in 1667.[89] By 1803 the parish was divided for purposes of poor relief into two townships, each presumably with its own overseer: one township comprised Horton village and Horton Hay and the other Blackwood Hill (presumably including Gratton) and Crowborough.[90] A parish house recorded c. 1807[91] probably stood on the road between Dams Lane and Blackwood Hill, where

the overseers had a cottage in 1816.[92] There were two poorhouses, possibly one for each township, when Horton became part of Leek poor-law union in 1837.[93]

CHURCH. A chapel at Horton was probably one of the dependent chapels granted with Leek church to Dieulacres abbey in the early 1220s. It was mentioned by name in Bishop Stavensby's confirmation of the grant between 1224 and 1228.[94] Horton was described as a parish in the earlier 1530s,[95] although in 1535 the church was recorded with others as a chapel of Leek and the grant of Leek rectory to Sir Ralph Bagnall in 1560 included what was described as Horton chapel.[96] In 1563 Horton was described as a church with cure but without institution, and in 1604 as a church annexed to Leek.[97] In 1612 the lay rector of Leek, Thomas Rudyard, conveyed Horton church and churchyard to Richard Edge of Horton Hall and William Hulme, and in 1721 Timothy Edge conveyed the church to John Alsop, his successor at Horton Hall.[98] Part of the west side of the parish was transferred to the new parish of Christ Church, Biddulph, in 1864.[99] The benefice was a perpetual curacy until 1868, when it was styled a vicarage.[1] The church was served by its own vicar until 1984 and thereafter by a priest-in-charge.[2]

By 1450 the vicar of Leek was responsible for providing a chaplain at Horton. The responsibility was transferred to Dieulacres abbey as rector, probably in 1450, and by the Dissolution the lessees of Horton tithes were responsible.[3] The patronage presumably passed with the church and churchyard to Richard Edge and William Hulme in 1612, and it was held by Edge's son Timothy in 1677.[4] By 1725, however, the patronage belonged to the lord of Horton manor, John Wedgwood, and it descended with the manor until 1791 when it was sold to Thomas Sutton of Leek. It was reunited with the lordship in 1807 when Sutton sold it to Edmund Antrobus.[5] In 1926 Crawfurd Antrobus transferred the patronage to the bishop of Lichfield.[6]

The curate received a stipend of 7 marks (£4 13s. 4d.) from the vicar of Leek in 1450.[7] The sale of Leek rectory to Thomas Rudyard in 1597 was subject to the payment of £5 6s. 8d. a year

76   B.R.L., Norton Colln. 638.
77   S.R.O., D. (W.) 1490/11, m. 3d.; D. (W.) 1490/44, m. 20; S.H.C. 1925, 157–62.
78   S.R.O., D. (W.) 1490/2, m. 14d.; D. (W.) 1490/47; P.R.O., SC 6/Hen. VIII/3350, m. 2.
79   P.R.O., SC 6/988/2, m. 4d.; S.R.O., D. (W.) 1490/10A.
80   S.R.O., D. (W.) 1490/17, ct. of 23 Oct. 1607.
81   Ibid. D. (W.) 1490/10A, m. 2; D. (W.) 1490/17, ct. of 23 Oct. 1607; D. (W.) 1490/47; W.S.L. 52/46.
82   S.R.O., D. (W.) 1490/6, mm. 17, 17d., 39; D. (W.) 1490/10B, mm. 7, 31; D. (W.) 1490/14/2B; D. (W.) 1490/15, ct. of 29 Apr. 1560. For farefee see Cart. Haughmond Abbey, ed. U. Rees, nos. 143, 300.
83   S.R.O., D. (W.) 1490/17, ct. of 14 Apr. 1616.
84   Ibid. D. (W.) 1490/22/51; D. (W.) 1490/43, m. 77.
85   Ibid. D. (W.) 1490/10B, m. 28; D. (W.) 1490/20/2; D. (W.) 1490/35, m. 19d.
86   Ibid. D. (W.) 1490/34, mm. 68d., 84d.; D. (W.) 1490/43, m. 79.
87   S.H.C. 1915, 130.
88   L.J.R.O., B/V/6/Horton, 1714.

89   S.R.O., D. 1040/5/2.
90   Abstract of Returns relating to Poor, H.C. 98, p. 472 (1803–4), xiii.
91   S.R.O., D. (W.) 1909/D/4/1, f. 8.
92   Ibid. D. 1535/1, p. 40 (no. 821); D. (W.) 1909/E/9/1.
93   Ibid. D. 699/1/1/1, pp. 1, 5.
94   Below, Leek: Leek and Lowe, churches.
95   S.H.C. 4th ser. viii. 34.
96   Valor Eccl. (Rec. Com.), iii. 123; Cal. Pat. 1558–60, 309.   97   S.H.C. 1915, 130.
98   Sleigh, Leek, 160; P.R.O., CP 25(2)/1062/7 Geo. I East. no. 7.   99   Lond. Gaz. 5 Feb. 1864, pp. 533–4.
1   Lich. Dioc. Ch. Cal. (1869).
2   Lich. Dioc. Dir. (1985 and later edns.).
3   L.J.R.O., B/A/1/10, f. 84; P.R.O., SC 6/Hen. VIII/3353, m. 34.
4   Sleigh, Leek, 160; B.L. Add. Ch. 41822.
5   L.J.R.O., B/A/3/Horton; S.R.O., D. (W.) 1761/A/4/253.
6   Lond. Gaz. 9 Nov. 1926, pp. 7227–8.
7   L.J.R.O., B/A/1/10, f. 84v.

to the minister of Horton, and that sum was fixed as a rent charge on the Horton Hall estate by Richard Edge, probably in 1612. A further charge of £14 13s. 4d. on the Horton Hall estate was bequeathed to the minister by Timothy Edge (d. 1683).[8] Both rents were still paid in full in 1830, but only £18 4s. was paid in 1841.[9]

By 1726 the curate also received a rent of £5 from 15 a. inclosed from the waste at Biddulph Moor.[10] In the late 1720s or early 1730s the 35-a. Denford farm, in Cheddleton, was bought for £300. The money came from a grant of £200 made in 1725 by Queen Anne's Bounty to meet benefactions of £100 raised by subscription and £100 apparently given by Charles Wedgwood, son of John Wedgwood of Harracles, in Longsdon. The land produced a rent of £20 in 1732.[11] When land on Wetley moor, in Cheddleton, was inclosed in the late 1730s, 9 a. was assigned to the curate of Horton as the owner of the Denford estate.[12] The living was worth £105 a year c. 1830.[13] In 1841 the Biddulph Moor land was let for £15 13s. 1d., the Denford estate for £44, and the Wetley moor land (10½ a.) for £10 18s.[14] A parliamentary grant of £76 6s. 9d. was made by 1849.[15] In 1862 the Ecclesiastical Commissioners gave £900 to meet benefactions of £400 given by the patron, J. C. Antrobus, £200 raised by subscription, £200 from the Poor Benefice Fund, and £100 from the Lichfield Diocesan Church Extension Society.[16] By 1869 the Commissioners also held for the curate's benefit £1,183 8s. 7d. from the sale of the Biddulph Moor land.[17] There was 50 a. of glebe in 1887, with an estimated rental of £69.[18]

A house for the perpetual curate was built north of the church by the patron, John Wedgwood, in 1753. It was held by trustees until 1935, when it was conveyed to the Ecclesiastical Commissioners.[19] It was sold in 1985.[20]

The curate Richard Mitchell (d. 1622) was described in 1593 as 'a country scholar and well trained in the scriptures'. In 1602, however, he was recorded as having no degree and in 1604 as being no preacher and of loose life.[21] A later minister, Robert Wood, was a signatory to the Presbyterian *Testimony* of 1648.[22] There were several endowed sermons: one on Good Friday founded by Elizabeth St. Andrew (d. 1644), daughter of John Wedgwood of Harracles;[23] one on 5 November founded by Timothy Edge (d.

1683);[24] one on 29 May founded by William Dudley (d. 1718);[25] and one at Candlemas founded by William Bostock (d. 1725), a Leek lawyer.[26] In 1830 there were Sunday prayers with a sermon in the morning and afternoon, and Communion was celebrated four times a year.[27] The attendance on Census Sunday 1851 was 50 in the morning and 90 in the evening.[28] When a new organ was acquired in 1883, a surpliced choir and altar candles were introduced. There was by then a Communion service every Sunday.[29]

St. Gabriel's mission church was opened in Whorrocks Bank Road in 1905. The site was left by Hugh Sleigh of Leek (d. 1901), who also gave £500 towards the cost of building the church. Designed in an Italianate style by J. T. Brealey, it consisted of a nave, with a tower on the east side, and an apse.[30] Because of the threat of subsidence the church was demolished in 1934.[31]

The church of *ST. MICHAEL*, so called by 1480,[32] is built of sandstone and consists of a chancel, an aisled nave of three bays, a south-west porch, and a west tower.[33] The tower and the north aisle date from the 15th century, having been added to an earlier nave, none of whose fabric survives. The chancel was rebuilt in the 16th century and retains evidence of a rood loft. A wooden screen dated 1618 separates the tower from the nave. The south aisle and porch were added when the church was restored by the Leek architect William Sugden in 1864.[34] The chancel was restored in 1878 at the expense of John Robinson of Westwood Hall, in Leek and Lowe.[35]

By 1484 seats in the church were assigned to particular houses in the parish. By 1740 there was a gallery at the west end, built to accommodate people living in the Horton Hay area.[36] A north gallery had been added by 1830.[37] It was removed in 1849, when the box pews were re-arranged to provide seating in the chancel for the minister and his family; at the same date additional seating was provided for the poor under the west gallery. Also in 1849 the wooden pulpit and reading desk were moved to the south side of the chancel arch.[38]

The restoration of 1864 included the removal of the west gallery and the replacement of the box pews in the chancel with open benches. New glass given in memory of Thomas Crompton of Dunwood House in Longsdon and his wife was

8 Ibid. B/V/6/Horton, 1693; W.S.L. 63/13/42; *S.H.C.* 1915, 130.
9 *S.H.C.* 4th ser. x. 88; L.J.R.O., B/V/6/Horton, 1841.
10 L.J.R.O., B/V/6/Horton, 1726.
11 Ibid.; ibid. 1732; Hodgson, *Bounty of Queen Anne*, pp. cxli, ccxcvii.
12 L.J.R.O., B/V/6/Horton, 1741, 1747.
13 *Rep. Com. Eccl. Revenues*, 482–3.
14 L.J.R.O., B/V/6/Horton, 1841.
15 Ibid. 1849.
16 Benefaction board in north aisle.
17 L.J.R.O., B/V/6/Horton, 1869.
18 *Return of Glebe Lands*, 65.
19 S.R.O., D. (W.) 1909/K/2/6/8; Lich. Dioc. Regy., Bp.'s Reg. W, p. 542.
20 Inf. from Lich. Dioc. Regy.
21 *S.H.C.* 1915, 130; L.J.R.O., B/C/11, Ric. Michell (1622).
22 *S.H.C.* 1915, 130.
23 L.J.R.O., B/V/6/Horton, 1693; S.R.O., D. 4069/2/1.

24 L.J.R.O., B/V/6/Horton, 1693, 1735, 1747.
25 Ibid. B/C/11, Wm. Dudley (1718).
26 Ibid. B/V/6/Horton, 1730, 1773, 1841; S.R.O., D. 4069/1/2, burial of 11 Mar. 1724/5.
27 *S.H.C.* 4th ser. x. 88.
28 P.R.O., HO 129/372/2/6.
29 W.S.L., Sleigh, ii, f. 118v.
30 *Staffs. Advertiser*, 23 Nov. 1901, p. 5; *Lich. Dioc. Mag.* xxvi (1905), 92; L. Porter, *Staffs. Moorlands* (Ashbourne, 1983), no. 68.
31 H. Pickford, 'Our Ancient Village of Rudyard', 8 (TS. in W.S.L.).
32 B.L. Add. MS. 34709, p. 2.
33 Below, plate 12.
34 *Staffs. Advertiser*, 17 Sept. 1864, p. 5.
35 Ibid. 29 June 1878, p. 7.
36 W.S.L., CB/Horton/1.
37 *S.H.C.* 4th ser. x. 87.
38 S.R.O., D. 4069/3/1; Lichfield Cath. Libr., Moore and Hinckes drawings, v, no. 20.

inserted in windows in the chancel and north
aisle. At the same date the organ was moved to
the east end of the new south aisle; it was
replaced by the present organ in the same position in 1883.[39] When the chancel was restored in
1878, the pulpit and reading desk were replaced
by a stone pulpit, given by J. C. Antrobus, and
a wooden prayer desk, given by Eliza Crompton
of Dunwood House.[40] A chancel screen, carved
by Bennett Blakeway, vicar of Horton 1879–
1919, was erected in 1900 as a memorial to
William Tellwright of Horton Lodge, also com-
memorated by the east window in the north
aisle.[41] A 17th-century oak communion table,
now in the north aisle, was replaced as the high
altar in 1931 by a medieval stone altar discovered
in the church.[42] The font dates from the 15th
century.[43]

The plate in 1553 included a silver chalice and
paten and a brass cross, pyx, and censer.[44] The
present silver chalice is dated 1640 and the silver
paten 1754. The latter was probably given by
the patron, John Wedgwood, also the donor of
a flagon, now lost.[45] There is a wooden poor box
dated 1714 at the south-west corner of the nave,
and in the south aisle there are royal arms of
1790.

In 1537 John Pyot of Leek left money for the
purchase of bells for Horton.[46] The three bells
mentioned in 1553, for which a debt of 20 marks
was still owed, were described as bought from
the king, possibly an indication that they had
come from Dieulacres abbey.[47] They were recast
in 1753 as a peal of six.[48]

The registers date from 1653 but those from
1684 to 1725 are missing.[49]

The churchyard was extended in 1864 and
1898.[50] A lychgate was erected in 1902 as a
memorial to John Munro of Fairview (d. 1900).[51]

NONCONFORMITY. Thirteen Roman
Catholics were recorded in Horton in 1635,
including John Biddulph of Dairy House and
his wife Mary.[52] Nine recusants named in a
return of 1641 included Richard Baddeley, his
wife Margaret, and their two sons, all of whom
were again returned in 1657. The sons only with
their wives were returned in 1678, along with
six other papists. Only two papists were listed
in 1706.[53]

William Yardley, the tenant at Dairy House,
became a Quaker in 1654, and in 1655 he was
imprisoned for speaking out in Leek parish
church. His house was used as meeting place for
Quakers in 1669. In 1675 he was fined for
preaching at a meeting in Leek.[54] John Whittakers
of Gratton was a Quaker by 1675, and the
Staffordshire Friends met at his house in 1685.[55]
Thomas Hammersley of Gratton attended the
Leek meeting in the mid 18th century,[56] and in
1770 John Fowler of Horton Hall was a trustee
of the meeting house in Leek.[57]

By 1784 a Methodist society of eight members
met at Steel House Farm. The society had
apparently lapsed by 1802, when no Methodist
services were held at Horton. By 1829, however,
there was a Wesleyan Methodist service every
Sunday, one week at Horton, presumably in or
near the village, and the next at Bank House at
the southern end of Whorrocks Bank.[58] Bank
House was the home of William Armett (d.
1842), a Methodist preacher who was encouraged by George Harvey, perpetual curate of
Horton 1831–6.[59] There may have been a chapel
by 1841 when there is mention of Chapel House,
the home of Armett's son Charles in 1851.[60] In
1862 a Wesleyan Methodist chapel was opened
east of Bank House.[61] It was replaced in 1912 by
a chapel in Lake Road, known as Rudyard
Methodist church in 1991.[62] The former building has been turned into a house.

A Wesleyan Methodist chapel was opened at
Gratton in 1822, and in 1829 there was a service
every Sunday. On Census Sunday 1851 the
attendance was 20 in the afternoon, besides
Sunday school children, and 45 in the evening.
The chapel, which was refronted in brick in the
late 19th century, was still in use in 1991.[63]

A Methodist congregation existed at Biddulph
Moor by 1803. A Wesleyan Methodist chapel
built in New Road on the Horton side of the
boundary by 1851 was replaced in 1887 by a
chapel on the same site, still open in 1991.[64]

Hugh Bourne, a pioneer of Primitive Methodism,
registered a house at Lask Edge for worship in
1807, when still a Wesleyan. In 1808 he preached
at Gratton, where in 1809 he registered a place
of worship, the first opened after his ejection
from the Wesleyan connexion. In 1810 he led a
camp meeting at Blackwood Hill.[65] A Primitive
Methodist chapel built at Lask Edge by 1856

39 *Staffs. Advertiser*, 17 Sept. 1864, p. 5; printed sheet on hist. of church (copy in W.S.L.).
40 *Staffs. Advertiser*, 29 June 1878, p. 7.
41 *Kelly's Dir. Staffs.* (1904).
42 S.R.O., D. 4069/3/4; *T.N.S.F.C.* xxxvii. 169.
43 *T.B.A.S.* lxviii. 21.   44 *S.H.C.* 1915, 130.
45 *T.B.A.S.* lxxvii. 65, 73; S.R.O., D. 4069/1/2, inside front cover.   46 L.J.R.O., B/C/11, John Pyot (1538).
47 *S.H.C.* 1915, 130; *T.N.S.F.C.* xix. 56.
48 Sleigh, *Leek*, 161.
49 Those not in current use are in S.R.O., D. 4069.
50 Lich. Dioc. Regy., Bp.'s Reg. Q, pp. 609, 733–7; U, pp. 322, 374–5.
51 Plaque on gate and memorial in churchyard.
52 *Staffs. Cath. Hist.* xxii. 22.
53 Ibid. ii. 97; v. 11; xiii. 27; xxiv. 20.
54 L.J.R.O., B/C/11, Ric. Yardley (1664); B/V/1/72, p. 15; A. G. Matthews, *Congregational Churches of Staffs.* (preface dated 1924), 90; below, Leek: Leek and Lowe, prot. nonconf. (Friends).
55 S.R.O., Q/SR/367, m. 23; S.R.O., D. 3159/1/1, f. 31.
56 Ibid. D. 3159/3/6/93.
57 Ibid. D. 3359/Condlyffe, draft deed of 19 July 1770.
58 D.R.O., D. 3568/4/1/1; Leek Libr., Johnson scrapbk. i (2), D/13/15.
59 Dyson, *Wesleyan Methodism*, 28, 82; S.R.O., D. 3155/1, 1825 and later years. For Armett see White, *Dir. Staffs.* (1834), 748; S.R.O., D. (W.) 1909/D/4/3; L.J.R.O., B/C/11, Wm. Armett (1842).
60 P.R.O., HO 107/1004; HO 107/2008; L.J.R.O., B/C/11, Wm. Armett (1842).
61 P.R.O., C 54/17558, mm. 17–18; G.R.O. Worship Reg. no. 15413.
62 G.R.O. Worship Reg. no. 45438; *Leek Wesleyan Methodist Circuit Yr. Bk. 1912*, frontispiece.
63 Leek Libr., Johnson scrapbk. i (2), D/13/15; P.R.O., HO 129/372/2/7; below, plate 58.
64 S.R.O., D. 3155/1; White, *Dir. Staffs.* (1851), 387; foundation stone in porch.
65 *S.H.C.* 4th ser. iii. 11, 18; H. Bourne, *Hist. of the Primitive Methodists* (Bemersley, 1835), 25; *Old Road to Endon*, ed. R. Speake (Keele, 1974), 58–9.

was replaced in 1875 by another on a site to the north-west, still open in 1991.[66]

EDUCATION. In 1700 a schoolmaster living in Horton was licensed to teach grammar. Another was licensed in 1714.[67] It is not certain that they taught in the parish, and there was no schoolmaster in 1732.[68] A schoolmaster, Thomas Shufflebotham, died at Horton in 1774, two years after the death of Sarah Shufflebotham, who was described as a schooldame.[69] The death of another schoolmaster was recorded in 1811.[70] A school was established in 1815, probably at Lea Laughton where the master, William Heath, was living by 1817. Heath had 30 pupils in 1818, when it was stated that there was inadequate provision for the poor.[71] In the earlier 1830s he had 83 pupils.[72] A new schoolroom was built in the later 1840s, and by then the school was affiliated to the National Society.[73] The building was enlarged in 1872 and again in 1894.[74]

The decision in 1930 that what was then called Horton Church of England school, an all-age school with 83 children on its books, should become a junior school probably took effect in the earlier 1940s, the senior children being transferred to schools in Leek.[75] Horton school took controlled status in 1954 as St. Michael's Church of England (Controlled) primary school.[76] In 1962 it was rebuilt on its present site at the north end of Whorrocks Bank Road, and the former school building was converted into the village hall.[77]

In 1830 there was a Church of England Sunday school with 30 children. There was also a non-conformist Sunday school in 1830. It was probably for Wesleyan Methodists, who in the earlier 1830s had a Sunday school with 80 children, apparently at their chapel at Gratton.[78] A Sunday school at Gratton chapel had 27 children on Census Sunday 1851; no Sunday school was recorded at the parish church that day.[79]

Hannah Plummer ran a private boarding school in the parish in 1888. It was in Rudyard village in 1892 and 1896.[80]

In 1950 a school for children with special needs was opened in Horton Lodge by Stoke-on-Trent education authority. Restricted from 1969 to physically handicapped children, the school was run by Staffordshire county council in 1991.[81]

CHARITIES FOR THE POOR. Elizabeth St. Andrew (d. 1644) left a rent charge of 6s. 8d. for distribution to the poor of Horton parish on Good Friday.[82] Timothy Edge (d. 1683) of Horton Hall left a rent charge of £10 10s., £5 to be spent on apprenticing or as a dole and £5 10s. on the distribution of bread to the poor of Horton every Sunday. In the earlier 1820s the churchwardens and overseers bought 12 loaves with £5 4s. and retained 6s. for administration. Thomas Jodrell (d. 1728) of Endon[83] left a third of the interest on £200 for the poor of Horton. The income in the later 1780s was £2 10s. By will of 1732 John Stonier of Crowborough left half the interest on £70 for distribution to the poor of Horton at Candlemas. The income in the later 1780s was £1 8s. John Wedgwood (d. 1757) of Harracles, in Longsdon, left half the interest on £120 for distribution to the poor of Horton at Candlemas. Horton's share was £3 in the later 1780s. From 1862 Fanny Bostock (d. 1875) of Cliffe Park gave £3 a year for the purchase of flannel to be given to poor women in Horton at the time of the parish wake. She bequeathed money to continue the distribution.[84] All the charities were united by a Scheme of 1936, and in 1993 £28 was distributed among seven elderly people.[85]

66 S.R.O., D. 4069/6/2/3; date stones on chapel.
67 L.J.R.O., B/A/4/13, [Oct. 1700]; B/A/4/14, 29 May and 19 July 1714.   68 W.S.L., S.MS. 424, f. 70.
69 S.R.O., D. 4069/1/3, ff. 22, 25.
70 Ibid. D. 4069/1/4, f. 24v.
71 Ibid. D. 4069/1/5, p. 21; P.R.O., ED 7/109/168; Educ. of Poor Digest, 861.
72 Educ. Enq. Abstract, 878; P.R.O., HO 107/1004.
73 P.R.O., ED 7/109/168; Nat. Soc. Inquiry, 1846–7, Staffs. 4–5.
74 Lich. Dioc. Ch. Cal. (1873), 92; Kelly's Dir. Staffs. (1896).

75 Staffs. C.C. Record for 1930, 867, 869.
76 S.R.O., CEH/197/1.
77 Ibid.; above, intro.
78 S.H.C. 4th ser. x. 88; Educ. Enq. Abstract, 878.
79 P.R.O., HO 129/372/2/7.
80 Kelly's Dir. Staffs. (1888; 1892; 1896).
81 Inf. from the head teacher, Mr. R. M. Orme.
82 Para. based on 13th Rep. Com. Char. 372–5; Char. Dons. 1152–3.   83 S.R.O., D. 4069/1/2, 27 Sept. 1728.
84 Benefaction board in south aisle of Horton church; Kelly's Dir. Staffs. (1880).
85 Inf. from the correspondent, Mrs. S. Clulow.

LEEK

THE ancient parish of Leek extending north to the county boundary with Cheshire consisted of the 12 townships of Leek and Lowe (including the town of Leek), Bradnop, Endon, Heaton, Leekfrith, Longsdon, Onecote, Rudyard, Rushton James, Rushton Spencer, Stanley, and Tittesworth.[1] The largest parish in Staffordshire, it was 33,254 a. (13,458 ha.) in area.[2] It had also included the chapelries of Cheddleton, Horton, and Ipstones until the 16th century, when the three became separate parishes.

The area is part of the Staffordshire Moorlands, known as the Moorland as early as 1329.[3] The town of Leek is built on Sherwood Sandstone, which is also found at Endon Bank. Elsewhere the underlying rock is sandstone of the Millstone Grit series. It outcrops as the Cloud in Rushton Spencer, 1,126 ft. (343 m.), and as the Roaches and Hen Cloud in Leekfrith, respectively 1,658 ft. (505 m.) and 1,350 ft. (410 m.), the highest points in the ancient parish. The Cloud produces the phenomenon of a double sunset when viewed from St. Edward's churchyard in Leek at the summer solstice.[4] The east side of the area is dominated by Morridge, a long ridge of high moorland which reaches 1,604 ft. (489 m.) on the northern boundary of Onecote. The northern boundary of the parish, which is also the boundary with Cheshire, followed the valley of the river Dane. On the east the boundary followed tributaries of the Dane and of the river Churnet, crossed Morridge, and then followed the river Hamps. Much of the southern boundary followed the Churnet and its tributaries. The western boundary was marked by ridges, culminating in the Cloud.

The grandeur of the scenery caught the imagination of Robert Plot when he visited the area c. 1680. He wrote enthusiastically of the rocks of the district, 'some of them kissing the clouds with their tops, and running along in mountainous ridges for some miles together'. At the sight of Hen Cloud and the Roaches 'my admiration was still heighten'd to see such vast rocks and such really stupendous prospects, which I had never seen before, or could have believed to be, anywhere but in picture'.[5] In 1708 Thomas Loxdale, the antiquarian vicar of Seighford and later vicar of Leek, visited Leekfrith 'to view some of our Moorland wonders' and found the Roaches 'one of the most *romantick* prospects in Nature, far beyond Dr. Plott's description'.[6] Such feelings were the exception before the end of the 18th century. Staffordshire's first county historian, Sampson Erdeswick, writing at the end of the 16th century, considered the area between the source of the Churnet and Dieulacres 'one of the barrenest countries I know'.[7] About the same time William Camden described the Staffordshire Moorlands as 'a tract so very rugged, foul, and cold that the snows continue long undissolved'.[8] A few years later Michael Drayton took a mixed view:[9]

> But Muse, thou seem'st to leave the *Morelands* too too long:
> Of whom report may speak (our mighty wastes among)
> She from her chilly site, as from her barren feed,
> For body, horn, and hair, as fair a beast doth breed
> As scarcely this great Isle can equal.

1 This introduction (written in 1994) draws together some of the topics which are treated in detail in the articles on the individual townships. Unless otherwise indicated, the sources for statements in the introduction are given in those articles.   2 *V.C.H. Staffs.* i. 327–8.
3 P.R.O., C 145/110, no. 22.

4 Plot, *Staffs.* 4–5; *Olde Leeke*, i. 52–7.
5 Plot, *Staffs.* 170–1 (spelling modernized).
6 W.S.L., S.MS. 237/E, no. 8.
7 Erdeswick, *Staffs.* 492.
8 Camden, *Brit.* (1722), i. 642.
9 M. Drayton, *Polyolbion* (1613), 207.

In the mid 18th century the antiquary Richard Wilkes enlarged on that description: Leek was 'seated on a hill in the northern and most barren part of the county, among large heaths and commons, whose soil is black with many loose naked stones standing on the tops and sides of the hills. These make the road to Buxton unpleasant and dismal.'[10] A feeling of awe was returning by the end of the century. William Pitt, the agronomist, visited the area in 1794 and considered the Roaches and Sharp Cliffe Rocks in Ipstones 'stupendous piles ... a sublime lecture on humility to the human mind'.[11] When Westwood Farm west of Leek town was offered for sale in 1804, its situation was described as commanding 'many beautiful, romantic, and extensive prospects'.[12] A view of Ball Haye north-east of the town published in 1813 showed it with the Roaches as a 'stupendously grand' background.[13]

The evidence of place names in the area suggests predominantly Anglo-Saxon settlement, with a Scandinavian element in the 10th or early 11th century in the north part of the parish.[14] A derivation from either Old English or Old Norse has been suggested for the name Leek itself. The centre of the area in the 10th century may have been at Rudyard, but by the 11th century Leek was the centre, with a church built perhaps *c.* 1000. Before the Conquest Leek belonged to the earl of Mercia, while thegns held Endon, Rudyard, and Rushton. All were held by the Crown in 1086, but by 1093 Leek had been granted to Hugh, earl of Chester. The entry in Domesday Book for Leek 'with the appendages' probably covered the site of the later town, Lowe to the south and west, Tittesworth, the area of the later townships of Bradnop and Onecote, and most of Leekfrith. Bradnop and Onecote became

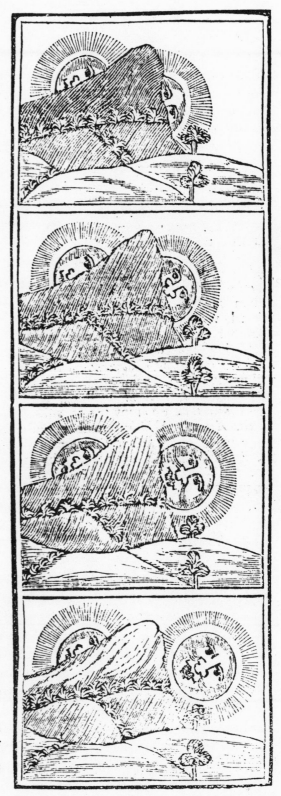

FIG. 13. THE DOUBLE SUNSET BEHIND THE CLOUD

10 *S.H.C.* 4th ser. xi. 91–2.
11 W. Pitt, *General View of Agric. of Staffs.* (1796), 199.
12 W.S.L., Sleigh scrapbk. ii, f. 57v.
13 J. Nightingale, *Staffs.* (Beauties of Eng. and Wales, xiii), 1021 and pl. facing p. 1168 (reproduced below, p. 236).
14 e.g. Berdeholm (later Bearda) and Swythamley, in Heaton; Middle and Upper Hulme, in Leekfrith.

separated from the rest apparently in the 12th century, and in 1218 manorial rights within that area were granted to Henry de Audley. The rest of the Domesday manor of Leek was enlarged to include part of Rudyard manor (the south-west part of the later Leekfrith township and probably Heaton township), and the northern half of Rushton manor (the later Rushton Spencer). As a result Leek manor comprised the tithings of Heaton, Leekfrith, Lowe, Rushton Spencer, and Tittesworth. The core of Rudyard manor remained separate. The southern half of Rushton manor (later Rushton James) became part of the manor of Horton, created by the Audley family and including Horton itself, Endon, Longsdon, and Stanley together with Bagnall, in the parish of Stoke-upon-Trent.

In 1207 the Crown confirmed to Ranulph, earl of Chester, a weekly market and a seven-day annual fair at Leek, and about the same time Ranulph established a borough there. The town has remained a market centre and also a centre of communications, with several medieval roads converging on it. By the early 13th century it was the centre of a fee which comprised the earl of Chester's estates in north-east Staffordshire.[15]

In 1214 Earl Ranulph founded a Cistercian abbey beside the Churnet a mile north of the town in Leekfrith, naming it Dieulacres. He granted Leek church to the monks in the early 1220s, and in 1232 he gave them the manor of Leek. The monks established granges in Leek and Lowe, Heaton, Leekfrith, and Tittesworth. The Cistercians of Hulton were granted Bradnop and Mixon in Onecote by their founder, Henry de Audley, in 1223, and they too established granges. The Cistercians of Croxden also had a grange at Onecote apparently by 1223. In the south-west part of the parish the Augustinian canons of Trentham had an estate by the early 13th century at Wall in Longsdon, where they established a grange. Leekfrith and Rushton Spencer lay in the earls' 'forest' of Leek, and the earls also had a hunting ground at Hollinhay in Longsdon.

Stock farming, which seems to have been important in Leek manor in the 1180s, flourished in the area in the 13th century, with Morridge and the Churnet valley providing pasture. In 1490 Dieulacres had a herd of just over 200 cattle at Swythamley in Heaton. Sheep farming too was important, and in the later 13th century Dieulacres was producing wool for export.

In 1552 the Crown granted what were described as the manors of Leek and Frith to Sir Ralph Bagnall. He asserted his rights against those of the burgesses of Leek, and the town lost its borough status. Otherwise there was a general absence of strong manorial control after the Dissolution, and the only part of the parish where the manorial lords pursued a policy of economic improvement was in the east. Successive Lords Aston attempted the inclosure of Morridge in the 17th and earlier 18th century as lords of Bradnop. Attempts were also made to exploit the limestone and mineral deposits at Mixon between the 17th and 19th centuries. In the late 20th century pasture still predominated, the farming being mainly dairy and sheep.

The usual building material from the 17th century onwards was stone. Most of the farmhouses were built of coursed rubble with ashlar dressings, though some of the wealthier builders made greater use of ashlar. Earlier buildings had often been of timber, and timber framing was used for internal walls well into the 18th century. Brick, which became widespread in the town in the 18th century, made an occasional appearance in the rural area, but stone continued as the main material

15 *Staffs. Studies*, v. 1 sqq.

throughout the 19th century. The parish contained some larger houses, notably Swythamley in Heaton, evidently rebuilt in the 17th century and enlarged in the 18th century, Ashenhurst in Bradnop, rebuilt in the mid 1740s and demolished in 1954, Ball Haye in Tittesworth, rebuilt about the end of the 18th century and demolished in 1972, and Westwood Hall, remodelled c. 1820 and further enlarged in 1851.

Protestant nonconformity was widespread in the later 17th century, with Presbyterians and Quakers particularly numerous. A Quaker meeting house was opened in Leek in the later 1690s, and in the earlier 18th century the Leek meeting appears to have been the largest in Staffordshire. The Presbyterians had a meeting house in the town by 1715. There was a Baptist centre in Rushton Spencer from the later 17th century.

By the 1670s silk working was established in Leek, and by the end of the 18th century the silk industry employed c. 2,000 people in the town and 1,000 in the neighbourhood. It was then still a domestic industry but became increasingly concentrated in factories in the town during the 19th century. A landscape of mills and streets of terraced houses appeared as the industry and the town expanded.

All the main roads through the parish were turnpiked in the early 1760s. The Caldon canal was opened through the south-west part probably in 1778, and a branch serving the town of Leek was opened in 1801. At the same time a reservoir for the canal was built on the boundary of Rudyard township and Horton parish, with a feeder running into the Leek branch. The railway arrived in 1849, when the Churnet Valley line was opened from Macclesfield to Uttoxeter with stations at Rushton Spencer, Rudyard, and Leek. A line was opened from Stoke-upon-Trent to the Churnet Valley line at Leekbrook in 1867. There was a station at Endon, and a residential area for commuters to the Potteries began to develop nearby. The opening in 1896 of a station at Stockton Brook to the south-west was followed by a similar development, which continued in Endon during the 20th century.

A body of improvement commissioners was set up in 1825 with responsibility for the town of Leek and an area outside within a radius of 1,200 yd. from the market place, increased to 1,500 yd. in 1855. The area covered included much of Leek and Lowe township and parts of Leekfrith and Tittesworth. In 1894 it became an urban district, which was enlarged in 1934. In 1974 the urban district became a parish in the new Staffordshire Moorlands district, which has its headquarters in Leek. The rest of the ancient parish, having been included in Leek rural district in 1894, likewise became part of Staffordshire Moorlands district in 1974.

In the late 20th century the area has been promoted for its tourist attractions, notably its scenery and outdoor activities such as walking, rock climbing, and sailing. Leek itself has been styled Queen of the Moorlands. Tourism was first promoted with the development of Rudyard canal reservoir as an attraction after the opening of the Churnet Valley railway in 1849. In 1850 the owners, the North Staffordshire Railway Co., landscaped the ground on the west side of the reservoir and in 1851 organized regattas on what was then called Rudyard Lake. The events attracted thousands of visitors until they were stopped by a local landowner later the same year. The Rudyard area, however, remained popular with visitors and was even promoted as 'the Switzerland of England' at the end of the century.[16] In the 1870s the owner of the Roaches, Philip Brocklehurst of Swythamley, acquired

[16]   Above, Horton, intro. (Rudyard Lake).

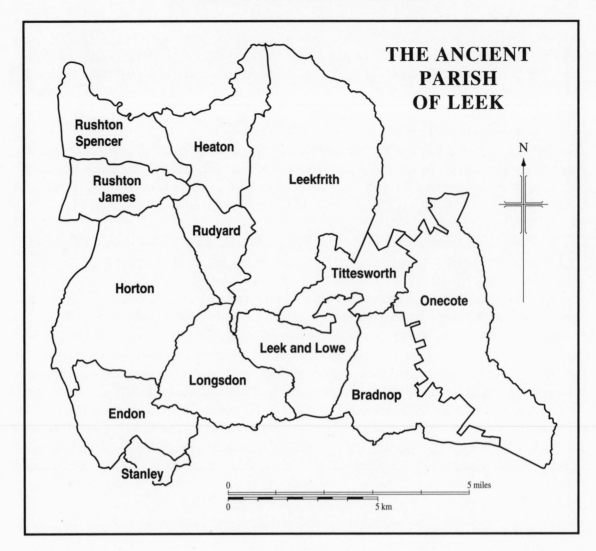

THE ANCIENT
PARISH
OF LEEK

Fig. 14

Hen Cloud and started to encourage visitors to the Roaches area by cutting footpaths and erecting bridges across streams. It became part of the Peak National Park created in 1951. Swythamley and Onecote were also included in the Park.

PARISH GOVERNMENT. The parish was divided into the quarters of Leek and Lowe (including the town of Leek), Bradnop (consisting of the townships of Bradnop and Onecote), Endon (consisting of Endon, Longsdon, and Stanley), and Leekfrith (consisting of Heaton, Leekfrith, Rudyard, Rushton James, Rushton Spencer, and Tittesworth). The division had been made by 1609,[17] and probably by 1553 when there were four churchwardens.[18] In the 1660s each quarter had its own local meeting place for the passing of its warden's accounts. In 1698, however, those accounts were passed at a general meeting of parishioners in the chancel of Leek parish church.[19] In 1654 the inhabitants of Rushton chapelry (covering the townships of Heaton, Rushton James, and Rushton Spencer) claimed exemption from serving the office of churchwarden for Leekfrith quarter on the ground that they already served as chapelwardens.[20] By 1725 the churchwardens were appointed

17 L.J.R.O., B/C/5/1609, Leek.
18 S.H.C. 1915, 146.
19 S.R.O., D. 1040/7, p. 24.
20 Ibid. Q/SO/6, f. 11.

by the vicar from lists of three names submitted in writing at Easter by the inhabitants of each quarter.[21] Only the Leek warden survived the creation of new parishes in the 19th century, with the office filled by the vicar from three names submitted by the St. Edward's vestry at its Easter meeting. The office of warden of Leek survived the appointment of district wardens following the creation of a team ministry for Leek in 1979.[22]

Each quarter had its own overseer of the poor by the 1660s.[23] By 1711 the movement of population into the town of Leek from the Leekfrith, Bradnop, and Endon quarters had created a burden on the Leek and Lowe quarter. That year the parishioners agreed that for a period of five years each quarter should be regarded as a separate parish for settlement purposes, an arrangement confirmed by the justices for Totmonslow hundred in 1712. Under the agreement the quarters outside the town were responsible for poor persons living in the town but having settlement in those quarters. In 1717 the overseers and several parishioners petitioned to have the arrangement made permanent.[24] Meanwhile in 1713 Leekfrith quarter was divided for purposes of poor relief into its constituent townships, each with its own overseer.[25] By 1743 Bradnop and Onecote townships too each had its own overseer.[26] Around 1700 money was collected for the poor and sick at celebrations of holy communion and distributed by the churchwardens; any such money not distributed was put in the poor's box.[27] There was a poorhouse in the parish by the 1740s.[28] It may have been in Derby Street in Leek, where by the late 1750s the vestry was renting a house from Lord Macclesfield for use as a poorhouse. In 1759 the vestry decided to end the lease.[29] A poorhouse on the east side of Ladderedge common in Longsdon in the mid 1770s was presumably for Endon quarter.[30] In 1768 a workhouse was built in Leek for Leek and Lowe township. All the townships were included in Leek poor-law union on its formation in 1837,[31] and a union workhouse was opened in Leek in 1839.

A few officers were appointed for the parish as a whole. There was a parish clerk by 1443.[32] By the late 1690s the clerk and the sexton were appointed by the vicar.[33] Besides fees the clerk then received seed oats, or money in lieu, from the parishioners at Easter.[34] In 1754 the vestry agreed to pay him a salary of £5 instead of oats, a figure raised to £10 in 1774.[35] By the late 1690s the sexton not only received burial dues but was paid £3 a year for looking after the bells and clock at St. Edward's and for cleaning the church every week.[36] He received 5s. for ringing the curfew bell at Leek. By the 1730s he was paid 4d. an hour for tolling the bell at Leek, Meerbrook, and Endon.[37] By 1725 the churchwardens were providing clothes for a dog whipper; by 1799 he was paid a salary.[38] In the late 18th century a mole catcher was paid 1s. a year by the churchwardens.[39]

21 Ibid. D. 1040/7, p. 78.
22 Docs. at St. Edward's ch., Leek, vestry min. bk. 1817–1959, pp. 156, 158, 162; *Leek Parish Church of St. Edward the Confessor* (Leek, earlier 1970s), p. xxxi; inf. from Mr. W. F. Brooks, warden of Leek.
23 *Leek Par. Reg.* 151–2.
24 B.L. Add. MS. 36663, ff. 396–400; S.R.O., Q/SO/11, M. 1711.
25 Leek Libr., Johnson scrapbk. ii (3), no. 12.
26 S.R.O., D. 3816/3/1.
27 Ibid. D. 1040/7, pp. 24, 28, 40.

28 Ibid. D. 1040/5/14, 4 June 1741, 3 Apr. 1742.
29 Ibid. D. 3359/Condlyffe, memo. 24 Nov. 1759.
30 Ibid. D. 4302/1/4; above, fig. 2.
31 Ibid. D. 699/1/1/1, p. 4.   32 *S.H.C.* N.S. iii. 163.
33 L.J.R.O., B/V/6/Leek, 1698.
34 S.R.O., D. 1040/5/3, f. 167; D. 1040/5/14.
35 Ibid. D. 1040/7, pp. 124, 172.
36 L.J.R.O., B/V/6/Leek, 1698.
37 S.R.O., D. 1040/5/3, f. 165v.
38 Ibid. D. 1040/7, pp. 79 sqq., 242.
39 Ibid. pp. 204, 208, 211.

LEEK AND LOWE

(THE TOWN OF LEEK)

THE township of Leek and Lowe, 2,722 a. (1,105 ha.) in area, included the town of Leek and a rural area to the east, south, and west. There were also three detached areas, one adjoining the Poolend area of Leekfrith, another on the east side of the Buxton road at Blackshaw Moor, and a small area on the south bank of the river Churnet north of the town.[40] A market centre by the 13th century and a centre of the silk industry from the 18th century, the town was described in 1793 as the capital of the Moorlands and in the later 19th century as both the metropolis and the queen of the Moorlands.[41] The style Queen of the Moorlands was used on the signs erected in 1992 on five roads entering the town.[42] In 1894 the built-up area was taken into the new Leek urban district and civil parish, and the area to the south became the civil parish of Leek and Lowe, renamed Lowe in 1895. The detached portions at Poolend and Blackshaw Moor were added to the civil parishes of Leekfrith and Tittesworth respectively, and the detached portion by the Churnet became part of the urban district. Lowe civil parish was taken into the urban district in 1934.[43] In 1974 the urban district became a parish in the new district of Staffordshire Moorlands. The present article deals with the former township, but for certain topics it also includes that part of the former Tittesworth township which has become a north-eastern suburb of Leek town. The detached portion at Poolend is treated in the article on Leekfrith, and that at Blackshaw Moor in the article on Tittesworth.

The boundary of Leek and Lowe township was formed by various watercourses except on the north-east: the Churnet on the north-west and west, Leek brook on the south, Kniveden brook, so named by the early 13th century,[44] on the east, and Ball Haye brook (now culverted) on the north. Ball Haye brook may be the earlier Church brook, mentioned in 1281 as 'kyrke-broke' and in 1569 as a tributary of the Churnet.[45] The name Leek may derive from either the Old English lece or the Old Norse loekr, both meaning brook.[46] The brook perhaps the stream called the Spout Water running down what is now Brook Street (formerly Spout Lane) and the north side of Broad Street, or its tributary which ran from a spring in St. Edward's churchyard down the west side of St. Edward Street (formerly Spout Street).[47]

The ground rises from below 500 ft. (152 m.) in the flat valley bottoms of the Churnet and Leek brook to 800 ft. (244 m.) on the eastern boundary around Kniveden. The town stands on a spur which is c. 2 miles east–west and c. 1 mile north–south. At the west end Westwood occupies a plateau at 625 ft. (191 m.) from which steep slopes run down to the Churnet on the north, west, and south. The plateau is linked to the higher ground on the east by a broad col from which the ground rises to the small hill occupied by the medieval town. St. Edward's church stands at the highest point, 649 ft. (198 m.), with a steep slope on the north down to Ball Haye brook. The market place and the main streets occupy gentler slopes running south and south-east to a small valley which includes Brook Street. The underlying rock in the western part of the area of the former township is Sherwood Sandstone, through which several of the approaches to the town are cut. In the eastern part the rock is sandstone of the Millstone Grit series. There is Boulder Clay over the rock in the Ball Haye Green area and alluvium along the Churnet. The soil is mostly loam, with sandy soil south of the town.[48]

In 1086 Leek had a recorded population of 28; in addition there is likely to have been at least one priest.[49] About 1220 there were 80½ burgages.[50] In 1327 eight people were assessed for tax in Leek 'cum membris' and 14 in Lowe, while in 1333 there were 33 in both combined.[51] In 1666 the number assessed for hearth tax was 76 in Leek and 17 in Lowe hamlet.[52] The population of Leek and Lowe township was 3,489 in 1801 and 3,703 in 1811. It rose to 4,855 in 1821 and 6,374 in 1831 and then grew steadily to reach 12,760 in 1891.[53]

The population of the urban district in 1901 was 15,484 and of the civil parish of Lowe 176. The figures were 16,663 and 192 in 1911, 17,214 and 255 in 1921, and 18,567 and 299 in 1931. The enlarged urban district had a population of 19,356 in 1951, 19,182 in 1961, and 19,452 in 1971. The population of Leek parish was 19,724 in 1981 and 19,518 in 1991.[54]

40 Census, 1881, 1891. A detached portion of 1 a. was transferred to Tittesworth under the Divided Parishes Act, 1882. This article was written in 1991–2, with some additions in 1993 and 1994. Mr. Paul Anderton of Newcastle-under-Lyme and others named in footnotes are thanked for their help.
41 P. Lead, Caldon Canal and Tramroads (Headington, 1990), 51; S. Lewis, Topog. Dict. Eng. (1831), iii. 49; Sleigh, Leek (1862), 1; Olde Leeke, i. 109. The name Queen of the Moorlands was used for a fire engine bought in 1898: below, public services.
42 Leek Post & Times, 20 May 1992, p. 5.
43 Below, local govt. (intro; improvement com. and urban dist. council); Leekfrith, intro.; Tittesworth, intro.
44 S.R.O., D. 5041, p. 129.
45 Ibid. D. (W.) 1761/A/4/168; B.L. Add. MS. 36665, f. 3.

46 N.S.J.F.S. xxi. 5–6.
47 Sleigh, Leek, 210 n.; S.R.O., D. 3359/Condlyffe, draft of deed 1746, Sutton and Goostrey; D. 3359/Strangman, deed of 2 Oct. 1764; D. 3359/Cruso, docs. relating to Spout Croft, 1787; below, local govt. (poor relief); public services (water supplies: drinking fountains).
48 Geol. Surv. Map 1/50,000, drift, sheet 111 (1978 edn.); solid with drift, sheet 124 (1983 edn.); Soil Surv. of Eng. and Wales, sheet 3 (1983).
49 Below, econ. hist. (agric.); churches (St. Edward's).
50 Below, local govt. (borough).
51 S.H.C. vii (1), 218–19; x (1), 115.
52 S.H.C. 1925, 164–6, 241–2.
53 V.C.H. Staffs. i. 328, which, however, gives 12,783 for 1891; Census, 1891, gives 12,760.
54 Census, 1901–91.

EARLY SETTLEMENT. The name Lowe may be derived from a burial mound. Two have been identified within the area of the former township. Cock Low, recorded as 'Catteslowe' in the later 16th century and as Cock Lowe or Great Lowe in 1723,[55] stood south- west of the town between Waterloo Road and Spring Gardens. In 1851, when it was described as 40 yd. in diameter and 18 ft. high, an excavation uncovered a flint implement and fragments of an urn and of human bone. The mound was destroyed in 1907 in the course of the development of the area, but an urn containing a cremation burial of the early or middle Bronze Age was discovered and also a heart-shaped carved stone.[56] In 1859 workmen digging in Birchall meadows west of the Cheddleton road broke into a mound where a cinerary urn was discovered.[57] A Roman road ran through the Leek area, and coins forming part of a hoard found 2 miles south of the town in the earlier 1770s were said to bear the inscription of the Gallic emperor Victorinus (269–71).[58]

THE MIDDLE AGES. Leek was probably an ecclesiastical centre c. 1000. In the later 12th and early 13th century it was a stopping place for the earls of Chester, the lords of Leek manor, who may have had a house there. Standing at the junction of several roads, the town was a commercial centre by the 13th century. In 1207 the king confirmed to Earl Ranulph a weekly market and an annual seven-day fair, and the earl established a borough probably about the same time. In 1214 he founded Dieulacres abbey beside the Churnet a mile north of the town and in 1232 granted Leek manor to the monks, who renewed the borough charter.

Until the 19th century the town consisted mainly of the area round the market place and of the streets leading off it, presumably the plan of the early 13th-century borough. Originally the market place probably extended to the west side of what is now St. Edward Street, thus forming the north-west corner of the town. The convergence of roads on the north-west, south-west and east sides of the town and the pattern of property boundaries suggest that the medieval town may have had a hard boundary, perhaps an earth bank pierced with gates.[59] The town was ravaged by fire in 1297,[60] but that presumably did not alter its plan.

There was also settlement along the road to Macclesfield on the north-west side of the town and the road to Newcastle-under-Lyme on the south-west. The first gave access to a mill by the Churnet, and the stretch by the mill was known as Mill Street by the earlier 16th century when a suburb had grown up there.[61] The steep part down from the town, also known as Mill Street by the earlier 19th century, was simply 'the hollow lane' in the later 17th century.[62] Abbey Green Road, which branches north from the Macclesfield road to cross the Churnet at Broad's bridge,[63] was presumably a road leading to Dieulacres abbey in the Middle Ages. It formed part of the road from Leek to Buxton (Derb.) until the later 18th century. A way evidently ran from the area of St. Edward's church down to Abbey Green Road along what is now Brow Hill footpath parallel to Mill Street and may have been another medieval route to the abbey. There was probably a medieval road to Westwood 1 mile west of the town, where Dieulacres had established a grange by 1291. Another probably linked the abbey and the grange along the present Kiln Lane, which continues Abbey Green Road across the Macclesfield road.

The Newcastle road, which crosses the Churnet at Wall bridge, was presumably the medieval Wall Street, where there was a burgage in the 13th century and where several people were living in the 1330s.[64] There may have been settlement at Woodcroft on the west side of the Newcastle road by the early 13th century, when there was mention of three bondmen at Wildecroft in the earl of Chester's fee of Leek.[65]

Moorhouse south-east of the medieval town may have been an occupied site by the 13th century.[66] By 1503 the house had passed by marriage from the Bailey family to John Jodrell of Yeardsley, in Taxall (Ches.), and it was still the home of the Jodrell family in 1700. Probably soon afterwards it passed to the Grosvenor family, which owned the 65-a. Moorhouse farm in the mid 19th century.[67] The farm survived in the earlier 20th century.[68]

In the area south of the town there was evidently settlement in the area of the present Ballington wood by the early 13th century, when Ralph of Baliden was a tenant in the fee of Leek.[69] Further south Dieulacres had established a grange at Birchall by 1246. Lowe Hill was probably an inhabited area by the earlier 14th century.[70] There was a farm at Kniveden to the north by 1535, when it was held of

55 Sleigh, *Leek*, 33 n.; *T.N.S.F.C.* lviii. 81; S.R.O., D. 3359/Cruso, deed of 22 Apr. 1587. Unless otherwise indicated, the sources for statements in this section are given in the relevant sections later in the article.
56 Staffs. C.C., Sites and Monuments Rec. 00350; T. Bateman, *Ten Years' Diggings* (1861), 183; *Memorials of Old Staffs.* ed. W. Beresford, 269–71.
57 Staffs. C.C., Sites and Monuments Rec. 00351; *Staffs. Advertiser*, 26 Nov. 1859, p. 5.
58 *Gent. Mag.* xlvi (1), 540, 591.
59 *Plan of Leek 1838.* Before turnpiking in the 1760s the road east from the town may have followed Fountain St.
60 C. Lynam, *Abbey of St. Mary, Croxden, Staffs.*, translation of chronicle, p. v.
61 S.R.O., D. 259/M/1; W.S.L., M. 540; P.R.O., SC

6/202/65, m. 3.
62 S.R.O., D. 3359/misc. deeds, deed of 17 Feb. 1662/3. *Acct. of Convincement and Call to the Ministry of Margaret Lucas, late of Leek, Staffs.* (1797), 80, mentions 'the precipice' below Overton Bank.
63 Its name was changed from Broad Bridge Rd. to Abbey Green Rd. c. 1860: *Staffs. Advertiser*, 13 Jan. 1855, p. 8; P.R.O., RG 9/1946. For the bridge see below, Leekfrith, intro.
64 Sleigh, *Leek*, 148; S.R.O., D. 1337/2, dorse.
65 *Staffs. Studies*, v. 8, 10.
66 Sleigh, *Leek*, 150; S.R.O., D. 1331/1, m. 5.
67 Sleigh, *Leek*, 32, 94; *S.H.C.* v (2), 191; S.R.O., D. 843/1/4.   68 *Kelly's Dir. Staffs.* (1932; 1940).
69 *Staffs. Studies*, v. 8.
70 *S.H.C.* x (1), 115; S.R.O., D. 1333/1, m. 5d.

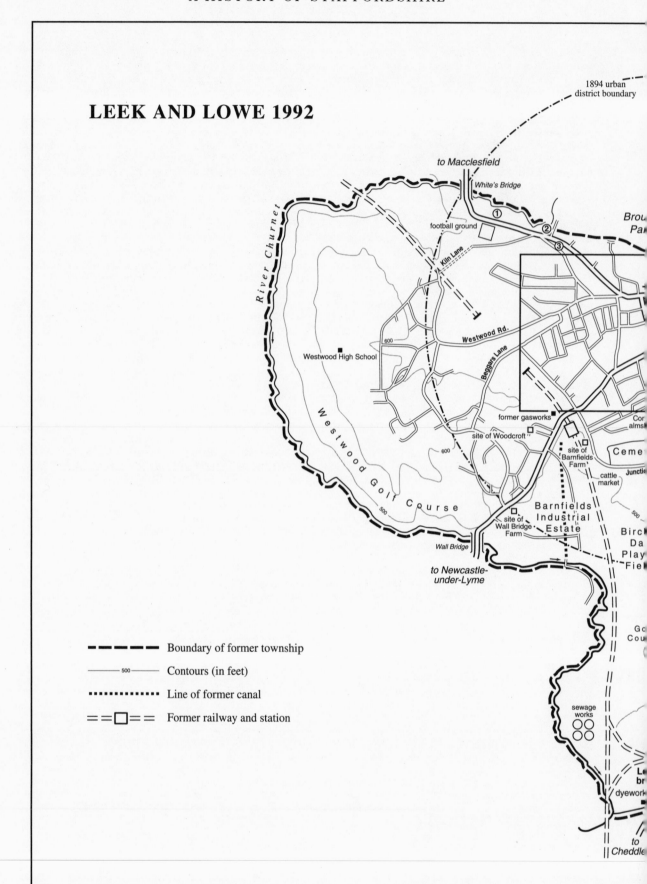

LEEK AND LOWE 1992

Boundary of former township
Contours (in feet)
Line of former canal
Former railway and station

FIG. 15

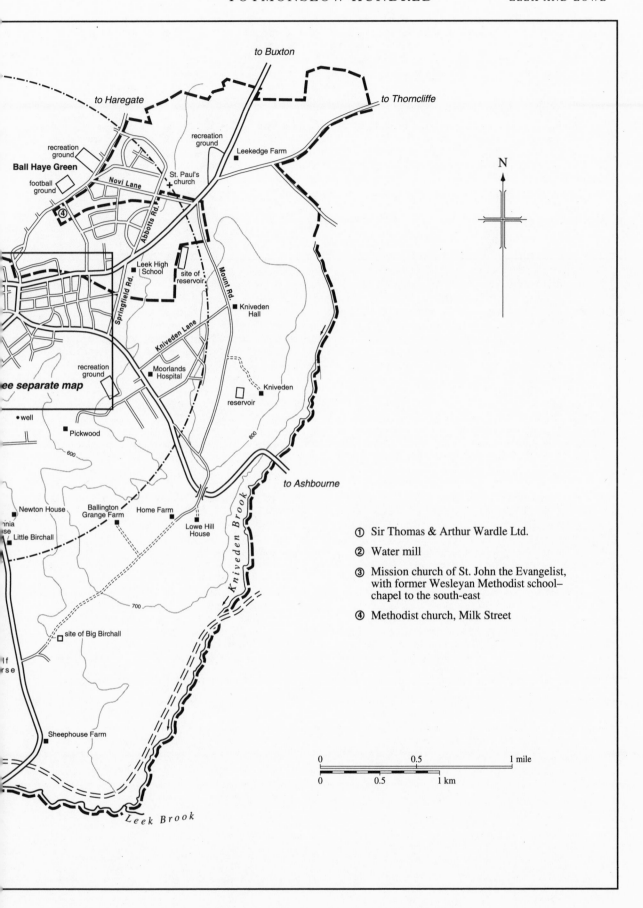

to Buxton

to Thorncliffe

to Haregate

recreation ground

recreation ground

Leekedge Farm

Ball Haye Green

football ground

Novi Lane

St. Paul's church

④

Abbotts Rd.

Leek High School

site of reservoir

Mount Rd.

Kniveden Hall

Springfield Rd.

Kniveden Lane

ee separate map

recreation ground

Moorlands Hospital

Kniveden

reservoir

800

• well

Pickwood

600

to Ashbourne

Kniveden Brook

Newton House

Ballington Grange Farm

Home Farm

nnia se

Little Birchall

Lowe Hill House

700

lf rse

□ site of Big Birchall

N

Sheephouse Farm

Leek Brook

① Sir Thomas & Arthur Wardle Ltd.

② Water mill

③ Mission church of St. John the Evangelist, with former Wesleyan Methodist school–chapel to the south-east

④ Methodist church, Milk Street

0		0.5		1 mile
0	0.5		1 km	

Dieulacres by Thomas Smith;[71] having bought it in 1562, the family remained there until the 1840s when they moved to the nearby Dee Bank Farm.[72] At the Dissolution Dieulacres had a farm called Sheephouse on the Cheddleton road near the southern boundary.[73]

The spring south of the town to the east of the Cheddleton road was evidently named in honour of Our Lady in the Middle Ages. The area was known as Lady Wall Dale in the late 16th century,[74] and the spring is now called as Lady o' th' Dale well. A 19th-century stone structure survives there. Within living memory the water was used by local people for healing purposes, and there was also a May Day procession to the site by children from St. Mary's Roman Catholic church.[75]

THE 16TH AND 17TH CENTURIES. Dieulacres abbey was dissolved in 1538, and the town's borough status seems to have been lost after the grant of most of the abbey's property, including Leek manor, to Sir Ralph Bagnall in 1552. At the beginning of the 17th century the town was noted for its market, which in the 1670s was one of the three most important in Staffordshire. On the other hand the buildings were then 'but poor and for the most part thatched'.[76]

It is likely that all or most of the surviving timber-framed buildings are of the 16th or 17th century, although later encased in stone or brick. Nos. 2–4 Clerk Bank and the Black Swan inn in Sheepmarket contain cruck frames. Nos. 2–4 Church Street on the north side of the market place incorporate the remains of a 16th-century timber-framed building, whose front was probably jettied. At the rear is another timber-framed building, originally detached, which has a large fireplace and may have been a kitchen. In the 17th century the front of the house was reconstructed in stone and a timber staircase turret and an attic floor were added. The work may well have been carried out for Thomas Parker, a lawyer, between 1662 and 1666.[77] The largest timber-framed building was probably the Hall House, later the Red Lion inn, on the east side of the market place. It was built, apparently in 1607, by Thomas Jolliffe, who like earlier members of his family had prospered in the wool trade. It contained an ornamented plaster ceiling

with a representation of the triumph of death, now preserved at the School of Art. It was later refronted, apparently in 1791.[78] The ornamental framing of the Roebuck inn of 1626 in Derby Street[79] and of the former Black's Head at the south end of the market place[80] suggests that the use of timber could be for display. Stone, however, had become the normal building material by the late 17th century.[81] Its use is visible in party walls, as at no. 47 Derby Street and no. 13 St. Edward Street. Another example of a stone house is no. 7 Stockwell Street, where despite an 18th-century brick façade a stone gable is visible. By the late 17th century, on the evidence of Greystones in Stockwell Street, a symmetrical stone front was fashionable, although the windows there still have stone mullions.

The streets around the market place can be traced by name from the 17th century only, those on the west side probably being encroachments. Church Street was so named by 1634.[82] St. Edward Street was formerly Spout Street, a name in use by 1637; the present name was adopted in 1866.[83] Sheepmarket was evidently a street by 1646.[84] Stanley Street was formerly Custard Street, a name which may have been derived from costard, a large kind of apple; it too was renamed in 1866.[85] East of the market place Stockwell Street (also known as Stockwood Street in the 1690s) and Derby Street were so named by the 1630s.[86] There were no streets in the area between them until the 19th century.

The earliest known inn is the Swan, in existence by the 1560s.[87] It may not, however, be identifiable with the present Swan on the corner of St. Edward Street and Mill Street, which existed as the Green Dragon by 1693 and was still so called in 1750. It was known as the Angel in 1781 and as the Swan in 1786.[88] The Roebuck in Derby Street is dated 1626, although the earliest known mention of an inn of that name is in 1773.[89] The Cock on the corner of the market place and Stockwell Street existed by 1666 and was sold by the Mellor family to John Toft of Haregate, in Tittesworth, in 1728.[90] In 1740 it had 18 rooms with one or more beds in them.[91] It was converted into a bank in the earlier 1820s, but a new Cock inn was opened nearby.[92] There was a Red Lion by 1698; its site is not known, but the Hall House in the market place had been turned into an inn of that name by 1751.[93]

71 S.H.C. 1912, 78; W.S.L., M. 540.
72 Sleigh, Leek, 56 n.; Leek Par. Reg. passim; P.O. Dir. Staffs. (1850); P.R.O., HO 107/1005; S.R.O., D. 1176/10/14, showing the Revd. Thos. Smith as owner of Kniveden in 1883. 73 W.S.L., M. 540.
74 S.R.O., D. 3359/Cruso, deed of 10 Sept. 1587.
75 Inf. from Mrs. L. W. Skellam of Leek.
76 R. Blome, Britannia (1673), 205.
77 Account based on Chronicles (autumn 1994), 38 sqq., with some of the details reinterpreted.
78 Sleigh, Leek, 33; Olde Leeke, ii. 102–5; S.R.O., D. 3272/1/4/3/25; Leek Libr., newspaper cuttings 1980 (2), p. 8; 1991, pp. 21–2.
79 Below, this sub-section.
80 Below, this section (18th cent.).
81 Plot, Staffs. 167.
82 S.R.O., D. (W.) 1702/1/14, deed of 20 June 1634.
83 Leek Par. Reg. 16; S.R.O., D. 3226/2, no. 1787; above, intro. 84 Leek Par. Reg. 66; B.L. Add. Ch. 46789.

85 J. Wright, Eng. Dialect Dict. i. 738; S.R.O., D. 3226/2, no. 1787.
86 Leek Par. Reg. 18, 20; L.J.R.O., B/C/11, Rob. Hulme (1634); S.R.O., D. 3359/misc. deeds, deed of 3 Apr. 1693.
87 Sleigh, Leek, 8, 123 n.
88 Olde Leeke, ii. 193; S.R.O., D. (W.) 1702/1/13, deeds of 14 Mar. 1692/3, 8 Jan. 1749/50; ibid. D. 4647/7.
89 S.R.O., D. 239/M/3849; below, plate 43. The statement in Sleigh, Leek, 10, that it was moved to Leek from a site in Shropshire seems improbable.
90 S.R.O., D. 1040/5/2, accts. of churchwarden of Bradnop quarter 1667; D. 3359/Toft-Chorley, deed of 9 Nov. 1728. 91 L.J.R.O., B/C/11, Wm. Statham (1740).
92 Leek & Moorlands Heritage, i, p. 4; Chronicles (spring 1988), 4–5; White, Dir. Staffs. (1834), 709; Plan of Leek 1838.
93 S.R.O., D. 1040/5/2, marriage of 28 Nov. 1698; D. 1040/7, p. 84; D. 3359/Condlyffe, deed of 12 Nov. 1751. The Hall House was still mentioned as such in 1730: D. 3272/1/4/33.

There was settlement on the west side of the town by the earlier 17th century, probably as a result of the piecemeal inclosure of Leek field, in progress by the end of the 16th century. Barngates and Beggars Way (presumably the later Beggars Lane) were inhabited areas by 1638,[94] and c. 1670 a few houses were built in Back of the Street (later Belle Vue Road) on the north-west side of the field.[95] Barnfields farm east of the Newcastle road evidently existed by 1675.[96] East of the Cheddleton road Ballington Grange Farm existed as Cowhay Farm by 1608.[97] The main part of the nearby Home Farm (formerly Bone Farm) carries the date 1628, although the cross wing is probably a little earlier. There was settlement on Leek moor east of the town by the 1630s.[98]

During the Civil War Leek, like the Moorlands generally, was strongly parliamentarian. A royalist force came into the Leek area in November 1642 but was driven away.[99] In February 1643 a band of Moorlanders mounted an unsuccessful attack on Stafford. They appealed to the parliamentary commanders in Cheshire and Derbyshire for assistance but received only an offer of a few men to be sent to Leek to help with training.[1] By May a parliamentary garrison had been established at Leek, and its commander, Lt.-Col. Peter Stepkin, and some of the Moorlanders played a prominent part in the capture of Stafford that month.[2] Royalist forces under Lord Eythin entered Leek in December.[3] By March 1644, however, a parliamentary committee had been set up there; it was one of three in Staffordshire, the others being at Stafford and Tamworth.[4] In May Col. John Bowyer of Knypersley in Biddulph was appointed governor of Leek.[5] When he took the garrison to help in the attack on Shrewsbury in February 1645, townships in Totmonslow hundred were ordered to send armed watchmen to guard Leek.[6] Arrangements were still being made in September 1647 for quartering troops in the Leek area.[7]

THE 18TH CENTURY. Although Samuel Johnson, visiting Leek in 1777, pronounced it 'a poor town',[8] the 18th century saw a marked increase in its prosperity. By the middle of the century there were seven annual fairs, with an eighth by the 1790s. The silk industry had reached the town by the 1670s and developed steadily in the 18th century, with buttons as the staple product. By the end of the century, though still a domestic industry, it employed some 2,000 people in the town and 1,000 in the neighbourhood. In the course of the century dyeing became established in the area at the junction of Mill Street and Abbey Green Road, using the water of the Churnet. Communications were improved with the turnpiking of the five main roads into the town in the earlier 1760s. In the course of the 18th century the town was supplied with water piped from two reservoirs on Leek moor.

The town was largely rebuilt in the 18th century with brick replacing stone as the dominant building material. The former grammar school of 1723 in Clerk Bank has a symmetrical ashlar front, but by the middle of the century red brick had become the fashionable material for frontages. In St. Edward's Street no. 64, with rain-water hoppers dated 1747, has a brick front which rises to three full storeys; it contrasts with no. 62, dated 1724, which has an ashlar front of two storeys with attics. The more important houses built after the middle of the century are generally of three storeys and have parapets. Most have a moulded stone cornice, whilst the smaller houses have a wooden cornice or no cornice at all.

By 1749 there was an inn at the south end of the market place known then and in 1764 variously as the Buffalo's Head and the Bull's Head. In 1764 the lane to the south-east running down to what is now Brook Street was called Blackmoreshead Lane, and the inn was known as the Blackmoor's Head by 1773.[9] Recorded as the Blackamoor's Head in 1818, it was the Black's Head by the early 1820s.[10] The timber-framed building[11] was rebuilt in the late 1850s to the design of William Sugden, and in 1931 the inn was converted into a 'fancy bazaar' by F. W. Woolworth & Co. Ltd.[12] The George, a coaching inn on the corner of Spout Street and Church Street, existed by 1776 and was probably built in the 1760s.[13] The Golden Lion in Church Street existed by 1786, and probably by 1756 when the house on the site was sold to the tenant, William Allen, described as an innholder.[14] Both the George and the Golden Lion were demolished in 1972 for the widening of Church Street.[15]

Pickwood farm south-east of the town evidently existed by 1705, and Samuel Toft, a button merchant, had cattle and goods there worth £29 at the time of his death, evidently in 1732.[16] Wall Bridge farm off the Newcastle road existed by 1775.[17]

Thomas Parker (1667–1732) was born at the

94 *Leek Par. Reg.* 23–4, 49, 51–2; Sleigh, *Leek*, 189 n.; S.R.O., D. (W.) 1702/1/14, 9 May 1640; B.L. Add. Ch. 41824.
95 P.R.O., E 134/6 Geo. I East./21; S.R.O. 3508/A/3/10; *Leek Par. Reg.* 220, 225, 249.   96 *S.H.C.* 1948–9, 103, 106–7.
97 *Leek Par. Reg.* 199.
98 Ibid. 8, 33, 42, 78, 84.
99 *Chronicles* (autumn 1994), 8.
1 Ibid. 9, 11–12; *S.H.C.* 4th ser. i, p. lxii.
2 *S.H.C.* 4th ser. i, p. lxiii.
3 Ibid. pp. lxiv, 8–9, 11, 14–15; *Chronicles* (autumn 1994), 14.   4 *S.H.C.* 4th ser. i, pp. xxiv, 61, 85.
5 Ibid. 121, 238, 242, 246; *S.H.C.* 1920 and 1922, 72–4.
6 *S.H.C.* 4th ser. i, pp. lxxi, 274–5.
7 D.R.O., D. 1232M/O73.
8 *Letters of Samuel Johnson*, ed. R. W. Chapman, ii, p.

226.
9 S.R.O., D. 3359/Strangman, deeds of 26 Jan. 1748/9, 2 Oct. 1764; D. 3359/Condlyffe, deed of 9 Jan. 1773. The lane was known as Pickwood Rd. by 1838: *Plan of Leek 1838*.
10 Parson and Bradshaw, *Staffs. Dir.* (1818), 125; Pigot, *New Com. Dir. for 1822–3*, 469.   11 Below, plate 42.
12 W.S.L., Sleigh scrapbk. i, f. 55; ii, f. 68; *Olde Leeke*, i. 169; G. A. Lovenbury, *Sugdens of Leek* (1975), 16; *Kelly's Dir. Staffs.* (1932); *Leek Post & Times*, 9 Oct. 1991, p. 6.
13 Sleigh, *Leek*, 10; *Chronicles* (autumn 1992), 24.
14 S.R.O., D. 3124/10 and 19.
15 Leek Libr., newspaper cuttings 1969–72, pp. 45, 67, 70.
16 S.R.O., D. 3359/misc. deeds, deed of 26 Mar. 1705; L.J.R.O., B/C/11, Sam. Toft (1732).
17 Above, fig. 2; below, plate 1.

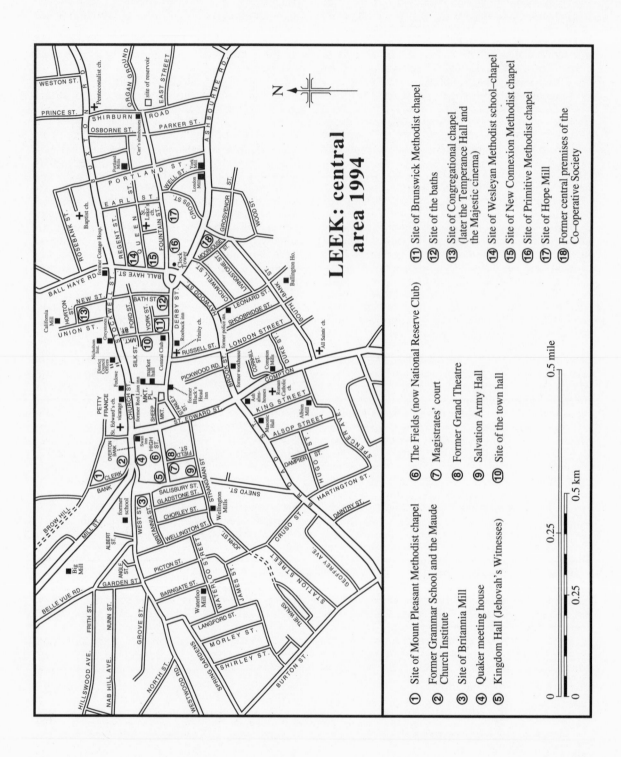

LEEK: central area 1994

① Site of Mount Pleasant Methodist chapel
② Former Grammar School and the Maude Church Institute
③ Site of Britannia Mill
④ Quaker meeting house
⑤ Kingdom Hall (Jehovah's Witnesses)
⑥ The Fields (now National Reserve Club)
⑦ Magistrates' court
⑧ Former Grand Theatre
⑨ Salvation Army Hall
⑩ Site of the town hall
⑪ Site of Brunswick Methodist chapel
⑫ Site of the baths
⑬ Site of Congregational chapel (later the Temperance Hall and the Majestic cinema)
⑭ Site of Wesleyan Methodist school–chapel
⑮ Site of New Connexion Methodist chapel
⑯ Site of Primitive Methodist chapel
⑰ Site of Hope Mill
⑱ Former central premises of the Co-operative Society

FIG. 16

house now nos. 2–4 Church Street, the son of Thomas Parker, a lawyer. Appointed Lord Chief Justice in 1710, he was created Baron Parker of Macclesfield in 1716 and earl of Macclesfield in 1721. He was Lord Chancellor from 1718 to 1725, when he was impeached for corruption and found guilty.[18] He bought the manor of Leek in 1723, and the same year he built the grammar school.

In 1715 several people in Leek declared for the Pretender, and the mob damaged the Presbyterian meeting house.[19] There is little evidence of such Jacobite sympathies in 1745 when Prince Charles Edward and his army passed through Leek on their way to Derby and again on their retreat north.[20] On 3 December a detachment under Lord George Murray passed through Leek on its way to Ashbourne. The main force with the prince arrived in Leek later the same day and took up quarters there, the prince staying at the house (later called Foxlowe) of William Mills, a lawyer. The Quaker meeting house was broken into and used as a stable. The troops began to leave for Ashbourne and Derby in the small hours of the 4th. Some remained behind and tried to seize the horses of people coming to the market; two of the soldiers were arrested and sent to Stafford gaol. The prince, retreating from Derby, was back in Leek on 7 December. The vanguard of his army went on to Macclesfield and the rest followed on the 8th. The houses of the principal inhabitants of Leek were reported as 'totally stripped and plundered', apparently in revenge for the arrest of the two horse thieves. The duke of Cumberland passed through Leek with the pursuing force on the 10th and was entertained in the market place.

THE EARLIER 19TH CENTURY. In the 1830s Leek was described as one of the handsomest market towns in Staffordshire.[21] Spout Street was the main residential street by the early 19th century and had several large houses. Derby Street had a few large houses and several smaller ones, and Stockwell Street contained c. 30 houses.[22] In 1826 a foreign visitor noted 'stone houses with gable windows decorated with balls and acroteria, thatched roof above. Brick buildings with attractive mouldings and brick gables.'[23]

The town's silk industry continued to develop in the earlier 19th century, and the first mills were established. A dyeworks was opened at Leekbrook in 1830 by Joshua Wardle. In the 1820s a fortnightly cattle market was introduced during part of the year and new fairs were started. In 1825 a body of improvement commissioners was set up for the town. A gas works was opened on the Newcastle road by the Leek Gas Light Co. in 1827. In 1837 Leek became the centre of a poor-law union. A branch canal was opened in 1801 from the Caldon canal in Endon to a wharf and basin off the Newcastle road; the part of the road from there to the town, known as Spooner's Lane by the 1660s,[24] was Canal Street by 1838.[25] The Churnet Valley railway was opened through the area west of the town in 1849 with a station on the Newcastle road.

By the 1820s the town was expanding on all sides. On the east a suburb grew up on either side of Fountain Street, an older road evidently taking its name from the 18th-century reservoir at its eastern end. It was linked with the Buxton road by the later 18th century, apparently along the line of what was called Osborne Street by 1838.[26] There were buildings along the Buxton and Ashbourne roads by 1820, and Cross Street and Well Street off the Ashbourne road were built up by then; there were also a few buildings in Fountain Street itself.[27] Ball Haye Street, Queen Street, Earl Street, and King Street (renamed Regent Street by 1834) had been laid out by 1826.[28] The part of Portland Street between Fountain Street and the Buxton road existed by 1834.[29] The Ashbourne road was known as London Road by 1838; it was renamed Ashbourne Road at the beginning of the 20th century.[30] An ecclesiastical parish centring on the suburb was created in 1845, and St. Luke's church was opened in 1848 on a site between Queen Street and Fountain Street, where a school had been opened in 1847.

Compton, the northern part of the Cheddleton road, was so named by 1817.[31] Two streets to the west, Albion Street and King Street, were laid out in the mid 1820s and consisted mainly of silk weavers' cottages; Albion silk mill was completed in the late 1820s. A silk mill was opened in Workhouse (later Brook) Street in 1823–4, and silk weavers' cottages had been built in London Street to the south by the 1830s. Roebuck Lane to the east had been renamed Russell Street by 1848.[32]

On the west side of the town, land at Barngates was advertised in 1815 as a suitable site for a large factory.[33] Two brothers, Samuel and William Phillips, were silk manufacturers there in 1818. They lived in the early 19th-century house known as the Field. Samuel died in 1851 and

[18] *Complete Peerage*, viii. 332–3; Sleigh, *Leek*, 26–7, 30; *Olde Leeke*, i. 165–7; *Leek Par. Reg.* 99, 137.

[19] Sleigh, *Leek*, 202.

[20] Rest of para. based on Sleigh, *Leek*, 203–10; *T.N.S.F.C.* lx. 57–69; F. L. McLynn, *The Jacobite Army in Eng. 1745*, 113–14, 116–19, 142–4; Hist. MSS. Com. 55, *Var. Colln.* viii, p. 138. For the damage to the meeting house see also S.R.O., D. 4812/1/1, 5 Dec. 1745.

[21] White, *Dir. Staffs.* (1834), 697.

[22] J. Corry, *Hist. of Macclesfield* (1817), 256, 258.

[23] K. F. Schinkel, '*The English Journey*', ed. D. Bindman and G. Riemann, 132.

[24] S.R.O., D. 4645/A/1/4, 8, and 14; White, *Dir. Staffs.*

(1834), 706; Pigot, *Nat. Com. Dir.* (1835), 413.

[25] *Plan of Leek 1838*.

[26] W.S.L., Sleigh scrapbk. ii, f. 114v.; *Plan of Leek 1838*; above, fig. 2.

[27] C. and J. Greenwood, *Map of County of Stafford* (1820).

[28] W.S.L., Sleigh scrapbk. ii, f. 114v.; White, *Dir. Staffs.* (1834), 706.

[29] White, *Dir. Staffs.* (1834), 710; *Plan of Leek 1838*.

[30] *Plan of Leek 1838*; *Kelly's Dir. Staffs.* (1900; 1904).

[31] Corry, *Macclesfield*, 257–8; Greenwood, *Map of County of Stafford* (1820).

[32] *Plan of Leek 1838*; S.R.O., D. 1176/A/11/8.

[33] Sherlock, *Ind. Arch. Staffs.* 46.

William in 1871, and the house passed to Thomas Whittles.[34] West Street existed by 1829.[35] Back of the Street had been renamed Belle Vue by 1841.[36]

On the north side of the town Union Street and New Street had been laid out off Stockwell Street by 1829, when four silk manufacturers had premises there.[37] The street linking them was at first called New Street but was renamed Horton Street in 1866.[38]

The period saw the beginnings of a suburb north-east of the town and partly in Tittesworth township. In 1824 the Leek Building Society began the erection of 42 houses on the north side of the Haregate road at Ball Haye Green, all of which were completed by 1829. There were buildings on the opposite side of the road there by 1832.[39]

From 1803 French prisoners of war, mostly naval and military officers, were held at Leek, the last group arriving in 1812. Many were exchanged for British prisoners, and 44 escaped; at any one time there seem to have been around 140 in the town. Some were accompanied by servants and a few by their families. Two companies of militia and a squadron of yeomanry were assigned to guard the prisoners, who enjoyed considerable freedom. They were on parole to stay within a radius of one mile from the market place and were welcomed into local society. Most left with the coming of peace in 1814. Some married locally and stayed in Leek, the last dying in 1874.[40] The tradition that they lived in the area north of St. Edward's church which was becoming known as Petty France by 1816 is improbable; the houses there were built by James Fernyhough after he had bought the land in 1808. The name Petty France may derive from the proximity of the part of the churchyard where several prisoners were buried.[41]

In 1817 four hundred workers from Manchester arrived at Leek on their way to London to present their grievances to the government. They were known as the Blanketeers from the blankets which they carried with them. They were not allowed to stay in Leek and continued towards Ashbourne. A few hours after their departure Edward Powys, the incumbent of Cheddleton and a magistrate, called out the Leek troop of yeomanry and went in pursuit of the marchers. He caught up with them at Hanging Bridge on the county boundary in Mayfield and dispersed them. They then tried to return to Leek. Only about 30 succeeded, and they were escorted to Macclesfield by some of the 400 special constables sworn in by Powys.[42]

There was unrest in the town in the 1830s and 1840s. Attempts by handloom weavers to defend and improve rates of pay for piecework led to at least one strike in 1834.[43] A short-lived silk operatives' union had been formed by May that year when over 400 men and women marched through the town with considerable ceremony at the funeral of a fellow member.[44] The mill hands struck against a pay cut in 1838. A government commissioner who came to Leek later that year and John Richards, a Chartist missionary who formed a political union in the town in 1839, found many of the hands poverty-stricken and resentful.[45] In January 1842 the Leek branch (1840–6) of the Anti-Corn Law League sponsored a petition to the queen from the women of Leek that drew attention to working-class distress in the town.[46]

Leek became involved in the Chartist unrest later in 1842.[47] On Saturday 13 August groups of young men arrived in the town, claiming to be strikers from neighbouring manufacturing towns, and they went round begging at houses. The following day the Leek magistrates were warned that several thousand men who were occupying Congleton were preparing to march on Leek. The magistrates swore in at least 350 special constables and sent to the Potteries for troops. They seem also to have organized a mounted patrol of the parish. On the morning of 15 August the Newcastle and Pottery troop of yeomanry cavalry arrived. Young men and boys, armed with bludgeons, were already drifting into the town from the direction of Congleton, but the main body of marchers, variously estimated at 2,000 and 4,000 men, did not arrive until 11 a.m. They were mainly from Congleton and Macclesfield, with a few from Stockport and Manchester.

Preceded by a band, they marched into the market place, where they were confronted by the magistrates, the yeomanry, and the specials. There was a brief altercation, but when the marchers assured the magistrates that no violence was intended, they were allowed to pass. Some begged through the town in groups for food and money. Others went round the silk mills and dyeworks, forcing those that had not already been closed by a strike to shut. The marchers then went to the cattle market for a meeting at which their leaders called on the Leek workers present to join a general strike. In the afternoon most of the marchers returned to Congleton, but some remained to organize a march on the Potteries the following day, 16 August. They slept in a plantation on the Ball Haye estate and were fed by local sympathizers.

There were riots in the Potteries on 15 August,

34 Parson and Bradshaw, *Staffs. Dir.* (1818), 121; Pigot, *New Com. Dir. for 1822–3*, 468; Pigot, *New Com. Dir.* [1829], 712; White, *Dir. Staffs.* (1834), 707; (1851), 734; *P.O. Dir. Staffs.* (1850 and later edns.); below, Bradnop, manor (Ashenhurst).
35 Pigot, *New Com. Dir.* [1829], 713.
36 P.R.O., HO 107/1005.
37 Pigot, *New Com. Dir.* [1829], 713.
38 S.R.O., D. 3226/2, no. 1896; D. 3226/47, no. 340.
39 J. Phillips and W. F. Hutchings, *Map of County of Stafford* (1832).
40 *Leek and Moorlands Heritage*, ii. 8; Poole, *Leek*, 51–5; Miller, *Leek*, 69–70; *Staffs. Advertiser*, 29 Aug. 1874, p. 4; *Plan of Leek 1838*; W.S.L., Sleigh scrapbk. i, ff. 4, 56v.

41 Inf. from Mrs. C. Walton of Leek, citing entries of 1816 and 1823 in St. Edward's par. reg. and docs. held by Staffs. Moorlands Dist. Council.
42 *Olde Leeke*, ii. 92–3.
43 *Reps. Assistant Com. Handloom Weavers, Pt. IV* [217], p. 345, H.C. (1840), xxiv.
44 *Staffs. Advertiser*, 17 May 1834.
45 *Reps. Assistant Com. Handloom Weavers, Pt. IV*, 345–7; M. Hovell, *Chartist Movement* (1925), 131.
46 Miller, *Leek*, 114–18.
47 For the next 4 paras. see P.R.O., HO 45/260, ff. 238–40, 244–6, 258, 263–9, 327, 475; S.R.O., D. 3359/Cruso, Leek Riots 1842; *Staffs. Advertiser*, 20 Aug. 1842; Miller, *Leek*, 107–10, 121.

and on the 16th the Newcastle and Pottery yeomanry returned from Leek before dawn to restore order. A few hours later the marchers who had remained at Leek overnight set off for the Potteries, accompanied by a large number of Leek workers. A troop of dragoons had already been called out to deal with looting in Burslem, and a magistrate, receiving news of the approach of the Leek and Congleton men, read the Riot Act. The marchers arrived and began to stone the dragoons, who opened fire. Several people were wounded, and Josiah Heapy, a 19-year-old Leek shoemaker, was killed. The dragoons then charged the crowd and dispersed it.

Later that day the leading inhabitants of Leek, fearing that their town would again be overrun, sent urgent appeals to the authorities for troops. In the evening they handed out a large amount of bread to the poor. On 17 August the district army commander agreed to send a company of the 34th Regiment of Foot and also the Lichfield troop of yeomanry, which was in Newcastle. The yeomanry may have reached Leek the same day; the infantry arrived early on the 18th. Heapy's funeral at St. Edward's later that day apparently led to no disorder, and the silk masters and dyers reopened their works the following morning. The troops were still at Leek on 20 August, but there seem to have been no further disturbances.

In September two Sunday school teachers were disciplined for involvement with the Chartists. Charles Rathbone, the master at St. Edward's Sunday school, had joined the march from Leek to Burslem. He expressed regret but was suspended for two months without pay.[48] Elizabeth Phillips, the mistress at the school, was reported as having declared her support for the Chartists. She refused to express regret and was dismissed.[49]

THE LATER 19TH CENTURY. The town continued to expand steadily. Its silk industry became concentrated in factories, and several large firms were established. Leek also increased its importance as a market town, with a new cattle market in 1874 and a covered butter market in 1897. A new body of improvement commissioners was established in 1855 with wider powers than its predecessor, and in 1894 it was replaced by an urban district council. A Leek parliamentary division covering north-east Staffordshire was created in 1885 as one of seven new divisions for the county. The town was the centre of Leek rural district, with offices

initially at the premises of Challinors & Shaw, solicitors of Derby Street, and in Russell Street by 1900.[50]

In the 1850s and 1860s streets were built over the area between Derby Street and Stockwell Street. Market Street, Silk Street, York Street, and Deansgate were laid out in 1855,[51] and Ford Street and Bath Street were completed in 1863. Ford Street was named after Hugh Ford (d. 1830), who had owned land, and Bath Street took its name from the baths opened at its junction with Derby Street in 1854. In 1863 the Leek and Moorlands Permanent Benefit Building Society, established in 1856, offered 44 building lots for sale in the two new streets and in Derby Street, Stockwell Street (which had been widened and raised to improve access), and Market Street.[52] In the 1890s plans for remodelling the east side of the market place aroused opposition and were modified to include only the butter market and a new fire station in Stockwell Street.[53]

The area south of the town centre was developed mainly in the 1870s. Workhouse Street, renamed Brook Street in 1867,[54] had been extended to London Road as Haywood Street by 1874. The extension provided a bypass round the town centre and also a direct link via Canal Street (renamed Broad Street in 1881)[55] between the railway station and the new cattle market in Haywood Street. The first part of Leonard Street running south from Haywood Street was built in the mid 1870s, and Shoobridge Street to the west in the late 1870s. The three streets were named after Leonard Haywood Shoobridge, who owned the land.[56] By 1878 three new streets had been laid out to the south-east, Cromwell Terrace, Livingstone Street, and Talbot Street,[57] linking with streets laid out over part of Moorhouse farm south of London Road. Moorhouse Street, so named by 1867, existed by 1863, Grosvenor Street by 1867, and Wood Street by 1872.[58]

Several silk manufacturers had their premises in Compton by the mid 19th century,[59] and the area on the east was being developed by then. Cornhill Street and Jolliffe Street were described as intended new streets in 1848, and Duke Street and South Street existed by 1856.[60] The west end of Southbank Street existed by 1871, and it was extended east c. 1881.[61] West of Compton, Alsop Street was laid out in the earlier 1850s over land belonging to James Alsop, a promoter of the Leek Benefit Building Society, which built the houses there.[62] Dampier Street

48 S.R.O., D. 3359/St. Edward's sch. acct. bk. 1834–66, mins. 1 Sept. 1842.
49 Ibid. 1 and 5 Sept. 1842.
50 Kelly's Dir. Staffs. (1896; 1900).
51 W.S.L., Sleigh scrapbk. ii, f. 37; S.R.O., D. 3226/1, no. 208.
52 W.S.L., Sleigh scrapbk. ii, ff. 37, 68; S.R.O., D. 3188/1/1, nos. 17, 19, 21–2; D. 3226/1, no. 1265; D. 3226/2, nos. 1514, 1528; D. 3359/Cruso, will of Hugh Ford, proved 1831.　　53 Chronicles (spring 1988), 13–16.
54 S.R.O., D. 3226/2, no. 1896; D. 3226/47, no. 340.
55 Staffs. Advertiser, 6 Aug. 1881, p. 7.
56 S.R.O., D. 538/B/2/3; D. 3679/5/1, roll of members 1875 and 1877; Staffs. Advertiser, 28 Feb. 1874, p. 1; 9 May 1874, p. 7; Kelly's Dir. Staffs. (1880); O.S. Map 1/500, Staffs. VIII. 10. 1 and 4 (1879 edn.); H. Bode, Visiting Leek, i (Leek,

1974), 20.
57 S.R.O., D. 538/B/2/2; D. 3226/2, nos. 2489, 2717; O.S. Map 1/500, Staffs. VIII. 10. 1 and 2 (1879 edn.).
58 W.S.L., Sleigh scrapbk. i, f. 75; ii, ff. 35, 60, 73; S.R.O., D. 843/1/5/1; D. 3188/1/1, nos. 40, 45–7, 74; D. 3188/1/2, nos. 244, 258, 261, 264; D. 3226/2, no. 2489; D. 3226/47, no. 361.　　59 White, Dir. Staffs. (1851), 740.
60 Staffs. Advertiser, 8 July 1848, p. 1; S.R.O., D. 3188/1/1, nos. 146, 165, 190, 202; D. 3226/1, no. 151; W.S.L., Sleigh scrapbk. ii, f. 52; P.R.O., RG 9/1946; O.S. Map 1/500, Staffs. VIII. 10. 5–6 (1879 edn.).
61 P.R.O., RG 10/2880; RG 11/2738; O.S. Map 6", Staffs. VIII. SW. (1889 edn.).
62 S.R.O., D. 538/B/2/3; D. 1176/A/11/22; P.O. Dir. Staffs. (1854); Staffs. Advertiser, 16 Mar. 1850, pp. 1, 6; 12 Apr. 1851, p. 4.

A HISTORY OF STAFFORDSHIRE

and Hugo Street were laid out in 1874–5.[63]
Hartington Street and Daintry Street had been
added by 1891 and 1893, and three houses were
designed for Spencer Street (later Spencer Avenue) in 1899.[64] Further south a cemetery was
opened at Cornhill Cross in 1857, and at the
same time Junction Road was laid out by John
Davenport of Westwood Hall across Barnfields
farm to link the Cheddleton and Newcastle
roads.[65] An Anglican school-church was opened
for the area in 1863.

On the west side of the town a suburb of mills
and workers' houses grew up around West
Street. Albert Street existed by 1850, when 13
building plots there were offered for sale.[66] Land
to the west between Belle Vue, West Street, and
the southern end of Garden Street had been laid
out as 24 building plots by 1851.[67] Angle Street
in the same area was in existence by 1857 but
was not so named until 1867.[68] A mill in West
Street became Britannia Mill after partial rebuilding c. 1850, and Britannia Street to the
south, in existence as a road by 1838, was so
named by 1851.[69] The first house in Westwood
Terrace linking West Street and Britannia Street
was built in 1851,[70] and in 1856 eight building
plots there were advertised as 'eligible sites for
a better class of houses'.[71] There were 10 households there in 1861.[72] Wellington Mills in
Strangman's Walk (later Strangman Street)
were built in 1853. Wellington Street linking
Britannia Street and Strangman's Walk had
been built by 1854, when four newly erected
houses there were advertised for sale.[73] Grove
Street further west and Westwood Grove, its
continuation, had been laid out with building
plots by 1879.[74] Chorley Street and Gladstone
Street east of Wellington Street had been built
by 1880 and 1881 on a recreation ground bought
for the purpose in 1878.[75] To the west Picton
Street existed by 1891 and Barngate Street by
1893 with Cruso Street running south to Broad
Street.[76] Waterloo Street presumably existed by
1894, when Waterloo Mills were built there.
Sneyd Street linking Strangman's Walk and
Broad Street existed by 1898.[77] The North
Street area and the corresponding part of Westwood Road represent further westward
development of the early 1890s.[78]

On the east there was further expansion between Buxton Road and London Road, notably
with the building and extension of silk mills
between Fountain Street and London Road
from the 1860s by J. and J. Brough, Nicholson
& Co. Brunswick Street dates from the earlier
1850s,[79] and Portland Street was extended south
to London Road c. 1889.[80]

The suburb on the north-east of the town
continued to develop from the 1850s. At Ball
Haye Green, Nelson Street was laid out in 1853
on part of the Ball Haye estate.[81] By 1857 Milk
Street, Prince Street, and Pump Street were
being built up, although they were not officially
named until 1867.[82] Park Road running from
Ball Haye Road to Abbey Green Road across the
Ball Haye estate was built in 1854.[83] Eleven
cottages making up Inkerman Terrace at its west
end were built shortly afterwards.[84] Vicarage
Road at the east end of Park Road was constructed c. 1894 to bypass the steeper Ball Haye
Road. It was named in 1910 after the nearby
vicarage house of St. Luke's parish.[85] Further
east Weston Street off Buxton Road and the
adjoining Victoria Street existed by 1856, the
first evidently taking its name from the owner of
the land,[86] and houses were built at the junction of
Abbotts Road and Novi Lane in the mid 1850s.[87]

Joshua Brough, of the silk-manufacturing firm
of Joshua and James Brough & Co., built Buxton
Villa on Buxton Road by its junction with
Abbotts Road at the time of his marriage in 1837
to the daughter of William Spooner Littlehales
of Erdington (Warws.).[88] In 1880 their son William Spooner Brough built a house on the
opposite side of Buxton Road and called it
Littlehales. He inherited Buxton Villa in 1885
and lived their until his death in 1917. He laid
out the Waste north of the junction of Buxton
Road and Novi Lane and gave it to the town for
recreational purposes. He also laid out a garden
next to Littlehales and opened it to the public.
In addition he planted an avenue of trees along
Buxton Road.[89]

The Broughs belonged to a group of men, of
differing religious and politcal persuasions, who
were prominent in the affairs of the town and
set their mark on its cultural life.[90] They included silk manufacturers such as Joshua

63 *Staffs. Advertiser*, 25 Apr. 1874, p. 1; S.R.O., D.
3226/2, no. 2186; D. 3272/1/4/3/79.
64 S.R.O., D. 3188/1/3, 31 Dec. 1891, 19 Jan. 1899; D.
3188/1/4, sale cat. 1893.
65 *Staffs. Advertiser*, 17 May 1856, p. 4; S.R.O., D.
3188/1/1, no. 168; D. 3226/30, no. 1; D. 3283, sheet 13.
66 *Staffs. Advertiser*, 1 June 1850, p. 8.
67 S.R.O., D. 1176/A/11/23.
68 Ibid. D. 3188/1/2, no. 81; D. 3226/2, no. 1931; D.
3226/47, no. 361; D. 3283, sheet 12; *Victorian Leek* (Staffs.
C.C. Educ. Dept., Local Hist. Source Bk. L. 26), 17–18.
69 White, *Dir. Staffs.* (1851), 734; *P.O. Dir. Staffs.*
(1854); *Plan of Leek 1838.*   70 S.R.O., D. 1273/4/1–2.
71 *Staffs. Advertiser*, 17 May 1856, p. 4.
72 P.R.O., RG 9/1946.
73 W.S.L., Sleigh scrapbk. ii, f. 63.
74 S.R.O., D. 3359/misc. deeds, plan of 1879.
75 *Kelly's Dir. Staffs.* (1880); P.R.O., RG 11/2740; Leek
Libr., Johnson scrapbk. iii, p. 195.
76 P.R.O., RG 12/2185; S.R.O., D. 3188/1/4, sale cat.
1893.
77 O.S. Map 6", Staffs. VIII. SW. (1900 edn.).
78 S.R.O., D. 3188/1/4, sale cat. 1889; P.R.O., RG

12/2185; date stone of 1895 on nos. 10–12 Westwood Rd.
79 *Staffs. Advertiser*, 18 June 1853, p. 8; 19 May 1855,
p. 2.
80 S.R.O., D. 3188/1/4, sale partics. 1889.
81 Ibid. D. 1176/A/2/8–9. For the estate see below,
Tittesworth, estates.
82 S.R.O., D. 3226/2, no. 1896; D. 3226/47, no. 340; D.
3283, sheet 9. Pump Lane at Ball Haye Green was mentioned
in 1861: P.R.O., RG 9/1946.
83 G. A. Lovenbury, 'A Certain Group of Men' (Leek,
1990), 4; S.R.O., D. 538/B/2/1, sale partics. of Ball Haye
estate 1853.
84 *Staffs. Advertiser*, 6 and 13 Jan. 1855, p. 8; P.R.O.,
RG 9/1946.
85 Leek Improvement Com. *Reps.* (1894), 32; *Staffs.
Advertiser*, 2 July 1910, p. 8.
86 S.R.O., D. 3188/1/2; D. 3283, sheet 13; W.S.L. 93/92.
87 *Staffs. Advertiser*, 20 May 1854, p. 8.
88 Lovenbury, 'A Certain Group of Men', 3; S.R.O., D.
538/C/2/2.
89 Lovenbury, 'A Certain Group of Men', 4, 16–18;
S.R.O., D. 3226/4, no. 3030.
90 Lovenbury, 'A Certain Group of Men'.

94

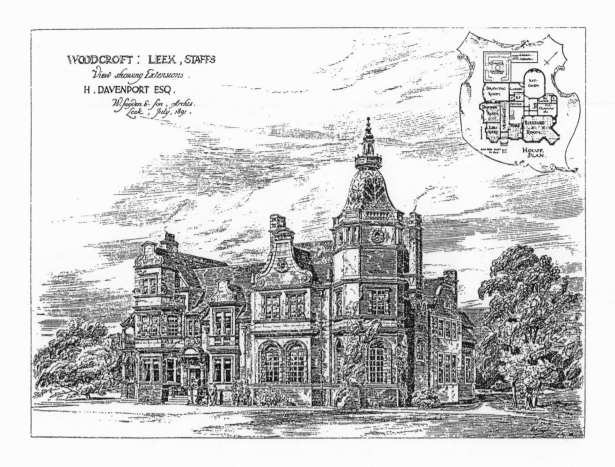

WOODCROFT: LEEK, STAFFS
View showing Extensions.
H. DAVENPORT ESQ.
W. Sugden & son, Archts.
Leek, July, 1891.

DRAWING
ROOM

LARDER

KIT-
CHEN

DINING
ROOM

CLOAK

LIB-
RARY

HALL

BILLIARD
ROOM

HOUSE
PLAN.

FIG. 17

FIG. 18. LITTLEHALES

Nicholson (d. 1885), Hugh Sleigh (d. 1901), and Sir Thomas Wardle (d. 1909), and professional men such as the lawyers William Challinor (d. 1896) and his younger brother Joseph (d. 1908).[91] Wardle brought William Morris to Leek in 1875 to experiment on dyes, and Wardle's wife Elizabeth founded the Leek Embroidery Society a few years later. Hugh Sleigh and Joseph Challinor promoted the building (1885–7) of All Saints' church in Compton, designed by Norman Shaw and decorated by members of the Arts and Crafts movement. Shaw had come to the area in the late 1860s to design the rebuilding of Meerbrook church in Leekfrith, and he also designed Spout Hall, Sleigh's house in St. Edward Street built in 1873.[92] Members of the Arts and Crafts movement also contributed to the decoration and furnishings of the William Morris Labour Church, opened in the Friends' meeting house at Overton Bank in 1896 chiefly through the influence of Larner Sugden, of the architectural firm of W. Sugden & Son.

Leek still owes much of its appearance to the work of Larner and his father William during the second half of the 19th century.[93] William Sugden came to Leek as architect and surveyor of the Churnet Valley railway line, opened in 1849. That year he set up on his own account. His buildings show a range of style. The West Street Wesleyan school (1854) is in a subdued Classical style, Rose Bank House (1857) in Rose Bank Street is plain, and Big Mill (by 1857) in Mill Street, though of an impressive size, is utilitarian and similar to many other mills in northern textile towns. He used a Gothic style for Brunswick Wesleyan Methodist chapel (1857) in Market Street and for the cemetery chapels (1857), and the Derby Street Congregational chapel (1863) is in a Decorated style. He introduced pointed windows into the Cottage Hospital (1870). Meanwhile he used an Italian style for the mechanics' institute (1862) in Russell Street. Larner was already working for his father by the time he was taken into partnership in 1881. He widened the practice and was responsible for the Queen Anne style of many of its later buildings, which also display considerable eclecticism. His own house at no. 29 Queen Street (1877) shows his liking for moulded brick, which is also seen in other houses such as nos. 33–35 Bath Street (1880) and Woodcroft, a house of the earlier 1880s[94] for which the firm designed additions in 1891. Moulded brick is also used at the ornate Ballington House, apparently of the later 1870s, to which the firm may have made additions.[95] At W. S. Brough's Littlehales (1880) Larner combined brick with timber framing. The District Bank (1883) in Derby Street incorporates tripartite windows whose design derives from buildings of c. 1600

in Ipswich (Suff.). The Nicholson Institute (1884) is in the Queen Anne style. The police station (1892) in Leonard Streeet has a main elevation derived from the Scottish Baronial style, the extension to J. and J. Brough, Nicholson & Co.'s Cross Street warehouse (probably 1892–3) is in a Classical style, and Sanders Buildings (1894) on the corner of Derby Street and Haywood Street show the influence of the Arts and Crafts movement. William died in 1892, and it seems that the architectural dominance of the practice was waning some years before Larner's death in 1901. Larner designed the co-operative society's central premises (1899) in the Ashbourne road and the extension (1900) of the Nicholson Institute. In the later 1890s, however, it was the less inventive J. T. Brealey who designed two important public buildings, the butter market (1897) and the fire station (1898).

THE 20TH CENTURY. Leek remained an industrial town concerned mainly with textiles, but in the course of the century new fibres, natural and man-made, became predominant and products became more varied. By the 1970s only one firm was still producing silk goods, and it ceased to do so in 1994. Leek also became the United Kingdom headquarters of Kerrygold Co. Ltd., the dairy products firm which took over the business built up by the Adams family from the 1920s. The largest employer in the town in the early 1990s was the Britannia Building Society, which evolved from the Leek and Moorlands Permanent Benefit Building Society of 1856 to become one of the country's leading building societies. Leek also remained a market centre, and in 1994 there were three general markets a week and two cattle markets. A large-scale antiques trade had developed in the town by the late 1980s, with showrooms and warehouses occupying converted buildings such as Cross Street Mill and Compton school.[96] In 1994 a weekly market was introduced specializing in crafts and antiques.

In 1974 the new Staffordshire Moorlands district was centred on Leek. Initially the council offices were at New Stockwell House in Stockwell Street and in the town hall in Market Street. Moorlands House off Stockwell Street was opened as the new headquarters in 1987; the council chamber was added in 1988.[97]

In the early 20th century the main expansion of the town was on the west. The growth of the area between Westwood Road and Broad Street continued with the laying out of Langford Street and James Street in 1901 by James Cornes, a Leek builder, who erected 50 workers' houses there specially designed by J. T. Brealey.[98]

91 For Sleigh see A. F. C. Sleigh, *Sleighs of Derbyshire and Beyond* (Bedhampton, priv. print., intro. dated 1991), 52; W.S.L. 495A/34, cutting of 20 Nov. 1901. For the others see below, econ. hist. (trade and ind.: silk ind.; professions: lawyers). For a portrait of Wardle see below, plate 67.
92 S.R.O., D. 4855/14/8; Sleigh, *Sleighs of Derb.* 52.
93 Para. based on G. A. Lovenbury, *Sugdens of Leek* (1975); *Town Scene* (Leek & Dist. Civic Soc., n.d.).
94 *Kelly's Dir. Staffs.* (1884).

95 Originally called Ballington View, it was Ballington House by 1888: ibid. (1880; 1884; 1888).
96 *Staffs. Life* (Christmas 1989), 44–7; *Leek Post & Times*, 21 July 1993, p. 1.
97 H. Bode, *Visiting Leek*, i (Leek, 1974), 5; Leek Libr., newspaper cuttings 1985 (1), p. 17; 1988 (1), p. 7; 1988 (2), p. 7; inf. from the Chief Executive, Staffs. Moorlands Dist. Council.
98 Anderton, *Edwardian Leek*, 65, 67–9; K. Parkes, *Windylow* (1915), 77; S.R.O., D. 3188/1/3.

Spring Gardens, Morley Street, and Station Street were laid out in 1905.[99] Shirley Street existed by 1911 and Burton Street by the early 1920s.[1] Meanwhile new streets of shops and commercial premises were built over the area west of St. Edward Street occupied by the Globe inn and the grounds of the house called the Field. In 1903 the council laid out Salisbury Street, Field Street, and the west end of High Street and offered 34 building plots there for sale. High Street was completed in 1904, the Globe having been demolished. In or soon after 1905 a post office was built on the corner of St. Edward Street and Strangman's Walk, the east end of which was widened and renamed Strangman Street.[2] The Field was used as a registration centre for those enlisting during the First World War and later became a social club called Leek National Reserve Club.[3] The north-west end of Belle Vue was widened in 1906 so that the street, renamed Belle Vue Road, opened into Mill Street. A route was thus provided from the foot of Mill Street to the railway station avoiding the town centre; a route was also provided into the town via West Street and High Street avoiding the steep climb up Mill Street.[4]

The eastern suburb expanded in the early years of the century as far as Shirburn Road, linking the Buxton and Ashbourne roads.[5] In 1924 work was begun on the Nicholson War Memorial, on the open space at the end of Derby Street then used as part of the cattle market. The memorial, a clock tower of white Portland stone designed by Thomas Worthington & Sons of Manchester, was given by Sir Arthur and Lady Nicholson, whose son Lt. B. L. Nicholson died in action in 1915. It was dedicated in 1925. In 1949 two bronze tablets were unveiled recording the names of those killed during the Second World War.[6]

The residential areas were greatly extended in the 1920s and 1930s, mainly by the building of council estates. The largest were the Abbottsville and Haregate estates in the north-east. Prince Street was extended south from Ball Haye Green to Buxton Road as part of the Abbottsville estate. The Glebeville estate off Junction Road was built in 1925, adjoining Sandon Road (later Sandon Street) where private development had begun by the early 1920s. A council estate was built in the Station Street area north of Broad Street in 1928.[7]

A 9-a. estate in Nab Hill Avenue and Hillswood Avenue on the north-west side of the town was built as a private initiative by Solomon Bowcock, the secretary of the Leek United and Midlands Building Society, to provide good houses for people of moderate means. Designed by Longden & Venables, the estate was begun in 1924 and completed in 1927. All 85 houses had two living rooms, a scullery, three bedrooms, a bathroom with a separate lavatory, and a front and back garden.[8] A number of large houses, also designed by Longden & Venables, were built at Big Birchall on the east side of the Cheddleton road in the mid and later 1920s.[9] By the later 1930s a private estate had been built west of the Newcastle road over the site and grounds of Woodcroft and over the grounds of Woodcroft Grange, another late 19th-century house. Houses had also been built in Beggars Lane, a continuation of Spring Gardens. Several large houses had been built on the Buxton road between Abbotts Road and Novi Lane.[10] Earlier large houses in Mount Road include Kniveden Hall, dated 1901.

During the Second World War many children were evacuated to Leek, mainly from Manchester, Liverpool, London, and Essex.[11] As part of the war effort St. Luke's church hall was fitted up in 1942 as a day nursery for 40 children aged from 2 to 5 in order to free their mothers for work.[12] The former Ball Haye Street schools were converted into a British restaurant, which continued apparently until 1951, having moved into the Primitive Methodist chapel in Fountain Street after that had closed in 1949.[13] In March 1941 a German bomber unloaded its bombs on the town, killing one man and damaging several buildings.[14] A number of aircraft crashed in the Leek area during the war, several of them on the Roaches, Hen Cloud, and Morridge. Most were on training exercises, but in 1941 a German bomber, hit during a raid on Liverpool, came down on the Roaches. In 1990 a board was unveiled in St. Edward's church commemorating the airmen who had been killed.[15] Thousands of American soldiers passed through the area in 1943 and 1944. Most were based at Blackshaw Moor in Tittesworth, but there was a camp for officers in the grounds of Ball Haye Hall with another for other ranks at Hencroft off Abbey Green Road.[16]

House building was resumed after 1945. Large council estates had been built by 1955 at Haregate and between Compton and Junction Road. The private Westwood estate was begun in the mid 1950s.[17] The private Wallbridge Park estate

99 Leek U.D.C. *Fifty Years of Municipal Govt. in Leek, 1855 to 1905* (Leek, 1905), 27; Leek Libr., newspaper cuttings 1954–7, p. 54; O.S. Map 6″, Staffs. VIII. SW. (1925 edn.).
1 S.R.O., D. 3188/1/3; O.S. Map 6″, Staffs. VIII. SW. (1925 edn.).
2 Leek U.D.C. *Fifty Years of Municipal Govt.* 27; *Leek Post*, 12 July 1913, p. 6 (extract in Leek Libr.); Leek Libr., newspaper cuttings 1969–72, p. 128; D.R.O., D. 247B/ES 400.   3 *Leek Post & Times*, 7 Oct. 1992, p. 10.
4 *Leek Post*, 12 July 1913, p. 6; W.S.L. 495A/34, cutting of Jan. 1904; ibid. 503/34, cutting of 13 Sept. 1906; D.R.O., 247B/ES400.
5 *Staffs. Advertiser*, 26 Aug. 1899, p. 5; *Kelly's Dir. Staffs.* (1908), 251; (1912), 256.
6 H. Bode, *Visiting Leek*, i. 8, 23–4.
7 O.S. Map 6″, Staffs. VIII. NW., SW. (1925 and prov. edns.).   8 *Leek News*, Dec. 1927; S.R.O., D. 3188/1/4.

9 S.R.O., D. 3188/1/4; D. 3188/2.
10 O.S. Map 6″, Staffs. VIII. SW. (1900, 1925, and prov. edns.).
11 *Chronicles* (Dec. 1989), 15–16, 45–52; ibid. (autumn 1992), 14–16; J. Whitehead, *Compton School* (Leek, 1988), 37, 99–110; N. Ramsay, *The Wasted Years? Leek High School 1934–1959* (Leek, 1992), 17–18, 27–8, 46; S.R.O., D. 782/1; D. 3133/3/2– 3; D. 3657/1/4 and 8.
12 *Leek Post & Times*, 19 Aug. 1992, p. 6.
13 Ibid. 31 July 1991, p. 2; S.R.O., CEH/83/1, 15 June 1950, 12 Mar. 1951; inf. from Miss J. Forrester of Trinity Church, Leek.
14 Bode, *Visiting Leek*, i. 10, 24; *Chronicles* (Dec. 1989), 12, 17, 24, 34.
15 M. S. Boylan, *A Moorlands Dedication* (Leek, 1992).
16 *Chronicles* (Dec. 1989), 13–14, 24–5, 42, 48.
17 S.R.O., CEH/83/1, 15 June 1954, 20 Mar. 1961.

to the south was begun in 1963 and was extended in the early 1970s.[18] Two industrial estates were developed from the later 1970s at Leekbrook and Barnfields. The latter includes the line of the canal, filled in in 1957, the site of the station, demolished in 1973, the site of Wall Bridge Farm, demolished in 1974, and the area of the pre-1934 sewage farm.[19] A Safeway superstore was opened on the site of the station in 1990.[20] Another smaller industrial estate was developed in Station Street on the former town yard in the earlier 1990s.[21]

In the later 20th century there was extensive demolition of old buildings in the town and some rebuilding. Slum clearance, begun in the 1930s, was resumed after the war. Most of the cottages in Mill Street were demolished between the late 1950s and the earlier 1970s, and flowers, shrubs, and trees were planted there in the mid 1970s.[22] Petty France was cleared in the 1960s.[23] In 1962

work began on a bus station and a shopping centre on the site of the former cattle market in Haywood Street.[24] Most of the buildings belonging to Brough, Nicholson & Hall west of Cross Street were demolished in 1968, and the county council's offices which occupy much of the site were opened in 1976.[25] In 1972 the south side of Church Street was demolished for road widening.[26] Much of the area west of Pickwood Road was cleared for the North Midland Co-operative Society's superstore opened in 1984.[27] Plans for the redevelopment of the area on the east side of the market place were put in hand in 1985 when the district council invited proposals. The scheme finally adopted in 1988 met with strong opposition, and at the local elections in 1991 the Ratepayers group won a number of seats from sitting councillors on both the parish and district councils. In 1994 a new scheme was still under consideration.[28]

COMMUNICATIONS

ROADS. It has been generally thought that a Roman road between Leek and Buxton followed the line of the present Leek–Buxton road. That road, however, seems to have been laid out in 1765–6 under a turnpike Act of 1765.[29] The line of the Roman road between Leek and Buxton has yet to be established, but it continued south through Cheddleton, Blythe Bridge, Hilderstone, and Stafford to join Watling Street at Pennocrucium (Stretton, in Penkridge).[30]

Before the 1760s the Leek–Buxton road left the town along Mill Street. It then ran through Leekfrith, via Abbey Green and Upper Hulme, and through Quarnford, in Alstonefield, via Flash, to Wallnook, in Hartington (Derb.), continuing to Buxton along the present route.[31] There may also have been a medieval road running east from Leek along what is now Fountain Street and turning north-east over Leek moor into Tittesworth.[32] The road south from Leek to Cheddleton was described in 1430 as part of the highway from Leek to Stafford.[33]

Leek stood on a medieval road called the Earl's Way, evidently because it linked estates of the earls of Chester. The stretch east of Leek formed the medieval road from Leek to Ashbourne as

far as Waterhouses, in Waterfall. North-west of Leek the Earl's Way followed the Macclesfield road through Rudyard as far as Rushton Spencer, where it turned west through Rushton James to Congleton (Ches.).[34] White's bridge, carrying it across the Churnet, was known as Conyngre bridge in 1430, presumably after a nearby rabbit warren. It was also known as White's bridge by 1636 after the family occupying Coneygray House on the Leekfrith side of the river.[35] It was then a stone bridge of two small arches, which were inadequate in times of flood. In 1649, by agreement between the inhabitants of Leek and Leekfrith, its rebuilding was begun as a bridge with a single arch, but its completion was delayed by the refusal of some of the inhabitants of Leekfrith to contribute.[36] A new bridge was built nearby in 1829[37] and was widened on both sides in 1931.[38] Another route from Leek to Macclesfield, recorded c. 1230 and still in use in the earlier 18th century, ran via Abbey Green and Gun, in Leekfrith, and entered Cheshire at Danebridge, in Heaton.[39]

The road to Newcastle-under-Lyme crosses the Churnet over Wall bridge. In 1244 the monks of Trentham gave the monks of Dieulacres permission to build a bridge there with

[18] Ibid. 14 Oct. 1963, headmaster's rep.; CEH/194/1, 2 June 1970, 9 Feb., 8 June 1971, 3 Oct. 1972; brochure for official opening of Woodcroft primary sch. 8 Oct. 1970.
[19] Leek Libr., newspaper cuttings 1972–8, pp. 78, 119.
[20] Ibid. 1990, p. 3.
[21] Ibid. 1972–8, p. 119; Leek Post & Times, 31 July 1991, p. 35; 4 May 1994, p. 8.
[22] L. Porter, Leek Thirty Years Ago (Clifton, Ashbourne, 1991), intro.; C. K. R. Pearce, Mission Church of St. John the Evangelist, Mill Street, Leek (Leek, 1975), 7–8; S.R.O., D. 3990/1/1, p. 114; Staffs. C.C. Educ. Dept., schools hist. service slides, no. 56.
[23] Anderton, Edwardian Leek, 58; Sherlock, Ind. Arch. Staffs. 49; Leek Libr., newspaper cuttings 1969–72, pp. 38–9.
[24] Leek Libr., newspaper cuttings 1960–8, pp. 22–3, 29.
[25] Ibid. 1972–8, p. 71.
[26] Ibid. 1969–72, pp. 45, 67, 70, 72.
[27] Ibid. 1982 (1), pp. 31, 40; 1984 (2), pp. 17, 24.
[28] Leek Post & Times, 12 Aug. 1992, p. 5; 9 June 1993, p. 3; inf. from Staffs. Moorlands Dist. Council.

[29] I. D. Margary, Roman Roads in Britain, ii. 45; Dodd, Peakland Roads, 31.
[30] City of Stoke-on-Trent Museum Arch. Soc. i. 10–17; inf. from Mr. R. A. Meeson, Staffs. C.C. Planning and Econ. Development Dept.
[31] Above, Alstonefield: Quarnford, intro. [roads]; below, Leekfrith, intro. [roads].
[32] Above, general hist. (earlier 19th cent.).
[33] S.R.O., D. 1333/2, dorse.
[34] Dodd, Peakland Roads, 53–5; V.C.H. Staffs. ii. 279; Earldom of Chester and its Charters (Chester Arch. Soc. lxxi), 56. For mention of the stretch of the Earl's Way in Leek manor in 1340 see S.R.O., D. 1333/1, m. 4.
[35] S.R.O., D. 1333/2; D. 3359/misc. deeds, deed of 1 Aug. 1710; Leek Par. Reg. 15, 191.
[36] S.R.O., Q/SO/5, pp. 271, 293, 322–3, 400.
[37] Ibid. Q/SO/30, f. 121; S.R.O., D. 745/1, 26 Jan. 1829 sqq.; Sandon Road acct. bk. 1821–69, acct. 1828–9 (in possession of Mr. R. Stones of Malpas, Ches., 1994).
[38] Inscription on bridge.
[39] Below, Leekfrith, intro. [roads].

free access for waggons and carts across Trentham priory's land at Wall in Longsdon township.[40] The Castle Way (*via castelli*) in the Wall bridge area mentioned in the mid 13th century[41] was presumably the Newcastle road. By the early 18th century the bridge was a wooden horse bridge with a dangerous ford adjoining it, and travellers suffered losses and delays from the frequent flooding of the river. In 1712, following a petition from 83 inhabitants of Totmonslow hundred, quarter sessions granted £60 to rebuild the bridge in stone for carts and carriages.[42] It was widened to the south in 1929.[43]

All the main roads from Leek were turnpiked in the earlier 1760s. The first were the road south via Cheddleton and the road to Macclesfield via Rudyard, which were turnpiked in 1762 as part of the road from Sandon to Bullock Smithy (later Hazel Grove) in Cheadle (Ches.).[44] A tollhouse was built that year on the Cheddleton road near Sheephouse Farm.[45] A bridge was built over Leek brook in 1786–7.[46] The stretch of the road between the Green Man inn in Compton and Big Birchall was realigned in 1839–40.[47] The Sandon to Bullock Smithy road was disturnpiked in 1878, and Sheephouse tollhouse was put up for sale.[48]

The road through Leek between Ashbourne and Congleton was also turnpiked in 1762.[49] It used the stretch of the Macclesfield road between Leek and Rushton Spencer and became entitled to a share of the tolls when a gate was erected at Rudyard in 1764.[50] In 1763 the trustees ordered a gate or chain to be placed at Lowe Hill south-east of the town. A tollhouse was built there in or just after 1765. It was sold in 1830 after a new line of road was built to the south in 1828, and it survives as part of a house. A bridge was built to carry the lane from Kniveden to Lowe Hill over the new road.[51] The cast-iron mileposts on the road date from 1834.[52] The road was disturnpiked in 1876.[53]

The road between Newcastle and Hassop (Derb.) via Leek and Longnor, in Alstonefield, was turnpiked in 1765, with a branch to Buxton.[54] The stretch north-east from Leek seems to have been largely a new road, laid out in 1765–6.[55] In 1766 the trustees ordered a gate and chain to be placed at the east end of Stockwell Street in Leek pending the building of a tollhouse.[56] The house was replaced, evidently in the early 1770s, by one at the Mile Tree on Leek moor.[57] It survives as a private house. The cast-iron mileposts on the Leek–Buxton road date from 1833, 11 being bought that year.[58] South-west of the town a tollhouse was built near the canal wharf probably soon after the opening of the canal in 1801.[59] The tollhouse went out of use in 1855 and was demolished for road widening in 1860.[60] It was replaced by one near Wall bridge.[61] The Buxton road was disturnpiked in 1875[62] and the Newcastle road in 1879.[63]

In 1767 the trustees of the Sandon to Bullock Smithy road announced that their road was completely finished and had 'genteel accommodations, good chaises, able horses, and careful drivers' at Leek as well as elsewhere. They also claimed that the road was the shortest route from London to Manchester.[64] The London–Manchester mailcoach route established in 1785, however, went to Leek via Ashbourne, while by 1803 Pickfords' wagons between London and Manchester also used that route or went via Buxton.[65] In the 1790s, besides the mail, coaches between London and Manchester ran daily through Leek in each direction from the George in Spout Street, and there were coaches twice a week to London from the Swan in Spout Street, and three times a week between Manchester and Birmingham in each direction from the Wilkes's Head in Spout Street.[66] By 1818 there were coaches daily to London, Birmingham, and Manchester, with the Red Lion in Market Place and the Roebuck in Derby Street evidently the main coaching inns.[67] In the late 1820s there was also a coach between Manchester and Nottingham daily in each direction from the Swan and in the mid 1830s one to Macclesfield three times a week from the Roebuck.[68] The mail ceased to run through Leek in 1837.[69]

With the coming of the railway in 1849 omnibuses were introduced from the Red Lion and the Roebuck to the station on the Newcastle road.[70] By the early 1870s they ran from the

40   *S.H.C.* N.S. ix. 359–60; S.R.O., D. 593/B/1/24/1/2 (calendared and wrongly dated as 1284 in *S.H.C.* xi. 333–4).
41   *S.H.C.* N.S. ix. 359.
42   S.R.O., Q/SO/11, E. and T. 1712; *Leek Par. Reg.* 15 (a weaver drowned there Dec. 1636); below, plate 1.
43   Inscription on bridge.
44   *S.H.C.* 4th ser. xiii. 102.
45   S.R.O., D. 706/1, 14 Apr. 1762, 23 Nov. 1763; above, fig. 2.
46   S.R.O., D. 706/1, 19 May 1786; D. 3359/Sandon Road acct. bk. 1783–1803, 1 Sept., 10 and 23 Oct. 1787.
47   Sandon Road cttee. order bk. 1839–45 3 June 1839 sqq. (in possession of Mr. Stones, 1994); Sandon Road acct. bk. 1821–69, accts. 1839, 1840.
48   Annual Turnpike Acts Continuance Act, 1872, 35 & 36 Vic. c. 85, sched. 8; S.R.O., D. 3359/Sandon Road order bk. 1843–89, 28 Feb., 23 July 1878, 27 Feb. 1879.
49   *S.H.C.* 4th ser. xiii. 103.
50   Below, Rudyard, intro. [roads].
51   *T.N.S.F.C.* lxxxiii. 53; lxxxiv. 57–9; S.R.O., Q/RDc 65, plan I.
52   *T.N.S.F.C.*. lxxxiii. 53; Sherlock, *Ind. Arch. Staffs.* 113, 125.
53   Annual Turnpike Acts Continuance Act, 1873, 36 & 37 Vic. c. 90, sched. 9.
54   *S.H.C.* 4th ser. xiii. 105.
55   S.R.O., D. 3359/Buxton Road order bk. 1765–1800, pp. 8, 10–11, 16–17, 21–2.
56   Ibid. pp. 5, 18, 23, 49, 55.
57   Ibid. 12 July 1771, 9 June 1772; D. 706/2, pp. 31, 36; S.R.O., Q/RDc 65, plan I.
58   Sherlock, *Ind. Arch. Staffs.* 113; Buxton Road. acct. bk. 1809–60, acct. 1832–3 (in possession of Mr. Stones, 1994).   59   S.R.O., Q/RUt 5/18.
60   S.R.O., D. 3226/1, 21 Aug. 1855, 30 Nov., 27 Dec. 1859, 10 Jan., 7 Feb. 1860; *Chronicles* (winter 1989), 23; *Staffs. Advertiser*, 31 Dec. 1859, p. 4; 14 Jan. 1860, p. 7.
61   P.R.O., RG 9/1946; RG 10/2883.
62   Annual Turnpike Acts Continuance Act, 1874, 37 & 38 Vic. c. 95, sched. 5; S.R.O., D. 3359/Leek, Buxton, and Monyash turnpike trust acct. bk. 1861–76, acct. 1875–6.
63   Annual Turnpike Acts Continuance Act, 1879, 42 & 43 Vic. c. 46, sched. 2.
64   S.R.O., D. 706/1, 4 Sept. 1767.
65   Dodd, *Peakland Roads*, 132, 137.
66   *Univ. Brit. Dir.* v [1798], 104.
67   Parson and Bradshaw, *Staffs. Dir.* (1818), 127.
68   Pigot, *New Com. Dir.* [1829], 713*; Pigot, *Nat. Com. Dir.* (1835), 414.
69   'Diary of Mary Elizabeth Cruso of Leek, Staffs., 1837', ed. A. W. Bednall (TS. in W.S.L.), 4 July 1837.
70   White, *Dir. Staffs.* (1851), 741.

Swan and the George also but by 1900 only from the Red Lion and the George.[71] Motor buses to Hanley, Ashbourne, Cheadle, and Buxton were introduced soon after the First World War. The service to the station from the two hotels had been reduced to market day (Wednesday) by 1924 and had ceased altogether by 1928. There was then a bus service to Butterton, and by 1932 services had been introduced to Macclesfield and Manchester and also to Calton and Longnor.[72] A bus station was opened on the former cattle market in Haywood Street in 1963.[73]

CANAL. The Trent & Mersey Canal Co. planned a branch canal to Leek from Etruria in 1773, and it seems later to have foiled a plan for a Leek canal by another company.[74] In 1801 it opened a branch canal running from the Caldon canal east of Endon to a basin and wharf on the Newcastle road in Leek and crossing the Churnet by an aqueduct. Traffic on the canal seems never to have been heavy. The transport of coal ceased in 1934, but tar was carried from Milton, in Norton-in-the-Moors, until 1939. The canal was abandoned under an Act of 1944. The stretch north of the Churnet aqueduct was bought by Leek urban district council in 1957 and filled in; the site became part of the Barnfields industrial estate.[75]

RAILWAYS. The Churnet Valley railway,

opened by the North Staffordshire Railway Co. in 1849 from its main line south of Macclesfield to Uttoxeter, had a station at Leek on the Newcastle road.[76] The company took over a house nearby and opened it in 1850 as the Churnet Valley Hotel.[77] Nab Hill tunnel through the high ground to the north was built to resemble a natural cavern in the rock, with no masonry at either entrance.[78] The station was rebuilt in 1880.[79]

A line was opened from Stoke-upon-Trent to the Churnet Valley railway at Leekbrook in 1867.[80] In 1905 a line was opened from Leekbrook to join the Leek & Manifold Valley light railway at Waterhouses. The light railway had been opened to Hulme End in Fawfieldhead, in Alstonefield parish, in 1904, and in the intervening year a steam-powered omnibus was run from Leek to Waterhouses to connect with it. Passenger services were withdrawn from the Leekbrook–Waterhouses line in 1935, a year after the closure of the light railway, and in 1943 the section between Cauldon and Waterhouses was closed.[81] Passenger services between Leek and Stoke and between Leek and Macclesfield ceased in 1960 and between Leek and Uttoxeter in 1965. The line north from Leek was closed for freight in 1964 and the line from Leek to Leekbrook in 1970. Leek station was demolished in 1973.[82] The lines from Leekbrook to Cauldon and to Stoke continued in use as mineral lines serving the Caldon Low limestone quarries until 1989.[83]

MANORS AND OTHER ESTATES

IN 1086 LEEK was held by the king, having been held before the Conquest by Alfgar, earl of Mercia. It was assessed at 1 hide 'with the appendages'.[84] By 1093 it had been granted to Hugh, earl of Chester,[85] and it then descended with the earldom. The earls may have had a house there by the later 12th century: Earl Hugh of Kevelioc issued charters at Leek c. 1170 and in the earlier 1170s and died there in 1181; his son and heir Ranulph de Blundeville issued a charter there c. 1210.[86] The manor was in the hands of the king in the 1180s, presumably because of Ranulph's minority.[87]

In 1232 Ranulph granted the manor to Dieulacres abbey, along with his heart for burial. The king confirmed the grant the day before Ranulph's death that year.[88] Ranulph's nephew

and heir John the Scot later granted the monks homage and services belonging to the manor which he had initially retained.[89] The manor remained with Dieulacres until the dissolution of the abbey in 1538. By 1291 it had been farmed out for £10 6s. 4d.[90]

In 1552 the Crown granted what were described as the manors of Leek and Frith with the site of Dieulacres and most of the former abbey's Staffordshire property to Sir Ralph Bagnall at a rent of £105 11s. 7½d.[91] A staunch Protestant, he was living in France in 1556, and later that year he was found guilty of treason, although he was pardoned in 1557.[92] He had conveyed the property to his brother Sir Nicholas, who in 1556 conveyed it to Valentine Brown.[93] Sir Ralph recovered it from Brown in

71 P.O. Dir. Staffs. (1872); Kelly's Dir. Staffs. (1900).
72 Kelly's Dir. Staffs. (1924; 1928; 1932).
73 Leek Libr., newspaper cuttings 1960–8, pp. 22–3, 29.
74 C. Hadfield, Canals of West Midlands, 33.
75 P. Lead, Caldon Canal and Tramroads (Headington, 1990), 51–5; below, Longsdon, intro.
76 R. Keys, Churnet Valley Rlwy. (Hartington, 1974), 9, 13–14; below, plate 44.
77 B. Jeuda, Memories of N. Staffs. Rlwy. (Cheshire Libraries, 1986), 91; White, Dir. Staffs. (1851), 738.
78 N.S.J.F.S. ii. 103 and pl. IXA; Leek in Maps (Staffs. C.C. Educ. Dept., Local Hist. Source Bk. L5), 1862/1.
79 B. Jeuda, Leek, Caldon & Waterhouses Rlwy. (Cheddleton, 1980), 27; Jeuda, N. Staffs. Rlwy. 31; G. Dow, N. Staffs. Album, 57.   80 V.C.H. Staffs. ii. 315.
81 Jeuda, Leek, Caldon & Waterhouses Rlwy. 17–19, 27, 30–1, 65–6.

82 N.S.J.F.S. iv. 79; Keys, Churnet Valley Rlwy. 22, 31.
83 R. Christiansen and R. W. Miller, N. Staffs. Rlwy. 285; Lead, Caldon Canal and Tramroads, 82; inf. from Brit. Rail, Stoke-on-Trent.   84 V.C.H. Staffs. iv. 39.
85 Charters of Earls of Chester, p. 4.
86 Ibid. pp. 180, 192, 346; Sleigh, Leek, 20; Complete Peerage, iii. 167.
87 Pipe R. 1183 (P.R.S. xxxii), 152; 1185 (P.R.S. xxxiv), 2; 1186 (P.R.S. xxxvi), 151; S.H.C. i. 131, 136, 141; ii (i), 3, 12; Complete Peerage, iii. 167.
88 Charters of Earls of Chester, pp. 387–8; Close R. 1231–4, 122.
89 Charters of Earls of Chester, p. 446; Complete Peerage, iii. 169.   90 Tax. Eccl. (Rec. Com.), 252.
91 Cal. Pat. 1550–3, 440–1.
92 S.H.C. 1917–18, 325–6; Cal. Pat. 1555–7, 318–19.
93 S.H.C. xii (i), 224; S.H.C. 1917–18, 346–7.

1560.[94] He was sheriff of Staffordshire in 1560–1.[95] In 1580, having sold much of the property, he was succeeded by his nephew Sir Henry Bagnall, who conveyed the manors of Leek and Frith in 1597 to Thomas Rudyard.[96] The manors then descended with Rudyard manor, passing in 1723 to Thomas Parker, earl of Macclesfield, on his second attempt to buy them.[97] A court was still held for the joint manors of Leek and Frith by the earl of Macclesfield in the mid 19th century.[98]

The rent of £105 11s. 7½d. reserved by the Crown in 1552 was in arrears to the amount of £446 3s. 9d. in 1572.[99] In 1609 it was granted to Sir Christopher Hatton and Sir Francis Needham. They sold small parts of it to John Rothwell of Leek in 1610 and Henry Wardle of Leekfrith in 1612.[1] Hatton's son Christopher, Baron Hatton, made a further sale to William Jolliffe of Leek in 1642–3.[2]

Within a few years of the foundation of Dieulacres abbey Ranulph son of Peter granted the monks all right in the land of *BIRCHALL*, an estate which he and his father had held.[3] By 1246 the monks had established a grange there, which was described in 1345 as the manor of Birchall Grange.[4]

The grange was included in the grant of the abbey's property to Sir Ralph Bagnall in 1552.[5] In 1563 Bagnall conveyed it to William Egerton of Fenton, in Stoke-upon-Trent.[6] It then descended with the Egerton family's share of Horton manor until 1623 when Timothy Egerton and his brother Thomas conveyed it to William Jolliffe of Leek.[7] Jolliffe died in 1669 and was succeeded by his son Thomas (d. 1693). Thomas was followed by his sons John, of Botham Hall in Cheddleton (d. 1694), and Benjamin, of Cofton Hackett, Worcs. (d. 1719). Benjamin's son and heir Thomas died unmarried in 1758.[8]

In 1765 Thomas's trustees conveyed what was then known as Great Birchall farm, with the nearby Sheephouse farm (also a property of Dieulacres abbey) and Barnfield (later Barnfields) farm (evidently in existence by 1675), to his nephews Michael, Benjamin, and Francis Biddulph.[9] In 1766 the Biddulphs sold the farms to Harry Lankford of Hurdsfield in Prestbury

(Ches.).[10] He was declared bankrupt in 1773, and in 1774 his assignees sold the three farms to Allwood Wilkinson of Chesterfield (Derb.), who was still alive in 1778.[11] Under Wilkinson's will of 1777 his estates passed to his eleven cousins, one of whom, Isaac Wilkinson, bought out the rest in 1786.[12] He died in 1831, and his heir was George Yeldham Ricketts, who under the terms of Isaac's will took the name of Wilkinson.[13] In 1841 he sold the three farms to John Davenport of Westwood Hall.[14] John's grandson George Davenport sold what had become known as Big Birchall to Howard Haywood in 1866[15] and Barnfields farm to Joseph Challinor of Leek in 1892.[16] A sewage farm was opened at Barnfields in 1899.[17] The farmhouse at Big Birchall was still standing in 1928 but was later demolished.[18]

Dieulacres abbey had established a grange at *WESTWOOD* by 1291 and possibly by 1246.[19] The estate may have been granted to the monks by Flora, daughter of William of Cockshut. In 1293 William's great-grandson Thomas, son of Robert of Olynleye (perhaps Hollinhay in Longsdon), claimed a toft and 120 a. at Westwood as William's heir, but a jury upheld the abbot's claim that William had enfeoffed Flora with the land before he died.[20]

The grange was included in the grant of the abbey's property to Sir Ralph Bagnall in 1552.[21] It later passed to Ralph Adderley of Coton in Hanbury, who was succeeded by his son William in 1595. In 1604 William conveyed it to Francis Trentham of Rocester.[22] Francis was succeeded in 1626 by his son Sir Thomas, and when Sir Thomas died in 1628 his widow Prudence went to live at Westwood.[23] Their son Francis, a minor in 1628, was succeeded in 1644 by his father's brother Sir Christopher (d. 1649) and Christopher by his brother William (d. 1652). William's heir was Francis's daughter Elizabeth, a minor, who by 1657 was the wife of Richard Cockayne, later Viscount Cullen.[24]

Westwood was the home of Ralph Lees in 1666, when he was assessed for tax on seven hearths.[25] By the early 18th century the farm was the property of William Jolliffe of Caverswall Castle. On his death in 1709 it passed to his daughter Lucy (d. 1742), wife of William Vane, in 1720 created Viscount Vane (d. 1734).[26] In

94 *S.H.C.* xiii. 207.
95 *S.H.C.* 1912, 284.
96 *S.H.C.* N.S. ix. 302–3; *S.H.C.* 1917–18, 326–7; Sleigh, *Leek*, 22–6.
97 Sleigh, *Leek*, 26; *Olde Leeke*, i. 166; S.R.O., D. 538/D/3/10, p. 46.
98 Below, local govt.
99 P.R.O., E 178/2075; Sleigh, *Leek*, 24 n.
1 S.R.O., D. 5017/5/89 and 306.
2 Sleigh, *Leek*, 59 n.
3 *S.H.C.* N.S. ix. 312. The grant was witnessed by Philip de Orreby, justiciar of Chester, who resigned that office in 1229: *Charters of Earls of Chester*, p. 387.
4 Below, econ. hist. (agric.); *Cal. Pat.* 1345–8, 84.
5 *Cal. Pat.* 1550–3, 440.
6 S.R.O., D. 3359/misc. deeds, deed of 20 Aug. 1563.
7 *S.H.C.* N.S. x (1), 42; Sleigh, *Leek*, 147, which states, at p. 44 n., that the Egertons sold Birchall to Thos. Jolliffe in 1674.
8 H. G. H. Jolliffe, *Jolliffes of Staffs.* (priv. print. 1892), 4–5, 8, 10–11, 18–20, 24, and pedigree following p. 232.
9 S.R.O., D. 3272/1/4/3/36 and 55. For Sheephouse and Barnfield see above, general hist. (Middle Ages; 16th and

17th cents.).   10 S.R.O., D. 3272/1/4/3/41–2.
11 Ibid. D. 3272/1/4/3/49–50, 54; D. 3359/misc. deeds, deed of 1 Sept. 1778.   12 Ibid. D. 3272/1/4/3/55.
13 Ibid. D. 3272/1/4/3/61.
14 Ibid. D. 3272/1/4/3/72.
15 Sleigh, *Leek*, 44 n.; S.R.O., D. 3272/1/4/3/77.
16 S.R.O., D. 3272/1/4/3/80.
17 Below, public services (public health).
18 S.R.O., D. 3188/2; O.S. Map 6", Staffs. VIII. SW. (1925 edn. and prov. edn. rev. 1937–8).
19 Below, econ. hist. (agric.).
20 *S.H.C.* vi (1), 220.
21 *Cal. Pat.* 1550–3, 440.
22 *S.H.C.* v (2), 3–5; xvi. 182–3; xviii (1), 44.
23 Ibid. v (2), 289; *Rocester Par. Reg.* (Staffs. Par. Reg. Soc. 1906), 51–2; below, Rom. Cath.
24 *S.H.C.* v (2), 289; Erdeswick, *Staffs.* 490–1 n.; *Rocester Par. Reg.* 49, 62–3, 68–9; *Complete Peerage*, iii. 562–3 (stating that Eliz. succeeded Sir Chris.); L.J.R.O., B/C/5/1663, Leek.
25 *S.H.C.* 1925, 165.
26 Jolliffe, *Jolliffes of Staffs.* 15–17; *Complete Peerage*, xii (2), 214.

1728 the farm, occupied by Caleb Morrice, covered 403 a., but the house was in a bad state of repair; there was also a 14-a. farm.[27] In 1759 William, Viscount Vane, son of William and Lucy, sold the reversion of what were described then and in 1735 as the manor or lordship of Westwood and the farm or grange called Westwood to Mary, countess of Stamford.[28] By the time of Lord Vane's death in 1789 she had been succeeded by her second son Booth Grey, who was succeeded by his son Booth in 1802.[29]

The younger Booth sold the estate in 1813 to John Davenport, a potter and glassmaker of Longport in Burslem and a native of Leek.[30] He died at Westwood in 1848 with his son John as his heir.[31] Both of them greatly enlarged the estate by buying neighbouring farms.[32] The younger John, who was appointed sheriff in 1854, died in 1862. His son George sold Westwood Hall with much of the estate to John Robinson in 1868.[33] Robinson was sheriff in 1882, the last to be accompanied by javelin men; the javelins were later kept at Westwood Hall. He died in 1902, leaving the house to his wife Helen with reversion to his three sons.[34] Helen Robinson continued to live at Westwood Hall until her death in 1908, and by 1912 it was the home of H. J. Johnson.[35] In 1920 he sold it to Staffordshire county council, which turned it into a school.[36]

In 1804 the farmhouse called Westwood was offered for sale with 212 a. as potentially 'a pleasant and convenient country residence'.[37] In 1818 John Davenport began improvements, and by 1834 the house, then known as Westwood Hall, was 'a neat mansion with extensive plantations and pleasure grounds'.[38] He added a new south entrance front and a wing to the northeast, employing James Elmes as his architect. The enlarged house, of two storeys with attics, was in the Elizabethan style with curved gables and mullioned and transomed windows.[39] In 1851 John Davenport the younger made further extensions, designed by Weightman, Hadfield & Goldie of Sheffield and including a great hall and tower at the west end of the south front and extensive buildings around a courtyard on the north-west. The extensions, which were in stone on the principal elevations and dark red brick elsewhere, were in a plain Elizabethan style, and the surviving elevations by Elmes were altered to conform to it.[40]

The improvements to the grounds made by John Davenport the elder included a terraced lawn to the east of the house with an ornamental retaining wall, entrance gates to the south-east, and a Gothick outbuilding with tower and spire to the south-west.[41] Further south-west are early 19th-century stables, which were used as farm buildings after coach houses and stables were built west of the house in the mid 19th century. By 1864 much of the plateau on which the house stands and the adjacent slopes had been landscaped with a mixture of small woods and fields. A lodge was built on the eastern drive in 1852,[42] and there was another at the entrance to the southern drive on the Newcastle road near Wall bridge by 1861.[43] Both survive as houses.

The endowments given to Chester abbey by Hugh, earl of Chester, in 1093 included all tithes from his manor of Leek.[44] In the earlier 1220s, however, Leek church was appropriated to Dieulacres abbey,[45] and the RECTORY was held by the monks until the dissolution of the abbey in 1538. In 1291 Leek church with a dependent chapel, presumably either Horton or Ipstones, was valued at £28.[46] In 1535 the rectory consisted of £1 4s. rent from the Leek glebe land, £18 3s. 8d. from the great tithes belonging to Leek church, £17 from the other tithes, £7 5s. 4d. from the Easter Roll, and £2 6s. 8d. from offerings.[47] In 1538–9 the rectory was valued at £63 4s. 8d.[48] There were then tithe barns at Birchall grange, at Fowlchurch grange in Tittesworth, at Endon, and evidently at Heaton and Longsdon.[49]

In 1560 the rectory was granted to Sir Ralph Bagnall at a fee-farm rent of £51 3s., given as the value of the rectory. The grant was made in recognition of his service and in consideration of all money owed him for his service in Ireland.[50] Sir Ralph sold most of the tithes to the owners of the property on which they were due.[51] His nephew and heir Sir Henry Bagnall sold what was called the rectory to Thomas Rudyard with the manor and the advowson of Leek in 1597, and the rectory still formed part of the Rudyard Hall estate in 1677.[52] In 1610 the Crown granted the fee-farm rent to Sir Christopher Hatton and Sir Francis Needham, to whom the fee-farm rent for Leek manor had already been granted. They sold small parts of both to John Rothwell of Leek later the same year.[53]

27 W.S.L., S.MS. 243/i, pp. 72–5.
28 Ibid. D. 1798/280; Complete Peerage, xii (2), 215.
29 W.S.L., D. 1798/281; Hist. Parl., Commons, 1754–90, ii. 551–2; 1790–1820, iv. 98–9 (noting confusion of the younger Booth with his cousin and brother-in-law Wm. Booth Grey, as in Sleigh, Leek, 46).
30 S.R.O., D. 3272/1/4/3/23; Sleigh, Leek, 46 n.; V.C.H. Staffs. ii. 230; viii. 136.
31 Olde Leeke, ii. 279; Sleigh, Leek, 47.
32 S.R.O., D. 3272/1/4/3/23.
33 Olde Leeke, ii. 280; Sleigh, Leek, 46–7; S.H.C. 1912, 293.
34 W.S.L. 495A/34, 12 July, 13 Sept. 1902; S.H.C. 1912, 294; S. A. H. Burne, A Legal Bi-centenary (Stafford, priv. print. 1960), 30.
35 W.S.L. 46/45, p. 62; Kelly's Dir. Staffs. (1912).
36 Below, educ.
37 W.S.L., Sleigh scrapbk. ii, f. 57v.
38 White, Dir. Staffs. (1834), 703.
39 H. Colvin, Biog. Dict. Brit. Architects, 292; below, plate 24.

40 150 Years of Architectural Drawings–Hadfield, Cawkwell and Davidson, Sheffield, 1834–1984 (cat. of exhibition at Mappin Art Gallery, Sheffield, 1984), 45; W.S.L., Sleigh scrapbk. ii, ff. 56–8 (1864 sale cat. and plans); date on rainwater heads; below, plate 25. Mr. G. R. Wiskin, head teacher of Westwood High sch., is thanked for his help.
41 Below, plate 24.   42 Date on building.
43 P.R.O., RG 9/1946; W.S.L., Sleigh scrapbk. ii, f. 58 (1864 sale cat. p. 16).
44 V.C.H. Ches. iii. 133.   45 Below, churches.
46 Tax. Eccl. (Rec. Com.), 243.
47 Valor Eccl. (Rec. Com.), iii. 123.
48 Sleigh, Leek, 69.
49 Below, econ. hist. (agric.); Endon, econ. hist. (agric.); Heaton, econ. hist. (agric.); Longsdon, econ. hist. (agric.); Tittesworth, econ. hist.
50 Cal. Pat. 1558–60, 308–9.
51 Sleigh, Leek, 22, 24; S.H.C. xiii. 243, 246–7; S.H.C. 1915, 146.   52 S.H.C. xvi. 167; S.R.O. 3508/A/1/4.
53 S.R.O., D. 5017/5/306; above, this section (Leek manor).

AGRICULTURE. In 1086 Leek manor had 12 ploughteams, and there were 15 *villani* and 13 bordars with 6 teams. There were 3 a. of meadow, and woodland measured 4 leagues in length and 4 in breadth. The value of the manor had increased from £4 in 1066 to £5 in 1086.[54]

At £5 the value of Leek manor in 1086 was relatively high for Staffordshire,[55] a fact which may indicate a well developed pastoral economy. Cattle farming appears to have been important in the late 12th century: in 1182–3 thirty-two cows were bought to complete the stocking of the manor.[56] Bee keeping too seems to have been important, with 5s. being raised by the sale of honey from the manor in 1184–5.[57] Dieulacres abbey, having acquired Leek manor, established a grange at Birchall by 1246 and possibly another at Westwood.[58] In 1291 Westwood grange consisted of 2 carucates worth £1 a year, and there was also 6s. 8d. a year from the sale of meadow.[59] The monks were evidently involved in arable farming at the granges c. 1500, with stock farming also at Birchall. There were 20 draught oxen at Birchall in 1490 and 10 with 2 heifers in 1501. In 1502 Birchall had 20 draught oxen, an unspecified number of cows (6 in 1508), and 200 sheep, while at Westwood there were 10 draught oxen.[60] By the 1530s both granges had been leased to the Brereton family of Westwood, Westwood grange then being known as the grange of Westwood and Woodcroft.[61] There was a tithe barn at Birchall at the Dissolution and in 1563.[62]

Leek's early 13th-century borough charter granted each burgess 1 a. in the fields.[63] In the late 16th century an open field called Leek town field extended from the Nab Hill area and Belle Vue Road to the east side of the Cheddleton road.[64] Piecemeal inclosure was then in progress there.[65]

By the later 17th century over 40 a. of common waste on the north side of the town field, consisting of Woodcroft heath, Westwood heath, and land at Nab Hill and Back of the Street (later Belle Vue Road), passed to the freeholders of Leek and Lowe township. The income from the rents charged for pasturing horses there and rents from houses built at Back of the Street was used for the repair of the highways and other public purposes. By 1711 the income was £2 15s. 6d.[66] Under the Leek inclosure Act of 1805 and the award of 1811 what were then known as the Town Lands were vested in seven freeholders as trustees who were to manage them and keep accounts. In addition 5 a. on Leek moor east of the town were assigned to them.[67] By 1849 over 10 a. had been lost, mainly through failure to collect the rents. The 34 a. remaining produced rents of £90 19s.[68] In 1878 the 64-a. Dee Bank farm in Mount Road was acquired from John Robinson of Westwood Hall in exchange for 19 a. at Westwood. The income of the Town Lands trust in 1990–1 was £7,334, derived from the rent of Dee Bank farm and from investments; £5,340 was spent on donations, mainly to local organizations, the income having to be used for the benefit of the inhabitants of Leek and Lowe.[69]

By 1708 freeholders were attempting action against incroachments on Leek moor east of the town.[70] In 1790 fifteen people with rights in the commons and waste of the manors of Leek and Frith signed an agreement to prosecute commoners who overloaded the commons and others without common rights who put sheep and cattle on the commons. The cost was to be divided according to the value of each signatory's holding, and a meeting of commoners was arranged at the Marquess of Granby inn at Leek.[71] The part of Leek moor which remained common waste was inclosed in 1811 under the Act of 1805.[72]

Of the 851 ha. in Leek civil parish returned in 1988, 732 ha. were grassland, 73 ha. rough grazing, and 42 ha. woodland. There were 1,869 head of cattle, including calves, and 444 sheep, including 204 breeding ewes and 212 lambs. Of the 35 holdings returned, 11 were full-time farms, 10 of them entirely devoted to dairying and the other mainly so. All were under 100 ha. in size, with only five of 50 ha. or more.[73]

In 1542 there was one free tenement in Leek and Lowe. Four other tenements, including Birchall Grange, owed rent, two capons worth 6d., one day's ploughing worth 3d., and one day's reaping worth 3d., while a fifth, Westwood Grange, owed rent, four capons, and two days of each work.[74]

A gardener named William Hyde was living in Leek in 1757, and there was another named Matthew Washington in Spout Street in 1762.[75] There were two gardeners and seedsmen in the

---

54 *V.C.H. Staffs.* iv. 39.   55 Ibid. vi. 2, 4.
56 *Pipe R.* 1183 (P.R.S. xxxii), 152.
57 Ibid. 1185 (P.R.S. xxxiv), 2.
58 Lambeth Palace Libr., Papal Docs. 40. The document is damaged, and the second grange could be Wetwood, in Leekfrith.
59 *Tax. Eccl.* (Rec. Com.), 252.
60 S.R.O. 4974/ADD 2.
61 *S.H.C.* N.S. ix. 72–3, 128–9; *S.H.C.* 1938, 73; S.R.O. 4974/ADD 1; W.S.L., M. 540.
62 Sleigh, *Leek*, 59 n., 62; S.R.O., D. 3359/misc. deeds, deed of 20 Aug. 1563.
63 Below, local govt. The 3 fields identified as in Leek by H. L. Gray, *Eng. Field Systems*, 497 (followed by *V.C.H. Staffs.* vi. 13), were in West Leake, Notts.: *Cartulary of Dale Abbey* (Derb. Rec. Soc. ii), pp. 22, 131–3.
64 *T.N.S.F.C.* lviii. 81 and pl. facing p. 79; S.R.O., D. 3359/Cruso, deeds of 22 Apr., 10 Sept. 1587; D. 3359/misc.

deeds, deed of 6 July 1589; L.J.R.O., B/V/6/Leek, 1685.
65 S.R.O., D. 3359/misc. deeds, deed of 16 Mar. 1601/2; L.J.R.O., B/V/6/Leek, 1612; B.L. Add. Ch. 46707.
66 *T.N.S.F.C.* lviii. 79–84; *Olde Leeke*, i. 263–4; P.R.O., E 134/6 Geo. I East./21; S.R.O. 3508/A/3/10.
67 45 Geo. III, c. 96 (Local and Personal); S.R.O., Q/RDc 65, no. 133 and plan I; *Olde Leeke*, i. 265.
68 *Rep. Cttee. Town Lands 1849*, 8–11; *T.N.S.F.C.* lviii, pl. facing p. 79.
69 Inf. from Mr. J. M. Hilton, secretary to the Leek Town Lands Trustees; Char. Com. file 244672.
70 D.R.O., D. 231M/B8, loose letter of 13 Apr. 1708.
71 S.R.O., D. 3359/misc. deeds, deed of 21 June 1790.
72 S.R.O., Q/RDc 65; 45 Geo. III, c. 96 (Local and Personal).   73 P.R.O., MAF 68/6128/63.
74 W.S.L., M. 540.
75 S.R.O., D. 3359/Strangman, deed of 22 July 1757; D. 3359/misc. deeds, will of Matt. Washington, 1762.

town in 1818.[76] Four listed in 1834 and 1851 included William Nunns, who landscaped the ground on the west side of Rudyard Lake in 1851. His nursery was at Barngates in 1849 when plants, rhubarb, and cabbages were stolen from it.[77]

Leek and District Agricultural and Horticultural Society held its first show in 1895 on a farm at Belle Vue.[78] The show lapsed in 1955 but was revived in 1962. In the early 1990s it was still held as an annual event at Birchall.[79]

WARRENS AND FISHERIES. There may have been a rabbit warren in the area south-east of the town in the 13th century.[80] There was evidently a warren at Westwood at some period. In 1728 Westwood farm included the 13-a. Cunney Greave and in 1804 a close called the Rabbit Warren. In 1864 three fields south-west of Westwood Hall and then part of Wallbridge farm were called Rabbit Burrow.[81]

A fishery in the Churnet formed part of the Birchall Grange estate in 1565.[82] In 1884 there was a protest that the river between Leek and Rocester was being contaminated by effluent from print and dye works and by Leek's sewage, with a consequent threat to the fishing.[83] Fish in the Leek–Cheddleton stretch of the river were eventually wiped out, but by the mid 1970s there was again good fishing there. In 1989 the National Rivers Authority, having released over 2,000 chub and dace into the Churnet at Leek and Cheddleton answered fears about their survival by stating that dyeworks effluent was then harmless and that the only danger was from the Leekbrook sewage works.[84] In 1992 the Leek and District Fly Fishing Club secured an out-of-court settlement from Severn Trent Water for the loss of fishing rights in the river between Kingsley and Alton since 1984 as a result of pollution from the sewage works. New treatment processes completed at the works in 1992 were designed to produce an improvement in the effluent discharged into the river.[85]

MILLS. Ranulph, earl of Chester, had a mill at Leek by the mid 12th century.[86] The borough charter granted by his grandson Earl Ranulph de Blundeville stipulated that the burgesses of Leek were to grind their corn at his mill 'immediately after that which shall be in the hopper', paying a toll of one twentieth of the grain

brought for grinding.[87] In the early 1220s Ranulph granted the mill to the monks of Dieulacres, c. 10 years before granting them the manor. He stated that his bailiffs would exact from the men of the manor suit at the mill on behalf of the monks and the customary work on the mill and its pool.[88] When the abbot renewed the borough charter after the grant of the manor, he included the clause relating to the grinding of the burgesses' corn.[89] The mill was valued at £1 in 1291.[90] At the Dissolution the abbey had two water mills at Leek.[91] One was evidently on the Churnet in Mill Street: that was the site of a mill in 1733, and Mill Street was so named by the earlier 16th century.[92] The other mill may have been at Birchall, where the abbey had a mill on the Churnet in the 13th century.[93]

In 1552 the Crown granted the mills with the manor to Sir Ralph Bagnall, who conveyed them to Ralph Rudyard in 1565.[94] In 1563 the jurors of the manor court stated that the tenants might grind their corn where they pleased,[95] but the Rudyards later challenged the claim. About 1615 Timothy Egerton of Wall Grange in Longsdon erected a horse mill at Birchall, but Thomas Rudyard forced him to abandon it. By 1632 Randle Ashenhurst of Ashenhurst in Bradnop had a horse mill in the town, and in 1635 Thomas Rudyard's son Thomas challenged his right, claiming that the inhabitants of the manor were obliged to grind at Thomas's mills at Leek and Dieulacres and pay a toll of one sixteenth. That claim was itself challenged in the subsequent inquiry, at least as far as corn bought outside the manor was concerned. It was also pointed out that the horse mill proved especially useful when the manorial mills were put out of action by floods or frosts.[96] The horse mill was probably in Derby Street where the Hollinsheads, the Ashenhursts' successors at Ashenhurst, had a horse mill in 1675, 1704, and 1721.[97]

The mill in Mill Street was rebuilt in 1752 by James Brindley, the engineer, who had set up as a millwright in Mill Street in 1742.[98] The mill remained in operation until the 1940s, and part of it was demolished for road widening in 1948. The building was bought in 1972 by a trust formed for the purpose. It was restored and in 1974 was opened as a working mill and a museum.[99]

L. Whittles & Son opened a steam mill in Strangman's Walk (later Strangman Street)

76 Parson and Bradshaw, *Staffs. Dir.* (1818), 124.
77 White, *Dir. Staffs.* (1834), 709; (1851), 737; *P.O. Dir. Staffs.* (1850); S.R.O., D. 3359/Cruso, Leek assoc. for prosec. of felons 1845–50, poster of 4 June 1849; above, Horton, intro. (Rudyard Lake).
78 *Staffs. Advertiser*, 7 Sept. 1895, p. 5.
79 *Leek Post & Times*, 24 July 1991, show special; 31 Dec. 1991, p. 4.
80 Sleigh, *Leek*, 150 (mention of Cuningrene, probably a mistranscription of Cuningreve).
81 W.S.L., S.MS. 243/i, p. 72; W.S.L., Sleigh scrapbk. ii, ff. 57v.–58.   82 *S.H.C.* xiii. 243.
83 *Staffs. Advertiser*, 2 Feb. 1884, p. 7.
84 Leek Libr., newspaper cuttings 1972–8, p. 76; *Leek Post & Times*, 13 Dec. 1989, p. 1.
85 *Leek Post & Times*, 17 June 1992, p. 1; 24 June 1992, p. 10.
86 *Charters of Earls of Chester*, p. 36.

87 Ibid. p. 348; cf. ibid. p. 382.
88 Ibid. p. 380.
89 Sleigh, *Leek*, 16 and pl. II following.
90 *Tax. Eccl.* (Rec. Com.), 252.
91 Sleigh, *Leek*, 17; P.R.O., SC 6/Hen. VIII/3353, m. 32d.
92 S.R.O., D. 3359/Badnall, abstract of title of Mrs. Badnall; above, general hist. (Middle Ages).
93 *S.H.C.* N.S. ix. 313.
94 *S.H.C.* xiii. 207, 240; *S.H.C.* N.S. ix. 9.
95 S.R.O., D. (W.) 1702/1/1/4.
96 P.R.O., E 134/11 Chas. I East./5; Sleigh, *Leek*, 17 n.
97 B.L. Add. Ch. 46793; D.R.O., D. 231M/B101; P.R.O., CP 25(2)/1062/7 Geo. I Hil. no. 7.
98 C. T. G. Boucher, *James Brindley* (Norwich, 1968), 32–4, 36–7; *T.N.S.F.C.* lxxiii. 56.
99 Boucher, *Brindley*, 32; J. Levitt, *The Brindley Mill at Leek* (Leek, 1974).

c. 1890. It ceased to be steam-powered *c.* 1930 but was still in operation in the mid 1970s.[1]

MARKETS AND FAIRS. In 1207 King John confirmed to Ranulph, earl of Chester, a market every Wednesday in the manor of Leek and a seven-day fair beginning three days before the feast of St. Edward (probably 20 June, the feast of the Second Translation of Edward the Martyr, or 13 October, the feast of the Translation of Edward the Confessor).[2] The borough charter granted by Earl Ranulph shortly afterwards stipulated that those coming to the market and the fair should pay only the same toll as was paid in the other free markets of Staffordshire.[3] About 1220 the earl received 20s. from tolls.[4] The right to a market and a fair passed to Dieulacres abbey, presumably with the manor in 1232, but the abbot's renewal of the borough charter made no mention of the payment of toll.[5] The fair was still held around the feast of St. Edward in the earlier 14th century,[6] but by the Dissolution it was held on the feast of St. Arnulf (18 July) and the seven days following.[7]

The right to a market and a fair was included in the Crown's grant of most of the former abbey's Staffordshire property to Sir Ralph Bagnall in 1552 and in the sale of the manor to Thomas Rudyard in 1597.[8] In 1629, however, the Crown granted Thomas Jodrell of Moorhouse in Leek the right to a three-day fair in May with a court of pie powder, tolls, and other dues.[9] The Jodrells acquired the market tolls as well. It was as bailiff of the town or of the market and collector of the market tolls that Thomas's great-nephew John Jodrell claimed a seat in the north aisle of the parish church in 1669, adding that his father, grandfather, and ancestors had held the seat by the same right.[10] John's son William succeeded in 1696, and *c.* 1700 he mortgaged the market and fair tolls to John Sutton and William Grosvenor, a Leek physician. Both sets of tolls were conveyed to Grosvenor in 1722.[11] By 1791 they were owned by his grandson Thomas Fenton Grosvenor (d. 1831) and Henry Manifold, vicar of Brackley,

Northants. (d. 1803); in 1792 Manifold offered to sell his half share to Grosvenor for 1,000 guineas.[12] The offer was evidently not accepted since in 1825 the owners were Grosvenor and Henry Townsend.[13] In 1855 the tolls were owned by Grosvenor's widow Mary, Edward Rooke, and the trustee of Grosvenor's will.[14] They were bought from Mrs. Grosvenor and Edward Rooke by the Leek improvement commissioners in 1859.[15]

The town was noted for its market *c.* 1600.[16] In the earlier 1670s, with a considerable trade in cattle, sheep, oats, and provisions, the market was ranked the third most important in the county, after Uttoxeter and Wolverhampton.[17] Wednesday was then still the market day, but in 1688 there was mention of Leek's 'new market day'.[18] Wednesday was the only market day in the late 18th century.[19] By 1822 a cattle market was held every alternate Wednesday from 28 July until Christmas.[20] It was held throughout the year by the later 1880s, and probably from 1867 when the Privy Council licensed a fortnightly cattle market at Leek.[21] It became a weekly market *c.* 1910.[22] There was a Saturday market by 1850, dealing chiefly in meat and vegetables; it evidently lapsed about the late 1880s.[23] Wednesday remains the main market day, but a Saturday general market had been introduced by the early 1960s and another on Friday by the early 1980s.[24] A Monday cattle market specializing in calves was started in 1994, following the closure of the smithfield at Newcastle-under-Lyme.[25] An outdoor Saturday market specializing in crafts and antiques was also begun in 1994.[26]

In the 17th century there were several fairs: there was a fair on All Souls' Day (2 November) in 1622,[27] the fair granted to Thomas Jodrell in 1629 was on 7, 8, and 9 May,[28] and 17 July was a fair day *c.* 1680.[29] By the mid 18th century Leek had seven fairs a year, on the Wednesday before 2 February, the Wednesday in Easter week, 7 May, the Wednesday after Whitsun, 22 June, 17 July, and 2 November; all the fixed dates moved on 11 days with the change in the calendar in 1752.[30] An additional fair on the

[1] *Kelly's Dir. Staffs.* (1892 and later edns.); Sherlock, *Ind. Arch. Staffs.* 177–8; H. Bode, *Visiting Leek*, i (Leek, 1974), 15.
[2] *Rot. Chart.* (Rec. Com.), 173.
[3] Below, local govt. (borough).
[4] *Staffs. Studies*, v. 20.
[5] *Plac. de Quo Warr.* (Rec. Com.), 714; Sleigh, *Leek*, 20; below, local govt.
[6] *Plac. de Quo Warr.* 714; S.R.O., D. 1337/1.
[7] Sleigh, *Leek*, 20.
[8] Ibid. 22, 25.
[9] P.R.O., C 66/2467, m. 31.
[10] L.J.R.O., B/C/5/1669, Leek (seat); P.R.O., CP 25(2)/724/19 Chas. II Mic. no. 29; Sleigh, *Leek*, 94. John's grandfather John Jodrell was described as 'baylie of Leek' in 1616: L.J.R.O., B/C/11, Wm. Rode (1616).
[11] Sleigh, *Leek*, 32, 94; P.R.O., CP 43/452, rot. 45.
[12] S.R.O., D. 3359/Fenton Grosvenor, letters from Manifold to Grosvenor 16 Jan. 1791 and to John Cruso 10 July 1792. For the Grosvenors see below (medical practitioners). For Manifold see *Admissions to St. John's Coll., Cambridge*, iii, ed. R. F. Scott, 139, 618.
[13] Act for lighting, watching, cleansing, and improving the town of Leek, 6 Geo. IV, c. 71 (Local and Personal), s. 89.
[14] Leek Improvement Act, 1855, 18 & 19 Vic. c. 132 (Local and Personal), s. 168; White, *Dir. Staffs.* (1851), 734.
[15] S.R.O., D. 3226/1, nos. 929, 935, 999; D. 3226/2, no. 1583; Leek Improvement Com. *Reps.* (1894), 22.
[16] Camden, *Brit.* (1607), 444.
[17] R. Blome, *Britannia* (1673), 201, 205–6.
[18] Ibid. 205; S.R.O., D. 3359/Condlyffe, Wm. Grosvenor's acct. bk. 1686–98, loose paper 20 Dec. 1688.
[19] *Bailey's Brit. Dir.* (1784), 388.
[20] Pigot, *New Com. Dir. for 1822–3*, 468.
[21] Miller, *Leek*, 43; W.S.L., Sleigh scrapbk. ii, f. 3.
[22] *Kelly's Dir. Staffs.* (1908; 1912).
[23] *P.O. Dir. Staffs.* (1850); *Olde Leeke*, ii. 75, describing it in 1889 as much smaller than the Wednesday market. Only the Wednesday market is mentioned in *Kelly's Dir. Staffs.* (1888).
[24] *Leek Official Guide* [early 1960s edn.], 19; K. Warrender, *Exploring Leek* (Timperley, 1982), 32.
[25] *Leek Post & Times*, 7 Sept. 1994, p. 5.
[26] Ibid. 24 Aug. 1994, p. 26; 7 Sept. 1994, p. 11.
[27] L.J.R.O., B/C/5/1623, Leek (slander of vicar).
[28] P.R.O., C 66/2467, m. 31.   [29] Plot, *Staffs.* 173.
[30] W.S.L., S.MS. 468, p. 101; P. Russell and O. Price, *Eng. Displayed* (1769), ii. 70; Pigot, *New Com. Dir.* [1829], 712.

Wednesday after 10 October was held by the late 1790s.[31] A fair on the first Wednesday in January was introduced in 1814, but the same year it was changed to the last Wednesday in December; it was a hiring fair by 1834.[32] Monthly cheese fairs were being held by 1820, but from 1821 they were reduced to three a year, in March, September, and November.[33] The fair on 3 July had dwindled to a fair for the sale of scythes by the mid 19th century, and even that was nominal by the later 1860s.[34] By 1867 the November fair included a hiring fair.[35] By 1887 the cheese fairs were held in February, August, and October, and the July fairs were changed to the first and last Wednesdays of that month early in the 20th century.[36] All the fairs were still listed in 1940.[37] The November hiring fair continued as a pleasure fair until 1960.[38] A pleasure fair formed part of the May fair by the mid 19th century[39] and was still held in the early 1990s.

The main venue for the markets and fairs was the market place, which probably once extended west to St. Edward Street. The names Sheepmarket and Custard (later Stanley) Street for the two streets linking the present Market Place with St. Edward Street suggest areas of specialized trading.[40] The market cross was mentioned regularly between 1654 and 1658 as a place where banns were published.[41] In 1671 a cross was erected at the south end of the market place by one of the Jolliffe family, probably Thomas. It was moved to Cornhill on the Cheddleton road in 1806 when a public hall was built on its site. In 1857 the Cornhill site was required for the chapels of the new cemetery, and the cross was re-erected in the cemetery on a new base. It was moved back to the market place in 1986.[42] The ground floor of the public hall of 1806 was left open for use by the market people, but they found it dark and inconvenient and soon abandoned it.[43] By the 1780s the stalls used at the markets and fairs were stored in a building in Derby Street known as the stall barn; it was still so used in 1863 when it was offered for sale.[44] A covered butter market designed by J. T. Brealey of Leek and Hanley was opened on the east side of the market place in 1897, and a poultry market was added in 1902. The building was again

extended in 1936, but soon after 1945 the two earlier portions were adapted to provide fixed lock-up stalls.[45]

Other parts of the town were also used. In 1586 the inhabitants of Leek were presented at quarter sessions for allowing fairs and markets to be held in the churchyard.[46] An open space at the east end of Derby Street bought by the trustees of the Town Lands from the earl of Macclesfield in 1827 was used for the fortnightly cattle market.[47] By the 1870s, however, animals offered for sale were clogging the streets of the town, and in 1874 the improvement commissioners opened a smithfield in Haywood Street, banning all livestock sales in the streets.[48] The site at the end of Derby Street continued to be used as an overflow smithfield and also as a fairground and a venue for travelling theatrical companies until the earlier 1920s when the Memorial Clock Tower was built there.[49] The Haywood Street smithfield was enlarged in 1894 by the addition of the land in Leonard Street occupied by the town yard. A building on the Ashbourne Road side of the smithfield was bought in 1877 and converted into a coffee tavern and a room for transacting business. In 1960 the cattle market was transferred to a 7-a. site off Junction Road in the south-west of the town, and a bus station and a shopping precinct were built on the Haywood Street site.[50] The May fair, having been held on the Haywood Street smithfield,[51] was also transferred to the new smithfield.

TRADE AND INDUSTRY. SILK. *The 17th and 18th centuries.* The suggestion that silk working was brought to Leek by French Protestant refugees after 1685 was based on a misreading of the Leek churchwardens' accounts.[52] Thomas Wardle, a leading figure in the industry in the 19th century, stated plausibly that the twisting of sewing silks came to Leek from Macclesfield (Ches.).[53] The first clear evidence of silk working in Leek dates from 1672. John Wood, a silk weaver of Derby Street, died that year possessing silk worth over £300, 'shop goods' worth £100, including ribbons known as galloons, and looms and wheels worth £4 1s.[54]

31 *Univ. Brit. Dir.* v [1798], 103; Pigot, *New Com. Dir.* [1829], 712.
32 *Staffs. Advertiser*, 25 Dec. 1813; 24 Dec. 1814; White, *Dir. Staffs.* (1834), 700.
33 *Staffs. Advertiser*, 23 Dec. 1820, p. 1; Pigot, *New Com. Dir. for 1822–3*, 468; *Derb. Arch. Jnl.* lxxxix. 38.
34 W.S.L., Sleigh scrapbk. ii, ff. 13–14, 81.
35 Ibid. f. 3.
36 Miller, *Leek*, 43; *Kelly's Dir. Staffs.* (1924); *Staffs. Advertiser*, 12 Sept. 1903, p. 5.
37 *Kelly's Dir. Staffs.* (1940).
38 L. Porter, *Leek Thirty Years Ago* (Clifton, Ashbourne, 1991), 7.
39 *Staffs. Advertiser*, 22 May 1852, p. 4; 25 May 1867, p. 7.
40 Sheepmarket was recorded in 1646: *Leek Par. Reg.* 66. Custard may have derived from the costard apple.
41 *Leek Par. Reg.* 95 sqq.
42 Sleigh, *Leek*, 33; *T.N.S.F.C.* viii. 6; S.R.O., D. 3226/1, no. 273; D. 3226/30, no. 38; Leek Libr., newspaper cuttings 1986, p. 29; below, plate 39. For Thos. Jolliffe see above, manors (Birchall).
43 *Olde Leeke*, i. 2.
44 S.R.O., D. 843/1/1; D. 843/1/5/1; D. 3226/1, no. 994; D. 3226/29, 20 Feb. 1860.

45 *Chronicles* (spring 1988), 13–16; Leek U.D.C. *One Hundred Years of Local Govt. in Leek 1855–1955*, 14.
46 *S.H.C.* 1927, 180–1.
47 *Rep. Cttee. Town Lands 1849*, 12–13; White, *Dir. Staffs.* (1834), 700.
48 W.S.L., Sleigh scrapbk. ii, ff. 97, 101; *Staffs. Advertiser*, 3 Oct. 1874, p. 1.
49 Leek Libr., newspaper cuttings 1979, p. 24; Anderton, *Edwardian Leek*, 78, 89, 105; below, social and cultural activities (theatres).
50 Leek U.D.C. *New Leek Cattle Market*, 9, 13, 15; Leek Improvement Com. *Reps.* (1894), 22–3; above, general hist. (20th cent.). For a view of the Haywood St. market see below, plate 41. 51 *Leek & Moorlands Heritage*, ii. 9.
52 Sleigh, *Leek*, 5; *Chronicles* (winter 1989), 11. Mr. P. Anderton of Newcastle-under-Lyme and Mr. A. W. Bednall of Macclesfield are thanked for generously making available the results of their research into the history of the Leek silk industry. Mr. Bednall has also supplied references from the *Macclesfield Courier* (from 1828 *Macclesfield Courier & Herald*).
53 *2nd Rep. Com. Technical Instruction, vol. iii* [C. 3981-II], pp. xxxii, xlvii, H.C. 1884, xxxi (2).
54 L.J.R.O., B/C/11, John Wood (1673); *Leek Par. Reg.* 191.

His son Jonathan was a silk weaver living in Leek in 1682,[55] and there are references to other silk weavers in the late 17th and early 18th century.[56] The ribbons among the stock of Mary Davenport, a Leek chapwoman, at her death in 1737[57] may have been made locally.

The wheels possessed by John Wood in 1672 may indicate that he was twisting his own yarn. In 1732 Leek joined with Manchester, Macclesfield, and Stockport in petitioning against the renewal of John Lombe's patent for his silk-throwing mill in Derby; the petitioners included manufacturers of silk and mohair yarn and twisters and twiners of mohair, cotton, worsted, and probably linen thread.[58] Joseph Myott of Church Street, described as a silk weaver in 1728, had a twisting alley next to his house in 1734.[59] It seems, however, that the twisting of mohair rather than silk predominated in Leek for much of the 18th century. In 1729 Joseph Jackson held a shed (locally known as a shade) for twisting mohair at Spout Gate at the south end of Spout Street (later St. Edward Street).[60] A Joseph Myott was twisting mohair in 1764 in a shade situated behind the Buffalo's Head inn at the south end of the market place and described in 1749 as newly erected. In 1773 it was used for stretching and drying mohair by Messrs. Phillips and Ford, button merchants.[61] William Badnall (d. 1760) of Mill Street worked as a dyer by 1734 and possibly by 1725, with dyehouses by the Churnet in Abbey Green Road at its junction with Mill Street. He was described as a mohair dyer in 1736. In 1758 he bought the bankrupt Richard Ferne's linen-thread works on the opposite side of Abbey Green Road, which included a dyehouse by Ball Haye brook. It is not known that he ever engaged in silk dyeing.[62] Ferne was described as a thread merchant in 1743 and as a threadmaker in 1754; his dyehouse was newly erected in 1743, when he also had 'poles for drying linen yarn' by the brook.[63] John Finney of Leek, who died in 1740, was then described as a cheese factor, but his house and shop contained flax, hemp, jersey, woollen and linen cloth, and woollen and worsted yarn. In addition there were hose for adults and children, caps, and a stocking frame.[64]

Buttons were the staple of Leek's textile industry until the later 18th century, consisting of moulds covered with various threads including mohair and silk. About 1680 the poor people of the area were said to employ themselves 'much in making of button'.[65] Buttons formed part of John Wood's stock at his death in 1672, and he was retrospectively described as a button man 10 years later.[66] Matthew Stubbs of Leek (d. 1692) combined trade with farming, and besides cloth his stock in 1692 contained a large quantity of buttons, including thread buttons, hair buttons, and braid buttons.[67] In 1721 Leek joined with several Cheshire towns in successfully petitioning on behalf of all employed in the manufacture of 'needle-wrought buttons' for the passing of an Act banning the wearing of cloth buttons and buttonholes.[68] Samuel Toft, a Quaker button merchant of Leek, had stock worth £634 6s. 'in the shops at Salop and Hereford' at the time of his death, evidently in 1732.[69] Richard Wilkes, a mid 18th-century Staffordshire antiquary, noted Leek's 'great trade of making buttons for men's clothes of hair, mohair, silk thread etc. . . . . Many hundreds of poor people are employed in this manufacture, get a good livelihood, and bring great riches to the gentlemen that procure materials to set them to work and patterns to please the wearer.'[70]

The improvement of communications in the later 18th century and the ban on the import of silk goods in 1765 encouraged the development of the Leek silk industry. Button making declined with the growth of the metal-button industry in Birmingham at the end of the century, but the production of ribbons increased. In 1760 the mayor of Coventry stated that he had sent materials to Leek as well as Congleton (Ches.) to be made up into ribbons.[71] Another Coventry man, Thomas Horton, is said to have introduced the weaving of figured ribbons in Leek c. 1800.[72] Five ribbon manufacturers were listed at Leek in 1784, two of them also making buttons and silk twist, and there were four other makers of buttons and twist, two of them also producing sewing silk.[73] By 1797 the shade behind the Buffalo's Head was used for stretching and drying silk as well as mohair.[74] The Badnall family's works was engaged in silk dyeing by the 1780s under the management of William's son Joseph. Thomas Ball was dyeing silk in the 1790s in Mill Street, and he was still in business in 1809.[75] In 1795 it was stated that Leek's considerable silk industry was producing sewing silks, twist, buttons, silk ferrets, shawls,

55 S.R.O., D. 3359/misc. deeds, deed of 15 May 1682.
56 Sleigh, *Leek*, 8; *Leek Par. Reg.* 251, 261; P. W. L. Adams, *Notes on some N. Staffs. Families* (Tunstall, priv. print., foreword dated 1930), 93, 94 n.; S.R.O., D. 1040/5/14, 5 Jan. 1697/8; D. 3159/3/1, no. 178; D. 3359/misc. deeds, deposition in Fernyhough and Myott v. Oakes and Cooke, 1720; apprenticeship indenture 8 July 1687 (in possession of Mr. R. Stones of Malpas, Ches., 1994); below, prot. nonconf. (Friends, Soc. of).
57 L.J.R.O., B/C/11, Mary Davenport (1737).
58 *C.J.* xxi. 840; *V.C.H. Derb.* ii. 372.
59 S.R.O., D. 3359/Badnall, abstract of title of Ric. Badnall to property at Clerks Bank, pp. 1–3.
60 Ibid. D. 3359/Cruso, deed of 1 May 1729.
61 Ibid. D. 3010/2, p. 5; D. 3359/Strangman, deeds of 26 Jan. 1748/9, 2 Oct. 1764.
62 S.R.O., D. 1040/5/14, 29 Nov. 1725, 14 Sept. 1735; D. 1040/5/15, 13 Dec. 1760; S.R.O., D. 3359/Badnall, abstract of title of Mrs. Badnall, p. 1; ibid. abstract of title of Ric. Badnall to the Brindley House, p. 31; ibid. abstract

ot title of Ric. Badnall to the Hencroft, p. 10; L.J.R.O., B/C/11, Sarah Badnall; *Staffs. Hist.* viii. 3; *Chronicles* (autumn 1994), 53.
63 S.R.O., D. 3359/Badnall, abstract of title of Ric. Badnall to the Hencroft, p. 10; *Admissions to St. John's Coll., Camb.*, iii, ed. R. F. Scott, 143.
64 L.J.R.O., B/C/11, John Finney (1740).
65 Plot, *Staffs.* 98.
66 L.J.R.O., B/C/11, John Wood (1673); S.R.O., D. 3359/misc. deeds, deed of 15 May 1682.
67 L.J.R.O., B/C/11, Matthew Stubbs (1692).
68 *L.J.* xxi. 498, 518, 535; *V.C.H. Staffs.* ii. 206.
69 L.J.R.O., B/C/11, Sam. Toft (1732); S.R.O., D. 3359/Toft-Chorley, record of marriage of Sam. Toft 1723.
70 W.S.L., S.MS. 468, p. 101.
71 *V.C.H. Staffs.* ii. 206–7.   72 Sleigh, *Leek*, 5.
73 *Bailey's Brit. Dir.* (1784), 388.
74 S.R.O., D. 3010/2, p. 14.
75 *Staffs. Hist.* viii. 4–5; xii. 15; S.R.O., D. 3359/misc. deeds, deed of 22 Sept. 1781.

and silk handkerchiefs. The industry, in which good fortunes had been made, employed *c.* 2,000 people living in the town and 1,000 in the neighbourhood.[76]

The earlier 19th century. The industry remained predominantly domestic or quasi-domestic until well into the 19th century, with manufacturers giving out the raw material to 'undertakers' to be woven or twisted and then receiving the finished products at their warehouses. There were seven mills in the town by 1835, but it was not until the later 19th century that factory working became fully established.

Weaving was organized by undertakers owning a number of looms and employing journeymen and apprentices.[77] The work was carried out on the second floor over groups of two or more houses, the space being lit by elongated windows and ventilated by means of sliding frames; the undertaker lived in one of the houses. Examples of such three-storeyed houses survive in Albion Street and King Street (1820s) and London Street (by the 1830s).[78] An earlier example may be the mid 18th-century houses in Derby Street (nos. 23 and 25), which have three- and four-light casement windows on the second floor. A further example was the group of six dwellings built in 1823 in what later became Wood Street by William Thompson, a broad-silk weaver, and demolished in 1968. Four of the dwellings, built as two back-to-back pairs, had a workshop on the top floor, which was not integrated with the living accommodation but had its own staircase and external door.[79]

In 1818 there were *c.* 200 ribbon weavers working engine looms and *c.* 100 working single handlooms. In addition there were between 50 and 60 broad-silk weavers, producing handkerchiefs, shawls, and silk varying in breadth between 18 in. and 1½ yd. There had been upwards of 100 such weavers in 1815, but since then prices and wages had fallen.[80] The easing of duties on imported silk and manufactured goods in the mid 1820s led to a further depression.[81] The increasing use of steam power in silk weaving meant the growth in the number of factories and the decline of domestic working. In 1818 there was only one factory, and that had only a few looms.[82] It stood in Mill Street and was run by Richard Badnall and William Laugharn, who appear to have been using steam power by 1816.[83] A foreign visitor in 1826 described it as a 'fine factory building, at the end of the town, quite new, most splendid position in the whole place'; he made sketches of the spinning apparatus, which he also described in

detail.[84] In 1835 there were seven mills (one unoccupied), with 119 power looms; they employed 744 people, 477 of them female.[85] In 1839 John Wreford had 50 looms in his mill in London Street established in 1823–4; Anthony Ward & Co., a firm dating from the early 19th century, had 10 in Albion Mill in Albion Street, completed in the late 1820s.[86]

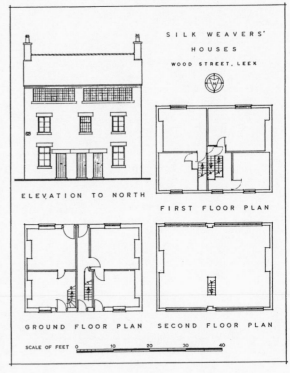

FIG. 19

On the domestic side in 1839 only half of the 150 or so broad looms and a third of the 180 engine looms were working full time. The domestic ribbon industry was mainly in the hands of the female members of the undertakers' families. The journeymen had moved into the mills, and apprentices were no longer being taken; children too were working in the mills. There were still some 40 broad-silk undertakers in 1839, with a large number of journeymen. As yet there were no powered broad looms in operation, but some were being erected.[87] Domestic weaving continued to decline. In 1863 the main products were coat bindings and sleeve facings.[88] In 1875 Robert Farrow, sanitary inspector to the improvement commissioners, stated that only a very little hand-loom weaving

76 J. Aikin, *Descrip. of Country from thirty to forty miles round Manchester* (preface dated 1795), 538.
77 *Reps. Assistant Hand-loom Weavers' Com., Pt. IV* [217], p. 344, H.C. (1840), xxiv.
78 Sherlock, *Ind. Arch. Staffs.* 51, 175–6; *2nd Rep. Com. Tech. Instruction, vol. iii,* p. xlix; *V.C.H. Staffs.* ii, pl. facing p. 210; S.R.O., D. 4645/A/1/30–1.
79 *Reps. Asst. Hand-loom Weavers' Com., Pt. IV,* 346; Sherlock, *Ind. Arch. Staffs.* 50, 52, 56; *V.C.H. Staffs.* ii. 210 (where the description by Samuel Bamford should be dated 1820).
80 *2nd Rep. Cttee. on Ribbon Weavers' Petitions,* H.C. 211 and 278, pp. 133–4, 136–8 (1818), ix.
81 *V.C.H. Staffs.* ii. 209.
82 *2nd Rep. Cttee. on Ribbon Weavers' Petitions,* 137.

83 *Staffs. Hist.* viii. 5; Miller, *Leek,* 48; S.R.O., D. 3359/Badnall, insurance policy of Badnall & Laugharn 26 Dec. 1816.
84 K. F. Schinkel, 'The English Journey', ed. D. Bindman and G. Riemann, 132–3.
85 *V.C.H. Staffs.* ii. 209.
86 *Reps. Asst. Hand-loom Weavers' Com., Pt. IV,* 344. For Anthony Ward & Co. see *V.C.H. Staffs.* ii. 207 (where the date in n. 21 and the corresponding part of the text should read 1798); Sherlock, *Ind. Arch. Staffs.* 175 and pl. facing p. 55; Leek Libr., newspaper cuttings 1960–8, p. 40; 1982 (1), p. 2; below, plate 48.
87 *Reps. Asst. Handloom Weavers' Com., Pt. IV,* 344, 346.
88 *5th Rep. Com. Child. Employment* [3678], p. 85, H.C. (1866), xxiv.

survived,[89] while in 1884 Thomas Wardle stated that there were few cottage hand looms to be found.[90]

Twisting continued longer as a domestic industry or at least as one carried out in shades which were not part of the mills. Thomas Ball, working in a shade behind St. Edward's church, is said to have introduced the twisting of sewing silk by means of a 'gate' c. 1800.[91] After the silk had been wound and doubled by women and children, it went to the twister working the gate. The threads to be twisted were attached to the gate and wound on bobbins. Each twister employed a boy, known as a helper or trotter. His job was to take a rod carrying the bobbins and run some 25 yd. to the other end of the shade; there he passed the thread round a 'cross' and ran back to the gate. He repeated the operation until the thread had reached the required thickness. In 1863 estimates of the distance run, barefoot, in the course of a day's work of 10 hours varied from over 16 miles to nearly 20. One twister commented that the boy who helped him, aged 10, 'was very tired always at the end of his day's work of 10 hours'. In 1841, however, Samuel Scriven, reporting to the Children's Employment Commission, stated that he had found no injury to the feet or ankles; on the contrary the boys were healthy and 'notorious for being long winded, and fast runners'. Even in the mills using steam power, twisting was still carried out by hand in 1863, only the winding engines being powered.[92]

A shade might occupy the top floor over several houses, as with the weaving shop. Thus in 1834 five newly built houses in Blackamoor's Head Lane (late Pickwood Road) were advertised for sale along with a silk shade extending over them.[93] More usually a shade was a separate building of one or more storeys. In 1841 Josiah Hastel, a twister, owned a terrace of five houses and a two-storeyed shade in London Street and lived in one of the houses. The upper floor of the shade consisted of a twisting room and also a winding room where Josiah and his wife employed ten 'piecers' and three 'doublers'. The ground floor was let to four twisters working for whom they wished and employing their own boys.[94] A three-storeyed shade in Clerk Bank, with four gates on each floor, was offered for sale in 1830.[95] A newly erected shade in Duke Street advertised for sale in 1855 consisted of four storeys, with the second floor used as a warehouse and winding room.[96]

In 1863 there were c. 300 out-twisters, each employing on average 5 people of whom 3 were aged between 9 and 16.[97] There were 251 workshops in 1868, devoted mainly to the production of sewing silk and employing 1,440 people.[98] By 1875 industrial and educational legislation had made it difficult to secure helpers, boys being at their most useful between the ages of 9 and 14 and turning to other work after 15 or 16.[99] As late as the 1930s, however, trotters were still employed.[1]

Dyeing also grew in the earlier 19th century. When Joseph Badnall died in 1803, his dyeworks was taken over by his son William and brother James. On William's death in 1806 a partnership was formed between James and his brother Richard and son Joseph. James died in 1813.[2] By 1826 the works was run by a partnership consisting of Richard's son Richard, F. G. Spilsbury, and Henry Cruso; the partners also manufactured silk and silk machinery. The partnership was dissolved that year.[3] The business was bought by James Badnall's son Joseph, on whose death in 1830 it passed to his sister Ann. She let the works to John Clowes, who died in 1833. Later that year the works was let to William Hammersley, a former employee of Richard Badnall, who by 1824 had opened a silk-dyeing works at Bridge End to the northwest on the Leekfrith side of the Churnet. The Hammersley firm remained in business in Mill Street and Bridge End until the early 20th century.[4]

Another dyeworks was established in 1830 by Joshua Wardle on Leek brook near its confluence with the Churnet. His firm, Joshua Wardle & Sons by the early 1860s, became Joshua Wardle Ltd. in 1927. A second works, adjoining the first and designed by Longden & Venables, was completed in 1929; it included the site of the Travellers' Rest inn, which was rebuilt on the opposite side of the Cheddleton road, also to the design of Longden & Venables.[5] In 1987 the firm was bought by a major customer, William Baird plc.[6]

Joshua Wardle's son Thomas claimed that the water of the Churnet and its tributaries was among the best dyeing water in Europe. In particular it produced the unique raven-black dye for which Leek was celebrated by the 1830s, so called because its rich blue-black resembled the bluest part of the raven's feathers.[7] Joshua Wardle was using raven black by 1835.[8]

Despite the competition from metal buttons

[89] Rep. Com. Factory and Workshops Acts, vol. ii [C 1443-I], p. 470, H.C. (1876), xxx.
[90] 2nd Rep. Com. Tech. Instruction, vol. iii, p. xxxiv.
[91] V.C.H. Staffs. ii. 207; Sleigh, Leek, 5; H. Bode, Visiting Leek, i (Leek, 1974), 31.
[92] 2nd Rep. Com. Child. Employment, App. Pt. I [431], pp. C 17–18 and c 96–9, H.C. (1843), xiv; 5th Rep. Com. Child. Employment, 75–6, 84–5; E. Mordaunt, Bellamy (1914), 29–39; R. K. Bacon, Life of Sir Enoch Hill, 18–23.
[93] Staffs. Advertiser, 27 Sept. 1834, p. 1.
[94] 2nd Rep. Com. Child. Employment, App. Pt. I, pp. c 96–7.
[95] S.R.O., D. 4675/2, p. 9.
[96] Staffs. Advertiser, 27 Sept. 1834, p. 1; 16 June 1855, p. 8.
[97] 5th Rep. Com. Child. Employment, 85.
[98] Rep. Com. Factory and Workshops Acts, 469–70.
[99] Ibid. 472–3.
[1] Leek Libr., newspaper cuttings 1986–7, p. 61; below,

plate 50.
[2] Staffs. Hist. viii. 5; S.R.O., D. 3359/Cruso, draft partnership agreement of 8 Oct. 1806.
[3] Staffs. Hist. viii. 4, 7; Lond. Gaz. 23 May 1826, p. 1231.
[4] Staffs. Hist. viii. 7–8; Miller, Leek, 35; Kelly's Dir. Staffs. (1916); below, this section (later 19th cent.: Wardle & Davenport).
[5] V.C.H. Staffs. ii. 209, 214; Staffs. Advertiser, 20 Apr. 1929, p. 5; S.R.O., D. 3188/2.
[6] Leek Libr., newspaper cuttings 1986–7, p. 27.
[7] T.N.S.F.C. x. 36; 2nd Rep. Com. Tech. Instruction, vol. iii, pp. l–li; Reps. Asst. Hand-loom Weavers' Com., Pt. IV, 344; Plot, Staffs. 98, noting c. 1680 that a stream coming from a sough belonging to a coal mine in Blue Hills in Heathylee dyed the moulds of the local button makers black.
[8] Science and Archaeology, vi. 20–1, 24.

FIG. 20. LEEKBROOK DYEWORKS IN 1879

the production of hand-made buttons persisted. In the earlier 19th century large quantities of Florentine buttons were made by several hundreds of women and children in the surrounding villages. The name was coined by Joshua Brough for buttons covered in a drab silk cloth mounted on moulds of wood, bone, or iron with a linen back. In the earlier 1880s buttons covered in a mixture of silk and mohair were still being produced by c. 300 people in Leek and the neighbouring villages, notably at Flash and Biddulph Moor.[9]

The later 19th century. The later 19th century, and especially the last quarter, saw the increasing concentration of the silk industry in factories.[10] New factories were built on a larger scale and were architecturally more self-conscious. Examples of 1853 are Wellington Mills in Strangman Street and London Mill on the corner of Ashbourne Road (formerly London Road) and Well Street.[11] California Mill, so named by 1892, illustrates the steady concentration of all processes on a single site. Standing in Horton Street, it is claimed to date from the 1820s and to be the oldest brick textile mill still in use in the north of England. It was occupied in the 1830s by Glendinning & Gaunt, who had 10 steam-powered looms there in 1839, having

earlier used Ball Haye brook to provide power. By the entrance there was a terrace of 10 back-to-back workers' cottages, evidently in existence by 1838. A shade was added on the Union Street side of the site in the mid 19th century and a dyeworks on the opposite side in the 1880s using water from Ball Haye brook. By 1878 there was a four-bedroomed house by the entrance, and it became the home of William Stannard after he acquired the mill in the early 1880s.[12] On an even larger scale was Big Mill in Mill Street, built by 1857 to the design of William Sugden and occupied from 1858 by Joseph Broster. It is 6 storeys high, 21 bays long, and 5 bays deep.[13] Waterloo Mills in Waterloo Street were built by William Broster & Co. in 1894 with J. G. Smith of Leek as architect; they resemble Big Mill in general design and in addition are of fireproof construction.[14]

The later 19th century also saw the growth of several large firms. Brough, Nicholson & Hall Ltd. became one of the largest, with premises covering several acres and employing 2,000 by the 1920s.[15] Its founder was John Brough, who was in business as a silk manufacturer in Leek by 1812.[16] He was in partnership with a Mr. Baddeley by 1815, with premises in Stockwell Street in 1818.[17] The partnership was dissolved in 1821, and John Brough continued to run the business alone until 1830.[18]

9 White, *Dir. Staffs.* (1834), 700; (1851), 721; *2nd Rep. Com. Tech. Instruction, vol. iii*, p. xlviii; above, Alstonefield: econ. hist. sections of Heathylee, Hollinsclough, and Quarnford; Horton, econ. hist. (trade and ind.).

10 W. Nithsdale, *Leek Past and Present* (1908); *5th Rep. Com. Child. Employment*, 85; K. Parkes, *Windylow* (1915), 13.

11 Sherlock, *Ind. Arch. Staffs.* 54–5, 177.

12 P. Anderton, 'Leek Silk Trail' (TS. in possession of Mr. Anderton); White, *Dir. Staffs.* (1834), 710; *Reps. Asst. Hand-loom Weavers' Com.*, Pt. *IV*, 344; *Kelly's Dir. Staffs.* (1880; 1884); *Plan of Leek 1838*; O.S. Map 1/500, Staffs. VIII. 6. 22 (1879 edn.); S.R.O., D. 538/B/2/2.

13 Sherlock, *Ind. Arch. Staffs.* 55, 176–7; S.R.O., D. 3283, sheet 8; below, plate 47.

14 Sherlock, *Ind. Arch. Staffs.* 55, 177; Leek Libr., newspaper cuttings 1960–8, p. 40; 1980 (2), p. 9.

15 *Brit. Industries Review*, July 1924 (copy in S.R.O., D. 4640/A/6/1); *V.C.H. Staffs.* ii. 208.

16 S.R.O., D. 538/C/2/26, John Brough's business accts.

17 Ibid. D. 538/C/2/27, John Brough's business accts.; Parson and Bradshaw, *Staffs. Dir.* (1818), 126. The premises have been identified by Mr. P. Anderton as the building now nos. 16 and 18, Stockwell St.

18 *Brief Hist. of Brough Nicholson & Hall Ltd.* (copy in S.R.O., D. 4382/8/1); S.R.O., D. 4241/4/1A.

FIG. 21. WELLINGTON MILLS

He had moved his premises to Union Street by 1829, when he built a house next to his silk warehouse there; he was then living in Tittesworth. He died in 1847.[19] In 1831 his sons Joshua, James, and John entered into partnership as Joshua and James Brough & Co.[20] A new factory was built in Union Street in 1844.[21]

James died in 1854.[22] In 1856 Joshua and John entered into partnership with Joshua Nicholson, who had joined the firm as a traveller in 1837,

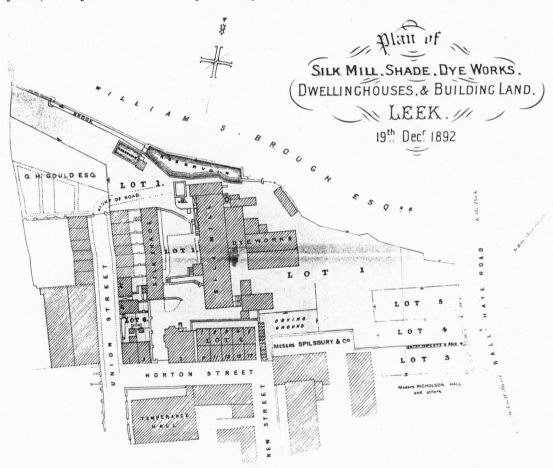

FIG. 22. CALIFORNIA MILL IN 1892

19 S.R.O., D. 538/C/2/2; Sleigh, *Leek*, 119.
20 S.R.O., D. 538/C/2/36, articles of partnership 1831; *Brough Nicholson & Hall Ltd.*

21 S.R.O., D. 538/C/2/27, bk. of payments on acct. of new silk factory.
22 Sleigh, *Leek*, 87.

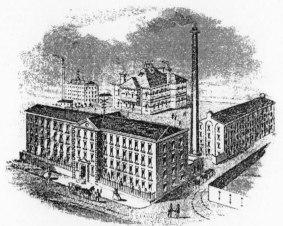

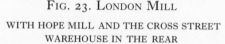

FIG. 23. LONDON MILL

WITH HOPE MILL AND THE CROSS STREET
WAREHOUSE IN THE REAR

FIG. 24. HOPE MILL

and B. B. Nixon, who had begun working for the firm in 1846 just before his 16th birthday.[23] The firm became J. and J. Brough, Nicholson & Co. in 1863.[24] Evidently in that year it moved to London Mill in Ashbourne Road,[25] and in the mid 1860s a warehouse was built on the east side of Cross Street with a shade behind it, both to the design of William Sugden.[26] In 1869, following the retirement of Joshua and John Brough, a new partnership was formed between Joshua Nicholson, B. B. Nixon, W. S. Brough (Joshua Brough's son), Arthur Nicholson (Joshua Nicholson's younger son), Edwin Brough (John Brough's son), and John Hall (apprenticed to the firm in 1854).[27] Hope Mill in Fountain Street, which had evidently been established by Thomas Carr & Co. in the 1820s, was acquired c. 1870 and doubled in size in 1875–6.[28] In 1871 the partnership was employing 470 persons; the number had risen to 630 by 1881.[29] W. S. Brough retired in 1881, the first of a succession of retirements from the partnership; Joshua Nicholson died in 1885. In 1891, after Nixon's retirement, the firm became Brough, Nicholson & Hall, with Arthur Nicholson (Sir Arthur from 1909) and John Hall as partners.[30] By 1898 the Cross Street building had been extended north to the junction of the street with Well Street, probably in 1892–3 to the design of Larner Sugden.[31] In 1898 a mill

was built on the east side of Well Street; it was named the Royal York Mill following a visit by the duke and duchess of York in 1900.[32] In the mid 1890s the firm took over the Cecily Mills in Cheadle.[33] By the 1920s it had a dyeworks at Bridge End.[34]

The firm became a private limited company in 1907 and a public company in 1946.[35] In 1956 it sold the Bridge End dyeworks to Sir Thomas & Arthur Wardle Ltd.[36] In 1962 it began a four-year modernization programme, with activities concentrated in Cross Street and at Cheadle. The knitting department was transferred to Job White & Sons Ltd. of Compton Mills, which took over London and York mills.[37] Most of the buildings west of Cross Street, including Hope Mill, were demolished in 1968.[38] In 1983 Cross Street Mill was taken over by Berisfords, the Congleton ribbon firm, but it was converted into an antiques showroom in the later 1980s.[39]

The firm of Wardle & Davenport was formed in 1867 as a partnership between Henry Wardle, keeper of the Britannia tavern in West Street and also described as a photographer, and George Davenport, a silk throwster. Wardle provided the capital, and Davenport ran the business.[40] Their premises were at first in West Street, but by 1872 they had moved to part of Big Mill in Mill Street, sharing it with William Broster &

23 S.R.O., D. 538/C/2/36, agreements of 1845, 1846, and 1856; Leek Libr., newspaper cuttings 1979, p. 1.
24 Brough Nicholson & Hall Ltd.
25 Brit. Industries Review, July 1924.
26 S.R.O., D. 3188/1/1, nos. 42 and 50; O.S. Map 1/500, Staffs. VIII. 10. 2 (1879 edn.).
27 S.R.O., D. 538/C/2/28, ff. 29v.–30; D. 4241/5/1; G. A. Lovenbury, 'A Certain Group of Men' (Leek, 1990), 3–4, 14; Leek Libr., newspaper cuttings 1979, p. 1.
28 S.R.O., D. 4241/4/2, ff. 23v., 24v.; Leek Libr., Johnson scrapbk. iii, p. 214. For the Carr firm in Fountain St. see Pigot, Nat. Com. Dir. [1829], 713; White, Dir. Staffs. (1851), 740 (with first mention of Hope Mill); P.O. Dir. Staffs. (1868); Plan of Leek 1838.
29 Under St. Edward Street in P.R.O., RG 10/2882; RG 11/2739.

30 S.R.O., D. 4241/5/2; Leek Libr., newspaper cuttings 1979, p. 1; Brough Nicholson & Hall Ltd.
31 S.R.O., D. 4241/5/104; O.S. Map 1/25,000, Staffs. VIII. 10 (1900 edn.).
32 Date on mill; Brit. Industries Review, July 1924.
33 V.C.H. Staffs. ii. 208.
34 Brit. Industries Review, July 1924.
35 Brough Nicholson & Hall Ltd. For an interior view of one of the mills probably in the 1890s see below, plate 49.
36 Below [Sir Thomas & Arthur Wardle Ltd.].
37 Leek Libr., newspaper cuttings 1960–8, pp. 80–2; below [Job White & Sons Ltd.].
38 Leek Libr., newspaper cuttings 1960–8, pp. 106–7.
39 Ibid. 1984 (2), p. 11; Staffs. Life (Dec. 1989), 46.
40 S.R.O., D. 1214/A/1/1, agreement of 1867; Leek Libr., newspaper cuttings 1960–8, p. 39; P.O. Dir. Staffs. (1868).

Co. and Frederick Hammersley & Co.[41] Davenport retired in 1875 and was succeeded by Henry Davenport; Wardle retired in 1879.[42] In 1882 Henry Davenport entered into a partnership with his brother George, who was already manager.[43] By 1888 there was a third partner, W. H. Rider. That year the three partners bought the whole of Big Mill from W. A. L. Hammersley, with another mill to the south-east in Belle Vue erected by Hammersley's father W. H. Hammersley and land adjoining the two buildings; the whole site occupied nearly 3½ a.[44] Henry Davenport died in 1895, and by 1899 his son Fred was the third partner. That year Wardle & Davenport became a limited company, with a workforce of upwards of 700.[45] An office and warehouse designed by G. H. Chappell was erected in Belle Vue behind Big Mill in 1900.[46] The mill in Belle Vue was enlarged c. 1920 to the design of R. T. Longden,[47] and in 1925 its western end was rebuilt as an office block, also designed by Longden.[48] The company took over several smaller concerns, including the dyeworks at Bridge End belonging to William Hammersley & Co., and by 1924 its various factories covered 15 a. and employed 2,500 people.[49] Big Mill in the meantime was transferred to a separate company for the production of mercerized cotton.[50] By the late 1960s Wardle & Davenport was suffering heavy losses, and in 1970 it went into receivership.[51] Belle Vue Mill was demolished in the 1970s, and a lingerie factory was built on the site.[52]

A. J. Worthington & Co. Ltd. of Portland Mills in Portland Street and Queen Street, though smaller than either of the latter two firms, was one of the larger firms in Leek by the 1920s, with a workforce of 400.[53] It is said to have originated in 1803 as James Goostrey & Co.[54] James Goostrey was a silk manufacturer in Portland Street in the mid 1830s, presumably at the mill there described as new when it was offered for sale in 1832.[55] Soon afterwards the business was taken over by James Hammond and Henry Turner. By 1838 Andrew Jukes Worthington, a friend of Turner, was a partner, and in 1839 he married the niece of Turner's wife.[56] He bought the Turners out, and the firm became A. J. Worthington & Co., evidently in

1845.[57] In 1861, when he was living in Spout Street, he was employing 200 people.[58] For some years before 1868 he was in partnership with Thomas Halcomb, evidently his brother-in-law. In that year Thomas withdrew, and Andrew's son Ernest became a partner. Andrew died in 1873.[59] Ernest and his brother Philip were in partnership with Henry Russell, a London silk agent, from 1875 until Russell's death in 1885. The brothers continued in partnership until Ernest's death in 1896, and when Philip died in 1902 the business was left in trust for his son Lancelot, a minor.[60] The firm became a private limited company in 1909 and was renamed A. J. Worthington & Co. (Leek) Ltd. in 1936.[61] It took over several firms after the Second World War, and a parent company A. J. Worthington (Holdings) Ltd. was formed in 1953; the group consisted of six companies in 1963.[62] In 1984 the group announced heavy losses, partly as a result of the closure of its subsidiary W. H. White & Sons of Old Bank Mill, Ball Haye Road, a firm dating from 1923. Turnover increased with the re-emergence of White & Sons, and Worthingtons showed a profit again in 1986.[63]

The silk-dyeing industry was also expanding in the later 19th century. Leek had three silk dyeing firms in 1851 and 5 in the later 1880s; 300–400 people were employed in 1884.[64] There were seven firms by 1912 and 11 by 1936.[65] A problem was created by the muddying of the Churnet when the Staffordshire Potteries Water Works Co. completed Tittesworth reservoir in 1858. Some firms switched to the water supplied by the improvement commissioners.[66]

A leading figure in dyeing as in other aspects of the silk industry was Thomas Wardle (Sir Thomas from 1897). Born in 1831, he was the son of Joshua Wardle, whose dyeing business at Leekbrook he joined at an early age.[67] In 1872 he bought from Samuel Tatton the Hencroft dyeworks in Abbey Green Road and the Mill Street dyeworks, which was renamed the Churnet works. Tatton had built Hencroft in the late 1840s and the second works in or soon after 1853; he remained at Hencroft as Wardle's tenant until 1875 when he moved to Britannia Street.[68] In 1881 Wardle's son Arthur joined the firm, which became a private limited company

[41] P.O. Dir. Staffs. (1868; 1872); S.R.O., D. 1227/A/6/16, p. 2.
[42] S.R.O., D. 1214/A/1/1, agreement of 1879 and note written on void bond.
[43] Ibid. agreement of 1883; D. 1227/A/6/16, p. 10.
[44] Ibid. D. 1227/A/6/16, pp. 1–3.
[45] Ibid. D. 1214/A/2/1, prospectus of 1899; D. 1227/A/6/1; D. 1227/A/3/4; D. 1227/A/6/16, p. 10.
[46] Ibid. D. 3188/1/3; date on building.
[47] S.R.O., D. 1214/A/3/2; D. 1227/G/8 and 14; D. 3188/1/3.
[48] Ibid. D. 1227/G/18; D. 3188/1/4.
[49] Leek Libr., newspaper cuttings 1960–8, p. 39; Drapers' Organiser, July 1924 (copy in S.R.O., D. 1214/A/3/6); below, plate 47. For the dyeworks see Kelly's Dir. Staffs. (1904; 1908); P. W. L. Adams, Notes on some N. Staffs. Families (Tunstall, priv. print. 1930), 93. [50] Below (20th cent.).
[51] The Times, 16 June 1970; Express & Star, 15 and 17 June 1970. [52] Leek Post & Times, 18 Mar. 1992, p. 8.
[53] V.C.H. Staffs. ii. 208.
[54] Leek Libr., newspaper cuttings 1972–8, p. 141.
[55] Pigot, Nat. Com. Dir. (1835), 413; Macclesfield Courier

& Herald, 25 Feb. 1832, p. 2. White, Dir. Staffs. (1834), 710, gives John Goostrey.
[56] P. W. L. Adams, Short Hist. of Worthington and Jukes Families (Tunstall, priv. print. 1902), 21–2; Plan of Leek 1838 (naming the firm as Worthington & Co.).
[57] Leek Libr., newspaper cuttings 1972–8, p. 141; S.R.O., D. 4316/8/4; D. 4316/10/1, pp. 1–3.
[58] P.R.O., RG 9/1946.
[59] S.R.O., D. 4316/4/1–2; P. W. L. Adams, Hist. of Adams Family of N. Staffs. 368.
[60] S.R.O., D. 4316/4/4 and 6; Adams, Adams Fam. 371.
[61] S.R.O., D. 4316/1/1–2.
[62] V.C.H. Staffs. ii. 208; Leek Libr., newspaper cuttings 1960–8, p. 39; 1972–8, p. 141.
[63] Leek Libr., newspaper cuttings 1960–8, p. 40; 1984 (2), p. 10; 1986–7, p. 27.
[64] White, Dir. Staffs. (1851), 739; Kelly's Dir. Staffs. (1888); 2nd Rep. Com. Tech. Instruction, vol. iii, p. xxxiv.
[65] Kelly's Dir. Staffs. (1912; 1936).
[66] Staffs. Advertiser, 26 July 1879, p. 6.
[67] D.N.B.; below, plate 67.
[68] Staffs. Advertiser, 26 July 1879, p. 6; P.O. Dir. Staffs. (1876).

in 1921 and a public company in 1949.[69] The Hencroft works was given up after the death of Sir Thomas in 1909.[70] The extension of the Churnet works, begun in 1938, continued after the Second World War.[71] In 1956, having bought Brough, Nicholson & Hall's Bridge End dyeworks, the firm established its subsidiary Leek Chemicals Ltd. there.[72] In 1967 Leek Chemicals became a subsidiary of Courtaulds.[73] Sir Thomas & Arthur Wardle Ltd. also became a subsidiary of Courtaulds; part of the premises was taken over by Courtaulds Jersey in 1982.[74]

From 1875 to 1877 William Morris was a frequent visitor to the Hencroft works, Wardle's brother-in-law George Wardle being the manager of Morris's works in London. With Morris Thomas Wardle revived indigo dyeing and restored vegetable dyeing to an important place in the industry. Their business association lasted until the early 1880s.[75] Thomas Wardle also promoted the use of Indian wild silks, especially that of the Tusser worm. It was dyed at the Churnet works under the supervision of his son Arthur, and the woven silk was printed at the Hencroft works under another son, Bernard.[76] Oscar Wilde, lecturing in Leek in 1884, paid tribute to Wardle's dyeing and to Leek's special contribution to the decorative arts.[77]

From the later 19th century there were important changes in the industry's products and technology. The introduction of the sewing machine in 1854 meant that silk was made in greater lengths and also involved spooling.[78] In the early 1880s the production of spun silk (thread made from silk waste) was introduced in Leek, apparently by William Watson & Co. Several local manufacturers, including Thomas Wardle, promptly combined to form the Leek Spun Silk Spinning & Manufacturing Co. About 1889 Brough, Nicholson & Co. introduced the Jacquard smallware loom, and in 1898 the first Sander & Graf crochet trimming loom in the country was installed in Leek. The first knitting machine using a latch needle was introduced in 1899, and within a few years flat knitting machines were being used. Some existing firms added knitted goods to their products, and new firms specializing in knitwear established themselves in the town.[79]

The 20th century. One of the first of the new knitwear firms was Job White & Sons Ltd. It started in 1909 as Trafford & White, a partnership between Herbert Trafford and Job White,

working at Victoria Mills in Ball Haye Road. The firm moved to Euston Mills in Wellington Street in 1911 and to Compton Mills in 1912 by exchange with Henry Bermingham & Son. William Davis replaced Trafford in 1914, and in 1918 the firm of White & Davis became a private limited company. On Davis's resignation in 1924 the firm was renamed Job White & Sons Ltd. It became a public company in 1962.[80] By 1964 the firm, one of the largest manufacturers of knitted headwear in the country, was employing some 600 people, over half at Compton and the rest at London and York mills, which it had acquired from Brough, Nicholson & Hall, and at Hope Mill in Macclesfield Road. That year Compton Mills were burnt down, but they were reopened in 1965.[81] The firm was acquired by Wardle & Davenport Ltd. in 1970 and went into liquidation later the same year.[82]

Early in the 20th century artificial silk was introduced, with Wardle & Davenport among the pioneers. The firm established a company at Tubize in Belgium in 1899 for the production of Chardonnet rayon, and *c.* 1905 it became the first in Britain to make artificial silk stockings. By 1912 mercerized cotton was being produced in Leek.[83] In 1920 Wardle & Davenport conveyed its manufacture of such cotton along with Big Mill to Peri-Lusta Ltd., established in 1919.[84] Peri-Lusta remained at Big Mill until 1992 when, having shed 40 members of its workforce of 90, it moved to premises in Belle Vue Road.[85]

In due course nylon and other man-made fibres were added to the materials used in Leek. Leek's importance as a centre for the production of knitted goods continued to grow, and it was estimated in 1957 that probably 75 per cent of the knitted scarves worn in Britain were made in the town. In 1970 Joshua Wardle Ltd. switched its dyeing from 90 per cent woven fabrics to 90 per cent knitted.[86] Leek remained the centre of the silk sewing thread trade in the 1950s, although the number of firms engaged in silk production was dwindling.[87] By the 1970s there was only one, Thomas Whittles Ltd., a family firm which operated at Wellington Mills in Strangman Street from the later 1860s.[88]

Numerous textile mills were closed in the late 1970s and early 1980s and adapted to other purposes. One of the mills formerly belonging to Brough, Nicholson & Hall was turned into an antiques showroom in the later 1980s, and in 1992 Albion Mill was an animal foods plant and Brunswick Mill was being converted into flats.[89]

69 Leek Libr., newspaper cuttings 1986–7, p. 27; *V.C.H. Staffs.* ii. 214.
70 D.R.O., D. 2614B/ES8; *Staffs. Advertiser,* 10 July 1909, p. 5. It is not listed in *Kelly's Dir. Staffs.* (1912).
71 Leek Libr., newspaper cuttings 1960–8, p. 78; K. Warrender, *Exploring Leek* (Timperley, 1982), 6; *Leek Official Guide* [late 1980s edn.], 21.
72 Leek Libr., newspaper cuttings 1960–8, p. 79.
73 *Leek Official Guide* [late 1980s edn.], 22.
74 Leek Libr., newspaper cuttings 1988 (1), p. 11.
75 J. W. Mackail, *Life of William Morris,* i. 313, 315–18, 324–7; ii. 331; *Staffs. Hist.* viii. 36–49.
76 D.R.O., D. 2375M/130/52.
77 *Staffs. Advertiser,* 1 Mar. 1884, p. 7.
78 *2nd Rep. Com. Technical Instruction, vol. iii,* p. l.
79 *V.C.H. Staffs.* ii. 211–12.

80 Leek Libr., newspaper cuttings 1960–8, pp. 40, 119; S.R.O., D. 1261/1/1; D. 3188/1/3, Oct. 1914.
81 Leek Libr., newspaper cuttings 1960–8, pp. 31–5, 55–7, 74–6, 119.
82 *Express & Star,* 15 and 17 June 1970.
83 *V.C.H. Staffs.* ii. 213.
84 S.R.O., D. 1262/B/1/1, pp. 1–2; D. 1262/B/3/1.
85 *Leek Post & Times,* 29 July 1992, p. 1.
86 Leek Libr., newspaper cuttings 1957–9, p. 63; 1980 (1), p. 11; *V.C.H. Staffs.* ii. 208.
87 *V.C.H. Staffs.* ii. 212–13; Leek Libr., newspaper cuttings 1957–9, p. 59.
88 H. Bode, *Visiting Leek,* i (Leek, 1974), 14, 32–4; *P.O. Dir. Staffs.* (1868), s.v. Bentley & Whittles.
89 Leek Libr., newspaper cuttings 1992–3, p. 29; *Staffs. Life* (Christmas 1989), 46.

Leek had about a dozen textile firms in 1992, involved mainly in dyeing, finishing, printing, and the production of knitwear, braids, and trimmings.[90] In 1994 Thomas Whittles Ltd. ceased to operate, and the silk industry in Leek came to an end.

Ancillary trades. Two ancillary trades had emerged in the town by the 1860s, the manufacture of bobbins and of cardboard boxes. The turning of wooden bobbins had become a full-time craft by 1861, and some at least of Leek's five wood turners in the late 1860s were probably engaged in the work.[91] By 1872 there were two bobbin turners, George Plant in Mill Street and William Wain in Buxton Road.[92] Wain was still in business in 1880, and the Mill Street works passed *c.* 1890 from George to Thomas Plant, who ran it for a short time.[93] Four new firms appeared in the earlier 1880s: Henry Brassington of Grosvenor Street, who was also a paper merchant and commission agent, Isaac Creighton of Cromwell Terrace and Shoobridge Street, John and Jabez Mathews of Buxton Road, who were also joiners and builders, and Murfin & Sons of London Mills, London Street.[94] Brassington had moved into London Mills by 1888 and had given up his other interests. The firm became Henry Brassington & Son at the beginning of the 20th century. By the time of its closure in the earlier 1960s it had become Brassington & Sons (Leek) Ltd., with its works in Cornhill Street, and it was then the only firm of bobbin manufacturers in the town.[95] At the beginning of the 20th century Isaac Creighton was succeeded by William Creighton, who moved to Westwood Terrace *c.* 1910. The firm had become Creighton & Co. of Sneyd Street by 1916, and it went out of business soon afterwards.[96] The firm of John and Jabez Mathews, which retained its links with the building trade until the 1890s, was still in business in the early 1920s.[97] In 1900 Matthew Swindells had a spool-making business in Queen Street, which by 1908 was run as M. Swindells & Co. In 1912 the firm had a second works at Portland Mills and had switched to the production of bobbins. It was still in business in Portland Street in 1940.[98]

Boxmaking in Leek seems to have made an uncertain start. Jabez Pickford was producing plain and ornamented boxes in Derby Street by 1860. The trade evidently died out in the mid 1860s but was revived after a few years. There were two boxmakers by 1872, four by 1876, and seven

by 1900. In 1940 there were 10, including G. H. Plant & Sons, a firm established in Mill Street in the later 1870s.[99] They also included Wardle & Davenport, which had its own boxmaking department before 1900 and built a factory in Hillswood Avenue in 1924 specially for the production of boxes.[1] In the early 1960s several of the larger textile firms had boxmaking departments, but there were also six independent box manufacturers.[2] In the early 1990s there were four packaging firms in the town.[3]

Local craftsmen probably made handlooms for domestic workers, and for a few years in the 1860s Henry Hubbard was in business as a 'loom and silk machine maker' in Union Street.[4] Otherwise there is no evidence that textile machinery was made in Leek. Much of the machinery introduced into the mills in the late 19th and early 20th century came from abroad and was installed by foreign workers.[5] In the early 1920s a few Leek firms sold and overhauled mill machinery,[6] and in the later 1930s there were five firms of textile engineers in the town.[7] In the earlier 1960s some of the small engineering works in Leek were ancillary to the textile trade.[8]

Between *c.* 1850 and 1939 a few silk brokers were in business in the town. They were at their most numerous in the 1880s and 1890s when there were five or six at any one time.[9]

Trade unions and manufacturers' associations. After various unsuccessful attempts trade unionism became established in the Leek silk industry in 1866 when the Amalgamated Society of Silk Twisters was formed with William Stubbs as secretary. Other societies followed, and in 1891 the Leek Federation of Local Trades Unions was formed. It promoted a series of lectures in 1892, including one by George Bernard Shaw on socialism. In 1907 seven of the existing unions formed the Leek Textile Federation. Its first and only secretary was William Bromfield, secretary of five of the unions; Stubbs was secretary of the other two. In 1919 seven unions amalgamated to form the Amalgamated Society of Textile Workers and Kindred Trades. The twisters' union remained separate, continuing until its dissolution in 1939. Bromfield, who in 1918 had been elected as Labour M.P. for the Leek division, became secretary of the new union. Foxlowe, the former home of the Cruso family in Church Street, became the union's headquarters. The union achieved a new importance in 1965 when the National Silk

[90] *The Independent*, 27 Aug. 1992, p. 5.
[91] *Leek in 1861*, ed. P. Anderton (Univ. of Keele, 1982), 39, 42; *P.O. Dir. Staffs.* (1868).
[92] *P.O. Dir. Staffs.* (1872).
[93] *Kelly's Dir. Staffs.* (1880 and edns. to 1892).
[94] Ibid. (1880; 1884).
[95] Ibid. (1888 and edns. to 1940); *Official Guide of Leek* [1961], 44; not listed ibid. [1965].
[96] *Kelly's Dir. Staffs.* (1900 and edns. to 1916); Wm. Creighton was also of Grove St. in 1904.
[97] Ibid. (1884 and edns. to 1916); E. F. Cope & Co. *Staffs. Dir.* (1921).
[98] *Kelly's Dir. Staffs.* (1900 and edns. to 1940); not listed in *Official Guide of Leek* [1961].
[99] *P.O. Dir. Staffs.* (1860 and edns. to 1876); *Kelly's Dir. Staffs.* (1880 and edns. to 1940).

[1] Leek Libr., newspaper cuttings 1960–8, p. 39; *Drapers' Organiser*, July 1924, p. x (copy in S.R.O., D. 1214/A/3/6); *Kelly's Dir. Staffs.* (1932); S.R.O., D. 3188/1/4.
[2] *Official Guide of Leek* [1961], 40, 43–4; [1965], 42, 44–5.
[3] *Yellow pages: Stoke-on-Trent 1992/93*, s.vv. cartons; packaging materials; contract packers.
[4] *P.O. Dir. Staffs.* (1860; 1864).
[5] E. Mordaunt, *Bellamy* (1914), 88 sqq., 116–17, 132; above (later 19th cent.).
[6] E. F. Cope & Co. *Staffs. Dir.* (1921); *Kelly's Dir. Staffs.* (1924).   [7] *Kelly's Dir. Staffs.* (1936; 1940).
[8] *Official Guide of Leek* [1961], 40, 44; [1965], 41, 44.
[9] *P.O. Dir. Staffs.* (1850 and later edns.); *Kelly's Dir. Staffs.* (1880 and edns. to 1940).

Workers' and Textile Trades Association merged with it.[10]

There was a Leek manufacturers' association for the prosecution of felons in the 1790s and the early 19th century.[11] A chamber of commerce, consisting mainly of silk manufacturers, was established in 1886 but did not flourish.[12] The Leek and District Manufacturers' and Dyers' Association was formed in 1913 after a successful strike that year. The first president was Sir Arthur Nicholson, who held office until 1929.[13] By the early 1980s its membership was declining, and it was dissolved in 1983.[14]

CLOCK AND WATCH MAKING. The earliest known clock makers in Leek were members of a Quaker family named Stretch. Samuel Stretch was making lantern clocks in 1670. His nephew Peter Stretch was also a Leek clock maker; he emigrated with his family to Philadelphia in Pennsylvania in 1702 and made long-case clocks there.[15] Randle Maddock, a prolific clock maker, was working in Stockwell Street by 1736 and was still living in Leek at his death in 1745.[16] A Leek watch maker named Richard Steen died in 1743.[17] There were several clock makers in Leek in the later 18th century, including a Thomas Ashton,[18] but in the 1790s John Ashton was the only clock and watch maker recorded there.[19]

He or a younger John Ashton was a clock maker in Sheepmarket in 1818, and a John Ashton aged 75 was working there in 1851.[20] A George Ashton was recorded as a watch maker in Sheepmarket in 1841 and a watch and clock maker the earlier 1860s. He had moved to Compton by 1868.[21] William Travis (1781–1875) started on his own account as a clock maker in Market Place when he came of age. He moved to other premises in Market Place in the late 1830s and remained there until his death. For many years he made a clock every week.[22] His son Samuel had his own business as a clock and watch maker in Market Place by 1851 and continued there until the early 1880s.[23]

THE CO-OPERATIVE SOCIETY. The Leek and Moorlands Co-operative Society opened a shop in a rented cottage in Clerk Bank in 1859. In 1860 the society moved the shop to Overton Bank.[24] It was known as the Leek and Moorlands Industrial Provident Society Ltd. from the mid 1860s until the mid 1890s when it reverted to its original name.[25] A branch shop and bakery were opened in Ashbourne Road in 1880, and other branches followed.[26] They included the shop on the corner of Picton Street and Britannia Street designed by W. Sugden & Son and opened in 1895.[27] In 1899 new central premises were built in Ashbourne Road. Also designed by Sugden & Son, they consisted of offices, a boardroom, a hall, a grocery, and a bakery. In the mid 1920s the bakery was replaced by one in Strangman Street designed by Longden & Venables.[28] In 1910 the Society built a department store in High Street, designed by R. T. Longden, and all trading was centred there by the 1970s.[29] It was replaced in 1984 by a superstore opened by the North Midland Co-operative Society Ltd. in Pickwood Road.[30]

DAIRY PRODUCTS. In 1922 Fred Adams started a butter-making business at Springfield farm, a small dairy farm bought by his father Fred from the earl of Macclesfield in the 1870s.[31] He installed a cold store in 1923, and in 1925 the business became one of the first in the country to introduce pre-packed butter.[32] In 1929 his son, another Fred, joined the firm, by then Adams Dairies (Wholesale).[33] A printing department was added in the 1930s to print the firm's butter wrappers and labels for customers.[34] In 1940 a second son, John, joined the partnership, and the firm became a private company called Adams Butter Ltd. It went public in 1965.[35] In 1964 a wrapper and box division was opened in a former silk mill in Queen Street, and an office block was built on a site adjoining the main factory.[36] In 1966 the company's fleet of refrigerated vehicles was concentrated at a depot on an 11½-a. site at Barnfields.[37]

In 1972 the Irish Dairy Board Co-operative Ltd., having acquired shares in the company in 1971, became a major shareholder and the company, with a growing diversification of interests,

[10] F. Burchill and J. Sweeney, *Amalgamated Soc. of Textile Workers and Kindred Trades* (Univ. of Keele, 1971); above, general hist. (earlier 19th cent.). For Shaw's lecture see *Staffs. Advertiser*, 2 Apr. 1892, p. 7.
[11] Below, public services (policing).
[12] Burchill and Sweeney, *Amalgamated Soc. of Textile Workers*, 39.
[13] Ibid. 53–6; Leek Libr., newspaper cuttings 1960–8, p. 39; S.R.O., D. 3838/1/1.
[14] S.R.O., D. 4121/1/2.
[15] Leek Libr., newspaper cuttings 1972–8, pp. 128–9; *Philadelphia*, ed. R. F. Weighley, 98.
[16] S.R.O., D. 3359/Cruso, deeds of 6 Sept. 1736 and 25 Mar. 1742; L.J.R.O., B/C/11 Randle Maddock (1745); *Olde Leeke*, ii. 35.   [17] L.J.R.O., B/C/11, Ric. Steen (1743).
[18] *Olde Leeke*, ii. 36, 38; Sleigh, *Leek*, 8; S.R.O., D. 3359/Condlyffe, deed of 28 Nov. 1757.
[19] *Univ. Brit. Dir.* v [1798], 104.
[20] Parson and Bradshaw, *Staffs. Dir.* (1818), 127; *Olde Leeke*, ii. 36; P.R.O., HO 107/2008.
[21] P.R.O., HO 107/1005; *P.O. Dir. Staffs.* (1860; 1864; 1868).
[22] *Olde Leeke*, ii. 39–40.
[23] P.R.O., HO 107/2008; W.S.L. 498/34, cutting of 28 Feb. 1902; *Kelly's Dir. Staffs.* (1880; 1884).
[24] Leek Libr., newspaper cuttings 1984 (2), p. 18; *Sou-*

venir Hist. of Leek and Moorlands Co-operative Soc. Ltd. 1859–1909, 9; R. Poole, *Around Leek in Camera* (Buckingham, 1990), 7–8.
[25] *P.O. Dir. Staffs.* (1864; 1868); *Kelly's Dir. Staffs.* (1892; 1896).
[26] *Leek and Moorlands Co-operative Soc.* 15.
[27] Leek Libr., newspaper cuttings bk. 1, p. 48; S.R.O., D. 3188/1/3.
[28] *Leek and Moorlands Co-operative Soc.* 5, 26; Leek Libr., newspaper cuttings 1980 (2), p. 2; S.R.O., D. 3188/1/3–4.
[29] Inf. from Mr. Ray Poole of Leek; date on the building.
[30] Leek Libr., newspaper cuttings 1982 (1), pp. 31, 40; 1984 (2), pp. 17, 24.
[31] *Leek Official Guide* [late 1980s], 22–3; Leek Libr., newspaper cuttings 1972–8, pp. 36, 38.
[32] Leek Libr., newspaper cuttings 1972–8, pp. 34–5; Adams Butter Ltd. *Forward into the 'Seventies*, 4.
[33] Leek Libr., newspaper cuttings 1972–8, p. 38; *Kelly's Dir. Staffs.* (1928).
[34] A. Rotherham and M. Steele, *Hist. of Printing in N. Staffs.* (N. Staffs. Polytechnic, 1975), 105 and plates 51–3.
[35] Leek Libr., newspaper cuttings 1972–8, p. 38.
[36] *N. Staffs. Chamber of Commerce Jnl.* (Sept. 1964), 23–4.
[37] Adams Butter Ltd. *Forward into the 'Seventies*, 4.

was renamed Adams Foods Ltd. In 1975 the company, then the largest butter selling organization in the United Kingdom, opened a warehouse and cold storage plant on the Barnfields industrial estate.[38] In 1978 the Irish Dairy Board Co-operative became the owner of the company, which in 1989 was taken over by another subsidiary of the co-operative, Kerrygold Co. Ltd.[39] Kerrygold opened its United Kingdom headquarters in Sunnyhill Road, Barnfields, in 1991; it also built a cheese-packing plant there and another for processed cheese. The Springfield Road site was put up for sale.[40]

METAL TRADES. When John Rothwell, a Leek mercer, died in 1623, his goods included 7 dozen scythes and 6 cwt. of bar iron in his 'iron seller',[41] and in 1667 an ironmonger named Thomas Brough was living in Leek.[42] In 1727 William Fallowfield of Leek obtained a patent for making iron with peat. He delayed putting it into operation 'because of a mighty bustle' by the Wolverhampton ironmaster William Wood, who was attempting to smelt with pit coal at Chelsea. Wood died in 1730, and by 1731 Fallowfield had a furnace near Leek, which was still working in 1735.[43] A Leek ironmonger named James Hall died in 1742.[44] In 1818 there were two forges in Leek producing edge tools.[45]

The firm of Woodhead & Carter, iron and brass founders, millwrights, and engineers, had a works near the railway station by 1860. It was known as Hope Foundry by 1872 and probably by the railway on the opposite side of Newcastle Road from the station, its situation in 1878. About then it was taken over by William Woodhead.[46] In 1886 a plan for extensions was prepared by W. Sugden & Son.[47] Woodhead sold it in 1899 to a Mr. Hitchcock of Ealing, presumably J. P. Hitchcock, an iron and brass founder, who was running the foundry in 1904.[48] By 1908 it was run by Churnet Valley Engineering Co., a firm of iron and brass founders, and by 1912 had been renamed Churnet Foundry. The firm was still running it c. 1916, having added the production of machine tools to its activities.[49] A firm of pump manufacturers, Moorlands Engineering Co. Ltd., opened a works by the canal wharf c. 1920.[50] Its closure c. 1960 left only one foundry in Leek, the works in Sneyd Street

belonging to Sneyd Engineering, a company in existence by the early 1920s. That foundry was closed in 1991 with the loss of some 16 jobs.[51]

PRINTING AND BOOKSELLING. A Leek bookseller named John Maddock died probably in 1766.[52] Joseph Needham was trading as a bookseller in Leek in 1778 and was recorded as a printer also in 1784 and 1785; his premises were on the corner of Derby Street and Market Place.[53] The story that Michael Johnson, father of Samuel, served his apprenticeship there to a Joseph Needham over a century before has been discounted, since Michael was apprenticed to a London stationer.[54] Three booksellers were listed in the 1790s. One of them, Francis Hilliard, went bankrupt in 1794, when he was described as a bookseller, printer, and stationer. He was in business as a printer at Scolding Bank by 1818 and was still there in the late 1820s. His son William Michael had taken over the business by 1834, with premises in Church Street.[55] He had moved to Market Place by 1841 and to Sheepmarket by 1850 and had added auctioneering to his business by 1854. He gave up business as a bookseller, stationer, and printer in 1866 and moved to Stockwell Street, where he was still in business as an auctioneer and appraiser in 1872.[56]

There was a second printer in the town from the late 1820s when George Nall set up a press in Spout Street. In the earlier 1830s he moved to Sheepmarket, where he introduced copperplate printing and also traded as a bookseller and stationer.[57] He moved to Custard (later Stanley) Street in 1843.[58] His son Robert joined the firm, which by 1860 was George Nall & Son. In 1865 Robert sold the business to William Clemesha, who had the first flatbed machine in Leek.[59] He had moved to St. Edward Street by 1880, and the firm was Clemesha & Clowes by 1888. A firm called Clowes & Co. had a printing works in London Street in the 1890s.[60]

By then there were several printers in the town. One of the most notable figures among them was Enoch Hill, who later became prominent in the building society movement. After being a twister's helper and a farm labourer he worked for two Leek printers and installed a press in his home.[61] He continued his printing business after joining the Leek United Permanent Benefit

38 *Leek Official Guide* [late 1980s], 23; Leek Libr., newspaper cuttings 1972–8, p. 34.
39 *Leek Official Guide* [late 1980s], 23; *Leek Post & Times*, 3 Jan. 1990, p. 9.
40 *Leek Post & Times*, 6 Dec. 1989, p. 3; 31 Oct. 1990, p. 3; 28 Nov. 1990, p. 7; 20 Mar. 1991, p. 1.
41 L.J.R.O., B/C/11, John Rothwell (1623); below, Tittesworth, estates (Fowlchurch).
42 L.J.R.O., B/C/11, Anne Thompson (1667).
43 *Gent. Mag.* i. 166–7, 452; *V.C.H. Staffs.* ii. 118; T. S. Ashton, *Iron and Steel in the Ind. Rev.* (1951), 25; *D.N.B.* s.v. Wood, Wm. Mr. P. W. King of Hagley (Worcs.) is thanked for his help.
44 L.J.R.O., B/C/11, Jas. Hall (1743); S.R.O., D. 1040/5/14, burial of 5 Dec. 1742.
45 Parson and Bradshaw, *Staffs. Dir.* (1818), 124.
46 *P.O. Dir. Staffs.* (1860 and later edns.); O.S. Map 6", Staffs. VIII. SW. (1889 edn.).
47 S.R.O., D. 3188/1/3.
48 *Kelly's Dir. Staffs.* (1900; 1904); *Staffs. Advertiser*, 19 Aug. 1899, p. 5.   49 *Kelly's Dir. Staffs.* (1908; 1916).
50 Ibid. (1924); O.S. Map 6", Staffs. VIII. SW. (1925 edn.).

51 *Leek Post & Times*, 6 Mar. 1991, p. 1; E. F. Cope & Co. *Staffs. Dir.* (1921).
52 S.R.O., D. 1040/5/115, 29 Dec. 1766; D. 5017/6/66.
53 Poole, *Leek*, 64; *Derby Mercury*, 7–14 Aug. 1778; S.R.O., D. 3359/Cruso, deed of 18 May 1785.
54 A. L. Reade, *Johnsonian Gleanings*, iii (priv. print. 1922), 6–7. Leek was given as the place by Boswell on the authority of Anna Seward of Lichfield.
55 *Univ. Brit. Dir.* v [1798], 105; *Olde Leeke*, i. 239–40 (stating that Francis appeared to have left Bristol and settled in Leek c. 1760); *Derby Mercury*, 25 Dec. 1794, p. 1 (ref. supplied by Mr. A. W. Bednall); Parson and Bradshaw, *Staffs. Dir.* (1818), 119; Pigot, *New Com. Dir.* [1829], 712; White, *Dir. Staffs.* (1834), 710.
56 Pigot, *Nat. and Com. Dir.* (1841), 25; *P.O. Dir. Staffs.* (1850 and edns. to 1872); W.S.L., Sleigh scrapbk. ii, f. 56v.
57 *Olde Leeke*, i. 240; Pigot, *New Com. Dir.* [1829], White, *Dir. Staffs.* (1834), 710.   58 Miller, *Leek*, 120.
59 *Olde Leeke*, i. 241; Poole, *Leek*, 65.
60 *Kelly's Dir. Staffs.* (1880 and edns. to 1896); he is not listed in *P.O. Dir Staffs.* (1872; 1876).
61 R. K. Bacon, *Life of Sir Enoch Hill*, 26–9, 31.

Building Society as a clerk in 1885 at the age of
20, and by 1892 he had moved it into a shop in
Cawdry Buildings, Fountain Street, where he
also had a bookselling and stationery business.[62]
He employed his three brothers in the printing
side of the business, and they and their father
took it over when Hill became secretary of the
building society in 1896.[63] In 1900 what had
become the firm of Hill Brothers moved to
Haywood Street. By then it owned the *Leek Post*,
and it installed the first linotype machine in
North Staffordshire. It took over the *Leek Times*
in 1934. The firm, now Hill Bros. (Leek) Ltd.,
moved into the former workhouse building in
Brook Street in 1968.[64]

George Hill started a stationery and printing
business in Stanley Street in the early 1880s. He
was joined by his sons John and William in the
1890s, and the firm became George Hill & Sons
in 1904. The sons were keen photographers and
in 1902 started to produce picture postcards
showing local scenes, an important side of the
business until the late 1920s. George died in
1922, and his sons retired in the early 1940s,
selling the business to John Myatt. The name
George Hill & Sons was retained until 1972
when Myatt sold the business.[65]

In 1901 Fred Hill started a stationery and
bookselling business in Derby Street with a print
works in Haywood Mill in Haywood Street.
About 1920 he bought three cottages in Getliffes
Yard off Derby Street opposite his shop and
converted them into a print works. He retired in
the late 1950s, and Albert Hughes, his brother-
in-law, took over the business. Hughes died in
1961, and his widow Hannah carried it on in
partnership with Ray Poole, who had been
Hughes's assistant. In 1971 Mr. Poole bought
Mrs. Hughes's share. He sold the printing side
in the later 1970s to John Hilton, who sold it *c.*
1980 to Getliffe Design & Print, the owners in
1993. Mr. Poole sold the bookshop in 1988, and
it was closed in 1993. Each Christmas from 1925
until 1938 Hill issued *Leek News*, an advertising
journal which was delivered free to every household in Leek.[66]

QUARRYING. About 1680 Robert Plot noted
that at Leek 'they build chiefly with a reddish
sort of stone' quarried locally.[67] In the Millstone
Grit of the Leek area there are outcrops of
sandstones known as crowstones with a high

silica content. Though not suitable for building,
they have been quarried for road metal and
walling stone.[68]

The mention in 1281 of Elyot 'le quarehour',
who formerly held land near Leek churchyard,
may indicate 13th-century quarrying.[69] In the
early 18th century building stone was dug in the
common land known as Back of the Street (later
Belle Vue Road).[70] In the later 18th and earlier
19th century stone was quarried at Ballington
south of the town for road repairs.[71] The cemetery
contractors were given permission in 1857 to get
stone in Thomas Sneyd's quarries in Ballington
wood,[72] and in 1861, during a trade depression,
the improvement commissioners provided work
for the unemployed in quarrying road stone
there.[73] Stone from Leek moor was used for
walling in the later 18th and earlier 19th century,[74]
and stone from Edge-end farm in Tittesworth was
used for road work in 1769.[75] There was quarrying at Kniveden in the earlier 19th century.[76]
Although the quarry there was not worked in
the late 1870s, All Saints' church, consecrated
in 1887, was built of Kniveden stone, and the
quarry was again worked in the early 1920s.[77]

ROPE MAKING. In the 1780s and 1790s Samuel
Goodwin, a Leek grocer, also made rope and
sacking.[78] There were four rope and twine makers in the town in 1818 and three in 1829. One
of them, Ralph Mountfort, worked in Derby
Street in 1818 and the early 1820s; his address
was given as Market Place in 1829 and Custard
(later Stanley) Street in 1834. By 1851 the firm
was styled Ralph Mountfort & Son and in 1854
was described as a firm of grocers and rope and
twine spinners (grocers and twine manufacturers
from 1868). It was still engaged in grocery and
twine manufacture in 1916 but in grocery only
by 1924.[79] In 1857 the Mountfords may have
owned the ropewalk then in operation at Ball
Haye Green; they were working it in 1871 and
1882.[80]

In 1841 James Rogers was making rope in
Buxton Road, probably at the ropewalk which
in 1838 was on the north side of Buxton Road
near its junction with Ball Haye Street. Simeon
Rogers was a ropemaker in Well Street in 1841.
James had moved to Spout Street by 1850 and
Simeon to Queen Street by 1860. Both contin-
ued at those addresses until *c.* 1890.[81]

There was a ropewalk off Abbotts Road in

62 Ibid. 41–2, 48–51, 54; *Kelly's Dir. Staffs.* (1892).
63 Bacon, *Hill*, 51, 55.
64 Ibid. 55–6; A. Rotherham and M. Steele, *Hist. of Printing in N. Staffs.* (N. Staffs. Polytechnic, 1975), 101 and pl. 56; *Kelly's Dir. Staffs.* (1900); below, social and cultural activities (newspapers).
65 *Picture Postcard Monthly* (Mar. 1992), 21–2 (copy in W.S.L., CB/Leek/38); *Kelly's Dir. Staffs.* (1884).
66 Rotherham and Steele, *Printing in N. Staffs.* 102–3; Poole, *Leek*, 67–8; *Kelly's Dir. Staffs.* (1924); Leek Libr., newspaper cuttings 1992–3, p. 42; inf. from Mr. Poole.
67 Plot, *Staffs.* 167.
68 *T.N.S.F.C.* N.S. v. 18.
69 S.R.O., D. (W.) 1761/A/4/168.
70 S.R.O. 3508/A/3/10.
71 Ibid. D. 706/1, 27 Dec. 1762, 6 Feb., 6 Mar. 1767; D. 706/4, p. 12; D. 3359, Sandon Road acct. bk. 1783–1803, 28 Apr. 1801.
72 Ibid. D. 3226/30, no. 30.
73 Leek Improvement Com. *Reps.* (1894), 28; S.R.O., D.

3226/1, no. 1290.
74 S.R.O., D. 706/1, 18 Apr. 1765; D. 1040/7, p. 191; *Staffs. Advertiser*, 12 Oct. 1839, p. 1.
75 S.R.O., D. 3359/Buxton Road order bk. 1765–1800, p. 98.
76 S.R.O., Q/RDc 65, plan I; D. 1040/4/3.
77 O.S. Map 6", Staffs. VIII. SW. (1888, 1925 edns.); below, churches.
78 *Bailey's Brit. Dir.* (1784), 388; *Univ. Brit. Dir.* v [1798], 105.
79 Parson and Bradshaw, *Dir. Staffs.* (1818), 126; Pigot, *New Com. Dir. for 1822–3*, 468; Pigot, *New Com. Dir.* [1829], 713; White, *Dir. Staffs.* (1834), 710; (1851), 739; *P.O. Dir. Staffs.* (1850, giving the firm as Ralph Mountford & Co., flax dressers; 1854; 1868); *Kelly's Dir. Staffs.* (1916; 1924).
80 S.R.O., D. 3283, sheet 9; W.S.L. 69/1/23, 1871, 1873; 69/2/23, f. 5; O.S. Map 6", Staffs. VIII. NW. (1888 edn.).
81 Pigot, *Nat. and Com. Dir.* (1841), Staffs. p. 25; *P.O. Dir. Staffs.* (1850; 1860); *Kelly's Dir. Staffs.* (1888); *Plan of Leek 1838*.

1857.[82] It may have been worked by Mark Abbott, a ropemaker with an address in Buxton Road by 1854 and still there in the early 1870s.[83]

OTHER TRADES AND INDUSTRIES. In the 1670s Leek was noted for its excellent ale.[84] Until the mid 19th century there is no evidence of wholesale brewing, as opposed to brewing for domestic and retail purposes. A brewer named Ralph Tatton was living in Stockwell Street in 1851,[85] but he is not known to have traded in Leek. In 1854 there two brewers in the town, Thomas Clowes, who kept the Pump inn in Mill Street, and George Walker, who had a brewery at the junction of Canal Street (later Broad Street) and Alsop Street.[86] Clowes had gone out of business by 1860,[87] but Walker's brewery was still in operation in 1908.[88] Bridge End brewery, on the Leekfrith side of the Churnet, was worked by William Brown Lea in 1860 and by Dixon & Johnson in 1864.[89] It probably closed in 1866: its stock, including beer, and movables were put up for sale that year, and the building and equipment were not in use when they were offered for sale in 1874.[90] There was a brewery attached to the Blue Ball in Mill Street in 1861. It was described as newly erected when advertised for lease in 1865. A month later the contents were put up for sale and were described as late the property of a brewer named Marriott.[91]

Soft drinks were made in the town in the later 19th and earlier 20th century. John Byrne, a house decorator, had established the North Staffordshire soda water works in Derby Street by 1864. By 1868 the business was run by Mrs. Caroline Byrne, who moved to Cross Street in the early 1880s and worked there until at least 1892. The business was evidently taken over by Moses Heapy, a Fountain Street grocer, who was producing bottled mineral water in Cross Street in 1896. He had moved the business to Fountain Street by 1900 and was still working there in 1904.[92] George Massey was making ginger beer in Shoobridge Street in 1880. By 1884 Richard Massey had taken over the business, moving it to Leonard Street where it remained until its closure in the later 1930s.[93] William Haywood, the landlord of the Golden Lion in Church Street, was making mineral water in Naylor's Yard, Clerk Bank, in 1896. By

1900 he was engaged solely in the production of mineral water and was still in business in 1928.[94] Mrs. Mary Burne was making soda water in Fountain Street in the late 1880s, and the Leek Mineral Water Co. had a works in London Street in the early 1920s.[95]

William Watson, a Leek grocer, had tobacco in stock at the time of his death in 1689.[96] John Oakes of Leek was trading as a tobacconist in 1711. He died in 1712 and was evidently succeeded by Thomas Oakes of Leek, described as a tobacconist in 1715 but as a grocer in 1718.[97] Joseph Grundy of Leek was described as a tobacconist at his death in 1733, and John Pott of Leek was trading as a tobacconist in 1744.[98] Samuel Grosvenor, a Leek grocer, had tobacco and spices in stock when he died in 1747.[99]

There were two chairmakers in Leek in the late 1790s, and the trade persisted until the 1850s, with members of the Booth family active throughout the period. Eight joiners and cabinet makers were recorded in 1818 and five cabinet makers in 1850.[1] Alfred Overfield, trading in 1850 as an upholsterer and cabinet maker in Sheepmarket, was in business the following year in Queen Street as a furniture broker and cabinet maker. He had moved to Russell Street by 1854, and his firm continued there until the 1920s.[2] The premises were burnt down in 1866 and rebuilt in 1868. They were extended in 1896 to the design of Larner Sugden and were described in 1910 as 'one of the most complete furnishing establishments in North Staffs.'[3] Sugden seems also to have designed furniture which Overfield & Co. made under his supervision.[4]

Leek had many makers of boots and shoes and of clogs and pattens throughout the 19th century. In the earlier 20th century numbers declined, and the last survivors were two clog-makers in business in the later 1930s.[5] The trade was evidently small-scale, domestic, and retail, with the exception of the International Crispin Patent Boot and Shoe Co. Ltd. A wholesale business, it was established in London Street by 1868 and was among the six most important boot and shoe manufacturers in Staffordshire before its closure by 1876. In the mid 1870s there were c. 650 factory hands and outworkers engaged in the town's shoe trade.[6]

There were two brickmakers in London Road in 1851 and three in 1861.[7] There were four

82 S.R.O., D. 3283, sheet 9.
83 P.O. Dir. Staffs. (1854; 1872).
84 R. Blome, Britannia (1673), 205.
85 P.R.O., HO 107/2008.
86 P.O. Dir. Staffs. (1854).
87 Ibid. (1860); S.R.O., D. 3283, sheet 12; O.S. Map 1/2,500, Staffs. VIII. 10 (1879 edn.).
88 Kelly's Dir. Staffs. (1908).
89 P.O. Dir. Staffs. (1860; 1864).
90 W.S.L., Sleigh scrapbk. ii, f. 56v.; S.R.O., D. 538/2/2, sale partics. 10 Sept. 1874.
91 P.R.O., RG 9/1947; W.S.L., Sleigh scrapbk. ii, ff. 45, 67.
92 P.O. Dir. Staffs. (1864 and later edns.); Kelly's Dir. Staffs. (1880 and later edns. to 1904); Chronicles (winter 1989), 15.
93 Kelly's Dir. Staffs. (1880 and later edns. to 1936); Chronicles (winter 1989), 15.
94 Kelly's Dir. Staffs. (1896 and later edns. to 1928).
95 Ibid. (1888); E. F. Cope & Co. Staffs. Dir. (1921).
96 L.J.R.O., B/C/11, Wm. Watson (1689); below, charities.
97 W.S.L. 132/2/47, nos. 15–17; S.R.O., D. 1040/5/14,

7 June 1712.
98 L.J.R.O., B/C/11, Joseph Grundy (1733); S.R.O., D. 4812/1/1, 5 July 1744.
99 L.J.R.O., B/C/11, Sam. Grosvenor (1747); S.R.O., D. 1040/5/14, 2 June 1747.
1 Univ. Brit. Dir. v [1798], 104–5; Parson and Bradshaw, Staffs. Dir. (1818), 124, 126–7; White, Dir. Staffs. (1834), 708, 710; (1851), 736, 738; Slater, Nat. Com. Dir. (1850), Staffs. p. 29.
2 P.O. Dir. Staffs. (1850; 1854); White, Dir. Staffs. (1851), 737–8; Kelly's Dir. Staffs. (1924).
3 W.S.L. 498/34, cutting of Nov. 1910; S.R.O., D. 3188/1/2, no. 106; D. 3188/1/3; C. M. Haywood and C. A. Parrack, Sugden & Son (Leek & Dist. Civic Soc. 1988).
4 K. Parkes, Windylow (1915), 113–14.
5 Parson and Bradshaw, Staffs. Dir. (1818), 123; White, Dir. Staffs. (1834), 708; (1851), 736; P.O. Dir. Staffs. (1850 and later edns.); Kelly's Dir. Staffs. (1880 and later edns.).
6 P.O. Dir. Staffs. (1868; 1872; 1876); J. A. Langford, Staffs. and Warws. Past and Present, i (2), pp. lxxvi–lxxvii.
7 White, Dir. Staffs. (1851), 736; P.R.O., RG 9/1947.

FIG. 25. THE MANCHESTER AND LIVERPOOL DISTRICT BANK

brickyards there in 1862 and the late 1870s but only one in 1898.[8] In the late 1870s there was also a brickworks east of Compton, along with sand and gravel working.[9]

PROFESSIONS. BANKS. The Leek Savings Bank was established in 1823, following meetings of leading inhabitants in 1822. It used a room in the town hall in Market Place and was open between noon and 1 p.m., at first every Monday and later two Mondays a month. In 1853 the trustees began building on the corner of Derby Street and Russell Street to the design of William Sugden, and the bank continued there until its closure in 1882.[10]

Two other banks were established in the 1820s. That of Fowler, Haworth & Gaunt in Market Place existed by 1825 and was presumably in the building on the corner of Market Place and Stockwell Street, formerly the Cock inn, part of which was the bank's premises in 1838. It was run in 1825 by a partnership consisting of Sarah Fowler of Horton Hall, John Haworth of Cliffe Park in Horton, and John and Matthew Gaunt, Sarah's sons by her first marriage. The bank closed in 1847.[11] The Commercial Bank, also in

Market Place, was opened in 1825 by a partnership consisting of Richard Badnall of Highfield House in Leekfrith, his son Richard of Ashenhurst in Bradnop, R. R. Ellis, Henry Cruso, and F. G. Spilsbury; all, except apparently Ellis, were connected with the silk industry. The partners were reduced in 1826 to the elder Badnall and Ellis. In 1827 the partnership was dissolved, and Ellis was left to close the bank at a heavy loss to himself.[12]

A Leek sub-branch of the Hanley branch of the Manchester and Liverpool District Bank was established in 1833. At first it was open on Wednesdays only, but from 1834 it opened daily.[13] When the lease of its Sheepmarket premises expired in 1841, it reverted to weekly opening in a room in Church Street. Daily opening was resumed in 1855 in premises in Custard Street, with a move to Derby Street in 1860. In 1861 the sub-branch became a main branch.[14] It moved temporarily into Gaunt House on the other side of Derby Street in 1881 while its premises were rebuilt. The new bank, designed by W. Sugden & Son, was opened in 1883. It is of brick with stone dressings; the interior of the portico has a frieze of tiles by William de Morgan. A notable feature is a

8 W.S.L. 93/92; O.S. Map 6", Staffs. VIII. SW. (1889, 1900 edns.).

9 O.S. Map 6", Staffs. VIII. NW. (1889 edn.).

10 T. J. Smith, *Banks and Bankers of Leek* (Leek, priv. print. 1891), 4–7; White, *Dir. Staffs.* (1851), 726; S.R.O., D. 538/D/3/10, p. 470; D. 3359, Leek Savings Bank min. bk. 1878–83, 4 Sept., 29 Dec. 1882.

11 Smith, *Banks and Bankers*, 11–13; *Lichfield Mercury*,

16 Sept. 1825, p. 4 (wrongly giving Haworth as Gaworth); Pigot, *New Com. Dir.* [1829], 712; *Plan of Leek 1838*; above, Horton. (manors).

12 Smith, *Banks and Bankers*, 11–12; *Lichfield Mercury*, 16 Sept. 1825, p. 4; *Lond. Gaz.* 1 Sept. 1826, p. 2140; 15 May 1827, p. 1064; W.S.L., Sleigh, ii, f. 241.

13 Smith, *Banks and Bankers*, 16.

14 Ibid. 27–8, 30.

first-floor oriel window surmounted by a pediment containing the bank's coat of arms; it is thought to have been copied from a building by Norman Shaw in Leadenhall Street, London.[15] The parent company (from 1924 the District Bank Ltd.) became a subsidiary of the National Provincial Bank Ltd. in 1962, and that in turn became part of the National Westminster Bank Ltd. in 1970.[16]

A branch of the Manchester-based Commercial Bank of England was opened in Derby Street in 1834. The bank failed in 1840.[17]

In 1857 a bank was opened by F. W. Jennings in a house in Stockwell Street enlarged for the purpose to the design of William Sugden. Jennings sold it in 1877 to the Warrington-based Parr's Banking Co. Ltd. In 1885 the bank moved to a building in St. Edward Street designed for it by W. Owen of Warrington. Parr's merged in 1918 with the London & Westminster Bank Ltd. to form the London County Westminster & Parr's Bank Ltd., from 1923 the Westminster Bank Ltd. The branch was closed after the formation of the National Westminster Bank in 1970.[18] In 1979 the building became a community centre occupied by the Citizens' Advice Bureau and voluntary services.[19]

The Mercantile Bank of Lancashire Ltd. opened a branch in Derby Street in 1898. The bank amalgamated in 1904 with the Lancashire & Yorkshire Bank Ltd., which was taken over by Martins Bank Ltd. in 1928. The Leek branch moved to the former Savings Bank building on the corner of Derby Street and Russell Street in 1964. Martins amalgamated with Barclays Bank Ltd. in 1969, and Martins' Leek branch was closed in 1972.[20]

There was a branch of the Cheque Bank Ltd. in Shoobridge Street at the end of the 19th century.[21] Williams Deacon's Bank opened a branch in Derby Street in 1920; it was closed in 1943.[22] Barclays Bank opened a branch in Derby Street in 1926; it moved to other premises in Derby Street in 1955 and to Haywood Street in 1960. The Midland Bank opened its branch in Derby Street in 1927. Lloyds Bank opened its branch in the Smithfield Centre in Haywood Street in 1964. A branch of the Trustee Savings Bank was opened in Market Place in 1986.[23]

A savings bank set up by the mechanics' institute in 1850 was open to the general public as well as to the members of the institute,[24] and by 1867 there was a branch of the Post Office savings bank in Leek.[25] The Leek Economic Loan Society was established in 1864 with its office in Silk Street, Ball Haye Green.[26]

BUILDING SOCIETIES. The first known building society in Leek was the Leek Building Society, a terminating society formed in 1824. Its 42 shares were to be paid for at the rate of 1 guinea a month over six years, and each subscriber was entitled to a house worth £80. Land was bought at Ball Haye Green, and it was arranged that 15 houses should be built there during the summer of 1824. By 1829 all 42 houses had been built.[27]

The Leek and North Staffordshire Benefit Building and Investment Society was formed in 1846, but the venture was unsuccessful.[28] Two terminating societies were launched within a few days of each other in 1850. The Leek United Benefit Building Society, which concerned itself with investment as well as building, successfully terminated in 1862, two years before its estimated term.[29] The Leek Benefit Building Society terminated in 1861, more than two years before its estimated term, having built Alsop Street, Westwood Terrace, and St. George's Row.[30]

The Leek and Moorlands Permanent Benefit Building Society was established in 1856 with its office at no. 1 Stockwell Street and with upwards of 120 members.[31] In 1879 it was incorporated as the Leek and Moorlands Building Society. New offices were built at no. 15 Stockwell Street in 1894–5 to the design of J. T. Brealey. Extended in 1924, they were replaced by the adjoining New Stockwell House, built on the site of Stockwell House in 1936–7 to the design of Briggs & Thornely of Liverpool.[32]

By that time the society was becoming nationally important. The growth was largely the work of Hubert Newton, who was appointed secretary in 1933 at the age of 29 and was later general manager, managing director, chairman, and president; he was knighted in 1968. The first of many mergers occurred in 1938 when the society took over the Longton Mutual Permanent Benefit Building Society. The merger with the London-based Westbourne Park Building Society in 1965 was the second biggest in the history of British building societies and produced the sixth largest building society in the country, renamed the Leek and Westbourne. The merger in 1974 with the Ipswich-based Eastern Counties Building Society resulted in a further change of name, to the Leek, Westbourne and Eastern Counties. In 1975, after the merger with the Oldbury Britannia Building Society in 1974, the society became the Britannia Building Society.

Meanwhile further office space was needed. In 1966 Milward Hall in Salisbury Street was

15 Ibid. 34–6; Leek Libr., newspaper cuttings 1980 (2), p. 4; S.R.O., D. 3188/1/3.
16 L. Richmond and B. Stockford, *Company Archives*, p. 250.
17 Smith, *Banks and Bankers*, 20–4.
18 Ibid. 28, 32–3; H. Bode, *Visiting Leek*, i (Leek, 1974), 12; Leek Libr., copy of hist. of National Westminster Bank, Leek; Richmond and Stockford, *Company Archives*, pp. 53, 255.   19 *Leek Post & Times*, 5 May 1993, p. 8.
20 Inf. from Barclays Records Services; Bode, *Visiting Leek*, i. 11.   21 *Kelly's Dir. Staffs.* (1896; 1900).
22 Inf. from the Royal Bank of Scotland plc.
23 Inf. from the managers of the respective branches.
24 Below, educ. (further and adult educ.: literary and mechanics' institute).
25 W.S.L., Sleigh scrapbk. ii, f. 3.

26 S.R.O., Q/RS 1/16.
27 R. Redden, *Hist. of Britannia Building Soc. 1856–1985*, 6–7; S.R.O., D. 1015/1/15/3; Leek Libr., box file labelled Leek Misc. Papers, envelope for Ball Haye Building Soc.
28 Redden, *Britannia Building Soc.* 7–8; *Staffs. Advertiser*, 23 Jan. 1847, p. 7.
29 P. Gallimore, 'Building Socs. and Housing Provision in N. Staffs. (1850–1880)' (Keele Univ. M.A. thesis, 1985), 100; *Staffs. Advertiser*, 15 Mar. 1862, p. 6.
30 Redden, *Britannia Building Soc.* 7; *Staffs. Advertiser*, 16 Mar. 1850, pp. 1, 6; 30 Mar. 1861, p. 7; W.S.L. 458/2/35, rules of Leek Benefit Building Soc.
31 Three paras. based on Redden, *Britannia Building Soc. passim*.
32 For the architects see Leek Libr., brochure for opening of New Stockwell House.

bought for the mortgage department. In 1968 no. 10 Stockwell Street was rented for the new computer department, which soon required larger premises and moved to St. Luke's church hall. Newton House on a 27-a. landscaped site on the east side of the Cheddleton road was opened as the society's new headquarters in 1970; it was designed by Adams & Green of Stoke-on-Trent. New Stockwell House was re-tained as the town-centre branch office but was sold in 1976 to Staffordshire Moorlands district council, a branch office having been opened in Derby Street. That was itself replaced in 1980 by a new building on the site of the baths on the corner of Derby Street and Bath Street. Newton House was extended in 1980, and in 1992 an-other large office building, Britannia House, was opened on the opposite side of the Cheddleton road.[33] In the early 1990s Britannia was Leek's largest employer.[34]

The Leek United Permanent Benefit Building Society was formed in 1863.[35] Its premises were at first in Russell Street,[36] but in 1871 it moved to St. Edward Street. It was incorporated in 1884. It moved to a new office in the same street in 1896 and to its present premises, also in St. Edward Street, in 1916. In 1919 it changed its name to the Leek United and Midlands Building Society.

LAWYERS. George Parker (d. 1675) of Park Hall in Caverswall was practising law at Leek in 1654.[37] The Thomas Parker who witnessed a marriage in the town in 1655[38] may have been George's elder brother, also a lawyer,[39] or George's second son, another lawyer, who was living in Leek in the 1660s and was the father of Thomas Parker, Lord Chancellor and earl of Macclesfield.[40] George Parker's son-in-law Richard Levinge was a lawyer apparently living in Leek in the later 1650s. Of his children baptized there, Richard (1656–1724) became attorney general for Ireland, chief justice of the Irish court of common pleas, and a baronet.[41] John Horsley, a Leek lawyer who died in 1695, probably came from a Bradnop family.[42]

Four generations of the Mills family practised law at Leek,[43] and the family is said to have taken over George Parker's practice.[44] Certainly they acted professionally for the earls of Macclesfield in the 18th century,[45] and in the middle of the century they were the town's leading lawyers. William Mills (d. 1695) was probably in practice by 1687.[46] His eldest son, also William (1689–1749), was practising by the 1720s,[47] and by 1738 he had been joined by his own son Thomas (1717–1802).[48] Thomas acquired the manor of Barlaston by marriage in 1742 and was sheriff of Staffordshire in 1754.[49] It was probably his son Thomas (1752–1821) who by 1783 was in part-nership with John Cruso. Later, probably in 1799, Mills and Cruso made their clerk, Henry Jones, a junior partner.[50] In 1806 Mills sold his interest in the firm to Cruso, and in 1807 Cruso and Jones took Sinckler Porter of Lichfield as partner. The partnership was evidently dis-solved in 1810.[51] In 1817 Jones and Porter had separate practices in Leek. Cruso had taken his son John into partnership, and that year his son-in-law Charles Coupland, a Leek attorney, joined the partnership.[52] Coupland left in 1824 or 1825.[53] When the elder John Cruso died in 1841, the younger moved from Spout Street to the house in Church Street which his father had bought in 1819 from Thomas Mills and which was known as Foxlowe by the early 20th cen-tury.[54] His younger brother Francis was practising as a solicitor in Stockwell Street by 1841.[55] Both were still practising in the earlier 1860s, Francis dying in 1864 and John in 1867.[56]

Another legal dynasty was the Condlyffe fam-ily.[57] William (1707–99) of Upper Hulme, in Leekfrith, was articled to a Richard Goodwin in 1723 and practised in Leek from the 1730s to the 1790s.[58] In 1757–8 he built a house in Derby Street which was to remain the family home.[59] His elder son John was working for him by the 1770s and seems to have been in at least nominal charge of the practice in the 1790s.[60] His health, however, was weak, and he was confined as a lunatic by the time of his father's death; he died in 1810.[61] His younger brother Joseph (1754–1839)

33 Inf. from Britannia Building Soc.; below, plate 51.
34 Leek Libr., newspaper cuttings 1992–3, p. 4.
35 Para. based on *Centenary Story of Leek United & Midlands Building Soc. 1863–1963.*
36 *P.O. Dir. Staffs.* (1864).
37 Keele Univ. Libr., Sneyd MSS., corresp. of Wm. Sneyd, no. 5; Erdeswick, *Staffs.* 246 n.; Sleigh, *Leek*, 27.
38 *Leek Par. Reg.* 99.
39 Sleigh, *Leek*, 27 (wrongly stating that he was sheriff of Staffs.).
40 Ibid.; *Leek Par. Reg.* 155–6, 161, 165, 173, 179, 181; above, general hist. (18th cent.).
41 *Leek Par. Reg.* 109, 111, 128, 137, 139; *Cal. Inner Temple Rec.* ed. F. A. Inderwick, ii. 319; *D.N.B.*
42 S.R.O., D. 1040/5/14, 28 Sept. 1695; Sleigh, *Leek*, 110.
43 Pedigree in Sleigh, *Leek*, 89.
44 Sleigh, *Leek*, 26; Challinor, *Lectures*, 9.
45 S.R.O., D. 3359/Condlyffe, Jas. Mallors to Wm. Condlyffe, 16 Oct. 1759; Sleigh, *Leek*, pl. facing p. 30.
46 S.R.O., D. 3359/misc. deeds, deed of 13 May 1687.
47 Sleigh, *Leek*, pl. facing p. 30; R. V. H. Burne, *Chester Cathedral*, 186–7.
48 J. Oldham, *Mansfield MSS. and Growth of Eng. Law in 18th Cent.* ii. 1083, 1089.
49 M. W. Greenslade, *Barlaston* (Univ. of Keele, 1966), 21–2; Sleigh, *Leek*, 88; *S.H.C.* 1912, 290.
50 S.R.O., D. 3359/misc. deeds, accts. of Thos. Mills and

partners 1784–1809.
51 Ibid.; D. 3359/Cruso, deeds of 31 Dec. 1806, 1 Jan. 1807.
52 *Clarke's New Law List* (1817), 145; *Lichfield Mercury*, 26 Dec. 1817; 'Diary of Mary Elizabeth Cruso of Leek, Staffs., 1837', ed. A. W. Bednall (TS. in W.S.L.), intro.
53 S.R.O., D. 3359/Cruso, copies of Sandon Road Turn-pike Act (1824) and Leek Improvement Act (1825) with names of Leek solicitors acting as agents; 'Diary of Mary Eliz. Cruso', intro.
54 'Diary of Mary Eliz. Cruso', intro.; S.R.O., D. 3359/Cruso, abstract of title 1870; above, this section (silk: trade unions).
55 Pigot, *Nat. and Com. Dir.* (1841), Staffs. p. 24.
56 *P.O. Dir. Staffs.* (1850; 1854; 1860); Challinor, *Lectures*, 9; 'Diary of Mary Eliz. Cruso', intro.
57 Pedigree in Sleigh, *Leek*, 121.
58 S.R.O., D. 3359/Condlyffe, draft articles 20 Sept. 1723; ibid. Wm. Condlyffe's personal accts. 1717–33; ibid. notes on Pedley v. Kidd 1736; ibid. deed of 22 May 1793. His portrait is in Sleigh, *Leek*, pl. facing p. 218.
59 S.R.O., D. 3359/Condlyffe, building accts. 1757–8.
60 Ibid. deed of ejectment in Dakin v. Lomas 15 Jan. 1773; *Univ. Brit. Dir.* v [1798], 104.
61 S.R.O., D. 3359/Condlyffe, Barbor & Browne to Wm. Condlyffe, 9 Sept. 1783; ibid. abstract of will of Wm. Condlyffe (d. 1799); ibid. letter from Jos. Condlyffe to Mr. Clulow 3 Jan. 1811.

worked for their father in the 1780s[62] but may have let the practice lapse after William's death. By the early 1820s the practice was being carried on by Joseph's son William (1796–1867), who was still active in the 1860s.[63]

Other 18th-century lawyers included Thomas Walthall (d. 1788), in practice in the 1750s and 1780s,[64] Thomas Gent, and John Davenport. When Thomas Mills became sheriff in 1754, he appointed Gent his undersheriff.[65] Davenport was articled to Gent in 1750, and he was in practice on his own account probably by the late 1750s and certainly by the earlier 1760s.[66] He inherited Ball Haye in Tittesworth in 1780 and died in 1786.[67]

Davenport's practice passed to William Challinor of Pickwood (1752–1800), who had been articled to him and by the early 1780s was his partner.[68] After Challinor's death the practice was carried on by his partner George Ridgway Killmister, who in 1807 went into partnership with William's eldest son, also William; they were still in partnership in the mid 1830s. Their office was at no. 10 Derby Street, a house dated 1760, where William was living in 1821 and where he died in 1839.[69] His eldest son William (d. 1896) and another son Joseph (d. 1908) went into partnership in 1850 or 1851 with William Beaumont Badnall; William was then living at Pickwood, Joseph at the Derby Street house, and Badnall in Church Lane.[70] In 1854 Badnall became the son-in-law of Francis Cruso, and he apparently took over most of the Cruso practice.[71] With his withdrawal from practice in the earlier 1860s the firm became Challinor & Challinor, and by 1868 it was Challinor & Co.[72] About 1890 it became Challinors & Shaw, Thomas Shaw having joined the firm in the earlier 1880s, and the name remains in use.[73]

MEDICAL PRACTITIONERS. There was a surgeon named John Hulme at Leek in 1658.[74] William Hulme, who owned Lower Tittesworth by 1673 and died in 1693, was a doctor of physic and a surgeon.[75] William Grosvenor of Leek was lic-

ensed to practise as a physician and surgeon in 1697, his certificate of fitness being signed by the vicar of Leek and by Thomas Beckett, a surgeon, and Benjamin Endon, a physician, probably of Dunwood House Farm in Longsdon.[76] Grosvenor was described in 1705 as an apothecary and in 1712 and 1723 as a physician.[77] He died in 1765 aged 101.[78] His son Joseph, who was supplying medicines in 1735 and the 1740s, practised in Cheadle. Joseph's son Joshua was described as a Leek apothecary in 1756 and was practising as a surgeon in Leek in the 1760s.[79] John Condliffe of Leek was described as a barber surgeon in 1705,[80] as was Benjamin Watson of Leek in 1723.[81] Robert Key, a member of a local Quaker family, practised as a physician in Leek in the late 1730s and the 1740s, having studied at Leiden. He moved to London but died at Leek in 1761.[82]

William Watson, a Leek grocer, had 'apothecary ware' amongst his goods at his death in 1689.[83] The goods of Gervase Gent, a Leek Quaker, as listed in 1690 after his death suggest that he was an apothecary and barber surgeon: they included drugs and allied equipment, a urinal, clyster pipes, razors, and 'some intruments of chirurgery'.[84] There was a Leek apothecary named Boller c. 1700, and one named William Thorpe died in 1707.[85] Eli Robinson (1693–1742) was practising as an apothecary in Leek by 1722 and was described as a surgeon and apothecary in 1728, when he attended the dying Thomas Jodrell of Endon.[86] Henry Fogg (1707–50), the son of a Stone butcher, was apprenticed to Robinson in 1722. Described in 1746 as an apothecary and surgeon, he had numerous clients in the Leek area and beyond. After his death the contents of his shop and his medical books were bought by Hugh Wishaw.[87]

A surgeon named Isaac Cope was living in Sheepmarket in 1760.[88] Three Leek surgeons were listed in 1784, F. B. Fynney, who was described as an apothecary also, and Eli and Isaac Cope; there was also a druggist, Benjamin

62 Ibid. memo. bk. 1787–91.
63 Ibid. brief in Rex v. Mellor 1823; ibid. A. Welby to Wm. Condlyffe, 19 Dec. 1864.
64 Ibid. memo. by John Watson 1757–9; S.R.O., D. 1040/5/15, 22 Aug. 1788; Bailey's Brit. Dir. (1784), 388.
65 S.R.O., D. 3359/Condlyffe, copy of sheriff's proclamation [1754].
66 Ibid. draft deed Davenport/Gent 1750; ibid. memo by John Watson 1757–9; ibid. papers in Cork v. Pegg 1763.
67 Below, Tittesworth, estates.
68 P. W. L. Adams, Notes on some N. Staffs. Families (Tunstall, priv. print., foreword dated 1930), 105, 108; D.R.O., D. 2375M/161/4.
69 Adams, N. Staffs. Families, 108–9, 115; Pigot, Nat. Com. Dir. (1835), 412. Pickwood was the home of T. F. Grosvenor in 1814: S.R.O., D. 3359/Grosvenor, abstract of title of G. N. Best to the Black Swan etc. p. 5.
70 Adams, N. Staffs. Families, 115–17; P.O. Dir. Staffs. (1850); White, Dir. Staffs. (1851), 735; S.R.O., D. 4855/2/14. For Wm.'s connexion with Charles Dickens and Bleak House see below, Onecote, intro.
71 Adams, N. Staffs. Families, 96, 117.
72 P.O. Dir. Staffs. (1864; 1868).
73 Kelly's Dir. Staffs. (1884; 1888; 1892).
74 Leek Par. Reg. 132.
75 S.R.O., D. 538/A/1/3 and 6; D. 1040/5/14, 24 Oct. 1693; L.J.R.O., B/C/11, Wm. Hulme (1693).

76 L.J.R.O., B/A/11/D; below, Longsdon, intro.
77 Sleigh, Leek, 8, giving him as 'aromatarius?', evidently a misreading of 'aromatarin'; S.R.O., D. 3359/Condlyffe, deeds of 23 Jan. 1711/12, 9 Dec. 1723.   78 Sleigh, Leek, 31.
79 Ibid.; W.S.L., Sleigh scrapbk. i, f. 70v. (a list of debts owing to Joseph, given as owing to James Fenton Grosvenor in Olde Leeke, i. 149); S.R.O., D. 3359/Grosvenor, abstract of title of G. N. Best to the Black Swan etc. p. 1; ibid. abstract of title of T. F. Grosvenor to Tofts meadow, p. 1.
80 L.J.R.O., B/V/6/Meerbrook, 1705.
81 S.R.O., D. 3359/Condlyffe, deed of 9 Dec. 1723. Sleigh, Leek, 8, gives a Wm. Watson of Leek as a barber surgeon in 1730.
82 W.S.L., Sleigh scrapbk. i, ff. 90, 107; ii, f. 5v.; S.R.O., D. 3359/Toft-Chorley, Haregate memo. bk. pp. 31, 33; Chain of Friendship: selected letters of Dr. John Fothergill of London, 1735–1780 (Cambridge, Mass., 1971), ed. B. C. Corner and C. C. Booth, 86, 93, 95, 97.
83 L.J.R.O., B/C/11, Wm. Watson (1689).
84 Ibid. Gervase Gent (1690).
85 D.R.O., D. 321M/B9, 16 Apr. 1709; S.R.O., D. 1050/5/14, 18 Jan. 1706/7.
86 Medical Hist. xxxvii. 188; L.J.R.O., B/C/11, Thos. Jodrell (1728).
87 Medical Hist. xxxvii. 187 sqq.; S.R.O., D. 3359/Cruso, deed of 27 Sept. 1746.
88 S.R.O., D. 3359/Grosvenor, deed of 5 Apr. 1760.

Challinor.[89] All were listed again in 1798; Fynney was then described as a surgeon and man midwife, as was a fourth surgeon, George Cope.[90] Fynney, who died in 1806, built Compton House in the Cheddleton road.[91] In 1818 six surgeons were listed, including three members of the Fynney family; druggists mentioned were Benjamin and Jesse Challinor and John Smith.[92] There were four surgeons in the earlier 1830s, a number which the vicar, T. H. Heathcote, considered too few for a town the size of Leek.[93]

They included Charles Flint, one of those listed in 1818; in the 1820s he moved from Stockwell Street to Compton House, where he died in 1864 at the age of 74, having practised in Leek for nearly 50 years.[94] Richard Cooper, a staunch Wesleyan Methodist who was born at Cheddleton in 1803, was admitted M.R.C.S. in 1825 and was in general practice in Leek until his death in 1872. He was also medical officer of the Leekfrith district of the Leek poor-law union from 1837.[95]

LOCAL GOVERNMENT

IN the later Middle Ages the area later covered by the township of Leek and Lowe was divided between the borough of Leek and a tithing of Leek manor apparently known as Lowe in 1327. The tithing was called Woodcroft by 1340, Lowe by 1429, and Leek by 1551.[96] With the disappearance of the borough after the Dissolution the whole area came within Leek manor and the township of Leek, called Leek and Lowe by the later 17th century.[97] The township formed one of the quarters of Leek parish, with its own churchwarden and its own overseer of the poor.[98] It had its own vestry meeting by the mid 19th century.[99] The built-up area was taken into the new Leek urban district in 1894, and the area to the south became the civil parish of Leek and Lowe, renamed Lowe in 1895. That too became part of the urban district in 1934.[1]

MANORIAL GOVERNMENT. Besides Leek and Lowe the manor of Leek included Heaton, Leekfrith, Rushton Spencer, and Tittesworth by 1340.[2] From the mid 16th century the manor was known as the manors of Leek and Frith, at that time still covering the same five townships.[3] All five were part of Leek constablewick in the later 17th century.[4] In 1827 the manors of Leek and Frith were described as covering the townships of Leek and Lowe, Leekfrith, and Tittesworth.[5] The manors, however, retained some vestigial control over Heaton and Rushton Spencer: in 1820 the court of Leek and Frith appointed a headborough for Heaton and a headborough and a pinner for Rushton Spencer.[6]

There was mention of the court of Leek in

1281,[7] and in the late 13th century land at Upper Tittesworth was held by suit at Leek court twice a year.[8] In 1293 the abbot of Dieulacres claimed view of frankpledge as lord of Leek in succession to Ranulph de Blundeville, earl of Chester.[9] Records of a small court survive from the earlier 14th century.[10] By 1340 each of the five townships making up the manor formed a tithing represented by one frankpledge at the twice-yearly view.[11] A twice-yearly great court and a three-weekly small court were still held at the Dissolution, with between 300 and 400 suitors attending the great court.[12] In 1744 the Green Dragon (later the Swan) inn at Leek was the meeting place of the court leet.[13] In the earlier 19th century a court leet was held at the Red Lion in Leek every October before the earl of Macclesfield's steward, and it was stated in 1834 that over 1,000 suitors usually attended.[14] In 1820 absentees who had not essoined were fined 6d. each, and an order was made for the compilation of a full list of suitors in time for the next court.[15] In 1831 the jurors assembled at 11 a.m. and after being sworn carried out 'a minute inspection of the town', making presentments of nuisances and encroachments. They returned about 4 p.m. for 'an ample and excellent dinner' and afterwards appointed the officers for the following year.[16] The court continued to be held until the early 1880s.[17]

Several officials were elected at a great court in January 1429/30: a constable, an ale taster, two meat tasters, and a bailiff ('catchpoll') with an associate (socius).[18] In 1538 the earl of Derby was steward of the manor as well as steward of the borough and of Dieulacres abbey; there was a single bailiff for all the abbey's manors.[19] In

89 Bailey's Brit. Dir. (1784), 388 (where F. P. Best is presumably an error for Fielding Best Fynney); L.J.R.O., B/V/6/Meerbrook, 1785. For the two Copes see also Olde Leeke, i. 145.

90 Univ. Brit. Dir. v [1798], 104.

91 Sleigh, Leek, 176.

92 Parson and Bradshaw, Staffs. Dir. (1818), 124.

93 W.S.L., S.MS. 43, Heathcote to Bd. of Health, 3 Sept. 1832; ibid. Keates to Bd. of Health, 17 July 1832; White, Dir. Staffs. (1851), 711.

94 Olde Leeke, i. 147; Pigot, New Com. Dir. for 1822–3, 468; Pigot, New Com. Dir. [1829], 713; Staffs. Advertiser, 26 Nov. 1864, p. 4.

95 Leek Wesleyan Meth. Circuit Yr. Bk. (1893), 15–16; Pigot, New Com. Dir. [1829], 713; P.O. Dir. Staffs. (1872).

96 S.H.C. vii (1), 219; S.R.O., D. 1333/1–3.

97 S.R.O., D. 1040/5/2; D. 1040/7, pp. 13, 19; W.S.L., Sleigh, ii, f. 38.

98 Above, Leek, par. intro. (par. govt.).

99 S.R.O., D. 706/3; D. 3226/34, 16 May 1853.

1 Below, this section (improvement com. and urban dist. council); Census, 1901.   2 S.R.O., D. 1333/1.

3 Sleigh, Leek, 17–18; P.R.O., SC 2/202/65; S.R.O., D. 1333/3; above, manors.   4 S.H.C. 1925, 164–72.

5 Act for better regulating supply of water in town of Leek, 7 & 8 Geo. IV, c. 37 (Local and Personal).

6 W.S.L. 490/34, pp. 3–4.

7 S.R.O., D. (W.) 1761/A/4/168.

8 S.H.C. 1911, 430.

9 Plac. de Quo Warr. (Rec. Com.), 714.

10 W.S.L., Sleigh, ii, f. 40; S.R.O., D. 1337/1–4.

11 S.R.O., D. 1333/1.

12 Sleigh, Leek, 18.

13 S.R.O., D. 3359/Condlyffe, notice for holding Leek court 1744.   14 White, Dir. Staffs. (1834), 701.

15 W.S.L. 490/34, pp. 3–4.

16 Ibid. p. 5.

17 White, Dir. Staffs. (1851), 719; Kelly's Dir. Staffs. (1880; 1884).   18 S.R.O., D. 1333/2.

19 F. A. Hibbert, Dissolution of the Monasteries, 242.

1820 the court appointed a constable, a deputy constable, and a headborough evidently for the whole manor, a combined beadle, 'bang beggar', and pinner for Leek and Lowe (with a rise in salary from 1s. to 3s. a week 'in case he executes his duty properly'), two market lookers, a pinner for Leekfrith, a headborough for Lowe, and two scavengers for the town of Leek, besides officials for Heaton and Rushton.[20] In the earlier 1830s the officials appointed consisted of a constable and a deputy, a headborough and a deputy, two market lookers, and a beadle, bang beggar, and pinner.[21] In 1831 a combined bailiff of the court and scavenger was appointed and two overseers of the highways for the town of Leek were reappointed.[22] Thomas Fernyhough was town crier at the time of his death in 1742,[23] and the manor court appointed a crier in 1837.[24] In the earlier 19th century there was a pinfold in Spout Street, apparently at the junction with Sheepmarket.[25]

THE BOROUGH. Between 1207 and 1215 Ranulph, earl of Chester, granted a charter to 'my free burgesses dwelling in my borough of Leek'. They were to be as free as 'the freer burgesses' of any other borough in Staffordshire. Each was to have ½ a. attached to his dwelling and 1 a. in the fields, with a right to timber and firewood in Leek forest and common of pasture for all cattle in Leek manor. The burgesses were to pay no rent for the first three years and thereafter 12d. each a year. They were also to be quit of all amercements relating to Leek for a payment of 12d. They were free to give or sell their burgages to anyone other than religious, subject to a toll of 4d. They were exempted from pannage dues in the manor, and they were granted privileged grinding at the earl's mills. The burgesses were exempted from tolls throughout Cheshire on all goods except salt at the wiches.[26]

The monks of Dieulacres renewed the charter, probably a short time after Earl Ranulph's grant of the manor to the abbey in 1232. The renewal omitted the clauses covering rights to timber, firewood, and pasture, exemption from pannage, and toll payable at the market and the fair. The 12d. rent was to be paid in two parts, 6d. on the feast of St. Edward in the summer (20 June) and 6d. at Martinmas (11 November). The ban on conveyance of burgages to religious was modified to allow conveyance to Dieulacres itself.[27]

About 1220 there were 80½ burgages; at the Dissolution there were 84.[28] Little is known about the organization of the borough. The earl of Chester's charter gave the burgesses the right

to choose their own reeve, subject to the approval of the earl or his bailiff, and the right was confirmed by the monks with a similar proviso. The town had its own bailiff by 1538 and probably by 1369; the earl of Derby was steward in 1538.[29] It is possible that the seat in the north aisle of the parish church occupied by the collector of the market tolls in the 17th century had once been the official seat of the borough bailiffs.[30] The moot hall in the town, which was held by a tenant in 1575 and 1677,[31] may earlier have been the meeting place of the borough court.

About 1530 the burgesses were in fear for their liberties because their charter had come into the possession of Thomas Rudyard, the lord of Rudyard manor.[32] Sir Ralph Bagnall, having secured the manors of Leek and Frith in 1552, proceeded to deny the burgesses their rights. In 1555 they asserted those rights, in particular the right to dispose of their tenements as they wished and the right to collect wood in the commons of the manor.[33] No later record of the borough has been found beyond the conveyance in 1622 of a moiety of a burgage[34] and the description of a house at Barngates in 1738 as a messuage or a burgage.[35]

IMPROVEMENT COMMISSIONERS AND URBAN DISTRICT COUNCIL. A body of 34 improvement commissioners was established by an Act of 1825 to light, watch, cleanse, and improve the town of Leek. The town was defined as a circle with a 1,200-yd. radius measured from the hall in the market place, and besides much of Leek and Lowe township the area included parts of Leekfrith and Tittesworth townships.[36] A new body of 24 commissioners with extended powers was set up under an Act of 1855, with responsibility for an area within a 1,500-yd. radius from the gas lamp in the centre of the market place.[37] Stones marking the boundary were erected on all the main roads and elsewhere,[38] and several survive.

In 1894 the commissioners were replaced by an urban district council of 24 members with powers covering the same area, 1,459 a. in extent. In 1934 the urban district was enlarged to 4,315 a. by the addition of Lowe parish and parts of the parishes of Cheddleton, Leekfrith, Longsdon, and Tittesworth; four wards were created.[39] From 1974 the former urban district was a parish in Staffordshire Moorlands district, with a town council of 12 members representing four wards and its chairman designated mayor of Leek. The parish is represented on the district council by 12 members.[40]

20 W.S.L. 490/34, pp. 3–4.
21 White, Dir. Staffs. (1834), 701.
22 W.S.L. 490/34, p. 5.
23 L.J.R.O., B/C/11, Thos. Fernyhough (1742); S.R.O., D. 1040/5/14.   24 Miller, Leek, 36.
25 Ibid. 82; Kelly's Dir. Staffs. (1888).
26 Charters of Earls of Chester, pp. 347–8.
27 Sleigh, Leek, 16–17 and pl. II.
28 Ibid. 17; Staffs. Studies, v. 9.
29 Hibbert, Dissolution of the Monasteries, 242; W.S.L., Sleigh scrapbk. ii, f. 87v.
30 Above, econ. hist. (markets and fairs).

31 P.R.O., E 178/2076; L.J.R.O., B/V/6/Leek, 1612; S.R.O. 3508/A/1/4.   32 P.R.O., C 1/651/52.
33 P.R.O., REQ 2/22/46; REQ 2/23/19.
34 S.H.C. N.S. x (1), 29.
35 S.R.O., D. 3359/Mills, deed of 15 July 1738.
36 6 Geo. IV, c. 71 (Local and Personal).
37 18 & 19 Vic. c. 132 (Local and Personal).
38 O.S. Map 6", Staffs. VIII. NW., SW. (1900 edn.).
39 Leek U.D.C. One Hundred Years of Local Govt. in Leek 1855–1955, 7; Census, 1901, 1931; Kelly's Dir. Staffs. (1936).
40 Leek Official Guide [late 1980s], 10–11.

In December 1855 the commissioners transferred their meetings from the public hall in the market place to a room in Derby Street. They moved to rented premises in Russell Street in 1862.[41] In 1881 the commissioners took over rooms in Union Buildings in Market Street, built as a concert hall in 1878 to the design of Alfred Waterhouse and others. In 1884 the commissioners bought the whole building, which then became the town hall. The Russell Street premises were reopened as the Liberal Club in 1882.[42] The town hall was demolished in 1988,[43] and the town council's offices moved to no. 15 Stockwell Street. Land in Leonard Street adjoining the cattle market of 1874 was used as a town yard for storing materials until 1894 when the yard was moved to Cruso Street.[44]

POOR RELIEF. In 1768 a workhouse for Leek and Lowe township was completed in Spout Lane, which was renamed Workhouse Street (and in 1867 Brook Street). The building was later enlarged, and by 1834 it was of four storeys and measured 75 ft. in length and 21 ft. in depth.[45] About 1800 nearly 3 a. of Leek moor on the Ashbourne road were inclosed as a garden for the workhouse.[46] In 1810–11 the governor of the workhouse was paid a salary of £42 and the matron one of £10.[47] The number of inmates averaged c. 54 in the earlier 1830s, maintained and clothed for 3s. 6d. each a week; the children were sent out to work in the silk mills.[48]

The Leek poor-law union was formed in 1837.[49] A union workhouse built on the Ashbourne road garden was opened in 1839; it was designed in a classical style by Bateman & Drury of Birmingham.[50] An infirmary block designed by J.T. Brealey was opened in 1898.[51] The buildings passed to the Stoke-on-Trent hospital management committee in 1948 and became Moorlands Hospital.[52] The former parish workhouse was put up for sale in 1839.[53] It was used as a dyeworks by 1868 and continued as such until it was taken over by the *Leek Post & Times* in 1968.[54]

In 1816 and 1841 distress funds were established by public subscription.[55] A soup kitchen was built in Stockwell Street by the improvement commissioners in 1868. They let it to a relief committee, which had been dispensing soup since the beginning of the year. The committee ran the kitchen until 1872.[56]

PUBLIC SERVICES

PUBLIC HEALTH. At the end of the 18th century Leek was described as a clean town with wide and open streets and a spacious market place.[57] In 1820 the manor court appointed two scavengers for the township of Leek and Lowe. It also ordered a 5s. fine for depositing filth, ashes, or rubbish in the streets of the town or on the highways or footpaths of the manor and failing to remove such deposits within three days after notice from the scavengers.[58] In 1831 the jurors of the court spent five hours inspecting the town and making presentments of nuisances and encroachments.[59]

At the end of 1831 a board of health was formed by the leading inhabitants in case of a cholera outbreak in the town. Poor families were visited and their needs ascertained; £110 was raised by subscription and distributed in bedding and coal. The board was legally constituted in 1832 and hired a building as a cholera hospital in case of need. Only one death in the town was recorded.[60]

In 1839 and 1841 government commissioners remarked on the cleanliness of the town and the workers' dwellings. The 1841 commissioner also recorded the prevalence of fever, which he attributed to 'the neglected state of the privies, ditches, and boglands, and lanes'. He described how a silk shade in London Street, itself very dirty, was in a yard behind a row of cottages, each with a privy emptying into the yard; there was only a shallow gutter to carry the filth to a cesspool, which was 'equally exposed and of itself enough to poison the whole neighbourhood'.[61] In 1849 the guardians of the Leek poor-law union appointed an inspector of nuisances, who was to inspect the town and report any nuisances to them.[62] A 'great mortality' in the town in 1856 led the improvement commissioners to set up a medical committee to report

[41] S.R.O., D. 3226/1, 7 Aug., 4, 18 Dec. 1855, and no. 1408; D. 3226/6, p. 37; W.S.L., Sleigh scrapbk. ii, f. 6; Leek Improvement Com. *Reps.* (1894), 25.
[42] S.R.O., D. 3226/6, pp. 36–8, 60, 89–90, 229; D. 3226/7, pp. 19, 131–2, 138; above, plate 38; below, social and cultural activities (public halls).
[43] Inf. from the Chief Executive, Staffs. Moorlands Dist. Council.   [44] Leek Improvement Com. *Reps.* (1894), 22.
[45] S.R.O., D. 3359/misc. deeds, deed of 28 June 1765; White, *Dir. Staffs.* (1834), 703; *Staffs. Advertiser*, 12 Oct. 1839, p. 1. For an earlier poorhouse in Leek see above, Leek, par. intro. (par. govt.). For Brook St. see above, general hist. (later 19th cent.).
[46] Act for inclosing lands in par. of Leek, 45 Geo. III, c. 96 (Local and Personal), s. 15; S.R.O., Q/RDc 65.
[47] S.R.O., D. 699/3/1.
[48] White, *Dir. Staffs.* (1834), 703.
[49] S.R.O., D. 699/1/1/1, p. 1.
[50] P. Walton, *A Peep into the Past* (Leek, n.d., dedication dated 1989), 2–6; below, plate 54.
[51] Walton, *A Peep into the Past*, 10–13.
[52] Ibid. 100.
[53] *Staffs. Advertiser*, 12 Oct. 1839, p. 1.
[54] *P.O. Dir. Staffs.* (1868), Leek commercial entries s.vv. Clowes & Stafford; S.R.O., D. 4310/2/2; Leek Libr., newspaper cuttings 1969–72, p. 73; 1980 (2), p. 3.
[55] S.R.O., D. 5343/1 and 2.
[56] Ibid. D. 3226/2, nos. 1988, 2042; D. 3359/Leek Soup Kitchen acct. bk.
[57] J. Aikin, *Descrip. of Country from thirty to forty miles round Manchester* (preface dated 1795), 537.
[58] W.S.L. 490/34, p. 4.
[59] Above, local govt. (manorial).
[60] W.S.L., S.MS. 43.
[61] *Reps. Assistant Handloom Weavers' Com., Pt. IV* [247], p. 347, H.C. (1840), xxiv; *2nd Rep. Com. Child. Employment, App. Pt. I* [431], p. C 17, H.C. (1843), xiv.
[62] *Staffs. Advertiser*, 1 Sept. 1849, p. 5.

on local conditions. The report, published in 1857, noted 'the vicious and intemperate habits of the people', inadequate ventilation in the factories, bad drainage, and an insufficient water supply. The Canal Street (later Broad Street) area was particularly insanitary, and a notable example of the inadequate provision of privies was to be found in 'Beard's houses' in Compton where there was only one privy for ten houses. Another group of houses in Compton known as O'Donnell's Square was described as 'a system of building outrageous to the sense of the 19th century'. Ball Haye brook had become an open sewer, and in no other town of similar size were 'filth and ordure more liberally bestowed'. A system of arterial sewers was recommended, as was the appointment of a medical officer of health.[63]

A complaint had been made in 1849 that the main sewers were too small to carry away all the sewage of the town.[64] About 1852 a brick sewer was constructed from the market place down Spout Street (later St. Edward Street) and Canal Street to discharge into a ditch.[65] In 1858, following the appointment of Charles Slagg as surveyor in 1857, the town was divided into two drainage districts, South and North. The sewerage of the South district, discharging into Birchall meadows, was completed in 1859 and that of the North district, apparently discharging at the bottom of Mill Street, in 1862. The sewage was distributed over large tracts of land and purified by broad irrigation before passing into the Churnet.[66] A medical officer of health was appointed by the commissioners in 1859 because of the high rate of mortality in the town.[67] In 1857 William Challinor had complained of Leek's notoriety compared with 'places less favoured by nature and circumstances but more by sanitary improvement'. At a conference in 1875 he was able to claim that Leek, from having been one of the worst towns in sanitary matters 20 years before, had become one of the best and that its death rate of about 30 in a 1,000 in 1860 had fallen to 15½ in 1874.[68]

By the later 1880s the pollution of the Churnet with sewage from the outfalls as well as with effluent from the dyeworks was causing concern, and in 1890 the county council threatened proceedings against the improvement commissioners.[69] The urban district council opened a sewage farm at Barnfields by the southern outfall in 1899.[70] Broad irrigation, however, continued north and west of the town until a new sewage works was opened at Leekbrook in 1934.[71] Improvements at Leekbrook, completed in 1992, introduced treatment processes claimed to be unique in Europe outside Italy.[72] In 1856 the surveyor had urged the adoption of water closets throughout the town. In 1873 there were 325 water closets as against 650 privies; by 1925 there were only 58 privies, 28 of them in outlying rural areas without sewers.[73]

FIG. 26 THE CEMETERY CHAPELS

Baths designed in an Elizabethan style by F. and W. Francis of London were opened at the east end of Derby Street in 1854.[74] Built by the Leek and Lowe vestry, they were taken over by the improvement commissioners in 1874 under the Public Health Act of 1872.[75] They were enlarged in 1897[76] and demolished in 1979 after being replaced in 1975 by swimming baths in Brough Park.[77]

In 1857 a cemetery was opened by the improvement commissioners on 5½-a. on the west side of the Cheddleton road at Cornhill Cross for the inhabitants of Leek and Lowe, Tittesworth, Rudyard, and Longsdon. Nearly 2½ a. were consecrated as a Church of England burial ground, and another part was set aside for Roman Catholics. The two mortuary chapels, linked by an archway surmounted by a tower and spire, were designed by William Sugden.[78] St. Edward's church and churchyard were closed for new burials in 1857, as were the graveyards attached to Mount Pleasant

[63] *Rep. of Medical Cttee. to the Commissioners acting under the Leek Improvement Act* (1857; copy bound into Ann. Reps. of Leek Benevolent Burial Soc. at the office of Leek Assurance Collecting Soc.). For the identification of O'Donnell's Square see *Staffs. Advertiser*, 5 Nov. 1859, p. 7.
[64] *Staffs. Advertiser*, 15 Sept. 1849, p. 3.
[65] S.R.O., D. 3226/1, no. 151.
[66] Ibid. nos. 151, 902–3; D. 3283; *Staffs. Advertiser*, 26 Nov. 1859, p. 5; *Leek Times*, 12 July 1913.
[67] S.R.O., D. 3226/1, no. 392; D. 3226/14, nos. 86, 88.
[68] Challinor, *Lectures*, 303, 311.
[69] S.R.O., D. 3226/31, 10 Apr. 1885, 17 May 1886; W.S.L. 495/34; *Staffs. County Council Rec. 1890*, 8, 34–5, 56–7, 72–4.
[70] W.S.L. 495/34, cutting from *Leek Times*, 24 June 1899; Leek U.D.C. *Fifty Years of Municipal Govt. in Leek,*

1855–1905 (Leek, 1905), 33.
[71] Leek U.D.C. *New Main Outfall Sewers and Sewage Disposal Works at Leekbrook.*
[72] *Leek Post & Times*, 24 June 1992, p. 10.
[73] S.R.O., D. 3014/10, cutting from *Leek Times*, 11 Oct. 1873; D. 3226/1, no. 151; Leek U.D.C. *Joint Rep. of M.O.H. and Sanitary Inspector for 1925*, 5 (copy in S.R.O., C/H/1/2/2/23).
[74] S.R.O., D. 3226/34, 16 May 1853; *Staffs. Advertiser*, 10 June 1854, p. 5.
[75] S.R.O., D. 706/3, p. 25; D. 3226/35, 5 Mar. 1874.
[76] Ibid. D. 3226/37, nos. 54, 68, 74, 81, 88, 100, 120, 145.
[77] Leek Libr., newspaper cuttings 1972–8, pp. 45–6; V. Priestman, *Leek Remembered* (priv. print. 1980), 3.
[78] *Staffs. Advertiser*, 8 Aug. 1857, p. 4; Lich. Dioc. Regy., Bp.'s Reg. Q, pp. 66–75.

Wesleyan Methodist chapel and Derby Street Congregationalist chapel; St. Luke's churchyard was closed in 1862.[79] The commissioners bought nearly 5 a. to the west of the cemetery in 1890, and just over 1 a. was consecrated by the bishop of Lichfield in 1893.[80] The cemetery was again extended in 1930.[81]

Robert Farrow (1822–1906), who settled in Leek in 1847 and evidently worked as a tallow chandler, became active in campaigns for sanitary reform. In 1867 he was appointed sanitary inspector by the improvement commissioners, and he continued to hold the post under the urban district council, retiring in 1905. He also served as supervisor of markets, school attendance officer, and secretary to the fire brigade.[82]

WATER SUPPLIES. In the 18th century there was a well in Mill Street west of the junction with Abbey Green Road.[83] In 1789 Joshua Strangman described his house on the west side of Spout Street as adjoining Holland's well. He also had the use of a well called the Dungeon near the lane later known as Strangman's Walk; the water was described in 1837 as 'pure and excellent' and never known to run dry.[84] In 1805 there was a well on the south side of Ashbourne Road;[85] Well Street, running north from Ashbourne Road, may have derived its name from the well.

By 1805 the town and places adjoining it were supplied with water piped from two reservoirs on Leek moor, at what are now the north end of Mount Road and the east end of Fountain Street. The Leek inclosure Act of that year, in confirming the earl of Macclesfield's ownership of the waterworks as lord of the manor, described the system as created by his ancestors.[86] An Act of 1827 obliged Lord Macclesfield and his heirs to supply the town from the reservoirs. It allowed him to charge up to £5 a year for each house supplied according to rented or rateable value; people requiring water for commercial purposes were to agree a charge with the earl.[87]

Complaints were made about the supply in 1849. Whereas the springs near Wall Grange, in Longsdon, provided a good supply to the Potteries, Leek's supply was inadequate and impure. The inhabitants were constantly annoyed by the bellman's calling out 'the water will be turned off all day tomorrow'. At the same time 'the reservoir and fountain' were 'full of

fish, frogs, toads, tadpoles etc.'[88] The reservoirs were enlarged in the early 1850s, and in the mid 1850s a reservoir was built at Blackshaw Moor, from which water was piped to the other two.[89] In 1856 the quality of the water was good but the reservoirs were in a filthy state so that 'the water is charged with vegetable matter and very unpure'. The needs of the town were estimated at an average of 90,000 gallons a day, but the supply was at the rate of 'only 2½ gallons per head per diem for the whole population'. Of the 2,117 houses within the improvement commissioners' district 1,263 paid a water rate. The main areas wholly or partially without a supply were the lower part of Mill Street, Belle Vue, Kiln Lane, Leek moor, and Ball Haye Green, and many people depended on polluted water from wells and the Churnet. The earl of Macclesfield's yearly income from the supply in 1855 was £586 and expenditure on repairs and maintenance was estimated at between £60 and £70; the commissioners' waterworks committee stated in 1856 that the income could be doubled if the powers given by the 1827 Act were fully used.[90]

One of the aims of the 1855 Improvement Act was that the new commissioners should take over the water supply, and in 1856 they bought the works for £11,000.[91] In 1859 they extended the main to Ball Haye Green, considered the unhealthiest part of the town.[92] Having bought land at Blackshaw Moor in 1864, the commissioners built a second reservoir there.[93] In 1872 the commissioners took a lease of springs at Upper Hulme, in Leekfrith; the urban district council bought the freehold before the lease expired in 1932.[94] The council opened a reservoir at Kniveden in 1931 mainly to supply the Ashbourne Road area.[95] In 1935 it built a pumping station at Poolend in Leekfrith linked to the Mount Road and Kniveden reservoirs.[96] The Mount Road reservoir was enlarged in 1964 and demolished in 1979.[97] The water undertaking is now owned by Severn Trent Water Limited.

In 1859 a drinking fountain was erected on the Buxton road south of its junction with Mount Road by Joshua Brough. Designed by William Sugden, it incorporated a spring which had long been used by the public, and it was intended for the refreshment of the many people who strolled out to the area in the summer.[98] In 1860 Charles Flint, a local surgeon, gave a drinking fountain

79 *Lond. Gaz.* 27 June 1856, p. 2246 (including order for closure of St. Luke's churchyard in 1857); 24 Mar. 1857, p. 1100; 10 June 1862, p. 2989.
80 Lich. Dioc. Regy., Bp.'s Reg. T, pp. 515, 530–4.
81 Leek Libr., newspaper cuttings, bk. 5, p. 52.
82 Anderton, *Edwardian Leek*, 107–11; Leek U.D.C. *Municipal Govt. in Leek*, 33; S.R.O., D. 3226/47, no. 360.
83 S.R.O., D. 3359/Badnall, abstract of title of Ric. Badnall to the Brindley House, pp. 32, 44; *Chronicles* (winter 1989), 3.
84 W.S.L. 329/21/40; S.R.O., D. 3359/Cruso, sale cat. for 27 Nov. [1837].
85 Act for inclosing lands in par. of Leek, 45 Geo. III, c. 96 (Local and Personal), s. 39; S.R.O., D. 843/1/5/1, lot 8.
86 45 Geo. III, c. 96 (Local and Personal), s. 39; S.R.O., Q/RDc 65, plan I.
87 7 & 8 Geo. IV, c. 37 (Local and Personal).
88 *Staffs. Advertiser*, 1 Sept. 1849, p. 3; 15 Sept. 1849,

p. 3; 22 Sept. 1849, p. 3.
89 White, *Dir. Staffs.* (1851), 722; S.R.O., D. 3014/10, cutting of 3 Feb. 1858; D. 3226/1, no. 146.
90 S.R.O., D. 3226/1, nos. 146, 151; *Staffs. Advertiser*, 21 Nov. 1857, p. 3.
91 S.R.O., D. 3226/1, nos. 180–1; above, local govt.
92 *Staffs. Advertiser*, 8 Oct. 1859, p. 7.
93 S.R.O., D. 3226/2, nos. 1578, 1586, 1601, 1660, 1736, 1834.
94 Ibid. nos. 2514, 2543, 2549; Leek U.D.C. *New Pumping Station at Pool End, Leek*, 7.
95 W.S.L. 501/34, Oct. 1931.
96 Leek U.D.C. *New Pumping Station at Pool End*; S.R.O., D. 3188/2.
97 Leek Libr., newspaper cuttings 1960–8, p. 42; *Leek Post & Times*, 25 Aug. 1993, p. 1.
98 *Staffs. Advertiser*, 22 Oct. 1859, p. 4; S.R.O., D. 3226/1, no. 865.

built into the wall of the town hall in the market place; it too was designed by Sugden. In 1872, with the demolition of the hall, the improvement commissioners re-erected the fountain in Canal (later Broad) Street.[99] Flint gave a second fountain in 1860, set in the wall of the churchyard at the west end of Church Street and fed by a spring.[1] A fountain given by William Challinor and designed by Joseph Durham was erected on the site of the hall in 1876. It was moved to Brough park in 1924, but the water was cut off in 1975 because the fountain was being vandalized. In 1988 it was moved to the forecourt of Moorlands House in Stockwell Street.[2]

MEDICAL SERVICES.

A dispensary was established in 1832 to provide medical and surgical help for the industrious working classes in their homes and attendance on poor married women during their confinements.[3] In 1851 adults paid 1d. a week and children ½d., and there were four surgeons available. Honorary subscribers paid 21s. a year, for which they could recommend 5 or 6 patients; midwifery cases counted as two ordinary cases.[4] In 1857 the Leek improvement commissioners' medical committee deplored the fact that the dispensary's annual income did not exceed £10 and urged greater publicizing of its work.[5] The dispensary still existed in 1898.[6]

The Leek Memorial Cottage Hospital at the east end of Stockwell Street was opened in 1870. It was built by Adelina Alsop in memory of her husband James (d. 1868) on land given by his nephews John and Robert Alsop. Designed by William Sugden, it consisted of a male ward of four beds, a female ward of three beds and two cots, and two private wards each with one bed. Mrs. Alsop managed and maintained the hospital until 1874 when she handed it over to a committee for three years. During that time she continued to maintain the building and contributed towards the running of the hospital, which was also supported by subscriptions and donations. In 1877 she handed it over to trustees.[7] An arched entrance gateway designed by W.

Sugden & Son was added in 1893. It was the gift of Mrs. Alsop, with gates given by John Robinson, the chairman of the committee. It was later removed to allow ambulances to drive up to the main door.[8] Four plots of land were added to the site in 1892, 1894, and 1897.[9] A wing designed by W. Sugden & Son was opened in 1909, the cost being met by a legacy of £1,000 from Elizabeth Flint and by public subscription. It contained a male and a female general ward, each with six beds, and two male and two female accident wards, each with one bed.[10]

In 1874 the improvement commissioners opened an isolation hospital in temporary premises on the west side of Ashbourne Road. They built a permanent hospital there in 1880; its four wards could accommodate 20 patients.[11] In 1938 it was taken over by the Newcastle and District joint hospital board.[12] It was closed in the 1950s and sold to the urban district council for conversion into dwellings. The council built old people's bungalows in the garden, and most of the original buildings had been demolished by the late 1980s.[13]

Leek Cripples' Aid Society, formed in 1921, worked at first in the Ball Haye Street schools and the Memorial Hospital. In 1927 the society opened a clinic in Salisbury Street designed by Longden & Venables.[14]

In 1948 the former union workhouse became Moorlands Hospital.[15] In 1990, after being refurbished and extended, it was opened as a community hospital, and the cottage hospital and the Salisbury Street clinic were closed.[16]

By 1921 Leek had a motor ambulance for non-infectious and accident cases and a horse-drawn vehicle for infectious cases. In 1924 the hospital convalescent committee presented a new motor ambulance to the town, and the existing ambulance was transferred to infectious cases.[17] There were seven ambulances by 1956, kept in the town yard. An ambulance station was opened in Haregate Road in 1957.[18]

The Leek branch of the Samaritans was established in 1966. At first it occupied a small room in Russell Street, and in 1976 it moved to Fountain Street.[19]

99 *Staffs. Advertiser*, 22 Oct. 1859, p. 4; 28 July 1860, p. 4; *Olde Leeke*, i. 147 and frontispiece; S.R.O., D. 3014/10, cutting from *Staffs. Sentinel*, 16 July 1873; D. 3226/2, no. 2515.
1 *Staffs. Advertiser*, 28 July 1860, p. 4; Sleigh, *Leek* (1862), 70; Leek Libr., newspaper cuttings 1969–72, p. 75; 1982 (1), p. 17; S.R.O., D. 3226/2, no. 2515.
2 S.R.O., D. 3226/4, no. 3007; Sleigh, *Leek*, 33 and pl. facing p. 32; Leek Libr., newspaper cuttings bk. 4, p. 18; bk. 5, p. 16; newspaper cuttings 1986–7, pp. 31–2; 1988 (2), pp. 5–6; inscrip. on fountain.
3 *Staffs. Advertiser*, 30 Mar. 1833, p. 3. For medical practitioners see above, econ. hist. (professions).
4 White, *Dir. Staffs.* (1851), 727.
5 *Rep. of Medical Cttee. to the Commissioners acting under the Leek Improvement Act* (1857), 14–15 (copy bound into Ann. Reps. of Leek Benevolent Burial Soc. at the office of Leek Assurance Collecting Soc.).
6 *Leek Annual* (1898), p. [18].
7 S.R.O., D. 3188/2, no. 251; D. 3359/Leek Memorial cottage hosp., rep. for 1874, pp. 3–5; rep. for 1877, pp. 3–4; ibid. vol. of copies of trust deeds etc. pp. 2–16.
8 Ibid. D. 3359/Leek Memorial Cottage Hosp., rep. for 1892, pp. 5, 6 n.; ibid. drawings of proposed gate, with extract from *Brit. Architect*, 1 Jan. 1892; Leek Libr., newspaper cuttings 1979, p. 18.

9 S.R.O., D. 3359/Leek Memorial Cottage Hosp., rep. for 1892, p. 4; 1894, p. 3; 1897, p. 5; 1898, p. 5.
10 Ibid. 1905, p. 5; 1906, p. 6; 1907, p. 5; 1908, pp. 5–7; 1909, p. 5. For plans for a new Memorial Hospital at Ball Haye Hall in the 1930s see below, Tittesworth, estates.
11 Leek U.D.C. *Fifty Years of Municipal Govt. in Leek, 1855 to 1905* (Leek, 1905), 17; *Kelly's Dir. Staffs.* (1884); S.R.O., D. 3226/2, nos. 2409, 2415, 2501; D. 3226/4, nos. 2910, 3221, 3263.
12 Leek U.D.C. *Ann. Rep. of M.O.H. and Sanitary Inspector for 1938*, 11 (copy in S.R.O., C/H/1/2/2/23).
13 P. Walton, *A Peep into the Past* (Leek, n.d., dedication dated 1989), 9.
14 W.S.L. 503/34, cutting of 1 Mar. 1928; *Kelly's Dir. Staffs.* (1932); S.R.O., D. 3188/1/4.
15 Walton, *Peep into the Past*, 100; below, plate 54.
16 *Leek Post & Times*, 3 Jan. 1990, p. 1; 2 May 1990, p. 31; 30 May 1990, p. 8.
17 *Rep. on Leek Rural Sanitary Dist. for 1921*, 9 (copy in S.R.O., C/H/1/2/2/22); Leek U.D.C. *Ann. Rep. of M.O.H. and Sanitary Inspector for 1934*, 7 (copy in S.R.O., C/H/1/2/2/23).
18 Leek U.D.C. *Ann. Rep. of M.O.H. for 1956*; 1957, 9 (copies in S.R.O., C/H/1/2/2/23).
19 *Leek Post & Times*, 2 Oct. 1991, p. 2.

POLICING. In 1293 the abbot of Dieulacres as lord of the manor claimed infangthief and right of gallows.[20] At the Dissolution the gallows stood 'at the end of the town', probably in Mill Street, and was stated always to have stood there.[21] In 1642 a group of inhabitants of Leek constable-wick agreed to build a cage or prison.[22] In 1651, however, the constable stated that the town had no pillory, cage, or other prison but only a pair of stocks, and quarter sessions ordered a levy on the constablewick for the provision of a cage and pillory.[23] A lock-up in the town was pulled down when the town hall in the market place was built in 1806 containing two cells.[24] In the earlier 19th century the stocks stood near the hall until their removal to a site beneath Overton Bank. Presumably as a replacement, steel stocks were set up in the market place opposite the Red Lion.[25] In the early 18th century a cucking stool stood by the Churnet off Abbey Green Road near Broad's bridge, apparently its site in the 1560s. A chair which may be part of a cucking stool is kept in St. Edward's church.[26] A scold's bridle was last used in 1824.[27]

By the beginning of the 18th century the sexton was paid 5s. for ringing the curfew.[28] In the later 1830s the sexton rang a bell at 6 a.m. and 1 p.m. each day.[29] He was still paid 5s. for ringing the curfew bell in 1857.[30]

A Leek association for the prosecution of felons was active in 1793.[31] What was evidently a new association was formed in 1802 covering the townships of Leek and Lowe, Leekfrith, and Tittesworth.[32] It was still meeting in 1898.[33] A separate association was formed for Leekfrith in 1819.[34] By the earlier 1790s a Leek manufacturers' association for the prosecution of felons had been formed to protect stock against theft, and that or a similar association was active in 1816. In 1838 silk manufacturers of Leek and its neighbourhood drew up a scheme for a new association for the prosecution of silk thieves.[35]

By 1818 there was a volunteer watch, which assembled at the town hall in the market place.[36] The improvement commissioners of 1825 were empowered to appoint watchmen and pay them, and they duly appointed four, each with a watch box.[37] By 1834 the commissioners' police force consisted of a superintendent (who was also clerk to the commissioners and to the Gas Light Co.), four constables, and some watchmen.[38] The manorial constable too still exercised policing duties in 1837.[39] A county police station was built at the junction of Mill Street and West Street in 1848; it included a dwelling for the inspector and three cells in place of the two in the town hall.[40] In 1851 the Leek county force consisted of a superintendent, an inspector, and 11 men.[41] A new station designed by W. Sugden & Son was opened in Leonard Street in 1892, with a superintendent's house attached.[42] That station was replaced by one in Fountain Street built in the late 1980s.[43]

By the 1830s petty sessions were held at the Swan every alternate Wednesday.[44] The police station of 1848 included a court room where petty sessions were held.[45] Courts were held in in part of the nearby West Street Wesleyan school by 1864 and continued there until 1879.[46] The magistrates then moved to Union Buildings in Market Street, later the town hall, and by 1884 they were also using a court room at the offices of Challinor & Co., solicitors of Derby Street.[47] In 1961 the courts were moved to part of the Methodist Sunday school building in Regent Street. In 1986 the Co-operative Society store on the corner of High Street and Field Street was converted into a court house.[48]

A Leek county court district was established in 1847, and in 1851 the court was held monthly at the Red Lion.[49]

FIRE PRECAUTIONS. The buckets provided and repaired by the churchwardens of Leek parish in the 18th century[50] were presumably for fire fighting and kept at St. Edward's church. By the earlier 1730s the town had a fire engine, given by the earl of Macclesfield, presumably after his purchase of the manor in 1723.[51] That too appears to have been maintained by the churchwardens.[52] A new engine, called Lord of the Manor, was given by one of the earls, probably in 1805.[53] From 1826 the Salop Fire

20 *Plac. de Quo Warr.* (Rec. Com.), 714.
21 Sleigh, *Leek*, 18.
22 S.R.O., Q/Sr 250, no. 19 (ref. supplied by Dr. P. J. Morgan of Keele University).
23 Ibid. Q/SO/5, p. 411.
24 S.R.O., D. 3359/Cruso, draft agreement of 7 Feb. 1806; below, social and cultural activities (public halls).
25 Miller, *Leek*, 80, 95, 97.
26 Sleigh, *Leek*, 20, 22; S.R.O., D. 3359/Badnall, abstract of title of Mrs. Badnall, p. 1; B.L. Add. MS. 36665, f. 3. Miller, *Leek*, 83, states that a chair then (1880s) in the tower of St. Edward's was not a cucking stool but was made for work on the tower.   27 *Olde Leeke*, ii. 224.
28 S.R.O., D. 1040/5/3, f. 167; D. 1040/5/14, terrier 1701; D. 1040/7, pp. 30–1, 36, 39.   29 Miller, *Leek*, 72.
30 L.J.R.O., B/V/6/Leek, 1857.
31 *Chronicles* (autumn 1992), 37.
32 S.R.O., D. 3359/Cruso, agreement of 12 June 1802.
33 Ibid. D. 3359, assoc.'s handbills 1851–70; *Leek Annual* (1898), p. [17].   34 Below, Leekfrith, intro.
35 Inf. from Mr. A. W. Bednall of Macclesfield, citing documents in his possession and *Macclesfield Courier*, 18 May 1816.
36 S.R.O., D. 3359/Condlyffe, Shufflebotham to Condlyffe

16 June 1818; Miller, *Leek*, 76.
37 6 Geo. IV, c. 71 (Local and Personal), ss. 35–40; Miller, *Leek*, 76.   38 White, *Dir. Staffs.* (1834), 701.
39 Miller, *Leek*, 11.
40 White, *Dir. Staffs.* (1851), 722; G. A. Lovenbury, 'A Certain Group of Men' (Leek, 1990), 7; *Olde Leeke*, i. 2.
41 White, *Dir. Staffs.* (1851), 722.
42 Staffs. C.C., *Record for 1891*, 53; *Leek Post & Times*, 15 Apr. 1992, p. 8; S.R.O., D. 538/D/33/10, p. 213; below, plate 40.
43 Leek Libr., newspaper cuttings 1985 (3), p. 3; *Leek Post & Times*, 17 Jan. 1990, p. 31.
44 White, *Dir. Staffs.* (1834), 700.
45 Ibid. (1851), 722.
46 Leek Libr., Johnson scrapbk. 3, p. 204; S.R.O., D. 1114/1, trust accts. 1876–9.
47 *Kelly's Dir. Staffs.* (1880; 1884; 1940).
48 Leek Libr., newspaper cuttings 1986, p. 28.
49 *Lond. Gaz.* 10 Mar. 1847, p. 1012; White, *Dir. Staffs.* (1851), 723.   50 S.R.O., D. 1040/7, pp. 72, 211.
51 Ibid. D. 5041, p. 33.
52 Ibid. D. 1040/7, p. 165.
53 Ibid. p. 252; Leek Improvement Com. *Reps.* (1894), 12.

Office paid £5 a year towards the cost of repairing the engine; two other offices were contributing £2 10s. each by the late 1840s. In 1827 the trustees of the Town Lands bought land at the east end of Derby Street as the site for an engine house. The land soon came to be used for the cattle market, and in the 1840s the engine was kept in rented premises.[54]

The improvement commissioners established in 1855 took over responsibility for the engine and paid for its manning. By the 1860s the engine house was on the open space at the end of Derby Street.[55] At that time the commissioners were exercising their power to ban the use of thatch as a roofing material.[56] In 1870 they appointed a fire brigade committee and set up a volunteer brigade in addition to the paid brigade. An engine was bought for the volunteer brigade the same year and housed in Stockwell Street. In 1871 the volunteers took charge of the fire escape belonging to the commissioners. The two brigades were merged as a single volunteer brigade in 1873. It was reorganized as a paid brigade in 1883 following the resignation W. S. Brough, captain of the volunteer brigade since 1870.[57]

In 1898 the urban district council opened a new fire station on the Stockwell Street site designed by J. T. Brealey.[58] At the same time a steam-operated engine was bought and named the Queen of the Moorlands.[59] A motor engine was bought in 1924 and named the Wilson after the chairman of the fire brigade committee; the steam engine was retained.[60] The Stockwell Street station was replaced by a new station in Springfield Road in 1971.[61]

GAS AND ELECTRICITY SUPPLIES.

In 1826 a group constituted the following year as the Leek Gas Light Co. bought land on the west side of the Newcastle road, and J. A. West of Durham, an engineer and the chief shareholder, built a gasworks there. An agreement was made in 1827 with the improvement commissioners to light c. 100 public lamps at £2 a year each from 29 September to 5 April. The lamps were to be lit from dusk, half until 2 a.m. and the rest until 6 a.m.; none was to be lit for three nights before a full moon and one night after it. There was a private supply to houses, factories, and shops. The dial of the clock in St. Edward's church tower was also lit, the improvement commissioners paying £7 a year by 1834.[62] A second gas holder was built in 1844.[63] In 1846 the undertaking was sold to the improvement commissioners and the company was dissolved.[64] The works ceased production in 1964.[65]

Electricity was supplied by the urban district council from 1904, with a generating station in Cruso Street.[66] The supply was extended to the Birchall area in 1931.[67] In 1955 most of the streets were still lit by gas, and the council was then planning systematic conversion to electricity.[68]

HOUSING.

The first houses provided by the urban district council were 12 wooden huts erected in 1920 in Junction Road on part of Barnfields farm, later the site of the cattle market. Faced with a housing shortage, the council bought the huts from the government, transported them, and converted them into temporary dwellings.[69] The council's first permanent estate was the 24-a. Abbottsville estate west of Abbotts Road, where 258 houses were built between 1920 and 1924; the estate was extended north to Novi Lane with another 72 houses in 1925 and 1926. In 1925 the council built 46 houses on the south side of the town. Most were in Glebeville off Junction Road on 2½ a. of glebe bought from the trustees of All Saints' church, but some were on the remainder of Barnfields farm. At the west end of the town 114 houses were built in Station Street, the Walks, and Morley Street in 1928. In the 1930s building continued north of Novi Lane on 29 a. at Haregate, where 104 houses were built in 1930 and 100 in 1933; another 156 were built in 1935 and 1936 to rehouse people displaced by slum clearance.[70]

Building was resumed after the Second World War, and by 1955 a further 557 houses and flats had been provided. They included 30 more in Novi Lane and Abbotts Road, 248 on the Compton estate including 9 flats in the adapted Compton House, and 268 on the Haregate estate, where the hall and 78 a. were acquired in 1948. A site of 3½ a. had also been acquired in Westwood Heath Road.[71] Slum clearance continued, and by 1961 283 dwellings had been demolished out of 450 scheduled for demolition.[72]

Leek's first housing-association project was Westwood Court in North Street, opened in 1980 and providing sheltered accommodation for the elderly. It was built by Anchor Housing Association and consists of 19 single flats, 9 for

54 *Rep. Cttee. Town Lands 1849*, 12–13, 17–18.
55 Ibid. 15–16; *P.O. Dir. Staffs* (1860; 1864; 1868); S.R.O., D. 3226/36, no. 5.
56 S.R.O., D. 3226/1, no. 1402; D. 3226/2, nos. 1450, 1487, 1504, 1766, 1857, 1865, 1951.
57 Ibid. D. 538/C/1/51, memo. of despatch of engine 22 Dec. 1870 and papers relating to Brough's retirement; D. 3226/36.
58 Ibid. D. 3188/1/3; D. 3226/37, nos. 116, 122, 131.
59 Ibid. D. 3226/37, nos. 112–13, 125; Leek Libr., newspaper cuttings 1969–72, pp. 28, 33.
60 Leek Libr., newspaper cuttings 1969–72, p. 31.
61 Ibid. p. 32.
62 S.R.O., D. 844/2, 13 May 1826, 19 Jan. and 30 Apr. 1827, 17 Feb. 1832, and agreement of 13 Jan. 1827 (loose); White, *Dir. Staffs.* (1834), 701.
63 S.R.O., D. 844/2, 17 Jan. 1844, 9 Jan. 1845.

64 Ibid. 22 Aug. 1845, 12 May 1846; D. 1047/15.
65 H. Bode, *Leek Canal & Rudyard Reservoir* (priv. print. 1984), 6.
66 Leek U.D.C. *Fifty Years of Municipal Govt. in Leek, 1855 to 1905* (Leek, 1905), 16.   67 *Leek News*, Dec. 1931.
68 Leek U.D.C. *One Hundred Years of Local Govt. in Leek 1855–1955*, 11.
69 Leek U.D.C. *Joint Rep. of M.O.H. and Sanitary Inspector for 1920*, 10 (copy in S.R.O., C/H/1/2/2/23); Leek Libr., newspaper cuttings 1954–7, p. 44.
70 Leek U.D.C. *Rep. on Provision of Houses, 1919–1930*; Leek U.D.C. *Ann. Rep. of M.O.H. and Sanitary Inspector for 1934*, 15, 21; *1936*, 3, 18 (copies in S.R.O., C/H/1/2/2/23).
71 Leek U.D.C. *One Hundred Years of Local Govt.* 9–10. Haregate Hall was converted into three dwellings.
72 Leek U.D.C. *Ann. Rep. of M.O.H. for 1961*, 32 (copy in S.R.O., C/H/1/2/2/23).

two persons, and 3 for three persons.[73] Another large scheme is Beth Johnson Housing Association's sheltered housing opened on the site of Mount Pleasant Methodist chapel in Clerk Bank in 1984 and consisting of 31 single flats and 8 double.[74] The same association completed the first phase of 40 pensioners' flats in Pickwood Close in 1990 and completed the scheme in 1993.[75] Horsecroft Grove, consisting of 10 bungalows built by the association, was opened in 1994.[76]

POST OFFICES AND TELEPHONE SERVICE. Leek had a postmistress by 1776[77] and was on the route of the London–Manchester mail coach introduced in 1785.[78] The post office was in the market place in the early 19th century but had moved to Spout Street (later St. Edward Street) by 1829 and to Custard Street (later Stanley Street) by 1834.[79] By 1838 George Nall, a bookseller, stationer, and printer in Sheepmarket, was also postmaster, and in 1843 he moved his business and the post office to Custard Street. The business was sold in 1865 to William Clemesha, who was postmaster in 1871.[80] In 1872 Samuel Tatton was appointed postmaster with his premises in Stanley Street.[81] He had moved to St. Edward Street by 1880 and to the former Savings Bank premises in Derby Street by 1884.[82] A post office was built on the corner of St. Edward Street and Strangman Street in or shortly after 1905.[83] A new post office was opened further north in St. Edward Street in 1964.[84] It was replaced in 1993 by a post office in part of the premises of Genies Lighting in Haywood Street.[85]

The National Telephone Co. opened an exchange in Stockwell Street in 1892. The exchange moved to Haywood Street in 1904 and to the post office in 1925. A new exchange was opened in the post office yard in Strangman Street in 1928. It was replaced in 1968 by a subscriber trunk dialling exchange on the site of the former post office in St. Edward Street.[86]

PARLIAMENTARY REPRESENTATION

A LEEK parliamentary division covering northeast Staffordshire was created in 1885 as one of seven new divisions for the county.[87] The first M.P. was a Liberal, but the Conservatives won the seat in 1886 and held it until 1906.[88] A Liberal won it that year and held it, with a Unionist interlude between the January and December elections in 1910, until 1918. That year William Bromfield, the secretary of the local textile union,[89] won the seat for Labour. He lost it to the Conservatives in 1931 but won it back in 1935. He was succeeeded in 1945 by Harold Davies, another Labour member, who held the seat until 1970; he was then created a life peer as Baron Davies of Leek. In 1970 a Conservative, D. L. Knox, gained the seat, which became Staffordshire Moorlands division in 1983. He won it for the seventh time in 1992 and was knighted in 1993.

CHURCHES

THE first known mention of a church at Leek is in the 13th century. There are, however, remains of pre-Norman crosses on the site,[90] and a church was built perhaps in the late 10th or early 11th century. Its dedication to St. Edward, recorded in 1281,[91] was evidently in use in 1207 when the king confirmed a fair at Leek at the feast of St. Edward.[92] The saint concerned was probably the English king, Edward the Martyr (d. 978 or 979), whose cult was officially promoted soon after his death: by the 1320s one of his feasts (20 June) was the day on which the burgesses of Leek had to pay the first half of their rent.[93] By the 1730s, however, Edward the Confessor was regarded as the patron saint.[94]

The church served a large parish which in the Middle Ages included dependent chapels at Cheddleton, Horton, Ipstones, Meerbrook, Onecote, and Rushton Spencer. Cheddleton, Horton, and Ipstones had become separate parishes probably by the mid 16th century,[95] and the chapels at Meerbrook, Onecote, and

73 Leek Libr., newspaper cuttings 1980 (1), pp. 22–5; *Leek Post & Times*, 10 Oct. 1990, p. 15.

74 Leek Libr., newspaper cuttings 1984 (1), p. 49.

75 *Leek Post & Times*, 3 Oct. 1990, p. 14; 17 Nov. 1993, p. 13.   76 Ibid. 12 Oct. 1994, p. 15.

77 *S.H.C.* 1934 (1), 120.

78 Above, communications.

79 Parson and Bradshaw, *Staffs. Dir.* (1818), 121; Pigot, *New Com. Dir. for 1822–3*, 468; Pigot, *New Com. Dir.* [1829], 712; White, *Dir. Staffs.* (1834), 706.

80 *Plan of Leek 1838*; White, *Dir. Staffs.* (1834), 708, 710; P.R.O., RG 10/2881; above, econ. hist. (trade and ind.: printing).

81 S.R.O., D. 3226/2, no. 2448; *P.O. Dir. Staffs.* (1872).

82 *Kelly's Dir. Staffs.* (1880; 1884); S.R.O., D. 3359/Leek Savings Bank min. bk. 1878–83, 29 Dec. 1882, 7 Aug. 1883.

83 Leek U.D.C. *Fifty Years of Municipal Govt. in Leek, 1855 to 1905*, 32; *Kelly's Dir. Staffs.* (1908); Poole, *Leek*, 28; W.S.L. 495A/34, Jan. 1904.

84 Leek Libr., newspaper cuttings 1960–8, p. 44.

85 *Leek Post & Times*, 24 Mar. 1993, pp. 1, 5; 30 June 1993, pp. 1, 5.

86 Leek Libr., newspaper cuttings 1960–8, pp. 100, 117–18.

87 *V.C.H. Staffs.* i. 273; *Kelly's Dir. Staffs.* (1888).

88 Rest of para. based on *McCalmont's Parl. Poll Book: Brit. Election Results 1832–1918*, ed. J. Vincent and M. Stenton, ii. 222–3; iii. 65; F. W. S. Craig, *Brit. Parl. Election Results 1918–1949*, 463; *1950–1970*, 489; *Dod's Parl. Companion 1984*, 542; *Leek Post & Times*, 15 Apr. 1992, p. 3; 16 June 1993, p. 1.

89 Above, econ. hist. (trade and ind.: silk: trade unions).

90 For the remains of pre-Norman crosses in the church and churchyard see below, this section. Grateful acknowledgement for help is made to Mr. W. F. Brooks, warden of Leek, and Mrs. B. C. Bunce, verger and clerk of St. Edward's.   91 Below, this section [churchyard].

92 Above, econ. hist. (markets and fairs). For the cult see S. J. Ridyard, *Royal Saints of Anglo-Saxon Eng.* 45, 154 sqq.

93 Above, local govt. (borough).

94 S.R.O., D. 5041, p. 1.

95 *S.H.C.* 1915, 60, 133; above, Horton, church.

Rushton Spencer had parishes assigned to them in the later 19th century. A chapel was built at Endon *c.* 1720, and that too became a parish church in 1865. A parish of St. Luke was formed in 1845, covering the eastern part of Leek town and the adjoining rural area. A parish of All Saints was formed out of St. Luke's and St. Edward's in 1889 to cover the southern part of the town and Longsdon.

In the earlier 1220s Ranulph, earl of Chester, granted the church of Leek to the monks of Dieulacres.[96] The grant was confirmed by William Cornhill, bishop of Coventry (resigned 1223), who instituted the monks into the vacant church. His confirmation mentioned dependent chapels, which were named as Cheddleton, Ipstones, and Horton in a further confirmation made by his successor Alexander Stavensby between 1224 and 1228.[97] Cornhill's confirmation stipulated the ordination of a vicarage; a Richard Patrick was vicar probably in the 1230s,[98] and there was a vicar with a deacon in 1241.[99] The advowson remained with Dieulacres until the Dissolution, and in 1560 the Crown granted it to Sir Ralph Bagnall.[1] It then descended with Leek manor until 1865 when Lord Macclesfield transferred it to the bishop.[2] In 1979 the parishes of St. Edward, All Saints, and St. Luke were united to form the parish of Leek, served by a team ministry composed of a rector and two vicars. The existing vicar of St. Edward's was named as the first team rector and the vicars of All Saints' and St. Luke's as the first team vicars. Thereafter the rector was to be appointed by the Leek Patronage Board, consisting of the bishop, the archdeacon of Stoke-upon-Trent, and three members chosen by the parochial church council of Leek parish. The vicars were to be appointed by the bishop and the rector jointly.[3] In 1983 the parish of Meerbrook was added to Leek, which became the parish of Leek and Meerbrook.[4]

In stipulating the ordination of a vicarage, the bishop fixed its value at 20 marks.[5] In 1288 the bishop settled a dispute between the vicar and the monks by ordering that the vicar was to have all annual oblations, the customary Lent offerings at Candlemas, casual perquisites, small tithes, tithe of hay from Endon, 6 marks a year from the monks, and the house by the church which it was customary for the vicar to have; the vicar had the duty of providing priests to serve the dependent chapels.[6] He was still in receipt of those dues and the 6-mark stipend in 1450, but the payment of £15 a year to the chaplains of Cheddleton, Ipstones, and Horton left him

with 14 marks.[7] It was probably then that the stipends of the chaplains were made a charge upon the rectory, as they were at the Dissolution.[8] In 1535 the vicar received £7 19s. 1½d. from offerings and other emoluments.[9]

The value of the vicarage was given as £10 a year in 1604.[10] In 1612 the vicar had a house, two little gardens, and arable in Leek field called the Vicars Croft (later Vicars Close), a shop at the west end of the moot hall let for 6s. 8d., and Easter payments of £9 in lieu of tithes.[11] By the later 17th century the Easter payments were at the rate of 1s. for a house with 20 a. or more attached (given as land worth £20 or more from 1701), 9d. for a house of lesser status occupied by a married man, and 7d. for one occupied by an unmarried or widowed person; 2d. was due for every boarder or child aged 16 and 1d. for every servant. Heaton, Rushton James, and Rushton Spencer were exempt from the Easter payments. The vicar also received a modus of 5s. 6d. a year for tithe of hay in Endon (8s. 6d. by 1730). It was further stated in 1698 that the churchyard had always belonged to him.[12] In 1705 the glebe was worth *c.* £6 a year; the Easter payments should have been worth nearly £30 a year, but because of the poverty of the people and the cost and trouble of collecting it in so large a parish its actual value was £20. Surplice fees could amount to nearly £15. The vicar complained that the dissenters and especially the Quakers 'do by their obstinacy draw the vicar into many tedious and expensive suits for the recovery of his just rights', with the result that the value of the vicarage was considerably reduced.[13] In 1708 it was stated that the vicars had always been allowed 12d. for every mile which they had to travel in the parish to baptize a child away from the church.[14] George Roades (d. 1713), rector of Blithfield and son of George Roades, vicar of Leek 1662–95, left the tithe corn from several plots of land in Leek to the vicar for ever.[15] James Rudyard of Dieulacres, by will proved 1714, charged his estate with an annual payment of £2 to the vicar.[16]

A grant of £200 was made from Queen Anne's Bounty in 1793 to meet two benefactions of £100 each made that year by Thomas Mills the younger and Mrs. Pyncombe's trustees. It was used to buy 25 a. in Ipstones, which were let for *c.* £18 by 1824. A further grant of £600 was made in 1824.[17] When Leek moor was inclosed in 1811, the vicar was assigned 8½ a. in respect of his glebe and in lieu of the tithe corn and rents from 20 a.[18] His income in 1836 was £191 1s. 4d., consisting of £60 14s. in rent from land and

96 *Charters of Earls of Chester*, p. 381.
97 *S.H.C.* N.S. ix. 311 (date indicated by the name of the see: *V.C.H. Staffs.* iii. 12). Cheddleton's status was disputed in the late 13th and early 14th cent.: *S.H.C.* vi (1), 191, 195, 199; x (1), 56; N.S. ix. 312; Sleigh, *Leek*, 51.
98 Sleigh, *Leek*, 17; *S.H.C.* N.S. ix. 312.
99 *S.H.C.* N.S. ix. 316.   1 *Cal. Pat.* 1558–60, 308–9.
2 *S.H.C.* xvi. 167; L.J.R.O., B/A/3/Leek; *Lond. Gaz.* 12 Sept. 1865, p. 4364.
3 Lich. Dioc. Regy., Bp's Reg. R, p. 440.
4 Ibid. Bp.'s Reg. S (Orders in Council), p. 37.
5 *S.H.C.* N.S. ix. 311 (giving the value as '20 monks').
6 S.R.O., D. 3508/A/2/6; D. 5041, pp. 9–10.
7 L.J.R.O., B/A/1/10, f. 84.
8 *Leek Par. Reg.* p. iv; P.R.O., S.C. 6/Hen. VIII/3353,

m. 34.   9 *Valor Eccl.* (Rec. Com.), iii. 126.
10 *S.H.C.* 1915, 146.
11 L.J.R.O., B/V/6/Leek, 1612, 1730.
12 Ibid. 1698, 1701; B/C/5/1703, Leek (tithes); S.R.O., D. 1040/5/3, f. 165v.
13 L.J.R.O., B/V/6/Leek, 1705. For the Quaker refusal to make Easter payments in 1704 see D.R.O., D. 231M/B8, loose letters of 4, 11, and 23 July 1704.
14 L.J.R.O., B/V/6/Leek, 1708.
15 S.R.O., D. 5041, p. 43. For Geo. Roades the elder see *S.H.C.* 1915, 148; L.J.R.O., B/A/3/Leek; for his son see *S.H.C.* 1919, 122.   16 L.J.R.O., Reg. of Wills C, ff. 196, 198.
17 Hodgson, *Bounty of Queen Anne*, pp. clxxviii, ccxcvii; L.J.R.O., B/V/6/Leek, 1824, 1832.
18 S.R.O., Q/RDc 65, nos. 80–1 and plan I.

sittings and in income from sermon endowments, £50 in Easter dues, £60 in fees, and £20 7s. 4d. in dividends from the 1824 grant.[19] In 1861 Queen Anne's Bounty made a grant of £150 to meet a benefaction of £300 from the earl of Macclesfield.[20] Vicars Close, consisting of 2½ a. on the Newcastle road, was sold in 1881, and in 1887 there was glebe of 35 a., with an estimated rental of £51.[21]

By the late 17th century the timber-framed vicarage house was in a ruinous state, and the parishioners rebuilt part of it when Thomas Walthall came as vicar in 1695. The rest was rebuilt in 1714 by George Jackson, vicar 1713–19, with the parishioners contributing c. £100. A summerhouse in the garden with a stable under it was built or rebuilt at the same time.[22] The house was enlarged by T. H. Heathcote after his institution in 1822 and again by his successor G. E. Deacon soon after his institution in 1861.[23]

By 1340 a chaplain was celebrating daily at the altar of St. Mary in Leek church; he held a messuage and a half and 12 a. in Leek for life by grant of William, vicar of Leek. William received royal licence in 1341 to use the property for the permanent endowment of a chantry at the altar.[24] The chapel of St. Mary was mentioned as a burial place in wills of 1545,[25] and the statue of Our Lady mentioned in 1543 presumably stood there.[26] In 1547 Robert Burgh of Leekfrith left 20d. to Our Lady's service at Leek.[27] In 1548 the chantry had lands worth more than £2 a year net and plate and ornaments worth 10s. It had its own wardens, who could dismiss the chaplain.[28] In 1549 the Crown sold the endowments, consisting of six messuages and land in Leek parish.[29]

By will proved 1537 Edmund Washington of Leek left £26 13s. 4d. to the new chapel of St. Catherine in Leek church to provide a stock chosen by the parish for the support of a priest to pray for the souls of Edmund's father and mother and for their children. Edmund directed that his son William 'shall sing for me if he will as long as the stock doth last' and that he was to be buried 'in my own form before St. Catherine'.[30]

Roger Banne, vicar 1569–1619, was described in the earlier 1590s as skilled in sacred letters and as a praiseworthy instructor of his flock. About 1603 he was stated to have no degree or licence to preach, but in 1604 there was a

stipendiary named Pott who held a licence.[31] In 1614 and 1616 there was a licensed preacher named Robert Wattes.[32]

Several sermons and lectures were endowed in the 17th and 18th centuries. In 1619 John Rothwell of Leek gave £1 8s. a year for four sermons.[33] Elizabeth St. Andrew (d. 1644), widow of William St. Andrew of Gotham (Notts.) and daughter of John Wedgwood of Harracles in Longsdon, left 6s. 8d. for a sermon every Good Friday.[34] Leek was one of 12 places in Staffordshire which benefited in rotation from the double lecture on the last Friday of each month founded by John Machin of Seabridge in Stoke-upon-Trent, a Presbyterian minister, and given from 1653 to 1660.[35] By will proved 1675 John Stoddard of Thorneyleigh Green Farm in Leekfrith (d. 1675) left £1 a year for a sermon on the third Wednesday in April, June, and September (May, July, and September by 1726).[36] Thomas Jolliffe (d. 1693) gave £4 a year for a lecture on the first Wednesday of every month.[37] By will proved 1718 William Dudley of the Fields in Horton, and formerly of Lyme House in Longsdon, left 6s. 8d. for a sermon on 29 May, the anniversary of Charles II's restoration.[38] John Naylor of Leek (d. 1739) left £5 for a sermon on his birthday, 12 October, and William Mills of Leek (d. 1749) left 20s. a year for a sermon on his birthday, 20 November; the dates were changed to 23 October and 1 December following the change of the calendar in 1752.[39]

Margaret Shallcross (d. 1677), daughter of Thomas Rudyard and widow of Edmund Shallcross (d. 1645), rector of Stockport (Ches.), left her husband's books to the vicars of Leek. She also gave a rent charge of 20s. to repair and augment the collection.[40] In 1701 the books were kept in a press in the vicarage house.[41] A catalogue of 1711 compiled by the vicar, James Osbourne, lists 44 folio volumes, 67 quarto, 17 octavo, and 41 bound in leather. Between 1713 and 1737 the next four vicars added another 34 volumes. Thomas Loxdale, who added 20 of them, stated that the library had been much diminished before coming into the vicar's hands and that less of the income had been spent than might have been expected.[42] The last vicar to add to the library was Richard Bentley (d. 1822).[43] The Leek inclosure award of 1811 re-

19 L.J.R.O., B/V/6/Leek, 1836.
20 Hodgson, Bounty of Queen Anne, suppl. p. lxvii.
21 L.J.R.O., B/C/12/Leek St. Edward; Return of Glebe Lands, 65.
22 S.R.O., D. 1040/5/3, f. 165v.; D. 5041, p. 154; date 1714 on the present house; L.J.R.O., B/V/6/Leek, 1714, 1718. Walthall was presented in 1695 (L.J.R.O., B/A/3/Leek) and not in 1698 as implied by D. 5041, p. 7, followed by Sleigh, Leek, 82.
23 Sleigh, Leek (1862), 83; Lich. Dioc. Regy., Bp.'s Reg. 29, p. 42; Reg. 32, p. 191.
24 S.H.C. 1913, 79–80; Cal. Pat. 1340–3, 180.
25 L.J.R.O., B/C/11, Wm. Gentte (1545), John Higginbotham (1545).
26 Ibid. Nic. Draycott (1543), expressing the wish to be buried 'afore Our Blessed Lady in the parish church of St. Edward of Leek'.   27 Ibid. Rob. Burgh (1548).
28 S.H.C. 1915, 146.
29 Cal. Pat. 1548–9, 414; B.L. Add. Ch. 46662.
30 T.N.S.F.C. lxvi. 36–7.
31 S.H.C. 1915, 146, 148; Derb. Arch. Soc. vi. 164;

E.H.R. xxvi. 342.   32 L.J.R.O., B/V/1/28.
33 S.R.O., D. 5041, p. 37.
34 Ibid. extract (loose) from will of Eliz. St. Andrew; J. C. Wedgwood, Hist. of Wedgwood Fam. (1908), 32 and corrections and addns.
35 A. G. Matthews, Congregational Churches of Staffs. (n.d., preface dated 1924), 30–1; D.N.B.
36 L.J.R.O., Reg. of Wills A, pp. 494–5; ibid. B/V/6/Leek, 1726; Leek Par. Reg. 198.
37 L.J.R.O., B/V/6/Leek, 1698; above, manors (Birchall).
38 L.J.R.O., B/C/11, Wm. Dudley (1718).
39 Ibid. B/V/6/Leek, 1744, 1747, 1755; S.R.O., D. 1040/5/14, 29 Jan. 1738/9, 13 May 1749.
40 S.R.O., D. 5041, pp. 41–2; L.J.R.O., B/V/6/Leek, 1730; Sleigh, Leek, 129; J. P. Earwaker, East Cheshire: Past and Present, i (1877), 386–8.
41 L.J.R.O., B/A/6/Leek, 1701.
42 Catalogue among docs. at St. Edward's; S.R.O., D. 5041, p. 42.
43 900th Anniversary Year: St. Edward the Confessor, Leek (Leek, 1966), 10; Sleigh, Leek, 84.

placed the rent charge with just over 1 a. of land at the junction of Mount Road and Kniveden Lane.[44] A trust was established in 1963, with the vicar and the warden of Leek as trustees, and the land was sold for £100 the same year.[45] About 10 years later most of the contents of the library were sold. The income of the trust, some £50 a year in the early 1990s, was then spent on books for use by the clergy of the team rectory.[46] By will proved 1724 Lady Moyer left a copy of Isaac Barrow's *Sermons* and one volume of John Foxe's *Book of Martyrs* to be kept chained in the church.[47]

At the end of the 17th century communion services were held on Palm Sunday, Good Friday, Easter Sunday, Low Sunday, Whit Sunday, Trinity Sunday, the Sunday before and after Michaelmas, the last Sunday in December, and the first Sunday in January. The highest number of communicants in 1700 was 62 on Easter Sunday, with 40 on Palm Sunday and 35 on Good Friday; the lowest was 16 on Whit Sunday.[48] In 1709 the vicar, Thomas Walthall, stated that he read prayers every morning.[49] As part of her endowment in 1717 of her charity school Lady Moyer assigned the vicar 20s. a year to catechize the children once a fortnight. In addition every Sunday after the sermon the children were to be allowed to sing hymns learnt at the school.[50] In 1751 there were two services on Sunday, at 10 a.m. and 2 p.m.; there were prayers on Wednesday, Friday, and Saturday and on all holy days. Children were catechized on Saturday evening during Lent. Communion was administered on the first Sunday in the month and on Christmas Day, Good Friday, Easter Sunday, the Sunday before or after Easter, Whit Sunday, and Trinity Sunday. The number of communicants at Easter and Whitsun was nearly 100 and at other times about 60.[51] In 1834 Jeremiah Barnes, assistant curate at St. Edward's and master of the grammar school, started a monthly lecture at the school. It was so well attended that he began a lecture and service in the church every Sunday evening later the same year. A subscription was started in 1835 to meet the cost, including a stipend of £30 a year for the lecturer; in addition a special sermon was preached annually to raise funds. Barnes also started cottage lectures. The Sunday evening lecture continued at least until 1888.[52] Attendances at the services on Census Sunday 1851 were 350 in the morning and 200 in the afternoon, besides Sunday school children, and 550 in the evening.[53] A weekly offertory was introduced in 1864 in place of an inadequate monthly offertory.[54]

In 1895 C. B. Maude, vicar 1887–96, established an institute in the former St. Edward's school in Clerk Bank, consisting of a working

men's club and a young men's union. In 1896, as archdeacon of Salop and vicar of St. Chad's, Shrewsbury, he conveyed the building to trustees, and the institute became the Maude Church Institute for men and women attending St. Edward's. The parishioners subscribed £191 in recognition of Maude's services, and the money was given to the trustees to pay off the mortgage.[55] The building, which was altered and enlarged in the mid 1970s,[56] was used in the early 1990s by various voluntary organizations. The mission church of St. John the Evangelist in Mill Street was opened in 1875 as a school-church. It was built at the expense of John Robinson of Westwood Hall, who also paid for extensions in 1881. Until 1906 the church was the particular responsibility of an assistant curate at St. Edward's. A detached recreation room was built in 1927–8. The school was closed in 1938, but the building continued in use as a mission church.[57]

The church of *ST. EDWARD THE CONFESSOR* is built of sandstone and consists of a chancel with a south aisle and a north vestry, a clerestoried nave which is aisled for three bays but continues west of the aisles as an area known as the parlour, a south porch, and a pinnacled west tower of two stages. In 1297 'the church of Leek was burnt down together with the whole town'.[58] It is possible, however, that the closely spaced circular piers of the south arcade which survived until the earlier 19th century were 12th-century. As rebuilt after the fire the nave was long and narrow, perhaps reproducing its earlier proportions, and was evidently fully aisled on both sides. Part of the western respond of the north aisle remains and is evidence that the aisle formerly extended the full length of the nave. The north arcade had octagonal piers, three of which survived until the earlier 19th century.[59] The lateral windows in the easternmost bays of both aisles are circular and filled with rose tracery of early to mid 14th-century design. The other aisle windows are of the same date, although much restored. The chancel was as wide as the nave, as is also the contemporary tower. Early in the 16th century the tower was remodelled and given a new top stage. At perhaps the same time the clerestory was added and the roofs of the aisles were renewed. In the early 1540s extensive work was carried out on the chancel. Fifty-nine loads of stone were used, and expenditure included £2 12s. 4d. on glass 'for the window' and £3 on plastering. Until the 1860s the chancel had a 16th-century east window.[60] The west end of both aisles appears to have been removed during the 16th century, with the arcades being replaced by walls. Date stones of 1556 in the south aisle and 1593 in the north are probably relevant to that work. The

44 S.R.O., Q/RDc 65, no. 84 and plan I.
45 W. F. Brooks, 'Margaret Shallcross Trust' (TS. at St. Edward's).
46 Inf. from Mr. Brooks.
47 S.R.O., D. 5041, p. 32; H. G. H. Jolliffe, *Jolliffes of Staffs.* (priv. print. 1892), 7 n.; below, educ. (primary and secondary schs.). 48 S.R.O., D. 1040/7, pp. 23, 27.
49 D.R.O., D. 231M/B9, 19 Apr. 1709.
50 S.R.O., D. 3359/misc. deeds, deed of 24 July 1717.
51 L.J.R.O., B/V/5/1751, Leek.
52 S.R.O., D. 1040/2/1.

53 P.R.O., HO 129/372/2/1.
54 W.S.L., Sleigh scrapbk. i, f. 127.
55 Docs. at St. Edward's, Maude Church Inst. min. bk. 1896–1939; below, plate 59. 56 Local inf.
57 C. K. R. Pearce, *Mission Church of St. John the Evangelist, Mill Street, Leek* (Leek, 1975).
58 C. Lynam, *Abbey of St. Mary, Croxden, Staffs.* translation of chronicle, p. v.
59 L.J.R.O., B/C/5/1816, Leek (faculty); ibid. 1838, Leek (faculty).
60 Sleigh, *Leek*, 74–5; W.S.L., Staffs. Views, v. 108.

east end of the south aisle was formed by a chapel known originally as the Abbot's chapel and later as Jodrell's chapel. In the mid 1760s there was mention of a seat called Jodrell's chapel. It was described in 1830 as an ancient canopied pew which was claimed by the occupiers of estates formerly belonging to Dieulacres abbey. It then evidently contained eight seats.[61] A church porch, presumably the south porch, was repaired in 1663.[62] The present south porch was built in 1670.[63] A north door was repaired in 1674.[64] The church had a spire in the 1660s and 1750s, but it was without one in 1795.[65]

A gallery described in 1704 as the new gallery was then being repaired.[66] It may have been the west gallery, which was stated in 1739 to have been in existence beyond living memory. A new west gallery was built that year extending over the unaisled part of the nave.[67] A gallery for 'the charity children' was erected in 1725–6.[68] A gallery over the south aisle was mentioned in 1807,[69] and one over the north aisle, in existence by 1813, was altered in or soon after 1816.[70] There was an organ gallery east of the chancel arch by the 1780s, probably erected when an organ was installed in the church in 1772.[71]

A vestry was built on the north side of the chancel in 1785. It had fallen down by 1816 and was then rebuilt.[72] A small porch was erected on the south side of the chancel in 1812 or 1813.[73] Eight pinnacles were placed on the tower in 1815 or 1816.[74]

The church was altered 1839–41 to the design of John Leech. The nave arcades were rebuilt as three bays where there had previously been four. Jodrell's chapel was removed and the side galleries were brought forward to the line of the arcades. The west end of the north aisle was remodelled to provide a porch with a stair to the west gallery. Besides private subscriptions grants were received from the Incorporated Church Building Society and the Lichfield Diocesan Church Building Society.[75] The timber ceiling of the nave was restored by Ewan Christian in 1856.[76]

The chancel was rebuilt 1865–7 to the design

of G. E. Street. A south aisle with an arcade of two bays was added for the organ and extra seating. At the same time the base of the tower, which had been walled off from the nave and used as a mason's workshop, was opened into the nave.[77] In 1874 the nave and aisles were reseated with open benches instead of box pews to a plan prepared by Street.[78]

The side galleries were removed in 1956.[79] In 1989–90[80] a floor was inserted in the tower to create a meeting room which extends under the west gallery and over the parlour. A kitchen and a lavatory were inserted on the ground floor of the tower.

In 1553 the plate consisted of a silver chalice and paten, and there was a brass cross.[81] In 1994 the plate includes a 14th-century silver-gilt North German chalice and a silver Swiss chalice dated 1641, both given in 1912 by Mrs. Barron (née Gaunt), two silver chalices and patens of 1777, one of the patens being the gift of Thomas Higginbotham, and a flagon of 1777 inscribed as the gift of F. M.[82] There is also a wooden cross which belonged to Emperor Maximilian of Mexico; it is inlaid with mother of pearl and inset with a reputed relic of the True Cross.[83] The church possesses several pieces of Leek embroidery, including three frontals designed respectively by Gerald Horsley, J. D. Sedding, and R. Norman Shaw.[84]

In 1553 there were two bells and a hand bell; a sanctus bell had been sold for 12s.[85] There were at least five bells in the later 17th century,[86] and one was recast at Nottingham in 1677.[87] The bells were recast in 1721 as a peal of six by Abraham Rudhall of Gloucester.[88] In 1863 two bells were added, cast by John Warner & Sons of London, and in 1926 two more, cast by Gillett & Johnson of Croydon.[89] A carillon made by Gillett & Bland of Croydon was installed by subscription in 1874; it consists of 14 tunes, one of which is played four times in the course of each day.[90] A clock was repaired in 1663.[91] In 1856 the improvement commissioners, who were already paying the cost of lighting the church clock, agreed to pay the cost of repairing

61 Sleigh, *Leek*, 78; W. F. Challinor, *St. Edward's Church, Leek*, 12, 22; *S.H.C.* 4th ser. x. 92; S.R.O., D. 593/B/1/24/9; docs. at St. Edward's, deed of 1 Sept. 1806; W.S.L., Sleigh, ii, f. 122.   62 *Leek Par. Reg.* 158.
63 S.R.O., D. 1040/5/2; date on porch.
64 S.R.O., D. 1040/5/2.
65 Ibid. accts. for 1669; D. 1040/7, pp. 28, 137; below, plate 1.
66 S.R.O., D. 1040/7, pp. 43–4.
67 Ibid. pp. 99–101; L.J.R.O., B/C/5/1738, Leek (faculty).
68 S.R.O., D. 1040/7, p. 80.   69 Ibid. p. 266.
70 Ibid. p. 290; L.J.R.O., B/C/5/1816, Leek (faculty); docs. at St. Edward's, vestry min. bk. 1817–1959, pp. 1–7; ibid., churchwardens' accts. 1817–91, f. 1.
71 S.R.O., D. 1040/7, p. 193; L.J.R.O., B/C/5/1816, Leek (faculty); below, this section [organs].
72 S.R.O., D. 1040/7, pp. 300, 305, 308–9; L.J.R.O., B/C/5/1785, Leek (faculty); ibid. 1816, Leek (faculty); docs. at St. Edward's, churchwardens' accts. 1817–91, f. 1.
73 S.R.O., D. 1040/7, pp. 286, 288; L.J.R.O., B/C/5/1816, Leek (faculty); below, plate 7.
74 S.R.O., D. 1040/7, p. 303; Pitt, *Staffs.* 248 (giving the date as 1816).
75 L.J.R.O., B/C/5/1838, Leek (faculty); docs. at St. Edward's, churchwardens' accts. 1817–91, cttee. acct. 1839–41.
76 Sleigh, *Leek*, 75; *T.N.S.F.C.* l. 71.

77 L.J.R.O., B/C/5/1865, Leek (faculty); *Staffs. Advertiser*, 20 July 1867, p. 7; *Lich. Dioc. Ch. Cal.* (1868), 94–5; *Olde Leeke*, i. 122.
78 L.J.R.O., B/C/5/1865, Leek (faculty); ibid. 1873, Leek (faculty); Sleigh, *Leek*, 76; *Staffs. Advertiser*, 12 July 1873, p. 2.   79 L.J.R.O., B/C/12/Leek, St. Edward.
80 Inf. from Mr. W. F. Brooks.
81 *S.H.C.* 1915, 145–6.
82 *T.B.A.S.* lxxvii. 59, 62, 65, 74, and pl. 8 (b); *Leek Parish Church of St. Edward the Confessor* (Leek, earlier 1970s), pp. xxvi–xxvii; inf. from Mrs. Bunce. One of the 1777 chalices is inscribed as the gift of George Roades, rector of Blithfield, in memory of his father George, vicar of Leek; the younger George, however, died in 1713: *S.H.C.* 1919, 122.
83 *Church of St. Edward the Confessor*, p. xxvii.
84 A. G. Jacques, *Leek Embroidery* (Staffs. Libraries, Arts & Archives, 1990), 51.   85 *S.H.C.* 1915, 145–6.
86 S.R.O., D. 1040/5/1, 1663; D. 1040/5/2, 1669, 1672, 1673.   87 Ibid. D. 1040/7, 1677.
88 Ibid. p. 64; C. Lynam, *Church Bells of County of Stafford*, 52.
89 Lynam, *Church Bells*, 52; *Church of St. Edward the Confessor*, p. xxviii.
90 *Church of St. Edward the Confessor*, p. xxviii; S.R.O., D. 3014/10.
91 S.R.O., D. 1040/5/1, 1663.

1. View from the south-west, with Wall bridge and Wall Bridge Farm in the foreground

2. View from the south

3. View from the north-east, with Ramshaw Rocks on the right

LEEK

4 and 5. Pre-Norman crosses
in the churchyard

6. Carving on a stone in the church
from a pre-Norman cross

7. View from the south-east in 1844

LEEK: ST. EDWARD'S CHURCH

8. View from the north-west

9. The interior

LEEK: ALL SAINTS' CHURCH

11. Warslow: St. Lawrence's church from the south-east in 1847

13. Alstonefield: St. Peter's church from the south-east in 1839

10. Longnor: St. Bartholomew's church from the south-east in 1847

12. Horton: St. Michael's church from the south-east in 1844

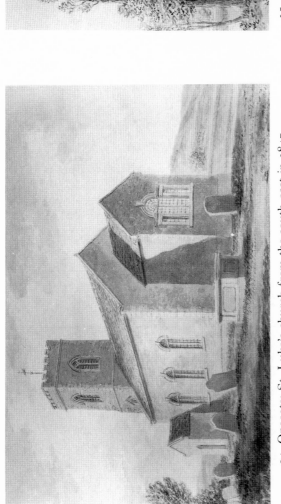

14. Onecote: St. Luke's church from the south-east in 1847

15. Rushton Spencer: St. Lawrence's church from the south-east in 1844

16. Meerbrook: St. Matthew's church from the south-west before 1870

17. Endon: St. Luke's church from the south-east in 1844

19. Rushton Spencer: the interior of St. Lawrence's church in 1857

18. Upper Elkstone: the interior of St. John's church in 1857

20. Sheen: St. Luke's church, the school, and the vicarage in 1857

22. Alstonefield: the south front of Beresford Hall (demolished in 1858)

23. Bradnop: the east front of Ashenhurst Hall (demolished in 1954)

21. Alstonefield: pulpit and Cotton family pew in St. Peter's church

24. View from the south-east *c.* 1835

25. The south front after the extensions of 1851

LEEK: WESTWOOD HALL

26. Horton: Horton Hall from the south-east in 1844

27. Leekfrith: the south front of Abbey Farm

28. Heaton: the west front of Swythamley Hall

30. Alstonefield: the east front of Stanshope Hall

32. Sheen: Broadmeadow Hall from the south-west

29. Alstonefield: the south front of Stanshope Hall

31. Longsdon: Harracles Hall from the north-west

34. Horton: Cliffe Park from the south-east

36. Endon: Endon Hall (demolished in the 1950s) from the south-east

33. Warslow: the former vicarage from the south

35. Warslow: Warslow Hall from the north-east

37. Ball Lane, Petty France
demolished in the 1960s

38. The town hall
demolished in 1988

39. The market place from the south

LEEK

40. The former police station in Leonard Street

41. The former cattle market in Haywood Street

LEEK

42. The south end of the market place in 1844, with the Black's Head inn
in the centre and the town hall on the right

43. Derby Street in 1844, with the Roebuck inn in the centre
and the Congregational chapel on the right

LEEK

44. Leek: the railway station of 1849

45. Fawfieldhead: the former railway station at Hulme End

46. Longsdon: the former pumping station of the Staffordshire Potteries Water Works Co.

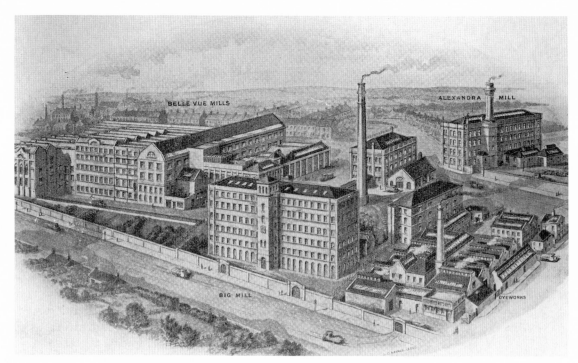

47. The mills of Wardle & Davenport Ltd.

48. Albion Mill

LEEK: THE SILK INDUSTRY

49. One of Brough, Nicholson & Hall's braid plaiting sheds, probably in the 1890s

50. Hand twisting at William Hill & Co.'s Star Silk Mills, Burton Street, in 1933

LEEK: THE SILK INDUSTRY

51. Leek: Britannia House, the headquarters of the Britannia Building Society

52. Quarnford: the former spinning mill at Gradbach, since 1984 a youth hostel

53. Leek: the Ash almshouses in 1844

54. Leek: Moorlands Hospital, formerly the Leek poor-law union workhouse

55. Alstonefield: the former workhouse

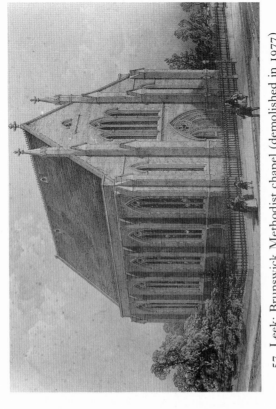

57. Leek: Brunswick Methodist chapel (demolished in 1977)

58. Horton: Gratton Methodist church

56. Leek: the Congregational chapel in Derby Street (since 1977 Trinity church)

59. Leek: Maude Church Institute and former grammar school

60. Hollinsclough: former schoolroom and former church of St. Agnes

61. Fawfieldhead: St. John's church, Reaps Moor

62. Meerbrook: the former school, since 1977 a youth hostel

64. Sheen: Brund mill bridge before 1891

65. Alstonefield: Viator's bridge and site of mill at Milldale

63. Alstonefield: Charles Cotton's fishing house

67. Sir Thomas Wardle

66. Sir George Crewe and his son John in 1828

68. A house of 1774 in Chapel Street

69. The former Methodist chapel

70. The market place, with the former market hall in the centre

LONGNOR

and attending it also. It was still their only public clock in 1894.[92] In 1874 they installed a clock by Gillett & Bland. Its mechanism was retained for the quarter and hour chimes when it was replaced by an electric clock in 1966–7.[93]

An organ made by Glyn & Parker of Manchester was installed in 1772. It was replaced in 1878 by an organ made by Jardine & Co. of Manchester.[94] In the early 19th century the organist was paid £30 a year, mostly from the rent of four plots of 'organ land' west of Mount Road which had been inclosed for the purpose before 1805.[95]

In 1837 the archdeacon noted that an old font had been moved into the church from outside.[96] It may have been the predecessor of the font installed in 1739.[97] In 1867 a font was given in memory of John Cruso, and the 18th-century font is said to have been transferred to Kirknewton church in Northumberland.[98] A pulpit with a reading desk and a sounding board was installed in 1718–19.[99] A three-decker pulpit was installed under a faculty of 1785 on a new site on the south side of the chancel arch.[1] It was moved to the north side during the alterations of 1839–41 and replaced by the present pulpit when the chancel was rebuilt 1865–7.[2]

The registers date from 1634.[3] An earlier register evidently existed in the 1730s, but it was lost by the early 20th century.[4]

The graveyard of St. Edward was mentioned in 1281.[5] It was walled by the 1660s, and there was mention of a little lich gate in 1672 and of the lich gate, the turn gate, and the new gate on the north side in the mid 1690s.[6] The arched and pinnacled stone gateway on the south is dated 1684. Three yews were planted in the churchyard in 1698 and some Worcestershire and mountain elms on the north side in 1727.[7] The churchyard was extended on the north in 1800 by 868 sq. yd. and in 1824 by ½ a.[8] The church and churchyard were closed for new burials in 1857 on the opening of the cemetery on the Cheddleton road.[9]

There are remains of several pre-Norman crosses in the church and churchyard. The rectangular-shafted cross south of the church was set up there in 1885 after lying for several years in three pieces against the east wall of the churchyard; it has a fragment of a runic inscription and may date from the early 9th century. The round-shafted cross south-east of the church is a particularly fine and well preserved example of its type, dating perhaps from the later 10th century. Inside the church are the remains of the wheel-head of a cross and also a stone from a rectangular shaft with a carving perhaps depicting Christ carrying the Cross or Christ wielding a cross as conqueror of sin.[10]

In 1845 a district of *ST. LUKE* was formed out of St. Edward's parish; it covered the eastern part of Leek and Lowe township, including most of the eastern side of Leek town, and also Tittesworth township.[11] The patronage of the perpetual curacy was vested in the Crown and the bishop alternately, with the Crown making the first presentation in 1845.[12] Benjamin Pidcock, minister 1845–82, at first held services in a room over a stable in the yard of the Black's Head inn in Derby Street. In 1846 land bounded by Queen Street and Fountain Street was bought as the site for a church and school, and with the opening of the school in 1847 services were transferred there.[13] The church was consecrated in 1848. The cost was met by subscriptions and grants from the Lichfield Diocesan Church Extension Society, the Incorporated Church Building Society, and Sir Robert Peel's Fund; money was also raised by the sale of land on the Ashbourne road left by Sarah Brentnall, née Grosvenor, as the site for a church.[14] The perpetual curacy was styled a vicarage in 1868.[15] In 1979 St. Luke's parish became part of the new Leek parish, with its vicar becoming a team vicar.[16]

When the district was constituted in 1845, the Ecclesiastical Commissioners agreed to pay the minister £100 a year, with a further £30 when a building was licensed for worship and a total of £150 on the consecration of a church. Fees and Easter offerings brought in a further £30 in 1851.[17] The vicar's income had risen to £265 by 1884.[18] In 1856 land on the Ball Haye estate was bought as the site for a house, which was begun

92 Ibid. D. 3226/1, no. 195; Leek Improvement. Com. *Reps.* (1894), 26; above, public services (gas and electricity supplies).
93 *Church of St. Edward the Confessor*, p. xxviii; *Staffs. Advertiser*, 7 Mar. 1874, p. 5.
94 S.R.O., D. 1040/7, pp. 169–70; *Olde Leeke*, i. 118–20; *Church of St. Edward the Confessor*, p. xxii; *Staffs. Advertiser*, 27 Apr. 1878, p. 4; *Lich. Dioc. Ch. Cal.* (1879), 76.
95 S.R.O., D. 1040/7, pp. 291–2, 299, 301; docs. at St. Edward's, churchwardens' accts. 1817–91, ff. 1, 3, 7, 14; ibid. vestry min. bk. 1817–1959, p. 18; L.J.R.O., B/V/6/Leek, 1841; Act for inclosing lands in par. of Leek, 45 Geo. III, c. 96 (Local and Personal), s. 8; S.R.O., Q/RDc 65, plan I.
96 *S.H.C.* 4th ser. x. 92.
97 S.R.O., D. 1040/7, pp. 99, 101.
98 *Leek & Moorlands Heritage*, ii. 4.
99 S.R.O., D. 1040/7, p. 80.
1 L.J.R.O., B/C/5/1785, Leek (faculty); ibid. 1816, Leek (faculty).
2 Ibid. 1838, Leek (faculty); ibid. 1865, Leek (faculty); Lichfield Cathedral Libr., Moore and Hinckes drawings, v, no. 24.
3 Printed 1634–95 in *Leek Par. Reg.* The registers of baptisms to 1849, marriages to 1837, and burials to 1791 are in S.R.O., D. 1040/5.

4 *Leek Par. Reg.* p. v; S.R.O., D. 5041, f. 7.
5 S.R.O., D. (W.) 1761/A/4/168.
6 Ibid. D. 1040/5/1 and 2; D. 1040/7, pp. 20, 51.
7 Ibid. D. 1040/7, pp. 22, 85.
8 L.J.R.O., B/A/2i/E, pp. 134–9; Lich. Dioc. Regy., Bp.'s Reg. G, pp. 648–56 (1st nos.), 611–29 (2nd nos.; *recte* pp. 711–29).   9 Above, public services (public health).
10 *T.N.S.F.C.* lxxx. 34–5, 48; lxxxi. 38–43; *Medieval Archaeology*, viii. 213–14; above, plates 4–7.
11 *Lond. Gaz.* 4 July 1845, 2020–2. Grateful acknowledgement is made to the Revd. K. R. Haywood, team vicar, and Mrs. Mavis Hudson for their help.
12 L.J.R.O., B/A/3/Leek St. Luke; S.R.O., D. 3867/6/1, p. 1.
13 Lich. Dioc. Regy., Bp.'s Reg. O, pp. 291–6; W.S.L. 498/34, 9 Sept. 1899.
14 Lich. Dioc. Regy., Bp.'s Reg. O, pp. 297–311; Reg. P, pp. 247–52; S.R.O., D. 3359/Grosvenor, memo. on Mrs. Brentnall's will; D. 3867/6/1, p. 2; *Staffs. Advertiser*, 23 Dec. 1848, p. 4.
15 *Lich. Dioc. Ch. Cal.* (1868; 1869).
16 Above, this section (St. Edward's).
17 *Lond. Gaz.* 4 July 1845, pp. 2020–2; P.R.O., HO 129/372/2/1.
18 S.R.O., D. 3867/2/8.

FIG. 27. ST. LUKE'S CHURCH FROM THE SOUTH-WEST,
AS COMPLETED IN 1854

in 1857.[19] A new house was built in Novi Lane in the mid 1970s.[20]

Attendances at St. Luke's on Census Sunday 1851 were 83 in the morning and 110 in the afternoon, besides Sunday school children.[21] Although all 650 sittings were free, a voluntary payment was made for some until 1859 when a weekly offertory was introduced instead.[22] A surpliced choir existed by 1856.[23] William Beresford, vicar 1882–1919, started a young men's society in 1884, and in 1903 he opened an institute and recreation room.[24] A parish magazine was started in 1882.[25] A parish hall was opened in 1930 in Organ Ground, the lane between Shirburn Road and Springfield Road; the site was given by the Challinor family in memory of William Challinor (d. 1926). The building became an annexe to the primary school in East Street in 1954.[26] The infants' school in Queen Street, closed in 1981, became the parish hall.

A school-church opened at Compton in 1863 was replaced in 1887 by the church of All Saints, for which a new parish was formed in 1889.[27] The school opened in Pump Street in Ball Haye Green in 1871 was soon used as a mission church also, known as St. Paul's by the 1930s.[28] A new St. Paul's church was built in Novi Lane in 1971; the Church Commissioners made a grant of £15,000 towards the cost of the building.[29] The Pump Street building survived in 1992 as a boy-scout headquarters. A school-church dedicated to the Good Shepherd was opened at Thorncliffe in Tittesworth in 1887.[30]

St. Luke's church consists of a chancel with a north vestry and a north organ chamber, an aisled nave of five bays with a south porch, and a west tower with a south-east turret. Built of sandstone in a Gothic style, it was designed by F. J. Francis of London.[31] When the church was consecrated in 1848, the tower had not been built beyond the first stage. It was completed in 1854 to the specifications of Francis and his brother Horace. At the same time a wall was built round the churchyard, which was closed for new burials in 1862.[32] In 1873 the chancel was extended by 10 ft., its floor was laid with Minton tiles, and a reredos of Caen stone was erected. The work was designed by J. D. Sedding of Bristol, and most of the cost was met by C. H. Joberns,

[19] Staffs. Advertiser, 22 Oct. 1853, p. 4; 7 June 1856, p. 4; 10 Oct. 1857, p. 5; S.R.O., D. 3867/2/6.
[20] Lich. Dioc. Regy., Bp.'s Reg. Y, pp. 183–4.
[21] P.R.O., HO 129/372/2/1.
[22] Ibid.; S.R.O., D. 3867/5/1; D. 3867/6/1, pp. 27–8 and accts. 1849–59; Staffs. Advertiser, 20 Oct. 1860, p. 4.
[23] S.R.O., D. 3867/6/1, pp. 20–1.
[24] R. Simms, Bibliotheca Staffordiensis (Lichfield, 1894), 54; Lich. Dioc. Mag. (1904), 33; W.S.L. 498/34, 9 May 1905.
[25] S.R.O., D. 3867/11/5.

[26] Ibid. D. 3188/1/5; W.S.L. 501/34, 20 Sept. 1930; below, educ. (primary and secondary schs.).
[27] Below, this section (All Saints').
[28] Lich. Dioc. Ch. Cal. (1873); S.R.O., D. 3867/2/12.
[29] Leek Post & Times, 17 June 1971, p. 14; Leek Libr., newspaper cuttings 1969–72, p. 57.
[30] Below, Tittesworth, church.
[31] S.R.O., D. 3867/6/1, p. 2.
[32] Ibid. pp. 5–7; D. 3867/3/3 and 4; Staffs. Advertiser, 23 Apr. 1853, p. 4; 13 May 1854, p. 4.

formerly an assistant curate.[33] The panelling in the chancel was given by Susannah Argles in 1891 and 1892. The choir stalls were given in 1892 by the family of A. J. Worthington, and the carved angels were added to them in 1897 in memory of Ernest Worthington by his brother and sisters.[34] The vestry was built in 1891.[35] In 1894 the organ, installed in 1861, was moved from the north aisle into the chancel.[36] The wooden chancel screen was erected in memory of William Challinor (d. 1926) and his daughter Mary Watson.[37] The church possesses several pieces of Leek embroidery, some designed by Sedding; one frontal is dated 1873.[38]

Henry Sneyd (d. 1859), incumbent of Wetley Rocks in Cheddleton, promoted a plan for a church in the Compton area, with a school and a house for the incumbent. By his death a site had been acquired in Compton, but there was not enough money for the full scheme. Instead a brick school-church, designed in a Gothic style by Robert Edgar, was opened on the site in 1863.[39] Variously known as Compton school-church and Christ Church, it was placed in the charge of an assistant curate at St. Luke's and by 1875 had its own wardens.[40] By 1885 it had been enlarged twice to more than double its original size.[41]

It was replaced as a church by *ALL SAINTS'* church on a site on the corner of Southbank Street and Compton, part of which was given by Joseph Challinor of Compton House, a Leek solicitor.[42] The foundation stone was laid in 1885, and the church was consecrated in 1887. Challinor contributed nearly one third of the cost, and grants were made by the Lichfield Diocesan Church Extension Society and the Incorporated Church Building Society. All the sittings were free.[43] The dedication to All Saints was chosen in 1885 because the earlier choice, St. Mary, was already the dedication of the nearby Roman Catholic church.[44] A parish was formed in 1889 out of St. Luke's and St. Edward's parishes and included the southern part of the town and the Longsdon area.[45] The patronage of the vicarage was vested in Joseph Challinor for life, with reversion to the bishop,

but Challinor transferred it to the bishop in 1896.[46] In 1979 All Saints' parish became part of the new parish of Leek, its vicar becoming a team vicar.[47]

The vicar was supported by grants and benefactions until 1896, when the Ecclesiastical Commissioners granted a stipend of £150 a year.[48] A bequest of £1,000 from Elizabeth Flint in 1905 increased the income to £210, besides grants from the churchwardens, fees, and Easter offerings.[49] In 1890 a house in Compton Terrace formerly occupied by Eliza Bradshaw was presented as a vicarage house in memory of her.[50] In 1902 a house in Compton adjoining the church was bought instead, and it remained the vicarage until 1972, when a new house was built next door.[51]

W. B. Wright, priest in charge from 1882 and vicar 1889–1921, described himself in 1887 as practising 'a quiet Catholic (as opposed to Protestant *and* Roman) ritual',[52] and All Saints' has continued in the High Church tradition. In 1889 the new parish took over from Endon church responsibility for the mission at Longsdon, for which a separate parish was formed in 1906.[53] In 1892 a house in Pickwood Road was used as a mission centre.[54] A monthly magazine was introduced in 1885.[55] A men's club was started in 1893 with a clubroom opposite the vicarage. It was closed in 1896 because there were too many rival attractions, but in 1897 a clubroom for the men and boys of the parish was opened south of the church.[56] A company of the Church Lads' Brigade was formed in 1894; a new company was formed in 1896 with a room in Shoobridge Street.[57]

The church, which stands on a sloping site, consists of a chancel with an undercroft used as a vestry, an aisled and clerestoried nave of four bays, a large north porch, and a low central tower.[58] Built of Kniveden stone,[59] it was designed in a Gothic style by R. Norman Shaw, who in 1891 described the church as 'always a favourite child of mine'.[60] The altar from the school-church, which was thought to have come from St. Edward's, was placed in the Lady chapel.[61] The bell too was brought from the school-church, but in 1900 a new bell, cast by

33 *Staffs. Advertiser*, 24 May 1873, p. 4; 13 Dec. 1873, p. 5; *Lich. Dioc. Ch. Cal.* (1874), 74 and pl. facing p. 73; (1875), 76.
34 Inscriptions in chancel; *Lich. Dioc. Mag.* (1894), 222.
35 *Lich. Dioc. Ch. Cal.* (1891), 163; (1892), 174.
36 S.R.O., D. 3867/3/5; D. 3867/6/1, p. 31; *Lich. Dioc. Mag.* (1894), 68.   37 Inscriptions on screen and in S. aisle.
38 A. G. Jacques, *Leek Embroidery* (Staffs. Libraries, Arts & Archives, 1990), 49.
39 S.R.O., D. 3359/Leek All Saints, printed circular 1859; *Staffs. Advertiser*, 25 Apr. 1863, p. 5; 22 Aug. 1863, p. 4; Sleigh, *Leek*, 101.
40 S.R.O., D. 4855/1/6; D. 4855/4/3; D. 4855/14/5.
41 Ibid. D. 4855/3/8A.
42 Ibid. D. 4855/5/29; *Lich. Dioc. Ch. Cal.* (1881), 73; *Staffs. Advertiser*, 30 July 1887, p. 6. For the school see below, educ. (primary and secondary schs.).
43 S.R.O., D. 4855/3/7 and 14; Lich. Dioc. Regy., Bp.'s Reg. T, pp. 133–7; *Staffs. Advertiser*, 30 July 1887, p. 6.
44 *Compton Ch. Monthly Mag.* Feb. 1885 (copy in S.R.O., D. 4855/11/1); *All Saints' Quarterly*, Jan. 1923 (copy in D. 4855/11/4).
45 *Lond. Gaz.* 23 Aug. 1889, pp. 4606–7.
46 Ibid. 4 Aug. 1896, pp. 4435–6; Lich. Dioc. Regy., Bp.'s Reg. T, pp. 129–32; ibid. Bp.'s Reg. 35, p. 167.
47 Above, this section (St. Edward's).

48 *Lond. Gaz.* 7 Aug. 1896, p. 4516; *Lich. Dioc. Mag.* (1896), 182–3; *All Saints' Ch. Monthly Mag.* Sept. 1896 (copy in S.R.O., D. 4855/11/1).
49 S.R.O., D. 4588/3/16, p. 28; D. 4855/3/39; *Lond. Gaz.* 19 Apr. 1907, p. 2657; 22 May 1908, p. 3786.
50 S.R.O., D. 4855/3/16, pp. 4–5; D. 4855/4/9.
51 Ibid. D. 4855/3/1/12; D. 4855/3/16, p. 26 and loose TS.; Lich. Dioc. Regy., Bp.'s Reg. Y, p. 162; *Lond. Gaz.* 2 May 1902, p. 2946.
52 S.R.O., D. 3359/Leek All Saints, Wright to Challinor, 4 Aug. 1887; D. 4855/3/16, pp. 4, 40, 49–50; D. 4855/3/51.
53 Below, Longsdon, church.
54 *All Saints' Ch. Monthly Mag.* Feb., Sept., Nov. 1892 (copies in S.R.O., D. 4855/11/1).
55 Bound set Feb. 1885–Nov. 1896 in S.R.O., D. 4855/11/1.
56 S.R.O., D. 4855/3/16, pp. 15, 22; *All Saints' Monthly Mag.* Feb. 1895; Sept. 1896.
57 *All Saints' Ch. Monthly Mag.* July 1894; Sept. 1895; S.R.O., D. 4855/3/16, p. 29.   58 Above, plates 8 and 9.
59 *All Saints' Quarterly*, Apr. 1923, 10 (copy in S.R.O., D. 4855/11/4).
60 S.R.O., D. 3359/Leek All Saints, Shaw to Challinor, 23 Aug. 1891. For Shaw's drawings see D. 3567/1–9.
61 *All Saints' Ch. Monthly Mag.* Aug. 1887.

Mears & Stainbank of Whitechapel, was installed.[62] The reredos, given by Hugh Sleigh, is a triptych showing the Crucifixion; the paintings are by R. Hamilton Jackson, and the frame was designed by W. R. Lethaby.[63] Most of the decoration in the church was carried out after 1887. The glass is mainly by Morris & Co. from designs by Sir Edward Burne-Jones; two windows in the south aisle are respectively by Gerald Horsley and J. E. Platt.[64] The wall paintings in the chancel are by Horsley and were given by Hugh Sleigh; those in the Lady chapel are by Horsley and by Platt.[65] The font and the pulpit are thought to have been designed by W. R.

Lethaby.[66] The church possesses many pieces of Leek embroidery, including a funeral pall designed by Horsley.[67] The plate includes a silver chalice and paten dated 1569 and given in 1963 under the will of Gilbert Tatton.[68] The processional cross incorporates a late-medieval crucifix from the Rhineland given in 1896 by the Revd. T. Barns. On the south-west tower column is a crucifix thought to be 16th-century Spanish and given in memory of W. G. Keyworth, vicar 1921–41. The oil painting of the entombment of Christ hanging over the vestry door is thought to be of the 17th-century Venetian School and was given in 1894 by Thomas Wardle.[69]

ROMAN CATHOLICISM

FOUR people in Leek parish were presented in 1589 for absence from church, three of them female members of the Comberford family.[70] Two recusants were recorded in the mid 1590s[71] and four in 1641.[72] Prudence, the widow of Sir Thomas Trentham, was living at the family's Westwood Grange when she compounded for recusancy in 1629; she conformed soon afterwards and attended the parish church.[73] Two ribbon weavers were the only papists in Leek parish returned in 1767, and in 1781 there were again only two papists returned.[74] In the early 19th century Louis Gerard, the emigré priest at Cobridge in Burslem, said mass at Leek for French prisoners of war and Irish workers. The usual place was a room in Pickwood Road, but in the 1820s the garret of a house in King Street belonging to William Ward, a solicitor, was sometimes used.[75]

About 1827 James Jeffries, the priest at Cheadle, started to say mass in Leek, probably in Ward's house, with a congregation of 15 or 16. He began building a chapel on the corner of Fountain Street and Portland Street in 1828 and opened it in 1829; the earl of Shrewsbury contributed £130 towards the cost of £700. Dedicated to St. Mary, it included an altarpiece depicting the Virgin and Child by Barney (probably Joseph Barney) and four paintings of saints brought from Lisbon by the Brigittine nuns who later settled at Aston Hall in Stone. Jeffries said mass on Monday morning, arriving from Cheadle on Sunday evening to stay with Henry Bermingham in London Road.[76] He built a presbytery adjoining the chapel in 1830, and a resident priest was appointed about the beginning

of 1832.[77] A Sunday school had been established by 1834, and a day school was opened in 1845.[78] The congregation appears to have declined in

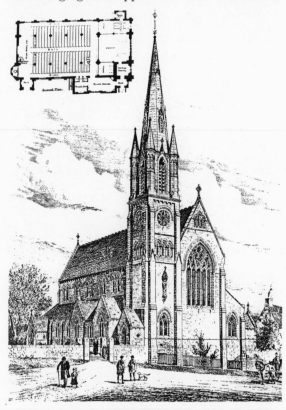

FIG. 28. ST. MARY'S ROMAN CATHOLIC CHURCH

62 S.R.O., D. 4855/3/11; D. 4855/5/38; T. S. Jennings, *Hist. of Staffs. Bells* (priv. print. 1968), 103.
63 *T.N.S.F.C.* 1888, 46–8.
64 P. M. Collins, *All Saints Church, Leek*; S.R.O., D. 4855/3/16, pp. 12–15, 27, 50; D. 4855/5/36.
65 Collins, *All Saints*; S.R.O., D. 4855/3/16, pp. 6–9, 17.
66 Collins, *All Saints.*
67 Ibid.; D. G. Stuart, *Hist. of the Leek Embroidery Soc.* 25–6; A. G. Jacques, *Leek Embroidery* (Staffs. Libraries, Arts & Archives, 1990), 50–1.
68 S.R.O., D. 4855/6/3, pp. 304, 306–7; D. 4855/4/16.
69 Collins, *All Saints*; S.R.O., D. 4855/3/16, pp. 16, 21, and loose TS.
70 *S.H.C.* 1929, 134. The Revd. A. J. Burns, parish priest of St. Mary's, and Mrs. Barbara Priest, a former parishioner, are thanked for help with this section.
71 *Cath. Rec. Soc.* lvii. 150; below, Rudyard, nonconf.

72 *Staffs. Cath. Hist.* v. 14; below, Rushton Spencer, nonconf.
73 *Staffs. Cath. Hist.* xviii. 10; L.J.R.O., B/C/5/1664, Leek.
74 *Staffs. Cath. Hist.* xvii. 26; House of Lords Rec. Office, Papists Returns, 1781.
75 *Staffs. Cath. Hist.* xx. 27; *Olde Leeke*, i. 224. The statement in J. Nightingale, *Staffs.* (Beauties of Eng. and Wales, xiii), 1051, that there was then 'an abbey of French nuns' on the site of Dieulacres may be a confusion with the Benedictine nuns from Ghent who settled at Caverswall in 1811: *V.C.H. Staffs.* viii. 272.
76 *Olde Leeke*, i. 224, 226; *Cath. Mag.* vi. 664 (reprinted in *Staffs. Cath. Hist.* xiv); *Staffs. Cath. Hist.* viii. 28; xx. 13; White, *Dir. Staffs.* (1834), 702; *Short Hist. of Rom. Cath. Church in Leek* [1956], 7, 10, 13, 17, 31.
77 *Cath. Mag.* vi. 664; *S.H.C.* 4th ser. iii. 143.
78 Below, educ. (primary and secondary schs.).

numbers in the 1830s: in 1839 it was stated that the many Irish who had formerly worked as broad-silk weavers in Leek had moved to Manchester and Macclesfield and that there were then few Irish in the mills.[79] On Census Sunday 1851 the congregation numbered 167 in the morning and 115 in the evening, besides Sunday school children.[80]

In 1860 Joseph Anderson, who had come as priest earlier in the year, established a small community of Irish nuns in the presbytery, and he himself went to live in lodgings. The nuns, who were members of the Institute of the Blessed Virgin Mary, took over the running of the school. They moved into a house in King Street in 1863.[81] Later the same year Anderson moved into an adjoining cottage. The owner, Mr. Bermingham (probably Henry Bermingham), gave the garden as the site for a new church. A building of brick and stone designed in a Gothic style by William Sugden, St. Mary's church was opened in 1864. The chapel and house in Fountain Street were sold, the chapel becoming a silk shade.[82]

A third St. Mary's was opened in 1887 east of the church of 1864, with the main approach from Compton. Designed in a Gothic style by Albert Vicars of London and built of Bath stone, it consists of a chancel with side chapels, an aisled nave of five bays with an organ gallery at the west end, and a lofty south-east tower and spire. There are sacristies in the south-east corner, and the north-east corner is occupied by the former nuns' chapel. The site was presented by J. H. Sperling; previously an Anglican clergyman, he was the father of A. M. Sperling, priest at Leek 1884–1923 (created a monsignor in 1916). Two bells, cast by Taylor & Co. of Loughborough, were given by the priest and his father. The church also possesses two pieces of Leek embroidery, an altar frontal and a cope.[83] The church of 1864 became part of the school and was later used as the parish hall; by 1991 it had stood empty for several years, and it was burnt down in 1994.[84] A new presbytery was completed north of the church in 1925.[85] The nuns moved from King Street to a smaller house in Alsop Street in the 1970s, and they left Leek in 1980.[86]

PROTESTANT NONCONFORMITY

IN 1648 the vicar of Leek, Francis Bowyer, signed the Staffordshire *Testimony* in favour of Presbyterianism.[87] His successor, Robert Fowler, from 1652 styled himself 'pastor' in the parish register,[88] possibly an indication of Presbyterian sympathy. Leek was one of the Staffordshire towns which benefited from the lectures endowed in 1653 by the Presbyterian John Machin of Seabridge, in Stoke-upon-Trent,[89] and Machin's friend Henry Newcome conducted and witnessed marriages in Leek in 1654 and 1655.[90] In a letter to Bishop Hacket in 1664 the vicar, George Roades, drew attention to his labours in 'these barren bogs and heathenish moors' where he met almost daily opposition from 'gainsayers'.[91] With the support of Anthony Rudyard of Dieulacres, in Leekfrith, Timothy Edge of Horton Hall, and William Jolliffe of Leek, all of them J.P.s, the members of the church at Leek developed Presbyterian sympathies,[92] and it was Presbyterians who in 1672 registered the first place of worship for nonconformists in the town, following the Declaration of Indulgence that year.

The magistracy was less sympathetic to the stirrings of Quakerism which followed George Fox's preaching at Caldon in 1651 or 1652 and the visit to Leek of the Quaker missionary

Richard Hickock in 1654.[93] On return visits in 1656 and 1658 Hickock disputed with Ranters, and in 1658 he confronted a woman member of the Family of Love.[94] Baptists and Ranters were numerous in the Leek area by 1660, when Quaker missionaries sought to convert them, with some success.[95] Although Quakers established meetings in the area, it was not until the mid 1690s that a meeting house was opened in the town.

An 'abundance of Presbyterians and Quakers and some Anabaptists' were noted in Leek parish in 1706.[96] More exact figures were given by the vicar in 1751. Out of 1,050 families in the parish, 20 were Quakers and 16 Presbyterians; there were also one or two 'reputed' Anabaptists. Some 30 or 40 people attended the Quaker meeting and a similar number the Presbyterian meeting, compared with about 60 who attended the monthly Anglican communion service at the parish church.[97] Methodists formed a society in Leek in 1755, and they opened a chapel in 1785. On Census Sunday 1851 there were adult attendances of 1,510 at the Wesleyan Methodist chapels, 276 at the Primitive Methodist chapel, and 288 at the Congregational chapel. In contrast there were 1,293 attendances at the two Anglican churches and 282 at the Roman Catholic church.[98]

79 *Reps. Assistant Hand-loom Weavers Com., Pt. IV*, [217], p. 345, H.C. (1840), xxiv.   80 *Staffs. Cath. Hist.* viii. 28.
81 *Rom. Cath. Church in Leek*, 13–14, 17.
82 Ibid. 17; *Staffs. Advertiser*, 7 May 1864, p. 4. Hen. Bermingham lived in King St.: *P.O. Dir. Staffs.* (1864).
83 *Rom. Cath. Church in Leek*, 19–20; A. G. Jacques, *Leek Embroidery* (Staffs. Libraries, Arts & Archives, 1990), 51; S.R.O., D. 538/D/3/10, pp. 68, 80.
84 *Leek Post & Times*, 25 Sept. 1991, p. 1; 13 Nov. 1991, p. 5; 24 Aug. 1994, p. 5.   85 *Rom. Cath. Church in Leek*, 23.
86 *St. Mary's Cath. Church, Leek: Centenary 1887–1987*; inf. from the Revd. A. J. Burns.
87 A. G. Matthews, *Congregational Churches of Staffs.* (preface dated 1924), 18 n.   88 *Leek Par. Reg.* 89.
89 Above, churches (St. Edward's: sermons).

90 *Leek Par. Reg.* 98–9.
91 Bodl. MS. Tanner 131, f. 9 (part of the letter is given in Matthews, *Cong. Churches of Staffs.* 54).
92 *S.H.C.* 1912, 334, 336; *S.H.C.* 4th ser. ii. 19; Matthews, *Cong. Churches of Staffs.* 25–7; *Autobiog. of Henry Newcome* (Chetham Soc. [1st ser.], xxvi), 42.
93 S.R.O., D. 3159/1/1, ff. 166–7; below, this section (Friends).   94 Matthews, *Cong. Churches of Staffs.* 39.
95 Friends' House Libr., London, Swarthmore MSS. i, no. 134.   96 *Staffs. Cath. Hist.* xiii. 29.
97 L.J.R.O., B/V/5/1751.
98 Above, churches (St. Edward's; St. Luke's); Rom. Cath.; below, this section (Congregationalists; Methodists). The figures are totals for all services held that day and include people who attended more than one service.

BAPTISTS. A chapel at 'Lower End', possibly at the bottom of Mill Street, was registered for Particular Baptists in 1815; it no longer existed by 1834.[99] Emmanuel Baptist church in Rosebank Street was registered for Old Baptists in 1934. The present Leek Baptist church on the same site was built in 1988.[1]

CONGREGATIONALISTS, formerly PRESBYTERIANS, later UNITED REFORMED CHURCH. The house of Thomas Nabes in Leek was licensed for Presbyterian worship in 1672.[2] Presbyterians may have met in Derby Street later in the century. Land there was owned in 1683 by Randle Sillitoe, a feltmaker and probably a relative of the Randle Sillitoe who signed the Cheshire Testimony in favour of Presbyterianism in 1648, and it may have been the site of two cottages which were apparently rented in 1695 by Josiah Hargrave (or Hargreaves), later recorded as a Presbyterian minister in Leek.[3] Presbyterians certainly had a meeting house in Derby Street by 1715, but they seem still in the 1690s to have met outside the town. A house registered for worship in 1695 at Dunwood, in Longsdon, may have been for Presbyterians, and a house registered in 1699 at Westwood, in Leek and Lowe, was almost certainly for them.[4] A house at Westwood was the home in 1701 of Josiah Hargrave, who was left £20 by Roger Morrice (d. 1702), ejected as vicar of Duffield (Derb.) in 1662 and later a London merchant. The bequest was conditional on Hargrave's continuing to preach at Westwood, or at any other place 'in the Moorlands', for at least two years after Morrice's death.[5] Hargrave was still living at Westwood in 1716. He was by then responsible for the Presbyterian meeting house in Derby Street, first recorded in 1715 when it was damaged by rioters. It stood on the west side of the Roebuck inn.[6]

The congregation numbered 250 'hearers' in 1717, but in 1751 it was estimated that only 30 or 40 people attended the meeting.[7] After the retirement of a Calvinist minister, James Evans, in 1782, a majority of the members chose a Unitarian, George Chadwick, as their minister. The choice caused a division in the church and a group of 36 members called Robert Smith to serve them. A lawsuit followed, and in 1784 Smith secured control. Although a trinitarian, Smith was not a Presbyterian, and under his leadership the Leek church became Congrega-

tionalist. In 1793, or possibly in 1780, a new chapel was built on the same site in Derby Street, with a graveyard in front.

In the early 19th century dissatisfaction with the ministry of James Morrow, on pastoral rather than doctrinal grounds, caused some members to attend Methodist services. In 1829 a large part of the congregation, with the support of the Congregationalist ministers of Staffordshire, seceded to form a new church. The seceders, who first met in a room behind the Black's Head inn in Derby Street, opened a chapel in Union Street in 1834. Morrow died in 1836, and the two congregations reunited, using the Union Street chapel and retaining the Derby Street chapel for a Sunday school and, until 1845, for mid-week services. Its graveyard was closed for new burials in 1857 on the opening of the cemetery on the Cheddleton road.[8]

On Census Sunday 1851 the Union Street chapel had congregations of 120 in the morning, besides Sunday school children, and 168 in the evening.[9] Numbers increased, and in 1860 it was decided to build a larger chapel on the Derby Street site. The new chapel was opened in 1863. Built of stone, it was designed in a Decorated style, with a tower and spire, by William Sugden, a member of the congregation.[10] The organ occupied an apse at the south end, and there was a north gallery. In 1872 a meeting hall and classrooms, also designed by Sugden, were built to the south in Russell Street.[11] The Union Street chapel was turned into a public hall by the town's temperance society in 1864.[12] A house at the north end of King Street, dated 1880 and probably built for William Broster, a silk manufacturer, was bought as a manse in 1898. It became a hall for the town's Freemasons in 1926.[13]

An evangelist was appointed in 1867, but he had little success. Another was engaged in 1878 to take services in a mission opened in Alsop Street school in 1876 and closed in 1935. There were also short-lived missions at Ball Haye Green (1882–93) and in Angle Street (1887–95).[14]

The congregation became Leek United Reformed Church in 1972. In 1977 it joined Leek Central Methodist Church to form Trinity Church, using the Derby Street chapel.[15] In 1981 the chapel was re-ordered internally, the organ being rebuilt with parts from an organ installed in Brunswick Methodist chapel in 1857, and the space under the gallery was converted into a vestibule.[16]

99 S.H.C. 4th ser. iii. 37; White, Dir. Staffs. (1834), 702. For the early hist. of Baptists in the Leek area see below, Rushton Spencer, nonconf.
1 G.R.O. Worship Reg. nos. 55492, 77631; inf. from Mr. G. Hitchins, a church member.
2 Cal. S.P. Dom. 1672, 379.
3 H. Woodhouse, Story of a Leek Church (Leek, 1988), 4–8.   4 S.H.C. 4th ser. iii. 109, 112.
5 P.R.O., PROB 11/463, f. 65v. The house at Westwood was occupied by Isaac Morris, possibly a relation of Morrice; and see above, manors (Westwood), for Caleb Morrice, living there in 1728.
6 Woodhouse, Story of a Leek Church, 8–11.
7 Ibid. 8; L.J.R.O., B/V/5/1751. The remaining paras. of this sub-section are based on Woodhouse, Story of a Leek Church.
8 S.R.O., D. 3679/5/1, hist. acct. of church; above,

public services (public health). For a view of the Derby St. chapel in 1844 see above, plate 43.
9 P.R.O., HO 129/372/2/1 (different figures are given in Woodhouse, Story of a Leek Church, 58).
10 Above, plate 56.
11 S.R.O., D. 3188/1/2, no. 318.
12 Below, social and cultural activities (public halls).
13 Woodhouse, Story of a Leek Church, 92; Kelly's Dir. Staffs. (1884); date stone with initials WB on house; below, social and cultural activities (Freemasons).
14 S.R.O., D. 3679/5/1, hist. acct. of church; G.R.O. Worship Reg. no. 29945; inf. from Mr. E. Everett of Trinity Church.
15 J. M. Forrester, Trinity Church, Leek (Leek, 1994), 22–3.
16 Leek Libr., newspaper cuttings 1981 (1), pp. 26–7; plaque on organ case.

FRIENDS, SOCIETY OF (QUAKERS). The first Quaker missionary to visit Leek and the Moorlands was Richard Hickock in 1654. He disrupted a service at St. Edward's church and was ejected by the congregation. The first converts included William Davenport of Fould Farm, in Leekfrith, Matthew Dale of Rudyard, and Thomas Hammersley of Basford, in Cheddleton, each of whom established a meeting at his home. Another convert, William Yardley of Dairy House, in Horton, was imprisoned in 1655 for speaking out in Leek church. When Hickock returned to Leek in 1656, the J.P.s placed armed men outside Quaker meeting places and put in the stocks those who travelled to hear him.[17] Hickock made a third visit in 1658, and in 1660 two other Quaker missionaries, Oliver Atherton and Richard Moore, visited Leek.[18] In 1675 William Yardley preached at a conventicle held at the house of Sarah Sleigh and Hannah Hay in Leek; he was fined £20 and the women £10 each.[19]

By 1680 Friends in the Leek area had joined together to form a monthly meeting.[20] Land at Overton Bank was acquired in 1694 from the daughters of Gervase Gent, a Friend, and a meeting house had been built by 1697.[21] A schoolmaster engaged by Friends in Staffordshire in 1697 was based in Leek.[22]

A separate monthly meeting held alternately at Whitehough and Bottom House, both in Ipstones, was amalgamated with the Leek meeting in 1712.[23] In 1721, as an experiment for the summer months, it was agreed to hold two meetings for worship at Leek on Sundays, one at 10.30 a.m. for both 'country' and 'town' members and another at 3 p.m. for 'town' members.[24] The meeting was evidently the largest in Staffordshire in the early 18th century: its contribution to national funds was normally twice that of Stafford's.[25] In 1735 the meeting comprised 125 adults and children, at least a third of whom lived outside the town.[26] In 1751 it was estimated that 30 or 40 attended meetings, which were held at noon on Sundays and Thursdays.[27] There was a library of some 200 books in 1736.[28]

There was a women's meeting by 1674, and minutes of it survive from 1709 to 1717.[29] It met irregularly by 1763, but it was on a sounder footing by 1776 and still existed in 1837.[30] An itinerant female minister, Frances Dodshon, was a member of the Leek meeting in the early 1770s.[31] By 1790 there was a resident female minister, Hannah West (d. 1809).[32]

From an early date the Leek Friends had connexions with Quaker settlements in America. Gervase Gent (d. probably 1690), apparently an apothecary, owned property in America,[33] and in 1702 Samuel Stretch, a clockmaker, emigrated to Philadelphia.[34] Stretch may have been associated with the plan in 1707 to send two children who were staying at John Stretch's home in Leek to Pennsylvania.[35] In 1754 Cornelius Bowman of Pennsylvania visited Leek, where his family were Friends; he remained in England and was still associated with the Leek meeting in 1770.[36] Links with America continued into the early 19th century. In 1804 the Leek meeting commended Henry Bowman and his family to the Quaker meeting at Oswego in New York state.[37]

Leading Quakers in the town in the 18th century included Joshua Toft of Haregate Hall, in Tittesworth, a button merchant, and his brother John, a silk weaver. Both men were also ministers.[38] Another Quaker button merchant, Joshua Strangman, who married Joshua Toft's niece Ann Toft in 1752 and lived at no. 62, St. Edward Street,[39] entertained his friend John Wesley in Leek in 1774.[40] Members of the Key family who were Quakers included several button merchants[41] and the physician Robert Key (d. 1761).[42]

The Leek Friends seem to have been tolerated in the 18th century.[43] Their separateness, however, was maintained and those who married outside the society were disowned.[44] By 1783 the meeting had so declined that it was decided to amalgamate it with the Stafford monthly meeting.[45] Leek Friends thereafter held a preparative meeting. That meeting was itself discontinued in 1843, when members joined a meeting in Stoke-upon-Trent. Sunday meetings for worship, however, were still held at Leek until 1846.[46] The Leek meeting was revived in 1880 but survived only until 1894.[47] Another revival took place in 1932. At first the Friends had to meet in private houses, the meeting house at Overton Bank having been let in 1896 to the William Morris Labour Church. The lease was evidently surrendered in 1936, and the Leek

---

17 S.R.O., D. 3159/1/1, ff. 144, 166–7; Matthews, *Cong. Churches of Staffs.* 38–9.
18 Matthews, *Cong. Churches of Staffs.* 39; Friends' House Libr., London, Swarthmore MSS. i, no. 134.
19 S.R.O., Q/SR/367, m. 23.
20 S.R.O., D. 3159/1/1, f. 25.
21 Ibid. D. 3159/2/49, pp. 10–11.
22 Below, educ. (private schs.).
23 S.R.O., D. 3159/3/1, no. 87.   24 Ibid. no. 176.
25 e.g. S.R.O., D. 3159/1/1, ff. 49, 56v.
26 Ibid. D. 4812/2.
27 L.J.R.O., B/V/5/1751.
28 S.R.O., D. 3359/Toft-Chorley, Haregate memo. bk., catalogue of 1736.
29 Ibid. D. 3159/1/1, f. 5; D. 3159/3/2.
30 Ibid. D. 4812/1/1, 11 Oct. 1763, 2 Feb. 1764; D. 4812/1/9–10.
31 Ibid. D. 3159/3/5/31–3; *Some Acct. of the Convincement and Religious Experience of Frances Dodshon* (Warrington, 1804).
32 S.R.O., D. 3159/1/2, 6 July 1790; D. 3159/2/2, 6 Mar.

1810.   33 L.J.R.O., B/C/11, Gervase Gent (1690).
34 Above, econ. hist. (trade and ind.: clock and watch making).   35 S.R.O., D. 3159/3/1, no. 29.
36 Ibid. D. 3159/3/5/4; D. 3359/Condlyffe, draft deed of 19 July 1770; D. 4812/2.   37 Ibid. D. 3159/2/2.
38 Ibid. D. 3159/1/2, 28 June 1768, 3 July 1770.
39 Ibid. D. 3359/Condlyffe, draft deed of 19 July 1770; D. 3359/Strangman, deed of 12 July 1757; D. 4812/1/1; W.S.L. 329/14/40; H. Bode, *Visiting Leek*, i (Leek, 1974), 17.
40 *Jnl. of John Wesley*, ed. N. Curnock, vi. 33.
41 Sleigh, *Leek*, 6; S.R.O., D. 3359/Condlyffe, draft deed of 19 July 1770.
42 Above, econ. hist. (professions: medical practitioners).
43 *Acct. of Convincement and Call to the Ministry of Margaret Lucas, late of Leek, Staffs.* (1797).
44 S.R.O., D. 3159/3/6/7–23, 56–87, 91–110.
45 Ibid. D. 3159/1/2, 21 Dec. 1783.
46 Ibid. D. 3159/2/3, 7 Mar., 18 July 1843, 26 Feb., 3 Mar., 21 July 1846.
47 Ibid. D. 3159/2/5, pp. 314, 320; D. 3159/2/6, pp. 138, 141; D. 4812/1/8.

meeting was re-established in 1937.[48] Meetings for worship were still held in 1992.

The meeting house of the mid 1690s at Overton Bank is built of stone; it had a gallery by 1708.[49] It was damaged by Jacobite troops in 1745.[50] In 1770 the croft on which it stood had recently been converted into a garden, and there was a new stable block for the use of Friends who attended the meeting from a distance. The buildings also included a 'house of ease'.[51] Land on the north side of the meeting house was used for burials, the last taking place in 1954.[52]

JEHOVAH'S WITNESSES. From 1942 to 1944 Jehovah's Witnesses met in a room in Globe Passage off High Street. They later met in King Street (1944–51), Barngate Street (1951–6), and Ball Haye Street (1956–64). The meeting then ceased, but it was revived in 1974, using a room in Ashbourne Road. The present Kingdom Hall, occupying the former Regal cinema at the corner of High Street and Salisbury Street, was registered in 1987.[53]

METHODISTS. WESLEYAN. A Methodist society of 24 members was formed in Leek in 1755. Preaching took place at Nab Hill, but there was no regular meeting place when John Wesley visited the town in 1772. By the time of Wesley's second visit in 1774, a room behind the Blackmoor's Head inn in Derby Street was used.[54] Wesley visited Leek for a third time in 1782, when he preached to a congregation of some 800 in the parish church on Easter Sunday, in both the morning and the evening. After the evening service there was a Lovefeast, described by Wesley as 'such a one as I had not seen for many years'.[55]

Membership of the Leek society numbered 30 in 1784, a year after it was included in the newly created Burslem circuit. A chapel was built at Mount Pleasant on the east side of Clerk Bank in 1785.[56] Wesley preached there in 1788, commenting that 'where for many years we seemed to be ploughing upon the sand . . . at length the fruit appears'.[57] The membership was then 96, sufficient to warrant the creation in 1792 of a circuit for the Leek area alone.[58] In 1811, when there were 178 members, a new chapel was built at Mount Pleasant with a graveyard attached.[59]

The old chapel was converted into houses, used by the circuit's preachers from 1833 until 1849 or 1850 when James Wardle, a Leek silk manufacturer, gave a house in Regent Street as a manse.[60] The graveyard at Mount Pleasant was closed for burials in 1857, on the opening of the cemetery on the Cheddleton road.[61]

A chapel was built at the corner of Ball Haye Street and Regent Street in 1828. The building was originally intended for use as a Sunday school only, but it was fitted with a gallery and an organ at the expense of James Wardle and was also used for services.[62] Two Sunday services were held there in 1829, and by 1832 it was known as Brunswick chapel.[63] At Ball Haye Green there was a fortnightly Sunday service in 1829, but apparently none by 1832.[64] Services were again held there from 1846, in a building between Prince Street and Pump Street opened as a Sunday school in 1845.[65]

On Census Sunday 1851 there were morning congregations of 294 at Mount Pleasant and 124 at Brunswick, afternoon congregations of 161 at Mount Pleasant and 60 at Ball Haye Green, and evening congregations of 517 at Mount Pleasant, 296 at Brunswick, and 58 at Ball Haye Green. There were also Sunday schools at all three places.[66]

Brunswick chapel was replaced by a chapel of the same name in Market Street in 1857. Built of brick with stone dressings, it was designed in a Gothic style by William Sugden and paid for by James Wardle.[67] A chapel was opened in Mill Street in 1871 as part of a building which also housed a ragged school,[68] and in 1894 a chapel was opened in Milk Street at Ball Haye Green.[69] By 1881 the Wesleyans had also opened a room in Haywood Street for the Hallelujah Band Mission, but the registration was cancelled in 1895.[70] In 1909 a building at the back of Mount Pleasant chapel was converted into a social centre called the Wesleyan Institute.[71]

From 1974 the congregations of Mount Pleasant and Brunswick used their chapels for joint services on alternate Sundays. They united as the Central Methodist Church in 1976, continuing to use both chapels.[72] In 1977 the congregation amalgamated with Leek United Reformed Church to form Trinity Church, using the United Reformed Church building in Derby Street.[73] Brunswick chapel was closed in 1976 and demolished in 1977.[74] Mount Pleasant

48 Ibid. D. 3159/2/61A; D. 5197/4; A. Walmesley, 'Reminiscences of Leek Friends' (TS. in W.S.L.); below, this section (Wm. Morris Labour Church).
49 S.R.O., D. 3159/3/1, no. 37.
50 Above, general hist. (18th cent.).
51 S.R.O., D. 3359/Condlyffe, draft deed of 19 July 1770.
52 Inf. from Mr. L. T. Stewart of the Leek Meeting.
53 G.R.O. Worship Reg. nos. 60011, 60813, 63243, 65751, 73645, 77354.
54 Dyson, Weslyan Methodism, 8–10, 14, 17; Wardle, Methodist Hist. 4.
55 Jnl. of John Wesley, vi. 346.
56 Dyson, Weslyan Methodism, 27–9; Wardle, Methodist Hist. 23.
57 Jnl. of John Wesley, vii. 372.
58 Dyson, Weslyan Methodism, 30, 32, 34.
59 S.R.O., D. 3155/1; hymn sheet for opening service, July 1811 (copy in S.R.O., D. 1114/1).
60 Dyson, Weslyan Methodism, 45, 47; Wardle, Methodist Hist. 51.

61 Above, public services (public health).
62 Dyson, Wesleyan Methodism, 46; Wardle, Methodist Hist. 50.
63 Leek Libr., Johnson scrapbk. i (2), D/13/15; S.R.O., D. 3156/1/1/24.
64 Leek Libr., Johnson scrapbk. i (2), D/13/15; S.R.O., D. 3156/1/1/24.
65 Wardle, Methodist Hist. 51; O.S. Map 1/500, Staffs. VIII. 6. 17 (1879 edn.).
66 P.R.O., HO 129/372/2/1.
67 Staffs. Advertiser, 1 Mar. 1856, p. 4; 21 Feb. 1857, p. 4; above, plate 57.
68 Staffs. Advertiser, 21 Jan. 1871, p. 4.
69 Ibid. 17 Feb. 1894, p. 5; S.R.O., D. 3188/1/3.
70 P.R.O., RG 11/2738; G.R.O. Worship Reg. no. 26722.
71 S.R.O., D. 1114/1, newspaper cutting of 15 Feb. 1909.
72 Leek Methodist News, nos. 25, 40–1 (copies in S.R.O., D. 4808/2/1).
73 Above, this section (Congregationalists).
74 Leek Libr., newspaper cuttings 1972–8, pp. 73, 105.

chapel was demolished in 1980, and sheltered flats were opened on the site.[75] Mill Street chapel was closed in 1990,[76] but the Milk Street church at Ball Haye Green remained open for worship in 1992.

NEW CONNEXION. A society of New Connexion Methodists was formed in Leek in 1856, meeting first in the Temperance Society's lecture room in Stockwell Street and then in the Friends' meeting house at Overton Bank. A chapel, designed by Robert Scrivener of Hanley, was opened in 1862 at the corner of Ball Haye Street and Queen Street.[77] It was known as Bethesda chapel by 1875.[78] Closed in 1941, the building was taken over in 1949 by the former Primitive Methodist congregation from Fountain Street. Again closed in 1963, the chapel was used for commercial purposes until its demolition in the late 1980s.[79]

PRIMITIVE. A Primitive Methodist chapel was built at the west end of Fountain Street in 1836. On Census Sunday 1851 there was a congregation of 59 in the morning, besides Sunday school children, and 217 in the evening.[80] The chapel was rebuilt in 1884.[81] In 1949 the congregation moved to the former New Connexion chapel in Ball Haye Street, and the Fountain Street building was used for various purposes until its demolition in the early 1970s.[82]

PENTECOSTALISTS. Pentecostalists first met in Leek in 1931, using the Congregationalists' hall in Russell Street before moving to premises in Globe Passage off High Street. In the early 1940s they moved to Strangman Street. The present church in Buxton Road was built in 1978.[83]

In 1987 the former pastor of the Buxton Road Pentecostalist church established a separate congregation called Oasis Ministries in the former Methodist school in West Street.[84] The congregation still met there in 1992.

PRESBYTERIANS, see CONGREGATIONALISTS.

QUAKERS, see FRIENDS, SOCIETY OF.

SALVATION ARMY. A Salvation Army barracks in Haywood Street was registered for worship in 1887.[85] Gen. William Booth addressed a meeting in the town hall in 1898 and in 1911.[86] The barracks was replaced in 1905 by a citadel in Union Street, itself replaced in 1912 by a hall in Ball Haye Road and that in 1914 by a hall in Ford Street.[87] A hall at the corner of Salisbury Street and Strangman Street, registered in 1936,[88] remained in use in 1992.

UNITED REFORMED CHURCH, see CONGREGATIONALISTS.

WILLIAM MORRIS LABOUR CHURCH. In 1881 the Leek architect Larner Sugden began to publish essays and lectures by various authors under the general title of Leek Bijou Freethought Reprints. They included, in 1884, *Art and Socialism* by William Morris, a frequent visitor to Leek in the later 1870s.[89] Chiefly through Sugden's influence, a Labour Church bearing Morris's name was established in Leek in 1896, the year of Morris's death. It leased the Friends' meeting house at Overton Bank, which underwent extensive redecoration. The walls were painted red with stencilled tracery designed by Walter Crane, and the woodwork was painted a translucent green. The windows were provided with blue velvet curtains in a Morris fabric. Other furnishings included a blue silk banner painted by Stephen Webb.[90] None of the decorations or furnishings survives. Services were moved probably *c.* 1910 to the Co-operative Society's hall in Ashbourne Road. They later ceased, although the church was still active politically in 1935.[91]

The church organized regular addresses by notable speakers on humanist, social, and religious subjects, which caused the local novelist Kineton Parkes to comment that 'a wave of intellectual and semi-intellectual activity flooded the town'.[92] Sugden died in 1901 and was cremated at Manchester, the first person from Leek to be cremated.[93] A fund was established in the same year to continue the addresses and provide an anniversary lecture in Sugden's honour. The last recorded address was given in April 1903.[94]

OTHER DENOMINATIONS. In 1822 John Jones, a Leek schoolmaster who by 1824 was a follower of Emanuel Swedenborg, registered his

75 Inf. from Miss J. M. Forrester of Trinity Church; above, public services (housing). For an undated interior view of the chapel see Poole, *Leek*, 48.
76 Inf. from Miss Forrester.
77 *Staffs. Sentinel*, 16 Aug. 1856, p. 1; *Staffs. Advertiser*, 26 Oct. 1861, p. 6; 16 Aug. 1862, p. 4.
78 G.R.O. Worship Reg. no. 22205.
79 Forrester, *Trinity Church, Leek*, 17–18; inf. from Miss Forrester. 80 P.R.O., HO 129/372/2/1.
81 S.R.O., D. 3156/2/1/6; L. Porter, *Leek Thirty Years Ago* (Clifton, Ashbourne, 1991), no. 89.
82 Inf. from Miss Forrester.
83 G.R.O. Worship Reg. no. 60272; Leek Libr., newspaper cuttings 1972–8, p. 84; inf. from the church secretary, Mr. J. Gregory.
84 Leek Libr., newspaper cuttings 1986–7, p. 77.
85 G.R.O. Worship Reg. no. 30427.

86 S.R.O., D. 1114/1, cards announcing meetings.
87 G.R.O. Worship Reg. nos. 41322, 45128, 46065.
88 Ibid. no. 56812.
89 There were only seven issues (1881–4): copies in Brit. Libr. For Morris's activities in Leek, see above, econ. hist. (trade and ind.: silk).
90 Leek Libr., newspaper cuttings 1972–8, p. 113; *Reformers' Yr. Bk., 1901*, 41, reprinted in *Jnl. of Wm. Morris Soc.* vi (1), 17.
91 Walmesley, 'Reminiscences of Leek Friends', p. 2; S.R.O., D. 5197/4, Wm. Bayley to Mrs. Lean, Nov. 1935.
92 Printed memo. of 21 June 1899 (copy in S.R.O., D. 538/D/3/9); K. Parkes, *Windylow* (1915), 110.
93 G. A. Lovenbury, *Sugdens of Leek* (1975), 12–14.
94 2nd Ann. Rep. of Larner Sugden Memorial, printed at end of E. Carpenter, *Art of Creation* (Hanley, 1903; copy in S.R.O., D. 4812/6/3).

schoolroom behind the Black's Head inn in Derby Street for worship by protestant dissenters. Swedenborgians still met there occasionally c. 1830.[95] A Swedenborgian missionary from Manchester gave lectures in Leek in 1859, but no society appears to have been formed.[96]

In 1864 the Friends' meeting house at Overton Bank was let to Christian Brethren.[97] Also known as Plymouth Brethren, they were presumably the 'persons who object to be designated by any distinctive sectarian appellation' who in 1867 registered the meeting house for worship. They had ceased to meet there by 1871, but Brethren were still active in the town in the 1880s.[98]

The Salvation Navy registered a harbour in London Street in 1882. The registration was cancelled two months later.[99]

The United Christian Army registered a mission hall in Strangmans Walk in 1883. The registration was cancelled later the same year.[1]

Spiritualists held services in the Friends' meeting house at Overton Bank in 1924, and in the mid 1930s they ran a Sunday school there. Services continued to be held there until the late 1950s.[2]

Seventh Day Adventists started to hold services in a private house in Leek in 1980. In 1982 they transferred their services to the Friends' meeting house, where they still met in 1992.[3]

SOCIAL AND CULTURAL ACTIVITIES

FOLK CUSTOMS. In the earlier 1830s a wake was held on the third Sunday in October, possibly in association with the feast of the Translation of Edward the Confessor (13 October), then regarded as the patron saint of the parish church.[4] It had probably been held at that time of the year at least since the early 18th century: horse races held in Leek in October 1708 were probably connected with the wake. In 1841 there was a four-day holiday following the Sunday wake, and horse racing took place on the Monday and Tuesday.[5] After the horse racing was stopped in 1851, many people went instead on the Monday to Trentham Gardens, Belle Vue in Manchester, or other attractions.[6] At the request of employers, the town's improvement commissioners abolished wakes week as a holiday in 1883, substituting the first Friday in August (Club Day) and the three following working days.[7] Wakes Monday, however, was still a school holiday in 1931.[8] From the earlier 1950s what was called Leek Mills (or Mill) holiday was taken on the first Monday in October. It evidently lapsed in the later 1960s.[9]

The custom of choosing a mock mayor for the town existed by 1758. The office-holder that year was John Sneyd of Bishton, in Colwich, who announced that he would hold a feast at the Cock inn in January 1759.[10] The occasion is probably identifiable with the annual Venison Feast recorded in 1837 when it was held early in October. The venison was supplied by the duke of Sutherland, the owner of Wall Grange Farm, in Longsdon. The feast was still held in 1889.[11]

The traditional sport of heaving in Easter week had apparently ceased by the later 19th century, but the custom of dragging a plough on Plough Monday (the Monday after Twelfth Night) was still observed.[12] Children went begging for soul cakes on All Saints' Day until the eve of the First World War.[13]

SUNDAY SCHOOL FESTIVAL. An annual procession of Sunday school children was first recorded in 1828, when it took place on the last Sunday in August. About 1,000 children from the Wesleyan Methodist Sunday school walked that day, and hymns were sung in the market place.[14] By the mid 19th century the event was known as Cap Sunday, from the caps worn by the girls until 1859. Because the crowds of onlookers attracted to the event were considered inappropriate for a Sunday, the procession was moved in 1859 to the afternoon of Club Day, the first Friday in August. By then the children walked with banners and flags and were accompanied by bands.[15] In 1860, evidently for the first time, children from the Church of England Sunday schools took part; they walked on their own, however, after the Wesleyans had finished singing in the market place. Children from the Congregational church seem not to have joined in the walking until 1867; from 1893 children from the Roman Catholic church also participated.[16] In the late 1890s Anglicans no longer walked on the same day as the nonconformists and Roman Catholics, but they again took part

95 S.H.C. 4th ser. iii. 57; Olde Leeke, i. 100–1, 170.
96 Staffs. Advertiser, 5 Nov. 1859, p. 4.
97 S.R.O., D. 3159/2/57.
98 G.R.O. Worship Reg. no. 17908; S.R.O., D. 3679/5/1, roll of members.   99 G.R.O. Worship Reg. no. 26594.
1 Ibid. no. 27012.
2 Kelly's Dir. Staffs. (1924); S.R.O., D. 5197/4; Walmesley, 'Reminiscences of Leek Friends', p. 3; inf. from Mr. L. T. Stewart of the Leek Society of Friends.
3 Inf. from Mrs. D. Price, a member of the congregation.
4 White, Dir. Staffs. (1834), 700; above, churches (St. Edward's).
5 2nd Rep. Com. Child. Employment, App. Pt. I [431], p. c99, H.C. (1843), xiv; below, this section (sport).
6 Staffs. Advertiser, 21 Oct. 1848, p. 5; 25 Oct. 1851, p. 4; 28 Oct. 1854, p. 4; 22 Oct. 1859, p. 4; 26 Oct. 1861, p. 4; 22 Oct. 1864, p. 4.

7 S.R.O., D. 3226/6, pp. 216, 222–3; St. Edward's ch., Leek, sch. log bk. 1876–1932, pp. 142–3, 154, 170. For Club Day see below, this section (friendly socs.).
8 S.R.O., D. 3657/1/3, pp. 9, 438; D. 3657/1/4, p. 234.
9 Ibid. D. 3133/3/3; D. 3657/1/5–6; D. 3990/1/1.
10 Olde Leeke, i. 261.
11 Staffs. Advertiser, 14 Oct. 1837, p. 3; 19 Oct. 1889, p. 7.
12 Sleigh, Leek, 218. For heaving see R. Chambers, The Book of Days (1869), i. 425, 429.
13 Sleigh, Leek, 217–18; T.N.S.F.C. xlix. 131.
14 Macclesfield Courier & Herald, 6 Sept. 1828, p. 3. This and other references to Macclesfield Courier & Herald have been supplied by Mr. A. W. Bednall of Macclesfield.
15 Staffs. Advertiser, 4 Sept. 1841, p. 3; 13 Aug. 1859, p. 2; Leek Wesleyan Methodist Circuit Yr. Bk. 1887, 31. For Club Day see below, this section (friendly socs.).
16 Staffs. Advertiser, 11 Aug. 1860, p. 4; 10 Aug. 1861, p. 4; 6 Aug. 1887, p. 5; 12 Aug. 1893, p. 7.

with the others from 1909. By then the procession took place on the third Saturday in July, the date having been changed probably in 1906. The change of date was probably made to dissociate the event from Club Day, with its secular entertainments, and the title Leek Sunday School Festival was in use by 1910.[17] Roman Catholic children could take part because the festival was not regarded as an act of worship, there being hymns but no prayers. The Lord's Prayer and Bible readings, however, were introduced in 1969.[18]

SPORT. Foxhunting in the Leek area was evidently organized by the Leek Hunt recorded in 1794. Hounds were then kept by Richard Badnall, a silk dyer.[19] In 1820 a pack called the Moorland Foxhounds hunted a country which covered Leek, Biddulph, and Draycott-in-the-Moors.[20]

Horse races at Leek were recorded in October 1708 and again in October 1748.[21] In 1803 a two-day meeting on Leek moor was advertised for the Monday and Tuesday after the third Sunday in October, and in 1833 racing took place on the same two days on a course at Birchall Dale on the west side of the Cheddleton road.[22] Races still took place at Birchall Dale in 1850, but in 1851 the owner refused permission for the use of the course and the races were cancelled.[23] Races were again held on the Birchall Dale course in 1863, 1864, and probably 1865.[24] No racing took place in 1866, but in 1867 races were held in the newly opened park at Highfield Hall, in Leekfrith, where they continued until 1870.[25]

From 1867 an additional meeting was held at Highfield park on the Monday and Tuesday following the town's Club Day on the first Friday in August. Known as the North Staffordshire Meeting by 1868, the races continued until 1870. There was a revival in 1883, the Birchall Dale course being used. The meeting evidently failed to attract visitors in 1889 and was not revived.[26]

There was land called the Bowling Green behind the Queen's Head inn in Spout Street (later St. Edward Street) in 1724,[27] and in 1766 there was evidently a bowling green in Stockwell Street.[28] A bowling green opened in Beggars Lane in 1911[29] was used by Leek Bowling Club

in 1992. A bowling green was opened in Brough Park in 1923. It has been used by Leek Park Bowling Club from the club's formation in 1928.[30]

In the mid 18th century the churchwardens tried to stop 'the lads' playing football in the churchyard, especially on Sundays. In 1783 the wardens engaged a man for 5s. a year to enforce the ban; he was still employed in 1786.[31] Leek Town Football Club originated in a club which was formed in 1873 and adopted Association rules in 1876.[32] By 1892 the club played on a pitch in the grounds of Highfield Hall, moving to its present ground in Macclesfield Road in the later 1940s.[33] In 1990 the club was the losing finalist at Wembley for the Football Association Challenge Trophy.[34] Ball Haye Green Football Club was formed in 1880. It has played on its present ground behind Ball Haye Green Working Men's Club since the later 1940s.[35] Leek Alexandra Football Club was formed by 1892 and still existed in 1927.[36]

Leek Rugby Union Football Club was formed in 1924. Discontinued during the Second World War, it was revived in 1946, playing on the ground at Birchall Dale still in use in 1992.[37]

A cricket club existed by 1838.[38] It was evidently re-organized in 1844 as the Leek and Moorlands Cricket Club, which at first played at Barnfields. Free use of a ground in Beggars Lane was given by John Davenport from 1852. In 1866 the club moved to a ground at Highfield Hall, also given free by the owner, Arthur Nicholson. A decision in 1874 to return to Beggars Lane led to a dispute, and a new club called Leek Highfield was formed by those who preferred not to move back. The two clubs were reunited in 1919 as Leek Cricket Club, using the Highfield ground for matches and that in Beggars Lane for practice.[39] Houses were built over the Beggars Lane ground c. 1990, but the Highfield ground continued in use.

Leek and Moorlands Bicycle Club, formed in 1876, changed its name in the earlier 1880s to Leek Cyclists' Club.[40] It still existed in 1992.

Leek Golf Club, formed in 1892, moved in 1923 to a course on the west side of the Cheddleton road, where it remained in 1992. The clubhouse was designed by Longden & Venables.[41] Westwood Golf Club on the north side of the Newcastle road near Wall Bridge was formed in 1923 and was at first for artisans. A

[17] Ibid. 11 Aug. 1900, p. 5; 3 Aug. 1901, p. 5; 12 Aug. 1905, p. 7; 28 July 1906, p. 4; 24 July 1909, p. 4; 30 July 1910, suppl. p. 2; S.R.O., D. 1114/1, festival plan, 1910.
[18] Inf. from the secretary of the festival cttee., Mr. G. Naden.
[19] Inf. supplied by Mr. Bednall from Badnall fam. papers in his possession.
[20] C. J. Blagg, Hist. of North Staffs. Hounds and Country, 1825–1902, 2.
[21] S.R.O., D. 538/D/3/10, p. 46; D. 3159/3/1, no. 40.
[22] Staffs. Advertiser, 30 Sept. 1803, p. 1; Leek Libr., vol. of accts. for Leek races, 1833–68.
[23] Staffs. Advertiser, 19 Oct. 1850, p. 1; 11 Oct. 1851, p. 1.
[24] Ibid. 24 Oct. 1863, p. 5; 22 Oct. 1864, p. 4; 14 Oct. 1865, p. 1.
[25] Ibid. 26 Oct. 1867, p. 5; below, this section (parks).
[26] Staffs. Advertiser, 10 Aug. 1867, p. 4; 8 Aug. 1868, p. 7; 13 Aug. 1870, p. 4; 11 Aug. 1883, p. 7; 11 Aug. 1888, p. 5.
[27] S.R.O., D. 3359/misc. deeds, abstract of Hen. Simpson's title, p. 1.

[28] Ibid. D. 3359/Condlyffe, deed of 19 May 1766.
[29] Staffs. Advertiser, 8 July 1911, p. 9; O.S. Map 1/2,500, Staffs. VIII. 9 (1925 edn.).
[30] Leek Libr., newspaper cuttings 1972–8, pp. 125–7.
[31] S.R.O., D. 1040/7, pp. 117, 132, 196–7.
[32] Poole, Leek, 112.
[33] Staffs. Advertiser, 9 Apr. 1892, p. 7; O.S. Map 6", Staffs. VIII. NW. (1900 and 1925 edns.); inf. from the club secretary.
[34] Leek Post & Times, 23 May 1990, p. 40.
[35] Inf. from Mr. D. Edge, the former club chairman.
[36] Staffs. Advertiser, 9 Apr. 1892, p. 7; Leek Libr., newspaper cuttings bk. 4, p. 19.
[37] Inf. from the club president, Mr. G. J. Bloore.
[38] Staffs. Advertiser, 30 June 1838, p. 3.
[39] T. Tipper, 80 Years of Leek Cricket 1844–1924, 11, 20, 34–5, 123, 174, 177, 417–18.
[40] Anderton, Edwardian Leek, 79–84; Leek Libr., newspaper cuttings, bk. 8, p. 40.
[41] S.R.O., D. 3188/2; inf. from the club secretary.

clubhouse, designed by David Horne of GCW Architects of Stoke-on-Trent, was opened in 1992.[42]

Abbey View Tennis Club was formed in 1913 with courts on the part of the Ball Haye Hall estate given that year for Brough Park.[43] The club still existed in 1992. Of the several tennis clubs associated with the town's churches the longest lived was probably that for St. Luke's, which may have existed before 1914. It certainly existed in 1921, and it survived until 1965.[44]

A gymnasium was opened next to the Nicholson Institute in 1901. Paid for by William Carr, it was designed by Larner Sugden and has external decoration and lettering by A. Broadbent. Carr gave the gymnasium to the urban district council, and in 1992 it was bought by Leek College.[45] A swimming pool was opened in Brough Park in 1975.[46] Squash courts were opened nearby in 1977, and a sports hall was added in 1986.[47]

PARKS AND RECREATION GROUNDS.

In 1867 a committee took a seven-year lease of the grounds at Highfield Hall, in Leekfrith, and opened them as a park for the town's working population. There was an entry charge of 1*d*. The committee provided facilities for bowling and croquet and encouraged athletics by staging sports days on the first Sunday of each month. The first such day, in June 1867, attracted 1,600 spectators. The park was also used for horse racing. The lease was surrendered in 1870, probably for financial reasons, and public use of the park was discontinued after that year's autumn horse races.[48]

It was presumably the loss of the Highfield park which caused the improvement commissioners in November 1870 to take a lease of land on the south side of Britannia Street for a recreation ground. That ground continued in use until 1878, when it was bought for housing and Gladstone Street and Chorley Street were laid out over the site.[49] Presumably to replace it the commissioners in 1879 laid out a 5-a. recreation ground between Westwood Road and Spring Gardens.[50] Pickwood recreation ground, also 5 a., was presented to the town by William Challinor of Pickwood on the occasion of Queen Victoria's jubilee in 1887.[51] Land called the Waste on the west side of the Buxton road on the outskirts of town was opened as a public

pleasure ground in the mid 1890s by W. S. Brough, who lived nearby at Buxton Villa.[52]

In 1913 Brough gave the urban district council 10½ a. of his Ball Haye Hall estate for use as a public park. Because of the First World War the conversion was postponed. The site was extended by 8½ a. given in 1921 by Joseph Tatton, and by 1923 it was called Brough Park. It was officially opened in 1924, and a bandstand was built the same year.[53]

A recreation ground at Ball Haye Green was laid out after 1919 as a war memorial.[54] In 1937 the urban district council bought 24 a. at Birchall Dale on the west side of the Cheddleton road, and playing fields were laid out for hire to local clubs.[55]

MUSIC.

From his appointment as choirmaster and organist at St. Edward's church in 1835 Benjamin Barlow encouraged the development of music in the town. He was the pianist when the Leek Philharmonic Society, established in 1839, gave the first in a series of subscription concerts in October that year in the assembly room at the Swan inn. The society still existed in 1857.[56] In 1842 Barlow arranged for Joseph Mainzer, the pioneer teacher of choirs according to the sol-fa method, to give lectures in Leek on congregational singing.[57] It was almost certainly Barlow who founded Leek Church Choral Society, in existence by 1857,[58] and he was probably involved in the formation in 1864 of Leek and District Association for Promoting Church Music, which sought to encourage congregational singing in Anglican churches.[59] Leek United Choral Society, also in existence by 1857,[60] was probably a nonconformist group.

Leek Amateur Musical Society, formed in 1866, gave concerts in the Temperance Hall until 1888, when it moved to the town hall in Market Street. It still existed in 1913.[61] In the 1930s two societies, Leek Choral Society and Leek Orchestral Society, gave joint concerts. After the Second World War there was no established choral society until the present Leek Choral Society was founded in the early 1970s under the direction of Keith Davis, the choirmaster at Brunswick Methodist church.[62]

Leek Amateur Opera Society was formed in 1893, usually staging its productions in the Grand Theatre. A performance in 1927 was

42 Leek Libr., newspaper cuttings bk. 5, p. 16; *Leek Post & Times*, 26 Aug. 1992.

43 Inf. from the club secretary, Mrs. J. M. Bennett.

44 Elinor Mordaunt, *Bellamy* (1914), 84; club min. bks. in possession of Challinors & Shaw, Derby St., Leek.

45 *Staffs. Advertiser*, 4 Aug. 1900, p. 5; 5 Oct. 1901, p. 7; below, educ. (further and adult educ.). For Carr see below, charities (other charities).

46 Above, public services (public health).

47 Inf. from Cllr. A. J. Hurst of Leek.

48 W.S.L., Sleigh scrapbk. ii, f. 2; *Staffs. Advertiser*, 8 June 1867, p. 5; 22 Oct. 1870, p. 4.

49 S.R.O., D. 3226/2, nos. 2309, 2655; W.S.L., Sleigh scrapbk. ii, f. 72v.; Leek Libr., Johnson scrapbk. iii, p. 195; above, general hist. (later 19th cent.).

50 Leek U.D.C. *Fifty Years of Municipal Govt. in Leek, 1855 to 1905* (Leek, 1905), 14.

51 Ibid.; programme for opening (copy in W.S.L. 46/45, p. 126).

52 *T.N.S.F.C.* xxix. 154; G. A. Lovenbury, 'A Certain

Group of Men' (Leek, 1990), 16.

53 *Leek Post*, 12 July 1913; W.S.L. 503/34, cuttings of 7 July 1923, 21 June 1924; O.S. Map 6", Staffs. VIII. NW. (1925 edn.).

54 Inscription on entrance.

55 Inf. from Staffs. Moorlands District Council.

56 Leek Libr., Johnson scrapbk. i (2), D/12/6; D/35/4; *Staffs. Advertiser*, 2 Nov. 1839, p. 3; 3 Oct. 1857, p. 4. For Barlow see below, educ. (private schs.).

57 S.R.O., D. 3359/St. Edward's Sunday Sch. acct. bk. 1834–66, min. of 1 Aug. 1842. For Mainzer see *D.N.B.* and *New Grove Dict. of Music and Musicians*, xi. 539–40.

58 *Staffs. Advertiser*, 3 Oct. 1857, p. 4; 24 Dec. 1859, p. 4.

59 Leek Libr., Johnson scrapbk. iii, p. 225; W.S.L., Sleigh scrapbk. i, f. 64v.

60 *Staffs. Advertiser*, 3 Oct. 1857, p. 4.

61 Ibid. 12 May 1866, p. 4; Leek Libr., Leek Amateur Mus. Soc. scrapbks. 1866–1913.

62 Inf. from Mr. Davis.

apparently its last.[63] An operatic society established at All Saints' church in 1927 was known from 1961 as All Saints' Amateur Operatic Society. Although the society still existed in 1992, no performance had been given since 1987 because of the lack of a suitable public hall for large-scale productions following the demolition of the town hall in 1988.[64] The Leekensian Amateur Operatic Society was formed in 1958. From 1960 until 1974 it used the Grand Theatre and then the town hall. Since 1988 performances have been given in Trinity church in Derby Street.[65]

A band led a parade by the town's friendly societies in 1830, and in 1834 one led the cortège at the funeral of a member of a silk operatives' union.[66] There was a drum and fife band by 1857, and in 1860 a similar band was formed by the recently established rifle volunteers.[67] Leek Harmonic Brass Band was formed in 1867 and held Friday evening concerts in the market place during the summer. It is probably identifiable as the band which played in the market place on Monday evenings in the early 1870s and was called Leek Promenade Band in 1873.[68] A band called the Talbot played on Thursday evenings in 1873 in the cattle market at the east end of Derby Street.[69]

Six Italian bagpipe players lodging in Leek in 1871 were presumably itinerant entertainers.[70]

DANCING ASSEMBLIES. A dancing master taught in Leek in 1714 and 1715.[71] By 1789 assemblies were held at the Swan in a room which survives at the back. Assemblies were still held at the Swan in the later 1820s, and a charity ball was held there in 1835.[72] In the late 1850s an annual town ball was held at the Red Lion.[73] One was apparently held at the town hall in the early 20th century.[74]

THEATRES. A room over a stable in the courtyard of the Golden Lion in Church Street had been used as a playhouse or club room for some years before 1782. In 1787 it was called the Long Room or Play Room.[75] A company led by Samuel Stanton included Leek in its circuit in 1789, and for the 1791–2 season it was based in the town while its theatre at Stafford was being rebuilt. On both occasions the company included Harriot Mellon, later duchess of St. Albans.[76] The venue was presumably the assembly room at the Swan, where a theatre mentioned in 1791 was still in use in 1834.[77] In 1832 an amateur performance took place at what was called the Theatre Royal, which occupied premises at the Red Lion.[78] The Grand Theatre and Hippodrome, built at the corner of High Street and Field Street in 1909, was at first used chiefly as a music hall. Even after it had become principally a cinema in 1915, performances by visiting professional companies and local amateur societies were occasionally given there.[79] By the 1960s the usual place for such performances was the town hall.

The tercentenary of Shakespeare's birth in 1864 was celebrated in Leek by readings from his works in the Wesleyan Methodist school in West Street.[80] Leek Amateur Dramatic Society had been formed by 1870 but seems not to have lasted.[81] In 1883 Leek Philothespian Club was founded to perform plays and give recitations. It performed in public twice yearly, usually in the Temperance Hall. Its last known production was in 1905.[82] A new Amateur Dramatic Society was formed in 1927; its last production was in 1958.[83] St. Luke's Players, in existence by 1948, were renamed Leek Players in 1991.[84]

John Snape's Travelling Theatre played at Leek in 1853, evidently during wakes week.[85] In the 1870s travelling companies played in the cattle market at the east end of Derby Street, and the Victoria Pavilion Theatre used that site in the early 20th century.[86]

CIRCUS. Wombwell's menagerie visited Leek in 1822.[87] On a visit in 1839 it engaged a local man, James Bostock of Horton, who married George Wombwell's niece, and from 1867 he managed the company. James was succeeded as manager by his son Edward, 'the British Barnum', who included Leek in the company's last tour c. 1930.[88]

CINEMAS. Moving pictures were shown at the Nicholson Institute by Messrs. Stokes and Watson of Manchester in 1898.[89] The Grand Theatre in High Street first included films among its entertainments in 1910, and from 1915 it was principally a cinema.[90] It was closed in the mid 1980s.

[63] Anderton, *Edwardian Leek*, 28–9; Leek Libr., Leek Amateur Opera Soc. scrapbk. 1913–27.

[64] Inf. from Mr. M. Birch, a member of the society.

[65] Inf. from Mr. Davis.

[66] *Macclesfield Courier & Herald*, 7 Aug. 1830, p. 2; *Staffs. Advertiser*, 17 May 1834, p. 3.

[67] *Staffs. Advertiser*, 29 Aug. 1857, p. 4; 30 June 1860, p. 4.

[68] Ibid. 20 July 1867, p. 4; 3 July 1869, p. 7; 16 July 1870, p. 4; S.R.O., D. 3226/2, no. 2580.

[69] S.R.O., D. 3226/2, no. 2571.

[70] P.R.O., RG 10/2882.

[71] *Acct. of Convincement and Call to the Ministry of Margaret Lucas, late of Leek, Staffs.* (1797), 7–8.

[72] *Derby Mercury*, 5 Nov. 1789; *Macclesfield Courier & Herald*, 17 Jan. 1829, 7 and 21 Mar. 1835.

[73] *Staffs. Advertiser*, 15 Jan. 1859, p. 4.

[74] W. K. Parkes, *The Money Hunt* [1914], 178 sqq.

[75] W.S.L., Sleigh scrapbk. ii, f. 106; S.R.O., D. 3124/20.

[76] M. Baron-Wilson, *Memoirs of Harriot, Duchess of St.*

Albans (1840), i. 97–8, 122.

[77] Leek Libr., newspaper cuttings 1960–8, p. 110; *Staffs. Advertiser*, 19 July 1834, p. 1.

[78] W.S.L., Sleigh, ii, f. 107.

[79] W.S.L. 503/34; Anderton, *Edwardian Leek*, 29–32; below, this section (cinemas).

[80] Leek Libr., Johnson scrapbk. ii (2), 5/7/1–2.

[81] *Staffs. Advertiser*, 15 Oct. 1870, p. 7.

[82] Club min. bk. (1883–8) and programmes in possession of Leek and District Hist. Soc.

[83] Inf. from Mrs. D. Newall, a former member.

[84] Inf. from the club secretary, Mrs. J. Herbert.

[85] *Staffs. Advertiser*, 29 Oct. 1853, p. 4.

[86] S.R.O., D. 3226/2, no. 2308; D. 3226/4, nos. 2886, 3295; Anderton, *Edwardian Leek*, 29–30.

[87] W.S.L., Sleigh, ii, f. 5v.

[88] E. H. Bostock, *Menageries, Circuses, and Theatres* (1927), 13–14; Leek Libr., Warrington scrapbk. i, p. 103.

[89] S.R.O., D. 1283/1, p. 233.

[90] Anderton, *Edwardian Leek*, 32.

Between 1910 and 1912 a roller-skating rink at the corner of High Street and Salisbury Street was converted to a cinema. Known first as the Salisbury Electric Picture Palace and in the 1920s and 1930s as the Picture Theatre, it was called the Regal by the 1960s. It then became a bingo hall, continuing as such until 1987, when it was taken over by the Jehovah's Witnesses as their Kingdom Hall.[91]

The Majestic cinema, occupying the former Temperance Hall in Union Street, was opened in the earlier 1920s. It was gutted by fire in 1961 and was not reopened.[92]

ARTS CLUB AND FESTIVAL. Leek and District Arts Club was founded in 1948 with support from the urban district council and the Arts Council of Great Britain. That year the urban district council converted the museum in the Nicholson Institute into a meeting and concert room for the club, and in 1949 the room was opened as an arts centre, one of the first six in the country to be recognized by the Arts Council.[93] A week of concerts and other entertainments organized by the club in 1977 led to the establishment in 1978 of the Leek Arts Festival. From 1990 it lasted for four weeks.[94]

FRIENDLY SOCIETIES. In 1803 there were eleven friendly societies in Leek, with a membership of 485.[95] Most were probably associated with inns: one was established at the Swan in 1807, and several met at other inns in the town in 1830.[96]

Societies which functioned as sick and burial clubs only and did not socialize in public houses included the Humane Society established in 1819 as a benefit society for men; it was reorganized in 1839 as the Leek Independent Male Humane Society.[97] Others were Leek Wesleyan Sunday School Society (1839),[98] Leek Benevolent Burial Society (1840), a society for members of the Congregational church (1840), societies for Anglican men (1842) and women (1846), and Leek and Moorlands Provident Association (1853). The Benevolent Burial Society was by far the largest, with 7,545 members in 1876.[99] It became a general insurance society known since 1950 as Leek Assurance Collecting Society, and still existed in 1992 with an office in Russell Street.[1] The only benefit society known to have been associated with a trade was the Leek Silk Twisters' Friendly Society, in existence by 1853.[2]

Clubs associated with the national friendly societies combined welfare and socializing and met in different inns in the town. The earliest in Leek were the Victoria Court of Foresters and the Loyal Westwood Lodge of Oddfellows (Manchester Unity), both formed in 1837. Others included the Moss Rose Lodge of Free Gardeners (1840), the Pacific Court of Foresters (1841), the Rising Sun Lodge of Druids (1845), the Prince Albert Lodge of Oddfellows (1853), the Highfield Moss Rose Lodge of Free Gardeners (1857), the Moorlands Lodge of Oddfellows (1857), and the Royal Victoria Lodge of Oddfellows (1859). It was estimated in 1865 that the clubs had nearly 1,700 members, almost a fifth of the town's population.[3] The three lodges of Oddfellows formed in the 1850s belonged to the Grand United Order and were amalgamated in 1901 under the name of the Moorlands Lodge. The lodge was closed in 1964.[4] The Pride of the Moorlands Lodge of the Order of Sisters, formed in 1846,[5] was affiliated to the Independent Order of Oddfellows (Manchester Unity) in 1912, and in 1974 it became part of the Unity's Loyal Westwood Lodge. In 1992 that lodge became an independent club called Leek Westwood Friendly Society.[6]

In 1829 two friendly societies, one for men and the other for women, celebrated a feast day on the first Friday in August. The members walked through the town, attended a sermon in St. Edward's church, and then had separate dinners in the Swan and Red Lion inns. Friendly societies which paraded in 1830 carried banners which displayed their emblems and were accompanied by a band. In 1831 the societies paraded on the last Thursday in July, and the town's factories were closed for the day. Celebrations probably continued on the Friday, as they did in 1833.[7] By 1846 the first Friday in August was the customary day for the parade, a date that was probably chosen to coincide with the Stoke wakes: the event attracted many people who came from the Potteries by canal boat. The lodges of the national friendly societies also took part in the parade by 1846. Known as Club Day by 1860, the occasion became more notable for an afternoon procession of Sunday school children, transferred in 1859 from its traditional date of the first Sunday in September. Only one friendly society paraded on Club Day in 1862, the others finding the cost too great, but in 1864 there was renewed participation. Some societies again paraded by 1882, but in later years their

91 Ibid. 28, 30–2; *Kelly's Dir. Staffs.* (1912 and edns. to 1936); inf. from Mr. Ray Poole of Leek.
92 *Kelly's Dir. Staffs.* (1924); V. Priestman, *Leek Remembered* (priv. print. 1980), 34. For a photograph of the exterior see L. Porter, *Leek Thirty Years Ago* (Clifton, Ashbourne, 1991), no. 47.
93 P. V. Smith, *Nicholson Institute, Leek* (Staffs. County Libr. 1984), 61; *Leek & District Arts Club 1948–58* (Leek, 1958). 94 *Leek Post & Times,* 2 May 1990, suppl.
95 *Abstract of Returns Relating to Poor,* H.C. 98, pp. 472–3 (1803–4), xiii.
96 S.R.O., Q/SO/24, f. 106v.; W.S.L., CB/Leek/51; *Macclesfield Courier & Herald,* 7 Aug. 1830, p. 2.
97 Printed announcement in S.R.O., D. 1114/1; *Rep. Chief Registrar of Friendly Socs. 1876, App. P,* H.C. 429-I, p. 403 (1877), lxxvii.

98 Printed announcement in S.R.O., D. 1183/1/6.
99 *Rep. Chief Registrar of Friendly Socs. 1876,* 403.
1 *Ann. Reps.* in society's office. Mr. J. Haywood, the office manager, is thanked for his help.
2 *Staffs. Advertiser,* 22 Oct. 1853, p. 4.
3 *Rep. Chief Registrar of Friendly Socs. 1876,* 403; *Leek Times,* 18 Mar. 1899 (cutting in W.S.L. 499/43); W.S.L., Sleigh scrapbk. i, f. 57.
4 *Staffs. Advertiser,* 13 June 1908, p. 6; inf. from the Grand United Order's head office, Manchester.
5 *Staffs. Advertiser,* 10 Jan. 1874, p. 5.
6 Inf. from the Independent Order's head office, Manchester, and from the secretary of the former Loyal Westwood Lodge, Mr. R. Pedlar.
7 *Macclesfield Courier & Herald,* 8 Aug. 1829, p. 2; 7 Aug. 1830, p. 2; 6 Aug. 1831, p. 6; 10 Aug. 1833, p. 2.

involvement seems to have become only occasional and was last recorded in 1901.[8]

FREEMASONS. In 1992 Leek had two lodges of Freemasons, St. Edward's formed in 1863 and Dieu-la-cresse formed in 1920. In 1926 the Congregational manse in King Street was converted into a masonic hall, which was extended in 1933 and was still used in 1992.[9]

TEMPERANCE SOCIETY. Leek Total Abstinence (later Temperance) Society was formed in 1836 by Charles Carus Wilson. The society established a Rechabite tent in 1839.[10] By 1856 it had a lecture room in Stockwell Street,[11] and in 1864 it converted the former Congregational chapel in Union Street into a general purpose hall.[12] The society supported the opening of a coffee house in the Haywood Street cattle market in 1878.[13]

NEWSROOMS. In 1817 a newsroom was established on the ground floor of the town hall in the market place. It remained there until 1871.[14] There was a commercial newsroom in Stockwell Street in 1850.[15] Newsrooms for working men were opened at Ball Haye Green in 1872, at no. 13 Market Place in 1873, and in the former soup kitchen in Stockwell Street in 1875.[16]

POLITICAL AND SOCIAL CLUBS. A Conservative Association was formed in 1872. In 1887 it moved to new premises on the site of the Church inn in Church Street, designed in a Tudor style by J. G. Smith. The club remained there until it was dissolved in 1947. The clubhouse was demolished in 1972.[17]

A Liberal Club was opened at no. 8 Russell Street in 1880. In 1882 it moved next door into a building recently vacated by the town's improvement commissioners and remodelled for the club by W. Sugden & Son. Known as Leek Central Liberal Club in 1897, it moved in 1898 into a former silk factory in Market Street, redesigned by Larner Sugden. Active politically until 1921, the club continued to function in 1992 as a social club called Leek Central Club.[18]

In the later 1890s a Liberal Club for working men was opened in Mill Street. By 1898 it occupied the former police station in West Street,[19] where it remained in 1992 as West Street Working Men's Club.

The opening of the Ball Haye Green newsroom in 1872 led to the establishment of a working men's institute by 1873.[20] It is not known where the institute first met, but in 1926 a clubhouse designed by Wilfred Ingram was built in Ball Haye Green Road opposite Prince Street. It remained in use in 1992 as Ball Haye Green Working Men's Club.[21]

Rules for a non-political and non-sectarian organization called the Union Club were drawn up on temperance principles probably in 1878; the club's meeting place was Union Buildings, opened that year in Market Street. The club presumably closed in 1884 when the premises were sold, if not earlier.[22] Leek Progressive Club was established possibly in the 1880s, with the architect Larner Sugden as its secretary. The club, which met in Silk Street, was short-lived.[23]

VOLUNTEERS. A troop of volunteer cavalry was raised in Leek in 1794 as part of the Staffordshire Regiment of Gentlemen and Yeomanry. It was supplemented by a troop of infantry, recorded in 1810 and probably first raised in 1804. The combined troop was disbanded in 1829 but was revived in 1842 following the Chartist disturbances earlier that year. Styled the Leek and Moorlands troop and later part of the Queen's Own Royal Yeomanry, it was disbanded in 1888.[24]

A company of rifle volunteers was formed in 1859.[25] By 1872 it had a drill room, known as the Armoury, in Ford Street, to which a reading room and gymnasium were added in 1877.[26] By 1894 the volunteers used the upper storey of a converted building in the Haywood Street cattle market.[27] Concern at the volunteers' lack of shooting skill led to the formation in 1872 of the Leek Volunteer Shooting Club, with butts on land south of Wall Grange Farm, in Longsdon.[28]

GARDENING SOCIETIES. Leek Operative Floral Society existed by 1848.[29] Also a horticultural society by 1851, it was known in 1859 as

8 *Staffs. Advertiser*, 15 Aug. 1846, p. 3; 11 Aug. 1860, p. 4; 9 Aug. 1862, p. 4; 13 Aug. 1864, p. 4; 5 Aug. 1882, p. 5; 3 Aug. 1901, p. 5; above, this section (Sunday Sch. Festival).
9 *Staffs. Advertiser*, 8 Aug. 1863, p. 4; inf. from the Provincial Grand Lodge of Staffs., Wolverhampton, and from the secretary of St. Edward's Lodge.
10 W.S.L., Sleigh scrapbk. ii, ff. 18, 29; Leek Libr., Johnson scrapbk. ii (2), 5/23; *Staffs. Advertiser*, 26 Oct. 1839, p. 3; 14 Aug. 1841, p. 3.
11 Above, prot. nonconf. (Methodists: New Connexion).
12 Below, this section (public halls).
13 *Staffs. Advertiser*, 16 Nov. 1878, p. 7; *Leek News*, Dec. 1933 (copy in Leek Libr.).
14 *Olde Leeke*, i. 2, 4; below, this section (public halls).
15 *P.O. Dir. Staffs.* (1850).
16 *Staffs. Advertiser*, 25 May 1872, p. 7; 31 May 1873, p. 7; 16 Oct. 1875, p. 7.
17 Ibid. 25 May 1872, p. 6; S.R.O., D. 1358/A/2/1/1; D. 1358/A/2/2/1, shares prospectus, 1886; Leek Libr., newspaper cuttings 1968–72, pp. 77–8.
18 S.R.O., D. 3188/1/3; *Leek Central Club* (Leek, 1980).
19 Leek Libr., newspaper cuttings 1980 (2), pp. 6, 11; *Leek Annual* (1898), p. [19].
20 W.S.L., Sleigh scrapbk. ii, f. 98; Leek Libr., Johnson scrapbk. iii, p. 235.
21 S.R.O., D. 3188/1/4.
22 W.S.L., CB/Leek/42; below, this section (public halls).
23 Leek Libr., Johnson scrapbk. i (2), D/6/4; iii, p. 229.
24 *Olde Leeke*, i. 179–80; ii. 89–95; P. Anderton and C. Walton, *Leek Volunteers* (Leek and Moorlands Hist. Trust, n.d.); *Staffs. Advertiser*, 3 Sept. 1842, p. 3; S.R.O., D. 1300/1/10–11.
25 *Staffs. Advertiser*, 31 Dec. 1859, p. 4; 25 Feb. 1860, p. 4.
26 Ibid. 24 Mar. 1877, p. 5; S.R.O., D. 3226/2, no. 2430.
27 Leek Improvement Com. *Reps.* (1894), 23; above, econ. hist. (markets and fairs).
28 *Staffs. Advertiser*, 18 May 1872, p. 4; O.S. Map 6", Staffs. VIII. SW. (1889 edn.).
29 S.R.O., D. 538/D/3/10, p. 163.

Leek Original Floral and Horticultural Society. From 1849 its annual show was held at the Blue Ball inn in Mill Street, still the venue in 1901.[30] Leek Horticultural Society existed in 1852 and was re-formed in 1854 as Leek Floral and Horticultural Society.[31]

A rose society was established in 1872 and a British fern society in 1892, the latter promoted by John Robinson of Westwood Hall. By 1902 the two societies had been amalgamated as Leek Rose and Fern Society.[32]

LEEK EMBROIDERY SOCIETY. As part of a national movement to improve methods of embroidery Elizabeth Wardle, the wife of the Leek silk dyer Thomas Wardle, established the Leek Embroidery Society (also known later as the Leek School of Embroidery) in 1879 or 1880. Using naturally dyed silks or other materials from the Wardle factory, the society produced both designs and finished articles. Its founders did not conceive it as a commercial business, but demand was such that some of the profit was used to employ embroideresses. Items were sold in London, at first through a short-lived shop in Bond Street opened in 1883 by Thomas Wardle and W. S. Brough, and later through agencies. There was also a shop in St. Edward Street, in Leek, next to the Wardles' home. Elizabeth Wardle died in 1902, and the society's output rapidly declined. Products which made use of the society's designs continued to be sold in the Leek shop until it was closed in the 1930s.[33]

CIVIC AND HISTORICAL SOCIETIES. Leek and District Civic Society was formed in 1978. It monitors the architectural heritage and development of the town and an area covering the former townships in Leek ancient parish, together with Bagnall, Cheddleton, Consall, Horton, and Ipstones.[34]

Leek and District Historical Society was formed in 1984, and since 1988 it has published a journal called *Chronicles*. Members of the society were involved in the establishment in 1989 of the Leek and Moorlands Historical Trust, one of whose aims is the opening of a heritage centre in the town.[35]

PUBLIC HALLS. In 1806 a public hall, com-monly known as the town hall, was erected at the south end of the market place on the site of the market cross. Designed and built by Robert Emerson, a joiner, and John Radford, a stone-mason, the building consisted of a basement with two lock-ups, a ground floor originally open for use by market people but converted in 1817 into a newsroom, and an upper room for meet-ings. The cost was met by subscribers, shareholders, and (for the lock-ups) the county quarter sessions.[36] The building was too small to be of much use for public gatherings, and it was considered to be architecturally undistin-guished. Nothing came of a plan in 1847 to replace it with a grander building on another site in the market place, and it survived until its demolition in 1872.[37]

In 1857 the town's temperance society planned to build a public hall. It later bought the former Congregational chapel in Union Street, which it converted and opened as the Temperance Hall in 1864.[38] The hall was enlarged in 1871 by the addition of an orchestra pit and changing rooms.[39] In the earlier 1920s it was converted into a cinema.[40]

Union Buildings in Market Street was built in 1878 'to supply rational recreation without the temptation of drink'. Designed by Alfred Waterhouse and others, it was principally a concert hall, but it also contained games rooms and a restaurant. The venture was evidently not a success, and in 1884 the building was bought by the improvement commissioners and con-verted into a town hall.[41] It continued to be used, however, for concerts and plays, and its demo-lition in 1988 left the town without a suitable place for large-scale musical or theatrical per-formances.[42]

LIBRARIES, MUSEUM, AND ART GAL-LERY. A subscription library was formed in 1791.[43] It was evidently refounded in 1828 as the Leek Book Society, with a membership re-stricted to 30.[44] The society was probably the same as the subscription library run in 1834 by George Nall, a printer and bookseller in Sheep-market. In 1843 Nall moved to Custard Street, where in 1850 he ran a subscription library and a public circulating library.[45] What was called the Leek and Moorlands Subscription Library in 1864 was run by Nall's son Robert, who retired in 1865. The library was taken over by

30 *Staffs. Advertiser*, 15 Sept. 1849, p. 4; 20 Sept. 1851, p. 4; 3 Sept. 1859, p. 4; 21 Sept. 1901, p. 7.
31 Leek Libr., box file labelled 'Leek misc. papers', list of subscribers, 1852; Johnson scrapbk. iii, p. 203.
32 *Staffs. Advertiser*, 13 July 1872, p. 4; Leek Libr., newspaper cuttings bk. 5, p. 72; W.S.L. 495A/34, newspaper cutting, retrospect of 1902, 26 July.
33 D. G. Stuart, *Hist. of Leek Embroidery Soc.* (Keele, 1969); A. G. Jacques, *Leek Embroidery* (Staffs. Libraries, Arts & Archives, 1990).
34 Inf. from the secretary, Mr. C. A. Parrack.
35 Inf. from the secretary of the hist. soc., Mrs. C. Walton.
36 *Olde Leeke*, i. 1–2; S.R.O., D. 3359/Cruso, draft building agreement 1806; W.S.L., vol. of Staffs. treas-urer's accts. 1774 and 1777–1832, acct. for 1806; above, plate 42.
37 *Olde Leek*, i. 3–6; *Staffs. Advertiser*, 8 Mar. 1845, p. 3; S.R.O., D. 3188/1/2, rep. on public meeting, 16 Dec. 1847.
38 S.R.O., D. 538/D/3/10, p. 79; *Staffs. Advertiser*, 1 Oct. 1864, p. 4.
39 *Staffs. Advertiser*, 14 Oct. 1871, p. 6; S.R.O., D. 3188/1/2, no. 299.
40 Above, this section (cinemas).
41 *Staffs. Advertiser*, 5 Oct. 1878, p. 7; S.R.O., D. 538/D/3/10, p. 106; *The Architect*, 19 Aug. 1887, p. 107.
42 Above, this section (music; theatres).
43 Miller, *Leek*, 103; W.S.L., Sleigh scrapbk. i, f. 37; ii, f. 104v.
44 Leek Libr., Johnson scrapbk. i (2), D/35/4; S.R.O., D. 538/D/3/10, p. 299.
45 White, *Dir. Staffs.* (1834), 708; *P.O. Dir. Staffs.* (1850); above, econ. hist. (trade and ind.: printing and bookselling).

and was open to all adults living within 6 miles of Leek. From 1887 it was supported from the rates, the town's improvement commissioners having adopted the Public Libraries Act of 1855. Open access to the books had probably been introduced by 1933. The urban district council remained an independent library authority, the smallest in Staffordshire, until local government reorganization in 1974, when the library service was handed over to the county council. From 1974 to 1980 the county council also ran the museum and art gallery under an agency agreement with Staffordshire Moorlands district council, which took direct control in 1980.[47] The museum exhibits and most of the paintings were put into store, where they remained in 1992.

The three-storeyed institute building, which stands back from the street and is partly masked by the 17th-century Greystones, is of brick with stone dressings and was designed in a Queen Anne style by W. Sugden & Son. It has a tower with a domed roof and lantern covered with copper; the base of the tower contains the main entrance, which is approached by a flight of stone steps. A large window in the façade incorporates a row of four stone portrait medallions carved by Stephen Webb. A three-storeyed extension was added in 1900 to house a high school and a silk school; it too was designed by Sugden & Son, with ornamental modelling and lettering by A. Broadbent.[48]

A library for the Anglican clergy of Leek originated in a bequest of 1677.[49] There was also a library for the members of the mechanics' institute established in 1837.[50]

FIG. 29. THE NICHOLSON INSTITUTE

another Leek bookseller, James Rider, who ran it from his shop in Derby Street. It appears to have been closed by 1880.[46]

The Nicholson Institute in Stockwell Street was presented to the town by Joshua Nicholson. Conceived c. 1875 as a monument to Richard Cobden, it was opened in 1884 and combined a free library, a museum, three picture galleries, and premises for Leek's school of art. The library contained c. 6,000 volumes chosen by J. O. Nicholson, eldest son of Joshua Nicholson,

NEWSPAPERS. The weekly *Leek Times* was founded in 1870 by M. H. Miller (d. 1909). The paper was politically neutral, although Miller was a Liberal.[51] A Conservative weekly, the *Leek Post*, was founded in 1884.[52] At first published by the North Staffordshire Newspaper Co. Ltd., the paper was acquired in the late 1890s by the Leek printing firm of Hill Brothers.[53] In 1934 that firm took over the *Leek Times*, and the papers were amalgamated as the *Leek Post & Times*.[54] That paper was still published by Hill Bros. (Leek) Ltd. in 1992.

EDUCATION

THE first known schoolmaster in the town was John Lumford, who was recorded in 1568.[55] Thereafter there were at least one or two schoolmasters at any one time.[56] A few may have offered grammar schooling: Lumford was a graduate and presumably competent to teach the classics, and a school held in the north aisle of the parish church in the late 16th and early 17th

century apparently included boys aged 14 and 15.[57] In 1697 the Staffordshire Quakers set up a boys' boarding school at Leek, which lasted c. 50 years. A charity English school was established in the town in 1713 but had ceased to function by the early 19th century. A grammar school was opened in 1720 but remained small and poor.[58] Boys from the Leek area who were

46 *Olde Leek*, i. 240–1; *P.O. Dir. Staffs.* (1864 and later edns.); *Kelly's Dir. Staffs.* (1880); S.R.O., D. 538/D/3/10, pp. 299–300.

47 P. V. Smith, *Nicholson Institute, Leek* (Staffs. County Libr. 1984).   48 Ibid.; *Staffs. Advertiser*, 4 Aug. 1900, p. 5.

49 Above, churches (St. Edward's).

50 Below, educ. (further and adult educ.).

51 Leek Libr., newspaper cuttings ii, f. 32. There is an incomplete run in the Brit. Libr.

52 *Kelly's Dir. Staffs.* (1900), adverts. p. 69.

53 Ibid. (1888; 1896; 1900); R. K. Bacon, *Sir Enoch Hill* (1934), 55. There is an incomplete run from 1890 in the Brit. Libr., and a complete run from 1911 in Leek Libr.

54 *Leek Post & Times*, 27 Oct. 1934. There are complete runs in Brit. Libr. and Leek Libr.   55 Sleigh, *Leek*, 6.

56 e.g. presentments in L.J.R.O., B/V/1/16–17, 23, 30, 32, 37, 57, 62, 77, 80, 84, 89A.

57 Ibid. B/C/5/1663, Leek; 1664, Leek.

58 Below, this section (primary and secondary schs.; private schs.).

intended for the universities continued to be sent to school elsewhere as they had been in the 17th century.[59]

Large-scale popular education in Leek came with the Sunday schools. In the earlier 19th century Leek was one of the small industrial towns where Sunday schools proved popular with the workers, and they provided most of the formal education in the town.[60] John Jones was appointed master of an Anglican Sunday school in 1787. He left Leek in 1791, and nothing is known about the school.[61] In 1797 a Methodist established a non-denominational Sunday school. The Anglicans co-operated in its work until 1813, when they set up their own Sunday school. The Congregationalists formed a Sunday school c. 1830, the Roman Catholics by 1834, the Primitive Methodists in or shortly after 1836, and the New Connexion Methodists evidently in 1857.[62] At the time of the Anglican withdrawal the non-denominational school was controlled by the Wesleyan Methodists, who built a schoolhouse in West Street in 1815 and another in Ball Haye Street in 1828. In 1841 Leek's six Sunday schools had 1,607 pupils on the books and an attendance of c. 80 per cent; there were 168 teachers.[63] The Wesleyans had the most pupils: in the late 1820s there were over 1,000 on the roll at their two schools, and in the 1830s and 1840s almost 1,000.[64] On the morning of Census Sunday 1851 a total of 1,049 Sunday school children attended the town's churches and chapels (523 Wesleyan Methodists, 336 Anglicans, 90 Congregationalists, 51 Primitive Methodists, and 49 Roman Catholics). In the afternoon 791 children attended; again the Wesleyan Methodists (404) and the Anglicans (278) predominated.[65] From the 1840s day schools were established in the town to supplement or replace the system of secular instruction offered at the Sunday schools. Reading and writing were still taught at West Street Sunday school in the 1850s, and reading at a Wesleyan Sunday school in Mill Street in 1866–7.[66] The important part which Sunday schools had played in the religious, educational, and social life of the town was still marked in the early 1990s by the children's annual procession.[67]

Rivalry between denominations and the generosity of a number of wealthy benefactors ensured that enough voluntary day schools were built in the town to make the formation of a school board for Leek unnecessary. There was a particularly vigorous period of building in the late 1860s, after the passage of the 1867 Workshops Regulation Act. A survey of 1861 had revealed that a large number of young children were employed in the Leek silk industry, many of them working at home or in other places not subject to factory inspection. After the Act the Leek improvement commissioners set about ensuring that all working children received some schooling.[68] In 1871, out of 2,072 children aged 5–13 living in the area covered by the Leek Improvement Act of 1855, 1,275 were at school full-time, 401 worked in factories or workshops and attended school half-time, 102 worked full-time in trades where there was still no legal obligation to ensure that child workers received some schooling, and 50 were 'street arabs'. Of those aged 11–13 there were 244 legally employed full-time in factories or in silk winding or throwing.[69] In 1882 the town's 12 public day schools had an average attendance of 2,043: 960 attended Anglican schools, 615 Wesleyan, 363 Congregationalist, and 105 Roman Catholic.[70]

From 1876 the improvement commissioners were represented on the school-attendance committee of Leek poor-law union, and between 1894 and 1902 the urban district council had its own school-attendance committee.[71] Teachers attributed some absenteeism to the fact that Leek had a large female labour-force: because mothers were at work all day in the mills children, especially girls, were kept at home to look after brothers and sisters and to run errands.[72]

Even before the county council became the local education authority in 1903 it supported further education in Leek and had made grants to a girls' high school in the town. In 1906 it took over a mixed high school, and Leek's first council school was built in 1914. For 20 years its work at Leek was hampered by the persistence of the half-time system. The number of children attending school half-time had greatly increased after 1867. Leek teachers complained from the 1870s about half-time attendance and about the pressure put on children by parents and employers to leave school for the mills.[73] In 1908 there still some 250 half-timers, but a suggestion that two schools should be set aside for their exclusive use came to nothing.[74] In 1913 Leek was the only place in the administrative county where children attended half-time,[75] and there were still half-timers in Leek schools until such attendance was brought to an end nationally in 1922.[76]

[59] *Admissions to Gonville and Caius Coll., Camb., 1559–1679*, ed. J. and S. C. Venn, 183; *Admissions to St. John's Coll., Camb.*, i, ed. J. E. B. Mayor, 38; ii, ed. Mayor, 14, 35; iii, ed. R. F. Scott, 128, 139, 143; J. Peile, *Biog. Reg. of Christ's Coll.* ii. 242; *Complete Peerage*, viii. 332.

[60] T. L. Laqueur, *Religion and Respectability: Sunday Schs. and Working Class Culture 1780–1850*, 100, 104.

[61] *Olde Leeke*, i. 98–9.

[62] T. E. Brigden, *Old Leek Sunday Sch. 1787–1897* (Leek, 1897), 26–7; *Staffs. Sentinel*, 21 Mar. 1857, p. 4.

[63] Brigden, *Old Leek Sunday Sch.* 15; *2nd Rep. Com. Child. Employment, App. Pt. I* [431], pp. C19 and c94, H.C. (1843), xiv.

[64] S.R.O., D. 1114/1, ann. reps.; Laqueur, *Religion and Respectability*, 46–7, 101.

[65] P.R.O., HO 129/372/2/1.

[66] Brigden, *Old Leek Sunday Sch.* 23; *Rep. and Accts. of Leek Ragged Sch. 1866–7* (copy in W.S.L., Sleigh scrapbk.

i, f. 128); below, this section (primary and secondary schs.).

[67] Above, social and cultural activities (Sunday Sch. Festival).

[68] *V.C.H. Staffs.* ii. 214.

[69] W.S.L., Sleigh scrapbk. ii, f. 71.

[70] S.R.O., D. 1141/1, newspaper cutting 1 Dec. 1883.

[71] Leek U.D.C. *Fifty Years of Municipal Govt. in Leek, 1855 to 1905* (Leek, 1905), 41.

[72] S.R.O., D. 3657/1/1, p. 166; D. 3657/1/3, pp. 206, 260–1, 300.

[73] Ibid. D. 3657/1/1 and 3, *passim*; D. 3657/5/1, cttee. mins. 10 Mar. 1870; *V.C.H. Staffs.* ii. 214.

[74] S.R.O., CEL/64/1, printed notice 18 Feb. 1908.

[75] G. Balfour, *Ten Years of Staffs. Educ. 1903–13* (Stafford, 1913), 77.

[76] S.R.O., D. 1167/3, pp. 194, 200, 205; D. 3657/1/4, pp. 146–7, 149, 151; S. J. Curtis, *Hist. of Educ. in Gt. Brit.* (1948), 247.

Leek was omitted from the county council's plans of 1919 for reorganizing elementary schools apparently because 'the denominational difficulty would be great'.[77] In 1931 the eight elementary schools in the town were reorganized as junior and senior schools.[78] When over the next few years the schools in neighbouring villages became junior schools, older children were brought into Leek by bus. With the closure of small country schools after the Second World War, many younger children were also brought into Leek, and harsh Moorland winters caused problems with transport.[79] Comprehensive secondary education was introduced in 1965. In 1981 Leek was one of the areas in which the county council adopted a three-tier system of schools, involving first schools for children under the age of 9, middle schools for children aged 9–13, and high schools for children aged 13–18. The system was still in force there in 1994.[80]

PRIMARY AND SECONDARY SCHOOLS.

ENGLISH SCHOOL. In 1713 Rebecca, wife of Sir Samuel Moyer, Bt., established an English school at Leek, the birthplace of her father John Jolliffe. The school was for 50 poor children of Leek and Cheddleton, who were to be given three years' tuition. A master was appointed, whom she instructed to pay strict attention to his pupils' morals and to ensure that they attended church every Sunday and holy day. She paid him £20 a year and undertook to provide new books every three years and to buy bibles as leaving presents for the children.[81]

In 1717 Lady Moyer gave in trust for the school a 90-year annuity of £25 and amplified her plan for the school. The master, who was to be a layman, was to receive £20 a year for teaching the 50 children to read and write. He and the children were to be chosen by a board of governors including the vicar and churchwardens. The children were to be admitted at the age of six and to remain at the school until they could read and write. The vicar was to be paid £1 a year for catechizing them, and £4 a year was to be spent on bibles, primers, and catechisms. Lady Moyer's will, proved 1724, confirmed the provisions and asked that the annuity should be used to buy land to endow the school, a request that was not carried out.[82] In 1751 the master was teaching 50 children the catechism and taking them regularly to church.[83] The school seems to have ceased by 1807, when the annuity expired, and it may have been wound up by 1786.[84]

LEEK GRAMMAR SCHOOL. In May 1720 a group of 22 townsmen, aware of the need for a grammar school, successfully petitioned the bishop to license as a grammar-school master Thomas Bourne, who had settled in Leek the previous January.[85] Lord Macclesfield built a house on Clerk Bank for the school in 1723.[86] In 1733 the *London Magazine* published a poem by 'H. C.', lauding Bourne's skill as a teacher of the classics.[87] He had some 40 pupils in 1751[88] and died in 1771.[89]

The school had no endowment. The earls of Macclesfield appointed Bourne's successors, presumably in return for having built the schoolhouse, and remained the owners of the building, the master paying a peppercorn rent and being responsible for the upkeep.[90] For many years his only income apart from fees came from the charity of George Roades (d. 1713), rector of Blithfield and son of a vicar of Leek, whose will provided for the establishment of an English school at Leek for poor children aged 6–10. Eventually enough money was received to buy £323 stock, the income from which was used to pay the master of the grammar school to teach poor children to read. By the early 19th century six children at a time were taught free.[91]

By then any attempt to maintain a purely classical syllabus had probably long been abandoned. In 1825 the school offered 'classical, mathematical, and commercial instruction'.[92] The school could generally support both a master and an usher only if one or both had other employment. Jeremiah Barnes, appointed master in 1832, employed as usher the organist at St. Edward's, where Barnes was assistant curate.[93] E. F. T. Ribbans, master in the 1850s, was also curate at St. Edward's and chaplain of the workhouse.[94] He left Leek in 1860 after well publicized accusations that he had fathered an illegitimate child.[95] His successor, P. N. Lawrence, was also workhouse chaplain and perpetual curate at St. Luke's.[96]

In 1865 Lawrence had 24 boys; 4 were boarders, and 6 or 7 of the others came from outside Leek. He taught six poor boys free in return for the income (£9 13s. 10d.) from Roades's bequest, but the arrangement was to end when Lawrence left. Himself a good teacher, he could not afford an assistant and dealt with boys of all ages, abilities, and requirements. The schoolhouse was in poor repair and no longer suitable. There was little demand in Leek for a traditional grammar-school education; parents who wanted one sent their sons elsewhere. Nevertheless the inspector for the royal commission on grammar

77 S.R.O., CEM/2/15, no. 52, p. 5.
78 Staffs. C.C. *Record for 1930*, 861, 866–9.
79 S.R.O., CEK/21/2, pp. 19–20; S.R.O., D. 3133/3/1, p. 171; D. 3133/3/3, prelim. pp.; *Leek Post & Times*, 26 Sept. 1990, p. 1; 15 Jan. 1991, p. 3; Leek and Dist. Schoolmasters' Assoc. *Which Way?* (1970), 21.
80 Leek Libr., newspaper cuttings 1982 (1), pp. 36–7; inf. from Staffs. C.C. Educ. Dept.
81 L.J.R.O., B/A/11B/Leek; G.E.C. *Baronetage*, iv. 185; H. G. H. Jolliffe, *Jolliffes of Staffs.* (priv. print. 1892), 6–7.
82 S.R.O., D. 5041, pp. 31–2; *13th Rep. Com. Char.* 383–4.
83 L.J.R.O., B/V/5/1751, Leek.
84 *13th Rep. Com. Char.* 383. The charity is not mentioned in *Char. Dons.* 1152–3.
85 L.J.R.O., B/A/4/28, 18 May 1720; B/A/11B/Leek.

86 Inscription on building. For the building see above, general hist. (18th cent.), and plate 59.
87 *Lond. Mag.* (1733), 583, reprinted with some errors in *Olde Leeke*, i. 135–7.   88 L.J.R.O., B/V/5/1751, Leek.
89 S.R.O., D. 1040/5/15, 11 June 1771.
90 *13th Rep. Com. Char.* 383; *Hist. of Leek High Sch.* (n.d. but 1960 or 1961), 4.
91 *13th Rep. Com. Char.* 383.
92 *Staffs. Advertiser*, 8 Jan. 1825.
93 Ibid. 2 Mar. 1861, p. 4; W.S.L., Sleigh scrapbk. ii, f. 97v.   94 White, *Dir. Staffs.* (1851), 723–5.
95 *Staffs. Advertiser*, 25 Feb. 1860, p. 5; 3 Mar. 1860, p. 7; 10 Mar. 1860, p. 7.
96 Ibid. 5 May 1860, p. 4; 5 Feb. 1870, p. 4; *P.O. Dir. Staffs.* (1864; 1868).

schools recommended that the school should continue as a feeder for a high school in some other town.[97]

Lawrence was succeeded in 1870 by Joseph Sykes, master of the private Leek Commercial School.[98] Shortly afterwards the income from the Roades charity was assigned to one of the town's National schools.[99] Joseph, and later John, Sykes ran the school for the next 30 years.[1] A department for girls and small boys was opened in or shortly before 1878 under Miss M. L. Sykes.[2] It was presumably the girls' grammar school which was being run in conjunction with the grammar school in 1889.[3] The grammar school had c. 65 pupils in the early 1890s and c. 45 in the later 1890s,[4] and it was closed in 1900.[5] In 1919 the earl of Macclesfield sold the building,[6] which in the early 1990s was used by various voluntary organizations.

WEST STREET WESLEYAN SCHOOL, later MOUNT METHODIST (CONTROLLED) FIRST SCHOOL. In 1797 Charles Ball, a Leek Methodist, began to hold a Sunday school in his house. Numbers soon became too great for the house: in 1800 there were 200 pupils and in 1801 c. 300, of whom 22 were being taught to write. The school moved successively to Mount Pleasant Methodist chapel, the grammar school, and the assembly room at the Swan inn. In 1815 the Wesleyans opened a schoolroom in West Street.[7] By 1817 the school, advertised as non-denominational, had 536 pupils, including 19 adults; there continued to be a few adult pupils until 1824. In 1826 over 900 children attended, and in the 1830s and 1840s, after another Wesleyan Methodist Sunday school had been opened in Ball Haye Street, there were still over 400 at West Street.[8] The school was rebuilt on a larger scale in 1854, and in 1855 a mixed day school was opened in the building. Reading and writing continued to be taught at the Sunday school until 1856.[9]

In 1855 the day school had 40 pupils, who paid 3d. or 4d. a week; the 4d. pupils were taught grammar besides reading, writing, and arithmetic. The school received a government grant.[10] The building was extended in 1881, and in 1885 West Street was a mixed and infants' school of 458 children.[11] In 1897–8 the building was remodelled and improved at government insistence.[12] In 1930 there were 440 on the books. West Street became a junior school in 1931. Although num-

bers were reduced, the building was inadequate, and in 1938 the managers proposed closure because they could not afford the improvements required. The outbreak of the Second World War foiled plans for alternative accommodation.[13] The school took controlled status in 1949 and shortly afterwards was renamed Mount Methodist school.[14] There were c. 300 on the books in the later 1950s and the later 1960s. Thereafter the school generally had c. 200 pupils until 1981, when it became a first school and numbers dropped to c. 100. It was closed in 1983.[15]

ST. EDWARD'S NATIONAL SCHOOLS, Clerk Bank. An Anglican Sunday school on the Madras system was established in 1813, and c. 100 children joined it from the non-denominational Sunday school. It was held in the grammar school and was supported by subscriptions and by collections at St. Edward's church. In 1834 Lord Macclesfield gave part of the grammar school's playground as a site, money was raised by subscription and grants from government and the National Society, and a two-storeyed brick building with stone dressings and some Gothick fenestration was erected to the design of William Rawlins. The trustees were authorized to admit poor children from Leek or any other place within 2 miles of Leek parish.[16] The new Sunday school was opened in 1835 with a salaried master and mistress, 34 monitors, and 265 children (141 girls and 124 boys). The unusual predominance of girls over boys may have arisen because the mistress as well as the master was allowed to teach writing.[17] A lending library for teachers, pupils, and parents was set up in 1836.[18] In 1837 there were 244 boys and 243 girls on the roll.[19]

In 1843 the trustees opened day schools for boys and girls in the building to supplement the Sunday school. The Chartist disturbances of 1842, in which the master and mistress of the Sunday school were marginally involved, seem to have strengthened the feeling that Anglican day schools for working-class children were needed in the town. A salaried master and mistress taught both the day and the Sunday schools.[20] The curriculum was to include reading, writing, and arithmetic, with some natural history and geography for certain children and knitting and sewing for girls; fees were to be 1d.–3d. a week.[21] The day schools united with the National Society in 1844.[22] In 1846, with grants from the society and government, the

97 *Rep. Schs. Enq. Com., vol. xv* [3966-XIV], pp. 425–6, H.C. (1867–8), xxviii (12).
98 *Staffs. Advertiser,* 5 Feb. 1870, p. 4; 19 Feb. 1870, p. 7.   99 *Staffs. Endowed Chars.* 80.
1 *P.O. Dir. Staffs.* (1872; 1876); *Kelly's Dir. Staffs.* (1880 and edns. to 1900).   2 *Staffs. Advertiser,* 5 Jan. 1878, p. 1.
3 Leek Libr., Johnson scrapbk. iii, p. 241.
4 *Kelly's Dir. Staffs.* (1892; 1896; 1900).
5 *Leek High Sch.* 9–10.
6 *Leek Post,* 12 July 1919.
7 S.R.O., D. 1114/1, copy of *Rep. Methodist Sunday Sch., Leek, 1800*; Brigden, *Old Leek Sunday Sch.* 9, 12, 15, 34.   8 S.R.O., D. 1114/1, *Reps.* 1817 sqq.
9 Brigden, *Old Leek Sunday Sch.* 18, 23, 25.
10 P.R.O., ED 7/109/206.
11 S.R.O., D. 1114/1, newspaper cutting 28 Dec. 1885, and handbk. for Japanese Bazaar Oct. 1898.
12 Ibid. notice for bazaar May 1898; S.R.O., CEL/64/1,

reps. of H.M.I. 1891–4, 1897.
13 Staffs. C.C. *Record for 1930,* 867–9; *1938,* 576.
14 S.R.O., D. 3990/1/1, loose papers.
15 Ibid. D. 3990/1/1–2, *passim.*
16 Ibid. D. 3359/St. Edward's Sunday sch. acct. bk. 1834–66, memo. of trust, subscription list, and building accts.; Wardle, *Methodist Hist.* 27; White, *Dir. Staffs.* (1834), 707. The date of the Anglican secession is given as 1812 in *Staffs. Advertiser,* 18 Sept. 1847, p. 5.
17 S.R.O., D. 3359/St. Edward's Sunday sch. acct. bk. 1844–66, mins. 1 Oct. 1835.
18 Ibid. mins. 7 Apr. 1836 sqq., 25 July 1844.
19 Ibid. mins. 28 Sept. 1837.
20 Ibid. mins. 8 Apr. 1842 sqq.; above, general hist. (earlier 19th cent.).
21 S.R.O., D. 3359/St. Edward's Sunday sch. acct. bk. 1834–66, mins 2 Feb. 1843.
22 Ibid. mins. 11 Apr. and 25 July 1844.

trustees bought three cottages and land adjoining the schoolhouse, the cottages for teachers' houses and part of the land for a playground.[23]

In 1847 the Sunday school ceased to teach writing; instead the master and two helpers gave writing lessons free on Friday evenings.[24] Numbers at the Sunday school then declined, partly, it was later suggested, because writing was no longer taught. In 1847 there was an average attendance of 343; in 1851 it was 257. Meanwhile the day schools grew slightly: average attendance was 126 in 1847 and 141 in 1851.[25] It is not clear when secular education at the Sunday school ended; the number of pupils was still falling in 1854.[26]

In 1853 the boys' and girls' day schools were merged and an infants' school was established in what had been the boys' schoolroom, beginning with 67 children.[27] A night school was started in 1860 and still existed in 1864.[28] The building was enlarged in 1862, and in 1863 separate boys' and girls' schools were again formed.[29] In 1886 the boys were moved to a new school in Britannia Street.[30] The Clerk Bank building was left to the girls and infants, and average attendance there over the next few years was c. 170.[31] It was closed in 1894–5, and the children were moved to Britannia Street.[32] The schoolhouse, the land, and the cottages were sold in 1895, and the Clerk Bank school building became the Maude Church Institute.[33]

WESLEYAN SCHOOL, Ball Haye Street. A Wesleyan Methodist Sunday school was opened in Ball Haye Street in 1828.[34] In 1840 the Wesleyans set up a day school in a room in Ball Haye Street, presumably the Sunday school. They employed a master, trained in the Lancasterian method, and a mistress. Early in 1841 there was an average attendance of 54. The children paid 6d. a week for reading, writing, and arithmetic, and 9d. a week if they were also taught grammar, history, and geography. Girls were offered free instruction in needlework, knitting, and marking clothes. The children's parents were millworkers and tradespeople. The master stated that they paid fairly regularly, although the fees were higher than in most schools.[35]

The project was probably too ambitious and expensive. The day school had apparently been closed by 1845, when an infants' school was

opened in the building. In 1859 it had an average attendance of 90. An evening school run by the organizers of the infants' school was then being held three nights a week. From 1860 the infants' school received a government grant.[36] The building was improved in 1865, when six new classrooms were built and the schoolroom was heightened.[37]

In 1872 a mixed day school with a government grant was opened on the upper floor of the building.[38] In 1878 both the mixed and the infants' schools were threatened with loss of their government grants unless the building was improved. Considerable alterations were duly made.[39] Further accommodation was provided in 1899.[40] Average attendance in 1901 was 200 in the mixed school and 83 in the infants' school.[41] Renewed government pressure for improvements to the building led to the closure of the schools in 1913.[42]

ST. MARY'S ROMAN CATHOLIC (AIDED) PRIMARY SCHOOL, Cruso Street. By 1834 there was a Sunday school connected with St. Mary's Roman Catholic chapel in Fountain Street. It had 40 pupils by 1841.[43] In 1845 a schoolhouse was built behind the chapel for a day school. It had separate rooms for boys and girls, but the children were taught together since there was scarcely enough money to pay even one teacher. The Roman Catholic priest commented: 'No books. No maps. No desks.'[44]

In 1860 a group of Irish nuns belonging to the Institute of the Blessed Virgin Mary took over St. Mary's school and its 50 pupils from the girl who had been running it. They also started an evening school and opened a private school with 17 children. When a church was opened in King Street in 1864 and the Fountain Street building was sold, the day and private schools were taught in various parts of the new church. A schoolhouse with rooms for boys, girls, and infants was built behind the church in 1871. From 1877 the school received a government grant. There was then an average attendance of 106, and the staff consisted of two nuns and three assistants.[45]

In 1930 St. Mary's was a mixed and infants' school with 194 on its books. It became a junior school in 1931.[46] It moved in 1937 to new buildings in Cruso Street, named the Monsignor A. M. Sperling Memorial School after the priest who had served at Leek from 1884 to 1923.[47] In

23 Ibid. mins. 4 Dec. 1845 sqq.; White, *Dir. Staffs.* (1851), 725.
24 S.R.O., D. 3359/St. Edward's Sunday sch. acct. bk. 1834–66, mins. 28 Jan. and 8 June 1847.
25 Ibid. mins. 19 Apr. 1851.
26 Ibid. mins. 28 Apr. 1854.
27 Ibid. mins. 2 July 1853 sqq.; P.R.O., ED 7/109/23.
28 S.R.O., D. 3359/St. Edward's Sunday sch. acct. bk. 1834–66, mins. 21 June 1860, 1 Feb. 1864.
29 Ibid. mins. 27 Feb. 1862 sqq.; *Lich. Dioc. Ch. Cal.* (1864), 147.   30 Below, this section (Leek par. ch. schs.).
31 *Kelly's Dir. Staffs.* (1888; 1892).
32 Docs. at St. Edward's ch., Leek, log bk. of St. Edward's girls' sch. 1878–94, p. 291; ibid. log. bk. of St. Edward's infants' sch. 1874–95, p. 345.
33 Docs. at St. Edward's ch., Maude Ch. Inst. min. bk. 1896–1939; W.S.L. 495A/34, Britannia St. sch. accts. 1896; above, churches (St. Edward's).
34 Above, prot. nonconf. (Methodists).
35 Leek Libr., Johnson scrapbk. i (2), D/3/4; *2nd Rep.*

Com. Child. Employment, App. Pt. I [431], p. c93, H.C. (1843), xiv.   36 P.R.O., ED 7/113/200.
37 S.R.O., D. 5123/1/18, 2 Mar. 1864 sqq.; W.S.L., Sleigh scrapbk. i, ff. 88v., 94.
38 P.R.O., ED 7/113/Leek, Brunswick Wesleyan mixed girls' sch.; S.R.O., D. 5123/1/18, 15 Dec. 1871 sqq.
39 S.R.O., D. 5123/1/18, 30 Sept. 1878 sqq.; D. 5123/1/19.
40 Ibid. D. 3133/2/1, pp. 367–70; D. 3188/1/3.
41 Ibid. D. 3133/1/4, 13 Mar. 1901.
42 Ibid. D. 3133/1/2, p. 159; D. 3133/1/5, pp. 57 sqq.; P.R.O., ED 7/109/195A.
43 *Staffs. Advertiser*, 27 Sept. 1834; White, *Dir. Staffs.* (1834), 702; *2nd Rep. Com. Child. Employment, App. Pt. I*, p. C19.
44 P.R.O., ED 7/109/198; White, *Dir. Staffs.* (1851), 724; *St. Mary's Catholic Church, Leek: Centenary 1887–1987.*
45 P.R.O., ED 7/109/198; S.R.O., D. 3188/1/2, no. 302.
46 Staffs. C.C. *Record for 1930*, 861, 867–8.
47 *Rom. Cath. Church in Leek*, 23–4; above, Rom. Cath.

1957 a separate infants' school was opened in Whitfield Street. The nuns continued to teach at both schools until they left Leek in 1980.[48]

WORKHOUSE SCHOOL. From 1839 until 1903 the Leek poor-law guardians maintained a school at the union workhouse for the children there. They employed a master and a mistress until 1854 and again from 1863 to 1868, but otherwise only a mistress. There were attempts at vocational training. In the 1840s boys were taught knitting and straw plaiting. In the late 1840s and early 1850s land was rented near the workhouse and the children were taught spade cultivation.[49]

CONGREGATIONALIST SCHOOL, Union Street. In 1845 the Congregationalists of Union Street chapel built a two-storeyed Sunday school next to the chapel. In 1846 they opened a day school for infants there, which they claimed to be the first in Leek. They obtained a mistress from the Infant School Society. After a year average attendance was c. 50, aged 2–6. The children paid pence, but the school was financed chiefly by donations and subscriptions. In 1873 it became a girls' and infants' school and began to receive a government grant.[50] In 1884 the girls at the Congregationalists' mixed school in Alsop Street were transferred to Union Street.[51] In the late 1880s and the late 1890s there was an average attendance of c. 140, which had dropped to c. 100 by c. 1910.[52] In 1908 the Board of Education considered that the building was no longer adequate,[53] and the school was closed in 1913.[54]

BALL HAYE GREEN WESLEYAN SCHOOL. A chapel used also as a Sunday school was opened by the Wesleyan Methodists at Ball Haye Green in 1846.[55] A day school was established in the building in 1870. In 1871, when there were c. 30 pupils, a certificated mistress was appointed and the managers applied for a government grant. Later that year or in 1872 the mistress, and apparently the pupils, were transferred to Brunswick Wesleyan school in Ball Haye Street.[56]

ST. LUKE'S NATIONAL SCHOOLS, later ST. LUKE'S C.E. (AIDED) PRIMARY SCHOOL, Fountain and Queen Streets. Day and Sunday schools for St. Luke's district were built in Fountain Street in 1847. Services were held in the building until the opening of St. Luke's church in 1848.[57] The promoters intended that the day school, initially for infants only, should admit older children if there were sufficient demand.[58] The school was financed by subscriptions, donations, and children's pence. Within a short time the mistress was probably teaching older girls as well as infants. From 1849 to 1852 the managers allowed a master to run his own school, presumably for boys, in a room in the building.[59] In 1851 the two schools had an average attendance of c. 150.[60]

In 1852 the managers gave the master notice to quit, and in 1853 they opened their own boys' school in the room which he had vacated. The schools then began to receive a government grant.[61] The new master, Joseph Sykes, enrolled some middle-class boys, who were charged higher fees and for additional payment were taught subjects such as Latin and algebra. Sykes took boarders, at one point jeopardizing the school's grant by not following government regulations.[62] In 1858 he engaged the school's first pupil teacher, William Beresford, later vicar of St. Luke's.[63] Sykes successfully demanded pay rises in 1854 and 1856.[64] In 1860 he resigned to open his own school.[65]

An evening school was being held at Fountain Street in 1861.[66] In 1863–4 the day schools had an average attendance of c. 200.[67] By the late 1860s the building was overcrowded and the schools were threatened with the loss of their government grant.[68] In 1872 a new boys' school designed by William Sugden was completed, with entrances in Queen Street and Earl Street.[69] The girls and infants, c. 150 in number, remained in the Fountain Street building. A separate infants' school was formed in 1873.[70] In 1894, after the boys' building had been remodelled, the girls' and boys' schools were merged there; the infants were left in Fountain Street.[71] In the early years of the 20th century the mixed school had over 300 children on its books and the infants' school over 200.[72]

In 1931 the mixed school became a junior school, with 256 on its books. Thereafter numbers dwindled in both the junior and the infants' schools. In 1943 the two were merged to form a junior and infants' school with 130 Leek children

48 Rom. Cath. Church in Leek, 27; St. Mary's Cath. Church in Leek: Centenary.
49 P. Walton, A Peep into the Past (Leek, n.d., dedication dated 1989), 71–5.
50 P.R.O., ED 7/113/197; Leek Libr., Johnson scrapbk. i (2), D/3/3; Staffs. Advertiser, 3 Apr. 1847, p. 5.
51 Below, this section (Hargreaves sch.).
52 Kelly's Dir. Staffs. (1888); Brit. and Foreign School Soc. 92nd Ann. Rep. (1897), 377; 106th Ann. Rep. (1911), 227.
53 S.R.O., CEL/64/1, printed notice 18 Feb. 1908.
54 P.R.O., ED 7/109/195A.
55 Above, prot. nonconf. (Methodists).
56 P.R.O., ED 7/113/Leek, Ball Haye Green Wesleyan sch.; ED 7/113/Leek, Brunswick Wesleyan mixed girls' sch.
57 S.R.O., D. 3657/5/1, mins. 12 July 1847; above, churches (St. Luke's).
58 S.R.O., D. 3657/5/4.
59 Ibid. D. 3657/5/1, mins. 12 July 1847, 25 Sept. 1849, 27 Sept. 1852; ibid. accts. 1847–8.
60 White, Dir. Staffs. (1851), 725.

61 P.R.O., ED 7/109/205; S.R.O., D. 3657/5/1, mins. 5 June 1855.
62 S.R.O., D. 3657/5/1, mins. 21 Mar., 29 June 1854, 5 June 1855, 15 Jan. 1856.
63 Ibid. mins. 30 Jan. 1858; Staffs. Advertiser, 14 Oct. 1922, p. 3.
64 S.R.O., D. 3657/5/1, mins. 19 Sept. 1854, 9 Aug., 27 Sept., 11 Nov. 1856.
65 Ibid. mins. 29 Mar., 23 Apr. 1860; below, this section (private schs.).
66 Staffs. Advertiser, 26 Jan. 1861, p. 4.
67 W.S.L. 495A/34, copy of sch. accts. 1863–4.
68 W.S.L., Sleigh scrapbk. ii, f. 20.
69 S.R.O., D. 3657/5/3; Staffs. Advertiser, 25 Feb. 1871, p. 7; 27 Jan. 1872, p. 8.
70 S.R.O., D. 3657/1/1, pp. 1, 4, 15, 60–1; D. 3657/5/1, mins. 10 Apr., 24 July 1873.
71 S.R.O., D. 3657/1/3, pp. 170–1, 179–81; Staffs. Advertiser, 28 July 1894, p. 7; 18 Aug. 1894, p. 4; Lich. Dioc. Mag. (1896), 53.
72 S.R.O., D. 3657/1/4, p. 47; D. 3657/1/7, pp. 180, 199.

and 12 evacuees on its books. Numbers recovered in the 1950s, but from the early 1960s there were never more than 100 on the books. The school was closed in 1981.[73]

ALL SAINTS' C.E. (AIDED) FIRST SCHOOL, Cheadle Road, formerly COMPTON SCHOOL. In 1863 a school-church was opened in Compton from St. Luke's, and the building continued to be used for worship until the opening of All Saints' church in 1887. The school was initially an infants' school and received a government grant as such, but by the early 1870s it was also taking older children. The building was extended in 1872, 1883, and 1891. There were over 400 pupils in the early 1900s. The building became overcrowded, and the managers were forced to cut numbers. In 1930 there were 361 on the roll. Compton became a junior mixed and infants' school in 1931. By the early 1960s there were fewer than 150 pupils. The managers were finding it increasingly difficult to maintain the building to the required standard, and parents were sending their children elsewhere. In 1965 the school moved into new buildings further south in Cheadle Road. It became a first school in 1981. A nursery class was opened in 1994.[74]

RAGGED SCHOOL, later MILL STREET WESLEYAN SCHOOL. In 1865 a ragged school was opened in a cottage in Belle Vue Road. Demand for places was great, and six weeks later the school was moved to two adjoining houses in Mill Street.[75] In 1866–7, when it was held on Sundays and for two hours every weekday evening, there were 120 on the books. On Sundays reading was taught by 20 unpaid teachers, and there was an average attendance of 80. At the night school a master and mistress, each paid £6 a year, taught writing and arithmetic, and the mistress also taught girls to sew.[76]

In 1869 the Leek Wesleyan Methodist quarterly meeting agreed to take charge of the school, following a request from the school's committee of management.[77] The school was moved into a newly built Wesleyan Methodist school-chapel in Mill Street in 1871, and in 1873 it became a public elementary day school known as Mill Street Wesleyan school.[78] It became an infants' school in or shortly before 1885. In 1909–10 it had an average attendance of 51.[79] It was closed in 1913, but the building continued in use as a chapel until 1990.[80]

ST. LUKE'S C.E. SCHOOL, Pump St., Ball Haye Green. From 1868 F. A. Argles of Haregate and his wife helped to maintain a day school run by an uncertificated teacher in a rented room at Ball Haye Green. In 1871 they built and settled in trust a mixed and infants' day school in Pump Street. The new building was soon used as a mission church also. The site included two cottages in Prince Street, which were assigned by Argles as residences for a teacher and a caretaker.[81] From 1871 the school had a certificated mistress. It soon had an average attendance of 51, and later in the year it began to receive a government grant.[82] During the winters of 1872–3 and 1873–4 the mistress ran a night school.[83] The building was extended in 1877–8 at Argles's expense.[84] Average attendance had risen to 125 by the late 1880s.[85] In 1930 the school was a mixed and infants' school with 142 on its books, and it was agreed that it should become a junior school in the general reorganization of Leek schools.[86] By 1940 it was an infants' school, and so remained until 1945 when it was closed. The staff and pupils were transferred to Beresford Memorial school, Novi Lane.[87] The building continued in use as a mission church.[88]

ST. JOHN'S C.E. SCHOOL, Mill Street. A school established in 1868 as a branch of St. Edward's schools became the school-church of St. John in Mill Street, opened in 1875. In 1876 it was made independent of St. Edward's schools and began to receive a government grant. The average attendance was then 66. The building was enlarged in 1881, and in 1882 a separate infants' department was established. In 1930 St. John's was a mixed and infants' school with 202 on the roll. It became a junior school in 1931 and was closed in 1938. The building continued in use as a church.[89]

BRITISH SCHOOL FOR BOYS, Union Street. In September 1868 a British school for boys was opened in two rooms in a rented building in Union Street. By December the master had c. 36 pupils, who paid from 2d. to 6d. a week, and from 1869 the school received a government grant.[90] Successive masters also ran a night school from 1869 to 1872, when it was abandoned for lack of support.[91] In 1871 average attendance at the day school was over 60, and a pupil teacher was appointed. By 1879 attendance sometimes exceeded 150, and an assistant master

73 Ibid. D. 3657/1/4, pp. 221 sqq.; D. 3657/1/5–6, passim; D. 3657/1/8, pp. 30, 78, 106–7, 171.

74 J. Whitehead, Compton School (Leek, 1988); Staffs. C.C. Record for 1930, 867–8; P.R.O., ED 7/109/21; Leek Post & Times, 14 Sept. 1994, p. 14; above, churches (All Saints').

75 Leek Wesleyan Methodist Circuit Yr. Bk. 1887, 33.

76 Rep. and Accts. of Leek Ragged Schol, 1866–7 (copy in W.S.L., Sleigh scrapbk. i, f. 128).

77 Leek Wesleyan Christian Sentinel, no. 2 (Jan. 1870), 5 (copy in Leek Libr., Johnson scrapbk. iii, p. 227).

78 P.R.O., ED 7/113/202; Staffs. Advertiser, 21 Jan. 1871, p. 4.

79 S.R.O., D. 1114/1, newspaper cutting of 28 Dec. 1885; Brit. and Foreign School Soc. 106th Ann. Rep. (1911), 227.

80 P.R.O., ED 7/109/195A; above, prot. nonconf. (Methodists).

81 P.R.O., ED 7/109/199; S.R.O., D. 3657/7/1, 21 Feb. 1903; Lich. Dioc. Ch. Cal. (1872), 91; Staffs. Endowed Chars. 79.

82 P.R.O., ED 7/109/199.

83 S.R.O., D. 3657/7/1, 5 Oct. 1872, 30 Oct. 1873.

84 Ibid. 6 Aug., 9 Nov. 1877, 7 Feb. 1878.

85 Kelly's Dir. Staffs. (1888).

86 Staffs. C.C. Record for 1930, 861, 867–8.

87 S.R.O., D. 782/1, pp. 92, 213–16.

88 Above, churches (St. Luke's).

89 P.R.O., ED 7/109/204; C. K. R. Pearce, Mission Church of St. John the Evangelist, Mill Street, Leek (Leek, 1975), 3–7; Staffs. C.C. Record for 1930, 867–9; 1938, 409; above, churches (St. Edward's).

90 P.R.O., ED 7/113/196; S.R.O., D. 1167/1, pp. 1–2; Leek Wesleyan Methodist Circuit Yr. Bk. 1887, 35.

91 S.R.O., D. 1167/1, pp. 15, 21, 30, 51–2, 54.

was engaged. In 1880 he started a night school. The day school was overcrowded, and in 1880 another room in the building was added.[92]

From the beginning the school's closest links had been with the Congregationalists,[93] and by the early 1880s they had taken over its management, running it in conjunction with their school in Alsop Street and the Congregationalist school in Union Street.[94] In 1882 they transferred the boys at the mixed school in Alsop Street to the British school, but in 1883 they closed it and moved the pupils to Alsop Street.[95]

HARGREAVES SCHOOL, later BRITISH SCHOOL, Alsop Street. In 1875 the Congregationalists opened a mixed and infants' school with 24 pupils in a building erected in Alsop Street in 1873–4 and perhaps named in honour of George Hargreaves, for many years a trustee of the Congregational chapel.[96] By 1880 the average attendance was 100.[97] In 1882 the boys in the mixed school were transferred to the British school in Union Street.[98] In 1884 the girls were transferred to the Congregationalist school in Union Street and the boys at the British school were moved to Alsop Street.[99] Thereafter the school, known first as the British school and from the beginning of the 20th century simply as Alsop Street school,[1] remained a boys' and infants' school. There were 100 on the roll in 1912 and 47 in 1920–1. The school was closed in 1921.[2]

LEEK PARISH CHURCH SCHOOLS, Britannia Street. A National school for boys, designed by J. G. Smith, was opened in Britannia Street in 1886.[3] The boys at St. Edward's National schools, Clerk Bank, were transferred there, with the girls and infants following in 1894–5.[4] Britannia Street then became a mixed school with an infants' class; a separate infants' department was re-established in 1909.[5] In 1930 the school had 454 on the roll. It became a senior mixed school in 1931.[6] Alterations in 1932 provided additional classrooms. In 1939 a new building, Milward Hall, was added in Salisbury Street adjoining the school. It comprised housecraft and handicraft rooms and an assembly hall which was also used as a gymnasium. The school became an aided secondary modern school under the 1944 Act. In 1950 there were 290 on the roll. A government inspector that year remarked unfavourably on the school's cramped town-centre site and considered the buildings inadequate.

The school was closed in 1965. The pupils were transferred to a secondary school built by the governors in Westwood Park Road and opened that year as part of the new comprehensive Westwood high school.[7] The Britannia Street building and Milward Hall were sold.[8]

LEEK HIGH SCHOOL FOR GIRLS, later LEEK CHURCH HIGH SCHOOL FOR GIRLS. The town's first secondary school for girls was a private school on Overton Bank run by Edith Milner in the later 1880s. When she decided to close it, a committee of Anglicans and nonconformists was set up to continue it as a non-sectarian high school. The new school, opened c. 1889, was evidently in Queen Street by 1892, and by 1896 it had moved to Russell Street.[9] In 1897 the county council made a grant for science teaching and appoined two representative governors.[10] The school was closed in 1900 when a mixed high school was opened at the Nicholson Institute. A group of Anglicans immediately opened Leek Church high school for girls in the Maude Institute, Clerk Bank, employing the staff of the defunct school. The Church high school began with 25 girls and had 45 by the end of the school year.[11] It became a maintained county high school for girls in 1919, when there were 66 pupils. It was closed in 1921.[12]

LEEK COUNTY HIGH SCHOOL, Springfield Road. In 1900 the urban district council opened a mixed high school in the Nicholson Institute. From 1901 the school used the adjoining Carr gymnasium for extra teaching space as well as for physical training. Although the school was intended mainly for older pupils, with an emphasis on science teaching, it also had preparatory and kindergarten departments. By summer 1902 there were 149 pupils. The school received county council and government grants, but for some years most of the running costs were paid by a few private benefactors. In 1905 the curriculum was widened in an attempt to attract more pupils. Instead numbers fell, and the managers decided to close the school. The county council persuaded them to keep it open, and in 1906 it became a county high school. The number of pupils began to increase, and additional accommodation was added in 1914 and 1920.[13]

In 1921 all the girls except those in the preparatory department were moved to the new girls' high school at Westwood Hall, with the

92 Ibid. pp. 46–7, 223, 230, 253, 268, 280, 284, 292–3, 297.   93 e.g. ibid. pp. 63, 75, 94.
94 Leek Wesleyan Methodist Circuit Yr. Bk. 1887, 35.
95 Below, this section (Hargreaves sch.).
96 P.R.O., ED 7/113/196; S.R.O., D. 1167/2, p. 1; D. 3226/2, no. 2575; inscription on building. For Hargreaves see H. Woodhouse, Story of a Leek Church (Leek, 1988), chaps. 7–9.   97 S.R.O., D. 1167/2, p. 81.
98 Ibid. D. 1167/1, pp. 316, 319; D. 1176/2, p. 116.
99 Ibid. D. 1167/1, pp. 356–8; D. 1167/2, pp. 129–30.
1 Kelly's Dir. Staffs. (1888; 1904).
2 S.R.O., D. 1167/2, p. 502; D. 1167/3, pp. 209, 222.
3 Ibid. D. 3559/St. Edward's par. ch. sch. cash bk., printed circular Mar. 1887; Staffs. Advertiser, 16 Jan. 1886, p. 7.   4 Above, this section (St. Edward's Nat. schs.).
5 Docs. at St. Edward's ch., log bk. of par. ch. infants' sch. 1909–31, p. 1.

6 Staffs. C.C. Record for 1930, 867–8, 1024.
7 Docs. at St. Edward's ch., log bk. of Leek par. ch. senior sch. 1932–65, pp. 1, 159, 281; below, this section (St. Edward's C.E. (aided) middle sch.).
8 Docs. at St. Edward's ch., new sch. building accts. 1963–9, public notice of sale 1966; below, this section (youth centres).
9 Hist. of Leek High Sch. (n.d. but 1960 or 1961), 6, 11; Kelly's Dir. Staffs. (1888; 1892, giving address as Queen St. (p. 201), and Clerk Bank (p. 206); 1896).
10 Staffs. C.C. Record for 1897, 243, 340.
11 Leek High Sch. 6–11, 14.
12 Staffs. C.C. Record for 1919, 296, 420; Leek Libr., vol. of Leek high sch. printed reps. 1906–34, rep. for 1920–1, 8.
13 Leek High Sch. Jubilee Mag. 1900–50, 5–6; Leek High Sch. 11–18; Staffs. C.C. Record for 1906, 109, 420. For the Carr gymnasium see above, social and cultural activities (sport).

Nicholson Institute housing a boys' high school and a mixed preparatory department.[14] By the later 1930s the premises were overcrowded, and in 1938–9 ninety of the boys had to be taught elsewhere in the town. In 1939 the boys' school was moved to a still unfinished building in Westwood Road. The preparatory department was divided. Boys under 8 and girls remained at the Nicholson Institute and became the responsibility of Westwood Hall girls' high school; the older boys went to Westwood Road. The building was completed in 1940. The part of the Nicholson Institute vacated by the high school was used from 1940 to 1943 by the boys of Parmiter's school, evacuated from the East End of London. Under the 1944 Act the high school became a grammar school. In 1948 it had 351 pupils.[15] Its preparatory department was closed in 1950.[16]

In 1965 the school was merged with two secondary modern schools in Springfield Road, Milner and Mountside, to form a mixed comprehensive secondary school on two sites. The Westwood Road building became the new school's Warrington Hall, named after T. C. Warrington, headmaster of the high school 1900–34.[17] When three-tier schooling was introduced in 1981, the number of children on the school's roll was reduced to 1,000, and the school was concentrated at Springfield Road, where the buildings were extended. The Westwood Road buildings became St. Edward's middle school.[18]

LEEK COUNTY FIRST SCHOOL, East Street, formerly LEEK COUNCIL SCHOOLS. Council schools were opened in East Street in 1914 with accommodation for 100 infants and 354 older children. Two silk manufacturers, John Hall and Sir Arthur Nicholson, paid half the cost of building the infants' school.[19] The buildings were extended in 1927.[20] The mixed school became a senior school in 1931, with 334 on the roll, and in 1937 it moved to new buildings in Springfield Road.[21]

The infants' school, which then had 150 children divided among three infant classes and a junior class, expanded into the vacated premises and became a full primary school. By 1943 there were 325 on the roll.[22] East Street became the town's largest primary school: there were over 400 on the roll in the later 1940s, and in 1954, as numbers continued to grow, St. Luke's church hall was hired to provide extra accommodation. In the later 1950s there were over 500 on the roll. Extensions, including an assembly hall, were added in 1966–7, and in 1969 the annexe at St. Luke's hall was closed. The school had been badly overcrowded in the earlier 1960s, but from 1969 the opening of new schools elsewhere in the town caused a steady reduction in numbers. By the later 1980s there were c. 200 on the roll.[23] East Street became a first school in 1981.

WESTWOOD HALL COUNTY HIGH SCHOOL FOR GIRLS. The county council bought Westwood Hall with 14 a. in 1920 and opened it as a girls' high school in 1921. It took the older girls from the mixed Leek county high school at the Nicholson Institute and the older pupils from the Church high school for girls at the Maude Institute.[24] In 1939 it became responsible for the children at Leek high school's preparatory department at the Nicholson Institute; the department was closed in 1950.[25] In 1965 Westwood Hall high school was merged with the newly built St. Edward's C.E. (aided) secondary school in Westwood Park Avenue to form the mixed comprehensive Westwood county high school.[26]

BERESFORD MEMORIAL C.E. (AIDED) FIRST SCHOOL, Novi Lane, also known as ST. PAUL'S SCHOOL, was opened in 1935 as a junior mixed school with 101 on the roll. During the Second World War its numbers declined, and in 1946 the staff and pupils of St. Luke's infants' school at Ball Haye Green were transferred to Novi Lane to create a junior mixed and infants' school with 128 on the roll.[27] It became a first school in 1981.

LEEK COUNTY SENIOR SCHOOL, Springfield Road, later MILNER COUNTY SECONDARY MODERN SCHOOL FOR GIRLS and MOUNTSIDE COUNTY SECONDARY MODERN SCHOOL FOR BOYS. A mixed senior school was opened in Springfield Road in 1937 with 483 on the roll.[28] In 1940 it was divided into Leek county senior school (boys) and Leek county senior school (girls).[29] They became secondary modern schools under the 1944 Act. The girls' school was renamed Milner school in 1955 after R. S. Milner, the founder of a local educational charity.[30] In 1959, when there were 476 on the roll, its building was extended.[31] The boys' school was renamed Mountside school in the late 1950s.[32] In 1965 the schools became the Milner Hall and the Mountside Hall of the mixed comprehensive Leek high school.[33]

[14] Leek Libr., vol. of Leek high sch. printed reps. 1906–34, reps. for 1920–1, 1921–2; Leek High Sch. 18.
[15] Leek High Sch. Jubilee Mag. 1900–50, 9–10; Chronicles (autumn 1992), 14–16.
[16] Leek High Sch. Mag. June 1951, 6.
[17] Leek Libr., newspaper cuttings 1982 (1), pp. 36–7; S.R.O., Survey of School Rec. 1979; Leek High Sch. 18.
[18] Leek Libr., newspaper cuttings 1982 (1), pp. 36–7; Leek Post & Times, 31 July 1991, pp. 7, 35.
[19] P.R.O., ED 7/109/195A; S.R.O., CEH/81/1, between pp. 79 and 80; Staffs. C.C. Record for 1914, 297.
[20] S.R.O., CEH/81/1, pp. 89, 91, 94.
[21] S.R.O., D. 3133/3/1, pp. 123, 171.
[22] S.R.O., CEH/81/1, p. 130; CEH/81/2, 21 June, 1 Nov. 1961.
[23] Ibid. CEH/81/1, pp. 160, 181; CEH/81/2, 1 Dec. 1952, 29 Mar., 28 June 1954, 12 Nov. 1956, 11 Nov. 1957, 12 May 1966; CEH/81/3, 22 Mar. 1967, 19 Feb. 1969; CEH/81/4, May 1988.
[24] Staffs. C.C. Record for 1920, 366, 597; 1921, 325; Leek Libr., vol. of Leek high sch. reps., rep. for 1920–1, 8.
[25] Above, this section (Leek county high sch.).
[26] Below, this section (Westwood county high sch.).
[27] S.R.O., D. 782/1, pp. 1, 209–10, 213–16. For variations of the school's name see e.g. ibid. D. 3657/1/6, pp. 178, 182, 244.   [28] Ibid. D. 3133/3/2, p. 1.
[29] Ibid. D. 3133/3/3, p. 1.
[30] S.R.O., CEK/22/1, 6 Mar. 1956, 11 Mar. 1958; below, this section (educ. chars.).
[31] S.R.O., CEK/22/1, 15 June, 6 Oct. 1959.
[32] S.R.O., D. 3133/3/3, pp. 112, 121.
[33] Leek Libr., newspaper cuttings 1982 (1), pp. 36–7; Leek Official Guide [1965], 18; above, this section (Leek county high sch.).

WESTWOOD COUNTY FIRST SCHOOL, Westwood Road, was opened in 1938 as Westwood Road junior mixed and infants' council school. From 1954 'Road' was gradually dropped from its title.[34] It became a first school in 1981.

ST. EDWARD'S C.E. (AIDED) MIDDLE SCHOOL, Westwood Road. The completion in 1965 of a new St. Edward's C.E. (aided) secondary school in Westwood Park Avenue to replace the parish church schools in Britannia Street coincided with the introduction of comprehensive secondary education in Leek. The planned school was merged with the nearby Westwood Hall high school, and its building was opened as the St. Edward's Hall of the comprehensive Westwood county high school. There was a common timetable and interchange of staff. The new building, however, was not handed over to the local authority, and St. Edward's remained a separate legal entity with its own board of governors.

The unusual status of a voluntary aided school which was also part of a maintained school continued until the further reorganization of Leek schools in 1981. The St. Edward's Hall building was then handed over to the county council for use by Westwood high school. The governors of St. Edward's Hall received in exchange Leek high school's Warrington Hall building, which was reopened that year as St. Edward's C.E. (aided) middle school. In 1990 there were 700 on the roll. A new wing was officially opened in 1992.[35]

WESTWOOD COUNTY HIGH SCHOOL, Westwood Park, was opened in 1965 as a mixed comprehensive high school on two sites, formed by the merger of Westwood Hall high school and St. Edward's secondary school.[36] A performing arts studio was opened in 1984 in what had once been Westwood Hall's banqueting room.[37] In 1981 Westwood Hall became the school's Old Hall and the former St. Edward's building its New Hall.[38]

HAREGATE COUNTY PRIMARY SCHOOL, Churnet View, was opened in 1969 and extended in 1974. It was closed in 1981, and its building was taken over by the new Churnet View middle school.[39]

WOODCROFT COUNTY FIRST SCHOOL, Wallbridge Drive, was opened as a primary school in 1969, initially taking infants only. The building was extended in 1972.[40] Woodcroft became a first school in 1981.

CHURNET VIEW COUNTY MIDDLE SCHOOL was opened in 1981 in the former Haregate county primary school, the building being modified and extended that year.[41]

PRIVATE SCHOOLS. In 1697, following a decision by the Society of Friends that there should be a Quaker schoolmaster in each county, the Staffordshire quarterly meeting decided to establish a school at Leek, with a master paid £15 a year. In 1700 the quarterly meeting allowed the master, Joseph Davison, to admit the sons of non-Quakers; their fees were to be used, with a grant from the quarterly meeting, to set up a fund to provide scholarships for the sons of poor Quakers.[42] Davison was imprisoned in 1700 and 1701 for teaching without a licence,[43] but the school survived. In 1711 the Leek monthly meeting was told that he was willing to be left 'to his liberty for some consideration, yet willing upon our request to serve us', and his salary was increased by £3 a year.[44] The school was described in 1732 as a grammar school where boys were boarded and were taught writing and accounts.[45] Davison died a prosperous man in 1747,[46] but the school apparently died with him.

Later private schools seem to have catered primarily for the children of townspeople and to have lacked wider appeal. They tended to be small and short-lived. Few were as short-lived as the girls' school opened c. 1719 by Margaret Brindley, later Margaret Lucas, and closed a year or two later amid family quarrels when she became a Quaker.[47] William Clowes, a Leek schoolmaster in 1758,[48] was renting part of Barnfield Farm in 1765 and using it as a schoolhouse.[49] He died in 1774; the schoolmaster of the same name who was buried at Leek in 1779 was perhaps his son.[50] John Jones, later Leek's pioneer Swedenborgian, kept a school from 1788 to 1791 with little success.[51] A Miss M. Nickson advertised her school in Spout Street in 1794, and a Miss Fynney kept a boarding school for girls in the later 1790s.[52] By 1813 Robert Hobson had opened a day and boarding school for boys, perhaps on Clerk Bank, where he was living in 1818. He or another member of the family was still there in the late 1820s, but the school had closed or moved from Leek by 1834.[53] Cornelius Brumby, who had been usher at the grammar school, opened his own school in 1826.[54] He still kept a school in 1841[55] and published locally his own system of shorthand.[56]

34   S.R.O., CEH/83/1; ibid. CEM/1/26, pp. 54, 78; Leek U.D.C. *One Hundred Years of Local Govt. in Leek, 1855–1955*, 15.
35   S.R.O., CEK/91/1; *Leek Post & Times*, 17 Oct. 1990, p. 1; 11 Mar. 1992, p. 5.
36   Leek Libr., newspaper cuttings 1972–8, p. 104; above, this section (St. Edward's C.E. middle sch.).
37   Leek Libr., newspaper cuttings 1984 (2), p. 27.
38   Inf. from the school.
39   S.R.O., CEH/193/1; ibid. CEL/78/1.
40   Brochure for official opening 8 Oct. 1970; S.R.O., CEH/194/1.   41   S.R.O., CEL/71/1, pp. 19–20.
42   S.R.O., D. 3159/1/1, ff. 44, 53v.
43   Ibid. f. 54v.; D. 3159/3/3, 20 Feb. 1699/1700, 3 Apr. 1701.   44   Ibid. D. 3159/3/1, 5 Apr. 1711.
45   Ibid. D. 3159/1/1, f. 99v.
46   Ibid. f. 109v.; L.J.R.O., B/C/11, Joseph Davison

(1747).
47   *Acct. of Convincement and Call to the Ministry of Margaret Lucas, late of Leek*, Staffs. (1797), 67, 75, 101–2.
48   L.J.R.O., B/A/21, CC 124093.
49   S.R.O., D. 3272/1/4/3/35–6.
50   Ibid. D. 1040/5/15, 9 Mar. 1774, 15 May 1779.
51   *Olde Leek*, i. 98–101; above, prot. nonconf. (other denominations).
52   *Chronicles* (autumn 1992), 37; *Univ. Brit. Dir.* v [1798]. 105.
53   *Staffs. Advertiser*, 6 Nov. 1813; Parson and Bradshaw, *Staffs. Dir.* (1818), 126; Pigot, *New Com. Dir.* [1829], 713; White, *Dir. Staffs.* (1834), 708.
54   *Staffs. Advertiser*, 8 Jan. 1825; 24 June 1826.
55   Pigot, *Nat. Com. Dir.* (1841), Staffs. 24.
56   R. Simms, *Bibliotheca Staffordiensis*, 84; Miller, *Leek*, 105.

From the 1830s to the 1860s there were usually about half a dozen private schools in the town; thereafter the number dwindled. They were middle-class schools, generally for older children. Some dame schools survived in the 1870s.[57] The longest-lived 19th-century school seems to have been a girls' school kept by the Mellor family. It existed by 1851 and survived until the 1890s.[58] James Morrow, minister of the Derby Street Congregational chapel, had by 1829 opened a boys' school, the Derby Street Academy, in a schoolroom built on to the chapel. It survived Morrow's death in 1836 but probably came to an end soon after 1840.[59] Joseph Sykes, master of St. Luke's National school, resigned in 1860 and opened a commercial school at Ball Haye Hall. In 1863 he moved the school to Stockwell Street, where it remained until he became master of the grammar school in 1870.[60] Leek's first secondary school for girls, in existence in the late 1880s, was a private foundation.[61]

Itinerant singing masters visited the town in the early 18th century.[62] In the early 1790s Thomas Entwhistle, band leader of a theatrical company which was temporarily based at Leek, gave violin and harpsichord lessons there.[63] From the 1830s there were generally a few music teachers, including some of the church organists. Benjamin Barlow, organist and choirmaster at St. Edward's from 1835 until his death in 1873, was well known in Leek and throughout Staffordshire as a musician, choirmaster, and music teacher.[64]

FURTHER AND ADULT EDUCATION.

LEEK LITERARY AND MECHANICS' INSTITUTE. A mechanics' institute with a circulating library was established in 1837.[65] A later claim that it succeeded an institute dating from 1781[66] seems to be unfounded. For some years it met in rented premises, at first in a school at the Derby Street Congregational chapel, from 1848 or 1849 in larger rooms at the chapel, and from 1854 in a building in Russell Street.[67] In 1862 it erected its own premises in Russell Street, a three-storeyed building designed in an Italian style by William Sugden.[68] It remained there until its closure in 1929. The founders of the mechanics'

institute, who were led by William France, a silk manufacturer, aimed their early publicity at working men who wished to better themselves. They described the 5s. subscription and the 2s. 6d. entry fee, both payable by instalment, as 'trifling'.[69] In October 1838 there were 145 members. They had a reading room, open three evenings a week, and a library of almost 500 books, pamphlets, and periodicals. The first lecture organized by the institute had been delivered in April at the Derby Street chapel. By late 1839 various classes had been started, including one in mutual improvement and another to help members with reading, writing, and arithmetic.[70] Outside speakers in the 1840s included John Murray, a lecturer on popular science, who gave at least four series of talks at Leek.[71] In 1847 the institute joined a Midlands union of literary and mechanics' institutions. By 1849 the institute had 226 members, and the library, then open six nights a week, had grown to c. 1,250 volumes.[72] The range of instruction broadened. Drawing classes began in 1843 or 1844 and survived at least until 1849.[73] By 1850 there were over 60 pupils attending classes; the subjects included singing, chemistry, and French.[74] That year a penny bank was set up at the institute for the 295 members and for the townspeople in general.[75]

The move from Derby Street in 1854 followed several years of quarrels over management. Some of the stricter nonconformist members objected to a proposal to buy novels for the library, tried to ban chess and draughts, and alleged that Sunday opening was being contemplated. Their opponents accused them of Calvinistic intolerance, stated that many of the library books were unread because they were too abstruse for a mechanics' institute, and claimed that much of the institute's educational effort had been of little use to 'the poor working boy'. They urged that future presidents should be men with a real interest in the institute and not merely local notables.[76] That point of view prevailed, and the institute moved away from the chapel precincts. There was, however, no schism, and the institute retained a strong nonconformist character.

In 1860 it had 287 members 'of all classes'.[77] Although it continued its educational work into

---

57 S.R.O., D. 1167/2, p. 1.
58 White, *Dir. Staffs.* (1851), 735; *Kelly's Dir. Staffs.* (1892).
59 Leek Libr., Johnson scrapbk. i (2), D/3/2; H. Woodhouse, *Story of a Leek Church* (Leek, 1988), 44, 56; *Staffs. Advertiser*, 30 Dec. 1837.
60 *P.O. Dir. Staffs.* (1860; 1864); *Staffs. Advertiser*, 4 Jan. 1862, p. 1; 3 Jan. 1863, p. 1; 27 June 1863, p. 1; 19 Feb. 1870, p. 7; S.R.O., D. 538/B/2/1, Ball Haye rent bk. 1851–78.
61 Above, this section (Leek high sch. for girls).
62 *Convincement and Call of Margaret Lucas*, 9.
63 M. Baron-Wilson, *Memoirs of Harriot, Duchess of St. Albans* (1840), i. 122–3; *D.N.B.* s.v. Mellon, Harriot. For the company see above, social and cultural activities (theatres).
64 W.S.L., Sleigh scrapbk, ii, ff. 70 (memorial card to Barlow), 97v. (newspaper obituary, misdated by Sleigh); above, social and cultural activities (music).
65 W.S.L., Sleigh scrapbk. ii, f. 6.
66 *Leek Post*, 29 Nov. 1924; Leek Libr., Literary and Mechanics' Institute (hereafter L.M.I.) folder, *88th Ann. Rep.*
67 W.S.L., Sleigh scrapbk. ii, f. 6; *Staffs. Advertiser*, 20

Oct. 1849, p. 4; 25 Mar. 1854, p. 4; 1 Apr. 1854, p. 3; 8 Apr. 1854, p. 3; 21 Oct. 1854, suppl., p. 2.
68 W.S.L., Sleigh scrapbk. ii, f. 6.
69 Ibid.; Leek Libr., L.M.I. folder, photocopy of handbill of 21 Dec. 1839.
70 Leek Libr., L.M.I. folder, photocopy of handbill 21 Dec. 1839; *Staffs. Advertiser*, 28 Apr. 1838, p. 3; 20 Oct. 1838, p. 4; 8 Mar. 1845, p. 3.
71 Leek Libr., L.M.I. folder, letters from Murray; *Staffs. Advertiser*, 11 Sept. 1847, p. 1; *D.N.B.* s.v. Murray, John (1786?–1851).
72 *Staffs. Advertiser*, 4 Sept. 1847, p. 7; 20 Oct. 1849, p. 4.   73 Ibid. 19 Oct. 1844, p. 2; 20 Oct. 1849, p. 4.
74 Ibid. 19 Oct. 1844, p. 2; 19 Oct. 1850, p. 5; J. W. Hudson, *Hist. of Adult Educ.* (1851), 230.
75 *Staffs. Advertiser*, 19 Oct. 1850, p. 5.
76 Ibid. 24 Apr. 1847, p. 2; 22 Oct. 1853, p. 4; 25 Mar. 1854, p. 4; 1 Apr. 1854, p. 3; 8 Apr. 1854, p. 3; 21 Oct. 1854, suppl., p. 2; 28 Oct. 1854, pp. 3–4; 4 Nov. 1854, p. 3; 11 Nov. 1854, p. 7; Leek Libr., L.M.I. folder, photocopy of handbill of Sept. 1854.
77 *Staffs. Advertiser*, 21 Apr. 1860, p. 4.

the 1880s, it gradually became little more than a middle-class social club with a circulating library. From the later 1850s it was generally known as the literary and mechanics' institute.[78] The number of working-class members in its early days is unknown. By the later 1860s there were fewer than there had been, and efforts were made to enrol more. The full annual subscription, still described by the managers as trifling, had been increased to 12s., and probably few of the new members were working men. Membership apparently peaked in 1873, at 305.[79] The institute's main attractions were its library and reading room,[80] but the opening of the Nicholson Institute in 1884, with its free library, made them less of a draw. In 1894 members considered but rejected a proposal to close the institute and to transfer its books to the Nicholson Institute.[81] By the early 1900s there were fewer than 100 members. Gifts and interest-free loans from well-wishers, fund-raising activities, and the opening of a billiard room in 1907 enabled the institute to survive. Billiards brought in new members and fees from players, and it also subsidized the library, which by then consisted mainly of popular fiction.[82] An appeal for new members in 1924 was apologetic about the old-fashioned word 'mechanics', while finding it necessary to assure working people that they would be welcome.[83] In 1928 the institute's trustees decided that it no longer had a useful function, and in 1929 it was closed. In 1930 the county court directed that its funds should be handed over to the urban district council, which was to invest the money and pay the interest to the Nicholson Institute.[84]

LEEK COLLEGE OF FURTHER EDUCATION AND SCHOOL OF ART, formerly LEEK SCHOOL OF ART and LEEK SCHOOL OF ART, SCIENCE AND TECHNOLOGY. From 1868 the government's Science and Art Department supported a school of art set up that year by the Leek mechanics' institute. A tutor, hired from the art school at Stoke-upon-Trent, held classes at the institute and apparently at the Union Street British school. Attendance was poor, and the classes were abandoned in 1870.[85] In 1874 the institute started new classes in science and art, again in connexion with the Science and Art Department. The art classes, taught by the headmaster of Hanley School of Art, were at first well attended.[86] In 1879 they were moved from the

institute to a hired room in Stockwell Street, which was large but badly lit and poorly ventilated. The Science and Art Department threatened to withdraw its grant unless better premises were found. In 1881, when average attendance had fallen to c. 30, Joshua Nicholson was persuaded to add accommodation for an art school to his projected institute at Leek. An independent committee was formed to manage the classes and to superintend their eventual move into the new institute.[87]

When the Nicholson Institute in Stockwell Street was opened in 1884, it included three large rooms for the art school, for which the school's managing committee paid a nominal rent. A headmaster was appointed, and the school was established on a permanent basis. Almost half the cost of the furniture and equipment was raised by a bazaar in the town hall; the rest came from donations, Science and Art Department grants, and the profits of a lecture given by Oscar Wilde.[88] Besides art classes some practical and technical instruction was offered, but in 1890-1 only a few of the 138 students took advantage of it.[89]

The Leek improvement commissioners set up a technical instruction committee in 1889, shortly after the passing of the Technical Instruction Act that year.[90] In 1891 they adopted the Act, and the committee started its own classes in the Nicholson Institute as Leek Technical School, complementing those offered by the committee of what had become Leek School of Art and Science. The Science and Art Department refused to sanction government grants to two separate committees running similar courses in the same building. The school of art and science and the technical school were accordingly merged in 1892, with the approval of the Science and Art Department, as Leek School of Art, Science, and Technology.[91] Average weekly attendance rose from 354 in 1892-3 to 694 in 1896-7. It was stated in 1897 that almost two-thirds of the pupils were artisans, clerks, warehousemen, and their children. Pupils included children from local elementary schools sent to the school for practical classes.[92]

An extension to the Nicholson Institute built in 1900 was partly for a county silk school, which was promoted by several leading mill owners. They were irked that Macclesfield had a technical school which provided instruction in silk throwing, spinning, and weaving, while all that

78 Ibid. 10 Oct. 1857, p. 4; *P.O. Dir. Staffs.* (1860).
79 W.S.L., Sleigh scrapbk. i, ff. 84, 106; ii, f. 97; Leek Libr., L.M.I. folder, *Rules* (1868).
80 Leek Libr., L.M.I. folder, photocopy of undated handbill.
81 Ibid. letter from W. S. Brough 21 Apr. 1894 and notice of A.G.M. 24 Apr. 1894; *Staffs. Advertiser*, 28 Apr. 1894, p. 5.
82 Leek Libr., L.M.I. folder, 20th-cent. ann. reps. and financial statements.
83 *Leek Post*, 29 Nov. 1924.
84 Leek Libr., L.M.I. folder, circular of 10 Dec. 1928 and letter from Enoch Hill to A. Newall 26 Apr. 1929; *Staffs. Weekly Sentinel*, 18 Jan. 1930 (ref. supplied by Mr. R. Poole of Leek).
85 P.R.O., ED 7/113/196; Leek Libr., L.M.I. folder, printed circular 24 Nov. 1868; W.S.L., Sleigh scrapbk. ii, f. 80.

86 Leek Libr., L.M.I. folder (A. A. Bradbury to W. S. Brough, 1 Aug. 1873; printed circular 6 Feb. 1875; *38th Ann. Rep.*; *39th Ann. Rep.*); W.S.L., Sleigh scrapbk. ii, f. 102; *Staffs. Advertiser*, 22 Aug. 1874, p. 4.
87 *Staffs. Advertiser*, 19 Nov. 1881, p. 6; P. V. Smith, *Nicholson Institute, Leek* (Staffs. County Libr. 1984), 9-10. For the Nicholson Inst. see above, social and cultural activities (libraries).
88 S.R.O., D. 538/D/3/10, p. 290; Smith, *Nicholson Inst.* 20, 27-30a, 44; *Staffs. Advertiser*, 1 Mar. 1884, p. 7.
89 Leek Sch. of Art, Science and Technology, *1st Ann. Rep. 1891-2* (Leek, 1893).
90 S.R.O., D. 3226/8, p. 326; D. 3226/31, 30 Oct. 1889; *Staffs. Advertiser*, 16 Nov. 1889, p. 7.
91 S.R.O., D. 1283/1, pp. 1-4, 23; *Staffs. Advertiser*, 16 May 1891, p. 7; 12 Dec. 1891, p. 7; Leek Sch. of Art, Science and Technology, *1st Ann. Rep. 1891-2*.
92 S.R.O., D. 1283/1, p. 181; Smith, *Nicholson Inst.* 46-8.

Leek offered was a class on the theories of silk dyeing.[93] In 1901 practical classes in silk dyeing and weaving were started at the new school, but despite the pressure and encouragement of employers they aroused little enthusiasm among employees. In 1912–13 the number of pupils on the register was the same as the average attendance in 1902–3, 25 in the weaving classes and 7 in the dyeing.[94] Classes continued as the County School of Hosiery Manufacture and Dyeing in the late 1930s.[95]

In 1938 control of the School of Art, Science and Technology passed from the urban district council to the county council.[96] By 1955 the school had been divided into a college of further education and a school of art and crafts, both housed at the Nicholson Institute.[97] The two were combined in 1981 to form Leek College of Further Education and School of Art.[98] By then there were annexes in Union Street and Russell Street,[99] and in 1986 a technology block and a business studies centre were opened in Union Street. There was also a subsidiary centre for further education at Biddulph by 1986.[1] In 1988–9 the college, one of the smallest in North Staffordshire and serving the Staffordshire Moorlands, had 260 full-time students, 848 part-time day students, 117 part-time day and evening students, and 1,740 students taking evening classes.[2] In 1992 it bought the Carr gymnasium, adjoining the Nicholson Institute, from the district council.[3] The college became self-managing in 1993, and responsibility for funding it passed from the county council to the Further Education Funding Council for England. In 1994 the interior of the 1900 building was remodelled to provide more study space and better reception facilities.[4]

OTHER INSTITUTIONS. Mutual improvement groups were organized in the 19th century by the churches and chapels[5] and by bodies such as the Leek branch of the Y.M.C.A., established in 1858.[6] In 1875–6 the town was involved in the short-lived Cambridge University extension scheme in North Staffordshire. Courses of lectures on chemistry and on history were given at Leek, and at the end of the session 13 people were awarded certificates by examination.[7] From 1884 the committee of the Nicholson Institute organized educational lectures there on literary, artistic, and scientific subjects. Some lectures

were also given there in connexion with an Oxford University extension scheme which ran in North Staffordshire from 1887 to 1892. In 1897 the institute provided a venue for a course of Cambridge University extension lectures on astronomy.[8]

A school of cookery was formed in 1876 in connexion with the national School for Cookery at South Kensington. It originally met in the rifle volunteers' hall in Ford Street. In 1877 it began to sponsor courses of lectures and cookery demonstrations at the Temperance Hall in Union Street. In 1878 it co-operated in a scheme which provided workers with hot mid-day meals, eaten at its new premises in Stockwell Street or taken away.[9]

SPECIAL SCHOOLS. From 1964 to 1970 there was a Leek area class for children with special educational needs, housed in part of Mount school, West Street.[10] A junior training centre established by the county council in Springfield Road in 1963 became Leek day special school in 1971 and was soon afterwards renamed Springfield special school. In 1992 it had 30 places and took children aged 2–19 with severe learning difficulties or physical handicaps.[11] Springhill hostel in Mount Road for adults with learning difficulties was opened in 1966. In 1994 it housed 31 people.[12]

DOMESTIC STUDIES. In the 1890s cookery classes were run by Leek School of Art, Science and Technology at Hargreaves school, Alsop Street, and those attending included children from local schools.[13] Ball Haye Domestic Subjects Centre, at which children from Leek schools were taught cookery, laundry, and household care, was opened in 1918 and still existed in 1926.[14] In 1939 the building of the former Hargreaves school was being used as a practical instruction centre and clinic for school-children.[15]

YOUTH CENTRES. A youth centre was opened in 1971 in Milward Hall in Salisbury Street, formerly part of the Leek parish church schools. By 1992 it was a youth and community centre used by all age groups.[16] Moorside youth centre in the grounds of Leek high school was opened in 1990.[17]

93 Smith, *Nicholson Inst.* 48–9.
94 G. Balfour, *Ten Years of Staffs. Educ. 1903–1913* (Stafford, 1913), 30, 36.
95 *Kelly's Dir. Staffs.* (1940).
96 S.R.O., CEM/1/26, pp. 112, 177; (2nd nos.), pp. 1, 204.
97 Leek U.D.C. *100 Years of Local Govt. in Leek, 1855–1955*, 15; *Leek Official Guide* [1961], 16.
98 Smith, *Nicholson Inst.* 56.
99 Leek Coll. of Further Educ. *Prospectus 1980–1*.
1   Leek Libr., newspaper cuttings 1985 (2), p. 95; Leek Coll. of Further Educ. and Sch. of Art, *Prospectus 1986–7*; *Prospectus 1988–9*.
2   *Prospectus 1988–9*; *Leek Post & Times*, 6 Dec. 1989, p. 5.
3   *Leek Post & Times*, 15 July 1992, p. 1.
4   Ibid. 29 June 1994, p. 10; inf. from the college.
5   e.g. W.S.L., Sleigh scrapbk. ii, ff. 2, 23, 84–5; Dyson, *Wesleyan Methodism*, 48.

6   *Staffs. Advertiser*, 6 Aug. 1859, p. 4; 8 Oct. 1859, p. 5; 5 Nov. 1859, p. 4; 3 Dec. 1859, p. 4.
7   Ibid. 16 Oct. 1875, p. 6; Leek Libr., Johnson scrapbk. iii, p. 239; T. Kelly, *Hist. of Adult Educ. in Gt. Brit.* 219 sqq.
8   Smith, *Nicholson Inst.* 40–1; *Hist. of Educ.* (Jan. 1972), 46.
9   *Staffs. Advertiser*, 30 Dec. 1876, p. 1; 5 Jan. 1878, p. 4.   10 S.R.O., D. 3990/1/1, pp. 120, 126–7, 204.
11 S.R.O., Charities Index; S.R.O., Survey of School Rec. 1979; *Leek Post & Times*, 8 Apr. 1992, p. 33.
12 *Leek Post & Times*, 28 July 1993, p. 8; 26 Oct. 1994, p. 15.
13 Smith, *Nicholson Inst.* 46.
14 Docs. at St. Edward's ch., Leek, log bk. of Leek Domestic Subjects Centre 1918–26.
15 S.R.O., CEM/1/26, p. 189 (2nd nos.).
16 Leek Libr., newspaper cuttings 1969–72, p. 47; *Leek Post & Times*, 18 Nov. 1992, p. 8.
17 *Leek Post & Times*, 3 Oct. 1990, p. 7.

EDUCATIONAL CHARITIES. Several small charities founded in the 18th and 19th centuries were for the support of individual Leek schools or were adapted for that purpose.[18] By will proved 1925 R. S. Milner established a general educational charity for Leek urban district. A Scheme of 1976 defined potential beneficiaries as persons living in Leek or attending an educational establishment there. In the early 1990s the charity's income, £3,500, was distributed mainly in interest-free loans to college and university students and in grants for pupils to study and travel in Great Britain and abroad in pursuit of their education.[19]

CHARITIES FOR THE POOR

WHEN Charity Commissioners visited Leek in 1824, they found the town's charities generally in good order but suggested some improvements in management.[20] A Leek branch of the Charity Organization Society was formed in 1879, with an office in Silk Street. It still existed in 1912.[21]

ALMSHOUSES. *Ash Almshouses.*[22] Elizabeth Ashe, daughter of William Jolliffe of Leek and widow of Edward Ashe, a London draper,[23] had eight almshouses built at the corner of Broad Street and Compton in 1676 or 1677.[24] The present building carries a plaque with the date 1696. The occupants were to be widows or spinsters aged at least 60, or in some way disabled, and resident in the parish. Each was to receive a weekly dole of 1s. 8d. from the vicar on Sunday, and every two years have a new gown of violet cloth, embroidered with the initials EA. As an endowment she gave a rent of £40 charged on land at Mixon, in Onecote.

The foundress chose the first almswomen and instructed that after her death one was to be chosen by her brother Thomas Jolliffe and his heirs, another by her son William Ashe and his heirs, and the other six by Jolliffe and Ashe jointly with the vicar, churchwardens, and overseers of the poor of Leek parish. Of those six, three were to come from the rural quarters of the parish, Bradnop, Endon, and Leekfrith. Elizabeth Ashe died in 1698.[25] Thomas Jolliffe and William Ashe and their heirs seem not to have exercised their right to nominate, and as late as 1727 there still had been no almswoman from Endon quarter and only one from Bradnop quarter. It was agreed that year that all the almswomen should be chosen by the vicar together with the churchwardens and overseers. It was also agreed in 1727 to put the names of the quarters over the doors of the houses assigned to them, and in 1992 the houses severally still bore those names and the names Jolliffe, Ash, and (in three instances) Leek.[26]

The division of the quarters in the later 19th century into new parishes caused uncertainty about the method of selection. The matter was settled by a Scheme of 1908: a body of 10 trustees, including the vicars of the three town churches, were to choose the almswomen for the Jolliffe and Ash houses; the vicars with their churchwardens and the overseers of Leek and Lowe were to choose the women for the Leek houses; and the vicar of St. Edward's with the appropriate vicars, churchwardens, and overseers were to choose women for the houses assigned to the former rural quarters.[27] A Scheme of 1980 restricted almswomen to residents of an area within 5 miles of Leek market place, preference being given to those living in one of the former townships of the ancient parish. It also renamed the charity the Ash Homes.[28]

The almshouses form an **L**-shaped building, with six dwellings facing Broad Street and two Compton. Originally a single-storey block, a second storey lit by dormer windows was added in the 18th century, possibly about the time of the 1727 agreement.[29] The houses were restored in 1911, when the work involved raising the roof by 2 ft. and extending the back walls.[30] A separate building comprising four flats for additional almswomen was built in Compton on the south side of the almshouses in 1985.[31]

Several charities have been established to support the almshouses. In 1678 Elizabeth Ashe's aunt Anne, the wife of Sir John Dethick, lord mayor of London,[32] gave £100, the interest to be spent on coal. In 1723 the capital was used, together with £100 left for the poor of Leek town by Thomas Jolliffe (d. 1693) and £10 similarly left by a Mrs. Haywood of Macclesfield (Ches.),[33] to buy 22½ a. at Oulton, in Rushton Spencer.[34] The almswomen were

[18] *Staffs. Endowed Chars.* 79–80.
[19] S.R.O., Charities Index; *Leek Post & Times*, 1 Apr. 1992, p. 2; inf. from the clerk to the trustees.
[20] *13th Rep. Com. Char.* 375–88.
[21] Leek Char. Organization Soc. *Ann. Reps. 1879–1912* (copies in Leek Libr.).
[22] Account based on *13th Rep. Com. Char.* 375–80; Sleigh, *Leek*, 91; deeds relating to the foundation, copied into the earliest surviving almshos. min. and acct. bk. 1830–1939, in possession, with later min. bks., of Challinors & Shaw, Derby St., Leek. Mr. R. F. Belfield, Mr. W. F. Brooks, and Mrs. D. F. Parker of Challinors & Shaw are thanked for allowing access to the records and providing information.
[23] H. G. H. Jolliffe, *Jolliffes of Staffs.* (priv. print. 1892), pedigree following p. 232; R. C. Hoare, *Modern Wilts.* (1822–43), Heytesbury hundred, 118; *Hist. Parl., Commons,* 1660–90, i. 557. The family name was later spelled Ash.
[24] The houses already existed at the time of their endowment on 13 Mar. 1676/7: S.R.O., D. 5235.
[25] P.R.O., PROB 11/449, ff. 1v.–2.
[26] S.R.O., D. 1040/9, pages at back of vol.; D. 5041, pp. 29–30. [27] Char. Com. Scheme, 7 Feb. 1908.
[28] Char. Com. Scheme, 18 Jan. 1980.
[29] Above, plate 53.
[30] Ash min. and acct. bk. 1830–1939, 17 May, 4 July 1907, 20 Nov. 1911, 8 July 1912.
[31] Ash min. bk. 1940–91, pp. 219, 222.
[32] Jolliffe, *Jolliffes of Staffs.* pedigree following p. 232.
[33] Given as Mr. Haywood in *13th Rep. Com. Char.* 377, but as Mrs. Haywood, widow, in deeds of 24 and 25 Mar. 1813 copied into Ash min. and acct. bk. 1830–1939.
[34] The acreage is given in deeds of 7 and 8 Aug. 1723 copied into Ash min. and acct. bk. 1830–1939.

entitled to $^{10}/_{21}$ parts of the rent from the land, the remainder being for the poor of Leek town. In the earlier 1820s the land was let at £25 a year, and a further £25 was received partly as the interest on money from the sale of timber in 1803 and partly from further occasional sales of timber and underwood. The land was sold in 1974.[35] In 1765 Rebecca Lowe, a relative of Thomas Jolliffe,[36] left £400 for the almswomen. It was invested in stock, which in the earlier 1820s produced an income of £13 1s. 7½d. By then a weekly dole of 2s. 6d. had for some time been paid to each almswoman. There was then no money to provide new gowns as directed by the foundress, but it was hoped that there would be enough to buy some in 1825. In 1876 the executors of Martha Babington gave £50, the interest to be spent on paying each almswoman 5s. a year on 1 January. Maria Jane Van Tuyl by will proved 1877 left £1,000 for the almswomen, Mary Flint (d. 1889) £500, George Sutton by will proved 1897 £200, and Elizabeth Flint by will proved 1905 £500.[37]

Condlyffe Almshouses. In 1867 Elizabeth Condlyffe (d. 1878) bought land at Cornhill Cross as the site for six almshouses. Eight were in fact built in 1882 in what later became Condlyffe Road. In two ranges joined by an arch, they are in an Arts and Crafts style designed by an architect named Lowe. Residence is restricted to men and women aged 50 years or over who are members of the Church of England. In 1966 each of the eight houses was divided into an upper and a lower self-contained flat.[38]

Carr's Almshouses. In 1893 Isabella Carr (d. 1899), daughter of Thomas Carr, a Leek silk manufacturer, had three almshouses built at the east end of Fountain Street in memory of her sisters Ellen and Rosanna Carr. Residence is restricted to men and women, whether married or single, who are members of the Church of England. A Scheme of 1981 renamed the charity the Carr Homes.[39]

Christian widows or spinsters resident in the area of the former Leek urban district are eligible to apply for a place at St. Joseph's Homestead, in Stratford-upon-Avon (Warws.), an almshouse founded in 1911 by Agnes and Rose Edith Carr-Smith, nieces of William Carr of Leek (d. 1903).[40]

THE TOWN DOLE. By the earlier 1820s several charities for the poor which were man-

aged by the churchwardens of Leek had been merged as the Town Dole.[41] It is uncertain whether some of the earliest charities were intended to benefit the whole of the ancient parish or only the township of Leek and Lowe or the town of Leek. By the earlier 1820s, however, the area was restricted to Leek and Lowe township.

The earliest known is the bequest of William Watson, a Leek grocer, who by will proved 1689 left to the poor of Leek the income from land near Barngates, with the tithe of corn from the land.[42] The income was £6 in the later 1780s but had increased to £15 10s. by the earlier 1820s.[43]

William Hulme, minister of Newton Solney (Derb.), left the interest on £26 13s. 4d. to the poor of Leek town and parish. The capital was given to a relative Robert Hulme, whose son John Hulme (d. 1690) of Thorncliffe, in Tittesworth, secured the charity by his will.[44] The income was £1 6s. in the later 1780s and the earlier 1820s.[45] John Hulme also left to the poor of Leek town and parish the rent from half the first crop from four days' mowing of a meadow called Leadbetters (later Poor's) meadow.[46] The rent, which was to be distributed at Christmas, was £1 10s. in the later 1780s, when it was charged on land called Craddock's meadow; in the earlier 1820s it was £1 15s. 10d.[47]

The poor of Leek town benefited from $^{11}/_{21}$ parts of the income from the land at Oulton, in Rushton Spencer, bought in 1723 with the bequests of Thomas Jolliffe and Mrs. Haywood.[48] The share was £27 5s. in 1823.[49]

Thomas Jodrell of Endon (d. 1728)[50] left a third of the interest on £200 for the poor of Leek. The share was £2 10s. in the later 1780s and the earlier 1820s.[51]

In the earlier 1820s the income from all the above charities, together with that from the charity of Anne Jolliffe,[52] was £85 12s. 10d., which was distributed in money, blankets, and linen at Christmas; coal was also sometimes given. To prevent people who lived outside Leek and Lowe township receiving any benefit, those eligible to share in the distribution were issued with tickets.[53]

Four other charities, originally administered separately, had been incorporated into the Town Dole by 1991. By will dated 1644 Elizabeth St. Andrew left a rent of 13s. 4d. charged on land in Gayton for distribution to the poor of Leek on Good Friday.[54] In the earlier 1820s the vicar distributed the dole weekly in the form of 16 quarts of soup to eight poor widows or families in Leek and Lowe township.[55] There was a soup kitchen supported by the charity in Mill Street in the later 1940s, when it was closed.[56]

35 Ash min. bk. 1940–91, p. 156.
36 Jolliffe, *Jolliffes of Staffs.* 6.
37 Notes in Ash min. and acct. bk. 1830–1939.
38 Condlyffe Char. min. bk. 1867–1976, in possession of Challinors & Shaw.
39 Carr's Almshos. Char. min. bk., in possession of Challinors & Shaw.
40 W.S.L. 498/34, cutting of 11 July 1903; *V.C.H. Warws.* iii. 282.   41 *13th Rep. Com. Char.* 380.
42 L.J.R.O., B/C/11, Wm. Watson (1689).
43 *Char. Dons.* 1152–3; *13th Rep. Com. Char.* 380.
44 L.J.R.O., John Hulme (1690); S.R.O., D. 1040/5/14, burial of 29 Aug. 1690; Sleigh, *Leek,* 92.

45 *Char. Dons.* 1152–3; *13th Rep. Com. Char.* 381.
46 L.J.R.O., B/C/11, John Hulme (1690).
47 *Char. Dons.* 1152–3; *13th Rep. Com. Char.* 381.
48 Above, this section (Ash almshos.).
49 *13th Rep. Com. Char.* 381.
50 Below, Endon, charities.
51 *Char. Dons.* 1152–3; *13th Rep. Com. Char.* 380.
52 Below, this section (other charities).
53 *13th Rep. Com. Char.* 381–2.
54 For the benefactress see above, churches (St. Edward's: sermons).
55 *13th Rep. Com. Char.* 383.
56 Inf. from Mr. W. F. Brooks of Challinors & Shaw.

By will proved 1668 Joan Armett of Thorneyleigh Hall Farm, in Leekfrith, left a rent of £2 13s. 4d. charged on land in Leekfrith to be distributed on Christmas Eve to the poor of Leek town, preference being given to those living in Mill Street. In the earlier 1820s the dole was given in sums of 1s. or less by the tenant of the land, prior notice of the distribution being given by the town crier.[57]

By will proved 1749 William Mills of Leek left the interest on £100, after payments of 20s. to the vicar of Leek for a charity sermon and 5s. to the parish clerk, for the distribution of bread on Sundays to poor widows of Leek and Lowe and of Leekfrith.[58] The poor's share in the earlier 1820s was £3 15s., which together with £2 15s. from James Rudyard's charity[59] was spent on a weekly dole of 36 bread rolls. The rolls were distributed by the organ-blower after Sunday-morning service; between six and eight rolls were taken to poor people too old to attend.[60] Bread was still left in the porch of St. Edward's church for collection by the poor in the mid 1970s.[61]

William Badnall, a Leek silk dyer (d. 1806), left the interest on £1,000 to be distributed in blankets, quilts, clothing, and other necessities such as coal but not food or drink on 5 November to 20 poor widows aged 60 or over; half the widows were to be residents in Leek town and half in Lowe. Because an insufficient number from Lowe were eligible, the number of town widows who benefited in the earlier 1820s was 13.[62]

In 1991 there was a distribution of c. £950 from the combined funds of all the charities included in the Town Dole. The money, given in small cash payments to individuals and families in need, was distributed by the warden of Leek in consultation with social agencies.[63]

OTHER CHARITIES. In 1619 John Rothwell of Leek (d. 1623) gave a rent of £10 10s. charged on land at 'Hellsend', probably Hillswood End in Leekfrith, and at Horsecroft, in Tittesworth, to provide a weekly dole of 7d. to six poor people in Leek, the residue going to the vicar for sermons. In the later 1780s the income was £9 2s. 6d. In the earlier 1820s £10 7s. 6d. was distributed by the vicar in a weekly dole to six poor widows.[64] In 1991 the charity was administered with those of James Rudyard and John Naylor (below) by the warden of Leek. A distribution of c. £200 was made that year in the form of parcels or vouchers to old people at Christmas.[65]

By will proved 1714 James Rudyard of Abbey Dieulacres, in Leekfrith, left a rent of £2 15s. charged on land in Leekfrith to endow a bread dole: 1d. loaves were to be distributed to 12 poor people at St. Edward's church every Sunday after evening service and on Christmas Day, Good Friday, and Ascension Day. Beneficiaries unable to come to church because of ill health were to be sent a loaf.[66] In the earlier 1820s the income was used along with £3 15s. from William Mills's charity to provide a weekly dole of 36 bread rolls.[67] In 1991 the charity was administered by the warden of Leek, together with those of John Rothwell and John Naylor.

In 1732 shortly before her death Anne Jolliffe, daughter of Thomas, Lord Crew, and widow of John Jolliffe of Cheddleton, gave the interest on £250 to be shared by the curate of Cheddleton (£4 a year), 12 poor widows of Cheddleton (£1 4s.), and poor widows of Leek (the remainder). The money was used to buy land at Compton and near Cornhill Cross. The income was £11 2s. in the later 1780s but had increased to £38 10s. by 1805.[68] The Cornhill Cross land was sold to the improvement commissioners in 1856 for part of the new cemetery, and in 1867 the trustees used the money to buy the 34-a. Pewit Hall farm, in Onecote. In 1873 the land at Compton was exchanged for the 36-a. Rock Tenement farm at Wetley Rocks, in Cheddleton. In 1992 a distribution of £35 was made to 39 Leek widows.[69]

John Naylor of Leek (d. 1739) directed his executors to secure an annuity of £50 for the poor of Leek town. The charity was established in the early 1740s. By 1783 the income had fallen to £44 3s. 8d., which was then distributed on 23 October. In the earlier 1820s the distribution was usually made every two years in the form of tickets for food or clothing, to be used in Leek shops.[70] In 1991 the charity was administered by the warden of Leek, together with those of John Rothwell and James Rudyard.

By will dated 1741 or 1742 William Grosvenor left the interest on £20 to be distributed on St. Thomas's Day (21 December) to poor householders of Leek town. The income was £1 in the later 1780s. The charity had been lost by the earlier 1820s.[71]

By will proved 1755 Thomas Birtles, a Leek button merchant, left the interest on £100 to be distributed on St. Thomas's day to poor householders of Leek town. In 1814 the capital was used to buy stock, and by the earlier 1820s a distribution of £5 was given to poor widows.[72] The charity still existed in 1911, when there was a distribution of £2 18s. 4d. made in 2s. doles.[73]

57 13th Rep. Com. Char. 384.
58 L.J.R.O., Reg. of Wills D, f. 343.
59 Below, this section (other charities).
60 13th Rep. Com. Char. 382–4.
61 Inf. from Mr. Brooks.
62 13th Rep. Com. Char. 385–6.
63 Inf. from Mr. Brooks. For the office of warden (held by Mr. Brooks in 1991) see above, Leek, par. intro. (par. govt.).
64 Char. Dons. 1152–3; 13th Rep. Com. Char. 382; Sleigh, Leek, 93.   65 Inf. from Mr. Brooks.
66 L.J.R.O., Reg. of Wills C, f. 196.
67 13th Rep. Com. Char. 382–3. For Mills's charity see above, this section (Town Dole).
68 S.R.O., D. 3359/misc. deeds, draft deed of 1767

(rehearsing deeds of 26 and 27 Jan. 1731/2); Jolliffe, Jolliffes of Staffs. pedigree following p. 232; Char. Dons. 1152–3; 13th Rep. Com. Char. 380–1.
69 Inf. supplied by Mrs. J. Pointon, trustee and clerk to the charity (now called the Charity of the Hon. Ann Jolliffe).
70 13th Rep. Com. Char. 386–8; S.R.O., D. 1040/5/14, 29 Jan. 1738/9. Before the change of calendar in 1752 the distribution day was probably Naylor's birthday, 12 Oct.: above, churches (St. Edward's: sermons).
71 Char. Dons. 1152–3; 13th Rep. Com. Char. 386.
72 L.J.R.O., B/C/11, Thos. Birtles (1755); 13th Rep. Com. Char. 384–5.
73 H. Henshaw, Ancient Charities of Leek (1911; copy in S.R.O., D. 4855/15/6).

Joseph Wardle of Leek (d. 1780) left an annuity of £5 to be distributed twice a year to the poor of Leek and Lowe township. The charity may not have taken effect: it was not recorded in the later 1780s.[74]

The Carr Trust was formed in 1981 by the amalgamation of the charities of Charles Carr, William Carr, and Elizabeth Flint.[75] Charles Carr (d. 1888) left the interest on £1,250 to be spent on the poor living in Leek town or within 5 miles. The charity became effective only after the death of an annuitant in 1903.[76] Charles's brother William (d. 1903), a Manchester businessman who retired to Leek, left his estate of c. £90,000 for charitable purposes in the town, subject to life interests which expired in 1926, 1939, and 1948. The first charitable disburse-

ment was made in 1928, when the beneficiaries were the almshouses established by his sister Isabella Carr, the cottage hospital, the cripples' clinic, and the Cruso Nursing Association. In 1929 part of the income was used to open a soup kitchen for school children in the Butter Market.[77] The charity of Elizabeth Flint of Leek was established by will proved 1905. The income was for general charitable purposes, including poor relief in Leek.[78] Much of the income of the Carr Trust was spent in 1991 on payments of £10 a month to some 100 persons, who also received a £20 Christmas bonus.[79]

In 1913 W. S. Brough of Leek (d. 1917) established a charity for the relief in kind of the poor of Leek. It still existed in 1929 but no later record has been found.[80]

OUTLYING TOWNSHIPS

BRADNOP

BRADNOP was formerly a township in Leek parish and later a civil parish 3,568 a. (1,444 ha.) in area.[81] It is pasture and shares with Onecote the south end of Morridge, formerly an area of extensive waste. There is a small village immediately north of the Leek–Ashbourne road, which runs diagonally across the township. Cartledge brook forms the northern boundary with Tittesworth, Kniveden brook the western boundary with Leek and Lowe, and Coombes brook part of the southern boundary with Ipstones. On the south-east the rest of the boundary with Ipstones follows the line of a medieval road called the Earl's Way.[82] The irregular eastern boundary with Onecote probably reflects a division of pasture rights on Morridge. The township included three detached portions, which were added in 1934 to the adjoining civil parishes: 53 a. including part of Thorncliffe village to Tittesworth, 385 a. centred on Hurdlow Farm to Heathylee, and 205 a. known as Cawdry to Butterton. At the same time 57 a. of Bradnop, mostly the wedge of land east of the Onecote–Ipstones road, were added to Onecote civil parish, and 417 a. of Onecote west of the road running along the top of Morridge were added to Bradnop from Onecote. As a result Bradnop civil parish was reduced to its present 3,285 a. (1,329.4 ha.).[83] This article deals only with the main part of the former township. The detached portions at Thorncliffe and Hurdlow

are treated in the articles on Tittesworth and Heathylee respectively, and that at Cawdry is reserved for treatment under Butterton in a later volume of this *History*.

The land beside Kniveden brook lies at 577 ft. (176 m.) near Ashenhurst Mill Farm and at 702 ft. (214 m.) near Pool Hall Farm. Bradnop village lies at 838 ft. (255 m.), and to the north-east the land rises to 1,331 ft. (407 m.) on Morridge. The underlying rock is sandstone of the Millstone Grit series. It is overlain by Boulder Clay, and the soil is mostly fine loam, with poorer quality soil on Morridge.[84]

Twelve people in Bradnop were assessed for tax in 1327 and 10 in 1333, the figures possibly including Onecote township which lay in Bradnop manor.[85] Eighty-two people in the manor were assessed for hearth tax in 1666 and a further 23 were too poor to pay.[86] The population of Bradnop township in 1811 was 420, rising to 489 by 1821. It was 467 in 1831, 447 in 1851, 445 in 1871, and 450 in 1891. By 1901 it had fallen to 405. It was 432 in 1911, 423 in 1921, and 384 in 1931. The population of the reduced civil parish was 315 in 1951, 283 in 1961, 275 in 197, 294 in 1981, and 305 in 1991.[87]

The name Bradnop, recorded in 1197, is derived from Old English words describing the broad (*bradan*) enclosed valley (*hop*) which opens to Cheddleton in the south-west.[88] Settlements existed in that part of the township by the later

74 L.J.R.O., B/C/11, Jos. Wardle (1780); *Char. Dons.* 1152.   75 Char. Com. Scheme, 14 Jan. 1981.
76 Carr's Char. min. bk. 1886–1890, in possession of Challinors & Shaw.
77 Wm. Carr's Char. min. bk. 1901–1992, in possession of Challinors & Shaw; W.S.L. 498/34, cuttings of 9 May and 11 July 1903.
78 W.S.L. 498/34, cutting of 6 Jan. 1906; Ashe Almshos. Char. min. and acct. bk. 1830–1939, entries for 17 Aug. and 30 Oct. 1906.   79 Inf. from Mr. Brooks.
80 S.R.O., Charities Index; Leek Libr., newspaper cuttings bk. 5, p. 68.
81 *V.C.H. Staffs.* i. 327. This article was written in 1992.

82 Below, this section [roads].
83 *Census*, 1931; Staffs. Review Order, 1934, p. 63 and map 1 (copy in S.R.O.). The township was named Bradnop and Cawdry in *Census*, 1881–1951.
84 Geol. Surv. Map 1/50,000, solid and drift, sheet 124 (1983 edn.); Soil Surv. of Eng. and Wales, sheet 3 (1983).
85 *S.H.C.* vii (1), 219; x (1), 115.
86 *S.H.C.* 1925, 172–4, 242.
87 *V.C.H. Staffs.* i. 327; *Census*, 1911–91. The figures up to 1931 include the detached portions, for which see above, Alstonefield: Heathylee, intro.; below, Tittesworth, intro.
88 R. W. Eyton, *Antiq. of Salop.* x. 367; *Eng. P.N. Elements*, i. 45, 259–60.

BRADNOP 1992

- ━ ━ ━ Boundary of former township
- ─ 800 ─ Contours (in feet)
- ═ □ ═ Former railway and station
- M✝ Methodist church
- ① Site of tollhouse
- ② Former Blacksmith's Arms inn
- ③ Sytch Farm
- ④ Golden Farm
- ⑤ Buckley Farm
- ⑥ Former school
- ⑦ Former Primitive Methodist chapel

FIG. 30

13th century at Ashenhurst, Apesford, and Revedge,[89] and apparently at Middle Cliffe and Wildgoose Farm.[90] There was a house at Longshaw by 1343.[91] Cliffe Farm has a doorhead dated 1679 with the initials of members of the Fernihough family,[92] and Revedge Farm has a date stone of 1691 with the initials possibly of Francis Hollinshead of Ashenhurst.[93] Longshaw Farm on the south side of the Leek–Ashbourne road is also of the 17th century. Lower Lady Meadows Farm on the south-eastern boundary is of the late 18th century.

Bradnop village stands in the centre of the Bradnop valley, north of the present Leek–Ashbourne road but on the line of the medieval Earl's Way.[94] The oldest house in the village is Sytch Farm, which incorporates at its east end a cruck truss that was part of a medieval hall. Buckley Farm is probably of the 17th century, and School Cottages, a pair of houses east of

Sytch Farm, is dated 1750. Golden Farm was built in the earlier 19th century. Brook Farm east of the village existed as Bent Head in 1690,[95] and the present house is probably of that date. South-west of the village is a cluster of houses called Stunsteads, a name recorded in the earlier 14th century as Tunstedes and meaning a farmhouse.[96] By 1834 there was an inn called the Hare and Hounds on the Ashbourne road; it still existed in 1868.[97] By 1850 there was another roadside inn, the Blacksmiths Arms; it was closed after a fire c. 1940.[98]

What was called 'the other Bradnop' in the mid 13th century and Upper Bradnop in the 1260s was evidently a settlement at the north end of the Bradnop valley.[99] Field House, recorded in that area in 1342, may have been an earlier name for Hare House, whose south front retains a 17th-century doorhead.[1] By 1343 Hulton abbey

89 P.R.O., SC 5/Stafford/3.
90 S.H.C. 1911, 428–30.
91 S.R.O., D. 3272/5/13/7.
92 For the Fernihoughs see B.L. Add. MS. 36664, f. 264.
93 Below, manor (Ashenhurst).
94 Dodd, Peakland Roads, 53–5; T.N.S.F.C. lxxxiii. 50–3.
For a plan of the village in 1775 see S.R.O., D. 1176/A/2/26.

95 W.S.L. 132/3/47, deed of 22 Sept. 1690.
96 S.R.O., D. 3272/5/13/5; Eng. P.N. Elements, ii. 199.
97 White, Dir. Staffs. (1834), 713; Staffs. Advertiser, 29 July 1854, p. 8; P.O. Dir. Staffs. (1868).
98 P.O. Dir. Staffs. (1850); local inf.
99 S.H.C. N.S. ix. 357; S.H.C. 1911, 438.
1 S.R.O., D. 3272/5/13/5.

had a grange at Upper Bradnop, and in 1345 it gave a tenant permission to build on land in the area called Colts moor.[2] In the earlier 16th century a house called the Grange was held by the Cokelee family of Coltsmoor,[3] and in 1666 what was called Coltsmoor House was assessed for tax on four hearths.[4] The Grange and Coltsmoor House probably stood near each other, but their sites are unknown; the present Coltsmoor Farm near the northern boundary was built after the waste there was inclosed in the later 18th century. Stile House Farm east of Hare House is of the 18th century and has an extension dated 1859.

There was a cottage called Pool Hall on the Ashbourne road north-west of Bradnop village by 1663.[5] It was rebuilt in Gothick style in the earlier 19th century for William Critchlow, the owner in 1839.[6] Lane End Farm further east along the Ashbourne road, mentioned in 1675, was an inn called the Red Lion in 1818; a coach house on the opposite side of the road is dated 1821 and has the initials of the innkeeper, John Cook.[7] It was still an inn in 1851 but no longer by 1860.[8] Houses at Morridge Side east of Lane End Farm and other houses to the south-west probably stand on the sites of cottages built on the waste in the 17th century and later.[9] One of the largest is Gooseneck Farm, which is partly of the 18th century.

The medieval Earl's Way, which formed part of the route between Leek and Ashbourne, entered Bradnop on the west near Pool Hall Farm. It continued east through Bradnop village and then turned south-east, leaving the township along the line of the boundary east of Lower Lady Meadows.[10] The road had evidently been replaced by the present line of the Leek–Ashbourne road by the 17th century, when the site of Lane End Farm was occupied. The Leek–Ashbourne road was turnpiked in 1762. There was at first a tollhouse over the Leek boundary at Lowe Hill; an improvement in the line of the road in 1828 included its replacement by a new tollhouse east of Pool Hall Farm, in Bradnop. Three cast-iron mileposts along the road form part of a series made in 1834. The road was disturnpiked in 1876. The Pool Hall tollhouse was demolished in the 1970s.[11]

A railway from Leekbrook, in Leek and Lowe, to Waterhouses was opened in 1905 with a station near Bradnop village. The station was closed in 1935 and later demolished, but the line remained open for the transport of limestone from quarries at Caldon Low until 1989.[12]

A spring called Egg well south-east of Ashenhurst Hall was believed to have curative powers. It was provided with an oval, or egg-shaped, stone surround bearing a Latin inscription praising the water's powers and the monogrammed initials of William Stanley, the owner of Ashenhurst between 1744 and 1752. In the 19th century the well was protected by a square wall, later roofed over.[13] The structure remained standing in 1992.

Bradnop village had a mains electricity supply by 1940 and was connected to a mains water supply in 1967.[14]

Part of the Coombes brook valley south of Apesford is included in a nature reserve, most of which lies in Ipstones. The reserve originated in 1961 with the scheduling of 26 a. owned by George Lovenbury at Clough Meadows, on the Ipstones side of the brook; a further 200 a., some of it in Bradnop, was bought by the Royal Society for the Protection of Birds in 1962. The reserve was open to the public and Mr. Lovenbury and his wife acted as honorary wardens. A salaried warden was appointed in 1969, and since 1970 he has lived at Sixoaks (formerly Ballfields) Farm, in Bradnop, where there is an information centre.[15]

A Women's Institute was formed in 1970.[16] In 1992 the former school in Bradnop village was used as a village hall.

MANOR AND OTHER ESTATES. In 1168–9 the Crown confirmed a grant to John Lestrange of Ness (Salop.) of unnamed pasture in Staffordshire,[17] probably at BRADNOP and held by grant of one of the earls of Chester. The earl seems to have objected when in 1197 John Lestrange's son, also John, gave land at Bradnop and at Mixon, in Onecote, to his cousin Margery (or Margaret) Lestrange and her husband Thomas Noel,[18] and in 1199 the earl was accused of trying to eject Lestrange and Noel.[19] There was no mention of overlordship when in 1218 Margery and her second husband, Thomas of Whitchurch, granted what were styled the manors of Bradnop and Mixon to Henry de Audley.[20] In 1223 Henry de Audley gave Bradnop and Mixon to his newly founded abbey of Hulton.[21] He renewed the grant after the death of Ranulph, earl of Chester, in 1232, requiring the monks to celebrate a daily mass for the earl and himself.[22] It was presumably because Ranulph was Henry's personal lord that the overlordship of the manors passed to the earl: in 1252 the Crown

2 Ibid. D. 3272/5/13/8; below, econ. hist. (agric.).
3 S.R.O., D. 3272/5/13/22.
4 S.H.C. 1925, 242 (occupied by Michael Nickolls); S.R.O., D. 3272/1/14/1/3 and 6.   5 B.L. Add. Ch. 46770.
6 S.R.O., D. 1176/A/2/27; stone with initials WC on house.
7 B.L. Add. MS. 36664, f. 149; Staffs. Advertiser, 4 Apr. 1818, p. 1; White, Dir. Staffs. (1834), 713.
8 White, Dir. Staffs. (1851), 730; P.O. Dir. Staffs. (1860).
9 J. Phillips and W. F. Hutchings, Map of County of Stafford (1832); above, fig. 2; below, econ. hist. (agric.).
10 Dodd, Peakland Roads, 53–5.
11 Above, Leek and Lowe, communications. For a photograph of the tollhouse see L. Porter, Staffs. Moorlands (Ashbourne, 1983), no. 20.

12 H. Bode, Visiting Bradnop (Ashbourne, 1973), 25–6; Porter, Staffs. Moorlands, no. 29; above, Leek and Lowe, communications.   13 Miller, Leek, 31.
14 Kelly's Dir. Staffs. (1940; s.v. Onecote); Leek R.D.C. Ann. Rep. of M.O.H. 1967 (copy in S.R.O., C/H/1/2/2/22).
15 Bode, Visiting Bradnop, 31.
16 Inf. from Staffs. Federation of Women's Institutes.
17 S.H.C. i. 55; Complete Peerage, xii (1), 348–9.
18 Eyton, Salop. x. 266, 367; for the cousinship see ibid. iii. 142; x. 262.   19 S.H.C. iii (1), 38, 49.
20 Eyton, Salop. iii. 132–4; Pipe R. 1218 (P.R.S. N.S. xxxix), 6.
21 S.R.O., D. 5041, p. 129 (a more accurate transcription of the grant than that in Dugdale, Mon. v. 715–16, which is followed by V.C.H. Staffs. iii. 235).
22 V.C.H. Staffs. iii. 235.

claimed the overlordship on the grounds that it had once belonged to Ranulph. The service then owed to the Crown by Hulton abbey comprised a rent of 5s. 2d. and four loads of hay to be delivered to the royal manor of Penkhull, in Stoke-upon-Trent. The service, however, was being withheld.[23] In 1275 it was stated that the abbey formerly held Mixon, presumably with Bradnop, of the Crown in fee farm for a rent of 5s., one cartload of hay, and an iron fork.[24] Penkhull manor had by then been absorbed into the royal manor of Newcastle-under-Lyme,[25] and the overlordship passed to the earls (later dukes) of Lancaster as lords of Newcastle; they were still the overlords in 1469.[26]

Hulton abbey was dissolved in 1538, and in 1546 the Crown granted Bradnop manor to Edward Agarde, a London speculator. In 1547 he was licensed to transfer it to Sir Edward Aston of Tixall,[27] in whose family (from 1628 Barons Aston) the manor descended, passing on the death in 1751 of James, Lord Aston, to his daughters Mary and Barbara jointly. Barbara married Henry Thomas Clifford, and Mary married Sir Walter Blount, Bt.[28] In 1770 an Act was secured to allow the division of their property,[29] and later the same year both parts of the manor were sold to John Sneyd of Bishton, in Colwich.[30] Sneyd was succeeded in 1809 by his son William (d. 1851). William's son, the Revd. John Sneyd, of Ashcombe Hall, in Cheddleton, still held the manor in 1868, but manorial rights were probably extinguished when a sale after his death in 1873 broke up the estate into its constituent farms.[31]

An estate at *ASHENHURST* was held by Henry of Ashenhurst in 1275.[32] Ranulph of Ashenhurst probably held it in 1318–19, and by 1327 it had probably passed to William of Ashenhurst.[33] The later descent is uncertain until the mid 16th century. John Ashenhurst, the owner in 1552, had been succeeded by his son, another John, by 1560, and the younger John was succeeded by his son Ralph in 1597.[34] Ralph died c. 1629, having settled Ashenhurst on his son Randle in 1616. Randle was still alive in 1662, when he was living at Glossop (Derb.).[35] He was succeeded by his son John, who sold the estate in 1667 to his cousin, Francis Hollinshead (or Hollingshed) of Gawsworth (Ches.).[36] Hollinshead's son, also Francis, held the estate in

1675[37] and was succeeded in 1717 or 1718 by his son Thomas, who died childless in 1744 with his nephew William Stanley as his heir.[38] William was succeeded in 1752 by his son Thomas, Thomas in 1765 by his brother Lawrence, and Lawrence in 1772 by his sister Frances, wife of the Revd. George Salt. George died in 1797 and Frances in 1808. She left Ashenhurst to her god-daughter, Margaret Leigh, who in 1824 sold it to Richard Badnall, son of Richard Badnall of Highfield Hall, in Leekfrith.[39]

Richard Badnall was declared bankrupt in 1826, and in 1828 the 143-a. Ashenhurst estate was bought by Samuel and William Phillips, brothers and Leek silk manufacturers.[40] Samuel died in 1851 and William in 1871. William's heir was his nephew Capt. (later Maj.-Gen.) Thomas Phillips.[41] Thomas died in 1913 and his widow Jessey in 1940, when a life interest passed to their daughter, Elsie Boynton. Elsie died probably in the early 1950s.[42] Her son Thomas had Ashenhurst Hall demolished in 1954, and its site and 72 a. were sold to the present owner, Mr. Isaac Hudson.[43]

In 1666 John Ashenhurst was assessed for tax on four hearths.[44] His house may have been rebuilt or remodelled by his successor.[45] A new house designed by Joseph Sanderson was built for William Stanley in or soon after 1745.[46] Facing east and approached from the north,[47] the house had an irregular plan which was partly concealed by symmetrical elevations on the north and east, giving it the appearance of a double-pile house. The earlier house may have survived behind the new elevations, for there was no direct relationship between the elevations and the arrangement or uses of the rooms behind them. The principal elevation was of seven bays with Corinthian pilasters at either end; the three central bays projected and were surmounted by a pediment. A central doorway on that elevation had been abandoned in favour of an entrance beneath a porch on the north elevation by the early 19th century. By then there were plantations around the house and a landscaped park to the north and east.[48] The north side of the house was remodelled in 1910 to the design of R. Scrivener & Sons of Hanley.[49]

Ashenhurst Hall Farm was built in 1981 on a site north of the former hall with stones from the dairy and one of the stable blocks. In 1992

23 *Bk. of Fees*, ii. 1286.   24 *S.H.C.* v (1), 117–18.
25 *V.C.H. Staffs*. viii. 184.   26 Below, local govt.
27 *V.C.H. Staffs*. iii. 237; *Cal. Pat.* 1547–8, 229–30.
28 *Complete Peerage*, i. 287 and n.
29 10 Geo. III, c. 57 (Priv. Act).
30 Keele Univ. Libr., Ashcombe Sneyd papers, partic. of Bradnop manor in box 2, parcel 2 (2); deed of 28 June 1770 in box 3, parcel 1 (1) (refs. supplied by Mrs. Sandra Burgess of Etruria, Stoke-on-Trent).
31 Sleigh, *Leek*, facing p. 172; *Staffs. Advertiser*, 9 Aug. 1873, p. 8; W.S.L., Sleigh scrapbk. ii, f. 35.
32 *S.H.C.* v (1), 118 (where 'Bradmore' is an error for Bradnop: P.R.O., SC 5/Stafford/3).
33 *S.H.C.* vii (1), 219; *S.H.C.* 1911, 434.
34 B.L. Add. Ch. 46664, 46668; Sleigh, *Leek*, 111; and see fig. 31 on facing page.
35 B.L. Add. Ch. 46725; *Visit. Derb. 1662–4* (Harl. Soc. N.S. viii), 68.
36 B.L. Add. Ch. 46783; Sleigh, *Leek*, 109, 111.
37 B.L. Add. Ch. 46792–3.
38 D.R.O., D. 231M/F372; Sleigh, *Leek*, 109.

39 Sleigh, *Leek*, 109; S.R.O., D. 3359/Phillips, abstract of title to Ashenhurst Hall, 1827.
40 *Lond. Gaz.* 8 Dec. 1826, pp. 2908–9; *Staffs. Advertiser*, 14 July 1827, p. 1; Sleigh, *Leek*, 106–7; sale cat. of 1827 (copy in S.R.O. 4675/1).
41 Sleigh, *Leek*, 11.
42 S.R.O., D. 3359/Phillips, docs. re appt. of public trustee for Phillips estate, 1938–9; abstract of title to Ashenhurst estate, 1942; copy opinion re Phillips Settled Estates, 1943.
43 Inf. from Mr. Hudson.
44 *S.H.C.* 1925, 172.
45 There was formerly in the house a stone dated 1675 with the initials of Fra. Hollinshead: Sleigh, *Leek*, 108. The rooms are described in an inventory of 1745: B.L. Add. MS. 36665, ff. 79–84v.
46 B.L. Add. MS. 36663, f. 564; H. Colvin, *Biog. Dict. of Brit. Architects, 1600–1840*, 717; above, plate 23.
47 S.R.O., D. 1176/A/2/26.
48 Sale cat. of 1827 (copy in S.R.O. 4675/1).
49 S.R.O., D. 1176/A/2/33; W.S.L. 105/1/2/77.

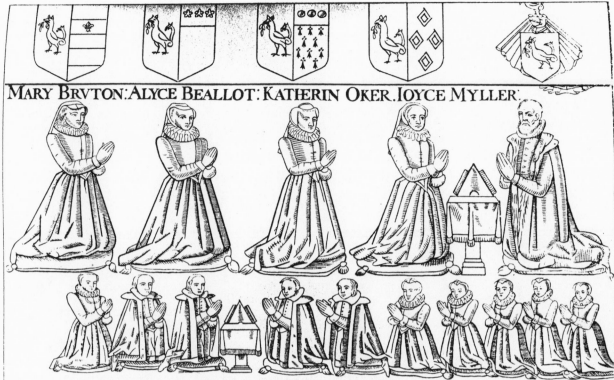

MARY BRVTON:ALYCE BEALLOT:KATHERIN OKER.IOYCE MYLLER.

HERE LYETH THE BODYES OF IOHN ASHENHVRST ESQVIRE, WHO HAD
4 WYVES VIZ IOYCE: ALYCE:KATHEREN: AND MARY: AND HAD ISSVE
BY IOYCE 2 SONNES:AND: 5°:DAVGHTERS: VIZ RALPHE & IOHN:DORO-
THIE :MARGARETT: ELIZABETH: ANNE: AND: IOYCE: AND BY ALYCE:HE
HAD ISSVE 2 SOÑES: THOMAS:AND LAVRANCE: &BY MARY HE HAD
ISSVE ONE DAVGHTER NAMED MARY: AND THE SAYD IOHN ASHEN-
HVRST DECEASED THE XXTH DAY OF OCTOBER ANNO DÑI 1597.

FIG. 31. THE ASHENHURST BRASS IN ST. EDWARD'S CHURCH, LEEK

the remaining stable block, which was originally a barn and retained its 17th-century roof, was being converted into a house.

ECONOMIC HISTORY. AGRICULTURE. Pasture on Morridge was included in Henry de Audley's endowment of Hulton abbey in 1223.[50] Its use was disputed by Dieulacres abbey, which had been established a few years earlier in Leekfrith and possibly resented Hulton's intrusion into the area. By an agreement made in the early 1230s Dieulacres was given pasture rights in the Birchall area, on the west side of Kniveden brook in Leek and Lowe, while Hulton was given pasture rights in the Bradnop valley, as long as it paid tithe to Dieulacres, as rector of Leek. For any land under cultivation on Morridge, Hulton was liable to pay great tithe to Dieulacres, along with a goodwill offering of 5s. at Easter.[51] By a further agreement, made in 1237 and relating chiefly to Hulton's grange at Mixon, in Onecote, Dieulacres was allowed pasture rights on Morridge for pigs 'without number' and in the summer for 200 dry cattle.[52]

By 1343 Hulton abbey had a grange in the north part of the township. It let it that year to William Gonne, along with pasture rights on Morridge for all animals except goats.[53]

A wood called Witherwood, which was included

50 S.R.O., D. 5041, p. 129.
51 S.H.C. N.S. ix. 357–8.
52 W.S.L., M. 539, no. 8.
53 S.R.O., D. 3272/5/13/9.

in Hulton's endowment of 1223, lay on the slope of Morridge south-east of Bradnop village: land called Weather Woods was recorded in 1827 near Lane End Farm.[54]

In the 1550s Sir Edward Aston, lord of Bradnop, tried to extinguish the rights of common claimed on Morridge by men from Grindon and Waterfall.[55] About 1634 Walter, Lord Aston (d. 1639), planned to inclose Morridge, then stated to cover 2,000 a.,[56] and in 1638 the Crown apparently gave permission.[57] The freeholders of Bradnop objected to such large-scale inclosure, although they agreed that the waste needed to be protected from outsiders. In 1653 they proposed that Walter, Lord Aston (d. 1678), should inclose 200 a. only and let it to them at 2s. 6d. an acre.[58] The rights of poor cottagers already settled on Morridge were protected in 1655 by the county justices, who ordered that each cottage was to have 4 a. of common allotted to it.[59] About 240 a. seems to have been inclosed, mainly at the south end of Morridge.[60] The Astons, however, remained intent on large-scale inclosure. In the early 18th century Thomas Hollinshead of Ashenhurst claimed that Lord Aston in 1660 had made an agreement with the freeholders not to inclose further and not to grant any right of pasture to people who had no land in the manor. Despite the alleged agreement Aston and his son Walter, Lord Aston (d. 1714), had in fact inclosed a further 600 a. and had settled cottagers on the land.[61] A draft agreement of 1688, evidently drawn up by the freeholders but not ratified, acknowledged Lord Aston's right to inclose up to 2,000 a., half of which was to be assigned to the freeholders.[62] Despite the Astons' efforts much of Morridge remained open, and full-scale inclosure did not take place until 1769 when 3,139 a. in Bradnop and Onecote were inclosed under an Act of 1766.[63]

To counter the problem of trespassers, or 'out men', using Morridge as pasture, the freeholders in 1653 proposed that a moor keeper be appointed; any fines that he collected were to be shared equally among Lord Aston, the poor of Bradnop manor, and the keeper himself.[64] In 1683 the freeholders further proposed that they should be allowed to prosecute trespassers in the Astons' name, although at their own expense.[65] A more complex means of policing was drawn up in 1691, whereby householders in both Bradnop and Onecote were divided into six groups of 20 (three for Bradnop and three for Onecote), each group providing by rota a hayward to deal with the trespassers; the haywards had the duty of inspecting the common at least once a month between 21 April and Michaelmas.[66]

In pursuing the policy of inclosure Lord Aston (d. 1714) was associated with others, including Humphrey Perry and William Greene, both of Stafford, George Gatacre of Cannock, and Joshua Potts of Park House Farm, in Leekfrith.[67] It is possible that those men arranged for cattle from other parts of the county to be pastured on Morridge and then sold them to butchers.

Of the 1,160 ha. of farmland returned for the civil parish in 1988, grassland covered 1,054 ha. and there were 85.5 ha. of rough grazing. The farming was chiefly dairy and sheep, with 2,441 head of cattle and 2,422 sheep and lambs. There were also 2,162 pigs and 1,847 hens. Of the 50 farms returned, 31 were under 20 ha. in size, 14 were between 20 and 49 ha., and 5 were between 50 and 99 ha. Woodland covered 10.2 ha.[68]

MILLS. About 1600 a mill at Ashenhurst was run by John Brindley of Wildgoose Farm.[69] Run by James Brindley in 1834, Ashenhurst mill apparently stopped working in the mid 1880s.[70]

Gorstead mill on Coombes brook east of Apesford was described in 1815 as lately built. It apparently stopped working in the late 1890s.[71]

INDUSTRY. Land called the Smelting Mill beside Kniveden brook in the south-west part of the township in 1687[72] suggests iron smelting at some date.

In 1825 Richard Badnall licensed a partnership of stone merchants to dig for stone on his estate at Ashenhurst. The quarry, whose site is unknown, produced stone suitable for the manufacture of cement. Work probably stopped with the sale of Ashenhurst in 1828.[73]

LOCAL GOVERNMENT. In the earlier 1370s the duchy of Lancaster, as overlord, held a great court for Bradnop manor attended by two frankpledges, one presumably representing Bradnop tithing and the other Onecote tithing.[74] The duchy still held a great court for Bradnop in 1469.[75]

The abbot of Hulton held a small court for his tenants at Bradnop in 1317, and a twice-yearly court in 1342.[76] The abbot still held a court at the Dissolution.[77]

A view of frankpledge for Bradnop manor was held by Walter, Lord Aston, as lord of the manor by the late 17th century.[78] In 1744 the customary

54 Ibid. D. 5041, p. 129; S.R.O. 4675/1, lot 5.
55 P.R.O., C 1/1381/50; ibid. STAC 4/9/8.
56 B.L. Add. MS. 36452, f. 157; W.S.L. 132/1/47, deed of 27 Sept. 1634.   57 D.R.O., D. 231M/E5038.
58 Ibid. D. 231M/E5029.
59 S.R.O., Q/SO/6, f. 23v.
60 D.R.O., D. 231M/E5030; B.L. Add. Ch. 46823.
61 B.L. Add. Ch. 46823.
62 D.R.O., D. 231M/E5044.
63 S.R.O., Q/RDc 31; S.R.O. 5116/1; 6 Geo. III, c. 29 (Priv. Act).   64 D.R.O., D. 231M/E5029.
65 Ibid. D. 231M/E5033.
66 Ibid. D. 231M/E5048.
67 B.L. Add. Ch. 46823. Aston also contracted with others to exploit mineral deposits in the manor: below, Onecote, econ. hist. (ind.).

68 P.R.O., MAF 68/6128/53.
69 Ibid. E 134/11 Chas. I East./5, m. 6; Leek Par. Reg. 8.
70 White, Dir. Staffs. (1834), 713; Kelly's Dir. Staffs. (1884; 1888).
71 Inf. from Miss M. F. Cleverdon, citing deed in possession of owner of Gorstead Mill Farm; Kelly's Dir. Staffs. (1896; 1900).
72 B.L. Add. MS. 36664, f. 174.
73 S.R.O., D. 3359/Badnall, draft agreement of Dec. 1825.
74 W.S.L., M. 541A; T. Pape, Medieval Newcastle-under-Lyme, 119, 191.   75 P.R.O., DL 30/233/8.
76 S.H.C. 1911, 433; S.R.O., D. 3272/5/13/5.
77 Valor Eccl. (Rec. Com.), iii. 107.
78 Humberside R.O., Beverley, DDCC/126/3–6 (refs. supplied by Dr. G. H. R. Kent of V.C.H. Yorks. E.R.).

meeting place was in Onecote.[79] The court was last recorded in 1868 when the lord, the Revd. John Sneyd, advertised a view with court leet and court baron for Bradnop to be held at the Blacksmiths Arms in Bradnop in November.[80]

Bradnop manor formed a constablewick by 1377 and still in the later 17th century.[81]

The township was part of the Bradnop quarter of Leek parish, and in the 1660s its poor were relieved by the quarter's overseer.[82] The township had its own overseer by 1743.[83] It became part of Leek poor-law union in 1837.[84]

CHURCH. People from Bradnop attended the church built in Onecote in the earlier 1750s, and the township was included in a parish created for Bradnop and Onecote in 1862. Services were also held in the school opened in Bradnop village in 1862.[85] The school was closed in 1978, but the building was still used for services until they were transferred in 1990 to the Methodist church in Bradnop village, where they were held fortnightly in 1992.[86]

NONCONFORMITY. Two Quakers from Bradnop, John Bloor and Ann Bottom, were married at a meeting of Friends at Whitehough, in Ipstones, in 1701.[87]

A Methodist society of eight members met at Stile House Farm in 1784. It still met there in 1790 but may later have used a house in Bradnop village which was registered for protestant worship in 1802.[88] Apparently later disbanded, the society had been revived by 1813, and in 1829 there was a weekly Sunday service in Bradnop.[89] A chapel was built in the village in 1840, and on Census Sunday 1851 the attendance was 32 in the afternoon and 40 in the evening, besides Sunday school children. Enlarged in 1890, the chapel was still open in 1992.[90]

Primitive Methodists apparently met in a barn at Cliffe Farm from the later 1830s. In 1890 they opened a chapel on the Ashbourne road. It was closed in 1970, and the building was derelict in 1992.[91]

EDUCATION. A schoolmaster was recorded at

Bradnop in 1681.[92] The pair of houses in Bradnop village called School Cottages is probably identifiable as the School House, so called in 1783.[93] In 1876 it was claimed that a school had been maintained in the township since the 1790s.[94] A school which in the earlier 1830s had 30 boys was by then endowed with a house and garden worth £5 a year. Also in the earlier 1830s there was a girls' school with 20 pupils and a Church of England Sunday school at which 23 children were taught free.[95] The Sunday school was possibly replaced by a school which was set up as a branch of Leek Sunday school in 1835 with an attendance of 43 children. That school still existed in 1861.[96]

A school-church was built in the village in 1862.[97] The site was given by the Revd. John Sneyd, the lord of the manor; the building and its furnishings were paid for by local subscribers, and free carriage of materials was provided by Bradnop farmers.[98] The school was run by a committee of local people as a public elementary school and was considered to be the successor to the earlier parish school. From 1876 the school received a government grant, and a board of managers was set up in 1904.[99] The decision in 1930 that what was then an all-age school with 30 children on its books should become a junior school took effect in 1937, the senior children being transferred to Leek.[1] Bradnop school took controlled status in 1959.[2] It was closed in 1978, and the children were transferred to Leek.[3] In 1992 the school building was used as a village hall.

CHARITY FOR THE POOR. By will of 1693 John (or Thomas) Stanley left the interest on £84 to be distributed after the death of his wife among the poor of Bradnop on 24 December each year. The beneficiaries were probably residents in the Bradnop quarter of Leek parish. In 1743 the capital was invested in 5 a. at Sheen, and it was agreed that the poor of both Bradnop and Onecote townships should benefit equally. The rent received from the land was £3 10s. in the later 1780s and had increased to £10 by the earlier 1820s.[4] By a Scheme of 1928 the charity was amalgamated with that of Joan Adsetts for Onecote, and the income in 1976 was £22.[5]

79 S.R.O., D. 3359/Condlyffe, notice for holding ct. 8 Oct. 1744.
80 W.S.L., Sleigh scrapbk. ii, f. 35.
81 S.H.C. 1925, 172, 242; S.H.C. 4th ser. vi. 8.
82 Above, Leek, par. intro. (par. govt.).
83 S.R.O., D. 3816/3/1.
84 Ibid. D. 699/1/1/1, p. 4.
85 Staffs. Advertiser, 21 June 1862, p. 4; S.R.O., D. 5047/1/11, letters of 26 June 1862; below, Onecote, church.
86 Inf. from the vicar, the Revd. S. G. Price.
87 S.R.O., D. 3359/Condlyffe, marriage declaration, 1701.
88 Wardle, Methodist Hist. 5; S.H.C. 4th ser. iii. 4.
89 S.R.O., D. 3155/1; Leek Libr., Johnson scrapbk. i (2), D/13/15.
90 Wardle, Methodist Hist. 40; P.R.O., HO 129/372/2/3.
91 Staffs. Advertiser, 19 Sept. 1889, p. 7; Bode, Visiting Bradnop, 12; S.R.O., D. 3156/2/1/6; G.R.O. Worship Reg.

no. 32257.
92 Leek Par. Reg. 218.
93 S.R.O., D. 3359/misc. deeds, draft deed of 1792 rehearsing deed of 24 Dec. 1783.
94 P.R.O., ED 7/108/39.
95 Educ. Enq. Abstract, 879.
96 S.R.O., D. 1114/1, ann. reps. of Leek Sunday sch. 1835–61.
97 Staffs. Advertiser, 21 June 1862, p. 4.
98 S.R.O., D. 5047/1/11, copies of subscription list and disbursements 1862, and letter from Dryden Sneyd 1899.
99 Ibid. Order of 30 Apr. 1904; P.R.O., ED 7/108/39.
1 Staffs. C.C. Record for 1930, 867, 869; S.R.O., CEL/68/2, pp. 118–19.
2 S.R.O., D. 5047/1/11, letters of 12 and 14 Oct. 1959.
3 Ibid. CEL/68/3, pp. 95–6.
4 Ibid. D. 3816/3/1; Char. Dons. 1152–3; 13th Rep. Com. Char. 388.
5 Char. Com. files 246426–7.

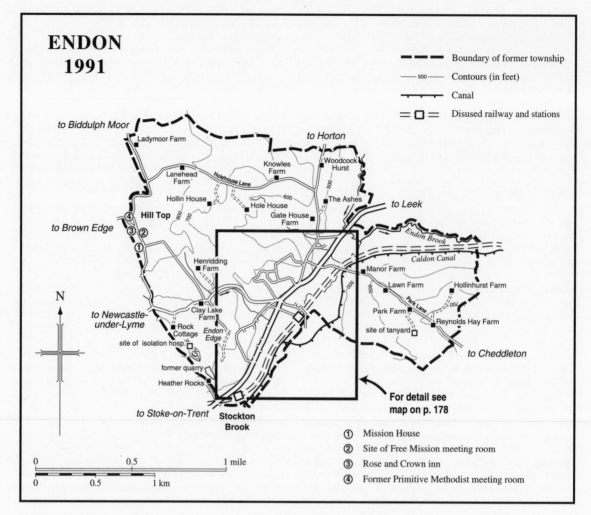

FIG. 32

ENDON

ENDON was formerly a township in Leek parish 2,303 a. (932 ha.) in area[6] and later part of a civil parish which included Longsdon and Stanley until 1894. That year a new civil parish called Endon and Stanley was formed, excluding Longsdon.[7] The area is mostly pasture, but there is much suburban housing in the south-west along the main road between Leek and the Potteries. The boundary follows brooks on the east and south[8] and ridges on the west. A boundary change in 1934 added 86 a. from Horton, with the loss of 2 a. to Biddulph.[9] A further boundary change in 1988 transferred a block of land along the west side of Endon to Brown Edge civil parish, whilst adding to Endon the Brown Edge part of Stockton Brook in the south-west. As a result the area of Endon and Stanley civil parish was reduced from 2,827 a. (1,144 ha.) to 2,682 a. (1,086 ha.).[10]

This article deals only with the former township of Endon.

The land lies at its highest, 900 ft. (274 m.), in the north-west part of the township. It falls gradually to the south-east and is 645 ft. (196 m.) at Endon Bank, a promontory in the centre of the township overlooking the valley of Endon brook. The land drops sharply beneath Endon Bank and is 482 ft. (146 m.) on the main Leek road. To the south-east it rises to 710 ft. (216 m.) at Reynolds Hay Farm. The underlying rock is sandstone of the Millstone Grit series, apart from Endon Bank which is Bunter Sandstone. There is Boulder Clay in the south-east part of the township and alluvium along the brooks. The soil is mostly fine loam, with an area of coarse loam in the east around Hollinhurst Farm.[11]

Forty people in Endon were assessed for hearth

[6] The acreage has been calculated by planimeter. This article was written in 1991.   [7] *Census*, 1901.
[8] For the boundary with Stanley see S.R.O., D. 1176/A/11/12.
[9] Staffs. Review Order, 1934, pp. 59, 63, and map 1

(copy in S.R.O.); *Census*, 1931.
[10] Staffs. Moorlands (Parishes) Order, 1988 (S.I. 1988 no. 292); *Census*, 1981–91.
[11] Geol. Surv. Map 1", drift, sheet 123 (1924 edn.); Soil Surv. of Eng. and Wales, sheet 3 (1983).

tax in 1666.[12] The population was 445 in 1821, 487 in 1831, 571 in 1841, and 658 in 1851.[13] The population of Endon and Stanley civil parish was 1,354 in 1901, 1,583 in 1911, 1,512 in 1921, and 1,471 in 1931. By 1951 it was 1,907. The population thereafter rose steadily, chiefly as a result of the building of housing estates in Endon: it was 2,697 in 1961, 3,792 in 1971, and 3,793 in 1981. In 1991, after the 1988 boundary change, the population was 3,288.[14]

A Bronze Age axe-head found at Henridding Farm on the west side of the township may indicate prehistoric settlement.[15] The site of a settlement called Endon in 1086 may have been in the area of Endon Bank, which is presumably the hill (*dun*) from which Endon takes its name.[16] By the later 13th century much of the township was parkland and settlement may have been limited: several tenants of Endon manor in 1308 were stated to have no houses attached to their land. The parkland had been converted to farmland by the mid 16th century, with a resulting pattern of scattered farmhouses.[17]

The oldest surviving house is Sutton House on the east slope of Endon Bank. Of the 16th century and possibly built for Richard Sutton (d. 1547),[18] the house was enlarged in the 17th and 18th centuries. It stands at the junction of a road which formed part of the route between Newcastle-under-Lyme and Leek before the early 19th century[19] and Hallwater Lane, so called in 1495.[20] To the east Hallwater Lane meets the present main Leek road and becomes Park Lane, a road which runs across the former parkland in the east part of the township. The earliest settlement in that area was possibly at Hollinhurst, on a hill north of the road near the eastern boundary. The site was occupied by 1574,[21] and the present Hollinhurst Farm retains a date stone of 1656. On Park Lane itself Reynolds Hay Farm, Lawn Farm, and Manor Farm are all of the 17th century, as is Hallwater Farm in Hallwater Lane. Manor Farm, probably the home of the Tomkinson family in 1607, was rebuilt in 1637 for Roger Tomkinson and his wife Mary.[22] The house was extended on the north side in the 18th century and remodelled in the early 19th century. Park Farm is of the early 19th century and may have been built for William Hand, a tanner, who lived there in 1816.[23]

In the former parkland in the north part of the township there was a house by the later 16th century called the Ashes, on the road to Horton. The present 17th-century house with early 18th-century additions was built either for John Bellot

(d. 1659), who was joint lord of Horton from 1625, or for his son Sir John (d. 1674).[24] Gate House Farm to the south-west is partly of the 17th century, and there was a house at Woodcock Hurst near the Horton boundary by the later 17th century.[25] West of the Horton road there was a house on the site of Hole House by 1561,[26] and one by 1607 in Holehouse Lane on the site of Knowles Farm.[27] Both the present houses are of the 19th century. Further west the site of Hollin House was occupied by the later 16th century, as was that of Ladymoor Farm on the north-western boundary.[28] The present Hollin House is of the 17th century; Ladymoor Farm was rebuilt in the 19th century. Lanehead Farm in Holehouse Lane was so called in 1648[29] and the present house is mostly of the 18th century.

Endon village grew up in the 17th century where the Newcastle–Leek road forded a brook north-east of Endon Bank: cottages of the 17th and early 18th century survive in Brook Lane and in a road called the Village. There was an inn, the Black Horse, by 1802.[30] It was moved to its present site on the new line of the Newcastle–Leek road east of the village presumably after that line was constructed between 1816 and 1820.[31]

By the 17th century there were houses elsewhere along the Newcastle–Leek road. One was recorded in 1607 at Woodhouse Green about ½ mile from where the road enters the township on the west; it was possibly on the site of Clay Lake Farm, so called in 1678.[32] East of Woodhouse Green the road drops into a valley, where it meets a road from Stanley at a place called Lane End in 1648. A house there then was probably the predecessor of the present Lane Ends House, which is mainly of the 18th century.[33] North-east of Lane End there was formerly a row of cottages where the road, as Church Lane, begins to climb Endon Bank. One cottage had a stone showing a skull and crossbones with the date 1663 and was possibly used as a stopping-place for funeral parties going to the parish church in Leek, before Endon acquired its own church in the early 18th century.[34] Another cottage was occupied by 1816 as the Plough inn,[35] whose present south-facing front is an extension of the original building and dates from after the construction of the new line of the Newcastle–Leek road. Half-way up Church Lane stands Bank House Farm, of the 18th century and possibly on the site of a house recorded at Endon Bank in 1677.[36] Bank House to the north-west on the summit of Endon Bank

---

12 *S.H.C.* 1925, 160–1.
13 *V.C.H. Staffs.* i. 327, where from 1861 the figs. are for Endon, Longsdon, and Stanley combined.
14 *Census,* 1901–91.
15 *T.N.S.F.C.* lxvi. 190–1.
16 *V.C.H. Staffs.* iv. 41. The meaning of the first element of the name is uncertain.
17 *S.H.C.* N.S. xi. 256; below, econ. hist. (warren and park).   18 L.J.R.O., B/C/11, Ric. Sutton (1547).
19 Below, this section (communications).
20 S.R.O., D. (W.) 1490/8, m. 11.
21 Ibid. D. (W.) 1490/15, ct. of 11 Oct. 1574.
22 Ibid. D. (W.) 1490/17, ct. of 23 Oct. 1607; *Leek Par. Reg.* 13, 25; date stone with initials RT and MT over former entrance on S. side of house.
23 Below, econ. hist. (trade and ind.).

24 Sleigh, *Leek,* 146; G.E.C. *Baronetage,* iii. 278.
25 *Leek Par. Reg.* 197.
26 S.R.O., D. (W.) 1490/14, m. 15d.
27 Ibid. D. (W.) 1490/17, ct. of 23 Oct. 1607.
28 *S.H.C.* N.S. ix. 42; W.S.L. 52/46.
29 *Leek Par. Reg.* 75.
30 S.R.O., D. 4302/5/1, p. 265; D. (W.) 1535/1, f. 67; D. (W.) 1909/E/9/1; Parson and Bradshaw, *Staffs. Dir.* (1818), villages section, p. 9.
31 Below, this section (communications).
32 S.R.O., D. (W.) 1490/17, ct. of 23 Oct. 1607; *Leek Par. Reg.* 207.   33 *Leek Par. Reg.* 75.
34 F. Stubbs, *Endon* (Leek, 1994), 3; below, church.
35 S.R.O., D. (W.) 1535/1, f. 87; D. (W.) 1909/E/9/1; Parson and Bradshaw, *Staffs. Dir.* (1818), villages section, p. 9.
36 S.R.O., D. 4069/1/1, f. 12.

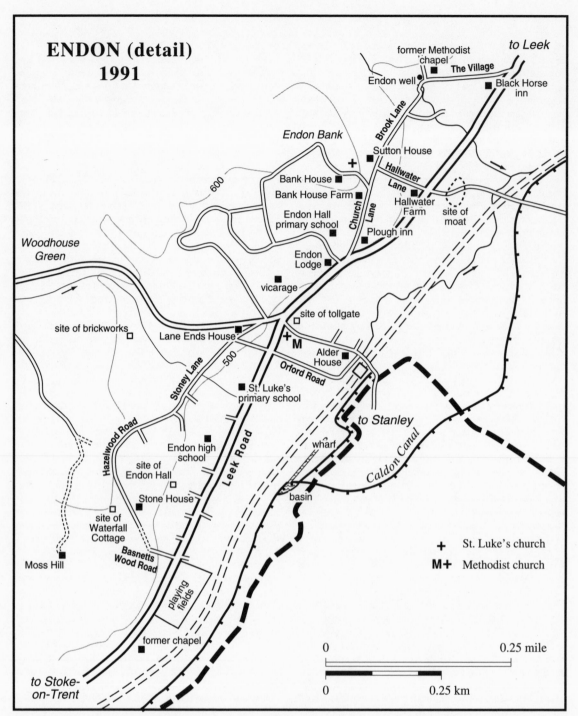

ENDON (detail)
1991

former Methodist chapel
to Leek
Endon well
The Village
Black Horse inn
Brook Lane
Endon Bank
Sutton House
Hallwater Lane
Bank House
Bank House Farm
Hallwater Farm
site of moat
Church Lane
Endon Hall primary school
Plough inn
600
Woodhouse Green
Endon Lodge
vicarage
site of tollgate
site of brickworks
Lane Ends House
M
Stoney Lane
Alder House
500
Orford Road
St. Luke's primary school
to Stanley
Hazelwood Road
Leek Road
Endon high school
wharf
site of Endon Hall
Caldon Canal
Stone House
basin
site of Waterfall Cottage
Moss Hill
Basnetts Wood Road
playing fields
✝   St. Luke's church
M✝ Methodist church
former chapel
to Stoke-on-Trent

0   0.25 mile

0   0.25 km

Fig. 33

almost certainly incorporates what in 1808 was called Endon House, then described as pleasantly situated on an eminence with gardens, nurseries, and fish ponds.[37] In 1815 it was the home of John Daniel, one of the owners of the New Hall pottery works in Shelton, in Stoke-upon-Trent.[38] Daniel was a free thinker, and when he died in 1821 he was buried without religious ceremony in unconsecrated ground near the house. His sister Alice was buried there

in the same manner in 1827.[39] In the later 19th century the house, then known as Endon Bank, was enlarged by a Leek solicitor, George Smith (d. 1892).[40]

In the south-west part of the township there was a house at Moss Hill called the Moss in 1750 and Moss Hall in 1772, and one in 1750 to the north at Endon Edge.[41] The former Waterfall Cottage in woodland at the south end of Endon Edge was occupied in 1841 by Elizabeth Basnett

37   Ibid. D. 4069/5/1, plan IV; Staffs. Advertiser, 27 Aug. 1808, p. 1.

38   S.R.O., Q/RDc 69, p. 67 and plan IV (no. 331); Ll. Jewitt, Ceramic Art of Gt. Brit. (1883), 484.

39   Staffs. Advertiser, 27 Jan. 1821, p. 4; 16 June 1827, p.

4; R. Garner, Suppl. to Natural Hist. of Staffs. (1860), 12.

40   P.O. Dir. Staffs. (1872); P.R.O., RG 11/2736; S.R.O., D. 4302/1/12, p. 98; O.S. Map 6", Staffs. VII. SE. (1900 edn.).

41   S.R.O., D. 4302/1/1, p. 66; D. 4302/7/1/3.

and in 1851 by James Basnett, a stone cutter and the owner of a beerhouse near the Caldon canal.[42] Rock Cottage to the north-west was built as a cottage ornée in 1846 for Abner Wedgwood, who died there in 1869. It was enlarged after being bought in 1890 by James Slater, director of art at the Doulton pottery works at Burslem. In 1983 a private nursing home was opened in the house, which was extended in 1984 and 1985.[43]

By the later 18th century there was a hamlet at Hill Top on the township's north-western boundary. In the earlier 19th century it was occupied chiefly by miners who worked in Brown Edge. The hamlet had a beerhouse in 1841, possibly on the site of the present Rose and Crown inn, recorded from 1871.[44]

The character of the south-western part of the township changed after the construction in the later 1840s of Leek Road and the opening of railway stations in 1867 and 1896.[45] The improved communications with the Potteries led to the building of detached and semi-detached houses. The former Endon Hall on the west side of Leek Road had been built by 1854, when it was occupied by James Bateman Wathen, the owner by 1864 of a pottery works in Fenton. It was remodelled in 1877.[46] Orford Road at the north end of Leek Road was laid out in the 1870s,[47] and was probably named after William Orford (d. 1897), for whom Endon Lodge near the Plough inn had been built by 1868.[48] In 1881 a house in Orford Road was the home of a ceramic artist and painter Herbert Wilson Foster (d. 1918).[49] The road to Stanley, running parallel to Orford Road on the north, was renamed Station Road, and Alder House at its east end was built in the late 1870s.[50] Houses were also built in the 1870s in Stoney Lane, running west from Lane Ends House, and on the Newcastle road to the north.[51] In 1896 five pairs of houses were built at Stockton Brook at the south end of Leek Road,[52] and a house called Heather Rocks on the road north from Stockton Brook to Brown Edge is dated 1901. A fountain was erected in 1898 at the top of Leek Road to commemorate Queen Victoria's Diamond Jubilee. It was demolished in the 1930s, apart from an inscribed stone which survives as the base of a seat.[53]

Suburban development was intensified after the First World War. Houses had been built by the earlier 1920s on the west side of Leek Road south of Basnetts Wood Road and by the later 1930s in side roads to the north, Spencer Avenue, Platts Avenue, and Brookfield Avenue.[54] Endon Hall was demolished in the later 1950s, and houses were built on its site in what became Kent Drive, named after the builder.[55] Houses were built on the east side of Leek Road from the 1950s. In the 1970s a large privately-built housing estate was laid out on the rising ground west of the Plough inn, along with smaller estates south-east of the inn and in Brook Side Drive in Endon village. The western stretch of Stoney Lane, later Hazelwood Road, is part of another large privately-built housing estate begun in the 1970s. From the summit of Hazelwood Road the estate continues down to Leek Road on either side of Basnetts Wood Road and includes the site of Waterfall Cottage. Railway Court and Dorian Way off Station Road were built c. 1990, and Station Road was then Endon's main shopping area.

Endon association for the prosecution of felons was formed evidently in 1801. It still existed in 1838.[56] Endon had a village policeman in 1847. His successor in 1851, William Hand, was still the policeman in 1871.[57]

A post office was opened in Endon village in 1853, possibly at the corner of Brook Lane and the Village, its site in the late 19th century.[58] By 1912 it was also a telephone call office.[59] There was a post office at Stockton Brook by 1898.[60]

An isolation hospital on the south-western boundary was opened for Leek rural sanitary district in 1894. Rebuilt in 1915, it was closed in 1931.[61]

Much of the township had a mains water supply by 1914. A sewerage scheme was completed in 1918, with a works in the west part of Longsdon; the works was rebuilt in 1970.[62] An electricity substation was opened at Stockton Brook in 1932, and by 1940 electricity was apparently available for the whole of Endon. There was a gas supply by 1940.[63]

COMMUNICATIONS. The road between Newcastle-under-Lyme and Leek crossed over Horton brook east of Endon village by a bridge in existence by 1367 and mentioned as a stone bridge in 1561.[64] The road was turnpiked in 1765. A tollgate was set up east of the junction with the road to Stanley in 1766, and by 1767

---

[42] P.R.O., HO 107/1005; HO 107/2008; O.S. Map 1", LXXII. NW. (1837 edn.); White, *Dir. Staffs.* (1851), 731; *Staffs. Advertiser*, 8 Mar. 1856, p. 1.

[43] J. C. Wedgwood, *Hist. of Wedgwood Family*, 207; *Staffs. Advertiser*, 22 May 1869, p. 5; *Rock Cottage Nursing Home Handbk.*

[44] P.R.O., HO 107/1005; ibid. RG 10/2878, naming the hamlet as Brown Edge; above, fig. 2.

[45] Below, this section (communications).

[46] S.R.O., D. 4302/1/2, p. 100; *V.C.H. Staffs.* viii. 220; above, plate 36, showing date stone of 1877.

[47] W.S.L. 458/5/35, plan of building land on Lane Ends Fm. 1868; O.S. Map 6", Staffs. XII. NE. (1888 edn.).

[48] *P.O. Dir. Staffs.* (1868); *Staffs. Advertiser*, 9 Jan. 1897, p. 5; O.S. Map 6", Staffs. VII. SE. (1890 edn.).

[49] P.R.O., RG 11/2736; F. Stubbs, 'Herbert Wilson Foster' (TS., copy in W.S.L.).

[50] *Staffs. Advertiser*, 1 Mar. 1879, p. 8.

[51] O.S. Map 6", Staffs. XII. NE. (1888 edn.).

[52] Date stone on central pair.

[53] *Staffs. Advertiser*, 16 July 1898, p. 7; *Old Road to Endon*, ed. R. Speake (Keele, 1974), pl. facing p. 145; local inf.

[54] O.S. Map 6", Staffs. XII. NE. (1925 and later edns.).

[55] *ARC News* (Stoke-on-Trent Mus. Arch. Soc.), no. 3 (Nov. 1983), p. 4.

[56] S.R.O., D. 3359/Cruso, draft agreement of 1801; *Staffs. Advertiser*, 24 Feb. 1838, p. 2.

[57] S.R.O., D. 4302/1/2, p. 82; P.R.O., HO 107/2008; ibid. RG 10/2878.

[58] *Staffs. Advertiser*, 17 Dec. 1853, p. 5; O.S. Map 6", Staffs. VII. SE. (1890 edn.).   [59] *Kelly's Dir. Staffs.* (1912).

[60] O.S. Map 6", Staffs. XII. NE. (1900 edn.).

[61] Leek Rural Sanitary Dist. *Ann. Rep. of M.O.H. 1894* (copy in S.R.O., C/H/1/2/1/5); *1915*; *1931* (copies in S.R.O., C/H/1/2/2/22).

[62] Leek Rural Sanitary Dist. *Ann. Rep. of M.O.H. 1914*; *1918* (copies in S.R.O., C/H/1/2/2/22); *Old Road to Endon*, 159.

[63] W.S.L. 103/2/71 (TS. hist. of Brown Edge), p. 24; *Kelly's Dir. Staffs.* (1940).

[64] S.R.O., D. (W.) 1490/1, m. 8; D. (W.) 1490/14/6.

there was a tollhouse.[65] Between 1816 and 1820 a new line was constructed from the Plough inn to the present Black Horse inn, avoiding the steep rise up Endon Bank.[66] The road was disturnpiked in 1879.[67] A cast-iron milepost dated 1821 originally stood at Woodhouse Green, where it marked the 7-mile point from Newcastle.[68] In 1991 it stood on Leek Road in front of Endon county high school. Other mileposts on the Newcastle–Leek road were replaced in 1879 by the present cast-iron posts.[69]

Leek Road, which enters the township at Stockton Brook and joins the Newcastle road at Lane End, formed part of a turnpike road from Stoke-upon-Trent. It was built under an Act of 1840 apparently in the later 1840s.[70]

The Caldon canal, opened probably in 1778, runs through Endon.[71] East of Park Lane the canal originally ran along the line of the later railway, but it was realigned to the south in the 1790s, in connexion with the building of a branch to Leek.[72] There was a wharf on the canal near Park Lane by 1860.[73] A basin and wharf south-west of Endon railway station were built probably in the 1910s, and in 1917 a mechanical chute was installed, designed to discharge stone brought by rail from Caldon Low.[74] Abandoned in 1961, the canal was reopened for leisure boats in 1974.[75]

A railway opened in 1867 from Stoke-upon-Trent to the Churnet Valley line at Leekbrook south of Leek ran through the south part of Endon, and there was a station on the road to Stanley.[76] Another station was opened at Stockton Brook in 1896; it was closed in 1956.[77] Endon station was closed in 1960 when passenger services were ended, but the railway continued in use as a mineral line until 1989.[78]

SOCIAL AND CULTURAL ACTIVITIES. A well-dressing festival was started in 1845.[79] That year Thomas Heaton[80] built a fountain in Endon village, and it was decorated to mark Oak Apple Day (29 May). By 1852 what had become an annual event began with an afternoon procession to the church, where a sermon was preached, followed by a visit to the fountain, which had been decorated with flowers; tea was then served, and there was dancing in Jaw Bone field on the east side of the Methodist chapel in the village. An estimated 300 people attended the event in 1852 and 400 in 1853, some of whom came from the Potteries. An organizing committee

had evidently been established by 1856, when admission to the grounds at Jaw Bone field was by 1s. ticket only. A quadrille band was engaged in 1861, and for many years from 1864 music was provided by Endon brass band.

There was an estimated attendance of 1,200 in 1864 and of over 2,000 in 1872. By then it was normal to keep the well decorated and the field open for a second day, and the festivities included a May queen and maypole dancing. In 1906 it was decided to hold the event over a weekend, beginning on the Saturday nearest 29 May and ending on the Monday. In 1916 there was a further change to Whit weekend. In 1991 the festival was held on the weekend of the spring bank holiday.[81]

By 1860 it was the custom to distribute the profits of the festival, by then some £25, among the poor of the area on St. Thomas's day (21 December).[82] The festival's growing popularity created problems for those arranging the event, especially as regards the disposal of the money raised. In 1868 Thomas Heaton, then of Alton, vested the fountain in a body of trustees, whose main function was to administer the funds. They were also to ensure that the festival was conducted in an orderly manner; it was Heaton's wish that the well-dressing should provide 'innocent recreation and enjoyment' for the inhabitants of Endon village and the neighbourhood 'without giving encouragement to any act of intemperance or vice'.[83] The trustees included the recently appointed vicar, James Badnall,[84] who emphasized the church's role in the festival by engaging visiting preachers to deliver sermons. Under the terms of the trust the profits were to be distributed in bread to the poor of Endon village and the immediate neighbourhood on 21 December and were also to be used for the Church of England Sunday school, the Wesleyan Methodist Sunday school, and 'the free grammar school' (Endon parochial school). A Scheme of 1974 reorganized what was by then called the Endon Well Dressing Festival Charity. The beneficiaries in 1991 included both Sunday schools and other youth groups and voluntary organizations in Endon.[85]

In 1854 James Basnett advertised the opening of his gardens and 'new pleasure grounds' at Waterfall Cottage during Stoke wakes' week, beginning on Monday 7 August. The main attraction was the woodland walk to a waterfall.

65 Ibid. D. 3359/Buxton Road order bk. 1765–1800, p. 53; D. 4302/1/1, f. 57; D. (W.) 1909/E/9/1; above, Leek and Lowe, communications.
66 S.R.O., D. (W.) 1909/E/9/1; S.R.O., Q/RUt 5/18; C. and J. Greenwood, Map of County of Stafford (1820).
67 Above, Leek and Lowe, communications.
68 Sherlock, Ind. Arch. Staffs. 113; above, fig. 2.
69 The date is visible only on the post near the Black Horse inn.
70 V.C.H. Staffs. viii. 178. Although the map of 1842 cited there shows the Burslem stretch, the road was completed only between 1845 and 1848: B.R.L., Norton 2294 (dated plan of proposed turnpike rd.); Staffs. Advertiser, 4 Nov. 1848, p. 4.
71 P. Lead, Caldon Canal and Tramroads (Headington, 1990), 19.
72 C. Hadfield, Canals of West Midlands, 199-200, with corrections by A. W. Jeffery of Longsdon pasted in copy in W.S.L.; S.R.O., D. (W.) 1909/E/9/1.
73 S.R.O., D. 4302/1/3, p. 15; P.R.O., RG 9/1945.

74 O.S. Map 6", Staffs. XII. NE. (1925 edn.); Lead, Caldon Canal, 16, 18, 37.
75 Lead, Caldon Canal, 40-1, 44, 50.
76 P.O. Dir. Staffs. (1868); above, Leek and Lowe, communications.
77 Staffs. Advertiser, 4 July 1896, p. 4; C. R. Clinker, Clinker's Reg. of Closed Passenger Stations and Goods Depots, 1830–1977 (1978), 129.
78 Above, Leek and Lowe, communications.
79 White, Dir. Staffs. (1851), 728; Old Road to Endon, 206. This and the next two paras. are based on reports in Staffs. Advertiser.
80 Below, econ. hist. (land surveyors).
81 Inf. on the changes of date from the clerk to the charity trustees, Mr. E. A. Durose.
82 Staffs. Advertiser, 2 June 1860, p. 4.
83 Trust deed in possession of trustees of Endon Well Dressing Festival Charity.
84 Lich. Dioc. Regy., Bp.'s Reg. 32, p. 282.
85 Inf. from Mr. Durose.

The opening apparently became an annual event: it still took place in 1867. In 1865 the grounds were also opened at the time of the well-dressing festival. Basnett's house became a private school in 1868, and the public use of the grounds presumably ceased.[86]

Endon friendly society was established in 1820. By 1876 it had 416 members and assets of nearly £3,800, derived partly from the tenancy of the Plough inn. The society acquired the tenancy in 1859 and surrendered it in the 1870s. By 1878 the society had a reading room, probably in the Plough inn.[87] The society still existed in 1899.[88] A Women's Institute was formed in 1920.[89] The Endonian Society, an all-male body devoted to record the history of the area, was established in 1961.[90]

A parish room opened in 1905 probably stood west of Alder House in Station Road: land there, with a building used as a parish room and later as a village hall, was given in 1915 to the Lichfield Diocesan Trust by E. W. Hollinshead of Endon.[91] A recreation ground south of the hall was acquired in 1927 as a war memorial.[92]

Endon had a cricket club in 1871, and by 1898 its ground was at the north end of Station Road. A ground near Moss Hill was used from c. 1950 until 1962 and one in Stanley from 1963.[93] A football club was established in 1876,[94] but nothing further is known about it. Endon Tennis Club existed by 1896,[95] and in 1991 its courts were on part of the former cricket ground in Station Road. Courts south of Moss Hill, in existence by the earlier 1920s,[96] were used in 1991 by Stockton Brook Tennis Club.

MANOR. Before the Conquest *ENDON* was held by Dunning and in 1086 by the king. It may have passed later to the earls of Chester and then back to the Crown in 1237.[97] By 1273 it had passed to John de Verdun of Alton, and in 1299 and 1308 Endon was held of Theobald, Lord Verdun, by homage only.[98] When Theobald died in 1316 he left four daughters as heirs, none of whom seems to have claimed the overlordship of Endon, and later the same year it was held by Margaret, Baroness Stafford, who received a rent of 5s. as service.[99] The Staffords were overlords of Horton, which was held by the same undertenant as Endon, and that presumably explains the change in overlordship. The Staffords remained overlords of Endon in

1411, when it was last mentioned as a separate manor.[1]

Henry de Audley evidently held Endon in 1246[2] and his son James was the undertenant in 1252.[3] The manor descended with the Audleys' adjoining manor of Horton.

There was evidently a manor house in 1246 when the bishop visited Henry de Audley at Endon.[4] It probably stood on the moated site at the north end of Park Lane.[5]

ECONOMIC HISTORY. AGRICULTURE. Endon was stated in 1086 to have land for one or two ploughteams.[6] In the early 14th century the lord of the manor had no arable in demesne, presumably because much of Endon was by then parkland.[7] The conversion of parkland into farmland by the mid 16th century resulted in the creation of small holdings: of the 590 a. held by customary tenants in 1607, half was in holdings of 25 a. or less.[8] Lady moor in the north-west part of Endon belonged to the lord of the manor in 1399. It was regarded as common waste by the early 17th century and was then being encroached upon.[9]

The 10s. which by the late 1460s the Audleys took each year from the works (*de operibus*) of Endon suggests the commutation of labour services. The sum was still demanded in 1509.[10] In the mid 16th century and in 1607 the Audleys also took 'worksilver' at Michaelmas from three tenements in Endon.[11]

Dieulacres abbey, the owner of the tithes of Endon as rector of Leek, had a tithe barn in Endon.[12]

Of the 762 ha. of farmland returned for Endon and Stanley civil parish in 1988, grassland covered 734.7 ha. and there were 16.3 ha. of rough grazing. Dairy farming predominated, with 1,761 head of cattle. There were 399 sheep and lambs and 3,000 hens. Of the 34 farms returned, 31 were under 49 ha. in size and 3 were between 50 and 99 ha.[13]

WARREN AND PARK. In 1252 James de Audley was granted free warren in Endon.[14] Endon park was mentioned in 1273, when its pannage and herbage were valued at 10 marks (£6 13s. 4d.).[15] The park was extensive, stretching across Endon to the south-eastern boundary. A reference in 1308 to the 'Old Park' suggests the existence of an additional area of parkland by that date;[16] in

86 *Staffs. Advertiser*, 29 July 1854, p. 1; 27 May 1865, p. 1; 3 Aug. 1867, p. 1; below, educ.
87 *Rep. Chief Registrar of Friendly Socs. 1876, App. P*, H.C. 429-I, p. 400 (1877), lxxvii; *Old Road to Endon*, 175, 177; S.R.O., D. 4302/9/1.
88 *Staffs. Advertiser*, 1 July 1899, p. 4.
89 Inf. from Staffs. Federation of Women's Institutes.
90 Inf. from Mr. F. Stubbs of Endon.
91 *Staffs. Advertiser*, 5 Aug. 1905, p. 4; S.R.O., D. 4302/10/1.
92 S.R.O., Charities Index.
93 H. R. Brown, 'Cricket in Endon, 1871–1981' (TS. in W.S.L.); O.S. Map 6", Staffs. XII. NE. (1900 edn.).
94 *Old Road to Endon*, 178.   95 *Kelly's Dir.* (1896).
96 O.S. Map 6", Staffs. XII. NE. (1925 edn.).
97 *V.C.H. Staffs.* iv. 41; below, Rushton James, manor.
98 *S.H.C.* N.S. xi. 242, 253, 256.
99 *Complete Peerage*, xii (2), 251; *S.H.C.* 1911, 338.

1 *Cal. Inq. p.m.* xix, p. 312; above, Horton, manors.
2 *S.H.C.* N.S. ix. 312.
3 *Cal. Chart. R.* 1226–57, 409.
4 Below, church.
5 Staffs. C.C., Sites and Monuments Rec. 00471.
6 *V.C.H. Staffs.* iv. 41.
7 *S.H.C.* N.S. xi. 256; below, this section (warren and park).   8 S.R.O., D. (W.) 1490/17, ct. of 23 Oct. 1607.
9 Ibid. D. (W.) 1490/2, m. 15d.; D. (W.) 1490/4, m. 2; D. (W.) 1490/19, m. 3.
10 P.R.O., SC 6/988/2, m. 4d.; SC 6/Hen. VIII/3350, m. 2.
11 W.S.L. 52/46; S.R.O., D. (W.) 1490/17, ct. of 23 Oct. 1607.   12 P.R.O., SC 6/Hen. VIII/3353, m. 34.
13 Ibid. MAF 68/6128/66.
14 *Cal. Chart. R.* 1226–57, 409.
15 *Cal. Inq. p.m.* ii, p. 67; *S.H.C.* N.S. xi. 242. The park was also called 'the chase of Horton' in 1273: *S.H.C.* vi (1), 59.
16 *S.H.C.* N.S. xi. 256.

A HISTORY OF STAFFORDSHIRE

1341 there was mention of Hanley park, which lay between Park Lane and Endon brook and extended into Cheddleton.[17] The name of Reynolds Hay farm at the south end of Park Lane may indicate an enclosure associated with the park, and Lawn farm was known in the earlier 17th century as the Laund, a name meaning woodland pasture and possibly referring to grassland reserved for deer.[18] A nest of sparrowhawks or falcons was stolen from the park in 1283, and Richard the parker was assessed for tax in Endon in 1333.[19] The parkland had been converted into farmland by the mid 16th century.[20]

MILL. There was a mill at Endon in 1273, and in 1276 it was stated to be in the park.[21] What was called Hanley mill in 1401 stood on Endon brook east of Endon village, and the bridge taking the Leek road over the brook was known as Mill bridge in 1679.[22] The mill no longer existed by 1732.[23]

TRADE AND INDUSTRY. There was a fulling mill on Endon brook near the site of Hanley mill in 1738 and 1756.[24] A dyer, William Whieldon, lived in Endon village in 1721, possibly in the cottage in Brook Lane which carries the date 1710 and the initials ww. There were two dyers, Richard Johnson and his son Richard, in Endon in the 1740s.[25] All three may have been associated with the fulling mill.

A tanner, Daniel Nickson, lived in Park Lane in 1721 and 1728.[26] In 1816 William Hand of Park Farm in Park Lane had a tanyard south of his house. It was still run by Hand when offered for sale in 1839.[27] The tanhouse owned by John Sutton in 1740[28] probably stood on the site of a tanyard in Hallwater Lane in 1816. When offered for sale in 1829, the yard included a barkmill with a new engine; there was also a warehouse, which survived in 1991 as Hallwater Cottages.[29]

In 1838 there was a quarry west of Moss Hill, producing stone which was used in the pottery trade and as ballast for railway tracks.[30] The quarry was still worked in the late 1930s.[31] Stone was probably quarried in the wood south of Endon Edge by 1851. Two stone masons and a stone quarryman then lived in a row of cottages there, which had possibly been built by a stone

cutter, James Basnett of the nearby Waterfall Cottage.[32] A quarry west of the cottages was disused by the late 1870s, but another quarry was then worked north of Waterfall Cottage; it was apparently disused by the early 1920s.[33]

A brickmaker named Thomas Potts lived at Endon Edge in 1859, and Charles and John Heath, also of Endon Edge, worked as drainpipe makers in 1861.[34] In the late 1870s there was a brickworks in Stonehaye Wood on the east side of Endon Edge. Run by Philip Kent in 1880, the works was closed between 1892 and 1896.[35]

LAND SURVEYORS. Charles Heaton, recorded as a surveyor in 1804, lived at Endon by 1815. He died there in 1859.[36] Two of his sons also practised as land surveyors: Thomas (d. 1875), who probably worked with his father, lived in Endon in 1856 but had moved to Alton by 1860;[37] Edwin, based in Leek in 1850 and in Cheddleton in 1860, moved between 1872 and 1876 to Hallwater House in Endon.[38] After Edwin's death in 1896[39] the practice moved to a house dated 1897 on the Leek road south-west of the Plough inn, where it continued in 1991 as E. Heaton & Sons.

A surveyor named Robert Cleminson lived at Hallwater House in 1868. When Edwin Heaton came to live there c. 1874, Cleminson moved to Springfield House in the Woodhouse Green area, where he remained in practice until his death in 1893.[40] A surveyor named Charles Trubshaw lived at Stockton Brook in 1839 and 1840,[41] and Francis Figgins, a surveyor and engineer, lived there in 1842.[42]

LOCAL GOVERNMENT. Endon manor had its own court in 1278, and in 1293 the lord, Nicholas de Audley, claimed view of frankpledge, assize of bread and of ale, waif, and infangthief.[43] In 1308, however, Endon was subject to the Audleys' court at Horton, sending a frankpledge to the twice-yearly view by 1351.[44] It was still part of Horton manor in 1795.[45]

Stocks at Endon were mentioned in 1694 as out of repair.[46] A pinfold, which apparently stood next to the tollgate near the Plough inn, was removed in 1889.[47]

The township was part of the Endon quarter

17 P.R.O., E 40/11269; S.R.O., D. (W.) 1490/3, m. 3. For Hanley mill in that area see below, this section (mill).
18 Leek Par. Reg. 49; Eng. P.N. Elements, ii. 17.
19 S.H.C. vi (1), 130; x (1), 116; S.H.C. 4th ser. vi. 25.
20 W.S.L. 52/46.   21 S.H.C. N.S. xi. 242, 244.
22 S.R.O., D. (W.) 1490/2, m. 11; D. (W.) 1490/27, m. 58; D. (W.) 1535/1, f. 98; D. (W.) 1909/E/9/1.
23 S.R.O. 3306, abstract of title to land at Dunwood, 1732.
24 Ibid. D. 4302/1/1, f. 37; D. (W.) 1490/41, m. 51d.
25 Old Road to Endon, 38; S.R.O., D. 3359/misc. deeds, draft settlement of estate of Ric. Johnson the elder.
26 Old Road to Endon, 38; L.J.R.O., B/C/11, Thos. Jodrell (1728).
27 S.R.O., D. (W.) 1535/1, f. 79 (nos. 2075, 2085); D. (W.) 1909/E/9/1; Staffs. Advertiser, 7 Dec. 1839, p. 1; T. J. Smith, Banks and Bankers of Leek (Leek, priv. print. 1891), 27.   28 L.J.R.O., B/C/11, John Sutton (1744).
29 S.R.O., D. (W.) 1535/1, f. 79 (no. 1436); D. (W.) 1909/E/9/1; Staffs. Advertiser, 14 Nov. 1829, p. 1.
30 Staffs. Advertiser, 20 Jan. 1838, p. 1; White, Dir. Staffs. (1851), 727.

31 O.S. Map 6", Staffs. XII. NE. (1945 edn.).
32 White, Dir. Staffs. (1851), 731; P.R.O., HO 107/2008.
33 O.S. Map 6", Staffs. XII. NE. (1888, 1925 edns.).
34 S.R.O., D. 4302/1/3, p. 11; P.R.O., RG 9/1945.
35 Kelly's Dir. Staffs. (1880; 1892; 1896); O.S. Map 6", Staffs. XII. NE. (1888, 1900 edns.).
36 S.R.O., D. 554/107A; D. 4069/5/1; memorial in Endon church.
37 P.R.O., HO 107/1005; S.R.O., D. 4069/6/2/1–4; P.O. Dir. Staffs. (1860; s.v. Alton); Staffs. Advertiser, 11 Dec. 1875, p. 5.
38 L.J.R.O., B/A/15/Upper Elkstone; P.O. Dir. Staffs. (1860; 1872; 1876).   39 Char. Com. file 243641.
40 P.O. Dir. Staffs. (1868); Kelly's Dir. Staffs. (1880; 1892); S.R.O., D. 4302/1/13, p. 98.
41 Staffs. Advertiser, 17 Aug. 1839, p. 3; S.R.O., D. 4302/1/2, p. 63.   42 S.R.O., D. 4302/1/2, p. 68.
43 S.H.C. vi (1), 243; vii (1), 16; ibid. N.S. xi. 245.
44 Above, Horton, local govt.
45 S.R.O., D. (W.) 1490/44, m. 20.
46 Ibid. D. (W.) 1490/32, m. 34.
47 Ibid. D. 4302/15/5; F. Stubbs, Endon (Leek, 1994), 34.

of Leek parish, and in the 1660s its poor were relieved jointly with those of Longsdon and Stanley by the quarter's overseer.[48] The poor were still relieved jointly in 1834, but separate assessments for each township were made by 1750.[49] Endon became part of Leek poor-law union in 1837.[50]

There was a surveyor of the highways for Endon in 1700. He was answerable to Horton manor court.[51]

CHURCH. The lord of Endon, Henry de Audley, had a chapel at Endon in 1246. That year Bishop Roger de Weseham granted him permission to have members of his family baptized in the chapel and to establish a chantry there. As Weseham took care to obtain approval from Dieulacres abbey, as rector of Leek, Endon chapel may have been more than a private oratory.[52]

The present church was built between 1719 and 1721 by the inhabitants of Endon and Stanley on land given by Thomas Jodrell.[53] It was dependent on the parish church at Leek until 1865, when the chapelry became a parish, also including Longsdon.[54] The benefice, at first a perpetual curacy, was styled a vicarage from 1868.[55] In 1889 most of Longsdon was transferred to All Saints' parish, Leek.[56]

It was not until 1730 that the bishop granted a faculty for the administration of the sacraments at Endon. The delay may have been caused by a dispute over fees, settled in 1731 by an agreement between the vicar of Leek and the curate and trustees of Endon chapel. The vicar retained payments made in respect of the Easter roll, the modus for the tithe of hay in Endon and Stanley, and other customary dues. He also retained fees for churchings, marriages, and burials conducted by the curate, but apparently not for baptisms. The payments were to be collected by the curate, who was also to forward within three days the names of those who had been baptized, married, or buried at Endon for entry into the register at Leek. The vicar was also to have 'all the advantages of mourning cloth' in Endon chapel, probably the income from hiring out a pall for funerals. Once a year (but not on Easter Sunday) the curate, having been given at least 10 days' notice, was obliged to assist the vicar in administering Communion at Leek.[57] By 1832 the curate retained half the fee for churchings and part of that for burials.[58]

John Daintry (or Daventry) subscribed as curate of Endon in 1724, having been nominated in 1723 by Thomas Jodrell and the chapel trustees. A rival candidate had been nominated by the vicar of Leek.[59] In 1737 the earl of Macclesfield nominated, evidently in his capacity as patron of Leek. The earls retained the patronage until 1892 when it was transferred to the vicar of Leek.[60]

In 1720 Queen Anne's Bounty gave £200 to meet a benefaction of £200 from Thomas Jodrell and others. A further bounty of £200 was given in 1727 to meet £150 given by Lady Holford and £50 by the earl of Macclesfield.[61] By 1738 some or all of the money had been used to buy a 39-a. farm at Oulton, in Rushton Spencer, and a 21½-a. farm at Dale Green, in Wolstanton.[62] Besides fees the curate then received a rent of 6s. 8d. a year left by William Dudley (d. 1718) of Lyme House, in Longsdon, for a sermon on 29 May;[63] a rent charge of £5 given by Thomas Jodrell;[64] the income from pasturage in the churchyard and from an adjoining croft given by Thomas Jodrell; and some of the pew rents from the chapel.[65] The living was worth £120 a year c. 1830.[66] In 1887 there were 99 a. of glebe, with an estimated rental of £140 4s.[67] The farm in Wolstanton was sold apparently in 1911 and that at Rushton Spencer in 1916, and the proceeds were invested.[68]

No house for the curate was included in the original endowment, and in 1732 John Daintry lived at Dunwood, in Longsdon. His successor, Enoch Tompkinson, lived in Park Lane at the time of his death in 1761.[69] The curate in 1851, Daniel Turner, lived at Hallwater House, where he died in 1864.[70] A vicarage house was built in 1914 off the Leek road south-west of the Plough inn; it was replaced in the later 1970s by a house built in the garden.[71]

In 1830 there were two Sunday services and Communion was celebrated five times a year.[72] On Census Sunday 1851 the attendance was 40 in the morning and 100 in the afternoon, besides Sunday school children.[73] The church had psalm singers and a band in 1815. The singers, still recorded in 1858, probably survived until 1862 when a harmonium was installed.[74] A surpliced choir took part in the opening service for the chancel in 1879.[75]

There was a mission room at Hill Top in 1881, and a mission church was built there in 1900. It was closed in 1978, and with the adjoining

48 Above, Leek, par. intro. (par. govt.).
49 S.R.O., D. 4302/7/1/3; White, *Dir. Staffs.* (1834), 712.
50 S.R.O., D. 699/1/1/1, p. 4.
51 Ibid. D. (W.) 1490/34, m. 81d.
52 *S.H.C.* N.S. ix. 312.
53 S.R.O., D. 5041, p. 165; *Old Road to Endon*, 37–8, where the statement that burials took place in the 17th cent. in the 'chancel of Endon' is based on a misreading of S.R.O., D. 5041, p. 176.
54 Lich. Dioc. Regy., Bp.'s Reg. 35, pp. 240–1, mentions the creation of 1865 for which no order-in-council has been traced.   55 *Lich. Dioc. Ch. Cal.* (1869).
56 *Lond. Gaz.* 23 Aug. 1889, pp. 4606–7.
57 S.R.O., D. 4302/1/1, at front of vol.; D. 4302/3/2; D. 5041, pp. 165–9.   58 L.J.R.O., B/V/6/Leek, 1832.
59 Ibid. B/A/3/Endon; B/A/4/29, 25 July 1724.
60 Ibid. B/A/3/Endon; Lich. Dioc. Regy., Bp.'s Reg. 35, pp. 240–1.

61 Hodgson, *Bounty of Queen Anne*, pp. cxxxiii, cxlii, ccxcvi; S.R.O., D. 4302/3/6.   62 S.R.O., D. 4302/3/3.
63 L.J.R.O., B/C/11, Wm. Dudley (1718).
64 S.R.O., D. 4302/3/3; plaque on west wall of church.
65 S.R.O., D. 4302/3/3.
66 *Rep. Com. Eccl. Revenues*, 476–7.
67 *Return of Glebe Lands*, 64.
68 S.R.O., D. 4302/5/3, Apr. 1911; D. 5003/2/3/2.
69 Ibid. D. 4302/1/1, pp. 3, 45.
70 White, *Dir. Staffs.* (1851), 731; *Staffs. Advertiser*, 19 Nov. 1864, p. 1; S.R.O., D. 4302/1/12, p. 8.
71 Lich. Dioc. Regy., Bp.'s Reg. V, p. 481; S.R.O., D. 4302/5/4; D. 5003/3/4/2/2–5.
72 *S.H.C.* 4th ser. x. 85.
73 P.R.O., HO 129/372/1/4.
74 S.R.O., D. 4302/5/1, pp. 19, 39; D. 4302/5/2; W.S.L., Sleigh, ii, f. 285.
75 *Staffs. Advertiser*, 18 Oct. 1879, p. 7.

caretaker's cottage it was later converted into a dwelling called Mission House.[76]

There was a chapelwarden by 1802.[77] A clerk, recorded in 1738, had his salary fixed at £5 in 1813, when he was also given a house with a garden.[78]

The present church of *ST. LUKE* dates mostly from the 1870s. It predecessor, of coursed rubble with stone dressings, consisted of a nave with a small sanctuary and a west tower.[79] There were two galleries in 1830, one presumably at the west end and approached through the tower by the external stairs which still survive.[80] In the 1850s the nave had box pews, and there was a two-decker pulpit at its south-east corner.[81] The church was rebuilt in ashlar in the later 1870s. The new church had a south aisle of three bays and a south-west porch, designed by Jeremiah and Joseph Beardmore of Hanley, who also designed a chancel arch. The chancel itself, with a sanctuary and north organ chamber, was designed by R. Scrivener & Sons of Hanley and was not completed until 1879. The box pews were removed and the pulpit was replaced by one of stone at the north-east corner of the nave.[82] Glass by Morris & Co. was installed in the east window in 1893 as a memorial to George Smith of Bank House.[83] A north aisle was added in 1899, the cost being met by Thomas Smith of Park Lane in memory of his wife.[84] A meeting room created under the tower in 1820 was extended to the south in 1970 to include lavatories.[85] A larger meeting room which adjoins the church on the north-west was built in the earlier 1980s. Called the Chapter House because of its octagonal shape, it was designed by Wood, Goldstraw & Yorath of Hanley.[86]

The church has a silver paten of 1638.[87] The single bell is dated 1726.[88] The furnishings include four altar frontals made in the late 19th century by the Leek Embroidery Society.

The registers date from 1731.[89]

The stone wall around the churchyard and the lychgate were built in 1874 at the cost of William Orford.[90] In 1898 the churchyard was enlarged on the north.[91]

NONCONFORMITY. The only papist returned for Leek parish in 1705 was Elizabeth, wife of Andrew Heath of Endon. She was again returned in 1706, along with Elizabeth, wife of Joseph Pedley of Park Lane.[92]

John Reynolds of Clay Lake was recorded as a Quaker in 1704, and he and his family were members of the Friends' meeting at Leek in 1735.[93]

Houses in Endon registered for protestant worship in 1805, 1814, and 1815 were probably used by Wesleyan Methodists, who had a society of 10 members at Endon in 1815.[94] John Heath of Bank Farm registered his house for worship in 1824,[95] and two years later the society moved to the home of his brother George in Endon village. Members also attended the chapel at Gratton.[96] A chapel was opened in Endon village in 1835. In 1851 the average attendance was 18 in the afternoon, besides Sunday school children, and 42 in the evening.[97] Following the suburban development of the Leek Road area, a larger and more conveniently sited chapel, designed in a Gothic style by William Sugden of Leek, was built in 1874 at the corner of Leek Road and Station Road. The former chapel was sold and converted into two cottages. The new chapel was itself replaced in 1991 by one on the same site, designed by Hulme, Upright & Partners of Hanley and incorporating a rose window and terracotta medallions from its predecessor.[98]

In 1832 Hugh Bourne opened a Primitive Methodist chapel at Hill Top; it occupied the north end of a low stone building, the rest of which probably consisted of cottages. Bourne was himself a member of the congregation. On Census Sunday 1851 the attendance was 45 in the afternoon and 50 in the evening.[99] In 1880 the congregation moved to a chapel on the Norton-in-the-Moors side of the boundary, known in 1991 as Hill Top Methodist Church.[1]

John Charlesworth, excluded from the Hill Top chapel in 1880, formed his own society called Brown Edge Free Mission. It had a mission room at Hill Top, served by both Wesleyan and Primitive Methodist preachers. The room was closed in 1963, and the site was occupied by a bungalow in 1991.[2]

A New Connexion Methodist chapel at the Stockton Brook end of Leek Road was registered in 1888. Re-registered as Trinity Methodist Church in 1937, it was closed in 1977.[3] It was reopened by Seventh Day Adventists in 1978. Services ceased in the 1980s, and in 1991 the building stood empty.[4]

76 P.R.O., RG 11/2736, naming the hamlet as Brown Edge; *Old Road to Endon*, 50, 75; plaques in Chapter House of Endon church.   77 S.R.O., D. 4302/5/1.
78 Ibid. D. 4302/3/3; D. 4302/5/1, p. 10.
79 Above, plate 17.   80 *S.H.C.* 4th ser. x. 85.
81 Lichfield Cath. Libr., Moore and Hinckes drawings, v, no. 8. An interior view of 1870 by H. W. Foster which hangs in the church is reproduced in F. Stubbs, *Endon* (Leek, 1994), facing p. 5, where it is wrongly dated c. 1850.
82 S.R.O., D. 4302/4/1/1; D. 4302/4/3/1; *Lich. Dioc. Ch. Cal.* (1877), 74; (1878), 76; (1880), 80; *Staffs. Advertiser*, 18 Oct. 1879, p. 7; *Old Road to Endon*, plans between pp. 40 and 41.
83 Pevsner, *Staffs.* 129. The design is attributed to Sir Edward Burne-Jones in *Kelly's Dir. Staffs.* (1896).
84 S.R.O., D. 4302/4/1/2; *Lich. Dioc. Mag.* (1899), 68; plaque in north aisle.
85 S.R.O., D. 4302/4/3/3; D. 4302/5/1, p. 261.
86 Ibid. D. 4302/4/1/10.
87 *T.B.A.S.* lxxvii. 65.
88 C. Lynam, *Ch. Bells of County of Stafford* (1889), 47.

89 All but the most recent are in S.R.O., D. 4302/1.
90 *Lich. Dioc. Ch. Cal.* (1875), 74, wrongly giving the donor's name as Oxford.
91 Lich. Dioc. Regy., Bp.'s Reg. U, pp. 251, 267.
92 *Staffs. Cath. Hist.* xiii. 29.
93 S.R.O., D. 3159/3/3, s.a. 1704; D. 4182/2.
94 Ibid. D. 3155/1; *S.H.C.* 4th ser. iii. 7, 35–6. Rest of para. based on *150th Anniversary of Methodism in Endon, 1835–1985*; *Old Road to Endon*, 59–62.
95 *S.H.C.* 4th ser. iii. 65.
96 Leek Libr., Johnson scrapbk. i (2), D/13/15.
97 P.R.O., HO 129/372/1/4.
98 Leek Libr., newspaper cuttings 1991, p. 12.
99 *Old Road to Endon*, 73–5; H. B. Kendall, *Origin and Hist. of Primitive Methodist Church* (1905), i. 120; P.R.O., HO 129/372/1/4.   1 *Old Road to Endon*, 75–6.
2 Ibid. 80–2; W.S.L. 103/2/71 (TS. hist. of Brown Edge), pp. 76–8.
3 G.R.O. Worship Reg. nos. 30801, 57541; O.S. Map 6", Staffs. XII. NE. (1925 edn.).
4 G.R.O. Worship Reg. no. 75103; local inf.

EDUCATION. In 1750 a school and a master's house were built on land adjoining the south-east corner of Endon churchyard. John Wedgwood of Harracles, in Longsdon, and James Sutton of Endon gave the land, and the freeholders paid for the building.[5] There were 35 pupils in 1751, taught at their parents' expense.[6] In 1781 Thomas Sherratt of Endon bequeathed the interest on £60 to endow free places, and in 1786 his brother William left the interest on £50 for the same purpose. The capital was held by the brothers' nephew, John Hand (d. 1799), and in 1825 John's son William, of Park Farm, paid £4 8s. as the interest. The number of pupils supported by the charity money varied; there were three in 1825, but earlier apparently as many as 10.[7] In 1797 the master was given a garden adjoining his house by Thomas Harding, lord of Horton manor.[8] In 1825 a further annuity of £2 10s. was paid out of the tolls collected at Endon tollgate, for which the master taught two pupils free.[9] By the earlier 1820s the master also received money for teaching poor children from Stanley out of the charity of the Revd. Richard Shaw.[10]

Only 12 boys and 8 girls were taught at the school in 1847.[11] In 1855 the management of what was then called Endon parochial school was reorganized under a body of trustees which included the curate. The school was to take children from Endon chapelry aged between 6 and 16 years, and weekly pence were to be charged.[12] A new schoolroom was opened on the site of the old one in 1871.[13] A government grant was paid from 1872, and a voluntary rate was levied from 1875. There were 50 children on the books in 1875.[14]

In 1930 it was decided that Endon parochial school, then an all-age school with 84 children on its books, should become a junior school. The decision took effect in 1939, when the present Endon county high school on Leek Road was opened as a senior school.[15] The junior school took controlled status in 1958 as St. Luke's Church of England (Controlled) primary school.[16] It was moved to its present site in Leek Road in 1963, and the former building was demolished in 1965.[17] Another junior school, Endon Hall county primary school in Hillside Avenue, off Leek Road, was opened in 1969.[18]

A Church of England Sunday school had been established by 1826,[19] and both Endon's Methodist chapels had Sunday schools by 1851. On Census Sunday that year there were attendances of 40 at the Church of England Sunday school and of between 30 and 33 at the Wesleyan Methodist school; there was apparently no school that day at the Primitive Methodist chapel, but the attendance was stated to average 47.[20]

The curate of Endon, John Salt (d. 1832), ran a private school in 1825.[21] There was a girls' school at Sutton House in 1851, run by John Minshull and the Misses Minshull.[22] In 1868 Mary Owen opened a girls' day and boarding school called Endon New Hall in the present Stone House in Basnetts Wood Road, and her husband John ran a commercial day school for boys in Endon.[23] The boarding school was taken over in 1875 or 1876 by John Bailey, who by 1881 had moved it to Orford Road, where he ran it with his wife and daughter mainly as a day school.[24] The school apparently no longer existed in 1884.[25] In 1940 a preparatory school was held in West End Villa at Stockton Brook.[26]

CHARITIES FOR THE POOR. Thomas Jodrell (d. 1728), the benefactor of Endon church, left a third of the interest on £200 for the poor of Endon chapelry. In the later 1780s the income was £2 10s. The same amount was disbursed in the earlier 1820s in 1s. doles.[27] John Boughey (d. 1749) of Little Chell, in Wolstanton, left the interest on £10 to be distributed on St. Thomas's day (21 December) to the poor of Endon chapelry. By the later 1780s the income was 8s., charged by 1888 on land at Endon Bank.[28] John Ball (d. probably 1749) of Endon gave the interest on £40 for the poor of Endon chapelry in the form of a weekly bread dole. In the later 1780s the income was £2. It was 30s. in the earlier 1820s, when it was charged on land at Blackwood Hill, in Horton. Bread worth 1s. was then distributed weekly, the shortfall in the cost of the bread being met from sacrament money. In 1888 the bread was distributed monthly.[29] John Wedgwood (d. 1757) of Harracles, in Longsdon, left half the interest on £120 for distribution to the poor of Endon chapelry at Candlemas (2 February). Endon's share in the later 1780s was £3. It was the same amount in the earlier 1820s and £1 16s. in 1888.[30] The Jodrell, Boughey, Ball, and Wedgwood charities were administered jointly by 1992, when six women each received £1.[31]

Francis Evans (d. 1824) of Lane Ends House

5 13th Rep. Com. Char. 395.
6 L.J.R.O., B/V/5/Endon, 1751.
7 13th Rep. Com. Char. 396.
8 Ibid. 395–6.
9 Ibid. 396.
10 Below, Stanley, charity.
11 Nat. Soc. Inquiry, 1846–7, Staffs. 6–7.
12 S.R.O., D. 5003/8/2/1.
13 P.R.O., ED 7/108/131; Old Road to Endon, 195–6; Bowyer and Poole, Staffs. Moorlands, ii. 53.
14 Staffs. Advertiser, 3 July 1875, p. 2; 10 July 1875, p. 5.
15 Staffs. C.C. Record for 1930, 419; Old Road to Endon, 200; S.R.O., D. 5048/1/1.
16 S.R.O., D. 5048/2/1, loose letter of 1 May 1959.
17 Old Road to Endon, 198–9.
18 S.R.O., CEH/306/1. It was opened officially in 1971: plaque in entrance hall.

19 S.R.O., D. 4302/5/1, p. 65.
20 P.R.O., HO 129/372/1/4.
21 Staffs. Advertiser, 25 June 1825, p. 1; 25 Feb. 1832, p. 4.   22 White, Dir. Staffs. (1851), 731.
23 Staffs. Advertiser, 7 Mar. 1868, p. 1.
24 Ibid, 16 Jan. 1875, p. 1; Leek Libr., Warrington scrapbk. i, p. 94; P.R.O., RG 10/2878; RG 11/2736.
25 Kelly's Dir. Staffs. (1884).
26 Ibid. (1940).
27 13th Rep. Com. Char. 373, 394; Char. Dons. 1152–3; S.R.O., D. 4302/8/1, p. 5; plaque in Endon church.
28 13th Rep. Com. Char. 396; Char. Dons. 1152–3; Old Road to Endon, 37; S.R.O., D. 4302/8/1, p. 1.
29 13th Rep. Com. Char. 395; Char. Dons. 1152–3; S.R.O., D. 4302/1/1, f. 27; D. 4302/8/1, p. 11.
30 13th Rep. Com. Char. 374, 395; Char. Dons. 1152–3; S.R.O., D. 4302/8/1, p. 9.
31 Char. Com. files 217911–12.

left £50 for the distribution of 30s. worth of bread to the very poor at Christmas.[32] Nothing further is known about the charity.

In 1850 Thomas Wood, son-in-law of Charles Heaton of Endon, spent £20 on the purchase of 1 a. of land near Lane Ends House to yield 20s. a year for the distribution of bread to the poor of Endon chapelry. The charity still existed in 1888, but nothing further is known about it.[33]

Elizabeth Turner (d. 1865) of Bank House left half the interest on £100 for the poor of Endon chapelry. In 1888 a distribution of £1 16s. worth of coal was made at Christmas. George Smith (d. 1892) of Endon Bank left £200, the interest to be distributed at Christmas to the poor living within one mile of Endon village. The first distribution was made in 1895 and amounted to £6 15s. By will proved 1896 Edwin Heaton of Hallwater House left the interest on £70 to be distributed at Christmas to the poor of Endon in blankets and flannel. The Turner, Smith, and Heaton charities were administered jointly by 1992, when £8.50 was added to a charitable distribution made by the churchwardens out of church funds.[34]

HEATON

HEATON was formerly a township in Leek parish and later a civil parish 2,689 a. (1,088 ha.) in area.[35] It is pasture, with a hamlet in the centre and Swythamley Hall in parkland in the north-east part. The northern boundary with Cheshire is formed by the river Dane. The boundary with Leekfrith on the south-east runs over a hill called Gun.

The hamlet of Heaton, an Old English name meaning a high settlement,[36] stands at 800 ft. (244 m.), and to the east the land on Gun rises to 1,000 ft. (305 m.). Beside the Dane it lies at 503 ft. (153 m.) on the west side of the township and 617 ft. (188 m.) in the north-east at Danebridge. There are two valleys, one in the north-east part of the township and the other south of Heaton hamlet; both are formed by streams which flow into the Dane. The underlying rock is sandstone of the Millstone Grit series. It is overlain by Boulder Clay, and the soil is mostly fine loam and clay.[37]

Ten people in Heaton were assessed for tax in 1327,[38] and forty-two were assessed for hearth tax in 1666.[39] In 1751 there were 179 people aged over 16 in the township.[40] In 1801 the population was 343, rising to 391 by 1821 and 430 by 1841. It had fallen to 405 by 1851 and 361 by 1871, and in 1881 it was 328. An increase to 371 in 1891 was followed by a further decline, to 359 in 1901 and 349 in 1911. The population was 355 in 1921 and 345 in 1931. It was 307 in 1951, 295 in 1961, 297 in 1971, 285 in 1981, and 274 in 1991.[41]

Part of an Anglo-Saxon circular cross shaft stands in a field north-east of Heaton hamlet.[42] The hamlet itself lies where a road from Rushton Spencer crossed a road which ran south to the main area of common waste in the township and north to the Dane.[43] Ivy Farm is of the 17th century, but most other houses in the hamlet are of the 19th century. By 1834 there was an inn,

the Black Horse, still recorded in 1871.[44] Heaton Hall Farm, so called by 1851, stands west of the hamlet on a site occupied by 1775 and was rebuilt in the 1860s.[45] When the waste was inclosed in 1820, a new road was laid out bypassing the hamlet.[46] Heaton House Farm at the west end of the inclosure road has a date stone of 1824, retained when the house was rebuilt in the 1840s, evidently for James Robins, a surgeon, who was living there in 1851.[47]

The earliest settlements outside the hamlet were mostly in the north part of the township. Wormhough Farm and Wormhill Farm on the north-western boundary stand in an area called Wurnuldehalth in the late 1240s.[48] There was a house there by the earlier 16th century,[49] possibly on the site of the present Wormhough Farm. Wormhill Farm is of the 19th century but probably replaced what was called the New House in 1702.[50] Brandy Lee Farm to the east, taking its name from words meaning a place in woodland cleared by burning, was an occupied site by the earlier 16th century.[51] At the same date there was a house to the north at Flashcroft beside the Dane.[52] East of Brandy Lee there were houses on the sites of Heaton Lowe and Hollinhall Farm by the earlier 16th century.[53] Heaton Lowe has a porch, ornamented with slender pyramids, which carries the date 1651 and the initials of William Nabs, joint lord of Heaton manor in 1654. Hollinhall Farm was largely rebuilt in 1896.[54]

There were houses in 1340 at a place called Berdeholm in the valley north-east of Heaton hamlet, where there was a mill possibly by 1327.[55] Bearda Farm on the north side of the valley retains the parlour wing of a 17th-century house, owned in 1666 by the Tunnicliffe family and then assessed for tax on five hearths.[56] The site of Hannel Farm on the south side of the valley was occupied by 1617.[57]

32 Plaque in Endon church.
33 S.R.O., D. 4302/8/1, p. 1; D. 4302/8/3/1.
34 Char. Com. files 242640, 243641–2; S.R.O., D. 4302/8/1, pp. 13, 38, 42.
35 V.C.H. Staffs. i. 327. This article was written in 1991.
36 Eng. P.N. Elements, i. 237–8; ii. 189–90.
37 Geol. Surv. Map 1", drift, sheet 110 (1968 edn.); Soil Surv. of Eng. and Wales, sheet 3 (1983).
38 S.H.C. vii (1), 219.   39 S.H.C. 1925, 169–70.
40 S.R.O., D. 1109/1, p. 87.
41 V.C.H. Staffs. i. 327; Census, 1911–91.
42 N.S.J.F.S. vi. 10 n.; Staffs. C.C., Sites and Monuments Rec. 00259.   43 Above, fig. 2.
44 White, Dir. Staffs. (1834), 714; P.R.O., RG 10/2884.
45 P.R.O., HO 107/2008; Staffs. Advertiser, 2 May 1868, p. 8; above, fig. 2.   46 S.R.O., D. 1176/A/8/5.
47 White, Dir. Staffs. (1851), 728, 732.
48 S.H.C. N.S. ix. 318.   49 W.S.L., M. 540.
50 S.R.O., D. 1260/1/1.
51 Eng. P.N. Elements, i. 47; ii. 18; W.S.L., M. 540.
52 W.S.L., M. 540.
53 Ibid.   54 Date stone on house.
55 S.R.O., D. 1333/1, m. 6; below, econ. hist. (mills).
56 S.R.O., D. 5017/1/16; D. (W.) 1702/1/2, deed of 30 June 1677; S.H.C. 1925, 169.
57 S.R.O., D. 5017/32/38.

Swythamley Hall in the north-east part of the township derives its name from an Old Norse word (*svitha*) meaning land cleared by burning and another Old Norse word (*holmr*), or its English equivalent, meaning raised ground in marsh land.[58] The hall, which stands on or near the site of a grange belonging to Dieulacres abbey by 1291, dates mostly from the 18th and 19th centuries and stands in parkland.[59] Hillylees Farm south of the hall was an occupied site by the earlier 16th century,[60] and Hangingstone Farm north of the hall, which takes its name from a rock perched on the nearby hillside, is of the 17th century. Part of Snipe Cottage, on the west side of Swythamley park and called Snipe Hall in 1756,[61] is possibly also of the 17th century. There was a house at the river crossing at Danebridge by 1708.[62] A hamlet which developed there in the late 18th and early 19th century in association with a cotton mill had a population of just over 50 in 1841.[63]

Hawksley Farm east of Heaton hamlet retains some fabric from a 17th-century house, as does the nearby Tofthall Farm. The latter was the home in 1741 of William Armett, sheriff of Staffordshire in 1764; he improved the house and laid out a walled garden. Known as Toft Hall in 1775, the house was remodelled and extended to the south in the mid 19th century.[64] Overhouses Farm south of Tofthall Farm is dated 1853 and stands west of a house of the same name in existence by 1656.[65] By 1291 Dieulacres abbey had a grange at Fairboroughs in the south part of the township.[66] The name means 'fair hills' and was perhaps coined by the monks.[67]

A medieval route between Leek and Macclesfield ran through the east side of the township over Gun, crossing the Dane into Cheshire at Danebridge. The crossing was recorded c. 1190 as Scliderford, meaning 'slippery ford'.[68] There was a bridge by 1357, known as Sliderford bridge in 1545. Rebuilt as a stone bridge of two arches in the early 17th century, it was washed away by a flood in 1631 and replaced the next year by a single-arch bridge.[69] The present bridge is dated 1869. The road formerly ran past Snipe Cottage and there was a steep descent to the river crossing. The present, more gentle route to the west existed by 1831 and may have been laid out primarily to serve traffic from the cotton mill at Danebridge.[70] In 1611 there was a ford on the west side of the township at Barleigh ford. There was a bridge there by 1752.[71]

A feeder for Rudyard Lake was constructed c. 1811, leaving the Dane half-way along its course in Heaton. It ran through Rushton Spencer and entered the lake at its north end in Rushton James.[72]

Heaton association for the prosecution of felons was formed in 1801.[73] The village hall on the east side of the township was converted from a school in 1982, and a post office was opened in an extension in 1985.[74] Heaton was connected to a mains water supply in the earlier 1970s.[75]

MANOR AND OTHER ESTATES. What became the manor of *HEATON* was probably included in the grant of Leek manor by Ranulph, earl of Chester, to Dieulacres abbey in 1232.[76] The abbey had granges at Fairboroughs and Swythamley by 1291, and in 1535 it held what was called the manor of Heaton.[77] After the Dissolution the Crown retained the manor until 1614 when it was sold to William Tunnicliffe of Bearda Farm and William Plant, also of Heaton. They sold it in 1629 to George Thorley of Heaton, from whom it was bought in 1631 by Francis Gibson of Wormhough. In 1654 Gibson sold the manor to William Trafford of Swythamley and William Nabs of Heaton Lowe.[78] One moiety then descended with the Swythamley estate. The other, still held by a member of the Nabs family in 1704, was later held by George Hunt (d. 1762), whose executors sold it to George Smith of Kingsley. In 1794 Smith sold his moiety to Edward Nicholls of Swythamley, and the reunited manor then descended with the Swythamley estate.[79]

Dieulacres abbey had a grange at *FAIRBOROUGHS* by 1291.[80] In 1546 the Crown sold the estate to William Fynney, who was succeeded in 1584 or 1585 by his son, also William. The younger William was succeeded in 1595 by his daughter Ann, widow of William Colmore of Birmingham, and Ann in 1598 by her son William.[81] In 1618 William Colmore sold the estate to George Thorley.[82] In the 1640s the house was occupied by John Pott. A man of the same name was living there in 1666, and his initials appear on a stone dated 1673, which survives on the front of the present house.[83] Another John Pott died at Fairboroughs in 1748.[84] John Potts of Fairboroughs (d. 1798) sold part of his estate to

58 *Eng. P.N. Elements*, i. 258; ii. 170; M. Gelling, *Place-Names in the Landscape*, 50–1.
59 Below, manor (Swythamley).
60 W.S.L., M. 540.
61 S.R.O., D. 1109/2, bapt. of 22 Feb. 1756.
62 Ibid. D. 1109/1, p. 9.
63 P.R.O., HO 107/1005; below, econ. hist. (trade and ind.).
64 B.R.L., Norton Colln. 282; S.R.O., D. 1109/2, bapt. of 10 Mar. 1752; *S.H.C.* 1912, 291; above, fig. 2.
65 Stone dated 1656 surviving in grounds of the present farmhouse. The 17th-cent. house was demolished in 1978: inf. from Mr. B. Needham of Overhouses Farm.
66 Below, manor (Fairboroughs).
67 Inf. from Dr. M. Gelling.
68 *P.N. Ches.* (E.P.N.S.), i. 166.
69 Dodd, *Peakland Roads*, 55–6; L.J.R.O., B/C/11, John Hyggynbothum (1545); S.R.O., Q/SO/4, f. 45v.

70 W.S.L., S.C. D/1/17; above, fig. 2.
71 *P.N. Ches.* i. 168; S.R.O., D. 1109/2, burial of 17 Mar. 1752.   72 Above, Horton, intro. (Rudyard Lake).
73 S.R.O., D. 3359/Cruso, draft agreement with declaration of 3 Feb. 1801.
74 Ibid. D. 4728/2/2, 8 Feb. 1982; inf. from the postmistress.
75 S.R.O., D. 4728/2/2, 9 Aug. 1972.
76 Above, Leek and Lowe, manors.
77 Sleigh, *Leek*, 18.
78 S.R.O., D. 5017/1/6, 14–15.
79 S.R.O. 4974/B/1/4; W.S.L., S.MS. 411.
80 *Tax. Eccl.* (Rec. Com.), 252.
81 *L. & P. Hen VIII*, xxi (1), p. 767; Sleigh, *Leek*, 175; P.R.O., C 142/344/77.
82 *S.H.C.* N.S. vii. 192.
83 *S.H.C.* 1925, 169; *Leek Par. Reg.* 41, 68.
84 S.R.O., D. 1040/5/14, burial of 14 Jan. 1747/8.

HEATON
1991

to Macclesfield
Danebridge
Hangingstone Farm
stone
Snipe Cottage
cross
Swythamley Hall
West Lodge
Hillylees Farm
Bearda Farm
River Dane
Hannel Farm
Barleighford Bridge
Hollinhall Farm
reservoir feeder
site of Flashcroft Farm
village hall
Wormhill Farm
Heaton Lowe
Wormhough Farm
Brandy Lee Farm
Gun End House
Hawksley Farm
Gun End
site of tanyard
Toothill Farm
former pinfold
Heaton
cross
Tofthall Farm
Heaton Hall Farm
to Rushton Spencer
former Methodist church
Heaton House Farm
Axstones Hill
Overhouses Farm
Gun
to Rushton Spencer
to Macclesfield
former quarry
Rad Brook
① Methodist church
② Site of mill
③ Former church
④ South Lodge
⑤ Site of mill
⑥ Site of paper mill
to Meerbrook
to Leek
Fairboroughs Farm

— · — · — County boundary
— — — Boundary of former township
—— 800 —— Contours (in feet)

0   0.5   1 mile
0   0.5   1 km

FIG. 34

the earl of Macclesfield in 1757,[85] and in the later 1860s a 159-a. farm at Fairboroughs was held as part of the earl of Macclesfield's Rudyard estate.[86] That estate was broken up in 1919, and after passing through various hands Fairboroughs farm was bought in 1966 by W. J. Lowe. His son Robert owned it in 1991.[87] The present house, which possibly contains part of a 16th-century house, was extended in 1673 and refronted in the mid 19th century.

Dieulacres abbey had a grange at SWYTHAM-

LEY possibly by 1246[88] and certainly by 1291.[89] In 1540 the Crown granted the estate to William Trafford of Wilmslow (Ches.), who was succeeded in or shortly before 1559 by his son Christopher.[90] Christopher was succeeded in 1572 by his brother Philip, Philip in 1621 by his son William, and William in 1627 by his son, also William.[91] The younger William, who was sheriff of Staffordshire in 1694, was succeeded in 1697 by his son William, sheriff in 1706.[92] His son, another William, succeeded in 1726 and

85 Ibid. D. 1109/4, burial of 25 Apr. 1798; W.S.L., M. 532, acct. for 1757–8.   86 S.R.O. 4974/B/5/20.
87 Ibid. D. 1176/B/11/1 (annotated copy of Rudyard estate sale cat. 1919); inf. from Mr. and Mrs. R. Lowe.
88 Lambeth Palace Libr., Papal Docs. 40 (damaged), a papal bull of 1246 confirming the abbey's estates and apparently including two granges at places with names ending '–leie'.
89 Tax. Eccl. (Rec. Com.), 252.
90 L. & P. Hen. VIII, xv, p. 342; Cal. Pat. 1554–5, 136–7; P.R.O., C 142/124/82.
91 P.R.O., C 142/165/177; C 142/391/12; C 142/431/77.
92 S.H.C. v (2), 288 and n.; S.H.C. 1912, 289; Sleigh, Leek, 19.

died in 1762, leaving as his heir a daughter Sarah, widow of William Nicholls. She was succeeded in 1785 by her son Edward, sheriff in 1818.[93] By 1828 Edward had taken the surname Trafford.[94]

In 1832 Trafford sold what was by then called Swythamley Hall to John Brocklehurst of Macclesfield, in Prestbury (Ches.).[95] John was succeeded in 1839 by his son William, who died childless in 1859 and was succeeded by his nephew Philip Lancaster Brocklehurst.[96] Created a baronet in 1903, Philip was succeeded in 1904 by his son, also Philip. The latter was succeeded in 1975 by his sister's grandson, John van Haeften, who broke up the estate in 1977.[97] The hall, with its parkland, was bought by the World Government for the Age of Enlightenment, followers of an Indian mystic, Maharishi Mahesh Yogi, and was opened as a training centre for teachers of Transcendental Meditation. It was sold in 1987 to Mr. R. M. Naylor.[98]

Assessed for tax on eight hearths in 1666, the house at Swythamley was possibly remodelled in the 1690s.[99] A section of wall incorporated in the present west front is probably from the 17th-century house, and it appears to have formed the south-west corner of what by the late 18th century was an irregular double-pile house. The 17th-century part of the house was damaged by fire in 1813, but a part recently added by Edward Nicholls survived.[1] The house was later enlarged by the Brocklehursts, and by 1862 a canted bay had been added to the room at the south-west corner and there was a billiard room at the north end.[2] The billiard room stood on the west side of what had been an open courtyard, on whose other sides were service quarters. The courtyard was covered over by Philip Brocklehurst c. 1860 for use as a dining room and ballroom by the tenantry at the twice-yearly estate audit.[3] The service quarters were removed in the early 20th century, when a large two-storeyed porch was added to the west front.[4] The outbuildings north-east of the house include a late 18th-century stable block, enlarged in 1860 to enclose a yard, and a tenants' hall of 1888.[5] After its purchase by Mr. Naylor in 1987, the house and outbuildings were divided into a number of separate residential units.

The house stands in parkland, which covered 80 a. in 1831 and was then stocked with deer.[6] In the later 18th century the approach was from the south, along a road which ran in front of the house and then along the north side of the park

to Snipe Cottage. By 1831 there was also a road along the south side of the park.[7] The present drive across the park existed by the later 19th century.[8] West Lodge at the west end of the drive is dated 1892, and the smaller South Lodge on the east side of the park was built probably c. 1905 in connexion with the nearby church.[9] An Anglo-Saxon circular cross shaft north-west of the house was brought from Wincle, in Prestbury (Ches.), c. 1874.[10]

Besides its granges at Fairboroughs and Swythamley, Dieulacres abbey owned other land in the township. Henry of Ford, son of Ligulf of Heaton, gave it 2½ bovates in the 1240s and Henry son of Adam of Tittesworth gave land at Wurnuldehalth (later Wormhough) in the late 1240s;[11] Robert of Heaton gave land in or before 1315.[12] At the Dissolution the abbey's property in Heaton included farms attached to houses at Bearda, Brandy Lee, Flashcroft, Heaton Lowe, Hillylees, and Hollinhall.[13]

ECONOMIC HISTORY. AGRICULTURE. Dieulacres abbey's grange at Swythamley comprised 2 carucates of land with meadow and its grange at Fairboroughs 1 carucate in 1291.[14] By the 1490s the abbey's cattle were managed from Swythamley, using land there and in the 'forest' in Leekfrith as pasture. In 1490 the herd consisted of 17 cows and a bull, 118 steers, heifers, and stirks, and 72 oxen and cows. The abbey also kept 10 draught oxen at Swythamley in the 1490s.[15] Payments and services owed to the abbey by free tenants in Heaton in the earlier 16th century comprised a money rent, the payment of two capons worth 6d., one day's ploughing worth 3d., and one day's reaping worth 3d.[16] The abbey probably had a tithe barn in the township: one mentioned in the sale of Heaton manor in 1614 probably stood on the road west of Heaton hamlet, where there was a house called Tithe Barn in 1820.[17]

The common waste lay south and east of Heaton hamlet.[18] Although parts had been inclosed by the earlier 17th century,[19] 476 a. of waste remained in 1820, when it was inclosed under an Act of 1816.[20]

Of the 706 ha. of farmland returned for the civil parish in 1988, grassland covered 601.4 ha. and there were 44.3 ha. of rough grazing. The farming was dairy and sheep, with 1,040 head of cattle and 1,304 sheep and lambs. There were

93 S.R.O., D. 1109/3, burial of 5 Apr. 1785; Sleigh, *Leek*, 19; *S.H.C.* 1912, 292.
94 S.R.O., D. 5017/1/33. For a portrait see W.S.L. copy of [P. L. Brocklehurst], *Swythamley and Its Neighbourhood* (priv. print. 1874), between pp. 74 and 75 (identified on p. 44).   95 S.R.O., D. 5017/1/36.
96 Sleigh, *Leek*, 141.
97 Leek Libr., newspaper cuttings 1972–8, pp. 100–2; W.S.L., S.C. C/3/34.
98 Inf. from Mr. Naylor.
99 *S.H.C.* 1925, 169; stones dated 1691 and 1697 with Trafford initials reset on the former stable block.
1 W.S.L., S.C. D/1/17; *Staffs. Advertiser*, 1 Jan. 1814, p. 4.
2 1862 plan of house in possession of Mr. Naylor; above, plate 28.
3 *Swythamley and Its Neighbourhood*, 40–1; W.S.L.

498/34, cutting of 14 May 1904; 1862 plan of house.
4 O.S. Map 6", Staffs. IV. NW. (1900, 1926 edns.).
5 Date stones on buildings.
6 W.S.L., S.C. D/1/17; S.R.O. 4974/A/1/4.
7 W.S.L., S.C. D/1/17; above, fig. 2.
8 O.S. Map 6", Staffs. IV. NW. (1888).
9 Ibid. (1900, 1926 edns.); below, church.
10 *T.N.S.F.C.* lv. 160; *V.C.H. Ches.* i. 282, 291.
11 *S.H.C.* N.S. ix. 318.
12 *Cal. Pat.* 1313–17, 332.   13 W.S.L., M. 540.
14 *Tax. Eccl.* (Rec. Com.), 252.
15 S.R.O. 4974/ADD 2; P.R.O., REQ 2/123/51, m. 3.
16 W.S.L., M. 540.
17 S.R.O., D. 5017/1/6; C. and J. Greenwood, *Map of County of Stafford* (1820).
18 Above, fig. 2.   19 S.R.O. 322/M10.
20 Ibid. Q/RDc 84; 56 Geo. III, c. 6 (Priv. Act).

also 10,550 hens. Of the 27 farms returned, 25 were under 50 ha. in size and 2 were between 50 and 99 ha. Woodland covered 39.8 ha.[21]

MILLS. A miller recorded at Heaton in 1327[22] may have held a mill on the stream which runs into the Dane near Bearda Farm: Dieulacres abbey had a mill at Bearda in the earlier 16th century.[23] Bearda mill ceased working apparently in the mid 1890s.[24]

There was a corn mill at Danebridge by 1652. It became a cotton mill evidently in or soon after 1783.[25]

TRADE AND INDUSTRY. A tanhouse was recorded at Heaton in 1640. It probably stood on the north-western boundary, where a tanyard was recorded in the earlier 19th century.[26]

By 1652 there was a paper mill on the Dane at Danebridge. It still existed in 1729 and apparently in 1742. It had ceased to operate by 1754, possibly having been replaced by the paper mill which by 1775 stood further downstream in Wincle on the Cheshire side of the river.[27] In 1671 there was also a fulling mill at Danebridge. It still existed in 1715 but not in 1742.[28]

The corn mill at Danebridge was let in 1783 to John Routh, a cotton manufacturer. It was presumably converted into a cotton mill, which existed there by 1829.[29] John and James Berresford were listed as cotton spinners at Danebridge in 1834, and in 1841 nine cotton workers were living near the mill.[30] By 1849 the mill had been closed,[31] but it was open again in 1851, when John Bennett, a pattern designer, lived at Danebridge cotton mill. The mill appears to have been closed again by 1861.[32] It was re-opened in the 1870s by John Birch, the owner of a dyeworks at Froghall, in Ipstones, and of a carpet manufactory at Wildboarclough, in Prestbury (Ches.). In 1876 his son Joseph used the Danebridge mill to make colours for the silk trade. The business was already in decline by the time of Joseph's death in 1898, and the mill was later used as a smithy. The building fell into disrepair and was demolished in 1976.[33]

Grindstone was quarried at Heaton c. 1680.[34] In 1820 there were several stone pits in the township, notably on the west side of Gun where a quarry was still worked in 1919.[35]

A brick and tile maker employing three men lived in Heaton hamlet in 1851.[36] His works may have been at the brick and tile yard recorded in 1866 south-east of Tofthall Farm.[37]

LOCAL GOVERNMENT. By the earlier 14th century Heaton was a tithing of Leek manor and sent a frankpledge to the twice-yearly view. It was still part of the manor in 1820, when the court appointed a headborough for the township.[38]

There was a view of frankpledge for Heaton in 1797, when it was stated that court records existed from 1697.[39] A court held in the mid 19th century by the owner of the Swythamley estate as lord of Heaton had been discontinued by 1874.[40] By the late 1870s a pinfold stood on the west side of Heaton hamlet,[41] where it survived in 1991.

The township was part of the Leekfrith quarter of Leek parish, and in the 1660s its poor were relieved by the quarter's overseer. The township had its own overseer by 1713.[42] A workhouse was built by the township at Danebridge in 1829. The intention may have been to accommodate unemployed workers from the cotton mill there. The upkeep of the workhouse was soon found to be too expensive, and in 1833 the township sold it to John Brocklehurst of Swythamley.[43] Heaton became part of Leek poor-law union in 1837.[44]

CHURCH. From the 18th century and presumably earlier people from Heaton attended St. Lawrence's church in Rushton Spencer.[45]

A plan by Philip Brocklehurst in the late 1870s to build a chapel near Swythamley Hall was abortive. Revived shortly before his death in 1904, the project was continued by his widow Annie and a memorial church licensed for services was completed in 1905. It was closed in 1977 and later converted into a house.[46] The church had a carillon worked by water power.[47]

NONCONFORMITY. A Methodist service held at Danebridge on alternate Sundays in 1798 took place in the cotton mill in 1806.[48] A Wesleyan Methodist chapel was opened at Danebridge in 1834, and on Census Sunday 1851 the attendance was 80 in the afternoon, besides Sunday school children, and 120 in the evening.[49] The chapel was known as Danebridge

21 P.R.O., MAF 68/6128/59.
22 S.H.C. vii (1), 219.   23 W.S.L., M. 540.
24 Kelly's Dir. Staffs. (1892; 1896); O.S. Map 6", Staffs. IV. NW. (1900 edn.).
25 S.R.O., D. 5017/40/41; below, this section (trade and ind.).
26 S.R.O. 322/M7; S.R.O., D. 848/6; O.S. Map 1", LXXXI. SW. (1842 edn.).
27 S.R.O., D. 3359/Condlyffe, Wm. Trafford to Mr. Brookes, 1 Oct. 1729; D. 5017/40/41–2, 64; above, fig. 2.
28 S.R.O., D. 5017/40/62, 639–40.
29 Ibid. D. 5017/40/641; S.R.O., Q/RUt 5/51.
30 White, Dir. Staffs. (1834), 712, 714; P.R.O., HO 107/1005.
31 S. Bagshaw, Hist. of County of Chester (1850), 260.
32 P.R.O., HO 107/2008; ibid. RG 9/1948.
33 Ibid. RG 11/2741; E. M. Lycett, 'The Birch Family Hist.' (TS. 1988, in Leek Libr.).
34 Plot, Staffs. 168.
35 S.R.O., D. 1176/B/11/1 (annotated copy of Rudyard estate sale cat. 1919); ibid. Q/RDc 84, plan I.
36 P.R.O., HO 107/2008.
37 Sale partics. 22 Feb. 1866 (copy in S.R.O., D. (W.) 1909/F/3).   38 Above, Leek and Lowe, local govt.
39 S.R.O., D. 5017/1/25.
40 Swythamley and Its Neighbourhood, 7.
41 O.S. Map 6", Staffs. III. SE. (1888 edn.).
42 Above, Leek, par. intro. (par. govt.).
43 S.R.O., D. 5017/13/74 and 157.
44 Ibid. D. 699/1/1/1, p. 4.   45 Ibid. D. 1109/1.
46 W.S.L. 498/34, cutting of 14 May 1904; S.R.O. 4974/B/8/12; Lich. Dioc. Regy., Bp.'s Reg. 36, pp. 450–2; Bp.'s Reg. U, pp. 696–700.
47 T. S. Jennings, Hist. of Staffs. Bells (priv. print. 1968), 107.
48 Dyson, Wesleyan Methodism, 40; Leek Wesleyan Methodist Circuit Yr. Bk. 1887, 19.
49 P.R.O., HO 129/372/3/2.

Methodist church in 1991. A Wesleyan chapel opened in 1816 on the township's western boundary was replaced by one in Rushton Spencer in 1899 and was later converted into a house.[50]

A Primitive Methodist chapel was built on the east side of the township in 1864.[51] It was closed in the late 1960s and was converted in 1985 into a private residence called Gun End House.[52]

EDUCATION. William Trafford (d. 1762) of Swythamley asked in his will that a school should be built on common land in Heaton.[53] There is no evidence that his request was fulfilled. In the earlier 1830s there were two schools in the township, one with 21 boys and the other with 25 girls.[54] A schoolmaster living at Heaton Lowe in 1851 may have taught in the township,[55] as may a schoolmistress who lived near Gun in 1871.[56] The Wesleyan Methodist Sunday school had an attendance of 45 on Census Sunday 1851.[57]

In 1902 a school was opened on the east side of the township to commemorate Edward VII's coronation. The site was given by Philip Brocklehurst of Swythamley, and the building was erected and furnished by Brocklehurst and his wife.[58] It was a Church of England elementary school until 1921, when it became Swythamley

council school.[59] From 1931 it was a junior school, senior children going to Rushton Spencer until 1940 and thereafter to Leek.[60] The school, which was rebuilt in 1960–1, was closed in 1981, and the building was converted into a village hall.[61]

CHARITIES FOR THE POOR. Sarah Nicholls (d. 1785) of Swythamley left the interest on £200 for distribution in woollen cloth, half to the poor of Heaton and half to the poor of Leekfrith. The recipients were to be chosen by Sarah's daughters, and after their deaths by the owner of the Swythamley estate. In 1788 the annual income was £10. By the earlier 1820s distributions each of 12 gowns and 12 coats for Heaton and Leekfrith were made once every three years.[62] The distribution ceased in 1940 but was revived in 1974. The charity was amalgamated that year with one established by Sir Philip Brocklehurst (d. 1904), who left the interest on £300 to be distributed in blankets and woollen clothing to needy tenants on the Swythamley estate.[63] A Scheme of 1981 provided for the income of what was then called the Nicholls and Brocklehurst charity to be distributed either in kind or in money equally among beneficiaries in Heaton and Leekfrith. In 1991 there was a cash distribution of £140.[64]

LEEKFRITH

LEEKFRITH was formerly a township in Leek parish and later a civil parish 7,542 a. (3,052 ha.) in area, including a detached portion of c. 10 a. to the east on the north side of Blackshaw moor.[65] It is pasture, with a village called Meerbrook in the centre beside the Meer brook. Dieulacres abbey, founded in 1214, stood near the river Churnet in the south part of the township, and its granges were among the earliest settlements in what was an area of wooded countryside; the 'frith' element of the township's name means a wood.[66] The short northern boundary with Cheshire follows the river Dane. On the east the boundary with Quarnford and Heathylee, in Alstonefield, follows a tributary of the Dane, Black brook, so called by the mid 13th century,[67] and Back brook, which flows south to the Churnet.[68] The Churnet itself forms the southern boundary with Tittesworth and with Leek and Lowe. The area was increased to 7,551 a. by the transfer under the Divided Parishes Act, 1882, of a detached portion of Tittesworth on Blackshaw moor.[69] In 1894 the south-western

corner of the the township, 127 a. at Abbey Green and Bridge End, was added to Leek urban district, and a detached portion of Leek and Lowe north-west of Bridge End was transferred to Leekfrith. As a result Leekfrith civil parish covered 7,534 a.[70] In 1934 Leekfrith was reduced to its present 7,016 a. (2,839 ha.) by the transfer of the detached portion of Leekfrith on Blackshaw moor to Heathylee civil parish and 508 a. in the south-west of Leekfrith to Leek urban district.[71] This article deals with the former township and the added parts of Leek and Lowe and of Tittesworth.

The township is dominated on the north-east by the Roaches and Hen Cloud, outcrops of Millstone Grit. The Roaches, rising to 1,658 ft. (505 m.), were so called by 1358 and derive their name from the French *roche,* meaning a rock or a cliff.[72] Hen Cloud to the south rises to 1,350 ft. (410 m.). Its name means a steep rock (*henge clud*) in Old English.[73] Gun, a hill on the west side of the township, rises to 1,263 ft. (385 m.). The valley between the Roaches and Gun is

50 Below, Rushton Spencer, nonconf.
51 *Gun End Methodist Church* (centenary brochure, 1964).   52 Inf. from the owner, Mrs. J. Brightmore.
53 S.R.O., D. 5017/1/20.
54 *Educ. Enq. Abstract,* 879.
55 P.R.O., HO 107/2008 (s.v. Low House).
56 Ibid. RG 10/2884.
57 Ibid. HO 129/372/3/2.
58 S.R.O., D. 3658/1, p. 1; *Staffs. Advertiser,* 26 Apr. 1902, p. 5; 27 Sept. 1902, p. 5.
59 S.R.O., D. 3658/1, pp. 1, 121.
60 Ibid. pp. 254, 269; Staffs. C.C. *Record for 1931,* 455.
61 S.R.O., D. 3658/2, pp. 182, 190–2; D. 3658/3, pp. 94–6.
62 *13th Rep. Com. Char.* 392, 394; *Char. Dons.* 1152–3.
63 A. N. Bebington, *St. Lawrence Parish Church* (1988),

11–12; *Kelly's Dir. Staffs.* (1912).
64 S.R.O., Charities Index; inf. from the correspondent, Mr. A. Needham.
65 *V.C.H. Staffs.* i. 328. This article was written in 1992.
66 Below, econ. hist. (woodland).
67 *S.H.C.* N.S. ix. 317.
68 Back brook was also known as Dane or Dain brook, after the mill at Upper Hulme: Sleigh, *Leek,* 86 n.; Challinor, *Lectures,* 301, 306–7, 309; below, econ. hist. (mills).
69 Below, Tittesworth, intro.
70 *Census,* 1901.
71 Ibid. 1931; Staffs. Review Order, 1934, pp. 60, 63 and map 1 (copy in S.R.O.).
72 *Eng. P.N. Elements,* ii. 86; *S.H.C.* xii (1), 162.
73 *Eng. P.N. Elements,* i. 101, 243.

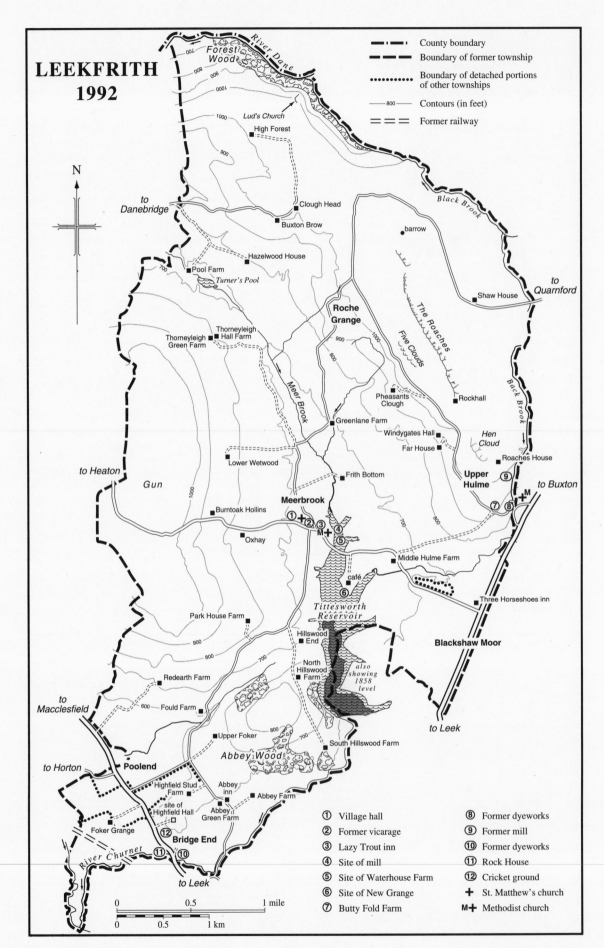

LEEKFRITH 1992

N

County boundary
Boundary of former township
Boundary of detached portions of other townships
—800— Contours (in feet)
=== Former railway

Forest Wood
River Dane
Lud's Church
High Forest
to Danebridge
Clough Head
Buxton Brow
barrow
Black Brook
Hazelwood House
Shaw House
to Quarnford
Pool Farm
Turner's Pool
Roche Grange
The Roaches
Five Clouds
Thorneyleigh Hall Farm
Thorneyleigh Green Farm
Meer Brook
Back Brook
Pheasants Clough
Rockhall
Greenlane Farm
Windygates Hall
Hen Cloud
to Heaton
Lower Wetwood
Far House
Roaches House
Gun
Frith Bottom
Upper Hulme ⑨
to Buxton
Meerbrook
⑦ ⑧ M✚
Burntoak Hollins
① ✚② ③ ④
Oxhay
M✚ ⑤
Middle Hulme Farm
café
Three Horseshoes inn
⑥
Tittesworth Reservoir
Park House Farm
Hillswood End
Blackshaw Moor
Redearth Farm
North Hillswood Farm
also showing 1858 level
to Macclesfield
Fould Farm
to Leek
Upper Foker
South Hillswood Farm
to Horton
Abbey Wood
Poolend
Highfield Stud Farm
Abbey inn
site of Highfield Hall
Abbey Green Farm
Abbey Farm
Foker Grange
⑫
Bridge End
⑪ ⑩
River Churnet
to Leek

① Village hall
② Former vicarage
③ Lazy Trout inn
④ Site of mill
⑤ Site of Waterhouse Farm
⑥ Site of New Grange
⑦ Butty Fold Farm

⑧ Former dyeworks
⑨ Former mill
⑩ Former dyeworks
⑪ Rock House
⑫ Cricket ground
✚ St. Matthew's church
M✚ Methodist church

0   0.5   1 mile
0   0.5   1 km

F ɪ ɢ. 35

drained by Meer brook, so called *c.* 1220.[74] Fed by Turner's pool, recorded in 1535,[75] the brook originally flowed into the Churnet, but since the mid 19th century it has flowed into Tittesworth reservoir. The reservoir originally lay mostly in Tittesworth, but it was extended *c.* 1960 and now lies mostly in Leekfrith.[76] At Meerbrook village the land lies at 682 ft. (207 m.), falling to 519 ft. (158 m.) at Abbey Green to the south-west. The Millstone Grit is overlain by Boulder Clay in the Meer brook valley and on Blackshaw moor, and the soil is mostly fine loam, with a mixture of clay, loam, and peat on Gun.[77]

In 1666 Leekfrith had 103 people assessed for hearth tax.[78] In 1751 there were 313 people aged over 16 in the township.[79] The population in 1801 was 697, rising to 806 by 1821, 873 by 1831, and 926 by 1841. It was 877 in 1851, 771 in 1871, and 792 in 1891. After the 1894 boundary changes it was 716 in 1901. In 1911 it was 614, falling to 598 by 1921 but rising to 625 by 1931. After the 1934 boundary changes the population was 514 in 1951. It continued to fall and was 452 in 1961, 362 in 1971, and 333 in 1981. In 1991 it was 350.[80]

A Neolithic or Bronze Age mace head has been found on the west side of Tittesworth reservoir, and two apparently Bronze Age vessels have been found near Hen Cloud.[81] There is a barrow at the north end of the Roaches, and another near Middle Hulme Farm beside the Churnet on the east side of the township.[82] The burial place (*sepulcrum*) of Thoni, mentioned in the bounds of the estate granted to Dieulacres abbey *c.* 1220 and lying at the south end of Gun, may have been a barrow.[83]

In 1214 the Cistercian monks at Poulton, in Pulford (Ches.), were transferred to a site in the grounds of the later Abbey Farm in the south part of the township. Their patron Ranulph, earl of Chester, had been instructed in a dream to settle them at 'Cholpesdale' on the site of the former chapel of St. Mary, itself possibly a hermitage. The name Dieulacres was fixed by the earl himself and means in French 'May God grant it increase'.[84] About 1220 the earl issued a charter granting the monks what was described as 'the land of Rudyard' on which to build their abbey.[85] The estate, covering the south-western part of Leekfrith township, stretched on the east as far as Meer brook, a name which means 'boundary brook' and may refer originally to the boundary of Rudyard manor.[86]

Abbey Green west of Abbey Farm probably originated as an open space at the abbey gate. It lies along a road which before the later 18th century formed part of the route between Leek and Buxton and of one to Macclesfield. Abbey Green Farm is of the 17th century, when it was owned by the Tunnicliffe family; it was assessed for tax on six hearths in 1666.[87] The Abbey inn east of the farmhouse has a lintel over the entrance with the date 1702 and the initials of the tenant John Allen and his wife.[88] By 1726 there was a bowling green at the house, which was known as Bowling Green House in 1770.[89] It was an inn by 1834, known as the Bowling Green.[90]

There was evidently a settlement at Meerbrook in the mid 13th century, when there was mention of Robert of Meerbrook, and by the earlier 16th century it had a chapel.[91] The former Water-house Farm on the east side of the village also existed by the earlier 16th century.[92] The siting of the village was probably determined by access to the upper part of the Meer brook valley and to Gun. A house at Burntoak Hollins west of the village, in existence by the earlier 16th century,[93] stood on what in the 18th century was a pack-horse way over Gun.[94] The nearby farmhouse called Oxhay may have been associated with the way: at the east end of the present house, which has date stones of 1754 and 1765, there is a large storage area, possibly for fodder. The Lazy Trout inn in the village centre existed as the Horseshoe by 1818 and the Three Horseshoes by 1834. There was another inn, the Fountain, to the south-east by 1834.[95] A post office was opened in the late 1890s.[96] In the later 1950s there was concern about possible pollution of Meer brook, which flows into Tittesworth reservoir, and the Staffordshire Potteries Waterworks Board compulsorily purchased nearly all the houses in the village. The reservoir was enlarged between 1959 and 1962, and the sites of the Fountain inn, Waterhouse Farm, and several houses were submerged. At the same time the road from Leek, which originally entered the village from the south-east, was replaced by a new line to the west. In the later 1970s the Board encouraged a return of population, and surviving houses were restored.[97] The village school, closed in 1969, became a youth hostel in 1977.[98]

By the mid 13th century there were settlements east of Meerbrook village called Nether, Middle, and Over Hulme, a name derived from Old Norse *holmr*, or its English equivalent, and meaning raised ground in marsh land.[99] Land at Nether Hulme was given by Ranulph of Wirral (otherwise Ranulph of Hulme) in the mid 13th century to Dieulacres abbey, which by 1291 had

74 *Charters of Earls of Chester*, p. 378.
75 S.R.O., D. 5017/1/2 (as Thornhurst pool).
76 Below, Tittesworth, intro.
77 Geol. Surv. Map 1/50,000, drift, sheet 111 (1978 edn.); Soil Surv. of Eng. and Wales, sheet 3 (1983).
78 *S.H.C.* 1925, 166, 242.
79 S.R.O., D. 1028/1/1, f. 67v.
80 *V.C.H. Staffs.* i. 328; *Census*, 1911–91.
81 *N.S.J.F.S.* iv. 28; viii. 70–2; W.S.L. 15/1/79.
82 Staffs. C.C., Sites and Monuments Rec. 00339, 04087.
83 *Charters of Earls of Chester*, p. 378.
84 *V.C.H. Staffs.* iii. 230.
85 *Charters of Earls of Chester*, p. 378.
86 *Staffs. Studies*, v. 4.
87 S.R.O., D. (W.) 1702/1/2, deed of 30 June 1677;

S.H.C. N.S. iv. 83; *S.H.C.* 1925, 168.
88 S.R.O., D. (W.) 1702/1/23, deed of 2 July 1726.
89 Ibid.; D. 3272/1/4/3/17B; H. Woodhouse, *Story of a Leek Church* (Leek, 1988), 21.
90 White, *Dir. Staffs.* (1834), 714.
91 *S.H.C.* N.S. ix. 317; below, church.
92 W.S.L., M. 540.   93 Ibid.
94 Dodd, *Peakland Roads*, 128; *V.C.H. Staffs.* ii. 278–9.
95 Parson and Bradshaw, *Staffs. Dir.* (1818), villages section, 15; White, *Dir. Staffs.* (1834), 714.
96 *P.O. Dir. Staffs.* (1900).
97 Leek Libr., newspaper cuttings 1972–8, p. 103; below, Tittesworth, intro.   98 Below, educ.
99 *S.H.C.* N.S. ix. 316; M. Gelling, *Place-Names in the Landscape*, 50–1.

built New grange at the confluence of the Churnet and Meer brook.[1] In 1666 there were two houses there, one occupied by John Hulme and assessed for tax on four hearths, and the other occupied by Thomas Mountford and assessed for tax on three hearths.[2] Both houses were submerged when Tittesworth reservoir was extended c. 1960. In 1974 adjoining land was laid out as Tittesworth Reservoir Amenity Area.[3]

The present Middle Hulme Farm was built in the early 17th century. It has the date 1118 and the initials TB on the east porch, placed there when the house was pebble-dashed in the later 20th century. The date is probably a misreading of 1718, which would fit the date of the kitchen wing and the occupation of the house by Thomas Brough.[4] In 1811 the road which originally ran north-east from the house to Upper Hulme was realigned to run south-east across Blackshaw moor.[5] By 1819 there was an inn where the new road met the Leek–Buxton turnpike road; it was called the Three Horseshoes by 1834.[6]

What was called Over Hulme in the mid 13th century is identifiable as the present hamlet of Upper Hulme on the township's eastern boundary. The original settlement was probably on the high ground west of Back brook, where Butty Fold Farm possibly stands on the site of one of two houses recorded at Over Hulme in the earlier 16th century.[7] The present farmhouse is of the early 18th century and has a 19th-century porch. It apparently replaced an earlier house occupied by the Condlyffe family in the 17th century: a date stone (possibly reconstructed) on an outbuilding has the date 1647 and the initials of William Condlyffe of Upper Hulme (d. 1664) and his wife Anne.[8] A hamlet grew up on the lower ground beside Back brook in the earlier 19th century, after the opening of a silk mill there.[9]

The earliest settlements elsewhere in the township were Dieulacres abbey's granges in the upper part of the Meer brook valley. Roche grange, in existence by 1246, probably stood north-west of the Roaches in the area of the present hamlet called Roche Grange. A grange at Wetwood, in existence possibly by 1246 and certainly by 1291, stood on the east side of Gun, probably on the site of Lower Wetwood, which is of the earlier 17th century and has an extension of 1671. At the Dissolution the abbey had a third grange at Foker, probably on the site of the farmhouse called Upper Foker north of the abbey site.[10] The name Foker, recorded in 1330s, means 'foul marsh'[11] and refers to an area of common waste in the south-west corner of the

township. Part of the waste was a detached portion of Leek and Lowe township, to which it had probably been assigned as pasture for use by inhabitants of Leek town.[12] A farmhouse on the southern edge of the waste was called Lower Foker in 1770 and Foker Grange, its present name, by the late 1890s.[13]

The sites of several other farmhouses were occupied by the earlier 16th century.[14] In the west part of the township they included the Sheephouse, renamed Fould Farm by 1673,[15] and Park House Farm, both on the Meerbrook road north of Abbey Green, and to the north-west of Fould Farm a house called Redearth. By the later 16th century there were two houses at Redearth, of which only one survives. Rebuilt in the 17th century, that house has a third storey with windows evidently inserted to provide light for weaving; in 1666 the house was occupied by a weaver, John Plant.[16] Two houses described in the earlier 16th century as lying 'under Wyndyat' probably stood on the sites of Far House and Windygates Hall on the east side of the township. Both houses are of the 17th century, and Windygates Hall has a date stone of 1634 on its porch. There was also a settlement by the earlier 16th century at the north end of the Meer brook valley at Thorneyleigh. The Armett family occupied a house there which probably stood on the site of Thorneyleigh Hall Farm, which is of the 17th century and has a doorhead dated 1691 reset over the garden entrance.[17] Thorneyleigh Green Farm dates from the 18th century but replaced a house occupied by John Stoddard (d. 1675), a benefactor of Meerbrook chapel and school.[18] Of other farmhouses in the Meer brook valley Greenlane Farm is first recorded in 1675[19] and Frith Bottom in 1695.[20]

The northern part of the township had been settled by the earlier 17th century. There was a house at Hazelwood by 1635. By 1640 there was one at Buxton Brow, then called Buckstone Brow, and another at Clough Head. The site of High Forest further north was also occupied by 1640.[21] Pool Farm near Turner's pool was built for William Armett in 1669.[22] In 1681 a family was living at Five Clouds, the name for rocks on the west side of the Roaches.[23] A cave at the south end of the Roaches inhabited by the early 17th century was known as Rockhall in 1770.[24] On the east side of the Roaches a scattered settlement of coal miners grew up in the 19th century around Shaw House.[25] Roaches House (originally Argyle Cottage) south-east of Hen Cloud was built in 1876.[26]

1 S.H.C. N.S. ix. 316; S.H.C. 1911, 186; below, econ. hist. (agric.).
2 S.H.C. 1925, 166; Leek Par. Reg. 175, 177.
3 Plaque in grounds.   4 Sleigh, Leek, 119.
5 S.R.O., Q/RDc 65.
6 S.R.O., D. 1028/1/4, p. 18; White, Dir. Staffs. (1834), 714.   7 W.S.L., M. 540.
8 L.J.R.O., B/C/11, Wm. Condlyffe (1664).
9 Below, econ. hist. (trade and ind.).
10 Below, econ. hist. (agric.).
11 S.R.O., D. 1337/3; Eng. P.N. Elements, i. 189 (ful); ii. 4 (ker); inf. from Dr. M. Gelling.
12 S.R.O., D. 1176/A/11/12; above, fig. 2.
13 S.R.O., D. 3272/1/4/3/17B; O.S. Map 6", Staffs. VIII. NW. (1900 edn.).   14 W.S.L., M. 540.
15 L.J.R.O., B/C/11, Wm. Davenport (1552); S.R.O., D.
(W.) 1702/1/11, deed of 29 Oct. 1673.
16 L.J.R.O., B/C/11, John Plant (1666); S.R.O., D. (W.) 1702/1/6–9.   17 Reliquary, vi. 196–7.
18 Leek Par. Reg. 198.
19 L.J.R.O., Reg. of Wills A, pp. 493–4.
20 S.R.O., D. 538/D/13/8, abstract of title to Mr. Wood's estate.
21 Leek Par. Reg. 4; L.J.R.O., B/C/11, John Johnson (1640); inf. from Miss M. F. Cleverdon, citing deed in possession of the owners of Buxton Brow.
22 S.R.O., D. 5017/8/104; date stone on house.
23 Leek Par. Reg. 217.
24 T.N.S.F.C. xviii. 21–2; S.R.O., D. 1028/1/2, bapt. of 27 Sept. 1770.   25 Below, econ. hist. (trade and ind.).
26 O.S. Map 6", Staffs. IV. SE. (1887 edn.); date stone on an upper storey (later removed) and now on garage.

A settlement on the township's south-western boundary where the Leek–Macclesfield road crossed the Churnet was known as Bridge End in 1641. It included Coneygray House, recorded in 1697 and named after a medieval rabbit warren.[27] The hamlet developed in the earlier 19th century after the opening of a dyeworks by 1824.[28] A row of seven houses dated 1850 stands to the east where the road to Meerbrook village crossed the Churnet. The former Highfield Hall north of Bridge End was built in the early 19th century.[29] Rock House, on the west side of the main road by the river crossing, was built in the earlier 1860s for Charles Ball, a Leek accountant.[30]

Before the later 18th century the road from Leek to Buxton ran via Abbey Green, Middle Hulme, and Upper Hulme. It crossed the Churnet by Broad bridge, so called in 1587 and rebuilt in the early 19th century.[31] It is now called Broad's bridge. From Upper Hulme the road ran north-west to a gap between Hen Cloud and the Roaches and on to Flash, in Quarnford, in Alstonefield.[32] The present Leek–Buxton road, which forms part of Leekfrith's eastern boundary, was laid out in 1765 and 1766 as a turnpike road. It was disturnpiked in 1875.[33] The Leek–Macclesfield road runs through the south-west corner of the township. Part of the medieval Earl's Way, the road was turnpiked in 1762, and in 1824 a tollhouse was set up at the north end of the Leekfrith stretch of the road at Poolend.[34] The road ran in front of Highfield Hall, but it was realigned to the west in the late 1820s.[35] It was disturnpiked in 1878, and the Poolend tollhouse was demolished in 1879.[36] There was formerly another route from Leek to Macclesfield, which branched from the Meerbrook road at Fould Farm and ran along the top of Gun, crossing into Cheshire at Danebridge, in Heaton. Recorded c. 1230, the road was still in use in the earlier 18th century.[37] In 1731 Robert Brough was murdered on Gun by his servant Joseph Naden as he travelled home along the road. After being sentenced at Stafford, Naden was hanged on Gun and his corpse gibbeted there.[38] The gibbet post was still standing in 1875.[39] A packhorse way ran east–west across Gun and passed through Meerbrook village and Middle Hulme.[40]

Leekfrith was included in an association for the prosecution of felons formed in 1802 and also covering the townships of Leek and Lowe and Tittesworth.[41] A separate association for Leekfrith was established in 1819 but evidently lapsed. The association was revived in 1833, and it still functioned in 1873.[42] The rural part of Leekfrith was connected to a mains water supply in the earlier 1970s.[43]

In the mid 19th century Meerbrook wake was celebrated at the end of September or the beginning of October.[44] Before the change in the calendar in 1752 it was probably held on the Sunday nearest 21 September, the feast of St. Matthew, the patron saint of Meerbrook church. By 1866 a wake was held in July at Abbey Green, and it was still held in 1919.[45] A village hall was built west of Meerbrook village in 1908 and rebuilt in 1988.[46] A Women's Institute was formed at Meerbrook in 1924.[47]

The Roaches and Hen Cloud impressed Robert Plot when he visited the area c. 1680.[48] He also noted Lud's Church, a ravine north-west of the Roaches, which has been suggested as the setting for the climax of the 14th-century poem, *Sir Gawain and the Green Knight*.[49] About 1862 the landowner, Philip Brocklehurst of Swythamley, in Heaton, placed a ship's figure-head in the form of a woman at the entrance of the ravine.[50] It was apparently intended to commemorate the supposed martyrdom of the daughter of a Lollard preacher, and it was still there in 1914.[51]

The Roaches were added to the Swythamley estate at the time of the inclosure of the area in 1811, and in the late 1890s Philip Brocklehurst acquired Hen Cloud. He encouraged visitors to the area by cutting footpaths and building bridges across streams. He also incorporated the Rockhall cave dwelling into a Gothic-style shooting lodge. The lodge became a tourist attraction, and in 1872 Princess Mary of Cambridge and her husband Francis, duke of Teck, were entertained there.[52] It later became a private dwelling, and it remained as such until 1989. It was then acquired by the Peak Park joint planning board, which had bought 975 a. of the Roaches in 1980, following the break-up of the Swythamley estate in 1977. In 1993 the lodge

27 *Leek Par. Reg.* 41; S.R.O., D. 3359/abstract of title to Geo. Vernon's estate, 1697–1801; below, econ. hist. (forest and warren).
28 P.R.O., HO 107/2008; *Staffs. Hist.* viii. 8.
29 Below, manor (Highfield Hall).
30 S.R.O., D. 3272/1/4/3/19; White, *Dir. Staffs.* (1851), 733; *P.O. Dir. Staffs.* (1860).
31 S.R.O., D. 3359/Cruso, deed of 22 Apr. 1587; S.R.O., Q/SO/25, f. 231.
32 Dodd, *Peakland Roads*, 174; *T.N.S.F.C.* N.S. iv. 37–8.
33 Above, Leek and Lowe, communications.
34 Ibid.; below, Rudyard, intro.
35 S.R.O., D. 706/4, p. 14; D. 1176/A/11/11; Sandon Rd. acct. bk. 1821–69, 13 Dec. 1828 and later accts. to 4 May 1830 (in possession of Mr. R. Stones of Malpas, Ches., 1994).
36 *Staffs. Advertiser*, 26 Oct. 1876, p. 8; S.R.O., D. 3359/Sandon Rd. order bk., 9 July 1878, 27 Feb. 1879; above, Leek and Lowe, communications.
37 Dodd, *Peakland Roads*, 55–6; *Charters of Earls of Chester*, p. 385; S.R.O., Q/RDc 65, plan V, showing the stretch south of Gun in 1811 as Macclesfield Old Road.
38 Sleigh, *Leek*, 199–201; *Gent. Mag.* i. 396; *Diary of James Clegg* (Derb. Rec. Soc. ii), 127; S.R.O. 4974/B/8/2.

39 *T.N.S.F.C.* lxxviii. 70.
40 *V.C.H. Staffs.* ii. 278–9 (based on W.S.L., D. 1798/617/76; D. 1798/681/15).
41 Above, Leek and Lowe, public services (policing).
42 *Macclesfield Courier & Herald*, 3 July 1819, p. 1 (ref. supplied by Mr. A. W. Bednall of Macclesfield); S.R.O., D. 1028/4/1 and 3.
43 S.R.O., D. 4728/2/2, 6 Feb. 1968, 9 Aug. 1972.
44 'Diary of John Plant of Hazelwood, 1849–53' (TS. in W.S.L., CB/Fam./Plant), 30 Sept. 1849, 5 Oct. 1851; S. W. Hutchinson, *Archdeaconry of Stoke-on-Trent* (1893), 98.
45 W.S.L., Sleigh, ii, f. 68; *Leek Par. Reg.* p. v n.
46 *Leek Post & Times*, 25 July 1990, pp. 8–9.
47 Inf. from Staffs. Federation of Women's Institutes.
48 Above, Leek, par. intro.
49 Plot, *Staffs.* 173; *N.S.J.F.S.* xvii, 20–49.
50 W.S.L. 498/34, cutting of 14 May 1904.
51 Anon. *Legends of the Moorlands and Forest in N. Staffs.* (1860), 66–76; W. K. Parkes, *The Money Hunt* [1914], 63, where 'Rock Chapel' is Lud's Church.
52 [P. L. Brocklehurst], *Swythamley and Its Neighbourhood* (priv. print. 1874), 46–51; W.S.L. 498/34, cutting of 14 May 1904; below, econ. hist. (agric.).

was made into a refuge by the British Mountaineering Club.[53] The area remains popular with walkers and rock climbers. A colony of wallabies there originated in the late 1930s, when some escaped from a private zoo kept by Col. H. C. Brocklehurst at Roaches House.[54]

Richard Caldwall (d. 1584), the physician, was born apparently at Upper Hulme.[55] The sculptor Richard Hassall (1831–68) was born at Pheasants Clough, a farmhouse on the west side of the Roaches.[56]

MANOR AND OTHER ESTATES. The manor of *FRITH* was first mentioned in 1552 when the Crown granted what were described as the manors of Leek and Frith with the site of Dieulacres abbey to Sir Ralph Bagnall. Frith manor descended with Leek manor.[57]

ABBEY FARM, which occupies part of the site of Dieulacres abbey, was the home in 1614 of Thomas Rudyard, lord of Leek manor.[58] His younger son Anthony lived there in 1638.[59] Anthony was succeeded in 1662 by his son Thomas.[60] The house was occupied by Edward Stubbs in 1666,[61] but the following year it was evidently the home of Anthony's brother John: a gateway into the garden on the west side of the house incorporates a stone with the date 1667 and the initials of John Rudyard and his wife.[62] Known as Abbey Dieulacres in 1673, the house and its estate were inherited that year or soon afterwards by John's nephew, James Rudyard. James died in 1712, leaving the estate in tail to his cousin John Rudyard, with reversion to his godson Ralph Wood, the son of another cousin.[63] John Rudyard evidently died childless, and the estate passed to Wood, who was living at Abbey Dieulacres in 1736 and died there in 1765.[64] The estate was later sold to the Misses Furnivall, of whom one was evidently the Anne Furnivall of the Abbey who in 1777 married John Daintry of Leek. Anne was succeeded in 1798 by her nephew John Smith Daintry.[65] In 1829 Daintry sold the estate in two separate shares to Theodosia Hinckes and John Davenport of Westwood Hall, in Leek and Lowe, either John (d. 1848) or his son John (d. 1862). The younger John

bought Theodosia's share in 1853.[66] In 1871 his son George sold what was then called Dieulacres Abbey Farm to James Searight,[67] whose executors sold it in 1892 to Capt. W. Jones Byrom of Leek.[68] On Byrom's death in 1897 it passed to George Renny, still the owner in 1940.[69] The owner in 1992 was Mr. A. E. Docksey.

Abbey Farm, which stands west of the site of the abbey church, is timber-framed on a sandstone course.[70] It is uncertain whether any part of the present fabric dates from before the 17th century. The house was assessed for tax on seven hearths in 1666.[71]

HIGHFIELD HALL, originally called Highfield House, was built in the 1810s by Richard Badnall, a Leek silk dyer, on land bought in 1801 by his father Joseph (d. 1803).[72] On Richard's bankruptcy in 1827 the house and 46 a. were sold to Sarah Fowler and her sons Matthew and Josiah Gaunt, all three members of a Leek banking family.[73] In 1870 the estate was bought by Charles Glover.[74] In 1885 E. Cliffe Glover sold it to Arthur Nicholson, a partner in the Leek silk company later known as Brough, Nicholson & Hall. Knighted in 1909, Nicholson was a noted breeder of shire horses and built a stud farm north-east of the house. The horses were paraded when George V and Queen Mary were entertained at Highfield in 1911.[75] Nicholson died in 1929, but his widow Marianne continued to live at the house until her death in 1937.[76] The house, to which Nicholson had by 1889 added a wing,[77] was of brick with stone dressings. It was sold in 1939 and demolished in 1940 or 1941.[78] Surviving outbuildings include the present Home Farm and the former stable block, also converted into a house.

ECONOMIC HISTORY. AGRICULTURE. About 1230 Ranulph, earl of Chester, granted Dieulacres abbey land on Gun and at Wetwood, besides the right to share with the earl's tenants pasture south of Gun and as far east as Meer brook.[79] Later in the 13th century local benefactors gave the abbey more land in the centre and east part of the township.[80] By 1246 the abbey had a grange on the west side of the Roaches (known

[53] *Leek Post & Times*, 20 Dec. 1989, p. 11; 3 July 1991, p. 3; 27 Jan. 1993, p. 1; 'King Doug' [D. Moller], *Wars of the Roaches* (Stoke-on-Trent, 1991); inf. from the Board.
[54] C. Lever, *Naturalized Animals of British Isles*, chap. 1.
[55] *D.N.B.*; Sleigh, *Leek*, 123.
[56] *Leek Post & Times*, 22 Aug. 1990, p. 12.
[57] Above, Leek and Lowe, manors.
[58] *S.H.C.* 4th ser. xvi. 109.
[59] *S.H.C.* v (2), 254; *Leek Par. Reg.* 22.
[60] *Leek Par. Reg.* 38, 144; W.S.L., S.D. Beck 126.
[61] *S.H.C.* 1925, 168; *Leek Par. Reg.* 170.
[62] S.R.O. 3508/A/3/2; Sleigh, *Leek*, 38.
[63] S.R.O. 3508/A/3/2; S.R.O., D. 1040/5/14, burial of 7 Nov. 1712; L.J.R.O., Reg. of Wills C, ff. 195v.–196.
[64] *Travels through Eng. of Dr. Richard Pococke*, i (Camd. N.S. xlii), 213 (where 'Mr. Rudson' is evidently a mistake for 'Mr. Rudyard'); S.R.O., D. 1040/5/14, 21 June 1736; D. 1040/5/15, 17 Aug. 1765.
[65] Sleigh, *Leek*, 9, 65; S.R.O., D. 1040/5/8, p. 169; marriage settlement of John Daintry and Anne Furnivall, 30 Aug. 1777 (in possession of Mr. R. Stones of Malpas, Ches., 1994).
[66] Sleigh, *Leek*, 65 (giving John the elder); S.R.O., D. 3272/1/4/3/23 (giving John the younger).
[67] S.R.O., D. 538/B/2/2, sale cat. 1871; Sleigh, *Leek*, 65.
[68] S.R.O., D. 538/B/2/3, sale cat. 1892; D. 538/D/3/10, p. 53.
[69] *S.H.C.* N.S. ix. 304; *Kelly's Dir. Staffs.* (1940).
[70] Above, plate 27; M. Fisher, *Dieulacres Abbey* (preface dated 1989), 45–6. It has not been possible to gain admission in order to make a detailed survey.
[71] *S.H.C.* 1925, 168 (occupied by Edw. Stubbs).
[72] S.R.O., D. 3359/Badnall, abstract of title of Jos. Badnall to Highfield Ho.; *Staffs. Hist.* viii. 5. Mr. A. W. Bednall of Macclesfield is thanked for supplying inf. from Badnall family papers in his possession.
[73] *Staffs. Advertiser*, 7 July 1827, p. 1; Sleigh, *Leek*, 7, 218 n.; above, Leek and Lowe, econ. hist. (professions: banks).
[74] *Staffs. Advertiser*, 22 Oct. 1870, p. 4.
[75] Leek Libr., newspaper cuttings 1972–8, p. 2; 1979, p. 1.
[76] *Staffs. Advertiser*, 16 Feb. 1929, pp. 9–10; 17 Apr. 1937, p. 8.
[77] W.S.L. 501/34, cutting of 8 Feb. 1929; O.S. Map 6", Staffs. VIII. NW. (1900 edn.).
[78] Leek Libr., Warrington scrapbk. i, p. 101; S.R.O., D. 4241/12/3.
[79] *Charters of Earls of Chester*, p. 385.
[80] *S.H.C.* N.S. ix. 316–17; *Cal. Pat.* 1313–17, 332.

as Roche grange by 1406) and possibly another at Wetwood.[81] There was certainly a grange at Wetwood by 1291 as well as a third, New grange, south-east of Meerbrook village. In 1291 Roche grange and New grange comprised 2 carucates each, and Wetwood 1 carucate.[82] The abbey may also have managed as a grange the land which it had by 1501 at Foker: the post-Dissolution tenant, Thomas Vigars or Vygers, held a house called Foker Grange in 1542.[83]

The common waste lay chiefly on Gun and the Roaches and was inclosed in 1811 under an Act of 1805. Most of the Roaches, 758 a., was sold by the inclosure commissioners to Edward Nicholls of Swythamley Hall, in Heaton.[84]

Sheep farming was important in the later 13th century when Dieulacres abbey produced wool for export.[85] A place called Woolhouses, recorded in Leek manor in the 1330s, was probably in Leekfrith, and in 1567 there was a building called the Woolhouse at Abbey Green.[86] In the late 15th century the abbey apparently concentrated on stock rearing and used land in the north part of the township as pasture for cattle belonging to the abbey's grange at Swythamley.[87] By 1535 most of the abbey's land in Leekfrith was leased to tenants, each paying a variable money rent, two capons worth 6d., one day's ploughing worth 3d., and one day's reaping worth 3d.[88]

In the early 19th century two farms which covered the Roaches area, Back Forest (312 a.) and High Forest (225 a.), were part of the 1,125 a. which formed the Leekfrith portion of the Swythamley estate.[89] What was called the Dieulacres Abbey estate in 1870, covering 1,193 a., was then owned by George Davenport, formerly of Westwood Hall, in Leek and Lowe. Its largest farms were Abbey farm (229 a.), Park House (161 a.), and North Hillswood (148 a.).[90]

Of the 2,840.7 ha. of farmland returned for the civil parish in 1988, grassland covered 1,936.3 ha. and there were 760 ha. of rough grazing. The farming was dairy and sheep, with 3,271 head of cattle and 7,621 sheep and lambs. There were 29,814 hens, mostly broilers. Of the 70 farms returned, 58 were under 50 ha. in size, 9 were between 50 and 99 ha., and 3 were between 100 and 199 ha.[91]

WOODLAND. The 'frith' element of the township's name indicates wooded countryside,[92] and woodland was recorded c. 1230 on Gun and at Wetwood and in 1340 at Hellis wood (later Hills wood) north-east of Dieulacres abbey.[93] Hills wood survives as Abbey wood, so called by the late 19th century.[94] Forest wood along the township's northern boundary is probably the result of planting in the early 19th century after inclosure.[95] The woodland returned for the civil parish in 1988 covered 108.5 ha.[96]

FOREST AND WARREN. The earl of Chester's forest of Leek was recorded c. 1170.[97] It was again mentioned when Earl Ranulph included in his charter to the burgesses of Leek, some time between 1207 and 1215, the right to collect timber and firewood in the forest.[98] The extent of the forest is unknown but it included Leekfrith, and when the earl gave Dieulacres abbey land on Gun and at Wetwood c. 1230, he reserved the right to hunt there himself with sparrowhawks. His foresters, however, were not to enter the abbey's land, where hunting was supervised by foresters of the abbey.[99] About the same time Henry, the son of William the forester and perhaps a forester himself, bound himself to serve the abbey for life. The abbey's foresters were again recorded in 1271–2 and 1429,[1] and its former servants in 1538 included Robert Burgh, described as forester of the forest of Leek. It was stated in the 1540s that the abbey's freeholders in Rushton Spencer and Heaton had once acted as foresters.[2] By the late 15th century the forest was used as pasture for livestock,[3] and it is likely that the main duty of the foresters was to prevent illegal grazing.

In 1282 Dieulacres abbey was granted free warren in its demesne lands in Leek manor.[4] There was evidently a rabbit warren in Leekfrith by 1430, when the bridge taking the Leek–Macclesfield road over the Churnet was called Conyngre bridge.[5] Land at Hen Cloud was set aside for use as a rabbit warren in or shortly before 1819.[6]

MILLS. In the early 1220s Ranulph, earl of Chester, granted Dieulacres abbey a mill at Hulme. It probably stood on Back brook at Upper Hulme, where the abbey had a mill at the Dissolution.[7] The mill, which was working in 1599, may have still existed in 1670.[8]

In the late 1560s Thomas Gent of Upper Hulme built a mill on Back brook, upstream from Hulme mill. In 1599 there was a complaint from the owners of Hulme mill that Gent's mill took water from their mill and drew some of its trade,[9] and Gent's mill was evidently demolished. In 1600 his grandson William Gent let the

81   Lambeth Palace Libr., Papal Docs. 40, naming Roche grange as the grange 'de Rupe' ('of the rock') and recording a grange at what may be 'Wetwood', in Leekfrith, or 'Westwood', in Leek and Lowe; W.S.L., Sleigh, ii, f. 87v.
82   Tax. Eccl. (Rec. Com.), 252.
83   S.R.O. 4974/ADD 2; W.S.L., M. 540; W.S.L., Sleigh scrapbk. ii, f. 107v.
84   S.R.O., Q/RDc 65; 45 Geo. III, c. 96 (Local and Personal).   85   V.C.H. Staffs. vi. 9.
86   S.R.O., D. 1337/3; D. (W.) 1702/1/4, deed of 21 Sept. 1567.   87   Above, Heaton, econ. hist. (agric.).
88   V.C.H. Staffs. iii. 233; W.S.L., M. 540.
89   S.R.O. 4974/B/7/1; 4974/B/8/3; W.S.L., S.C. D/1/17.
90   S.R.O., D. 538/B/2/2.
91   P.R.O., MAF 68/6128/67.
92   Eng. P.N. Elements, i. 190.
93   Charters of Earls of Chester, p. 385; S.R.O., D. 1333/1,

m. 2; D. (W.) 1702/1/20, deed of 1 May 1613.
94   O.S. Map 6", Staffs. VIII. NW. (1888 edn.).
95   W.S.L., S.C. D/1/17.
96   P.R.O., MAF 68/6128/67.
97   Charters of Earls of Chester, p. 181.
98   Ibid. p. 348.   99   Ibid. p. 385.
1   S.H.C. iii (1), 19; S.R.O., D. 1333/2, ct. of 8 Oct. 1429.
2   Sleigh, Leek, 20, 69.
3   Above, Heaton, econ. hist. (agric.).
4   Cal. Chart. R. 1257–1300, 264.
5   S.R.O., D. 1333/2.
6   Staffs. Advertiser, 9 Oct. 1819, p. 2.
7   Charters of Earls of Chester, p. 380; W.S.L., M. 540.
8   S.R.O., D. 3359/Cruso, deed of 1 Apr. 1670; below (next para.).
9   D.R.O., D. 2375M/142/13; P.R.O., E 134/41 Eliz. I East./14.

site to two brothers, John and William Hind, and the mill had been rebuilt by 1602.[10] The tenant in 1610 was Robert Deane,[11] and the mill was known in the 18th century as Deans (later Danes or Dains) mill.[12] It stopped working c. 1946.[13]

There was a mill on Meer brook east of Meerbrook village in 1676.[14] A mill there built probably in the mid 1850s stopped working c. 1890.[15]

There was a mill at Turner's pool in 1595 and apparently in 1795.[16] Thomas Rudyard had a mill at Dieulacres in 1635; it was called Abbey mill in 1677 and probably stood on the Churnet.[17]

TRADE AND INDUSTRY. A smith named Jordan was living in Leek manor in the earlier 1330s, and a locksmith named Alexander was accused in the manor court in 1340 of cutting down the lord's timber.[18] Both men may have lived in Leekfrith and made use of the woodland there. An ironworks and a pool in Leek and Frith manors were granted to Stephen Bagot by Sir Ralph Bagnall in 1564.[19]

A bark house and bark pit recorded in the earlier 16th century at a place called Sury south of Abbey Green[20] probably indicate the existence of a tanyard.

Walk Mill pool recorded in the earlier 16th century as formerly belonging to Dieulacres abbey may have been associated with a walk (or fulling) mill in Leek manor mentioned in 1548.[21] The mill was possibly in Leekfrith. Certainly there was a fulling mill at Abbey Green in 1677, and it may have been the walk mill in Leek parish mentioned in 1752.[22]

A silk throwster named William Lowndes was living at Upper Hulme in 1824,[23] and by 1831 there was a four-storeyed silk mill with a house and four workers' cottages.[24] No silk workers were recorded at Upper Hulme in 1841, but by 1851 another silk throwster, George Parker, ran a mill there, employing 18 workers. By 1860 John Beardmore used the works for spinning flax and for dyeing.[25] In 1869 the mill was sold to William Tatton, the son of a Leek silk dyer, and he opened a dyeworks there. From 1924 the works also wound rayon filament yarn, and in 1928 warping machines were introduced. The company also had warping machines in rented premises in Shoobridge Street in Leek until 1931, when a new factory

was built at Upper Hulme to house all the machines. In 1970 production was moved from Upper Hulme to the firm's premises in Buxton Road, Leek.[26] The premises at Upper Hulme were converted to other industrial uses. Roaches (Engineering) Ltd., established in 1974, designs and manufactures matrices for textile laboratories, and small-scale machines for the same market are made by a sister company, Roaches (Fabrication) Ltd. Hillcrest Engineering Instrumentation Ltd., established in 1986, makes instruments for measuring temperatures in industrial processes.[27] There was also a furniture-making business, J. S. and R. Hine, in 1992. The surviving mill buildings include offices dated 1891.

The digging of coal was included in the licence granted in 1596 or 1597 by Sir Henry Bagnall, lord of Leek manor, to Thomas Jolliffe, a Leek mercer, to exploit the waste in Leek and Leekfrith, and coal pits recorded in Leek manor in the early 18th century were probably in Leekfrith.[28] Six colliers lived in the area around Shaw House on the east side of the Roaches in 1841, but only one in 1871.[29] A colliery there was disused by 1878.[30]

In 1704 the lords of the manor licensed William Gravenor and Ralph Hood, both of Leek, and Jeremiah Condlyffe and Emmanuel Wood, both of Leekfrith, to dig for lead and copper ore on the waste near the Roaches.[31] There was a stone quarry on the Roaches in 1811 and evidently another on Gun in 1839.[32]

LOCAL GOVERNMENT. By the earlier 14th century Leekfrith was a tithing of Leek manor and sent a frankpledge to the twice-yearly view. The tithing was then called Roche, a name still used in 1430. It was called Frith by 1548. Leekfrith was still part of the manor in 1820, when the court appointed a pinner for the township.[33]

The township was part of the Leekfrith quarter of Leek parish, and in the 1660s its poor were relieved by the quarter's overseer. The township had its own overseer from 1713,[34] and there was a poorhouse at Thorneyleigh in 1775.[35] The township became part of Leek poor-law union in 1837.[36]

CHURCH. There was a chapel at Meerbrook by 1537. It may have been supported by a

10 D.R.O., D. 2375M/57/1, 12 Oct. 44 Eliz. I; D. 2375M/281/13.
11 Ibid. D. 2375M/106/27, Staffs. leases, 1 Apr. 1610.
12 Ibid. D. 2375M/70/5, Heathylee, p. 7; above, fig. 2.
13 Inf. from Mr. H. Ball of Upper Hulme.
14 S.R.O., D. 583/2, abstract of title to estate of John Hughes.
15 S.R.O. 4974/B/7/32; Kelly's Dir. Staffs. (1888; 1892).
16 S.R.O., D. 5017/5/69; D. 5017/8/87.
17 S.R.O. 3508/A/1/4; above, Leek and Lowe, econ. hist. (mills).
18 S.R.O., D. 1337/1-2. 19 S.H.C. xiii. 236, 239.
20 W.S.L., M. 540; Leek Par. Reg. 3 n.
21 P.R.O., SC 2/202/65, m. [3]; SC 11/603.
22 S.R.O., D. 1040/5/14, burial of 21 Dec. 1752; D. (W.) 1702/1/2, deed of 30 June 1677.
23 Ibid. D. 1028/1/4, p. 33.
24 Macclesfield Courier & Herald, 13 Aug. 1831, p. 2 (ref.

supplied by Mr. A. W. Bednall of Macclesfield).
25 White, Dir. Staffs. (1851), 732; P.O. Dir. Staffs. (1860, s.v. Hulme, Upper); P.R.O., HO 107/2008.
26 M. A. Tatton, A Staffs. Centenary: William Tatton of Leek, 1869–1969.
27 Inf. from the respective firms.
28 Sleigh, Leek, 118 n.; S.R.O. 3508/A/2/2.
29 P.R.O., HO 107/1005; ibid. RG 10/2884.
30 O.S. Map 6", Staffs. IV. NE. (1887 edn.).
31 S.R.O., D. 3359/Condlyffe, articles of agreement, 1 Aug. 1704.
32 S.R.O., Q/RDc 65, plan IV; Staffs. Advertiser, 12 Oct. 1839, p. 1.
33 S.R.O., D. 1333/1-2; P.R.O., SC 2/202/65, m. 2; above, Leek and Lowe, local govt.
34 Above, Leek, par. intro. (par. govt.).
35 S.R.O., D. 1040/5/15, burial of 26 May 1775.
36 Ibid. D. 699/1/1/1, p. 4.

fraternity dedicated to St. Antony: in 1545 William Gent bequeathed 2s. to the stock of St. Antony at Meerbrook for the maintenance of God's service there.[37] Chapel House, probably a house for a priest serving the chapel, was mentioned in the earlier 16th century.[38] In 1547 Robert Burgh, probably the former forester of Dieulacres abbey's forest of Leek, left a rent of 13s. 4d. to God's service at Meerbrook. There seems to have been a doubt whether the chapel would survive: Robert's son Edmund was to have the rent if the service stopped.[39] The chapel still existed in 1553; chapel goods recorded that year included a silver chalice with a paten, and there was a bell.[40]

Sir Ralph Bagnall later rebuilt the chapel, and in 1565 he gave it to trustees, with a small endowment for a minister. His intention was not only to provide services for the inhabitants of Leekfrith but also to have prayers said for himself and his family on Sundays and feast days by the priest 'preaching the word of God' there.[41] The inhabitants of the chapelry were also expected to contribute a levy towards the upkeep of the chapel and the minister's stipend. After a disagreement between them and the trustees, it was decided in 1568 that the levy should be set by four men chosen jointly by both parties at Michaelmas.[42] The income was inadequate for a curate, and in 1597 the chapel was served only by a reader, John Bullocke. The bishop suspended services that year until a sufficient stipend had been raised to support a curate.[43] A reader c. 1603 was paid £4, together with food and drink; in 1604 he got 'what the people will given him'. The reader in 1604, William Smallwood, was described as tainted with 'vile sins' and denounced as a drunkard. Stated to conduct unlawful marriages 'to the great hurt of the country', he remained at the chapel despite complaints to the church authorities.[44] There was a curate in 1614 and presumably in 1623, when several inhabitants were presented for withholding his stipend.[45]

After new endowments of 1668 and 1675,[46] the chapel was licensed for baptisms in 1677 and burials in 1679; marriages were performed by 1698. Prior permission to conduct those services was necessary from the vicar of Leek, who retained all the fees.[47] From the mid 1790s the curate, James Turner, appears to have resented having to collect fees, and he determined only to request and not demand them. In 1797 he noted: 'I am advised not to concern or interest myself at all about Leek in future.' In 1799,

however, he paid the fee for the baptism of his own son Daniel. In 1800 he again expressed his decision not to collect anything for the vicar until they had come to a new agreement. The vicar still claimed fees for baptisms and burials in 1832.[48]

The curate was nominated by the trustees of the chapel lands in 1724, by the vicar of Leek in 1728 and again in 1735, and by the principal inhabitants of the township in 1790. Thereafter the right of the vicar of Leek to nominate appears to have gone unchallenged.[49] The chapelry, which was coterminous with the township, became a parish in 1859.[50] The benefice, at first a perpetual curacy, was styled a vicarage from 1868.[51] The church was served by a resident priest-in-charge from 1973 until 1979. There followed a vacancy until 1983, when the parish became part of a new parish of Leek and Meerbrook with services conducted by one of the Leek team ministry.[52]

Sir Ralph Bagnall's endowment of 1565 comprised a house for the minister, a garden and two crofts adjoining the chapel yard, two crofts at Gunside, another croft elsewhere in the township, and a rent charge of 2s. from a house in Leek.[53] He also gave 1 a. at Middle Hulme, which had been lost by 1693.[54] In 1647 the committee for plundered ministers granted the curacy £25 from the sequestered rectory of Stowe.[55] By will proved 1668 Joan Armett of Thorneyleigh Hall Farm left a rent charge of £2 13s. 4d. for the support of 'a sufficient and able minister' at Meerbrook; if there was no resident minister, the money was to be used to pay a preacher to give two sermons every quarter.[56] By will proved 1675 John Stoddard of Thorneyleigh Green Farm left a rent charge of £4 to be paid to a graduate minister for preaching in Meerbrook chapel on Sundays or monthly at the trustees' discretion.[57] By will proved 1680 Edmund Brough gave the minister of Meerbrook the reversion of a rent charge of £2 10s.[58]

The curate's income in 1718 was £13.[59] In 1723 Queen Anne's Bounty gave £200 to meet benefactions of £100 given by John Ward and £100 collected from the inhabitants of the chapelry. Of the money £320 was used by 1730 to buy 27 a. at Roche Grange, which in 1735 was let for £15 10s.[60] Shortly before 1747 the remaining £80 was used to buy 12 a. near Hazelwood House.[61] William Bostock (d. 1725) left the reversion of the tithes from two fields in Horton to the curate for preaching a sermon at Candlemas.[62] In 1792 Queen Anne's Bounty

37 L.J.R.O., B/C/11, John Fyssher (1538); Wm. Gentte (1545).   38 W.S.L., M. 540.
39 L.J.R.O., B/C/11, Rob. Burgh (1548); above, econ. hist. (forest and warren).
40 S.H.C. 1915, 147.   41 S.R.O., D. 4849/1/2.
42 Ibid. D. 1028/3/5.   43 L.J.R.O., B/V/1/23.
44 S.H.C. 1915, 147–8 (which mistranscribes the third quoted passage: E.H.R. xxvi. 342).
45 L.J.R.O., B/V/1/28 and 46.
46 Below, this section [endowments].
47 S.R.O., D. 5041, pp. 95–9; L.J.R.O., B/V/6/Leek, 1698.
48 S.R.O., D. 1028/1/2, esp. entries for 1 Mar. 1797 (and n. at foot of page), 4 May 1800; L.J.R.O., B/V/6/Leek, 1832.
49 L.J.R.O., B/V/3/Meerbrook; P.R.O., Inst. Bks., Ser. C, i (1), f. 89 (1735 nomination).

50 Lond. Gaz. 11 Mar. 1859, pp. 1086–7.
51 Lich. Dioc. Ch. Cal. (1869), where it is mistakenly styled a rectory.
52 Lich. Dioc. Dir. (1974, 1979); above, Leek and Lowe, churches.   53 S.R.O., D. 4849/1/2.
54 L.J.R.O., B/V/6/Meerbrook, 1693, 1722.
55 S.H.C. 1915, 148–9.
56 L.J.R.O., B/C/11, Joan Armett (1668).
57 Ibid. Reg. of Wills A, pp. 488–98.
58 Ibid. B/C/11, Edmund Brough (1680).
59 Ibid. B/A/11A, 2nd list.
60 Hodgson, Bounty of Queen Anne, pp. cxxxviii, ccxcvii; L.J.R.O., B/V/6/Meerbrook, 1730, 1732, 1735, 1824.
61 L.J.R.O., B/V/6/Meerbrook, 1747, 1751.
62 Ibid. 1755, 1805; S.R.O., D. 4069/1/2, burial of 11 Mar. 1724/5.

gave £200, which was used in 1800 to buy c. 10 a. near Turner's pool.[63] When the commons were inclosed in 1811 the commissioners assigned 7 a. to the curate.[64] Another grant of £800 was made by Queen Anne's Bounty in 1822. Half was used in 1835 with a further grant of £200 made in 1830 and benefactions of £100 each from the curate, James Turner, and a Mrs. Pyncombe to buy an additional 28 a. at Roche Grange.[65] In 1845 James Turner gave a further 5 a. near Roche Grange as an endowment, requiring future curates to preach on Sunday evenings in summer.[66] The living was worth £97 a year c. 1830.[67] In 1887 there were 71 a. of glebe, with an estimated rental of £92.[68] The land at Roche Grange was sold in 1920.[69]

The other half of the £800 granted by Queen Anne's Bounty in 1822 was used in 1827 to rebuild the curate's house.[70] It was destroyed by fire in 1927 and again rebuilt.[71] The house was sold soon after 1979.[72]

In the later 1720s the vicar of Leek, Thomas Loxdale, wrote to the bishop stating that the inhabitants of Leekfrith were negligent in bringing their children to be baptized and that he seldom heard about the sickness of 'any poor people on the Moors' until they were dead. A curate appointed in 1724 had soon left, and Loxdale asked the bishop to ordain Henry Royle, the schoolmaster at Meerbrook.[73] The request was not granted, and in 1728 a new curate, Richard Legh, was appointed. He died in 1733.[74] Daniel Turner was appointed curate in 1735, later also becoming curate of Quarnford, in Alstonefield, and of Rushton. He lived at Meerbrook, where he died in 1789, and was succeeded by his son James. On his retirement in 1826 James was succeeded by his son, also James (d. 1863).[75] In 1830 there was one Sunday service at Meerbrook and Communion was celebrated four times a year.[76] In 1851 the average Sunday attendance was 50 when the service was in the morning and 120 when in the afternoon or evening, besides Sunday school children.[77] Psalm singers were mentioned in 1754.[78] They may have survived until 1864 when new liturgical practices were introduced by James Turner's successor, John Clarke.[79] By Easter Sunday that year the church band had been replaced by a

harmonium, and a harvest festival was held for the first time later in the year.[80]

There was a chapelwarden in 1553, and from 1698 he usually signed the terriers with the curate. It was the custom by 1809 for the curate to nominate the warden.[81] There was a clerk for the chapel by 1730. His salary was £1 in 1754 and £2 in 1830.[82]

Roger Morrice (d. 1702) left half the interest on £100 for the purchase of bibles for the poor of Leekfrith. A distribution of 10 or 12 bibles was still made in the earlier 1820s.[83]

The present church of ST. MATTHEW dates from the 1870s. Its smaller predecessor, of coursed rubble with ashlar dressings, consisted of a chancel, nave, and west tower. An external stairway on the south side of the tower was probably built to provide access to a room apparently used as the school until 1778.[84] There was a west gallery by 1830, lit by a dormer window on the south side of the nave.[85] In the 1870s the church was rebuilt in ashlar to a design by R. Norman Shaw. The first stage, in 1870, was the addition to the existing church of a chancel, north vestry, and central tower. The cost was met by Elizabeth Condlyffe (d. 1878). In 1873 the nave was rebuilt and was given a south-west porch; the west tower was demolished. The church has a stone pulpit and font carved by Edward Ash of Meerbrook, the nephew and pupil of the sculptor Richard Hassall of Leekfrith, and there are pieces of Leek embroidery designed by Shaw. An organ, also paid for by Elizabeth Condlyffe, was installed in 1879.[86] The single bell is dated 1818.[87]

The registers date from 1738.[88]

The graveyard was enlarged in 1901 and 1968.[89]

NONCONFORMITY. John Tompson was described as not 'conformable to the religion now established' in 1623, when he taught a school at Meerbrook.[90]

William Davenport of Fould Farm was converted by the Quaker Richard Hickock in 1654 and established a meeting at his home. It had 30 members in 1669, many of whom presumably lived in Leek.[91]

John Wood, a nonconformist who had been

63 Hodgson, *Bounty of Queen Anne*, p. ccxcvii; L.J.R.O., B/V/6/Meerbrook, 1805, 1809.
64 L.J.R.O., B/V/6/Meerbrook, 1828.
65 Ibid. 1832, 1836; S.R.O., D. 4849/1/8; Hodgson, *Bounty of Queen Anne*, pp. ccxi, ccxcvii.
66 L.J.R.O., B/V/6/Meerbrook, 1845.
67 *Rep. Com. Eccl. Revenues*, 488–9.
68 *Return of Glebe Lands*, 65.   69 S.R.O., D. 4849/1/7.
70 L.J.R.O., B/V/6/Meerbrook, 1832.
71 W.S.L. 503/34, cutting of 7 Mar. 1927.
72 Inf. from Lich. Dioc. Regy.
73 L.J.R.O., B/A/3/Meerbrook, 1724, 1728.
74 Ibid. B/A/4/29, 10 Sept. 1728; S.R.O., D. 1040/5/14, burial of 16 Oct. 1733.
75 P.R.O., Inst. Bks., Ser. C, i (1), f. 89; L.J.R.O., B/V/5/Meerbrook, 1751, 1772–3; S.R.O., D. 1028/1/2, burial of 14 Oct. 1789; Lich. Dioc. Regy., Bp.'s Reg. 29, p. 104; *Staffs. Advertiser*, 7 Nov. 1863, p. 4.
76 *S.H.C.* 4th ser. x. 94.
77 P.R.O., HO 129/372/3/1.
78 S.R.O., D. 1029/1/1, reverse pages at back of vol., chapelwarden's acct. 1754.
79 Lich. Dioc. Regy., Bp.'s Reg. 32, p. 268.

80 *Staffs. Advertiser*, 8 Oct. 1864, p. 4; *Lich. Dioc. Ch. Cal.* (1865), record of dioc. p. ii.
81 *S.H.C.* 1915, 147; L.J.R.O., B/V/6/Meerbrook.
82 L.J.R.O., B/V/6/Meerbrook, 1730; S.R.O., D. 1028/1/1, f. 64; *S.H.C.* 4th ser. x. 94.
83 P.R.O., PROB 11/463, ff. 64–5; *13th Rep. Com. Char.* 394. For Morrice see below, nonconf.
84 Above, plate 16; below, educ.
85 *S.H.C.* 4th ser. x. 93.
86 L.J.R.O., B/C/5/Meerbrook; W.S.L., Sleigh scrapbk. ii, ff. 9–10; *Lich. Dioc. Ch. Cal.* (1871), 75; (1875), 76; (1880), 80; A. G. Jacques, *Leek Embroidery* (Staffs. Libraries, Arts & Archives, 1990), 48–9; memorial plaque of Eliz. Condlyffe in chancel.
87 C. Lynam, *Ch. Bells of County of Stafford* (1889), 53.
88 All but the most recent are in S.R.O., D. 1028.
89 Lich. Dioc. Regy., Bp.'s Reg. U, pp. 446–7, 449; Y, pp. 40, 83.
90 L.J.R.O., B/V/1/45.
91 A. G. Matthews, *Congregational Churches of Staffs.* (preface dated 1924), 90; above, Leek and Lowe, prot. nonconf. (Soc. of Friends).

FIG. 36. ST. MATTHEW'S CHURCH FROM THE SOUTH-EAST, AS COMPLETED IN 1873

ejected from his fellowship at St. John's College, Cambridge, in 1662 and had preached in the Staffordshire Moorlands, was in 1690 recommended as a minister for a congregation to be based at Meerbrook, but he died later the same year. The recommendation came from Roger Morrice (d. 1702), vicar of Duffield (Derb.) until his ejection in 1662 and later a London merchant. He presumably had connexions with Leekfrith, where he was living when he made his will in 1701.[92] The house of John Cartwright of Upper Hulme was licensed for worship by protestant dissenters in 1693.[93]

A Methodist service was held fortnightly on Sundays at Roche Grange in 1798.[94] In 1805 the curate of Meerbrook claimed that there were 'scarcely any Methodists' in his chapelry and in 1809 that there was only one, a widow.[95]

Wesleyan Methodists, however, continued to meet at Roche Grange, and an afternoon congregation of 20 was recorded there on Census Sunday 1851. Sunday services were last held at the farmhouse in 1921.[96] Fortnightly Sunday services held in 1829 at Thorneyleigh and at Meerbrook had ceased by 1832.[97] A Wesleyan chapel at Meerbrook was opened in 1862 and remained in use in 1992.[98] Another at Upper Hulme is in the Heathylee part of the hamlet.[99]

EDUCATION. John Tompson, a licensed schoolmaster in Leek parish in 1616, probably then taught at Meerbrook. He certainly taught there in 1623, even though his licence had been withdrawn.[1] John Comylach of Meerbrook subscribed as a schoolmaster in 1621.[2] Ralph Poulson,

92 Matthews, *Cong. Churches of Staffs.* 95–8; *Calamy Revised*, ed. A. G. Matthews, 355, 541; *Freedom after Ejection*, ed. A. Gordon, 98.   93 L.J.R.O., B/V/1/89A.
94 Dyson, *Wesleyan Methodism*, 40.
95 L.J.R.O., B/V/6/Meerbrook, 1805, 1809.
96 P.R.O., HO 129/372/3/1; S.R.O., D. 3457/1/5.
97 Leek Libr., Johnson scrapbk. i (2), D/13/15; S.R.O., D. 3156/1/1/24.
98 G.R.O. Worship Reg. no. 15414.
99 Above, Alstonefield: Heathylee, nonconf.
1 L.J.R.O., B/V/1/33 and 45.
2 Ibid. B/A/4/18/1, 7 Nov. 1621.

licensed in 1662 to teach at Foker, was probably the man of the same name who was a schoolmaster of Mill Street, Leek, at his death in 1691.[3]

By will proved 1675 John Stoddard of Thorneyleigh Green Farm gave a rent charge of £10 for a master to teach 20 poor children.[4] Roger Morrice (d. 1702) left half the interest on £100 for the master at Meerbrook to teach eight poor children, provided that the master was able to teach Latin.[5] Henry Royle became the master in 1722 and continued to teach at Meerbrook until his death in 1769.[6] In 1818 the master teaching the 28 free children also taught 12 fee-paying children.[7] The school was apparently held in a room in the church tower until 1778, when a schoolroom was built in Meerbrook village. A house for the master was added in 1839, and in 1871 the schoolroom was enlarged. There were 30 children on the books in 1874.[8]

The decision in 1930 that Meerbrook Church of England school, then an all-age school with 63 children on its books, should become a junior school took effect in 1940, the senior children being transferred to Leek.[9] The school took controlled status in 1957 as St. Matthew's Church of England (Controlled) primary school.[10] It was closed in 1969, and the children were moved to a new school at Blackshaw Moor, in Tittesworth.[11] The former school building at Meerbrook was converted into a youth hostel in 1977.[12]

Two dame schools at Meerbrook, with a combined attendance of 16 in 1818, evidently still existed in the earlier 1830s.[13] A Church of England Sunday school established in 1825 had 50 children in the earlier 1830s but an average of only 30 in 1851.[14]

CHARITIES FOR THE POOR. By will proved 1668 Joan Armett left a rent charge of £1 to be distributed on Christmas Eve at Meerbrook chapel to the poor of the chapelry, especially those living 'along the side of Gun'. In the earlier 1820s nine people received 2s. each, a tenth 1s., and 1s. was paid to the landlord of the public house where the money was distributed.[15]

By will proved 1675 John Stoddard left a rent charge of £2 for the poor living at Gunside. In the earlier 1820s it was paid to between three and six people.[16]

By will proved 1680 Edmund Brough left a rent charge of £1 to be distributed at Candlemas to the poor living at 'Roachside' and in the Hazelwood area in the north of the township. In the earlier 1820s four people shared the 17s. which was received after land tax had been deducted.[17]

By will of 1760 Thomas Wood left the interest on £30 to be distributed in bread to the poor of Leekfrith every Sunday at Meerbrook chapel. The interest in the later 1780s was £1 10s. In the earlier 1820s the bread was given out on Sundays between November and March.[18]

Sarah Nicholls (d. 1785) left the interest on £200 for the poor of Leekfrith and Heaton. The charity was later amalgamated with one established by Sir Philip Brocklehurst for Leekfrith and Heaton.[19]

By will proved 1832 James Mobberley left the reversion of rents from three cottages at Meerbrook and from 1 a. on Gun to provide bread for the poor of the chapelry; it was to be distributed at the chapel every Sunday between 1 October and 1 May. The charity had taken effect by 1860. The cottages came to be treated as poorhouses, let at low rents, but were sold in 1925 to increase the charity's income.[20]

Elizabeth Turner (d. 1865), daughter of James Turner, curate of Meerbook 1789–1826, left half the interest on £100 for the poor of Leekfrith.[21]

By a Scheme of 1979 all the above charities, except for the Nicholls and Brocklehurst charity, were united as Leekfrith Relief in Need charity.[22]

LONGSDON

LONGSDON was formerly a township in Leek parish 2,708 a. (1,096 ha.) in area and later part of a civil parish which included Endon and Stanley until 1894. That year Longsdon became a separate civil parish.[23] The area is mostly pasture, but there is suburban housing in the east along the road to Leek. The boundary followed in part the river Churnet and Endon and Horton brooks on the east, south, and west respectively. A boundary change in 1934 transferred 580 a. in the east to Leek urban district and so reduced Longsdon civil parish to its present 2,128 a. (861 ha.).[24] This article deals with the former township.

The land lies at c. 450 ft. (137 m.) beside Endon brook and c. 490 ft. (149 m.) beside the Churnet and Horton brook. It rises towards the north, reaching 779 ft. (237 m.) at Little Longsdon on top of the long hill (dun) from which Longsdon takes its name. At its south end the hill forms a ridge called Ladderedge by the earlier 16th century.[25] The underlying rock is

3 Ibid. B/A/4/5, 26 Sept. 1662; S.R.O., D. 1040/5/14, burial of 19 Mar. 1690/1; S.R.O., D. (W.) 1702/1/5, deed of 15 May 1697.   4 L.J.R.O., Reg. of Wills A, pp. 488–98.
5 P.R.O., PROB 11/463, ff. 64v.–65; 13th Rep. Com. Char. 394.
6 L.J.R.O., B/A/4/29; S.R.O., D. 1040/5/15, burial of 23 Feb. 1769.   7 Educ. of Poor Digest, 862.
8 Reliquary, iii. 59; P.R.O., ED 7/109/207.
9 Staffs. C.C. Record for 1930, 861, 867; S.R.O., D. 4849/6/1, p. 12.   10 S.R.O., D. 4849/6/1, pp. 59–60.
11 S.R.O., CEH/100/1.
12 Leek Libr., newspaper cuttings 1972–8, p. 103; above plate 62.
13 Educ. of Poor Digest, 862; Educ. Enq. Abstract, 879.
14 Educ. Enq. Abstract, 879; S.H.C. 4th ser. x. 94; P.R.O.,

HO 129/372/3/1.   15 13th Rep. Com. Char. 384, 392–3.
16 Ibid. 393; L.J.R.O., Reg. of Wills A, pp. 488–98.
17 13th Rep. Com. Char. 393–4; L.J.R.O., B/C/11, Edmund Brough (1680).
18 13th Rep. Com Char. 394; Char. Dons. 1150–1.
19 Above, Heaton, charities.
20 S.R.O., D. 4849/5/1; P.O. Dir. Staffs. (1860).
21 Staffs. Advertiser, 11 Mar. 1865, p. 5; S.R.O., D. 4302/8/1, p. 13.
22 Char. Com. file 216091, where no details of distribution are given.
23 Census, 1901. This article was written in 1991.
24 Census, 1931; Staffs. Review Order, 1934, p. 60 and map 1 (copy in S.R.O.).
25 P.R.O., SC 2/202/63, m. 1.

sandstone of the Millstone Grit series. It is overlain by Boulder Clay, and there is alluvium along Endon brook. The soil is fine loam, except for an area of coarse loam in the south-east corner of the township at Wall Grange.[26]

Twenty-eight people in Longsdon were assessed for hearth tax in 1666.[27] The population was 350 in 1821, rising to 428 by 1851.[28] From 530 in 1901 it rose to 650 in 1911, 715 in 1921, and 903 in 1931. The population of the reduced civil parish was 691 in 1951, 639 in 1961, 588 in 1971, 581 in 1981, and 565 in 1991.[29]

Two farmhouses, Great Longsdon and Little Longsdon, on top of Longsdon hill are probably successors of a settlement called Over Longsdon in 1278.[30] Harracles Hall, an 18th-century house at the north end of the hill, stands on a site occupied probably by the later 13th century. The name incorporates words meaning hoar (*har*) and land added to an estate (*ecels*).[31] Rowley Gate Farm south of Harracles probably stands on or near land called 'Throwleyate' in 1515. The present house is mainly of the later 17th century and has a porch with a doorhead bearing the name Anne Hulme and the date 1686, now illegible.[32] Lyme House, under the brow of the hill west of Rowley Gate Farm, was possibly an inhabited site by 1414 when John of Lyme had a house in Longsdon. There was certainly a house there by 1515.[33] Bradshaw Farm to the south stands on a site occupied probably by the later 14th century.[34] Longsdon pool on the hill east of Bradshaw Farm may have been created in the later 16th century when a stream was diverted from 'Lyme well' to power Harracles mill on the Horton side of the boundary.[35] The pool certainly existed by 1775.[36]

A settlement called Nether Longsdon in 1278 and Dunwood in the early 17th century lay on the west side of Longsdon hill, south of Bradshaw Farm.[37] The oldest surviving house there is Dunwood House Farm, which has a brick front with the date 1678 and the initials BE, presumably those of Benjamin Endon (d. 1699).[38] Dunwood Farm is of the 18th century, and Dunwood House of the mid 19th century. On a promontory to the south-east stands Stonelowe Hall, a mainly 17th-century house on a site occupied probably by the early 13th century.[39]

The road south from Dunwood hamlet forks at Taylor's Green, mentioned in 1482.[40] The western branch runs to the Leek road past Upper Dales, formerly a cottage but rebuilt in

the mid 1980s as a house in 17th-century style.[41] The name is presumably taken from the Dale family, which had a house in the area in the early 18th century.[42] Another Dunwood House, to the south-west, was called New House in 1736.[43] It was rebuilt in the mid 19th century, possibly for Thomas Crompton, who lived there in 1861.[44] Trees Farm at the junction with the Leek road is of the early 19th century. The eastern road from Taylor's Green meets the Leek road at Bryan's Hay, where there was a cottage in 1611.[45] A farmhouse there is partly of the 17th century. From Bryan's Hay the Leek road formerly ran south-east to Bank End, where there is another 17th-century farmhouse. Dunwood Lodge Farm on the north side of the Leek road west of Bryan's Hay is of the 18th century. It was bought in 1870 by Thomas Hulme of Bank House in Endon, who built Dunwood Hall next to the farmhouse in 1871. Designed by Robert Scrivener of Hanley, Dunwood Hall retains its original features, including a central hall paved with Minton tiles.[46]

There was an estate by the early 13th century at Wall on the township's eastern boundary. It was then owned by Trentham priory, which established a grange there.[47] Wall probably takes its name from the Old English word for a well or spring.[48] A spring, called Coena's well in the 1870s,[49] still feeds a pool between the river and the Caldon canal, south-west of Wall Grange Farm. A meadow there was called Signe Walles in 1627. The name 'signe' may be a corruption of St. Agnes or St. Ann: in 1849 the well was called St. Ann's, Senus, or Sinners Well.[50]

In the south part of the township Endon brook is crossed at Denford, recorded in 1341 as Derneford.[51] The word means a hidden or secret ford, presumably in contrast to a more open or accessible ford nearby.[52] There was a bridge at Denford by 1529.[53] Keghton ford, mentioned in 1438, may have been to the east where Horse bridge existed by 1603.[54] The Ladderedge area to the north was settled after the common waste there was inclosed in 1815. The New inn at the junction of the Leek road and Denford Road had been opened by 1817,[55] and the Wheel inn to the north-east at the junction with Sutherland Road was opened c. 1850 as the Waterworks inn.[56] There are late 19th-century houses at the north end of Sutherland Road, which had by then become the main centre of Longsdon. By 1888 there was a post office, probably near the later

[26] Geol. Surv. Map 1", drift, sheet 110 (1968 edn.); sheet 123 (1924 edn.); Soil Surv. of Eng. and Wales, sheet 3 (1983).
[27] *S.H.C.* 1925, 160, 162.
[28] *V.C.H. Staffs.* i. 327, which gives figures only for 1821–51.   [29] *Census*, 1901–91.
[30] Below, manors (Longsdon).
[31] Ibid. (Harracles); *Eng. P.N. Elements*, i. 145, 234.
[32] S.R.O., D. (W.) 1490/10B, m. 9d.; *S.H.C.* 1925, 160; inf. from the owner.
[33] S.R.O., D. (W.) 1490/6, m. 2d.; D. (W.) 1490/10B, m. 10.   [34] Below, manors (Bradshaw Farm).
[35] Above, Horton, econ. hist. (mills).
[36] Above, fig. 2.
[37] *S.H.C.* N.S. x (1), 29; N.S. xi. 245.
[38] S.R.O., D. 1040/5/14, burial of 28 Apr. 1699.
[39] Below, manors (Stonelowe Hall).
[40] S.R.O., D. (W.) 1490/6, m. 58.
[41] Inf. from the owner.
[42] S.R.O. 3306, abstract of title to land at Dunwood,

1819.
[43] Ibid. D. 1535/1, f. 98; D. (W.) 1909/E/9/1; D. 4302/1/1, p. 7.   [44] P.R.O., RG 9/1945.
[45] S.R.O., D. (W.) 1490/17, ct. of 21 Mar. 1610/11.
[46] *People of the Potteries*, ed. D. Stuart, i. 127–8; inf. from the owner, Dr. R. Vincent-Kemp.
[47] Below, manors (Wall Grange).
[48] *Eng. P.N. Elements*, ii. 250.
[49] O.S. Map 6", Staffs. VIII. SW. (1889 edn.).
[50] S.R.O., D. 593/H/14/3/24; D. 593/T/1/2/9, plan of proposed pipes and reservoir.
[51] P.R.O., E 40/11269 (wrongly given as 'Berneforde' in *Cat. Anct. D.* v, A 11269).
[52] As at Darnford near Lichfield: *V.C.H. Staffs.* xiv. 275–6.   [53] S.R.O., D. (W.) 1490/10B, m. 25.
[54] Ibid. D. (W.) 1490/6, m. 23; *S.H.C.* 1940, 45.
[55] S.R.O., D. 4302/1/2, p. 9.
[56] P.R.O., HO 107/2008; O.S. Map 1/2,500, Staffs. VIII. 13 (1899 edn.).

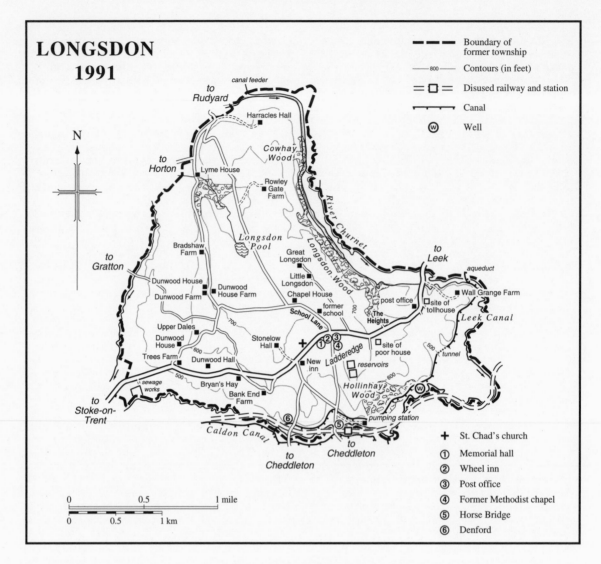

LONGSDON
1991

Boundary of
former township

Contours (in feet)

Disused railway and station

Canal

Well

to
Rudyard

canal feeder

N

Harracles Hall

to
Horton

Cowhay
Wood

Lyme House

Rowley
Gate
Farm

River Churnet

to
Leek

aqueduct

Bradshaw
Farm

Longsdon
Pool

Longsdon Wood

Great
Longsdon

Little
Longsdon

Wall Grange Farm

to
Gratton

Dunwood House

Dunwood
House Farm

Chapel House

post office

site of
tollhouse

Leek Canal

Dunwood Farm

former
school

The
Heights

School Lane

Upper Dales
Dunwood
House

Stonelow
Hall

site of
poor house

tunnel

Trees Farm

Dunwood Hall

New
inn

Laddersedge

reservoirs

sewage
works

Bryan's Hay

Hollinhay
Wood

Bank End
Farm

pumping station

to
Stoke-on-
Trent

Caldon Canal

to
Cheddleton

to
Cheddleton

+ St. Chad's church

① Memorial hall

② Wheel inn

③ Post office

④ Former Methodist chapel

⑤ Horse Bridge

⑥ Denford

0   0.5   1 mile

0   0.5   1 km

Fig. 37

St. Chad's church, its site in 1898. It was moved to its present site opposite the Wheel inn at the north end of Sutherland Road, probably when St. Chad's was built in 1905.[57] Houses and bungalows at the south end of Sutherland Road were built in the 1920s and 1930s.[58]

East of Longsdon village houses were built along the main road and in side roads from the 1920s,[59] and a post office for the area was opened in the 1930s.[60] An estate of 24 detached houses called the Heights was built in the late 1980s on the site of a brickworks.

The road between Newcastle-under-Lyme and Leek crossed the Churnet by a bridge at Wall, apparently first built in or soon after 1244. The road was turnpiked in 1765.[61] A tollgate was erected that year near the Longsdon end of the bridge; it had been removed by 1816 when a tollhouse there was sold.[62] The road was disturn-

piked in 1879.[63] Two cast-iron mileposts of 1879 survive on the road, one near Dunwood Hall and the other 2 miles to the east. The present line of the road east of Bryan's Hay, bypassing the former route via Bank End, was constructed in the 1930s.[64]

A branch canal to Leek was opened from the Caldon canal west of Denford in 1801. It also linked the canal with a feeder from Rudyard Lake, in Horton. The Longsdon stretch of the branch was abandoned in 1961, with the main canal, but was reopened for leisure boats in 1974.[65] It was closed in 1980 for repairs to a tunnel south of Wall Grange Farm and reopened in 1985.[66]

A railway opened in 1867 from Stoke-upon-Trent to the Churnet Valley line at Leekbrook south of Leek ran through the south side of Longsdon. A station called Wall Grange (later

57 Kelly's Dir. Staffs. (1888); O.S. Map 6", Staffs. VIII. SW. (1900 edn.).   58 S.R.O., D. 3188/2.
59 Ibid.
60 O.S. Map 6", Staffs. VIII. SW. (1945 edn.).
61 Above, Leek and Lowe, communications.
62 S.R.O., D. 593/B/1/24/7; D. 3359/Buxton Rd. order

bk. 1765–1800, pp. 4, 27–8, 31; above, fig. 2.
63 Above, Leek and Lowe, communications.
64 O.S. Map 6", Staffs. VII. SE. (1945 edn.).
65 P. Lead, Caldon Canal and Tramroads (Headington, 1990), 40–1, 44, 50, 53.
66 Leek Libr., newspaper cuttings 1985 (1), pp. 4, 6.

Wall Grange and Longsdon), just over the boundary in Cheddleton, was opened in or shortly before 1876 and closed in 1956. The railway continued in use as a mineral line until 1989.[67]

The Staffordshire Potteries Water Works Co. built a pumping station in 1849 at the south end of Ladderedge. The station pumped water from springs to a reservoir on the east side of Sutherland Road.[68] A second reservoir was built to the north as a replacement in 1963. The pumping station was closed in the 1980s, after new boreholes had been dug to supply water direct to the reservoir.[69]

Longsdon had a mains water supply from the later 1950s.[70] A sewage works in the west end of the parish initially served Endon.[71] Sewers for the Ladderedge area of Longsdon were laid in 1937.[72] A mains electricity supply was introduced from Leek in 1930.[73]

A lodge of the United Ancient Order of Druids met at the New inn from 1846. It still met there in 1876, when it had 103 members.[74] Longsdon Memorial Hall, on the Leek road west of the Wheel inn, is dated 1920. A Women's Institute was formed in 1926.[75] Longsdon Amateur Dramatic Society was established in 1945.[76]

MANORS AND OTHER ESTATES. In the early 13th century *LONGSDON* was held with Rushton and Ipstones of the earl of Chester by Nicholas de Verdun.[77] The overlordship passed to the Crown with the earldom of Chester in 1237.[78]

In 1242–3 Nicholas's daughter and heir Rose (d. 1248), widow of Theobald Butler, held Longsdon with Rushton and half of Ipstones by service of providing a knight for the garrison of Chester castle for 40 days.[79] Rose's son and heir John de Verdun held Longsdon in 1274, and as Over Longsdon it was recorded as part of the lordship of the Verduns and their successors until 1409.[80]

James de Audley held Longsdon in 1252.[81] The estate was by then in two parts,[82] called Over Longsdon and Nether Longsdon in 1278 and described as manors in 1316.[83] Over Longsdon at least descended with the Audleys' manor of Horton until 1400,[84] but the descent thereafter

is not known. Over Longsdon probably centred on Great Longsdon and Little Longsdon farmhouses, and Nether Longsdon on Dunwood hamlet.

A house at Great Longsdon was owned by John Bateman in 1666, when it was assessed for tax on six hearths.[85] Bateman, who was still alive in 1680, was succeeded at Longsdon by his daughter Mary, wife of the Revd. Richard Jackson: their son, another Revd. Richard Jackson (d. 1782), devised the estate to Trinity College, Cambridge, to endow what came to be called the Jacksonian Professorship in Natural Philosophy.[86] The college sold the farm in 1919 to the tenant, John Knight.[87] In 1946 it was bought by William Heath (d. 1978), whose son Charles and his wife Elizabeth were the owners in 1991.[88] The farmhouse is mainly of the 19th century.

Little Longsdon was owned in 1816 by William Sneyd.[89] It was bought in 1851 by John Davenport of Westwood Hall, in Leek and Lowe, whose son George sold it in 1868 as part of the Westwood estate to John Robinson.[90] In the mid 1950s the Critchlow family bought the farm, and Mr. Harold Critchlow owned it in 1991.[91] The farmhouse is partly of the 17th century.

By the early 13th century Trentham priory owned an estate at Wall which was later known as *WALL GRANGE*. It had presumably been granted to the priory by one of the earls of Chester, who were patrons of the priory:[92] in the early 13th century Ranulph, earl of Chester, freed the priory from the service of a foot soldier (or possibly a messenger) which it owed him for its land at Wall.[93] The estate was enlarged in 1275 when Henry de Audley gave it Threapwood and land called Ametshaw[94] and in 1312 when William of Cocknage gave the priory a half virgate at Wall.[95] In 1293 the prior claimed to hold a manor court at Wall, and in 1339 Wall was described as a manor.[96] A grange was established, the name Wall Grange being in use by 1510 and possibly by 1439.[97]

Trentham priory was dissolved in 1537, and in 1538 Wall Grange was included in the grant of the priory's estates to Charles, duke of Suffolk. He sold them soon afterwards to Sir Thomas Pope, who in 1540 sold them to James Leveson of Wolverhampton.[98] Wall Grange then descended in the Leveson, later Leveson-Gower,

67 *T.N.S.F.C.* xi. 5; C. R. Clinker, *Clinker's Reg. of Closed Passenger Stations and Goods Depots, 1830–1977* (1978), 140; above, Leek and Lowe, communications.
68 *Pure & Wholesome Water for One Hundred Years, 1849–1949*; S.R.O., D. 593/T/1/2/9, plan of proposed pipes and reservoir; above, plate 46.
69 Inf. from Mr. A. D. Moore of Severn Trent Water (Stoke District).
70 Leek R.D.C. *Ann. Rep. of M.O.H. 1957* (copy in S.R.O., C/H/1/2/2/22).   71 Above, Endon, intro.
72 Leek U.D.C. *Ann. Rep. of M.O.H. and Sanitary Inspector, 1937* (copy in S.R.O., C/H/1/2/2/23).
73 Leek Libr., newspaper cuttings, bk. 5, p. 52.
74 *Rep. Chief Registrar of Friendly Socs. 1876, App. P,* H.C. 429-I, p. 403 (1877), lxxvii.
75 Inf. from Staffs. Federation of Women's Institutes.
76 Inf. from the secretary, Mrs. S. Edwards.
77 *Staffs. Studies,* v. 2.   78 *V.C.H. Ches.* ii. 6.
79 *Bk. of Fees,* ii. 970; *Complete Peerage,* xii (2), 246–7.
80 *S.H.C.* 1911, 160; *Complete Peerage,* xii (2), 246–7; *Cal. Inq. p.m.* xviii, pp. 155–6 (where John de Verdun is wrongly named as John de Horton); xix, pp. 213, 215.

81 *Cal. Chart. R.* 1226–57, 409.
82 *Bk. of Fees,* ii. 970.
83 *S.H.C.* N.S. xi. 245; *S.H.C.* 1911, 110–11.
84 *Cal. Inq. p.m.* xviii, pp. 155–6.
85 *S.H.C.* 1925, 160; *Leek Par. Reg.* i. 153.
86 *S.H.C.* 1919, 269; A. L. Reade, *Reades of Blackwood Hill* (priv. print. 1906), 55 n.; P.R.O., PROB 11/1101, ff. 285v.–291.
87 *Kelly's Dir. Staffs.* (1916); inf. from the librarian, Trinity Coll.   88 Inf. from Mrs. Heath.
89 S.R.O., D. (W.) 1535/1, f. 97; D. (W.) 1909/E/9/1.
90 Ibid. D. 3272/1/4/3/23; Sleigh, *Leek,* 46–7.
91 Inf. from Mr. Critchlow.
92 *V.C.H. Staffs.* iii. 255–6.
93 *Charters of Earls of Chester,* pp. 314–15, where Wall is wrongly identified as Wales. The original charter is S.R.O., D. 593/B/1/24/1/1.   94 *S.H.C.* xi. 334.
95 *S.H.C.* 1911, 310–11; *Cal. Pat.* 1307–13, 494.
96 S.R.O., D. 593/B/1/24/1/4; below, local govt.
97 *S.H.C.* N.S. iii. 150; *L. & P. Hen. VIII,* i (1), p. 228.
98 *V.C.H. Staffs.* iii. 259; *L. & P. Hen. VIII,* xiii (2), pp. 492, 495; xv, p. 284.

family[99] until 1911 when it was sold to the tenant, Robert Bennison.[1] The owner in 1991 was Mr. S. G. Clowes.

By the late 15th century the estate was evidently leased to members of the local gentry, some of whom lived there. Hugh Egerton, apparently the lessee in 1484, was presumably the Hugh Egerton (d. 1505) who built his principal house at Wrinehill, in Madeley.[2] William Egerton seems to have been the lessee in 1509–10.[3] The tenant in 1537 was Lawrence Savage, younger son of Sir John Savage, lord of Rushton Spencer, and husband of Mary Egerton of Wall Grange, perhaps William's daughter.[4] Lawrence was living at Wall Grange in 1556, when Sir Richard Leveson granted Sir Ralph Egerton of Wrinehill and William Egerton of Fanton a 40-year lease from 1558.[5] Sir Ralph (d. 1596) was Hugh Egerton's great-grandson, and William was descended from the Egertons of Wrinehill.[6] William was living at Wall Grange in the later 1560s and died there, apparently in 1570.[7] His son Thomas in 1571 settled the lease on his son Timothy and Timothy's intended wife Margaret Aston.[8] Timothy, alive in 1578, died without issue, and by 1584 the estate was held by Margaret's second husband Edward (from 1603 Sir Edward) Tyrrel.[9] The lease was evidently renewed, and after Tyrrel's death in 1606[10] the estate passed first to Timothy Egerton's cousin, Thomas Egerton of Adstock (Bucks.), and then to Thomas's son Timothy. In 1620 Timothy held 460 a. at Wall.[11] He died in 1628 and was presumably succeeded by his son Thomas, who was apparently living at Wall in 1638. Thomas died unmarried, probably in the 1640s, and his heir was his cousin, another Thomas Egerton. In 1649 the lessee was a Mrs. Egerton, presumably a widow.[12] The estate was later sequestrated, and in 1654 it was held by a parliamentarian, Col. Edward Downes, who was still living there in 1666.[13]

William Jolliffe of Leek acquired the lease in 1668 and was succeeded in 1669 by his son Thomas (d. 1693).[14] The lessee in 1694 was Simon Debank (d. 1701), followed by his widow Mary (d. 1709) and their son John (d. 1750). John's successor at Wall Grange was a younger son Simon, who remained the lessee until 1758.[15] He was replaced that year by Thomas Royles (or Royle), who died in 1790 and was succeeded by Vernon Royle (d. 1824).[16] Later lessees were

Henry West (1825–55) and another Henry West, presumably his son (1859–91).[17]

The house at Wall Grange assessed for tax on eleven hearths in 1666 comprised a central range with cross wings.[18] The present house was built c. 1715 by John Debank.[19] Of ashlar, it has a double-pile plan, and the west front of five bays has tall windows.

An estate centred on *BRADSHAW FARM* existed by 1371 when Roger of Bradshaw issued a charter at Bradshaw.[20] By 1473 William Bradshaw held the estate, which passed to William Rode, possibly c. 1490 when Bradshaw granted Rode land in Rushton James.[21] Rode died c. 1517 and was succeeded at Bradshaw by his son John.[22] John, still alive in 1581, had been succeeded by 1586 by his son William, and William was succeeded in 1616 by his nephew John Rode.[23] John died in 1669, and the estate passed to his son Thomas (d. 1683), to Thomas's son John (d. 1698), to John's son James (d. by 1759), and to James's daughter Hannah.[24] Hannah, later the wife of John Davenport of Ball Haye, in Tittesworth, died childless in 1808. One third of the Bradshaw estate passed to William, Hannah, and Frances Astley, the children of Hannah Davenport's half-sister; one third to a servant, Susannah Mellor, for life, and then to her daughter Elizabeth Jones, Hannah's god-daughter; and the remaining third to John Davenport's great-nephew, John Davenport Rhodes Hulme, Hannah's godson.[25] By 1857 the farmhouse and 71 a. were owned by a Mr. Astley.[26] In 1991 the farm was owned by Mr. J. W. Heath. The present farmhouse is mainly of the late 18th century, but part of a 17th-century house survives on the west side, where there is a doorhead with the date 1623 and the initials of John Rode and his wife Mary.

An estate called *HARRACLES* was evidently held by Henry de Audley (d. 1276), lord of Horton: his widow Lucy held it as dower in 1279.[27] In the earlier 1470s Harracles was held by John Shaw, whose daughter Margaret, wife of John Wedgwood of Blackwood, in Horton, had succeeded by 1477. Margaret was still alive in 1490 and John in 1494; their heir was their son Richard.[28] He had died probably by 1526, leaving a son John, who was still alive in 1546.[29] John was succeeded apparently by 1556 by his son John, who died at Blackwood in 1572.[30] In

99 For the fam. (later Barons and Earls Gower, marquesses of Stafford, and dukes of Sutherland) see *Complete Peerage*, vi. 36–8; xii (1), 199–201, 563–9.
1 S.R.O., D. 593/G/1/23/30.
2 Sleigh, *Leek*, 147; *Visit. Ches. 1580* (Harl. Soc. xviii), 97–8.   3 *L. & P. Hen. VIII*, i (1), p. 228.
4 Ibid. xiii (2), p. 492; *Visit. Ches. 1580*, 204.
5 S.R.O., D. 593/B/1/24/2, deed of 18 May 1556.
6 *Visit. Ches. 1580*, 97–8; Sleigh, *Leek*, 147.
7 Sleigh, *Leek*, 147; S.R.O., D. 5041, p. 176.
8 Sleigh, *Leek*, 155–6.
9 Ibid. 147; W. A. Shaw, *Knights of Eng.* ii. 106; S.R.O., D. 593/G/2/1/1 and 4.   10 *V.C.H. Bucks.* iv. 245.
11 Sleigh, *Leek*, 147; S.R.O., D. 593/B/1/24/2, deed of 1 Mar. 1609/10; D. 593/H/14/3/1; D.(W.) 1702/2/30.
12 Sleigh, *Leek*, 147; S.R.O., D. 593/G/1/13.
13 S.R.O., D. 593/G/1/14–15; *S.H.C.* 1925, 162.
14 S.R.O., D. 593/I/1/23, 27–44; D. 593/I/3/3A; H. G. H. Jolliffe, *Jolliffes of Staffs.* (priv. print. 1892), pedigree following p. 232.
15 Sleigh, *Leek*, 149; S.R.O., D. 593/G/1/1/46–60; D.

593/G/2/3/1–37; D. 593/G/2/4/1.
16 S.R.O., D. 593/G/2/4/2–28; D. 593/G/2/5/1–3; D. 1040/5/15, burial of 18 Jan. 1790; *Staffs. Advertiser*, 20 Nov. 1824, p. 4.
17 S.R.O., D. 593/G/2/5/3–6; D. 593/G/2/6/73–8.
18 Ibid. D. 593/H/3/380; *S.H.C.* 1925, 162 (occupied by Edw. Downes).   19 S.R.O., D. 4092/C/2/65.
20 Ibid. D. (W.) 1761/A/4/165.
21 Ibid. D. (W.) 1702/1/15, copy deed of 6 June 1473; below, Rushton James, manor.
22 *S.H.C.* 1938, 43.
23 *S.H.C.* xv. 136; *S.H.C.* 1927, 130; Sleigh, *Leek*, 85; L.J.R.O., B/C/11, Wm. Rode (1616).
24 S.R.O., D. 538/A/5/42; Sleigh, *Leek*, 85.
25 Sleigh, *Leek*, 85, 113; S.R.O., D. 983/1/25 and 52.
26 S.R.O., D. 983/1/23.   27 *S.H.C.* vi (1), 100.
28 J. C. Wedgwood, *Hist. of Wedgwood Family*, 8; J. C. Wedgwood and J. G. E. Wedgwood, *Wedgwood Pedigrees* (Kendal, 1925), 28–30.
29 S.R.O., D. (W.) 1702/2/2–4.
30 Wedgwood, *Wedgwood Fam.* 10–13, 22.

1559 John settled Harracles on his son, another John, a London draper who had been joint lord of Horton manor since 1554.[31] The younger John, who was living at Harracles by 1572, was succeeded in 1589 by his son John (d. 1658). The younger John's heir was his grandson William Wedgwood, who was succeeded in 1677 by his son John.[32] John died in 1757, leaving three daughters as his heirs, of whom Susannah, widow of John Fenton, survived until 1790. The estate then passed to Sir Brooke Boothby, Bt., the son of John's great-niece, Phoebe Hollins (d. 1788), and her husband Sir Brooke Boothby, Bt.[33] In 1791 Boothby sold what was by then called Harracles Hall farm to Thomas Mills, a Leek solicitor.[34] Mills was succeeded in 1802 by his son, another Thomas (d. 1821).[35] His heir at Harracles was Catherine Mills, his great-niece, who in 1821 married John Cave-Browne. In 1827 they sold the hall and 232 a. to John Davenport of Westwood Hall, in Leek and Lowe.[36] In 1868 his grandson George Davenport sold Harracles as part of the Westwood estate to John Robinson.[37] Harracles was again sold, probably in the early 20th century, to the Woolliscroft family, tenants by the early 19th century[38] and still the owners in 1991.

In 1666 William Wedgwood was assessed for tax on seven hearths at Harracles.[39] The present Harracles Hall, built in the early 18th century, is of brick with stone dressings. The north front of seven bays has a central pediment containing the Wedgwood family's arms, rusticated end pilasters, and a doorcase surmounted by a broken segmental pediment.[40] There are remains of walled gardens to the north and south, and extensive stone farm buildings survive to the west.

An estate centred on *STONELOWE HALL* probably existed in the early 13th century, when there is mention of Randle of Stanlowe.[41] In 1327 and 1333 William of Stanlowe headed lists of those assessed for tax in Endon and Longsdon, and he was alive in 1338.[42] The owner of the estate in 1434 was apparently Richard Sherard,[43] probably the ancestor of Richard Sherratt, who owned Stonelowe in the earlier 16th century. Sherratt's heir was his daugher Joan, the wife of Richard Bulkeley.[44] Thomas Bulkeley was living at Stonelowe in 1556 and his son Arthur in 1600.[45] Arthur's heir was his son John, who was succeeded in 1666 by his son Thomas (d. 1675).[46] Thomas's heir was his son

John, who died in 1697.[47] John was succeeded by Thomas Bulkeley (d. 1736), and his heir may have been James Bulkeley (d. 1761).[48] In 1816 Henry Bulkeley owned an 89-a. farm at Stonelowe.[49] The owner in 1866 was probably Editha Pigot.[50] Dennis Fernyhough and his sister Gladys Fernyhough bought the 96-a. farm in 1952 and were still the owners in 1991.[51] The house, assessed for tax on five hearths in 1666[52] and now called Stonelow Hall, is mainly of the 17th century. The façade, which includes mock crenellations, is probably the result of the restoration undertaken in 1866 by Editha Pigot, whose name is on the dated pediment over the main door.

ECONOMIC HISTORY. AGRICULTURE. Trentham priory's estate at Wall included arable and meadow in the early 13th century: in 1257 four named fields and two named meadows there were said to be long established. In the 1250s the priory was apparently bringing more land at Wall into cultivation, and in 1291 it had 1 carucate of land there.[53]

The priory claimed that its land at Wall was tithe-free, and in 1257 Dieulacres abbey, the owner of the tithes of Longsdon as rector of Leek, agreed not to take small tithes or tithes of young animals there. The exemption, however, was restricted to land newly brought into cultivation, and Dieulacres insisted on still taking tithes from established arable and meadow.[54] The abbey evidently had a tithe barn on Longsdon moor. In 1560 the Crown granted the rectory to Sir Ralph Bagnall, who in 1562 sold the Longsdon tithes and tithe barn to John Wedgwood of Harracles.[55] The barn possibly stood at Little Longsdon, where there was a late 16th-century barn which incorporated re-used medieval cruck trusses and had been recased in stone. It was demolished in 1984.[56]

The common waste on Longsdon hill was inclosed in 1815 under an Act of 1808. It was then in two parts, Longsdon moor covering 310 a. and Ladderedge common 280 a.[57] Soon afterwards the land at Ladderedge, having been limed, was producing grain and turnips.[58]

Of the 547.4 ha. of farmland returned for the civil parish in 1988, grassland covered 492.7 ha. and there were 16.2 ha. of rough grazing. The farming was predominantly dairy and sheep, with 804 head of cattle and 555 sheep and lambs.

31 S.R.O., D. (W.) 1702/2/6; above, Horton, manor.
32 Wedgwood, *Wedgwood Fam.* 22, 25–6, 29, 36, 42–4; Erdeswick, *Staffs.* 494.
33 Wedgwood, *Wedgwood Fam.* 44–5; G.E.C. *Baronetage*, iii. 83; S.R.O., D. (W.) 1761/A/4/236.
34 S.R.O., D. 3359/Gaunt, handbill for auction on 11 Nov. 1790; D. (W.) 1761/A/4/241.
35 Ibid. D. (W.) 1702/1/24; Sleigh, *Leek*, 89.
36 Sleigh, *Leek*, 89; G.E.C. *Baronetage*, ii. 95; S.R.O., D. 3272/1/4/3/21.   37 Sleigh, *Leek*, 46–7.
38 L.J.R.O., B/C/11, Wm. Woolliscroft (1821); P.R.O., HO 107/2008.   39 *S.H.C.* 1925, 160.
40 Above, plate 31.
41 *S.H.C.* xi. 332.
42 Ibid. vii (1), 217; x (1), 116; S.R.O., D. (W.) 1761/A/4/12.
43 *Cal. Fine R.* 1430–7, 190.
44 Sleigh, *Leek*, 152.
45 *S.H.C.* v (2), 64; *S.H.C.* 1935, 245.
46 *S.H.C.* v (2), 64–5; *Leek Par. Reg.* 164, 199.
47 *S.H.C.* v (2), 65; S.R.O., D. 1040/5/14, burial of 26 Mar. 1697.
48 S.R.O., D. 1040/5/14, burial of 21 May 1736; D. 1040/5/15, burial of 5 Dec. 1761.
49 Ibid. D. (W.) 1535/1, ff. 64–5.
50 Below (this para.).
51 Inf. from Miss Fernyhough.
52 *S.H.C.* 1925, 160.
53 *S.H.C.* N.S. ix. 359; *Tax. Eccl.* (Rec. Com.), 252.
54 *S.H.C.* N.S. ix. 359.
55 P.R.O., SC 6/Hen. VIII/3353, m. 34; S.R.O., D. (W.) 1702/8/8; above, Leek and Lowe, manors (rectory).
56 Staffs. C.C., Sites and Monuments Rec. 580–89/84.
57 S.R.O., Q/RDc 69; 48 Geo. III, c. 132 (Local and Personal).
58 Pitt, *Staffs.* 248.

Cereal and horticultural crops were grown on 10.6 ha. Of the 24 farms returned, 22 were under 50 ha. in size and two were between 50 and 99 ha.[59]

WOODLAND. A wood called Dunwood in 1275 was worth 20s. a year in 1278. It was again mentioned in 1313, together with a wood at Harracles.[60] Threapwood, added to Trentham priory's estate at Wall in 1275, means disputed wood, presumably a reference to a conflict over ownership or pasture rights.[61] Hollinhay wood on the south-eastern slope of Ladderedge common covered 50 a. in the early 18th century, when there was also woodland called Soyle wood along the Churnet in the south-east corner of the township.[62] The woodland returned for the civil parish in 1988 covered 21.7 ha.[63]

CHASE AND WARREN. In the early 13th century the earl of Chester had a chase at Hollinhay, in the area of the later Hollinhay wood. Its fence was maintained by men from estates in the earl's fee of Leek.[64] The area was presumably included in a grant of free warren in 1252 to James de Audley as lord of Longsdon.[65] In 1251 Trentham priory was granted free warren at Wall, where in the early 18th century there were closes around Wall Grange Farm whose names indicate the existence of a former rabbit warren.[66]

MILL. There was a mill at Longsdon in 1325.[67] Its site is unknown.

INDUSTRY. Timothy Cooke of Leek was presented in 1604 for carrying away stone from Ladderedge and similarly Thomas Brindley of Leek in 1638.[68] Brindley may have been related to Lawrence Brundley, recorded as a mason in Longsdon in 1659 and as a stone worker at his death in 1664.[69] There were several quarries in the early 19th century, notably at Ladderedge, where one was still worked in the late 1890s.[70]

There were brick kilns at Ladderedge in the early 19th century, some of them evidently on the east side of the common where by 1832 there was a cluster of houses called Brick Bank.[71] John Alcock and his son John worked as brickmakers there in 1834, and the younger John was making bricks in 1841 with two other members of his family, Peter and Thomas Alcock. Richard and Thomas Hargreaves also worked as brickmakers at Ladderedge in 1841.[72] William and Solomon

Alcock built a brickworks there shortly before 1863, presumably on the site of the works recorded at Brick Bank in the late 1870s.[73] William and his son John still worked as brickmakers at Longsdon in 1881. The Brick Bank works survived in 1898 but was apparently superseded soon afterwards by a larger works, in existence by 1892, just over the Cheddleton boundary south of Horse Bridge.[74]

Limekilns recorded at Denford in 1816 were probably worked by the Caldon Lime Co. The kilns were no longer worked in the late 1890s.[75]

LOCAL GOVERNMENT. Longsdon had its own court in 1278.[76] By 1351, however, Longsdon was subject to the Audleys' court at Horton and sent a frankpledge to the twice-yearly view there.[77] It was still part of Horton manor in 1795.[78]

In 1293 the prior of Trentham claimed to hold a court at Wall.[79] Although no records survive, the claim was probably justified: no matters relating to Wall occur in the records of either Horton or Leek manor court in the Middle Ages. Wall Grange, however, was in Horton constablewick in the later 17th century.[80]

The township was part of the Endon quarter of Leek parish, and in the 1660s its poor were relieved jointly with those of Endon and Stanley by the quarter's overseer.[81] The poor were still relieved jointly in 1834, but separate assessments for each township were made by 1750.[82] The township became part of Leek poor-law union in 1837.[83]

The township was responsible for its own roads by 1726.[84]

CHURCH. People from Longsdon attended the church built at Endon c. 1720, and the township was added to Endon parish in 1865.[85] A mission church dedicated to St. James and used also as a school was opened from Endon in 1871.[86] It stood in School Lane at the south end of Longsdon hill on a site given by John Robinson of Westwood Hall, in Leek and Lowe; Dorothy Crompton of Dunwood House gave £500 as an endowment. The parishioners subscribed £10 a year to defray the cost of Sunday evening services.[87] The mission was transferred to the new parish of All Saints', Leek, in 1889.[88]

59 P.R.O., MAF 68/6128/80.
60 S.H.C. ix (1), 43; xi. 334; ibid. N.S. xi. 245.
61 Eng. P.N. Elements, ii. 212; above, manors (Wall Grange). 62 S.R.O., D. 593/H/3/380.
63 P.R.O., MAF 68/6128/80.
64 Staffs. Studies, v. 7.
65 Cal. Chart. R. 1226–57, 409.
66 S.H.C. xi. 304–5; S.R.O., D. 593/H/3/380.
67 Cal. Inq. p.m. vi, p. 356.
68 S.R.O., D. (W.) 1490/17, ct. of 12 Apr. 1604; D. (W.) 1490/20/19A. 69 Leek Par. Reg. 138, 156.
70 S.R.O., Q/RDc 69, plan V; O.S. Map 6", Staffs. VIII. SW. (1900 edn.).
71 S.R.O., D. (W.) 1909/N/1; J. Phillips and W. F. Hutchings, Map of County of Stafford (1832).
72 White, Dir. Staffs. (1834), 714; P.R.O., HO 107/1005.
73 Staffs. Advertiser, 10 Jan. 1863, p. 8; O.S. Map 6", Staffs. VIII. SW. (1889 edn.).
74 P.R.O., RG 11/2736; O.S. Map 6", Staffs. VIII. SW.

(1889, 1900 edns.); Kelly's Dir. Staffs. (1892; s.v. Cheddleton).
75 S.R.O., D. (W.) 1535/1, ff. 66 (no. 1853), 86 (no. 1920); O.S. Map 6", Staffs. VII. SE. (1900 edn.); P. Lead, Caldon Canal and Tramroads (Headington, 1990), 25–7.
76 S.H.C. N.S. xi. 245.
77 Above, Horton, local govt.
78 S.R.O., D. (W.) 1490/44, m. 20.
79 S.H.C. vi (1), 243.
80 Above, Horton, local govt.
81 Above, Leek, par. intro. (par. govt.).
82 S.R.O., D. 4302/7/1/3; White, Dir. Staffs. (1834), 712.
83 S.R.O., D. 699/1/1/1, p. 4.
84 Ibid. D. (W.) 1702/1/16, declaration of 9 Aug. 1726.
85 Ibid. D. 4302/1/1; above, Endon, church.
86 Lich. Dioc. Ch. Cal. (1872), 171; (1873), 92; framed photo. at St. Chad's church, Longsdon, of interior of mission church.
87 Kelly's Dir. Staffs. (1884).
88 Lond. Gaz. 23 Aug. 1889, pp. 4606–7.

In 1899 Robinson gave land off the Leek road for a burial ground and redeemed the mortgage on a house which had been bought for a curate. In 1901 he gave land adjoining the burial ground as the site for a new church, which was opened in 1905. At the same time the house was enlarged and a parish room added to it. The provision of church, burial ground, house, and parish room was described as 'one of the most complete gifts that the diocese of Lichfield has ever known'.[89] A parish was created in 1906.[90] The patronage of the vicarage was vested in John Robinson's three sons, with reversion to the bishop after the last of them had died. The bishop first exercised the patronage in 1938.[91]

The church of *ST. CHAD*, of rough ashlar and designed in a 14th-century style by Gerald Horsley,[92] consists of a chancel with a north vestry and an organ chamber, a nave of three bays, a north aisle, a baptistery under a west tower, and a south porch. The tower has a broach spire. The fittings are in the Arts and Crafts style and include metal chancel gates and foliated brackets on the organ case. Altar coverings include three frontals, one of them designed by Horsley and all worked by the wife of the first vicar, S. P. Warren.[93] The west window has stained glass in memory of members of the Warren family, made in 1986 by John Hardman Studios of Birmingham.

NONCONFORMITY. In 1695 a house at Dunwood was registered for protestant worship, possibly by Presbyterians, who were then strong in Leek. The house was owned by Thomas Bulkeley, probably the man of that name who was heir to the Stonelowe Hall estate.[94]

John Whittaker (or Whittakers) of Rowley Gate Farm was recorded as a Quaker in 1704. He may have been the man of that name who lived at Gratton, in Horton, in 1685. Whittaker's house at Rowley Gate was registered for worship by Quakers in 1713.[95]

A house at Ladderedge was used in 1821 for preaching by Wesleyan Methodists, and by 1825 a society had been formed there.[96] In 1851 a chapel was opened in School Lane on the site occupied by Chapel House in 1991.[97] The chapel was replaced in 1887 by a larger one at the north end of Sutherland Road.[98] That chapel was closed in or shortly before 1980 and converted into a private house.

Hugh Bourne, the founder of Primitive Methodism, registered a house for worship at Denford in 1806, when still a Wesleyan. He later registered three houses in Longsdon as a Primitive Methodist: Joseph Corbishley's at Taylor's Green in 1815, Joseph Armett's at Dunwood in 1817, and John Alcock's at Ladderedge in 1818.[99] A Sunday service was held by Primitive Methodists at Dunwood in 1874. The meeting place is not known, and the service was no longer held by 1879.[1]

EDUCATION. There was a schoolhouse at Dunwood c. 1807.[2] In 1841 a schoolmistress lived at Dunwood and a schoolmaster near Great or Little Longsdon. In 1861 a schoolmistress lived at Ladderedge, as did another in 1871.[3] The Anglican mission church opened in School Lane in 1871 was also used as a day school, and there were c. 40 children on the books in 1876. A master's house was built next to the school in 1882.[4] Enlarged in 1884, 1890, and 1893, the school-church was used solely as a school after the opening of St. Chad's church in 1905.[5]

The decision in 1930 that Longsdon Church of England school, then an all-age school with 80 children on its books, should become a junior school took effect in 1939, the senior children being transferred to Endon.[6] Longsdon school took controlled status, apparently in 1954, as St. James C. E. (Controlled) primary school. It was closed in 1981.[7]

CHARITY FOR THE POOR. By will proved 1899 Joseph Corbishley gave the interest on £50 for distribution to poor people living at Ladderedge. In 1972 the income was being allowed to accumulate.[8]

[89] S.R.O., D. 4855/3/16, pp. 25, 27; *Staffs. Advertiser*, 7 Oct. 1905, p. 3; *Lich. Dioc. Mag.* (1905), 167–8.
[90] *Lond. Gaz.* 15 May 1906, p. 3330.
[91] Lich. Dioc. Regy., Bp.'s Reg. 36, pp. 452–60; Reg. 40, p. 385.
[92] *Staffs. Advertiser*, 7 Oct. 1905, p. 3.
[93] A. G. Jacques, *Leek Embroidery* (Staffs. Libraries, Arts & Archives, 1990), 23–4, 52.
[94] *S.H.C.* 4th ser. iii. 109.
[95] Ibid. 118; S.R.O., D. 3159/3/3, s.a. 1704; above, Horton, nonconf.
[96] S.R.O., D. 3155/1; Wardle, *Methodist Hist.* 41.
[97] *Staffs. Advertiser*, 15 Nov. 1851, p. 4.

[98] S.R.O., D. 3156/1/5/2.
[99] *S.H.C.* 4th ser. iii. 8 (where 'Genford' is evidently a mistake for Denford), 36, 40, 43.
[1] S.R.O., D. 4087/1/1–2.
[2] Ibid. D. (W.) 1909/D/4/1.
[3] P.R.O., HO 107/1005; ibid. RG 9/1945; RG 10/2878.
[4] Ibid. ED 7/109/220; *Kelly's Dir. Staffs.* (1884).
[5] *Kelly's Dir. Staffs.* (1896); S.R.O., D. 4855/3/16, p. 11.
[6] Staffs. C.C. *Record for 1930*, 419; S.R.O., D. 3665/1, p. 51.
[7] S.R.O., D. 3665/1, pp. 136–7; D. 3665/2, p. 70.
[8] Char. Com. file 243245.

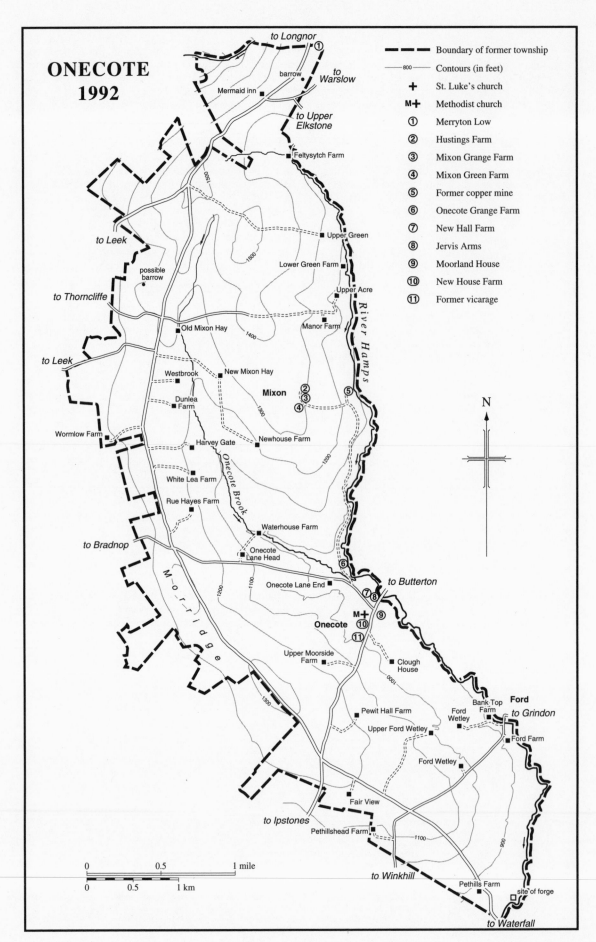

ONECOTE
1992

to Longnor
to Warslow
barrow
Mermaid inn
to Upper Elkstone
Feltysytch Farm
to Leek
Upper Green
Lower Green Farm
possible barrow
Upper Acre
to Thorncliffe
Manor Farm
Old Mixon Hay
to Leek
Westbrook
New Mixon Hay
Mixon
Dunlea Farm
Wormlow Farm
Harvey Gate
Newhouse Farm
White Lea Farm
Rue Hayes Farm
Waterhouse Farm
to Bradnop
Onecote Lane Head
to Butterton
Onecote Lane End
Onecote
Upper Moorside Farm
Clough House
Ford
Bank Top Farm
to Grindon
Pewit Hall Farm
Ford Wetley
Ford Farm
Upper Ford Wetley
Ford Wetley
Fair View
to Ipstones
Pethillshead Farm
to Winkhill
Pethills Farm
site of forge
to Waterfall

River Hamps
Onecote Brook
Morridge

	Boundary of former township
—800—	Contours (in feet)
+	St. Luke's church
M+	Methodist church
①	Merryton Low
②	Hustings Farm
③	Mixon Grange Farm
④	Mixon Green Farm
⑤	Former copper mine
⑥	Onecote Grange Farm
⑦	New Hall Farm
⑧	Jervis Arms
⑨	Moorland House
⑩	New House Farm
⑪	Former vicarage

N

0   0.5   1 mile
0   0.5   1 km

FIG. 38

ONECOTE

ONECOTE was formerly a township in Leek parish and later a civil parish 4,936 a. (1,998 ha.) in area.[9] It is pasture and shares with Bradnop the south end of Morridge, formerly an extensive area of waste. A small village stands on the east side of the township where the Ipstones–Butterton road crosses the river Hamps. The township's boundary followed the Hamps on the east and was marked in the north-east corner by a barrow called Merryton Low, a name meaning in Old English a barrow (*hlaw*) by a boundary lane (*gemaere lone*).[10] The irregular western boundary with Bradnop and Tittesworth townships probably reflected the division of pasture rights on Morridge. Boundary changes in 1934 transferred 880 a., mostly on the west side of the road running along the top of Morridge, to neighbouring civil parishes: 433 a. to Tittesworth, 417 a. to Bradnop, and 30 a. to Heathylee. At the same time 57 a. of Bradnop were added to Onecote in the south. The resulting area of Onecote civil parish was 4,114 a. (1,665 ha.).[11] This article deals with the former township.

The land lies at 804 ft. (245 m.) at the southern tip of the township, and Onecote village to the north stands at 920 ft. (280 m.). On top of Morridge south-west of the village the land lies at 1,224 ft. (373 m.), rising to 1,604 ft. (489 m.) on the northern boundary at Merryton Low. The underlying rock is mostly sandstone of the Millstone Grit series, with an area of Carboniferous Limestone rising to 1,356 ft. (413 m.) at Mixon north of Onecote village. The land is drained by Onecote brook, which joins the Hamps north of Onecote village. The soil on Morridge is clay and loam with some peat; at Mixon and around Onecote village it is more permeable.[12]

The population of Onecote township in 1811 was 464, rising to 585 by 1821. It was 456 in 1831, 438 in 1851, 392 in 1871, and 401 in 1891. Thereafter it fell steadily and was 389 in 1901, 364 in 1911, 337 in 1921, and 332 in 1931. The population of the reduced civil parish was 301 in 1951, 229 in 1961, 214 in 1971, 203 in 1981, and 247 in 1991.[13]

There is a Bronze Age barrow at Merryton Low, another a short distance to the south, and possibly one on the north-west side of the township.[14] There may have been a barrow on the western boundary near Wormlow Farm, whose name apparently incorporates the Old English word *hlaw*.[15]

The name Onecote, recorded in 1199, means

a remote cottage.[16] The original settlement was possibly at the confluence of the Hamps and Onecote brook, where Croxden abbey had a grange apparently by 1223.[17] Mixon, a name recorded in 1197 and meaning a midden or dung hill, was originally a settlement at the north end of the Onecote brook valley, where by 1237 Hulton abbey had a grange on or near the site of Old Mixon Hay.[18] The valley includes Dunlea Farm, on a site occupied by 1510 and probably standing on land called Duncowleye in 1405,[19] White Lea Farm, on a site occupied by the late 1530s,[20] Waterhouse Farm, dated 1639 but replacing a house recorded in 1609,[21] and Rue Hayes Farm, which is partly of the 17th century. Farmhouses at Harvey Gate and Westbrook are of the 19th century but stand on sites occupied by 1710.[22]

Onecote village grew up where a road from Bradnop over Morridge met a road between Ipstones and Butterton near the Hamps. Moorland House on a site there occupied by 1634 is probably of the later 17th century. By the later 18th century it was an inn, called the Dog and Partridge by 1850, and it remained an inn until *c*. 1930.[23] Another inn, called the Sneyd Arms in 1818, possibly stood on the site of the present Jervis Arms, a name used by 1834 and probably a reference to the Jervis family of Darlaston Hall, in Stone, which owned land in Onecote township.[24] New Hall Farm on the north-west side of the village is of the later 19th century but evidently replaced an earlier house: some outbuildings date from the late 18th or early 19th century. There was a village post office by 1888.[25]

By the 17th century there were houses on the Bradnop road north-west of Onecote village. A cottage south of Onecote Grange Farm is dated 1677, and Onecote Lane End Farm existed probably by 1641 and certainly by 1690.[26] Onecote Lane Head further west was so called by 1670.[27] New House Farm on the Ipstones road south of the village is dated 1680, and Clough House to the south-east stands on a site occupied by 1663.[28] Farmhouses at Upper Moorside and Pewit Hall are probably of the early 19th century.

A settlement at Ford on the Grindon side of the Hamps south-east of Onecote village spread into Onecote township. A bridge there made of wood and straw was recorded in 1621.[29] Bank Top Farm is of the late 16th or early 17th century. Its ground floor has two main rooms divided by a plank wall which has carved designs on alternate planks. The original fireplace, beneath

9   *V.C.H. Staffs*. i. 328. This article was written in 1992.
10   S.R.O., D. 5041, p. 128 (giving the 13th-cent. spelling as 'Meriloneslowe'); *Eng. P.N. Elements*, i. 248–9; ii. 33.
11   *Census*, 1931; Staffs. Review Order, 1934, p. 63 and map 1 (copy in S.R.O.).
12   Geol. Surv. Map 1/50,000, drift, sheet 111 (1978 edn.); Soil Surv. of Eng. and Wales, sheet 3 (1983).
13   *V.C.H. Staffs*. i. 328; *Census*, 1911–91.
14   Staffs. C.C., Sites and Monuments Rec. 00354, 04180, 04186.
15   The name Wormlow is first recorded only in 1768: S.R.O., D. 3359/misc. deeds, deed of 25 Mar. 1768.
16   *S.H.C*. iii (1), 168–9; *Eng. P.N. Elements*, i. 10.
17   Below, manor (Onecote Grange Farm).

18   Ibid. (Mixon); *Eng. P.N. Elements*, ii. 41.
19   S.R.O., D. 3272/5/13/12; D.R.O., D. 2375M/27/3, m. 2.   20   Below, manor (White Lea Farm).
21   W.S.L. 132/20/47, deed of 1 June 1609.
22   S.R.O., D. 1203/D/1/1–2.
23   *P.O. Dir. Staffs*. (1850); deeds in possession of the owner, Mr. G. A. Burton.
24   Parson and Bradshaw, *Staffs. Dir*. (1818), villages section, p. 16; White, *Dir. Staffs*. (1834), 715; L.J.R.O., B/A/15/Onecote.   25   *Kelly's Dir. Staffs*. (1888).
26   S.R.O., D. 1040/5/14, burial of 5 Sept. 1690. A doorhead on the W. front of the house appears to be dated 1641.   27   *Leek Par. Reg*. 185.
28   Ibid. 151.   29   S.R.O., Q/SO/2, f. 111v.

a smoke hood, was in the southern room. Ford Farm is of the 18th century. A house of the late 19th century called Ford Wetley probably stands on a site occupied by 1666.[30] Two nearby farmhouses, one also called Ford Wetley and the other Upper Ford Wetley, are probably of the 18th century.

Land called Pethills at the south end of the township was recorded in 1251, and there was a house there by 1539.[31] The present Pethills Farm is dated 1799. Outbuildings dated 1793 and 1799 on the opposite side of the road belonged to a house in existence there by 1775 but not longer standing in the late 1870s.[32] Fair View, near the southern boundary east of the Ipstones road and so called in 1873,[33] was the home in 1901 of Ralph de Tunstall Sneyd (d. 1947); he built the low, crenellated wall around the house as protection against expected enemy attack during the First World War. A poet, philosopher, and Arthurian enthusiast, Sneyd converted a stable block into a sanctuary which included Buddhist artefacts.[34]

The valley of the Hamps north of Onecote village was probably the last part of the township to be settled. Lower Green Farm, dated 1773, stands on a site occupied by 1650, when the house was called the Green or Threewall Green.[35] The site of Upper Acre was occupied by 1775.[36] Manor Farm (so called in 1913 but formerly known as Lower Acre)[37] is dated 1826 and Upper Green 1830. Feltysytch Farm to the north is also probably of the earlier 19th century. Mixon hamlet on the east side of the Mixon spur existed by 1775 and was occupied chiefly by copper miners in the earlier 19th century.[38]

Blakemere House on Morridge at the north end of the township existed by 1638 and possibly stands on the site of a house recorded as at Blakemere in 1348.[39] In the 18th century a packhorse way ran past the house. Rebuilt on a nearby site in the earlier 19th century, the house was an inn by 1851.[40] It was known by 1863 as the Mermaid, a name derived from a legend that a mermaid inhabited the nearby pool which lies to the north in Heathylee, in Alstonefield parish.[41]

A highway on Morridge mentioned in 1413 was probably the road which runs the length of the township and which may have originated as a prehistoric ridgeway.[42] A bridge mentioned in 1619 took the Ipstones–Butterton road over the Hamps.[43] The road was turnpiked in 1769 as part of a route from Cheadle to Buxton (Derb.), and

a tollgate was set up in Onecote village in the earlier 1770s.[44] A two-arched stone bridge built over the Hamps in 1777 was replaced by the present single-arched bridge probably in 1831.[45] The road was disturnpiked in 1878.[46]

A lodge of the Grand United Order of Oddfellows was established in 1866, meeting at the Dog and Partridge. It still existed in 1992.[47] In 1925 the vicar, the Revd. Henry Johnson, built and furnished a room in the village, primarily for church use but also for social activities. It still existed in 1949.[48] A Women's Institute was formed in 1985.[49]

Staffordshire Gliding Club, established in 1962, moved from its original base at Meir airfield in Stoke-on-Trent to a site in Onecote south of the Mermaid inn in 1973. The rough ground, the poor weather conditions, and the proximity of commercial airways forced the club to move in 1992 to the former Seighford airfield near Stafford.[50]

A dispute in the 1840s between members of the Cook family of Onecote Lane End Farm provided Charles Dickens with ammunition for his attack on the workings of Chancery in *Bleak House* (1852–3). Thomas Cook (d. 1816) bequeathed £300 to his second son, Joseph, to be paid after the death of Thomas's wife Mary. She died in 1836, and in 1844 Joseph began a Chancery suit to obtain his money. Four years later the case had made virtually no progress and costs of £800 or £900 had been incurred. William Challinor, a Leek solicitor who was involved in the case, published the details (but not the names of the parties) in a pamphlet urging Chancery reform. He sent a copy of the pamphlet to Dickens when the first instalment of *Bleak House* appeared, and the details, little altered, occur as the case of Gridley in chapter xv of the novel.[51]

MANOR AND OTHER ESTATES. Land at *MIXON* was part of an estate granted by John Lestrange to his cousin Margery (or Margaret) Lestrange and her husband Thomas Noel in 1197.[52] The grant appears to have ignored the claim of Adam of Gratton that he had inherited a carucate at Mixon from his father Ranulph, and in 1203 Adam sued Margery and Thomas for the land, then described as 15 bovates. He was evidently unsuccessful, and his son Ralph still claimed it in 1275.[53] In 1218 Margery and her second husband, Thomas of Whitchurch,

30 *Leek Par. Reg.* 168.
31 *S.H.C.* N.S. ix. 358; *L. & P. Hen. VIII*, xiv (1), p. 591.
32 Above, fig. 2; O.S. Map 6", Staffs. XIV. NW. (1888 edn.).
33 *Staffs. Advertiser*, 11 Oct. 1873, p. 7.
34 *County Biographies. 1901 (Staffs.)*, ed. F. B. Ludlow, 62–4; Leek Libr., newspaper cuttings bk. 3, p. 25; newspaper cuttings pasted into W.S.L. copy of Sneyd's *Poems* (Chesterfield, 1929).
35 B.L. Add. Ch. 46751; O.S. Map 6", Staffs. VIII. NE. (1887 edn.).   36 Above, fig. 2.
37 W.S.L., S.C. F/4/24.
38 Above, fig. 2; below, econ. hist. (ind.).
39 *Leek Par. Reg.* 22; S.R.O., D. (W.) 1761/A/4/164 and 167; D.R.O., D. 2375M/67/23, plan of Blakemere farm, 1827.
40 *V.C.H. Staffs.* ii. 278–9 (based on W.S.L., D. 1798/617/76; D. 1798/618/15); Dodd, *Peakland Roads*, 128;

White, *Dir. Staffs.* (1851), 732.
41 *Reliquary*, iii. 183; above, Alstonefield: Heathylee, intro.
42 Dodd, *Peakland Roads*, 18; *Procs. before J.P.s*, ed. B. H. Putnam, 326.   43 S.R.O., Q/SO/2, f. 95v.
44 *S.H.C.* 4th ser. xiii. 109; S.R.O., D. 239/6/26, 11 Apr. 1772; above, fig. 2.
45 S.R.O., D. 239/6/2, building agreement with plan, 4 Jan. 1777; D. 239/6/8, copy letter of 6 Apr. 1831.
46 Ibid. D. 239/M/14/63, cert. of 25 Nov. 1878.
47 Inf. from the Order's head office, Manchester.
48 S.R.O., D. 5047/1/13.
49 Inf. from Staffs. Federation of Women's Institutes.
50 Inf. from the club secretary, Mr. P. Gill.
51 P.R.O., C 14/204, no. 59; Challinor, *Lectures*, 201–6, 243–4; *Dickensian*, xiii. 16–17; *Letters of Chas. Dickens*, ed. G. Storey and others, vi, pp. xi, 623 n.
52 Above, Bradnop, manor.
53 *S.H.C.* iii (1), 53, 122, 125; vi (1), 64, 69.

granted what were styled the manors of Bradnop and Mixon to Henry de Audley, and in 1223 he gave them to the abbey which he had founded at Hulton.[54] The abbey had established a grange at Mixon by 1237,[55] on or near the site of Old Mixon Hay, where there is a small farmhouse of the 18th century or earlier.

Hulton abbey was dissolved in 1538, and Mixon was presumably included in the Crown's grant of Bradnop manor in 1546 to Edward Agarde, a London speculator, and in Agarde's grant of the manor in 1547 to Sir Edward Aston of Tixall.[56] In 1610 Sir Walter Aston sold land called Mixon Hay on either side of Onecote brook to William (later Sir William) Bowyer of Knypersley, in Biddulph.[57] Sir William died in 1641, and in 1644 his son John sold Mixon Hay to William Jolliffe of Leek.[58] Jolliffe died in 1669, and the land at Mixon passed to his daughter Elizabeth, widow of Edward Ashe, a London draper. In 1677 she charged the land with a rent to support the almshouses which she had founded in Leek.[59] In 1710 a 300-a. farm at Mixon Hay (later Old Mixon Hay), together with farms at Westbrook and Harvey Gate and probably others in that area, were owned by Elizabeth's grandson William Ashe, a London merchant.[60] William was succeeded in 1742 by his daughter Bridget. She died unmarried in 1776, and her estate was divided between William Pierce Ashe A'Court and Charles Penruddock.[61] Both moieties were sold in 1808 to a syndicate,[62] which broke up the estate, selling the largest part, 200 a., in 1821 to Sir Thomas Constable, Bt.[63] In 1843 Constable's son, also Sir Thomas, sold the land to the Revd. John Sneyd, from 1851 lord of Bradnop manor.[64]

Sneyd already owned 465 a. in Onecote, comprising Upper Acre and Manor farms (158 a. and 183 a.) and Feltysytch farm (124 a.), and in 1851 he inherited Onecote Grange farm from his father William.[65] John died in 1873, and his Onecote estate, then 879 a., was put up for sale.[66] Land at Mixon amounting to 243 a. was bought by John Philips of Heybridge, in Checkley,[67] who built New Mixon Hay farmhouse in 1879.[68]

Croxden abbey had an estate at Onecote apparently by 1223. The grange of Onecote then mentioned in the bounds of Henry de Audley's charter endowing Hulton abbey with land at Mixon was evidently not Hulton's;[69] Croxden

certainly owned land in Onecote in 1251, and it had a grange there by 1291.[70] Croxden abbey was dissolved in 1538, and in 1543 the Crown granted its Onecote estate to Sir Edward Aston of Tixall. Aston acquired Bradnop manor in 1547, and what became *ONECOTE GRANGE FARM*, 210 a. in 1839, descended with the manor until 1873 when it was offered for sale.[71] The owner from the earlier 1930s was George Critchlow. He was succeeded in 1990 by his daughter Janet, wife of John Stone.[72] The present farmhouse is dated 1884 and was built for William Finney, presumably the owner.[73] It stands on the site of an earlier house,[74] which was probably of the later 17th century and was of two storeys with end stacks and gabled attic dormers.[75] A date stone of 1654 on an outbuilding possibly comes from a still earlier house.

A 90-a. estate which Croxden abbey acquired from Hulton abbey c. 1330 may have been centred on *WHITE LEA FARM*: in the late 1530s Croxden had two houses at Whitelee.[76] The land was included in the Crown's grant of Croxden's Onecote estate to Sir Edward Aston in 1543.[77] The present house is dated 1786.

ECONOMIC HISTORY. AGRICULTURE. In 1237, after a dispute between Hulton abbey and Dieulacres abbey over pasture rights on Morridge, Dieulacres confirmed Hulton's possession of Mixon, along with a sheepfold around which Hulton was allowed to inclose 240 a. Half of that land was to be brought into cultivation within three years, and tithe from it was to be paid to Dieulacres, as rector of Leek, even if Hulton did not in fact cultivate the land. Tithe was also due from the other half, but only if Hulton decided to cultivate it. Dieulacres reserved the right to pasture its cattle on the entire 240 a. once any corn or hay had been removed.[78] When the agreement was renewed in 1252, presumably after a further dispute, Hulton was required to give Dieulacres a yearly goodwill offering of ½ mark for as long as the 240 a. remained inclosed.[79] There was a large herd of cattle at Mixon in the earlier 1260s, when the sheriff illegally took 40 head and drove them to Chartley castle, in Stowe.[80] In 1291 Hulton's grange at Mixon consisted of 1 carucate. At the same date

54 Above, Bradnop, manor.
55 Below, econ. hist. (agric.).
56 Above, Bradnop, manor.
57 B.L. Add. Ch. 46718; W. A. Shaw, *Knights of Eng.* ii. 165.
58 S.R.O., D. 3359/misc. deeds, deeds of 2 Nov. and 5 Dec. 1644; J. Ward, *Borough of Stoke-upon-Trent* (1843), pedigree following p. 562.
59 H. G. H. Jolliffe, *Jolliffes of Staffs.* (priv. print. 1892), pedigree following p. 232; above, Leek and Lowe, charities (almshos.).
60 S.R.O., D. 1203/D/1/1–2; R. Colt Hoare and others, *Hist. of Wiltshire* (1822–43), Heytesbury, 118.
61 S.R.O., D. 1203/D/1/19, 26, and 31.
62 Ibid. D. 1203/D/1/22 and 30; *Staffs. Advertiser*, 26 Sept. 1807, p. 1.   63 S.R.O., D. 1203/D/2/4.
64 Ibid. D. 1203/D/3/4.
65 Ibid. D. 3359/Sneyd, copy of 1839 survey of Onecote township; below, this section (Onecote Grange Farm).
66 *Staffs. Advertiser*, 9 Aug. 1873, p. 8; Sleigh, *Leek*, facing p. 172.
67 S.R.O., D. 1176/A/12/8; D. 1203/D/2/2.
68 Date stone on house.
69 S.R.O., D. 5041, p. 129; above, Bradnop, manor.
70 *V.C.H. Staffs.* iii. 226; *Tax. Eccl.* (Rec. Com.), 253 (wrongly giving the name as Housecote).
71 *L. & P. Hen. VIII*, xv, p. 561; xviii, p. 200; S.R.O., D. 3359/Sneyd, copy of 1839 survey of Onecote township; above, Bradnop, manor.
72 Inf. from Mr. Stone.
73 *Kelly's Dir. Staffs.* (1888); date stone with initials WMF on house.
74 O.S. Map 6", Staffs. VIII. SE. (1887, 1900 edns.).
75 Photo. (in possession of the present owners of the farm) of an untraced 18th-cent. painting of the house.
76 *Cal. Pat.* 1330–4, 224; P.R.O., SC 6/Hen. VIII/3353, m. 47v.
77 *L. & P. Hen. VIII*, xviii, p. 200.
78 W.S.L., M. 539, no. 8; above, Bradnop, econ. hist. (agric.).   79 *S.H.C.* N.S. ix. 356–7.
80 *S.H.C.* v (1), 121. The sheriff named there was in office in 1263: *S.H.C.* 1912, 276.

Croxden abbey's grange at Onecote, together with a grange at Caldon, consisted of 3 carucates.[81]

A complaint made in 1373 related to damage done to pasture and crops in a 'spacious field' at Onecote adjoining Morridge.[82] Much of the extensive waste of Morridge, however, remained common until 1769.[83]

Of the 1,315.7 ha. of farmland returned for the civil parish in 1988, grassland covered 1,258.8 ha. and there were 51.2 ha. of rough grazing. The farming was dairy and sheep, with 1,634 head of cattle and 3,775 sheep and lambs. Of the 43 farms returned, 37 were under 50 ha. in size, 5 were between 50 and 99 ha., and 1 was between 100 and 199 ha.[84]

MILLS. Hulton abbey's grange at Mixon included a mill in 1291.[85] A mill at Onecote in 1743 probably stood on Onecote brook near Onecote Grange Farm, where there was a mill in 1775.[86] By the later 1870s the mill stood to the east on the river Hamps. It was disused by 1898.[87]

INDUSTRY. A 'stonegetter' was living at Mixon in 1639, and when John Bowyer sold Mixon Hay to William Jolliffe in 1644 the sale included stone and other mines.[88] Limekilns mentioned in the Morridge area in 1683 and 1701 were presumably at Mixon, where the underlying rock is limestone.[89] In the early 1770s the limestone was used to build walls along parts of the turnpike road through Onecote. It was probably as a favour to the manorial lord, John Sneyd, that in 1774 the trustees of the turnpike road decided to charge him a reduced toll when his men used the road to carry lime between Onecote village and the Leek–Ashbourne road at Bottom House, in Ipstones.[90] Limestone was still quarried at Mixon Hay and elsewhere in the township in the early 19th century, and a limekiln east of Westbrook farmhouse was apparently still in use in the late 1870s.[91]

In 1718 Walter, Lord Aston, the lord of the manor, granted six gentlemen a 21-year lease to exploit a deposit of lead ore which had been found in the manor, probably at Mixon. Aston was to receive either ⅛ of the ore or 10s. 6d. per ton. Within the first three years of the lease the contractors were also allowed to dig for copper ore and coal.[92] In 1730 Ann Bosvile, who held land at Mixon possibly as a mortgagee, licensed Robert Bill of Stone and Thomas Gilbert of Cotton, in Alton, to dig for lead or copper ore at Mixon for a term of 21 years. She was to receive ½ of all the ore, or its value in money,

month by month. To insure that she received her share and that the mines were worked properly, the contractors had to employ someone of her choosing to oversee operations.[93] In 1771 Bridget Ashe licensed Hugh Serjeant of Wetley Rocks, in Cheddleton, to dig for lead and copper ore on her land at Mixon Hay for a term of 21 years, giving her ⅑ of the ore every three months. Mining was to stop if her share of the ore each year was not worth at least 10 guineas more than the money which she had paid to her tenants to recompense them for damage done to their land.[94]

John Sneyd, the owner of land at Mixon as part of his purchase of Bradnop manor in 1770, evidently had a mine at Mixon by 1775: that year mining equipment was borrowed from the nearby copper mine at Ecton, in Wetton, for use at 'Snead's mine'.[95] In 1780 there was a copper mine east of Mixon Grange Farm. Still productive in 1817, it was closed c. 1824. Attempts to resume profitable exploitation were made by Sneyd's sons in the later 1820s and early 1830s, but without success. Mining equipment at Mixon was offered for sale in 1834, although ore was apparently still being extracted in 1841. Nine copper miners were then living at Mixon, with another near Onecote village. There were 10 at Mixon in 1851, even though production had probably stopped by then; possibly they travelled to work at Ecton.[96] A company called Mixon Great Consols Copper Mine Co. was established in 1853 to resume digging at Mixon; it failed in 1858.

A kiln at Onecote mill in 1743 was evidently used for smelting iron: the millowner, Ralph Hall, had 77 bars of iron worth £26.[97] By 1758 George Critchlow, a whitesmith, had built a forge near the river Hamps east of Pethills Farm: he made a weathercock for Leek church that year. He died in 1780, and the forge was continued by his son, also George (d. 1782).[98] Worked by Francis Gosling in 1793, it apparently no longer existed by 1820.[99]

LOCAL GOVERNMENT. Onecote was probably a tithing in Bradnop manor in the Middle Ages.[1] It was part of the Bradnop quarter of Leek parish, and by the 1660s its poor were relieved by the quarter's overseer.[2] The township had its own overseer by 1743, and in 1766 he was a signatory to an agreement to open a workhouse in Ipstones.[3] The township became part of Leek poor-law union in 1837.[4]

81 *Tax. Eccl.* (Rec. Com.), 252–3.
82 *S.H.C.* xiv (1), 136.
83 Above, Bradnop, econ. hist. (agric.).
84 P.R.O., MAF 68/6128/70.   85 *Tax. Eccl.* 252.
86 L.J.R.O., B/C/11, Ralph Hall (1743); above, fig. 2.
87 O.S. Map 6", Staffs. VIII. SE. (1887, 1900 edns.).
88 *Leek Par. Reg.* 32; S.R.O., D. 3359/misc. deeds, deed of 2 Nov. 1644.
89 D.R.O., D. 231M/E5033; B.L. Add. Ch. 46823.
90 S.R.O., D. 239/6/26, 21 Dec. 1771, 25 June and 30 July 1774, 3 June 1775.
91 J. Farey, *General View of Agric. and Minerals of Derb.* i (1811), 410–11; O.S. Map 6", Staffs. VIII. NE. (1887 edn.).
92 S.R.O., D. 3359/Condlyffe, articles of agreement, 15 Sept. 1718.
93 Ibid. D. 240/D/299; *V.C.H. Staffs.* ii. 268 n.

94 S.R.O., D. 1203/D/1/13.
95 Para. based on *Bull. Peak Dist. Mines Hist. Soc.* iv. 260–70; *Aris's Birmingham Gaz.* 5 June 1780, p. 2; *V.C.H. Staffs.* ii. 267; J. Phillips and W. F. Hutchings, *Map of County of Stafford* (1832).
96 P.R.O., HO 107/1005; HO 107/2008; White, *Dir. Staffs.* (1851), 788.
97 L.J.R.O., B/C/11, Ralph Hall (1743).
98 Ibid. Geo. Critchlow (1780, 1782); Sleigh, *Leek*, 76; above, fig. 2.
99 Sheffield City Archives, Bagshawe C. 3277; C. and J. Greenwood, *Map of County of Stafford* (1820).
1 Above, Bradnop, local govt.
2 Above, Leek, par. intro. (par. govt.).
3 S.R.O., D. 925/5/25; D. 3816/3/1.
4 Ibid. D. 699/1/1/1, p. 4.

CHURCH. There was a chapel at Onecote by 1524.[5] In 1553 it had a chapelwarden, and the church goods included a bell in a steeple, a sacring bell, and a silver chalice and paten. In 1604 the chapel was stated to be in Grindon parish, and it probably stood near Onecote Old Hall on the Grindon side of the boundary north of Onecote village: land there was called Chapel Yard in the early 20th century.[6] In 1604 the chapel was served by Ralph Salt, described as no preacher and a lewd young man who 'out of all good order wears a feather in his hat'. Thomas Miles was appointed minister by the committee for plundered ministers in 1648 with a grant of £20 a year from the sequestrated rectory of Ellastone.[7] Nothing further is known about the chapel.

The present church in Onecote village was built in the earlier 1750s, the cost being met by subscription.[8] The chapelry, which covered Onecote and Bradnop townships, became a parish in 1862 with the vicar of Leek as patron,[9] and the perpetual curacy was styled a vicarage from 1868.[10] The church retained its own vicar until 1976 and was later served by the vicar of Ipstones as a priest-in-charge. The benefice was united with that of Ipstones in 1983, but the parishes remained separate. The patronage was vested jointly in the bishop of Lichfield as patron of Ipstones and the team rector of Leek.[11]

Queen Anne's Bounty endowed the living with four grants of £200 in 1783, 1784, 1789, and 1797. It made a further grant of £1,400 in 1824.[12] The living was worth £99 a year c. 1830,[13] and the endowments comprised the churchyard (4 a.), a smallholding called Ten Acres south-west of Ford Wetley (18 a.), Pethillshead farm (17 a.), a farm at Moorside (10 a.), and land called Chapel field (7 or 8 a.). By 1845 the endowment also included 27 a. at Pill Will in the north-west part of the township.[14] In 1862 Queen Anne's Bounty gave £200 to meet a benefaction of £200 raised by subscription and a grant of £200 from the Lichfield Diocesan Church Extension Society.[15] There was glebe of 82 a. in 1887, with an estimated rental of £90 10s.[16] In 1899 the Bounty gave £360 to meet a benefaction of £600, comprising £300 from diocesan societies, £200 from subscriptions, and a donation of £100.[17]

In 1830 the incumbent apparently served Onecote himself though he lived at Butterton, of which he was also curate. In 1831, however, he em-

ployed an assistant curate at Onecote with a salary of £35.[18] In 1851 the assistant, Harling Richardson, lived at Golden Farm in Bradnop village, and he continued to live there after he became the incumbent in 1859.[19] A house was built in Onecote village for the newly appointed incumbent in 1864, the cost being met by the vicar of Leek.[20] When the benefice was united with that of Ipstones in 1983, the vicarage house at Ipstones was designated the place of residence. The house at Onecote was sold and converted in 1984 into a home for the elderly.[21]

There was one Sunday service in 1830, and Communion was celebrated four times a year.[22] In 1851 the average Sunday attendance was 20 when the service was held in the morning and 70 when it was held in the evening.[23]

The church of ST. LUKE, which is built of ashlar, was originally a single cell building with a wooden bellcot. In 1837 it was given a chancel, probably reusing a Venetian window from the original east end, a south-west porch, and a west tower.[24] Also in 1837 a west gallery replaced one on the north side.[25] The organ in the west gallery dates from 1904.[26] The box pews were removed during a restoration in 1906–7, the panelling being used to make the present benches.[27]

The furnishings include royal arms of 1754 and a commandments board of 1755; both hang on the west wall. There is a single undated bell.[28]

The registers date from 1755.[29]

Burials took place from 1782.[30] Small additions to the churchyard were made in 1897 and 1979.[31]

NONCONFORMITY. John Forde of Onecote, a blacksmith, and his wife were recorded as papists in 1706.[32]

In 1815 Hugh Bourne, the founder of Primitive Methodism, registered a room in Onecote for preaching, and a Primitive Methodist chapel was opened in the village in 1822.[33] On Census Sunday 1851 there was an evening congregation of 54.[34] A porch was added in 1934, and the chapel was enlarged in 1955.[35] It was known as Onecote Methodist church in 1992. Primitive Methodists also held services at Mixon from 1863 until 1904.[36]

By 1823 there was a Wesleyan Methodist society in Onecote. The room registered there for worship by protestant dissenters in 1826 was probably for that society, and in 1829 a Wesleyan

5 L.J.R.O., Reg. of Wills 1, p. 84.
6 S.H.C. 1915, 199; W.S.L., S.C. E/1/15.
7 S.H.C. 1915, 199–200; Sleigh, Leek, 110.
8 S.H.C. 4th ser. x. 95–6; S.R.O., D. 3186/1/1.
9 Lond. Gaz. 5 Sept. 1862, p. 4358.
10 Lich. Dioc. Ch. Cal. (1869).
11 Lich. Dioc. Dir. (1976); Lich. Dioc. Regy., Bp.'s Reg. S (Orders in Council), p. 46.
12 Hodgson, Bounty of Queen Anne, p. ccxcvii.
13 Rep. Com. Eccl. Revenues, 492–3.
14 L.J.R.O., B/V/6/Onecote, 1824; S.R.O., D. 3816/2/3; Staffs. Advertiser, 26 Sept. 1807, p. 1.
15 Hodgson, Bounty of Queen Anne, suppl. pp. lii, lxvii.
16 Return of Glebe Lands, 66.
17 Docs. at St. Edward's church, Leek, bdle. O/1, letter of 23 Mar. 1899.
18 S.H.C. 4th ser. x. 79, 96; Rep. Com. Eccl. Revenues, 492–3.
19 P.R.O., HO 107/2008; ibid. RG 9/1947; Lich. Dioc. Regy., Bp.'s Reg. 32, p. 168.

20 Lich. Dioc. Regy., Bp.'s Reg. 32, p. 267; P.O. Dir. Staffs. (1868).
21 Lich. Dioc. Regy., Bp.'s Reg. S (Orders in Council), p. 46; inf. from the owners of the house.
22 S.H.C. 4th ser. x. 96. 23 P.R.O., HO 129/372/2/4.
24 S.H.C. 4th ser. x. 95–6; S.R.O., D. 3186/2/1; above, plate 14. 25 W.S.L., Sleigh, ii, f. 239v.
26 Alstonfield Par. Mag. June 1904.
27 Lich. Dioc. Mag. (1906), 187; (1907), 150; Bowyer and Poole, Staffs. Moorlands, ii. 114.
28 C. Lynam, Ch. Bells of County of Stafford (1889), 55.
29 All but the most recent are in S.R.O., D. 3186.
30 S.R.O., D. 3186/1/1.
31 Lich. Dioc. Regy., Bp.'s Reg. U, p. 222; Y, pp. 249–50. 32 Staffs. Cath. Hist. xiii. 29.
33 S.H.C. 4th ser. iii. 38; White, Dir. Staffs. (1851), 729.
34 P.R.O., HO 129/372/2/4. 35 Date stones on church.
36 W. H. Simcock, 'Primitive Methodism in the Leek Moorlands' (TS. in Leek Libr.), p. 22; S.R.O., D. 4087/1/1 and 31.

service was held at Onecote every Sunday.[37] The society still existed in 1843 but apparently not in 1844.[38]

EDUCATION. A Wesleyan Methodist Sunday school was established in Onecote in 1827, and it had 25 boys and 23 girls in the earlier 1830s.[39] In 1839 it was said that few parents could afford to pay for their children's education, and it was proposed to raise £10 or £12 a year by subscription to hire a master who would teach 10 or 12 poor children free.[40] A school seems to have been opened, but in 1861 what was called Onecote school house was occupied by a labourer.[41] The only teacher recorded in the township in 1851 was the woman tollgate keeper, who presumably ran a dame school,[42] but there was a Primitive Methodist Sunday school which had an attendance of 18 pupils on Census Sunday that year.[43]

A National school was built in 1872, and there were 46 children on its books in 1875.[44] A school board was formed voluntarily in 1878.[45] A teacher's house was built in 1880.[46] Until 1909 a few children from Butterton and Grindon attended the school, but when those parishes refused to contribute towards the cost of an extension, the school was restricted to children from Onecote.[47]

The decision in 1930 that Onecote council school, then an all-age school with 47 children on its books, should become a junior school took effect in the earlier 1940s, the senior children being transferred chiefly to Leek.[48] As Onecote county primary school it was closed in 1984, and most of the children were transferred to Leek.[49] In 1992 the school building was used as a village hall.

CHARITIES FOR THE POOR. In 1788 Joan Adsetts of Mayfield left the interest on £30 to poor widows in Onecote, and in 1794 the money was used to buy 1½ a. near Ford. The income was £1 in 1839, when it was distributed at Christmas among five widows.[50] The poor of Onecote shared with those of Bradnop in the charity of John Stanley, established by will of 1693. In 1928 the two charities were amalgamated, and a distribution was still made in 1976.[51]

RUDYARD

RUDYARD was formerly a township in Leek parish and later a civil parish 1,435 a. (581 ha.) in area.[52] It extends from a hill called Gun on its east side to Rudyard Lake, a reservoir formed in 1799 by damming the brook which marked the western boundary with Horton.[53] A hamlet on which the township centred in the 18th century was gradually deserted in the 19th century. It was replaced by the present Rudyard village in Horton, which grew up to cater for tourists visiting Rudyard Lake. Rudyard township was amalgamated with Horton parish in 1934 to form Horton civil parish.[54] This article deals with the former township.

The land lies at 600 ft. (183 m.) beside Rudyard Lake and rises to 1,000 ft. (305 m.) on Gun. The underlying rock is mostly Bunter Pebble, with sandstone of the Millstone Grit series in the north and west parts of the township. Boulder Clay overlies the Bunter Pebble, and the soil is coarse loam, except on Gun where it is clay and loam with some peat.[55]

Six people in Rudyard were assessed for tax in 1327 and eight in 1333,[56] and seventeen were assessed for hearth tax in 1666.[57] The population was 109 in 1801, rising to 117 by 1831 but then falling to 72 by 1881. It was 81 in 1901 and 1911, and 78 in 1921. It was 112 in 1931, the last time that Rudyard's population was separately recorded.[58]

Rudyard has been identified as an estate called Rudegeard in the early 11th century. The name is derived from Old English words meaning the shrub rue and an enclosure.[59] The oldest surviving building is the 17th-century Rudyard Hall.[60] By the later 18th century there was a hamlet in the south-west part of the township on the road between Leek and Macclesfield. It declined after the road was turnpiked in 1762 with a new line to the east.[61] There are four farmhouses in the area of the former hamlet, Rudyard Manor (formerly called Green Farm)[62] and Rudyard House (formerly called Greentree Farm),[63] both of the 18th century, Highgate Farm on a site occupied by 1677,[64] and Willgate Farm on a site occupied by 1669.[65] Hunt House Farm to the north of the hamlet was so called by 1636. The road linking it to the hamlet, formerly part of the Leek–Macclesfield road, was stopped up in 1827.[66] Barnswood Farm on the township's

37 S.R.O., D. 3155/1; Leek Libr., Johnson scrapbk. i (2), D/13/15; S.H.C. 4th ser. iii. 68.
38 S.R.O., D. 3156/1/1/2.
39 Educ. Enq. Abstract, 880.
40 S.R.O., D. 3186/2/1, notes about teacher, 1839.
41 P.R.O., RG 9/1947.   42 Ibid. HO 107/2008.
43 Ibid. HO 129/372/2/4.
44 Ibid. ED 7/109/241; Staffs. Advertiser, 11 Mar. 1871, p. 2.
45 List of Sch. Boards, 1902 [Cd. 1038], p. 638 (1902), lxxix.   46 S.R.O., CEB/18/1, pp. 1–4.
47 S.R.O., D. 4165/1/1, pp. 144, 175, 191–2, 200–1.
48 Ibid. D. 4165/1/3, pp. 224, 231; D. 5067/1/12, letter of 27 Jan. 1944; Staffs. C.C. Record for 1930, 1027.
49 S.R.O., D. 4165/1/5, pp. 145–6.
50 Ibid. D. 3186/2/1, acct. for Adsetts' Dole; D. 3816/3/2.
51 Above, Bradnop, charity.
52 V.C.H. Staffs. i. 328. This article was written in 1991.
53 Above, Horton, intro. (Rudyard Lake).
54 Census, 1931.
55 Geol. Surv. Map 1", drift, sheet 110 (1968 edn.); Soil Surv. of Eng. and Wales, sheet 3 (1983).
56 S.H.C. vii (1), 223; x (1), 115.
57 S.H.C. 1925, 203.
58 V.C.H. Staffs. i. 328; Census, 1911–31.
59 Eng. P.N. Elements, i. 198; ii. 88; below, manor.
60 Below, manor.
61 S.R.O., D. 1176/A/16/2; J. Phillips and W. F. Hutchings, Map of County of Stafford (1832); O.S. Map 6", Staffs. VII. NE. (1887 edn.); above, fig. 2; below (next para.).
62 S.R.O., D. 1176/A/16/2.
63 It formerly had a date stone of 1717: inf. from the owner.   64 S.R.O. 3508/A/1/4.
65 Leek Par. Reg. 184.
66 Ibid. 12; S.R.O., Q/SB Trans. 1827.

northern boundary stands on or near a site occupied by the early 17th century.[67]

The Leek–Macclesfield road was turnpiked in 1762,[68] taking a new line which ran through the middle of the township east of Rudyard hamlet. A tollgate was set up near a milepost at Packsaddle Cottage in 1764, and a tollhouse was built in 1767.[69] Under the 1762 Act a share of the tolls from the Packsaddle gate was paid to the trustees of the Ashbourne–Congleton turnpike road because of the joint use of part of the Macclesfield road through Rudyard.[70] In 1808 the Macclesfield road was again rerouted, the new line leaving the old one north of the tollhouse to run west past Hunt House Farm and Barnswood Farm and rejoining it in Rushton Spencer.[71] The tollhouse at Packsaddle was replaced in 1824 by one at Poolend, in Leekfrith.[72] The road was disturnpiked in 1878.[73]

The North Staffordshire Railway Co.'s Churnet Valley line between Leek and Macclesfield, opened in 1849, ran along the west side of the township. Rudyard station south of Rudyard Lake was opened in 1850. Renamed Rudyard Lake station c. 1925, it was closed for passengers and freight in 1960 and the building was demolished.[74] A miniature railway follows the old line for nearly a mile north from the site of the station along the side of Rudyard Lake. Its track was laid in the later 1970s and remade in 1985.[75]

MANOR AND ANOTHER ESTATE. Between 1002 and 1004 the thegn Wulfric Spot devised to Burton abbey a place called Rudegeard, which has been identified as *RUDYARD*. The abbey either failed to gain possession of the estate or soon lost it. Before the Conquest Rudyard was held by Wulfmaer. In 1086 it was held by the king.[76]

By the mid 12th century the Verduns of Alton were the overlords of Rudyard. About 1200 a fee-farm rent of 22s. was owed to Norman Pantun, son of Alice de Verdun. It was still paid c. 1800 to the earl of Shrewsbury, the Verduns' successor at Alton.[77]

Ulf held the manor in the mid 12th century, and c. 1200 Norman Pantun confirmed Ulf's grandson, Ranulph of Tittesworth, in possession of the vill of Rudyard. Norman's mother, Alice de Verdun, with the agreement of her other son

William Pantun, had earlier confirmed Rudyard to Ranulph of Tittesworth with all its liberties in return for a payment of 5 marks, together with fines of 37s. for herself and 20s. for William.[78] Ranulph was succeeded by his son, Thomas of Rudyard, and Thomas by his son Richard.[79] Richard was still alive in 1293–4.[80] Randal of Rudyard, alive in 1302, was lord of Rudyard in 1315.[81] Ranulph of Rudyard, who headed the list of those assessed for tax there in 1327, and Richard of Rudyard, who headed a similar list in 1333, were probably lords of the manor.[82] In 1366 the widow of the same or another Richard of Rudyard claimed dower in the manor against John of Rudyard, probably her son. John, lord in 1370, was succeeded by his son Thomas, and Thomas by his son Ralph, alive in 1411. Richard Rudyard was evidently the lord in 1418.[83]

Thomas Rudyard was lord in 1507.[84] Still alive c. 1530,[85] he was succeeded by his nephew Ralph Rudyard, who was lord later in the 1530s and in 1564 or 1565.[86] He was succeeded by Thomas Rudyard, probably his son, who died in 1572 or 1573 with his son, another Thomas, as his heir.[87] He was succeded in 1626 by his son, also Thomas. The younger Thomas was succeeded in 1638 by his brother Ralph, and Ralph in 1653 by his son Thomas.[88] Thomas, sheriff of Staffordshire in 1682,[89] was alive in 1683 but dead by 1691. In 1695 his son, another Thomas, settled the manor on trustees for the benefit of his four daughters, Margaret, Mary, and Mercy Rudyard and Elizabeth, wife of Charles Gibbons.[90] Thomas died probably soon afterwards and certainly before 1709.[91] Elizabeth died in 1716 and Mary in 1717.[92]

In 1723 Margaret Rudyard and her sister Mercy, by then the wife of William Trafford of Swythamley, in Heaton, sold Rudyard with the manor of Leek to Thomas Parker, earl of Macclesfield.[93] The earls of Macclesfield retained the estate until it was broken up in 1919. A 418-a. farm centred on Rudyard Hall was then bought by the tenant, Nathan Buxton.[94] He sold it in 1927 to John Wain. In 1966 the farm was bought by Frank Robinson.[95]

Rudyard Hall is mainly of the earlier 17th century, and a stone with the date 1635 and the initials TR and MR survives inside the house. The house was assessed for tax on seven hearths in 1666.[96] A garden wall around the house, with an

67 Below, manor (Barnswood Farm).
68 Above, Leek and Lowe, communications.
69 S.R.O., D. 706/1, 3 May 1764, 4 Feb. and 4 Dec. 1767; D. 1176/A/16/2.
70 2 Geo. III, c. 42, pp. 95–6; Sandon Rd. acct. bk. 1821–69 (in possession of Mr. R. Stones of Malpas, Ches., 1994), where payment ceases after 1825.
71 S.R.O., D. 607/1, 30 May 1806; D. 3359/Sandon Rd. acct. bk. 1803–21, 24 Dec. 1807, 19 Jan., 28 May, and 4 July 1808.
72 Sandon Rd. acct. bk. 1821–69, July–Sept. 1824.
73 Above, Leek and Lowe, communications.
74 R. Keys, *Churnet Valley Railway* (Hartington, 1974), 9, 36; B. Jeuda, *Rudyard Lake Golf Club, 1906–1926* (Leek, 1993), 4.   75 Local inf.
76 *Charters of Burton Abbey*, ed. P. Sawyer, pp. xxxi, 55; *V.C.H. Staffs.* iii. 199, 201; iv. 41 (giving Wulfmaer as Wlmar).
77 S.R.O. 3508/A/1/1; W.S.L., M. 532.
78 S.R.O. 3508/A/1/1.
79 *S.H.C.* vi (1), 205; ibid. N.S. ix. 313.

80 *S.H.C.* 1911, 225.   81 Ibid. 433.
82 *S.H.C.* vii (1), 223; x (1), 115.
83 Ibid. xiii. 58; xvii. 61; ibid. N.S. iv. 179; D.R.O., D. 2375M/126/2/6.
84 S.R.O. 3508/A/1/2.
85 P.R.O., C 1/651/52.
86 Ibid. C 1/882/33; Sleigh, *Leek*, 65 n.
87 S.R.O. 3508/A/3/1.
88 *Reliquary*, vii. 214–15; *Leek Par. Reg.* 90.
89 *S.H.C.* 1912, 288.
90 S.R.O. 3508/A/1/6; 3508/A/3/5. For Chas. Gibbons see L.J.R.O., Reg. of Wills C, f. 198.
91 S.R.O., D. 3359/misc. deeds, deed of 26 Mar. 1709.
92 *Reliquary*, vii. 215.
93 Sleigh, *Leek*, 26; S.R.O. 3508/A/3/6.
94 *Staffs. Advertiser*, 14 June 1919, p. 2; S.R.O., D. 1176/B/11/1 (annotated copy of Rudyard estate sale cat. 1919).
95 *Staffs. Advertiser*, 14 Jan. 1928, p. 2; inf. from Mr. Robinson.
96 *S.H.C.* 1925, 203.

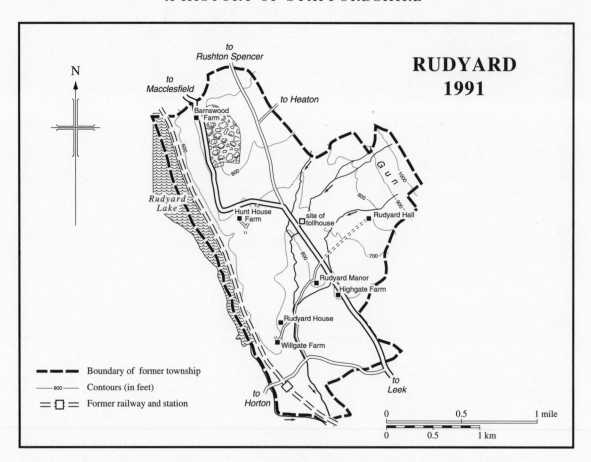

Fig. 39

imposing gateway on the north side, is probably of the late 17th century. The farm buildings include a stone barn dated 1657.

An estate centred on *BARNSWOOD FARM* probably originated in the grant of land which the lord of Rudyard, Thomas son of Ranulph of Tittesworth, gave to William son of Richard of Rushton in the early 13th century.[97] William later gave the land to his brother Ranulph, who by 1246 had given it to Dieulacres abbey.[98] After the Dissolution it became part of Rudyard manor: in 1606 the Rudyard family owned a house called Barnswood and adjoining land in Rudyard.[99] The farm was sold in 1919 to the tenants, J. and J. S. Fletcher. In the later 1920s it was bought by the family of the present owner, Mr. F. A. Brown.[1]

Nothing remains of the house at Barnswood which was assessed for tax on four hearths in 1666.[2] It may have been demolished when the new line of the Leek–Macclesfield road was constructed in 1808: the present house, which lies on the west side of the road, dates from that time.

ECONOMIC HISTORY. In 1086 the area known as Rudyard had land for one or two ploughteams.[3]

When the earl of Macclesfield's Rudyard estate was broken up in 1919 there were six farms: Rudyard Hall (418 a.), Greentree (208 a.), Green, later Rudyard Manor (181 a.), Barnswood (178 a.), Willgate (158 a.), and Hunt House (143 a.). They were principally dairy farms and included 808 a. of pasture and 306 a. of arable. There were also 132 a. of woodland in the township, the main area being 55 a. at Barnswood, still a wood in 1991.[4]

Fields called Near and Far Rabbit Bank on the east and south-east sides of Rudyard Hall in 1731[5] may indicate the site of a rabbit warren.

LOCAL GOVERNMENT. Rudyard was subject to the overlord's manor court at Alton, where a headborough for Rudyard tithing was sworn at least between 1732 and 1823.[6] Rudyard remained part of Alton constablewick in 1851.[7] In 1507 the lord of Rudyard claimed to hold a small court of his own at Rudyard.[8]

The township was part of the Leekfrith quarter of Leek parish, and in the 1660s its poor were relieved by the quarter's overseer. The township

97 *S.H.C.* N.S. ix. 313.
98 Ibid. 314; Lambeth Palace Libr., Papal Docs. 40.
99 S.R.O., D. 3359/misc. deeds, deed of 1 Jan. 1605/6.
1 Inf. from Mr. Brown.
2 *S.H.C.* 1925, 203.   3 *V.C.H. Staffs.* iv. 41.
4 S.R.O., D. 1176/B/11/1 (annotated copy of Rudyard

estate sale cat. 1919); *Staffs. Advertiser*, 14 June 1919, p. 2; 14 Jan. 1927, p. 2.
5 S.R.O., D. 1176/A/11/9.
6 Ibid. D. 240/E(A)1/144 and 344.
7 White, *Dir. Staffs.* (1851), 765.
8 S.R.O. 3508/A/1/2.

had its own overseer from 1713.[9] It became part of Leek poor-law union in 1837.[10]

CHURCH. From the 17th century and presumably earlier people from Rudyard attended the parish church at Leek.[11]

NONCONFORMITY. The Jane Rudyard who was recorded as a recusant in the mid 1590s was possibly the mother of the lord of the manor Thomas Rudyard (d. 1638), who was himself returned as a recusant in 1616.[12]

Matthew Dale of Rudyard was converted by the Quaker missionary Richard Hickock in 1654, and he established a meeting at his home. The Richard Dale who suffered impris-

onment in 1655 for his beliefs as a Quaker may also have lived in Rudyard.[13] Joshua and Mary Dale of Rudyard were recorded as Quakers in 1708, as was Thomas Finney of Rudyard in 1709 and 1716.[14] Another Thomas Finney of Rudyard and two members of the Dale family attended the Leek meeting of Friends in 1735.[15]

Methodist preachers held regular services in the 19th century at Rudyard Hall, the home of a class leader, Robert Needham (d. 1887).[16]

EDUCATION. No evidence.

CHARITIES FOR THE POOR. None known expressly for the township.

RUSHTON JAMES

RUSHTON JAMES was formerly a township in Leek parish and later a civil parish 1,390 a. (563 ha.) in area.[17] It is pasture, with scattered settlement along the Leek–Congleton road, which runs across the north part of the township, and at Newtown on the former waste in the south-west part. The township was coterminous with the manor of Rushton James, the boundary of which in the early 14th century followed Cress brook on the north, Rad brook on the east, Hay brook on the south, and a ridge called Long Edge on the west. The boundary was also then marked by three sites whose names incorporate the Old English word *hlaw*, meaning a hill or barrow: Holclowe on the north, Wolfelowe on the north-west, and Gledelowe on the west.[18] In 1934 the civil parish was amalgamated with Rushton Spencer to form Rushton civil parish, 3,250 a. (1,315 ha.) in area.[19] This article deals with the former township.

In the west part of the township the land lies at 1,050 ft. (320 m.) on Long Edge. To the east it slopes down gradually to 575 ft. (175 m.) at Ryecroft Gate, where the Leek–Macclesfield road crosses Rad brook. Dingle brook flows through the centre of the township. It was dammed in 1799 to form Rudyard Lake, whose north end lies in the township.[20] The underlying rock is sandstone of the Millstone Grit series. It is overlain by Boulder Clay, and the soil is fine loam.[21]

Twenty-eight people in Rushton James were assessed for hearth tax in 1666.[22] In 1751 there were 153 people aged over 16 in the township.[23] The population in 1801 was 264, rising to 354

by 1821 and falling to 273 by 1861. It was 281 in 1871, 267 in 1881, 242 in 1891, 229 in 1901, 237 in 1911, and 231 in 1921. It was 234 in 1931, the last time that Rushton James's population was separately recorded.[24]

The name Rushton originally described a settlement at Rushton Marsh in what became Rushton Spencer after the division of Rushton manor by the 13th century.[25] The suffix James, recorded in the early 14th century,[26] was presumably taken from the name of the lord of the manor, James de Audley (d. 1272). Rushton James manor house probably stood on the site of Rushton Hall Farm in the centre of the township, where the Leek–Congleton road was crossed by a road between Rushton Spencer and Horton.[27] The present farmhouse is of the 17th century, and Fold Farm and New Hall Farm to the east are of the 18th century. Other farm-houses stand along the Leek–Congleton road, which in the Middle Ages was part of the Earl's Way.[28] They include Earlsway House on the west side of the township on a site occupied by 1350,[29] and Wolf Lowe Farm further west is of the 18th century.

Wolf Dale on the east side of the township is mainly of the 18th century but probably occupies a medieval site: a house was recorded in Wolf dale in the early 1320s.[30] A farmhouse at Rye-croft Gate north of Wolf Dale is partly of the 17th century.

There was encroachment on the common waste in the south-west part of the township before its inclosure in 1773.[31] A farmhouse called Pyat's Barn is presumably named after the Pyatt

9 Above, Leek, par. intro. (par. govt.).
10 S.R.O., D. 699/1/1/1, p. 4.
11 Leek Par. Reg. passim.
12 Cath. Rec. Soc. xviii. 308; lvii. 150; L.J.R.O., B/V/1/33.
13 S.R.O., D. 3159/1/1, f. 144.
14 Ibid. D. 3159/3/1, entries for 2 Dec. 1708, 3 Nov. 1709; D. 3159/3/4/36.
15 Ibid. D. 4812/2.
16 Leek Wesleyan Methodist Circuit Yr. Bk. 1887, 44.
17 V.C.H. Staffs. i. 328. This article was written in 1991.
18 S.R.O., D. (W.) 1761/A/4/19; Eng. P.N. Elements, i. 248–9.
19 Staffs. Review Order, 1934, p. 67 and map 1 (copy in

S.R.O.).
20 Above, Horton, intro. (Rudyard Lake).
21 Geol. Surv. Map 1", drift, sheet 110 (1968 edn.); Soil Surv. of Eng. and Wales, sheet 3 (1983).
22 S.H.C. 1925, 159.   23 S.R.O., D. 1109/1, p. 87.
24 V.C.H. Staffs. i. 328; Census, 1911–31.
25 Below, manor; Rushton Spencer, intro.
26 S.H.C. 1911, 437; S.R.O., D. (W.) 1761/A/4/12.
27 Below, manor.
28 For the Earl's Way see above, Leek and Lowe, communications.
29 S.R.O., D. (W.) 1761/A/4/13.
30 S.H.C. 1911, 437.
31 Below, econ. hist. (agric.).

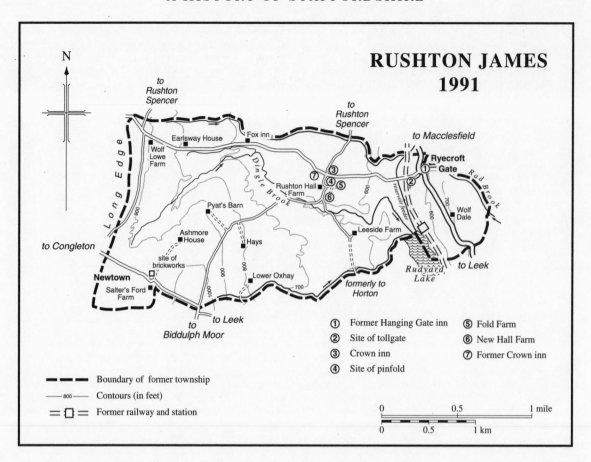

FIG. 40

or Pyott family recorded in the late 16th century.[32] Ashmore House to the south-west stands on the site of a house called Ashmoor Hay in 1688,[33] and there was a farmhouse at the Hays in 1756 and one at Lower Oxhay in 1768.[34] The waste was settled most densely at Newtown, so called by 1701. In 1783 there were several cottages, mainly on the south side of a road running between Leek and Congleton via Horton.[35] Salter's Ford Farm there possibly stands on a packhorse way.[36]

The Crown inn at the road junction north of Rushton Hall Farm existed by 1805. It replaced an earlier inn, also called the Crown, which stood to the south-west.[37] The Fox inn, further west along the Congleton road, was recorded as the Fox and Paw in 1749 and as the Fox in 1783.[38] There was an inn by 1841 at Ryecroft Gate. Known as the Hanging Gate by 1851, it was closed in 1972.[39]

In the early 14th century a cross called 'le cunstablecross' stood beside the Leek–Congleton road at the west end of Rushton

James, presumably where it was crossed by a road which runs along Long Edge.[40] The cross had gone by 1611.[41] The Congleton road was turnpiked in 1762;[42] a tollgate was set up at the Crown inn in 1805.[43] The road originally left the Leek–Macclesfield road in Rushton Spencer ¼ mile east of Ryecroft Gate. After the Macclesfield road was realigned in 1808,[44] the Congleton road left it at Ryecroft Gate itself, and a tollgate had been set up there by 1820.[45] The road was disturnpiked in 1876.[46] South of Rushton Hall Farm the road to Horton past Leeside Farm was stopped up on the Horton side of the boundary when the Cliffe Park estate there was created in the early 19th century.[47]

The North Staffordshire Railway Co.'s Churnet Valley line between Leek and Macclesfield, opened in 1849, ran through the east side of the township. A station was opened at the north end of Rudyard Lake in 1905, chiefly to give access to the company's newly laid-out golf course at Cliffe Park in Horton. At first called Rudyard Lake station, the name was changed to

32 S.H.C. xiv (1), 213; S.H.C. 1930, 97.
33 S.R.O., D. (W.) 1761/B/3/18.
34 Ibid. D. 3566/3/1.
35 Ibid. D. 1109/1, p. 3; W.S.L., M. 684.
36 V.C.H. Staffs. ii. 278–9.
37 S.R.O., D. 423/M/B/1, 13 May 1805; D. 1109/4, baptisms of 8 Nov. 1807, 13 Aug. 1809; D. (W.) 1535/6–7, no. 236.   38 Ibid. D. (W.) 1761/B/3/73; W.S.L., M. 684.
39 P.R.O., HO 107/1005; HO 107/2008; Bowyer and

Poole, Staffs. Moorlands, 21; local inf.
40 S.R.O., D. (W.) 1761/A/4/19.
41 P.R.O., E 134/9 Jas. I Hil./5, m. 4.
42 Above, Leek and Lowe, communications.
43 S.R.O., D. 423/M/B/1, 13 May 1805, 15 Mar. 1806.
44 Above, Rudyard, intro.
45 S.R.O., D. (W.) 1535/7.
46 Above, Leek and Lowe, communications.
47 Above, Horton, intro.

Cliffe Park *c.* 1925. It was closed for passengers in 1960 and for freight in 1961.[48]

Rushton association for the prosecution of felons, in existence in 1813, possibly served both Rushton James and Rushton Spencer.[49]

MANOR. Before the Conquest *RUSHTON*, which covered the later manors of Rushton James and Rushton Spencer, was held by Wulfgeat, possibly the landholder of that name with extensive interests in Cheshire. The king held it in 1086.[50] The overlordship passed to the earls of Chester, possibly in the late 11th century, and then to the Crown with the earldom of Chester in 1237.[51]

Ranulph, earl of Chester (1129–53), gave Rushton to Norman de Verdun of Alton, and in the early 13th century Nicholas de Verdun held Rushton with Longsdon and Ipstones of the earl of Chester.[52] In 1242–3 Nicholas's daughter and heir Rose (d. 1248), widow of Theobald Butler, held Rushton with Longsdon and half of Ipstones by service of providing a knight for the garrison of Chester castle for 40 days.[53]

By the early 13th century the northern part of Rushton became a separate manor, known later as Rushton Spencer.[54] The Verduns' overlordship was thereafter confined to the southern part, known later as *RUSHTON JAMES*, presumably after the Verdun's tenant there, James de Audley (d. 1272).[55] In 1273 Rushton James was held with other manors of John de Verdun as ½ knight's fee, and in 1283 on its own of Theobald, Lord Verdun, as ¹⁄₂₀ fee.[56] The overlord in 1308 was said to be Edmund, Baron Stafford; he was overlord of Horton, which was held by the same undertenant as Rushton James.[57] There are no further references to the overlordship.

The Audleys' intermediate lordship descended with their manor of Horton, and the lords of Horton still exacted suit of court from Rushton James in the late 18th century.[58]

In 1308 Richard of Rushton held what was called the hamlet of Rushton of the Audleys for a rent of 10s.[59] Richard is presumably identifiable as Richard 'le loverd', who in the early 14th century, as lord of Rushton, granted Rushton James to his nephew Henry of Bradshaw, in Longsdon.[60] Henry's heir was his son William, alive in 1372.[61] The later descent is unknown until 1490, when William Bradshaw sold lands and rents in Rushton James to William Rode of Congleton, in Astbury (Ches.). Rode

apparently believed that the sale included the manor, which was still held by Bradshaw in 1512 when Rode petitioned for it.[62] Rode died *c.* 1517[63] and was succeeded at Rushton James by his son William. William's son, another William, had succeeded by 1588 when he settled his lands on his son Ralph.[64] Ralph was alive in 1611, having settled the manor on his son William in 1609.[65] William was succeeded in 1673 by his son James, who was succeeded in 1689 or 1690 by his son Christopher.[66]

Christopher Rode, who lived at Eaton, in Astbury (Ches.), died in 1731,[67] his four sons having predeceased him.[68] Under his will his estates were settled in trust for his daughters, Isabella, wife of a Mr. Herryman, and Jane, a spinster. From 1739, however, manor courts were held in the name of Anna Maria Rode, the infant daughter of Christopher's eldest son, also Christopher.[69] Her claim to the estate was dismissed by Chancery in 1740, although manor courts continued in her name until 1748. That year, both Isabella and Jane having died without sons, Chancery decreed that the lord was Thomas Rode, son of William Rode, brother of Christopher Rode (d. 1731). In 1752 Thomas sold his Staffordshire and Cheshire estates to George Lee, a London goldsmith.[70]

Lee died in 1773,[71] leaving his estates to his sister's son-in-law Richard Ayton, who added Lee to his surname. In 1800 Richard and his son George agreed to sell their estates to Edmund Antrobus, a London banker.[72] Edmund appears to have been acting on behalf of his brother Philip Antrobus of Congleton, lord of Rushton James in 1805.[73] Philip died probably in 1816[74] and was succeeded by his brother Edmund, created a baronet in 1815. Sir Edmund had bought the neighbouring manor of Horton in 1804, and Rushton James descended with Horton.[75] Manorial rights were presumably extinguished when the lord sold all his freehold land in the township between 1917 and 1926.[76]

The medieval manor house probably stood on the site of Rushton Hall Farm. The lord's house was assessed for tax on six hearths in 1666 and was known as Rushton Hall by 1730.[77] The present farmhouse is of the late 17th century and has 19th-century alterations.

ECONOMIC HISTORY. AGRICULTURE. In 1086 Rushton, including what was later Rushton Spencer, had land for two ploughteams.[78]

48 B. Jeuda, *Memories of the N. Staffs. Railway* (Chester, n.d. [1986]), 30; R. Keys, *Churnet Valley Railway* (Hartington, 1974), 9, 36.   49 Below, Rushton Spencer, intro.
50 *V.C.H. Ches.* i. 324; *V.C.H. Staffs.* iv. 41 (giving Wulfgeat as Ulviet).   51 *S.H.C.* iv (1), 109; *V.C.H. Ches.* ii. 6.
52 *S.H.C.* iv (1), 109; *Staffs. Studies*, v. 2.
53 *Bk. of Fees*, ii. 970; *Complete Peerage*, xii (2), 246–7.
54 Below, Rushton Spencer, manor.
55 *S.H.C.* vi (1), 58–9; ibid. N.S. ix. 261.
56 Ibid. N.S. xi. 242, 247.   57 Ibid. 254–5.
58 Below, local govt.
59 *S.H.C.* N.S. xi. 255 (wrongly transcribing 'hamlet' as 'halimote': *Cal. Inq. p.m.* v, p. 28).
60 S.R.O., D. (W.) 1761/A/4/19.   61 *S.H.C.* xiii. 92–3.
62 S.R.O., D. (W.) 1761/A/4/1 and 40.
63 *S.H.C.* 1938, 43.
64 S.R.O., D. (W.) 1761/A/1/1; Sleigh, *Leek*, 85.

65 S.R.O., D. (W.) 1761/A/1/2A; P.R.O., E 134/9 Jas. I Hil./5, m. 5.
66 Sleigh, *Leek*, 85; L.J.R.O., B/C/11, Wm. Rhodes (1673); S.R.O., D. (W.) 1761/C/3.   67 S.R.O., D. 1109/1, p. 63.
68 Rest of para. based on ibid. D. (W.) 1909/B/1/10.
69 Ibid. D. (W.) 1535/Rushton James cts.
70 W. T. Prideaux, *List of Wardens of the Worshipful Company of Goldsmiths since 1688*, 13.
71 G. Ormerod, *Hist. of County Palatine and City of Chester* (1882), iii. 29.   72 S.R.O., D. (W.) 1909/B/1/3 and 10.
73 Ibid. D. (W.) 1909/D/1/1; Ormerod, *Hist. Ches.* iii. 563.   74 *Gent. Mag.* lxxxvi (1), 277.
75 Above, Horton, manor.
76 S.R.O., D. (W.) 1909/F/7/1; F/9/1; F/11; F/13/1 (sale partics. 1917, 1920, 1921, and 1926).
77 *S.H.C.* 1925, 159; S.R.O., D. (W.) 1761/A/1/22.
78 *V.C.H. Staffs.* iv. 41.

A HISTORY OF STAFFORDSHIRE

Selions recorded in Rushton James in 1617 presumably indicate open-field agriculture.[79] In 1643 the lord of the manor compensated those with rights on the common waste after he had inclosed part of it, and further inclosures were made by freeholders and cottagers. Some 134 a. had been inclosed in that way by 1753, when an abortive attempt was made to inclose what remained.[80] Inclosure eventually took place in 1773 under an Act of 1772. The waste then covered 544 a., principally in the south-west part of the township, with a smaller area east of Wolf Dale.[81] Before 1773 the lord of the manor owned 311 a. in Rushton James, about a third of the freehold land; after inclosure he held 614 a. The farms in 1783 were nearly all between 67 a. and 49 a., and there were several smallholdings under 21 a., notably at Newtown. The 153-a. Rushton Hall farm was the only large farm.[82]

From the 1740s two or three officials called burleymen or haywards were appointed by the manor court, probably annually; they were recorded until 1769. Each was paid 10s. a year in 1769, and more 'if that does not satisfy'.[83] Nearly every farm tenanted from Philip Antrobus in 1805 had a cowhouse, in all providing accommodation for over 120 cows.[84] The farming in 1988 was dairy and sheep.[85]

MILL. There may have been a mill near Rushton Hall Farm in the mid 18th century. A man was presented at the manor court in 1746 for pounding up water in that area,[86] and a farmhouse there was known as Rushton Mill in 1851.[87]

INDUSTRY. In 1692 the lord of the manor, Christopher Rode, licensed Thomas Endon to dig for limestone on the waste in Rushton James for a term of 23 years. During the first two years Endon was to be allowed to take 40 tons of stone a year to test its quality; if he continued to dig thereafter, he was to pay 4d. a ton and give Rode 30 tons a year free.[88] A penalty laid by the manor court in 1714 on all people who dug for limestone in the manor may have been intended to protect Endon's rights.[89] A similar licence was granted in 1776 by the lord, Richard Ayton Lee, to John Hancock and Richard Wincomb, both coalmasters. After a six-month period of investigation they were to be allowed to dig and burn limestone for a year without payment, thereafter paying 1s. a ton for 10 years. A minimum output of 1,000 tons a year was stipulated.[90]

Bricks were probably made in Rushton James in 1755 and 1756 when 12,500 were sold to various buyers.[91] A brick and tile maker was recorded in 1861, and a brick and pipe maker lived at Newtown in 1881.[92] In 1917 there was a brickyard at Newtown in a field on the north side of the Congleton road.[93]

LOCAL GOVERNMENT. Rushton James was subject to the Audleys' court at Horton, sending a frankpledge to the twice-yearly view by 1351.[94] It was still part of Horton manor in 1781.[95] In the earlier 1670s the lord of Rushton James, William Rode, stated that he held no courts of his own.[96] By 1689, however, his son James held small courts, which were still held in 1772.[97]

In 1574 the Horton manor court presented that the stocks at Rushton James were out of repair. A new pair was made in 1699; they were out of repair in 1732.[98] A pinfold was recorded in 1578.[99] In the later 1870s one stood east of Rushton Hall Farm.[1]

The township was part of the Leekfrith quarter of Leek parish, and in the 1660s its poor were relieved by the quarter's overseer. The township had its own overseer from 1713.[2] There was a poorhouse in 1837. That year the township became part of Leek poor-law union.[3]

CHURCH. From the 18th century and presumably earlier people from Rushton James attended St. Lawrence's church in Rushton Spencer.[4]

NONCONFORMITY. There was a Wesleyan Methodist society in Rushton James in 1833. It still existed in 1875.[5]

EDUCATION. A day school for 12 boys and girls was recorded in Rushton James in the earlier 1830s.[6] It may have been a dame school.

CHARITY FOR THE POOR. In 1725 Elizabeth Hulme, in fulfilment of the wishes of her father, Thomas Higginbotham of Rushton James, settled land at Woodhouse Green in Rushton Spencer on trustees, to produce an income of £13 10s. Most was to go to charities in Cheshire, but £4 was to be distributed in clothing to six poor people in Rushton James on 16 October (Thomas's burial day).[7] By 1788 Rushton James's share had increased to £6,

79 S.R.O., D. (W.) 1761/B/3/16.
80 Ibid. D. (W.) 1761/A/4/123; D. (W.) 1761/B/3/81, 83, and 90.
81 Ibid. D. (W.) 1535/9; 12 Geo. III, c. 24 (Priv. Act).
82 S.R.O., D. (W.) 1761/B/3/64–5; W.S.L., M. 684.
83 S.R.O., D. (W.) 1535/Rushton James cts., 1742 sqq.
84 Ibid. D. (W.) 1909/D/1/2.
85 Below, Rushton Spencer, econ. hist. (agric.).
86 S.R.O., D. (W.) 1761/B/3/76.
87 P.R.O., HO 107/2008.
88 S.R.O., D. (W.) 1761/B/3/59.
89 Ibid. D. (W.) 1535/Rushton James cts., 6 May 1714.
90 Ibid. D. (W.) 1761/B/3/60.
91 Ibid. D. (W.) 1909/K/2/6/4.
92 P.R.O., RG 9/1948; RG 11/2741.

93 S.R.O., D. (W.) 1909/F/7/1 (sale partics. 1917), lot 12A.　　94 Above, Horton, local govt.
95 S.R.O., D. (W.) 1490/44, m. 16.
96 Ibid. D. (W.) 1761/B/3/130–1.
97 Ibid. D. (W.) 1535/Rushton James cts.
98 Ibid. D. (W.) 1490/15, ct. of 11 Oct. 1574; D. (W.) 1490/41, m. 26d.; D. (W.) 1761/B/3/1.
99 Ibid. D. (W.) 1490/15, ct. of 6 Oct. 1578.
1 O.S. Map 6", Staffs. III. SE. (1888 edn.).
2 Above, Leek, par. intro. (par. govt.).
3 S.R.O., D. 699/1/1/1, p. 5.　　4 Ibid. D. 1109/1.
5 Ibid. D. 3155/1; D. 3156/1/1/4.
6 Educ. Enq. Abstract, 880.
7 S.R.O., D. (W.) 1761/B/3/128; 13th Rep. Com. Char. 390–1.

apparently paid by Charles Armett, the owner of Elizabeth Hulme's estate in Rushton James.[8] By the earlier 1820s the charity was again financed by the charge on the Woodhouse Green land, and the money was spent on gowns and cloaks.[9] In 1972 the income was being allowed to accumulate.[10]

RUSHTON SPENCER

RUSHTON SPENCER was formerly a township in Leek parish and later a civil parish 1,860 a. (753 ha.) in area.[11] It is pasture, with a village on the east side spread out along the Leek–Macclesfield road. The northern boundary with Cheshire is formed by the river Dane. Most of the western boundary, also with Cheshire, runs along the top of the Cloud, an outcrop of rock. The boundary on the Cloud was marked in the early 17th century by a monolith called the Stepmother Stone and by a mound called Mystylowe, possibly the name then used for the Neolithic chambered tomb now called the Bridestones and lying on the Cheshire side of the boundary.[12] The southern boundary with Rushton James followed streams, called Cress brook and Rad brook in the early 14th century.[13] In 1934 the civil parish was amalgamated with Rushton James to form Rushton civil parish, 3,250 a. (1,315 ha.) in area.[14] This article deals with the former township.

The highest point in the township is the Cloud, which rises to 1,126 ft. (343 m.). The name is derived from the Old English *clud*, meaning a rock.[15] From the Cloud the land falls sharply on the north into the valley of the Dane, where it lies at 390 ft. (119 m.) on the west side of the township at Lymford bridge and 472 ft. (144 m.) to the east at Hug bridge. A church stands on a bluff on the south-east side of the township at 600 ft. (183 m.), and beneath the bluff the land drops to 515 ft. (157 m.) in the valley of a brook which flows north to the Dane. Wall Hill Farm on a bluff on the east side of the valley also stands at 600 ft. The underlying rock is sandstone of the Millstone Grit series with an area of Bunter Pebble in the east. There is Boulder Clay over much of the rock, and the soil is mostly fine loam.[16] In 1962 the National Trust acquired 135 a. on the Cloud, of which 26 a. lie in Staffordshire.[17]

Twenty-seven people in Rushton Spencer were assessed for hearth tax in 1666.[18] In 1751 there were 132 people aged over 16 in the township.[19] The population in 1801 was 294, rising to 362 by 1811. It was 359 in 1821 and 358 in 1861. It then fluctuated and was 315 in 1901, rising to 333 by 1911 and 360 by 1921. It was 375 in 1931, the last time that Rushton Spencer's population was separately recorded.[20]

The name Rushton is Old English and means a settlement by rushes,[21] a reference to marsh land in the valley on the east side of the township. The suffix Spencer, recorded in the early 14th century,[22] is taken from the Despensers, lords of the manor. What was called Rushton Marsh in the mid 17th century[23] was probably a hamlet on the Leek–Macclesfield road in the area of the present village, where the oldest house is Hammerton House, of the late 17th or early 18th century. In the later 18th century a school was built in a side road to Heaton,[24] and the Royal Oak inn at the road junction existed by 1818.[25] There was a village post office by 1872.[26] Lane End Farm on the main road ¼ mile north of Hammerton House was so called in 1707.[27] By 1818 there was another inn, the Golden Lion, ¼ mile further north still.[28]

The medieval church was known in 1673 as 'the chapel in the wilderness', probably a reference to its solitary position.[29] Hall House Farm to the north was so called in 1600.[30] Wall Hill Farm in the north-east part of the township retains a timber-framed core of two bays of *c.* 1600, to which a wing was added in 1621[31] to provide a parlour.

There may have been a settlement in the Middle Ages in the south part of the township at Oulton Farm. Although the name has been found only from 1651 for a close, it is probably derived from words meaning an old farmstead (*ald tun*).[32] The nearby hamlet of Woodhouse Green probably existed by 1413, when there was mention of tenements at Wodehouse.[33] Two farmhouses there are each called Woodhouse Green Farm. That on the east side of the hamlet is partly of the early 17th century. The other, to the west, includes an early 18th-century wing added to an earlier house.

The site of Cloud House north-west of Woodhouse Green was probably occupied in 1451 by William Sutton of the Cloud; the Sutton family certainly owned the house in 1596.[34] The present house is dated 1612 and has a small 18th-century extension on the north. Raven's Clough to the

8 *Char. Dons.* 144–5, 1152–3; W.S.L. 25/6/46, abstract of title of Chas. Armett's estate.
9 *13th Rep. Com. Char.* 391–2.
10 Char. Com. file 501221.
11 *V.C.H. Staffs.* i. 328. This article was written in 1991.
12 P.R.O., E 134/9 Jas. I Hil./5, m. 4; *V.C.H. Ches.* i. 43.
13 Above, Rushton James, intro.
14 Staffs. Review Order, 1934, p. 67 and map 1 (copy in S.R.O.).
15 *Eng. P.N. Elements*, i. 101.
16 Geol. Surv. Map 1", drift, sheet 110 (1968 edn.); Soil Surv. of Eng. and Wales, sheet 3 (1983).
17 Inf. from National Trust, Mercia Regional Office.
18 *S.H.C.* 1925, 168–9.
19 S.R.O., D. 1109/1, p. 87.
20 *V.C.H. Staffs.* i. 328; *Census*, 1911–31.

21 *Eng. P.N. Elements*, ii. 85.
22 S.R.O., D. (W.) 1761/A/4/19.
23 *Leek Par. Reg.* 127.
24 Below, educ.
25 Parson and Bradshaw, *Staffs. Dir.* (1818), villages section, p. 17.
26 *P.O. Dir. Staffs.* (1872).
27 W.S.L. 25/3/46, deed of 17 July 1707.
28 Parson and Bradshaw, *Staffs. Dir.* (1818), villages section, p. 17.
29 L.J.R.O., B/V/6/Rushton, copy deed of 1 Dec. 1673.
30 W.S.L. 25/1/46, copy deed of 21 Jan. 1599/1600.
31 *T.N.S.F.C.* lxxxvi. 112.
32 S.R.O., D. (W.) 1761/A/4/151; *Eng. P.N. Elements*, i. 8; ii. 188.
33 S.R.O., D. (W.) 1761/A/4/24.
34 Ibid. D. (W.) 1761/A/4/29 and 149.

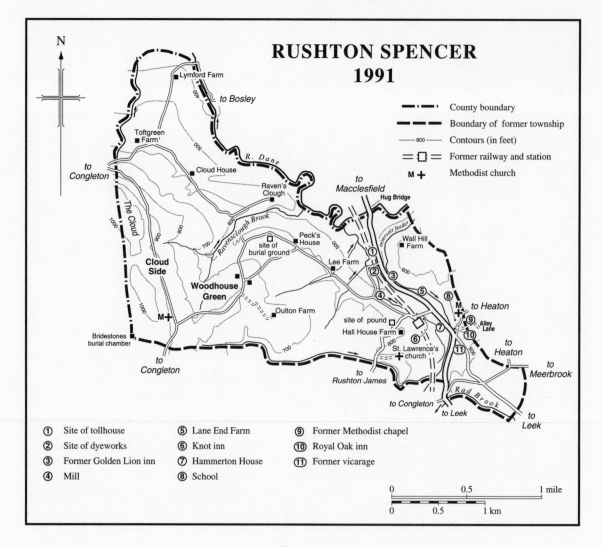

FIG. 41

east was so called by 1596.[35] North of Cloud House there was evidently a settlement at Lymford in 1333, when there was mention of Henry of Lymford.[36] Lymford House, recorded in 1596,[37] possibly stood on the site of the present Lymford Farm, which is of the 18th century. By the later 18th century there were houses at Toft green at the road junction north-west of Cloud House, and also a settlement called Cloud Side on the east side of the Cloud.[38]

Peck's House on the road descending into Rushton Marsh from Woodhouse Green was so called in 1662.[39] Lee Farm further down the road is of the early 18th century. An adjoining house called the Lee was built in 1793, and its south front was remodelled in 1852.[40] In 1848 there was an inn called the Hope and Anchor in the valley bottom. It was replaced in 1853 by the

Railway inn, built near the station opened in 1849.[41] It was known in 1991 as the Knot inn.

The Leek–Macclesfield road through the east side of the township crosses the Dane over Hug bridge, so called in the early 13th century and then giving its name to the manor.[42] Repaired c. 1550, the wooden bridge was destroyed by flood c. 1620 and replaced by a stone one.[43] The present bridge is of the 18th and early 19th century. The road was turnpiked in 1762.[44] In 1769 an order was made for tolls to be taken at the bridge, and there was probably a tollhouse nearby. A tollhouse was built ¼ mile south of the bridge in 1826.[45] The road formerly entered Rushton Spencer from Rudyard in the south-east. It was realigned in 1808[46] and thereafter entered the township in the south, crossing Rad brook and rejoining the former line at the Royal

35   Ibid. D. (W.) 1761/A/4/149.
36   S.H.C. x (1), 115.
37   S.R.O., D. (W.) 1761/A/4/149.
38   Above, fig. 2.   39   Leek Par. Reg. 147.
40   Deeds in possession of the owners, Mr. and Mrs. W. Oliver.
41   Staffs. Advertiser, 26 Feb. 1848, p. 4; 30 Apr. 1853, p. 1; below, this section [railway].

42   Below, manor.
43   V.C.H. Staffs. ii. 280; S.H.C. 1915, 147.
44   Above, Leek and Lowe, communications.
45   S.R.O., D. 706/1, 7 Apr. 1769; Sandon Rd. acct. bk. 1821–69, acct. 1826–7 (in possession of Mr. R. Stones of Malpas, Ches., 1994); J. Phillips and W. F. Hutchings, Map of County of Stafford (1832).
46   Above, Rudyard, intro.

Oak. The road was disturnpiked in 1878 and the tollhouse near Hug bridge was demolished.[47]

The Dane was also crossed at Lymford, where there was a bridge by the later 18th century.[48] The road there was turnpiked in 1770 as part of the route from Tunstall to Bosley, in Prestbury (Ches.). By 1861 there was a tollgate apparently between Toftgreen Farm and Lymford Farm.[49]

The North Staffordshire Railway Co.'s Churnet Valley line between Leek and Macclesfield, opened in 1849, ran through the east side of the township. From its opening there was a station in Rushton Spencer, enlarged in the mid 1890s. Closed for passengers in 1960 and for freight in 1961, the station later became a house.[50]

Rushton association for the prosecution of felons existed in 1813,[51] possibly serving both Rushton Spencer and Rushton James. A police officer lived near the railway station in 1851 and at Rushton Marsh from at least 1871 until the mid 1920s.[52] A police station was opened north of Hammerton House c. 1960, but it was no longer occupied by an officer in 1991.[53]

A wake was mentioned in the later 1760s. Before the change in the calendar in 1752 it was held probably on or near the feast of St. Lawrence (10 August), the patron saint of the church. In the later 19th century it was held on the Sunday nearest Old St. Lawrence's Day.[54] The custom of begging for soul cakes on All Souls' Day, noted in 1856, survived in 1914.[55] By 1867 well-dressing took place at a spring known variously as St. Helen's or St. Daniel's well, south of the vicarage house at Rushton Marsh. From 1897 the ceremony involved a May Queen. The well was last dressed in 1933.[56]

Rushton Friendly Society was established in 1859; by 1876, and probably earlier, it met at the Royal Oak.[57] Nothing further is known about it. A lodge of the Grand United Order of Oddfellows was established in 1897 and dissolved in 1953.[58] A Women's Institute was formed in 1937.[59]

MANOR. Originally the northern part of a manor called Rushton,[60] Rushton Spencer had emerged by the early 13th century as a separate manor called HUGBRIDGE. It was then held by Sir Hugh le Despenser of the earl of Chester for a chief rent of 1 lb. of pepper.[61] By 1251 the same rent was paid to Dieulacres abbey,[62] which probably acquired the overlordship when Earl Ranulph granted Leek manor to the abbey in 1232. Dieulacres still demanded the rent for Rushton Spencer manor at the Dissolution.[63]

Sir Hugh le Despenser was succeeded in 1238 by his son Sir Hugh (d. 1265). The latter's son Hugh, created earl of Winchester in 1322, was executed in 1326, and in 1327 the king granted *RUSHTON SPENCER* to Sir Roger Swynnerton.[64] Swynnerton also acquired the Despensers' share of Alstonefield manor.[65] Rushton Spencer descended with that share until 1446, when Richard Peshall lost it to his half-brother John Savage.[66] John was succeded in 1463 by his son John, knighted in 1471. Sir John was succeeded in 1495 by his grandson John Savage, knighted in 1497. That Sir John died in 1528 and was succeeded by his son, another Sir John, who died later the same year. The younger Sir John's heir was his son John, knighted in 1547.[67] Sir John died in 1596,[68] soon after he had conveyed Rushton Spencer to trustees in order to convert the manor's copyhold estates into freehold, and in 1599 the freeholders acknowledged his son, also Sir John, as lord.[69] By 1620, however, five of the freeholders had become joint lords of the manor.[70] There were still five joint lords in 1841, Francis Johnson of Cloud House, John Lockett of Hall House Farm, Thomas Yardley of Wall Hill Farm, Charles Harwar of Congleton (Ches.), and the devisees of John Webb of Cowley, in Gnosall.[71]

ECONOMIC HISTORY. AGRICULTURE. In 1086 Rushton, including what was later Rushton James, had land for two ploughteams.[72] In 1329 there were 4 freeholders in Rushton Spencer, together with 6 villeins, each holding a house and a bovate of land, and 13 tenants-at-will, each holding a house and 16 a.[73] There were 319 a. of common waste in the township in 1777, when it was inclosed under an Act of 1776. Most of the waste lay in the Rushton Marsh area.[74]

Of the 1,131 ha. of farmland returned for Rushton civil parish in 1988, grassland covered 1,036.3 ha. and there were 29 ha. of rough grazing. The farming was dairy and sheep, with 2,034 head of cattle and 1,443 sheep and lambs. There were 770 hens. Of the 51 farms returned, 47 were under 50 ha. in size and 4 between 50 and 99 ha. Woodland covered 61.4 ha.[75]

47 *Staffs. Advertiser*, 26 Oct. 1878, p. 8; above, Leek and Lowe, communications.   48 Above, fig. 2.
49 *S.H.C.* 4th ser. xiii. 109–10; P.R.O., RG 9/1948.
50 R. Keys, *Churnet Valley Railway* (Hartington, 1974), 9, 36; White, *Dir. Staffs.* (1851), 730; S.R.O., C/Rd/5/3.
51 *Macclesfield Courier*, 11 Sept. 1813, p. 1 (ref. supplied by Mr. A. W. Bednall of Macclesfield).
52 P.R.O., HO 107/2008; ibid. RG 10/2884; RG 11/2741 (s.v. Heaton); *Kelly's Dir. Staffs.* (1892; 1924).
53 Local inf.
54 S.R.O., D. 3566/3/1, chapelwarden's acct. 1766–7; S. W. Hutchinson, *Archdeaconry of Stoke-on-Trent* (1893), 98.
55 T. W. Norwood, *Acct. of the Ancient Chapel of Rushton* (Leek, 1856), 16; *T.N.S.F.C.* xlix. 117.
56 Plot, *Staffs.* 49; A. N. Bebington, *St. Lawrence Parish Church* (Rushton P.C.C., n.d. but 1988), 43.
57 *Rep. Chief Registrar of Friendly Socs. 1876, App. P*, H.C. 429-I, p. 406 (1877), lxxvii.
58 Inf. from the Order's head office, Manchester.
59 Inf. from Staffs. Federation of Women's Institutes.
60 Above, Rushton James, manor.
61 *Staffs. Studies*, v. 5.
62 *S.H.C.* iv (1), 244–5.   63 Sleigh, *Leek*, 18.
64 *Complete Peerage*, iv. 259–66; *S.H.C.* 1913, 22; *Cal. Pat.* 1327–30, 33.
65 Above, Alstonefield: Alstonefield, manors (Philippa Malbank's share).
66 *S.H.C.* N.S. iii. 171, 174–5, 177.
67 G. Ormerod, *Hist. of County Palatine and City of Chester* (1882), i. 712–16; W. A. Shaw, *Knights of Eng.* ii. 29, 60.   68 Ormerod, *Hist. Ches.* i. 716.
69 S.R.O., D. (W.) 1761/A/4/149; D. 3359/Condlyffe, abstract of title of Thos. Armett to one-fifth of Rushton Spencer manor, and draft appt. to stewardship 1828.
70 *S.H.C.* N.S. vii. 212; N.S. x (1), 66.
71 S.R.O., D. 3359/Condlyffe, Rushton Spencer cts. 19 Oct. 1841.   72 *V.C.H. Staffs.* iv. 41.
73 *S.H.C.* 1913, 22.
74 S.R.O., Q/RDc 39; 16 Geo. III, c. 24 (Priv. Act).
75 P.R.O., MAF 68/6128/81.

MILL. A mill was recorded in Rushton Spencer from 1329.[76] It probably stood on the site of the water mill which in 1775 stood on the east side of the township.[77] A mill there has been powered by electricity since the late 1950s, when the mill pond was filled in.[78]

TRADE AND INDUSTRY. In 1791 a pool on the west side of the Leek–Macclesfield road south of Lane End Farm was let to two Cheshire men, John Burgess of Wilmslow and Thomas Percival of Bosley, with licence to use the water to power a cotton mill, which they built the same year. It was run evidently by William Maskrey, a cotton manufacturer, dealer, and chapman in the later 1790s and certainly by Peter Goostry in 1805.[79] Goostry, who used the mill to supply cotton weft for the Manchester market, still worked it in 1818.[80] In 1821 the pool was acquired by a Leek silk manufacturer, Richard Gaunt.[81] He may also have acquired the mill, which was worked in 1831 by John Wild, a silk spinner. The mill was offered for sale that year.[82] Nothing further is known about it.

By 1827 there was a silk mill on a site down-stream from the corn mill.[83] In 1851 it was run by a dyer, James Cook, who in 1861 employed 30 people and was assisted by a relative, William Cook. William ran the mill in 1881, when he was described as a 'manufacturing chemist'.[84] The manufactory was run by James Cook & Co. in 1940 but was closed soon afterwards.[85]

Cotton spinners living near Lymford Farm in 1841, 1851, and 1861 presumably worked at the cotton mill in Bosley on the Cheshire side of the Dane.[86]

A nailer, Richard Mitchell, recorded in Rushton Spencer in 1834, was living at Cloud Side in 1841.[87] James Mitchell, a nail manufac-turer, lived at Cloud Side in 1871,[88] and Stephen Mitchell of Cloud Side was recorded as a nail maker between 1884 and 1908.[89]

There was a quarry at the southern end of Cloud Side in 1777.[90] Two stonemasons lived in that area in 1851, one of whom was still working as a mason in 1861.[91] In the mid 1870s there was a disused quarry at Cloud Side, one east of Peck's House, and one south of Rushton Marsh.[92]

LOCAL GOVERNMENT. By the earlier 14th century Rushton Spencer was a tithing of Leek manor and sent a frankpledge to the twice-yearly view. It was still part of the manor in 1820, when the court appointed a headborough and a pinner for the township.[93] The lords of Rushton Spencer held their own court by 1772. Recorded until 1841, the court was by then chiefly a social event.[94]

There was a pinfold near Hall House Farm in the late 1870s. It had apparently been removed by the late 1890s.[95]

The township was part of the Leekfrith quarter of Leek parish, and in the 1660s its poor were relieved by the quarter's overseer. The township had its own overseer from 1713.[96] It became part of Leek poor-law union in 1837.[97]

CHURCH. There was a church at Rushton Spencer in 1368, when the bishop licensed the inhabitants to have services in their chapel.[98] It had a silver-gilt chalice and a paten in 1553; another chalice, along with a bell, had been sold a few years earlier to raise money to repair Hug bridge.[99]

The chapel was dependent on the parish church at Leek until the 19th century, despite having developed claims to parochial status by the late 17th century. The curate then remitted to the vicar fees for burials and marriages but retained those for baptisms and churchings of women. Moreover, the inhabitants of Rushton chapelry did not pay Easter offerings to the vicar.[1] In 1742 the curate alleged that he was not required to assist the vicar and that when he had refused to do any parish duty the vicar had not pressed the matter.[2] In the early 19th century the inhabitants attempted to have the chapel declared independent and so to free themselves from paying fees and from contributing to the repair of Leek parish church.[3] It was probably as a result of the inhabitants' need to prepare their case that records were apparently removed from the chapel: at a visitation of 1841 the archdeacon of Stafford ordered Mr. Yardley, probably Thomas Yardley of Wall Hill Farm, 'to surrender the old parish chest'.[4] The chapelry, which by the 18th century included the townships of Heaton, Rushton James, and Rushton Spencer, became a parish in 1865, and the perpetual curacy was styled a vicarage from 1868.[5] The church retained its own vicar until

76 S.H.C. 1913, 22; S.R.O., D. (W.) 1761/A/4/149; W.S.L. 25/3/46, deed of 6 Apr. 1711.   77 Above, fig. 2.
78 Inf. from the owner, Mr. J. Cook.
79 S.R.O., Q/RDc 39; S.R.O., D. 3359/Cruso, deed of 11 Feb. 1797 (re Maskrey); D. 3359/Phillips, abstract of title to silk dyehouse.
80 J. Nightingale, Staffs. (Beauties of Eng. and Wales, xiii), 1051; Parson and Bradshaw, Staffs. Dir. (1818), p. cxxiii.   81 W.S.L. 25/6/46, deed of 26 Mar. 1821.
82 Macclesfield Courier & Herald, 19 Feb. 1831, p. 1 (ref. supplied by Mr. A. W. Bednall of Macclesfield).
83 S.R.O., D. 706/4, p. 17.
84 P.R.O., HO 107/2008; ibid. RG 9/1948; RG 11/2741; O.S. Map 6", Staffs. III. SE. (1888 edn.).
85 Kelly's Dir. Staffs. (1940); inf. from Mr. J. Cook of Rushton corn mill.
86 P.R.O., HO 107/1005; HO 107/2008; ibid. RG 9/1948; J. Phillips and W. F. Hutchings, Map of County of Stafford (1832); S. Bagshaw, Hist. of County of Chester (Sheffield, 1850), 195.

87 White, Dir. Staffs. (1834), 715; P.R.O., HO 107/1005.
88 P.R.O., HO 107/2008; ibid. RG 10/2884.
89 Kelly's Dir. Staffs. (1884; 1908).
90 S.R.O., Q/RDc 39.
91 P.R.O., HO 107/2008; ibid. RG 9/1948.
92 O.S. Map 6", Staffs. III. NE., SW., and SE. (1888 edns.).   93 Above, Leek and Lowe, local govt.
94 W.S.L. 490/34, pp. 6–12, 24; S.R.O., D. 3359/Condlyffe, Rushton Spencer cts.
95 O.S. Map 6", Staffs. III. SE. (1888, 1900 edns.).
96 Above, Leek, par. intro. (par. govt.).
97 S.R.O., D. 699/1/1/1, p. 4.
98 S.H.C. N.S. viii. 42–3.   99 S.H.C. 1915, 147.
1 L.J.R.O., B/V/6/Leek, terriers of 1698, 1705, 1735, 1744; B/V/6/Rushton, terrier of 1698.
2 S.R.O., D. (W.) 1761/B/3/110.
3 Ibid. D. 3566/3/1, acct. for 1806–7; White, Dir. Staffs. (1834), 713.   4 S.H.C. 4th ser. x. 98.
5 S.R.O., D. 1109/1; Lond. Gaz. 19 May 1865, p. 2634; Lich. Dioc. Ch. Cal. (1869).

1970. Since then it has been served by a priest-in-charge.[6]

The right to nominate a curate was claimed in 1673 by James Rode, the lord of Rushton James, who had endowed the living that year. The curate in 1718, Thomas Meakin, stated that he had been nominated by the vicar of Leek, but in 1742 his son and successor, William Meakin, claimed that both of them had been nominated by the trustees of land given to the chapel in 1660.[7] The vicar of Leek presented in 1750 and 1790, and in 1804 his nominee was appointed rather than a man nominated by the trustees. Thereafter the vicar's right to present went unchallenged.[8]

In 1604 the church was evidently served by a reader, who was paid only what the inhabitants gave him.[9] In 1660 Thomas Turnock, formerly of Heaton, vested a house and 10¼ a. in Heaton (later known as Toothill farm) in trustees 'for the encouragement of a preaching minister'. The estate was worth £9 10s. a year in 1698.[10] In 1673 James Rode, lord of Rushton James, gave the trustees 6 a. in Rushton James, in fulfilment of his father's wish, to provide an income for a resident preaching minister at Rushton; when there was no resident minister, the income was to remain with the Rode family. The land was worth £4 a year in 1698.[11] In 1725 Queen Anne's Bounty gave £200 to meet benefactions of £110 given by John Ward and £90 left by a Mrs. Baron. The money was used to buy the 22½-a. Flashcroft farm in Heaton; the income in the mid 1730s was £17 a year.[12] In 1810 the Bounty gave another £200 and in 1816 £1,000. The money was used in 1826 to buy 24 a. at Wormhill, in Tideswell (Derb.).[13] The living was worth £91 a year c. 1830, and the assistant who served the cure for the non-resident curate received a salary of £46 in 1835.[14] The Bounty gave £200 in 1854 to meet benefactions of £400 raised by subscription and £200 given by the Lichfield Diocesan Church Extension Society.[15] There was glebe of 82 a. in 1887, with an estimated rental of £109.[16] Grants of £100, £450, and £100 were made respectively in 1896, 1907, and 1912 by the Ecclesiastical Commissioners to meet benefactions.[17] A house for the curate was built at Rushton Marsh in 1854–5. It was sold in 1973.[18]

The perpetual curate appointed in 1750, Daniel Turner, was also curate at Meerbrook, Leekfrith, and at Flash in Quarnford, in Alstonefield. He lived at Meerbrook, where he died in 1789.[19] In the early 19th century Rushton chapel was served for the absentee curate, George Mounsey, by Turner's son James and later by James's son Daniel. Both were based at Meerbrook.[20] Mounsey died in 1852 and was succeeded as curate in 1853 by William Melland, the first curate to reside for over 100 years.[21] In 1830 there was one Sunday service, and Communion was celebrated four times a year.[22] In 1851 the average Sunday attendance was 50 when the service was held in the morning and 150 when held in the afternoon, besides Sunday school children.[23]

In the 18th and earlier 19th century the church had a society of psalm singers, who occupied a west gallery. They were accompanied, at least from the later 18th century, by a church band. The gallery's 18th-century benches bear the carved initials of members of the society. One set, with the date 1719, belong to Uriah Davenport (d. 1784), the compiler of a text book on the teaching of metrical psalms, *The Psalm-Singer's Pocket Companion* (1755). Davenport evidently had considerable influence in the chapelry: its financial support of both singers and instrumentalists was exceptional in Staffordshire.[24]

By will of 1764 John Thornely, curate of Bosley, in Prestbury (Ches.), arranged for the distribution of a bible every year in Rushton Spencer, evidently to a poor household. The gift was possibly still being made in 1850.[25] A distribution of bibles and prayer books was instituted in 1854 by the curate of Meerbrook, James Turner. The gift, presumably for the poor, was still recorded in 1940.[26]

There was a chapelwarden by 1597.[27] In 1757 a clerk for Rushton chapel was chosen jointly by the curate and the vestry. He had a salary of 10s. and was provided with clothes. In 1778 the vestry raised his salary to 30s. but withdrew the supply of clothes. Furthermore, he was forbidden to go 'begging' at Christmas or at any other time to increase his salary. It seems, however, that he continued to do so, causing the vestry from 1801 to allow him an extra £1 11s. 6d. a year in lieu of his 'Christmas box'.[28]

The church of *ST. LAWRENCE*, which is built of sandstone but retains medieval timber framing, has a chancel with a north chapel, a nave of three bays, undivided from the chancel, with a north aisle and a west gallery, a south porch, and a west vestry surmounted by a timber bell turret. The low nave has a partly renewed late-medieval crown-post roof, and the principal posts survive on its north side. The original walls may have been plank-filled. The frame of the

6 *Lich. Dioc. Dir.* (1970–1 and later edns.).
7 S.R.O., D. (W.) 1761/B/3/110 and 112; L.J.R.O., B/V/5/1718, Rushton. For the trustees see next para.
8 L.J.R.O., B/V/3/Rushton.   9 *S.H.C.* 1915, 149.
10 L.J.R.O., B/V/6/Rushton, undated memo. and terriers of 1698, 1705; S.R.O., D. 3566/2/2.
11 L.J.R.O., B/V/6/Rushton, copy deed of 1 Dec. 1673 and terrier of 1698.
12 Hodgson, *Bounty of Queen Anne*, pp. cxli, ccxcviii; L.J.R.O., B/V/6/Rushton, terriers of 1730, 1735, 1744.
13 Hodgson, *Bounty of Queen Anne*, p. ccxcviii; Sleigh, *Leek*, 138.   14 *Rep. Com. Eccl. Revenues*, 496–7.
15 Hodgson, *Bounty of Queen Anne*, suppl. p. lxviii.
16 *Return of Glebe Lands*, 66.
17 Lich. Dioc. Regy., Bp.'s Reg. U, p. 118; V, pp. 109, 349.

18 S.R.O., D. 3566/1/2, front endpaper; inf. from Lich. Dioc. Regy.
19 S.R.O., D. 1109/2, memo. of 8 June 1750; above, Leekfrith, church.
20 S.R.O., D. 3566/1/1 and 3; *S.H.C.* 4th ser. x. 97; above, Leekfrith, church.
21 S.R.O., D. 1109/4, front endpaper; Lich. Dioc. Regy., Bp.'s Reg. 31, p. 312.   22 *S.H.C.* 4th ser. x. 97.
23 P.R.O., HO 129/372/3/4.
24 *West Gallery* (Newsletter of West Gallery Music Assoc.), v (summer 1993), 7–13 (where the date 1758 on p. 7 should read 1755).
25 Bagshaw, *County of Chester*, 195–6.
26 *Kelly's Dir. Staffs.* (1884; 1940).
27 L.J.R.O., B/V/1/23.
28 S.R.O., D. 3566/3/1.

south doorway is of timber and has a flat ogee head.[29] The church was rebuilt in stone in the 17th century, and extended on the north side. The east wall of the chancel is dated 1690. The north chapel contains a 17th-century pew for the Trafford family of Swythamley, in Heaton. The chapel was formerly entered through a doorway, now blocked, in the east wall. The vestry doorway is dated 1748,[30] when it and the turret may have been added or rebuilt. The oak pulpit dates from the later 17th century, and a 17th-century communion table in the nave has the initials GS above the letter W, which possibly stands for 'warden'.

In 1830 the archdeacon of Stafford recommended that the church should be demolished and a new one built at Rushton Marsh. He was supported by 'some of the more respectable parishioners', and he repeated the recommendation in 1841.[31] It was decided, however, to repair the building. In 1842 dormer windows were set in the south roof and buttresses placed against the east wall, and in 1848 the south wall of the nave was rebuilt. In 1898 the box pews were replaced by open seats and the stone flagged floor by wooden blocks, while the pulpit was moved from the south-east to the north-east corner of the nave and the organ from the chancel to the place vacated by the pulpit.[32] An altar of carved oak was installed in 1923.[33]

The large stone font at the west end of the nave dates probably from the 13th century.[34] In 1991 the plate included a silver-gilt paten of 1706 given by Thomas Higginbotham in 1709 and a silver chalice bought, apparently by subscription, in 1727.[35] There is a bell dated 1686.[36] Royal arms of Queen Anne's reign hang on the north wall of the nave.

The registers date from 1700.[37]

The churchyard was extended in 1872, 1913, and 1942.[38]

NONCONFORMITY. Two popish recusants were returned in 1607, Anne, wife of Edward Sutton of Hall House, and their daughter Alice Eardley. Alice was returned with her husband John in 1616, when three other women, all labourers' wives, were also returned. Anne Sutton

was again returned in 1635, along with another woman, and Alice Eardley in 1641.[39]

Two Anabaptists, Thomas and William Goodfellow, who were recorded in Leek parish in 1665, were members of the Goodfellow family of Wall Hill Farm.[40] In 1699 the same or another Thomas Goodfellow registered a meeting place in Leek parish for protestant worship.[41] The place was probably the farmhouse on the east side of Woodhouse Green hamlet where Baptists held services from the later 17th century. By 1688 there was a Baptist burial ground north-east of Woodhouse Green; it was last used in 1780. Baptists continued to hold occasional services at Woodhouse Green Farm until 1828.[42]

Methodist services were held fortnightly on Sundays at Rushton in 1798, and in 1816 a Wesleyan Methodist chapel was opened in Alley Lane, just over the Heaton boundary.[43] By 1829 services were held there every Sunday.[44] In 1851 there was an afternoon attendance of 86, besides Sunday school children, and an evening attendance of 70.[45] The chapel was replaced in 1899 by a larger one, built of brick, on a site to the west in Rushton Spencer.[46] It was known in 1991 as Rushton Methodist church.

From 1821 another Wesleyan Methodist congregation met at what in 1851 was called Diglake Sunday school, near the Leek–Macclesfield road at Rushton Marsh. Services held there on Census Sunday 1851 were attended by 50 adults in the afternoon and 80 in the evening; a Sunday school had met in the morning.[47] Nothing further is known about the congregation.

Hugh Bourne, the founder of Primitive Methodism, preached at Cloud Side in 1811, and a Primitive Methodist chapel was opened there in 1815. Only the attendance of Sunday school children was recorded on Census Sunday 1851. The stone building was extended in brick in 1958 and was known as Cloud Methodist church in 1991.[48]

EDUCATION. There was a schoolmaster in the chapelry in 1631.[49] Seats at the west end of Rushton chapel were fitted for a school in 1770–1.[50]

A school was built by subscription at Rushton Marsh in 1772.[51] The first teacher may have been

29   Above, plates 15 and 19. For plans of the church see *Vernacular Architecture*, xiv. 31–4.
30   *T.N.S.F.C.* xvi. 19.
31   *S.H.C.* 4th ser. x. 97–8.
32   *Staffs. Advertiser*, 27 Aug. 1898, p. 7. A photograph of the church interior before 1898 is reproduced in Bebington, *St. Lawrence Parish Church*, 24.
33   L.J.R.O., B/C/12, Rushton Spencer.
34   *T.B.A.S.* lxviii. 17.
35   Ibid. lxxvii. 68–9, 71; S.R.O., D. 1109/1, p. 24.
36   C. Lynam, *Ch. Bells of County of Stafford* (1889), 56.
37   All but the most recent are in S.R.O., D. 1109.
38   Lich. Dioc. Regy., Bp.'s Reg. R, pp. 619, 653; V, pp. 428, 435–6; X, pp. 34, 67; inf. from Lich. Dioc. Regy.
39   *Staffs. Cath. Hist.* iv. 13; v. 14; xxii. 23; L.J.R.O., B/V/1/33. For the family relationship see S.R.O., D. 3359/Condlyffe, abstract of title of Thos. Armett to one-fifth of Rushton Spencer manor, and deeds of 21 Jan. 1599/1600 and 8 Jan. 1601/2.
40   L.J.R.O., B/C/11, Thos. Goodfellow (1662), mentioning his sons Thos. and Wm.; B/V/1/72, p. 17.

41   *S.H.C.* 4th ser. iii. 112.
42   *Trans. Congregational Hist. Soc.* iii. 6; A. G. Matthews, *Congregational Churches of Staffs.* (preface dated 1924), 82–3; J. M. Gwynne Owen, *Records of an Old Association* (Birmingham, 1905), 164–6.
43   Dyson, *Wesleyan Methodism*, 40; *S.H.C.* 4th ser. iii. 39; P.R.O., HO 129/372/3/2 (s.v. Heaton).
44   Leek Libr., Johnson scrapbk. i (2), D/13/15.
45   P.R.O., HO 129/372/3/2 (s.v. Heaton).
46   *Leek Wesleyan Methodist Circuit Yr. Bk. 1899*, 8–16.
47   P.R.O., HO 129/372/3/2 (s.v. Heaton). For Diglake see ibid. HO 107/2008; ibid. RG 9/1948.
48   H. B. Kendall, *Origin and Hist. of Primitive Methodist Church* (1905), i. 114, 123, 126, 172; *Hist. of Congleton*, ed. W. B. Stephens (Manchester, 1970), 252; P.R.O., HO 129/372/3/4.
49   L.J.R.O., B/V/1/51, f. 127.
50   S.R.O., D. 3566/3/1.
51   Plaque on school. A contemporary tablet has a Latin text, adapted from Ovid, *Ars Amatoria*, ii. 269–70, which may be translated as: 'Work at your books while you are young and strong/My children; time like water slips along.'

Uriah Davenport, who in 1773 lived at School House in Alley Lane, just over the Heaton boundary.[52] The master in 1794 was also the chapel clerk.[53] Between 40 and 50 children were taught at the school in 1818 and 35 in the earlier 1830s.[54] In 1834 the school received £3 from the rent of land adjoining the building; reduced to £2 by 1871, the rent ceased when the land was made into a school playground in the earlier 1890s.[55] The building was enlarged several times in the later 19th century.[56] An all-age school with 104 children on its books in 1930, it became a junior school c. 1940, senior children being transferred to Leek.[57] The school, which had taken controlled status by 1958,[58] was known as Rushton Church of England (Controlled) primary school in 1991.

By 1851 there were Sunday schools for the Anglicans, the two Wesleyan Methodist congregations, and the Primitive Methodists. The attendances on Census Sunday that year were 40 at the Church of England school, 36 at the Wesleyan Methodist school in Alley Lane, 46 at the Wesleyan Methodist school at Diglake, and 40 at the Primitive Methodist school at Cloud Side.[59]

CHARITIES FOR THE POOR. By will of 1744 Mary Sydebotham left the interest on £11 for distribution to poor widows in Rushton Spencer. At an unknown date Alice Yardley gave £12, the interest to be distributed in bread to the poor on the first Sunday of each month. In 1753 the combined capital of the two charities was laid out in the purchase of a cottage and 1½ a. in the township, which were let for 23s. a year. Out of that income 11s. was paid to the chapelwarden and the overseer of the poor a week before St. Thomas's day (21 December), presumably for distribution as a dole on that day; the remaining 12s. was paid to the same officers to buy a dozen loaves to be distributed once a month on a Sunday to poor churchgoers. In the later 1780s the income was £3. It had increased to £6 5s. by 1823. A third of the money was then given to poor widows, there being 8 recipients that year; the remainder was spent on the monthly distribution of loaves, for which there were usually 8 or 9 recipients.[60] Bread continued to be distributed until 1972. The property was sold in 1983, and the capital invested in the name of the Rushton Relief in Need charity, established by a Scheme of 1984. In 1993 £992 was spent on grants to needy people and on treats for the elderly.[61]

STANLEY

STANLEY was formerly a township in Leek parish 441 a. (178 ha.) in area[62] and later part of a civil parish which included Endon and Longsdon until 1894. That year a new civil parish called Endon and Stanley was formed, excluding Longsdon.[63] There is a small village on the west side of the township. The boundary with Endon on the north and east sides follows streams.[64] The boundary with Bagnall, in Stoke-upon-Trent, on the west also follows a stream, which was dammed in 1786 to form a canal reservoir called Stanley Pool.[65]

Most of the land lies between 500 and 600 ft. (152 and 182 m.). The underlying rock is sandstone of the Millstone Grit series. It is overlain by Boulder Clay, except in the west part of the township where there is alluvium. The soil is fine loam.[66]

Seven people in Stanley were assessed for hearth tax in 1666.[67] The population was 113 in 1821, 122 in 1841, and 108 in 1851.[68]

The Stanley family, recorded in the late 12th century,[69] probably took their name from an existing settlement. The name means a clearing in stony ground[70] and is probably a reference to the site of the present village. The oldest house there is Lower House Farm, of c. 1700 and probably on the site of the medieval manor house. The village grew up in the 19th century in connexion with flint mills. Rows of cottages were built in the 1860s, probably for mill workers, and one row contained a beerhouse called the Travellers Rest, a name still used in 1991 for an inn there. Two larger houses, Tudor House opposite the Travellers Rest and Spilsbury House at the west end of the village, were also built in the 1860s.[71] A post office was opened in the earlier 1880s.[72] Several detached and semi-detached houses were built in parts of the village between the two World Wars and from the 1960s.

Clough House on the township's eastern boundary was so called by 1602,[73] and there were houses in that area at the Acres by 1700,[74] Stanley Head by 1743,[75] and Newhouse by 1751.[76] From the early 1960s Stanley Head was let as a children's outdoor education centre to Stoke-on-Trent city council, which bought it in 1967. On the reorganization of local government in 1974 ownership was transferred to Staffordshire

52 S.R.O., D. 1109/3, baptism of 13 May 1773. Davenport is to be distinguished from his namesake the psalm singer.   53 Ibid. D. 1109/4, burial of 4 May 1794.
54 Educ. of Poor Digest, 862; Educ. Enq. Abstract, 880.
55 White, Dir. Staffs. (1834), 713; Kelly's Dir. Staffs. (1896); P.R.O., ED 7/109/261.
56 Lich. Dioc. Ch. Cal. (1860), 122; Kelly's Dir. Staffs. (1884; 1896; 1908).
57 S.R.O., CEQ/2/200/1.
58 Lich. Dioc. Dir. (1959).
59 P.R.O., HO 129/372/3/2 (s.v. Heaton) and 4.
60 13th Rep. Com. Char. 389–90; Char. Dons. 1152–3.
61 Char. Com. file 515569.
62 The acreage has been calculated by planimeter. This article was written in 1991.   63 Census, 1901.

64 S.R.O., D. 1176/A/11/12.
65 Below, this section.
66 Geol. Surv. Map 1", drift, sheet 123 (1924 edn.); Soil Surv. of Eng. and Wales, sheet 3 (1983).
67 S.H.C. 1925, 161.
68 V.C.H. Staffs. i. 327, which gives figures only for 1821–51.   69 Below, manor.
70 Eng. P.N. Elements, ii. 21, 144.
71 P.R.O., RG 10/2878; below, econ. hist.
72 Kelly's Dir. Staffs. (1884); O.S. Map 6", Staffs. XII. NE. (1900 edn.).
73 W.S.L. 132/18/47, deed of 10 Aug. 1654.
74 Ibid. 141/36.
75 S.R.O., D. 4302/1/1, p. 17.
76 Ibid. p. 30.

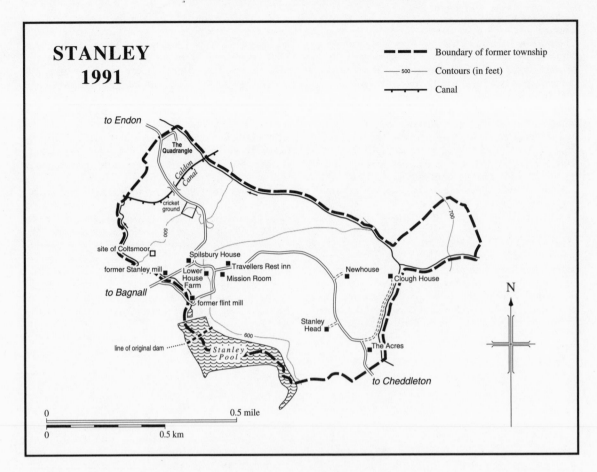

STANLEY
1991

- - - - Boundary of former township
——500—— Contours (in feet)
—•—•— Canal

to Endon

The Quadrangle

Caldon Canal

cricket ground

site of Coltsmoor

Spilsbury House

former Stanley mill

Travellers Rest inn

Lower House Farm

Mission Room

Newhouse

Clough House

to Bagnall

former flint mill

Stanley Head

line of original dam

Stanley Pool

600

The Acres

to Cheddleton

N

0   0.5 mile

0   0.5 km

FIG. 42

county council, which still ran the centre in 1991.[77]

By 1750 there was a house called Coltsmoor at Stanley Moss, low-lying ground in the north-west part of the township. The house still existed c. 1830.[78] Houses of the 1930s on the east side of the Endon road north of Stanley village are an extension of the residential development in Endon. An estate of 26 council houses there called the Quadrangle was built in the early 1950s.

Stanley Pool was constructed in 1786 as an 8-a. reservoir for the Caldon canal, which was opened through Stanley probably in 1778.[79] It was enlarged to 33 a. in 1840, when a new dam was built to the north.[80] Still a reservoir in 1991, it was also used for sailing and fishing.

MANOR. There was presumably an estate at STANLEY in the late 12th century when there was mention of Adam of Stanley.[81] There was certainly an estate there c. 1200 when Adam de

Audley, lord of Horton, gave Stanley to Adam of Stanley's son William. In 1272 the estate was held by Walter of Stanley, alive in 1282 but dead by 1285. His heir was his son William, who was succeeded probably in the early 1320s by his son John (d. c. 1330). John's heir was his son William, the forester of Wirral forest (Ches.). In 1359 the estate was styled a manor.[82] William was succeeded in 1360 by his son, another William (d. 1398). His heir was his son William, knighted c. 1400, who took part in the rebellion of Henry Percy in 1403 but was later pardoned. Sir William was succeeded in 1428 by his grandson William Stanley (d. 1466). William's son and heir, another William, knighted c. 1484, died in 1512 and was succeeded by his son William, knighted in 1513.[83] That Sir William, alive in 1528–9, was succeeded by his son William (d. 1546). William's heir was his brother Roland, knighted in 1553.[84] Sir Roland was succeeded in 1613 by his great-grandson William Stanley, and William in 1644 or 1645 by his son William. In 1652 William leased the manor, probably as part

77 Inf. from the warden, Mr. David James.
78 S.R.O., D. 4302/7/1/3; O.S. Map 1", LXXII. NW. (1834 edn.).
79 S.R.O., D. 1798/H.M. 37/19, Trent & Mersey Canal Co. balance sheet, June 1786, and rep. to proprietors, Sept. 1787; S.R.O., D. (W.) 1535/1, ff. 101 (no. 2181), 130 (no. 2391); D. (W.) 1909/E/9/1; P. Lead, Caldon Canal and Tramroads (Headington, 1990), 19. The identification ibid. 21, of Stanley Pool as the 17-a. reservoir constructed near Bagnall in 1787 is mistaken. That reservoir, in Bagnall SW.

of Stanley Pool, was defective and was soon abandoned.
80 Inf. from Mr. I. P. Selby of British Waterways (Pennine and Potteries Waterway), Marple, Ches.
81 Para. based on Trans. Hist. Soc. of Lancs. and Ches. cv. 47–61; Complete Peerage, xii (1), 243–8; G. Ormerod, Hist. of County Palatine and City of Chester (1882), ii. 411–16.
82 B.L. Add. Ch. 47942.
83 W. A. Shaw, Knights of Eng. ii. 42.
84 Ibid. 68.

of an arrangement which led to its sale to Thomas Fernihaugh in 1660.[85]

Fernihaugh was living at Stanley in 1666 but no longer by 1688, when his house there was bought by John Shaw, rector of Swettenham (Ches.).[86] Shaw was succeeded in 1715 by his son Richard, an Anglican clergyman who died unmarried in or shortly before 1754. In 1760, in accordance with Richard's wishes, the house, then known as Lower House, and 70 a. were settled on trustees to endow a charity for the poor of the township. The estate had been sold by 1963.[87] The present Lower House Farm is of c. 1700 and has an outbuilding dated 1776.

business, Corinthian Stone Ltd., established in 1990.[91]

A flint mill was built upstream from the corn mill, probably in the late 1770s.[92] Powered later by Stanley Pool, it still existed as a flint mill in 1835, but its site was submerged when the reservoir was extended in 1840. In 1835 there was another mill, worked as a flint, glaze, and colour mill, between the corn mill and the flint mill.[93] Still a flint mill in the late 1870s, it had been turned into a gelatine works by the late 1890s. The works was disused by the early 1920s, and the building was converted into a house.[94]

FIG. 43. STANLEY MILL

ECONOMIC HISTORY. There was a mill in Stanley in the earlier 16th and in the later 17th century.[88] It probably stood on the stream on west side of the village, north of the Bagnall road, where there was a corn mill in 1816.[89] In 1865 that mill was both a corn mill and a flint mill.[90] Stanley mill was rebuilt in 1887 as Hercules mills by Harrison & Son, who used it for grinding potters' materials, notably black manganese, until its closure c. 1970. In 1991 the mill and associated buildings were occupied by small commercial enterprises, including a stone-cutting

LOCAL GOVERNMENT. Stanley was subject to the Audleys' court at Horton, sending a frankpledge to the twice-yearly view by 1351.[95] It was still part of Horton manor in 1795.[96] Stocks in Stanley were mentioned in 1722 and 1731.[97]

The township was part of the Endon quarter of Leek parish, and in the 1660s its poor were relieved jointly with those of Endon and Longsdon by the quarter's overseer.[98] The poor were still relieved jointly in 1834, but separate assessments for each township were made by

85 John Rylands Univ. Libr. of Manchester, Ch. 1804–5; T.N.S.F.C. lxviii. 168.
86 S.H.C. 1925, 161; T.N.S.F.C. lxviii. 167–8.
87 A. L. Reade, Reades of Blackwood Hill (priv. print. 1906), 54 n. and pedigree XXIV; below, charity.
88 P.R.O., C 1/1273, no. 7; C 1/1507, no. 44; S.R.O., D. 1040/5/1, p. 162; Leek Par. Reg. 176, 220.
89 S.R.O., D. (W.) 1535/1, f. 110 (no. 2211); D. (W.) 1909/E/9/1.
90 Staffs. Advertiser, 6 May 1865, p. 8.
91 Date stone on mill; local inf.

92 13th Rep. Com. Char. 398.
93 S.R.O., D. (W.) 1535/1, ff.102 (no. 2182A), 110 (no. 2183A); D. (W.) 1909/E/9/1; Staffs. Advertiser, 19 Dec. 1835, p. 1.
94 O.S. Map 6", Staffs. XII. NE. (1888, 1900, 1925 edns.).
95 Above, Horton, local govt.
96 S.R.O., D. (W.) 1490/44, m. 20.
97 Ibid. D. (W.) 1490/39, m. 28d.; D. (W.) 1490/40, m. 23.
98 Above, Leek, par. intro. (par. govt.).

1750.[99] Stanley became part of Leek poor-law union in 1837.[1]

CHURCH. Stanley was part of Endon chapelry and later of Endon parish. By 1851 an evening service or lecture was occasionally held at Stanley, where a mission room was opened in the village in 1868.[2] The room was known as St. Agnes's mission by 1872.[3] Services were still held there in 1991.

NONCONFORMITY. Mary Dunnell, a Methodist preacher, took a service at Stanley in 1810. A society was formed for which the Primitive Methodists took responsibility, the Wesleyans having refused to accept it. It had been disbanded by 1814.[4]

EDUCATION. There was a dame school at Stanley in the earlier 1820s, and some children from Stanley were supported with charity money to attend school at Endon.[5]

CHARITY FOR THE POOR. In 1760 the 70-a. estate centred on Lower House Farm was settled on trustees in accordance with the wishes of the late owner, the Revd. Richard Shaw. The trustees, after repairing the farm buildings, were to use the profit for the benefit of poor householders in Stanley not in receipt of parish relief and in apprenticing poor children from Stanley. The income was £36 in the later 1780s. In the earlier 1820s, when the income was £73 10s., a weekly dole of 11s. 6d. was divided among four poor people and £13 10s. was used to support an apprentice. The trustees also paid £10 or £11 to the schoolmaster at Endon for teaching poor children from Stanley.[6] The estate had been sold by 1963 and the money invested. In 1994 a distribution of £78 was made to four needy people, together with £60 in Christmas gifts.[7]

TITTESWORTH

TITTESWORTH was formerly a township in Leek parish and later a civil parish.[8] The area was originally 1,659 a. (671 ha.). That was reduced by the transfer of a 9-a. detached portion at Blackshaw Moor north-east of the township to Leekfrith under the Divided Parishes Act, 1882, although at the same time a 1-a. detached portion of Leek and Lowe at Blackshaw Moor was added to Tittesworth.[9] In 1894 much of the south-west part of the township was transferred to Leek urban district, and the part of Blackshaw Moor which was a detached part of Leek and Lowe was added to Tittesworth; the area of Tittesworth was reduced to 1,514 a. (613 ha.).[10] In 1934 a detached portion of Bradnop, 53 a. in area and including part of Thorncliffe village, was added to Tittesworth, along with 433 a. from Onecote; at the same time 146 a. at Haregate in the south-west part of Tittesworth were transferred to Leek urban district. As a result of the changes the area of the civil parish was increased to 1,854 a. (750 ha.).[11] The present article covers the former township together with the added parts of Blackshaw Moor and Thorncliffe. For certain topics the more recent history of the parts of Tittesworth added to Leek urban district is treated in the article on Leek and Lowe.

The boundary of the township followed the river Churnet on the west and a tributary, Ball Haye brook, on the south-west. Cartledge brook, recorded as Easing brook in 1223,[12] formed the south-east boundary. The irregular boundary with Onecote on the east was probably the result of the division of pasture rights on Morridge. A tributary of the Churnet forms the north-east boundary of the part of Blackshaw Moor added in 1894. Tittesworth brook, a tributary of the Churnet, runs west through the middle of the former township. The ground reaches 1,298 ft. (395 m.) on Morridge on the eastern boundary, while what was formerly the south-west corner of the township lies at 515 ft. (160 m.) by the Churnet. The underlying rock is sandstone of the Millstone Grit series, and it is overlain by Boulder Clay at Blackshaw Moor and south of Thorncliffe. The soil is mostly fine loam over clay.[13]

In 1542 there were 10 tenants holding 10 houses in Tittesworth, two in Thorncliffe holding two houses, and two in Easing holding three houses.[14] Twenty-nine people in Tittesworth township were assessed for hearth tax in 1666.[15] In 1801 the population of the township was 274. It rose from 288 in 1821 to 447 in 1831 with the development of Ball Haye Green in the south-west part of the township as a suburb of Leek. The continued growth of that area accounts for the increase of the township's population to 606 in 1851, 1,227 in 1861, and 1,524 in 1891.[16] By 1901, after the boundary changes of 1894, the population of Tittesworth had shrunk to 121, including 9 people in the added part of Blackshaw Moor. It was 96 in 1911, 120 in 1921, and 157 in 1931. In 1951,

99 S.R.O., D. 4302/7/1/3; White, *Dir. Staffs.* (1834), 712.
1 S.R.O., D. 699/1/1/1, p. 4.
2 P.R.O., HO 129/372/1/4; *Staffs. Advertiser,* 28 Mar. 1868, p. 7.
3 *Lich. Dioc. Ch. Cal.* (1872), 171. For an interior view c. 1900 see F. Stubbs, *Endon* (Leek, 1994), facing p. 4.
4 *N.S.J.F.S.* ix. 67; H. B. Kendall, *Origin and Hist. of Primitive Methodist Church* (1905), i. 115–16, 118; J. Petty, *Hist. of Primitive Methodist Connexion* (1864), 38–9.
5 *13th Rep. Com. Char.* 399.
6 Ibid. 396–9; *Char. Dons.* 1152–3.

7 Char. Com. file 217340.
8 This article was written mainly in 1992.
9 *Census,* 1891.
10 Ibid. 1901.
11 Ibid. 1931, 1951; Staffs. Review Order, 1934, p. 63 and map 1 (copy in S.R.O.).
12 S.R.O., D. 5041, p. 129.
13 Geol. Surv. Map 1/50,000, drift, sheet 111 (1978 edn.); Soil Surv. of Eng. and Wales, sheet 3 (1983).
14 W.S.L., M. 540.   15 *S.H.C.* 1925, 170.
16 *V.C.H. Staffs.* i. 328; *Census,* 1891.

after the addition of the Thorncliffe part of Bradnop and the establishment of a Polish re-settlement camp at Blackshaw Moor, the population was 957. It was 444 in 1961, 333 in 1971, 298 in 1981, and 281 in 1991.[17] The Bradnop portion of Thorncliffe had a population of 46 in 1841, which had declined to 27 by 1891.[18]

The place-name Tittesworth is an Old English compound of a personal name, thought to be Tet, and the word for an enclosed settlement.[19] A local family took its name from the place by the beginning of the 13th century.[20] By the latter part of the century there were two main settlements, Upper Tittesworth mentioned in the 1250s and Lower Tittesworth mentioned in 1292.[21] In 1353 Upper Tittesworth lay on the north side of Tittesworth brook and extended from Thorncliffe on the east to the Churnet on the west; to the north-east a ditch separated its fields from 'the moor of Tittesworth', presumably Blackshaw Moor.[22] The farmhouse called Upper Tittesworth by the mid 19th century[23] dates from c. 1700. Lower Tittesworth lay to the north-west, with its fields adjoining those of Upper Tittesworth in 1353.[24] By the 1770s Lower Tittesworth was the name of a house with 180 a. attached.[25] It had been renamed Troutsdale Farm by 1859[26] and was rebuilt in the later 20th century.

Thorncliffe was an inhabited area by the 1230s.[27] It was at first spelled as 'Thorntileg' or variants, an Old English name meaning a clearing amid thorn trees.[28] By the end of the 16th century the present name was in use,[29] presumably reflecting the situation of the village on the south side of a deep ravine formed by Tittesworth brook and known in 1353 as 'le coppedlowesclogh'.[30] Ley Fields on the Morridge road north-east of the village is a house of 17th-century date. Underbank off the Blackshaw Moor road dates from the late 18th century but has an outbuilding which is probably of the 17th century. The building occupied as the Red Lion inn carries the date 1787; it was known as the Reform inn by 1851 and was renamed c. 1860.[31] A Primitive Methodist chapel was built in

1839.[32] A school was started in 1884, and an Anglican school-chapel was opened in 1887.[33]

Easing south of Thorncliffe was evidently inhabited by the early 1230s when there was a family of that name.[34] A house and land at Easing belonging to the family was mentioned in 1291.[35] Easing Farm, rebuilt evidently in 1910 after a fire, retains a doorway probably of the 17th century[36] and may be the successor of the house in Tittesworth where Thomas Mountford was assessed for tax on two hearths in 1666.[37] The Ashes, formerly known as Easing,[38] has a door-head carrying the initials ID:ED and a date which is probably 1642; John Dale was living at Easing in 1642 and was assessed for tax on three hearths in Tittesworth township in 1666.[39] Easing Moor Farm and Ankers Lane Farm existed by 1841,[40] and Easing Villa, offered for sale in 1867 with 16 a., was then described as newly erected.[41]

By the late 16th century there was settlement to the west on the edge of Leek moor near the southern boundary. Pool House stood there by 1596 and was described as at Leek Moorside in 1648. It was known variously as Leek Moorside and Pool House in the late 17th century, as the Edge in the 18th century, and as Leek Moorside again by 1821.[42] The present house appears to date from the 17th century. Edge-end further to the west was formerly timber framed but was remodelled in stone in the 17th century, with later additions in stone and brick.

The south-west part of the township remained rural until the 19th century. By 1246 Dieulacres abbey had established a grange at Fowker, later Fowlchurch. There was a farm at Haregate by the Dissolution and another at Ball Haye by 1565.[43] Horsecroft Gate, inhabited by 1639,[44] was presumably in the area of Horsecroft Farm, a 19th-century building on earlier foundations. Rose Bank farm, in existence in the earlier 18th century, was presumably south-west of Ball Haye in the area of Rose Bank Street, in existence by 1851.[45] By the later 1730s the area south of Ball Haye was the home of the Nall family; it was known as the Hole, presumably because of its position by Ball Haye brook with the ground

17 *Census*, 1901–91.
18 P.R.O., HO 107/1005; ibid. RG 12/2186. The figures include Underbank farm, formerly called Little Birches and Birchenbank, which was in the detached portion of Bradnop but was recorded separately from Thorncliffe.
19 *Eng. P.N. Elements*, ii. 273–5; inf. from Dr. Margaret Gelling.
20 *S.H.C.* iii (1), 93, 99; Sleigh, *Leek*, pl. II between pp. 16 and 17; above, Rudyard, manor.
21 *S.H.C.* vi (1), 205; *S.H.C.* 1911, 428.
22 B.L. Add. Ch. 46881.
23 P.R.O., HO 107/2008.
24 B.L. Add. Ch. 46881.
25 S.R.O., D. 538/C/13/8.
26 *Staffs. Advertiser*, 26 Nov. 1859, p. 8; 6 Oct. 1860, p. 8; W.S.L. 69/1/23; it was still called Lower Tittesworth on O.S. Map 6", Staffs. VIII. NW. (1888 edn., surv. 1878).
27 *S.H.C.* 1911, 423.
28 Ibid. 428; *Eng. P.N. Elements*, ii. 18–19, 204–5. The name is mistranscribed in *S.H.C.* N.S. ix. 319, as 'Yomberley' and variants.
29 Sleigh, *Leek*, 189; *S.H.C.* 1935, 320; D.R.O., D. 2375M/142/13.
30 B.L. Add. Ch. 46881.
31 P.R.O., HO 107/2008; ibid. RG 9/1946; *P.O. Dir.*

Staffs. (1860), 877.
32 Below, prot. nonconf.
33 Below, church; educ.
34 *S.H.C.* 1911, 423.
35 *S.H.C.* vi (1), 202.
36 Inf. from Mr. F. Gilman, the owner; date stone, probably of 1910, on doorway.
37 *S.H.C.* 1925, 170. The Mountfords held an estate at Easing by the earlier 16th cent. and were still there in the 1690s: *S.H.C.* xiii. 247; *S.H.C.* 1912, 77–8; *Leek Par. Reg.* 216; P.R.O., CP 25(2)/873/3 Wm. and Mary Mich. no. 10; W.S.L., S.MS. 411.
38 O.S. Map 6", Staffs. VIII. NE. (1887 edn.).
39 *Leek Par. Reg.* 44; *S.H.C.* 1925, 170. The Dales were at Easing by 1548 and were still there in the 1690s: *L. & P. Hen. VIII*, xxi (1), p. 779; *Leek Par. Reg.* 259; W.S.L., S.MS. 411.   40 P.R.O., HO 107/1005.
41 W.S.L., Sleigh scrapbk. ii, f. 60.
42 S.R.O., D. 3359/Toft-Chorley, deeds of 10 Aug. 1596, 30 Dec. 1648, 1 Oct. 1674, 3 Nov. 1675, 30 Sept. 1687, 30 Sept. 1724; W.S.L. 329/13/40; 329/18/40; L.J.R.O., B/C/11, Mary Chorley (1821). It was also known as Moorside in 1775: above, fig. 2.   43 Below, estates.
44 *Leek Par. Reg.* 29, 147.
45 W.S.L., S.MS. 243/i, pp. 76–7; P.R.O., HO 107/2008.

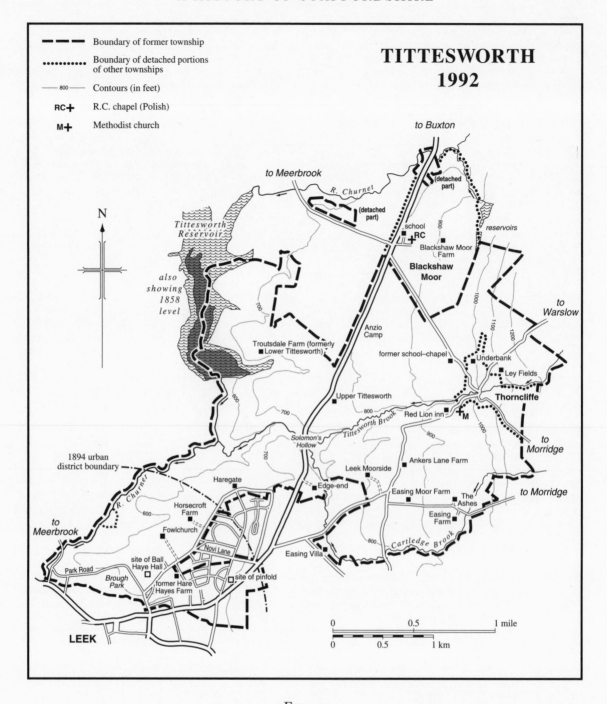

Boundary of former township
·········· Boundary of detached portions of other townships
— 800 — Contours (in feet)
RC✛ R.C. chapel (Polish)
M✛ Methodist church

TITTESWORTH
1992

FIG. 44

rising steeply on either side of the brook.[46] By 1775 there was settlement on the north side of the Buxton road in the area of what was known by the early 19th century as Youngs Road; both the road and a building at the end of it survived until the Abbottsville housing estate was laid out in the earlier 1920s.[47] Hare Hayes farm east of Ball Haye evidently existed by 1811; the house was also known as Ball Haye Cottage in 1838.[48] The present road from Leek town to Haregate via the area known as Ball Haye Green by 1820 was set out when the waste was enclosed in 1811,[49] but it is not known whether there was an earlier road. Another road was set out in 1811 running from the Buxton road to Ball Haye Green and was then known as Ball Haye Road; it was called Novi Lane by 1854.[50] In 1811 Abbotts Road (then known as Abbots Road and later as Abbotts Lane) running from the Buxton road to Novi Lane was described as an ancient

46 S.R.O., Q/RDc 65, plan II; S.R.O., D. 1040/5/14, 28 Feb. 1736/7, 15 Oct. 1740; L.J.R.O., B/C/11, Eliz. Nall (1737), John Nall (1741).
47 Above, fig. 2; S.R.O., Q/RDc 65, plan II; O.S. Map 6", Staffs. VIII. NW. (1925 and prov. edn.); above, Leek and Lowe, public services (housing).
48 S.R.O., Q/RDc 65, plan II; Leek Libr., Johnson scrapbk. ii (3), no. 11.
49 S.R.O., Q/RDc 65, award and plan II; C. and J. Greenwood, Map of County of Stafford (1820).
50 S.R.O., Q/RDc 65, award and plan II; Staffs. Advertiser, 20 May 1854, p. 8.

highway. Formerly it had probably continued north to Haregate, as it was made to do with the building of Queen's Drive after 1948.[51] From the 1820s the area developed as a suburb of Leek. Its core was at Ball Haye Green where the Leek Building Society erected 42 houses between 1824 and 1829. A number of houses were built in Park Road in the south-west corner in the mid 1850s. The Ball Haye Green suburb was further extended in the 20th century by the building of housing estates.[52]

In the 1250s there was mention of the moor between Scarpschaw and Blakeshaw.[53] Blackshaw Moor was an inhabited area by the 1640s. A pauper family was living at Blackshaw Moorside in 1640.[54] Richard Plant and his family were described as of Blackshaw Moor in 1644, and the Plants may have been settled there in the 16th century, three farms in Tittesworth being held by three members of the family in 1542.[55] The moor, which extended west into Leekfrith, was inclosed in 1811. There was probably a track running north-west across the moor from Thorncliffe before inclosure, but the present road between Thorncliffe and the Leek–Buxton road dates from the inclosure.[56] Blackshaw Moor farm existed by 1841.[57] A transit camp for anti-aircraft battalions from the United States of America was opened on the east side of the Buxton road in 1943.[58] In 1946 it was taken over by Polish troops from Italy, and other Polish troops arrived later. The camp continued as a Polish civilian settlement until 1964 when those remaining there were rehoused on a new estate ½ mile to the north.[59] The camp site was cleared in the early 1980s, and in 1983 Anzio Camp was opened there as a training camp for use by the regular army, territorials, and scouts.[60]

There was mention in 1353 of 'Stokkenbrugg' on Tittesworth brook,[61] perhaps a bridge carrying a road from Leek to Upper Tittesworth. The Leek–Buxton road, turnpiked in 1765, runs through the area. Before then the route from Leek to Buxton ran further west through Leekfrith, and it appears that all or most of the route through Tittesworth was a new road laid out by the turnpike trustees in 1765 and 1766.[62] It included a bridge over the brook in Edge End Hollow (later Solomon's Hollow).[63] In the 18th century a packhorse way ran over Blackshaw Moor, crossing the north-east boundary stream by a stone bridge.[64]

In 1858 the Staffordshire Potteries Water Works Co. (later the Staffordshire Potteries Water Board) dammed the Churnet in the north-west part of the township to create the 51-a. Tittesworth reservoir. In 1959 work was begun on an extension which increased the area to 189 a. and the capacity from 222 million gallons to 1,417 million. The work also included the provision of plant for treating effluent from the dyeworks at Upper Hulme, in Leekfrith. The enlarged reservoir was inaugurated by Princess Margaret in 1962.[65]

In 1802 Tittesworth was included in the area covered by the Leek association for the prosecution of felons.[66]

ESTATES. In 1565 Sir Ralph Bagnall, lord of Leek manor, granted a house called *BALL HAYE* with appurtenances in Leek and Lowe and in Tittesworth to Henry Davenport, who was already in possession.[67] Henry was succeeded in 1584 by his son Ralph, who was followed by his son Henry in 1597. Henry died in 1680 aged 93 and was succeeded by his grandson John Davenport. John was succeeded in 1726 by his son Henry, who was followed by his son John in 1753. John was succeeded in 1780 by his son, another John, who died childless in 1786. His heir was his nephew James, son of his sister Sarah and James Hulme of Tittesworth, born in 1772.[68]

John left half the income from the estate to his widow Hannah for life and a quarter to Lucy, daughter of Isaac Cope, a Leek surgeon and one of John's trustees. The remaining quarter was for the education of James, the heir, who had to assume his uncle's name and arms.[69] Hannah Davenport died in 1808.[70] In 1811 James granted Lucy Cope a rent charge of £75 a year for life as her share.[71] He seems to have continued to use the surname Hulme.

James rebuilt the house and in 1807 bought more land.[72] He was at Ball Haye in 1811, but for much of his life he lived elsewhere.[73] In 1818 Ball Haye and 80 a. were advertised for letting, and in 1819 James mortgaged the estate.[74] He died in 1848.[75]

In 1814 a Chancery suit was begun against James and his wife Elizabeth on behalf of six of her children by her first husband. James was even imprisoned for a time in 1828 for disobeying an order of the court. That year a settlement was reached vesting the estate in trustees who had

51 S.R.O., Q/RDc 65, award and plan II; S.R.O., D. 3283, sheets 9–10; *Staffs. Advertiser*, 20 May 1854, p. 8; O.S. Map 6″, Staffs. VIII. NW. (1900, 1925 edns.); above, Leek and Lowe, public services (housing).
52 Above, Leek and Lowe, general hist. (earlier 19th cent.; later 19th cent.; 20th cent.). 53 *S.H.C.* 1911, 428.
54 *Leek Par. Reg.* 34.
55 Ibid. 55; W.S.L., S.MS. 540.
56 S.R.O., Q/RDc 65; above, fig. 2.
57 P.R.O., HO 107/1005.
58 *Chronicles* (Dec. 1989), 13, 17.
59 Inf. from Mr. E. Lejman of Hanley; albums relating to Blackshaw Moor at the Polish Catholic Social Centre, Longton.
60 Leek Libr., newspaper cuttings 1983, p. 1.
61 B.L. Add. Ch. 46881.
62 Above, Leek and Lowe, communications.
63 S.R.O., D. 3359/Buxton Road order bk. 1765–1800,

pp. 21–2.
64 Above, Alstonefield: Heathylee, intro.
65 *Staffs. Advertiser*, 26 July 1879, p. 6; brochure for inauguration 4 July 1963.
66 Above, Leek and Lowe, public services (policing).
67 Sleigh, *Leek*, 86 n.
68 Ibid. 87; *Leek Par. Reg.* 202; for John Davenport (d.1786) see above, Leek and Lowe, econ. hist. (professions: lawyers).
69 *Olde Leeke*, i. 284. 70 Sleigh, *Leek*, 87.
71 S.R.O., D. 538/A/1/14.
72 Ibid. D. 538/A/1/72, pp. 9–15.
73 Ibid. D. 538/A/1/14; D. 538/A/1/72, pp. 9, 24; J. Nightingale, *Staffs.* (Beauties of Eng. and Wales, xiii), 1168 n.; Sleigh, *Leek*, 117.
74 *Staffs. Advertiser*, 28 Mar. 1818, p. 4; S.R.O., D. 538/A/1/72, p. 33.
75 *Olde Leeke*, i. 147.

FIG. 45. BALL HAYE

power to sell it.[76] It was unsuccessfully offered for sale in 1830 and 1840.[77] By 1851 the two families were again involved in Chancery proceedings, and new trustees were appointed in 1852. In 1853 they sold the house and 43 a. to Joshua and John Brough, James's nephews, John Birch, and Richard Hammersley.[78] Birch died in 1857, and Hammersley conveyed his quarter share to the Broughs in 1862. In 1873 John Brough conveyed his share to William Spooner Brough, Joshua's son, who in 1880 bought the Birch share. On his father's death in 1885 he succeeded to the remaining share.[79]

Meanwhile the house, which became known as Ball Haye Hall, was let. Work had to be carried out in the later 1850s to make it habitable.[80] Some of the rooms were occupied from 1854 to 1870 by successive tenants of the adjoining Ball Haye farm, and another part was let from 1860 to 1863 to Joseph Sykes, who kept a school there.[81] A. E. Worthington of Portland Mills took a lease of the hall in 1870. He died in 1873,

and his widow continued at the hall for a few years.[82] In 1880 it was unoccupied, but Worthington's son Ernest was there in 1881.[83] John Hall, a partner in the firm of J. and J. Brough, Nicholson & Co., took a lease in 1882 and remained at the hall until his death in 1930.[84]

W. S. Brough died unmarried in 1917, and the estate passed to his nephew, H. H. Brindley.[85] In 1931 Brindley sold the hall and 27 a. to the trustees of the Leek Memorial Cottage Hospital, whose plans for a new hospital in the grounds of the hall were suspended on the outbreak of the Second World War. From 1946 the trustees allowed the hall to be used as a Polish club.[86] It was later converted into flats. It finally became derelict and was demolished in 1972.[87]

In 1666 Henry Davenport was assessed for tax on three hearths.[88] The house as rebuilt by James Hulme was a three-storeyed brick building faced with stone. The entrance front was of seven bays and had a hood porch on steps.[89] The stone is said to have been taken

76 S.R.O., D. 538/A/1/73, pp. 5 sqq.
77 *Staffs. Advertiser*, 3 Apr. 1830, p. 1; Miller, *Leek*, 110; S.R.O., D. 1176/A/2/6(i); for an attempted sale in 1826 see *Staffs. Advertiser*, 2 Dec. 1826, p. 1.
78 S.R.O., D. 538/A/1/80; Sleigh, *Leek*, 87.
79 S.R.O., D. 538/A/1/80 and 85.
80 Ibid. D. 538/B/2/1, Field to Brough, 6 Feb. 1858, and Sugden to Brough, 29 June 1860; ibid. Ball Haye estate acct. bk. 1853–9, 8 Feb. 1855.
81 Above, Leek and Lowe, educ. (private schs.).
82 S.R.O., D. 538/B/2/1, Ball Haye rent bk. 1851–78; P.R.O., RG 10/2880; P. W. L. Adams, *Hist. of Adams Family of N. Staffs.* (Tunstall, priv. print., foreword dated 1930), 372; *P.O. Dir. Staffs.* (1876).

83 *Kelly's Dir. Staffs.* (1880); P.R.O., RG 11/2738.
84 S.R.O., D. 538/B/2/1, Hall to Brough, 13 Feb. 1882; *Kelly's Dir. Staffs.* (1884; 1928); Lovenbury, 'A Certain Group of Men' (Leek, 1990), 14.
85 Lovenbury, 'A Certain Group of Men', 4, 18. For Brough's gift of 10½ a. for a public park see above, Leek and Lowe, social and cultural activities (parks).
86 S.R.O., D. 3359, papers relating to Leek Memorial Cottage Hospital.
87 *Evening Sentinel*, 15 June 1971; Pevsner, *Staffs.* 172; L. Porter, *Staffs. Moorlands* (Ashbourne, 1983), no. 40.
88 *S.H.C.* 1925, 172.
89 Min. of Town and Country Planning, *Leek U.D.: prov. list of buildings* (1948), 2.

from the bed of Back brook at Upper Hulme, in Leekfrith.[90] James Hulme also laid out a lawn, plantations, and pleasure grounds and created a large fish pool.[91]

By 1246 Dieulacres abbey had established a grange at *FOWLCHURCH*, then called Fowker.[92] In 1552 what was called Fowchers grange was granted by the Crown to Sir Ralph Bagnall with most of the abbey's property.[93] His son Sir Henry sold it in 1597 to John Rothwell, a Leek mercer.[94] On Rothwell's death in 1623 the grange passed to his great-nephew John Hulme, son of John Hulme of New Grange in Leekfrith.[95] The younger John Hulme died in 1636, and in 1648 his executors sold what was called Fouchers House to the tenant, Thomas Washington,[96] whose family appear to have lived there at least since the beginning of the 16th century.[97] Thomas died in 1661, leaving half the Fowlchurch estate to his wife Margery and half, with the reversion of Margery's share, to their daughter Ellen, wife of William Stonhewer (or Stonyer).[98] Margery was presumably the Widow Washington who was assessed for tax on two hearths in Tittesworth in 1666; she died in 1686.[99] In 1694 Ellen Stonhewer, then a widow, was living at what was called Fowkers or Fowker Grange, and she died in 1699, with her son Thomas apparently her heir.[1] The name Fowchurch was coming into use by the later 1630s, and Foulchurch was used in 1677.[2]

By 1749 Fowlchurch was owned by Joshua Stonhewer of Leek, who died that year leaving it to his grandson William Stonhewer Hall.[3] William died in 1772.[4] The estate passed to his wife Catherine, but by 1791 it was owned by his nephew, also W. S. Hall. It was bought in 1799 by William Challinor, of Pickwood in Leek and Lowe, another estate left by Joshua Stonhewer to his grandson in 1749.[5] Challinor died in 1800 with his son William as his heir. In 1835 the 35-a. farm was sold to John Brough, who conveyed it to his son Joshua in 1843. Fowlchurch then descended with the Ball Haye estate, and Joshua's son William lived there in the later 1870s.[6] In 1918 it was sold to the tenant, T. H. Sillito, from whom it was bought in 1969 by Leek urban district council. It passed in 1974 to Staffordshire Moorlands district council. The house was sold to the tenants, Mr. and Mrs. J. H. Hine, in 1989.

The house appears to date from *c.* 1700, but the front was remodelled in 1849.[7]

A house in Tittesworth called the *HAREGATE* and land belonging to it were owned by Dieulacres abbey and passed to Sir Ralph Bagnall in 1552.[8] In 1565 he sold the estate to Thomas Wardle.[9] Wardle was living there in 1594, but his son John had succeeded him by 1616.[10] In 1620 John sold Haregate to Ralph Bayly of Bradnop, but Widow Wardle, probably John's wife Elizabeth, was living there at the time of her death in 1634.[11] By 1657 Ralph had been succeeded by Thomas Bayly of Bradnop, evidently his son, who sold Haregate in 1679 to Samuel Bromley of Mixon Hay, in Onecote.[12] Samuel was still living at Mixon Hay in 1701 but had moved to Haregate by 1713.[13]

In 1720 he sold Haregate to Joshua Toft, a Leek button merchant who was living there by 1724.[14] Haregate was also the home of his elder brother John, a Quaker like Joshua.[15] Some of Prince Charles Edward's troops were given a meal at Haregate in 1745, having first been made to leave their arms outside, and John Toft was given a receipt for hay and oats for the horses.[16] On Joshua's death in 1769 Haregate passed to his daughter Mary, widow of Charles Chorley.[17] She died in 1821, evidently at Haregate.[18] The estate was divided among her two surviving sons, Edwood Chorley of Doncaster (Yorks. W.R.) and Toft Chorley of Leek, and two of her grandchildren, Joshua Chorley of Manchester and Sarah Rawlinson of Haregate. In 1821 Joshua Chorley conveyed his share to his uncle Toft.[19] Haregate, however, had evidently passed to Joshua by the time of his death in 1837, when he was living there. His heir was his brother Edwood, a Manchester merchant, who was living at Haregate in 1851 and died childless in 1853.[20] Toft's heir was evidently his sister Elizabeth, wife of Tobias Atkinson. She died a widow in 1867, and her heir was her daughter Susannah, wife of Frank Atkinson Argles.[21]

In 1861 and 1871 Haregate was occupied by a farm bailiff, but Argles lived there on occasion

90   Sleigh, *Leek*, 86 n. (calling the brook by its other name, Dane brook).   91   S.R.O., D. 538/A/1/72, pp. 27, 29.
92   Lambeth Palace Libr., Papal Docs. 40.
93   *S.H.C.* N.S. ix. 140–1; *S.H.C.* 1938, 174.
94   S.R.O., D. 3359/Toft-Chorley, deed of 14 Jan. 1596/7.
95   Ibid. deed of 19 Aug. 1619.
96   Ibid. deed of 28 Mar. 1648; *Leek Par. Reg.* 14.
97   S.R.O. 4974/ADD 2; D. 3359/Toft-Chorley, deeds of 14 Jan. 1596/7 and 19 Aug. 1619; W.S.L., M. 540; *Leek Par. Reg.* 12, 53; for other tenants in the 1530s and 1540s see *S.H.C.* N.S. ix. 141–2; *S.H.C.* 1938, 174–5.
98   L.J.R.O., B/C/11, Thos. Washington (1661).
99   Ibid. Margery Washington (1686); *S.H.C.* 1925, 170.
1   S.R.O., D. 538/A/1/40; L.J.R.O., B/C/11, Ellen Stonehewer (1698/9).
2   *Leek Par. Reg.* 20, 27, 34, 42, 53; S.R.O. 3508/A/1/4.
3   L.J.R.O., B/C/11, Joshua Stonhewer (1749).
4   Rest of para. based on inf. provided by Miss M. F. Cleverdon from Fowlchurch deeds in possession of Staffs. Moorlands dist. council; for the Broughs and the Challinors see above, Leek and Lowe, econ. hist. (trade and ind.: silk, later 19th cent.; professions: lawyers).
5   L.J.R.O., B/C/11, Joshua Stonhewer (1749).
6   *T.N.S.F.C.* 1878, 29; *Kelly's Dir. Staffs.* (1880).

7   Date stone on front.
8   W.S.L., M. 540; above, Leek and Lowe, manors.
9   S.R.O., D. 3359/Toft-Chorley, deeds of 25 Apr. 1565, 20 Jan. 1568/9.
10   Ibid. deeds of 14 Jan. 1593/4, 28 Dec. 1616, 8 Jan. 1616/17.
11   Ibid. deed of 1 Nov. 1620; *S.H.C.* N.S. vii. 226; *Leek Par. Reg.* 1.
12   S.R.O., D. 3359/Toft-Chorley, deeds of 30 Dec. 1648, 16 Mar. 1656/7, 12 June 1679.
13   Ibid. deeds of 16 May 1701, 30 May 1713.
14   Ibid. deeds of 4 May 1720, 30 Sept. 1724.
15   Ibid. D. 3159/1/2, 28 June 1768, 3 July 1770; D. 3159/3/3, 1726; W.S.L. 329/15/40; Friends' House Libr., London, Dict. of Quaker Biog. s.vv. Toft, John, Joshua.
16   Sleigh, *Leek*, 203, 205, 206 n.
17   W.S.L. 329/13/40; 329/15/40; 329/16/40; S.R.O., D. 3159/1/2, 3 July 1770; Sleigh, *Leek*, 115.
18   S.R.O., D. 3359/Toft-Chorley, deed of 7 Aug. 1821; L.J.R.O., B/C/11, Mary Chorley (1821).
19   S.R.O., D. 3359/Toft-Chorley, deeds of 7 Aug. 1821, 23 Jan. 1822; Sleigh, *Leek*, 115.
20   W.S.L. 329/24/40; Sleigh, *Leek*, 115; White, *Dir. Staffs.* (1851), 734.   21   Sleigh, *Leek*, 115.

in the 1870s.[22] Thereafter the house was let. In 1880 and 1881 it was occupied by W. E. Challinor.[23] Ernest Worthington moved to Haregate from Ball Haye Hall in the early 1880s and remained there until his death in 1896.[24] Frank Argles died in 1885 and his widow in 1895, and their son Thomas was living at Haregate by 1900.[25] He moved to his estate in Westmorland c. 1916, but it was his custom to spend a week or two at Haregate every summer. He died in 1923, and Haregate passed to his first cousin, R. M. Argles.[26] In 1948 the house and 78 a. were acquired by Leek urban district council. The house was converted into three dwellings, and a council estate was laid out on the land.[27]

The main range of the house dates from the 17th century or earlier.[28] Built of ashlar, it consists of one storey with attics. A parlour block of red brick was added at the east end in the 18th century. Of two storeys with attics, it was re-modelled in the 19th century but retains some original interiors. At the back of the main range is a low two-storeyed service wing of the 18th and early 19th century. A group of red-brick farm buildings stands to the west of the house.

ECONOMIC HISTORY. Tittesworth was part of Leek manor, and in the mid 13th century the services owed by tenants there to the abbot of Dieulacres as lord of Leek manor included ploughing, reaping, and payment of a rent of chickens.[29] At the Dissolution all 15 farms in Tittesworth, Thorncliffe, and Easing were held by rent, two capons worth 6d., one day's plough-ing worth 3d., and one day's reaping worth 3d.[30] Tenants appear to have owed suit of mill at Hulme mill at Upper Hulme, in Leekfrith.[31]

The abbey's grange at Fowlchurch, established by 1246,[32] consisted in 1291 of 2 carucates and meadow.[33] At the end of the Middle Ages the grange was used for cattle farming. There were 18 cows there in 1490, 15 with a bull in 1501, 17 with a bull in 1502, and 13 in 1508.[34]

Each of the vills of Upper and Lower Tittes-worth had its own fields in the mid 14th century.[35] Those of Upper Tittesworth may have survived into the 18th century: in 1728 a farm at Thorncliffe included a field called Town field and parcels in the Middle field and the Lower field.[36] Oats were grown at Fowlchurch in the mid 16th century.[37] In 1868 the land at Thorncliffe was used mainly for pasture, but a few oats were grown.[38]

There was a tithe barn at Fowlchurch grange at the Dissolution.[39]

In 1811 the remaining common waste was inclosed under an Act of 1805.[40]

Of the 621.6 ha. of farmland returned for the civil parish in 1988, grassland covered 541.4 ha. and there were 55 a. of rough grazing. The farming was dairy and sheep, with 903 head of cattle and 1,677 sheep and lambs. There were also 1,100 pigs, with one farm devoted to pigs and poultry. Of the 16 farms returned, 12 were under 50 ha. in size, 3 were between 50 and 99 ha., and 1 was between 100 and 199 ha. Wood-land covered 20.6 ha.[41]

In 1563 and 1565 the Haregate estate included an iron forge by the Churnet.[42] Quarrying on the same estate was indicated by land there in 1821 called Quarry Plantation.[43] In 1823 there was mention of Tittesworth stone quarry, which was perhaps the quarry near the Buxton road south-east of Haregate in the late 1890s.[44] There was quarrying at Edge-end farm in 1749 and at Thorn-cliffe in 1860 and 1885, probably on the east side of the road to Blackshaw Moor.[45]

LOCAL GOVERNMENT. By the earlier 14th century Tittesworth was a tithing of Leek manor and sent a frankpledge to the twice-yearly view. It was still regarded as a part of the manor in 1827.[46]

The township was part of the Leekfrith quarter of Leek parish, and in the 1660s its poor were relieved by the quarter's overseer. From 1713 it had its own overseer of the poor, with the office rotating among 14 tenements.[47] It became part of Leek poor-law union in 1837.[48] By the early 1870s a Tittesworth vestry was meeting at the Red Lion in Thorncliffe. On the occasion of the election of an assistant overseer in 1872 the attendance was so large that the meeting had to be held in the Primitive Methodist chapel.[49]

There was a pinfold in Abbotts Road in the south-west part of the township by 1857.[50] The Leek improvement commissioners agreed to its removal in 1872 and accepted an offer of £5 for the materials in 1873.[51]

[22] P.R.O., RG 9/1946; RG 10/2880; *P.O. Dir. Staffs.* (1872; 1876).
[23] *Kelly's Dir. Staffs.* (1880); P.R.O., RG 11/2738.
[24] *Kelly's Dir. Staffs.* (1884; 1896); above, Leek and Lowe, econ. hist. (trade and ind.: silk).
[25] Burke, *Land. Gent.* (1952), 54; *Kelly's Dir. Staffs.* (1900).
[26] *S.H.C.* 1915, p. v; 1916, list of members; *Staffs. Advertiser*, 28 July 1923, p. 6; Burke, *Land. Gent.* (1952), 54.
[27] Above, Leek and Lowe, public services (housing).
[28] It has not been possible to gain admission to that part of the house in order to make a detailed survey.
[29] *S.H.C.* N.S. ix. 319.
[30] W.S.L., M. 540.
[31] D.R.O., D. 2375M/142/13.
[32] Above, estates.
[33] *Tax. Eccl.* (Rec. Com.), 252.
[34] S.R.O. 4974/ADD 2.
[35] B.L. Add. Ch. 46881.
[36] W.S.L., S.MS. 243/i, p. 78.
[37] *Cal. Pat.* 1558–60, 309.

[38] *P.O. Dir. Staffs.* (1868).
[39] P.R.O., SC 6/Hen. VIII/3353, m. 34; S.R.O., D. 3359/Toft-Chorley, deed of 14 Jan. 1596/7.
[40] S.R.O., Q/RDc 65; 45 Geo. III, c. 96 (Local and Personal). [41] P.R.O., MAF 68/6128/75.
[42] S.R.O., D. 3359/Toft-Chorley, deeds of 2 Dec. 1563, 25 Apr. 1565, 1 Nov. 1626.
[43] Ibid. deed of 7 Aug. 1821.
[44] Buxton Rd. acct. bk. 1809–60, acct. 1823–4 (in pos-session of Mr. R. Stones of Malpas, Ches., 1994); O.S. Map 6", Staffs. VIII. NW. (1900 edn.).
[45] *Staffs. Advertiser*, 14 July 1860, p. 7; S.R.O., D. 3226/7, p. 308; O.S. Map 6", Staffs. VIII. NE. (1887 edn.); above, Leek and Lowe, econ. hist. (trade and ind.: quarrying).
[46] Above, Leek and Lowe, local govt. (manorial govt.).
[47] Above, Leek, par. intro. (par. govt.); S.R.O., D. 3359/Toft-Chorley, Haregate memo. bk. 1733.
[48] S.R.O., D.699/1/1/1, p. 4.
[49] W.S.L., Sleigh scrapbk. ii, ff. 93, 98.
[50] S.R.O., D. 3283, sheet 10.
[51] W.S.L., Sleigh scrapbk. ii, f. 75; S.R.O., D. 3014/10, cutting of 16 July 1873; D. 3226/2, no. 2490.

CHURCH. A school-chapel dedicated to *THE GOOD SHEPHERD* was opened in 1887 on the Blackshaw Moor road north-west of Thorncliffe. It was served from St. Luke's church in Leek, Tittesworth having become part of St. Luke's parish on its formation in 1845. A building of local stone, the chapel was designed by J. G. Smith of Leek and consisted of a chancel, a nave, a west bellcot with a bell, and a wooden porch at the west end. The site was given by Susannah Argles in fulfilment of the wishes of her husband F. A. Argles (d. 1885). The cost of nearly £600 was met by subscriptions, grants from church societies, and gifts of furnishings. Mrs. Argles gave £100 and the churchyard gates, and her son Thomas gave the bell. Local farmers provided team work. Although the school was closed in 1968, the chapel continued in use until 1984. It had been converted into a house by 1992.[52]

ROMAN CATHOLICISM. A hut on the Polish camp established at Blackshaw Moor in 1946 was used as a Roman Catholic chapel, and there was a resident chaplain. The Poles were rehoused on a new estate to the north in 1964, and a former bath house there was converted into a chapel. The chaplain was also the Polish chaplain for the whole North Staffordshire area, and in 1974 his base was moved to the Polish centre at Longton. The chaplain continued to celebrate mass at the Blackshaw Moor chapel on Sundays and holy days until 1993 when the chapel was closed because of the decreasing size of the congregation. Instead the chaplain began celebrating a Polish mass at St. Mary's Roman Catholic church in Leek.[53]

PROTESTANT NONCONFORMITY. There was a Wesleyan Methodist class at Thorncliffe by 1827. Sunday services were held every fortnight in 1829 but had ceased by 1832.[54] A small Primitive Methodist chapel and Sunday school was built there in 1839.[55] On Census Sunday 1851 there was an afternoon congregation of 21, with 21 Sunday school children.[56] The chapel is now Thorncliffe Methodist chapel.

EDUCATION. A public elementary school was started at Thorncliffe in 1884. At first it was held in the Primitive Methodist chapel, but the vicar of St. Luke's in Leek had the right to give religious instruction.[57] The chapel was declared unfit for a school by the Education Department, and by 1885 the teacher, Mrs. Burnett, was holding the school in her cottage as a temporary measure pending the building of a school-chapel at Thorncliffe.[58] She had given up the school by the beginning of 1886, and a building was found on a farm.[59] A school-chapel was opened in 1887.[60] It was decided in 1930 that Thorncliffe Church of England school, then an all-age school with 40 children on its books, should become a junior school, the senior children being transferred to Leek; the decision had taken effect by 1948.[61] The school was replaced in 1969 by Blackshaw Moor Church of England (Controlled) primary school, which became a first school in 1981.[62]

A nursery school was run for the Polish community settled at Blackshaw Moor after the Second World War. It was closed when the Poles were rehoused in 1964.[63]

CHARITIES FOR THE POOR. None known expressly for the township.

[52] *Leek Times*, 19 Feb. 1887 (cutting in S.R.O., D. 3014/10); S.R.O., D. 3359/Leek, All Saints, copy of pastoral address and accts. 1884–5 for St. Luke's, Leek, pp. 6–7; D. 4855/11/7, Aug. 1886; Thorncliffe school subscribers' and managers' mins. 1884–99, pp. 9–11 (photocopy in W.S.L.); Lich. Dioc. Regy., Bp.'s Reg. 35, p. 86. For the Argles family see above, estates (Haregate).
[53] Inf. from the Revd. F. Smalcerz, chaplain at the Polish Catholic Social Centre, Longton; *Leek Post & Times*, 9 June 1993, p. 7; 23 June 1993, p. 2.
[54] S.R.O., D. 3155/1; D. 3156/1/1/24; Leek Libr., Johnson scrapbk. i (2), D/13/15.
[55] Date stone on chapel.
[56] P.R.O., HO 129/372/2/2.
[57] S.R.O., D. 4855/11/5, May 1884.
[58] Subscribers' and managers' mins. 1884–97, pp. 1–5 (photocopy in W.S.L.).
[59] Ibid. pp. 6–8, 11.   [60] Above, church.
[61] Staffs. C.C. *Record for 1930*, 867, 869, 1024; S.R.O., CEQ/2/242/2.
[62] S.R.O., CEH/290/1–2; brochure for official opening of Blackshaw Moor sch. 14 May 1970; above, Leek and Lowe, educ. (intro.).
[63] Inf. from Mrs. W. Hryciuk of Blackshaw Moor.

N

SHEEN
1994

① Former reading room
② Lower House
③ The Palace
④ Cross Farm
+ St. Luke's Church

to Longnor
Upper White
Knowsley
Under Whitle
Over Boothlow
Top Farm
Sheen Moor
Broadmeadow Hall
Pilsbury Bridge
Lower Boothlow
1000
Ridge End Farm
900
Sheen Hill
High Sheen
Harris Close
Stonepit Hill
800
Slate House Farm
b
Manor Farm
1000
Sprink
former mill
Brund
Sheen
④ +
former school
The Old Vicarage
to Fawfield-head
b
① ② ③
New House Farm
Staffordshire Knot inn
Fold Farm
Drumbus
former Methodist chapel
Pool Hall Bridge
Bridge-end
site of school
Newfield
b
Lowend
800
Scaldersitch
Beresford Manor
to Hartington
Hartington Bridge
Raikes Farm
Hulme End
site of Titterton tollgate
Bank House Farm
800
to Warslow
inn
to Alstonefield   to Alstonefield   to site of Beresford Hall

R. Manifold

River Dove

— · — · — County boundary
— — — Boundary of ancient parish
— 800 — Contours (in feet)
b   barrow

0   0.5   1 mile
0   0.5   1 km

FIG. 46

SHEEN

THE ancient parish of Sheen lies in the north-east of the county on the boundary with Derbyshire. It was originally 2,893 a. in area, but an adjustment of its western boundary with Fawfieldhead civil parish in 1934 reduced it to 2,875 a. (1,164 ha.).[1] Three and a half miles from north to south and at its widest 2 miles from east to west, the parish is bounded on the east by the river Dove, which forms the county boundary, and on the west by the river Manifold. The shorter northern and southern boundaries run along minor valleys.

Sheen, which remains rural in character, has been described as 'one immense hill'.[2] The land rises from 711 ft. (271 m.) at Hulme End in the south-west corner to 1,116 ft. (340 m.) at Knowsley in the north on the ridge forming Sheen moor. The ridge has a steep escarpment to the Dove on the east, but the land falls less steeply to the Manifold on the west. Sheen Hill at the south end of the ridge rises to 1,247 ft. (380 m.). It is the uppermost of a series of hard bands of sandstone, known as the Sheen Beds, in the Millstone Grit which underlies the parish.[3]

[1] Census, 1931; Staffs. Review Order, 1934, p. 63 and map 1 (copy in S.R.O.). This article was written in 1994. The Revd. A. C. F. Nicoll, vicar of Sheen, and others named

in footnotes are thanked for their help.
[2] Annals of Dioc. of Lichfield (1859), 23.
[3] Geol. Surv. Map 1/50,000, drift, sheet 111 (1978 edn.).

The land continues to slope steeply to the Dove in the southern part of the parish, with a spur projecting south-westward and providing the site of Sheen village. The soil is loam over clay, and there is alluvium along the Manifold.[4] In 1611 it was stated at the manor court that Sheen was mostly 'cold, stony, barren ground' and during the winter was 'commonly so troubled with winds, frosts, and snow as cattle cannot endure to stay thereupon'.[5] Stone is the usual local building material.

Eight people were assessed for tax in 1327.[6] In 1666 thirty-three were assessed for hearth tax,[7] and in 1751 there were 58 families in the parish.[8] The population was 362 in 1801 and had risen to 429 by 1821, with a drop to 366 by 1831. It had reached 458 by 1871 but thereafter declined, falling to 321 in 1911 and 304 in 1921. It had risen to 331 by 1931 but was down to 279 in 1951, 260 in 1961, 238 in 1971, and 220 in 1981. It had risen to 225 by 1991.[9]

There are two Bronze Age barrows near Brund on the west side of the parish, another south of Townend, and possibly one west of Sheen village.[10] There was evidently a settlement at Sheen by the early 11th century.[11] The name probably derives from the Old English *sceon*, meaning shelters, perhaps a reference to shelters for herdsmen pasturing animals there.[12] An alternative suggestion derives the name from the Old English *sceone*, meaning beautiful and possibly referring to one of the rivers.[13]

The present village, which lies along the road running north-south through the parish, probably existed by 1175 when there was mention of a chapel at Sheen,[14] presumably on the site of the present church. The farms in the village, though rebuilt entirely or in part in the 19th century, are on the sites of earlier buildings. Lower House has an outbuilding with a doorhead inscribed TW 1621. The Palace has a date stone inscribed WM 1673 on the lintel of the main doorway. By 1699 there was a house on the site of Cross Farm,[15] which takes its name from the cross, probably of medieval origin, on the opposite side of the road. Manor Farm has a doorway which may date from c. 1700, and there was a house on the site of Fold Farm by 1716.[16] Four of the farms on the outskirts of the village can be traced from the 17th century. Two stand beneath Sheen Hill north of the village, Slate House, mentioned in 1611,[17] and High Sheen, which was the home of the Mort family by 1620.[18] High Sheen was evidently rebuilt by Thomas Mort in 1663: a stone bearing his name

and the date has been reset by the present entrance. His widow Mary was assessed for tax on three hearths in 1666.[19] The hall and parlour end survive from a three-roomed house of coursed rubble stone with ashlar dressings; there is a richly ornamented entrance doorway inside the present entrance, and the hall has moulded ceiling beams and a broad segmental arch over the fireplace. Lowend to the south of the village beyond Townend has a barn with a date stone inscribed IS 1666, and there was a house at Newfield east of Townend by 1677 and probably by 1615.[20] There was settlement at Drumbus north-west of Townend by 1785,[21] and Harris Close by the roadside north-east of the village is dated 1842.

By 1834 there was a beerhouse in the village run by Edward Woolley, a blacksmith.[22] It was probably the inn there which by 1850 was called the Horse Shoe and was run by John Woolley, also a blacksmith.[23] In 1851 it was run by Elizabeth Woolley, who was still there in 1868.[24] By 1872 it had been renamed the Staffordshire Knot.[25] Known as Ye Olde Spinning Wheel in the 1970s,[26] it was the Staffordshire Knot in 1994. It forms part of a building of various dates; much is 19th-century, but there is a lintel dated 1666 on a part occupied as a cottage.

In the 1850s A. J. B. Hope, the heir to the Beresford estate in Alstonefield and Sheen, set about making Sheen into an 'Athens of the Moorlands'. Having acquired the patronage of the church, he rebuilt it and provided a new house for the incumbent, a new school, and a reading room. He also restored the village cross.[27] He had plans for letting some of the land as building plots for villas to someone 'of means and religion' and thus bringing Sheen 'into the market as a religious watering place', but the scheme was not carried out.[28]

There is scattered settlement throughout the parish. Whitle at the north end of the eastern escarpment was a settled area by the early 15th century; by 1711 there was a house at Under Whitle, and the name suggests another by then on the site of Upper Whitle.[29] The present houses date from the 19th century. There was a house on the site of the 17th-century Broadmeadow Hall by the Dove to the south-east by the later 16th century,[30] and one at Sprink further south by 1755.[31] Nether Boothlow at the north end of the western escarpment existed by 1573; that name too suggests the existence by then of Upper Boothlow, recorded in 1611.[32] The houses now called Lower Boothlow and

4 Soil Surv. of Eng. and Wales, sheet 3 (1983).
5 P.R.O., DL 30/53/657.
6 S.H.C. vii (1), 222.
7 S.H.C. 1925, 203-4.
8 L.J.R.O., B/V/5/1751, Sheen.
9 V.C.H. Staffs. i. 329; Census, 1911-91.
10 Staffs. C.C., Sites and Monuments Rec., 00137-8, 00168, 04193.
11 Below, manor.
12 Eng. P.N. Elements, ii. 106-7.
13 P.N. Surr. (E.P.N.S.), 65-6.
14 Below, church.
15 S.R.O., D. 3596/1/1, p. 84.
16 Ibid. p. 86.
17 P.R.O., DL 30/53/657.
18 L.J.R.O., B/C/11, Ric. Mort (1620).

19 S.H.C. 1925, 203.
20 S.R.O., D. 4952/1-3.
21 Ibid. D. 3596/1/1, pp. 89-90.
22 White, Dir. Staffs. (1834), 761.
23 P.O. Dir. Staffs. (1850).
24 Ibid. (1868); White, Dir. Staffs. (1851), 787.
25 P.O. Dir. Staffs. (1872).
26 Inf. from Mr. Nicoll.
27 Staffs. Advertiser, 7 Aug. 1852, p. 8.
28 H. W. and I. Law, Bk. of the Beresford Hopes, 182-90.
29 D.R.O., D. 2375M/1/1, ct. of 2 and 3 Hen. V, 2nd ct. 29 Hen. VI; S.R.O., D. 3596/1/1, p. 86; below, church [curate's income].
30 Below, manor.
31 S.R.O., D. 3596/1/1, pp. 70, 72.
32 P.R.O., DL 30/51/631, m. 2d.; DL 30/53/657.

Over Boothlow date from the 19th century. There was a farm at Ridge End to the south by 1648;[33] the house was rebuilt in coursed stone by William Edensor in 1744.[34] Most of the other farms on the western escarpment and below it existed by 1716, although all have been rebuilt. In 1716 there was also a house on the site of Top Farm on Sheen moor.[35] There was another at Knowsley further north by 1733,[36] and nearby are the remains of a cross, re-erected near its former site in 1897. It was a tradition in the 1830s that the cross had formerly had 'a dial for the country people to mark the hour'.[37]

At Brund on the west side of the parish the Riley family had a house in the early 16th century.[38] A mill on the Manifold nearby, described as new in 1602, may have been on the site of a mill in existence c.1250.[39] Brund hamlet consists of three houses and a huddle of cottages and outbuildings, the earliest features of which date from the 17th century. New House Farm was built in 1645–6 and rebuilt in coursed stone in 1830, in each instance by a George Critchlow.[40]

There was settlement in the south-east of the parish by the 17th century. Beresford Manor, formerly Bank Top House, dates from then; built of coursed stone with ashlar dressings and extended in the 19th century, it was originally a three-bayed house and seems to have had an end lobby entrance. For a few years after 1917 it was the home of Prince Serge Obolensky and his family.[41] By 1651 there was a farm at Raikes, then also known as Bartine Edge;[42] the present Raikes Farm dates from c. 1800. Scaldersitch is a 19th-century building but incorporates a date stone inscribed IOM 1661. There was a house at Bridge-end on the escarpment south-west of Pool Hall bridge by 1772;[43] the present house dates from c. 1800.

At Hulme End in the south-west corner of the parish there was a house by 1775 on the north side of the road between Warslow, in Alstonefield, and Hartington (Derb.).[44] The three-storeyed Hulme End Farm on the site was bought in the late 1880s by A. T. Hulme, a medical practitioner, who moved there from Bank Top. He enlarged the house and renamed it Bank House. In 1967 his grandson, Robert Bury, rebuilt the older part, which was suffering from subsidence.[45] A building on the south side of the road by 1775

at the junction with the Alstonefield road[46] had become the Jolly Carter inn by 1834.[47] Renamed the Waggon and Horses by 1850, the inn was the Jolly Carter again by 1860 and Hulme End inn by 1879.[48] By 1912 it had been renamed the Light Railway hotel, the Leek & Manifold Valley light railway having been opened in 1904 to a terminus on the other side of the Manifold in Fawfieldhead.[49] It became the Manifold Valley hotel in the earlier 1980s.[50] The central section of the building may be the building which was there by 1775.

The Warslow–Hartington road was turnpiked in 1770.[51] It had until then crossed the Manifold at Archford bridge and continued to Hulme End through the northern end of Alstonefield township. With its turnpiking it was realigned to cross the river further upstream by a new bridge at Hulme End.[52] By 1795 there was a tollgate at Hulme End, probably the building which stands at the north-east corner of the bridge.[53] A second gate, Titterton gate, was erected between 1841 and 1851 at the junction with the more easterly of the two roads to Alstonefield.[54] The Warslow–Hartington road originally passed north of Raikes Farm, but it was diverted to run south of the farm c. 1840.[55] It was disturnpiked in 1878.[56] The road crosses the Dove at Hartington bridge, which was the joint responsibility of Sheen and Hartington in 1620 and was still such in the late 1720s.[57] By 1758 it had become the responsibility of Staffordshire and Derbyshire, and it was rebuilt as a cart bridge shortly afterwards.[58] The present single-arch stone bridge dates from c. 1819.[59]

The present footpath running south-east from Sheen village was evidently once the route from the village to Hartington, crossing the Dove at Pool Hall bridge, so named by the early 17th century.[60] There was evidently a bridge there by 1506 when there was mention of pasture in the area called the Bregende.[61] In the 1770s Sheen paid half the cost of repairing Pool Hall bridge,[62] the other half presumably being the responsibility of Hartington parish. Another footpath running west from Sheen village suggests a road to Brund and the bridge over the Manifold at Brund mill.

In the 18th century a packhorse way entered Sheen from Warslow, presumably following the

33 Date on rear doorway of barn.
34 Date stone inscribed E/WG 1744 over main doorway; D.R.O., D. 395Z/Z33; Sheen par. accts. 1720–1803, p. 88.
35 S.R.O., D. 3596/1/1, p. 86.   36 Ibid. p. 59.
37 J. P. Sheldon, *Ancient Cross in Par. of Sheen* (reprinted from *Leek Times*, 28 Nov. 1897; copy among docs. in Longnor church 1994); W.S.L. 148/34; 149/34; inscription on base.   38 P.R.O., DL 30/49/588.
39 Below, econ. hist.
40 Date stone on main front; inf. from the owner, Mrs. M. L. Critchlow, citing deeds and date stone in cellar inscribed GC 1645.
41 Nicoll, *Sheen*, 77–8 and pl. facing p. 78; S.R.O., D. 3596/1/1, p. 71; P.R.O., RG 9/1949.
42 W.S.L., M. 381.
43 Sheen par. accts. 1720–1803, overseers' accts. 1771–2; for the bridge see below, this section.
44 Above, fig. 2.
45 Inf. from Mr. R. Bury; P.R.O., RG 11/2742; RG 12/2188.   46 Above, fig. 2.
47 White, *Dir. Staffs.* (1834), 761.
48 *P.O. Dir. Staffs.* (1850; 1860); O.S. Map 6", Staffs.

IX. NE. (1884 edn.).
49 *Kelly's Dir. Staffs.* (1908; 1912); above, Leek: Leek and Lowe, communications.   50 Inf. from the hotel.
51 *S.H.C.* 4th ser. xiii. 110–11.
52 Above, Alstonefield: Fawfieldhead, intro.
53 Sheen par. accts. 1790–1803, headborough's accts. 1794–5; O.S. Map 1", sheet 81 SE. (1840 edn.).
54 P.R.O., HO 107/1007; HO 107/2008; two fields by the road junction are still called Titterton Gate and Far Titterton: inf. from Mr. Bury.
55 O.S. Map 1", sheet 81 SE. (1840 edn.); L.J.R.O., B/V/15/Sheen, map.
56 S.R.O., D. 239/M/14/63, cert. of 25 Nov. 1878.
57 S.R.O., Q/SO/2, ff.79, 102v.; Sheen par. accts. 1720–1803, pp. 17–18.
58 S.R.O., Q/SO/15, f. 116; Sheen par. accts., headborough's accts. 1758, 1761.   59 S.R.O., Q/SO/27, f. 119v.
60 Chatsworth House (Derb.), map 2063, dated 1614.
61 *Duchy of Lancaster's Estates in Derb. 1485–1540* (Derb. Arch. Soc. rec. ser. iii), 75.
62 Sheen par. accts. 1720–1803, headborough's accts. 1772, 1773, 1778.

Hartington road.[63] Another packhorse route evidently branched from the first to enter Sheen by Brund mill bridge and continued north-east to cross the Dove by Pilsbury bridge south-east of Broadmeadow Hall, a joint responsibility of Sheen and Hartington.[64] It was stated in 1859 that old people in Sheen could remember mule stables attached to certain farms with doorways large enough to admit salt-laden animals.[65]

Brund mill bridge and Ludford bridge, probably further up the Manifold near Ludburn in Fawfieldhead, were maintained by Sheen and Alstonefield jointly until the 18th century. In 1735 or 1736 Sheen took over Ludford bridge, rebuilding it in 1837; Alstonefield took over Brund mill bridge, which was rebuilt in 1890–1.[66]

There was a post office in Sheen village by 1868, run by George Harrison, a grocer; his wife Elizabeth was the postmistress at least between 1871 and the early 1900s.[67] By the early 1930s there was a bus service between Ashbourne and Buxton via Hulme End; in 1991 there was also a twice-weekly service between Sheen village and Longnor, in Alstonefield.[68] Electricity was available in the parish by 1940.[69] A waterworks was built at Hulme End on the road to Sheen village in 1961, and a piped supply became available in the 1960s.[70] There is also a reservoir on the high ground at Knowsley.

SOCIAL AND CULTURAL ACTIVITIES. Before the change in the calendar in 1752 the wakes were held on the Sunday before 18 October, the feast of the patronal saint of the parish, St. Luke. Thereafter they were held on 29 October.[71] By the early 20th century they lasted for a week at the end of October.[72] By 1994 a social gathering was held during the week following Wakes Sunday.[73]

In 1856 A. J. B. Hope opened a parochial lending library and reading room at Sheen with a paid librarian in order to 'provide intellectual occupation, including chess, for a population that has hitherto boozed at the public house'. In 1859 it was open two evenings a week, had c. 50 subscribers from the parish and its neighbourhood, and contained 555 volumes. It was run by the schoolmaster in 1867, when it was still open two evenings a week. It was closed in 1889 for lack of support.[74] In 1905 the vicar, E. E. Ward, opened a reading room in the vicarage three nights a week for reading and games.[75] By 1918 the county council had established a centre at Sheen school for its circulating library service.[76] A reading room was erected south of the village centre in 1912. The corrugated iron building was repaired by volunteers in 1959 but was sold in the earlier 1980s.[77]

A festival of vocal and instrumental music by Handel in Sheen church was advertised for Monday 27 October 1794, perhaps in connexion with the wakes. The orchestra was to be 'a numerous company, selected from the best country choirs', and a newly installed organ was to be inaugurated by a Mr. Slater of Ashbourne.[78] There was a Sheen band in 1860 and a Sheen and Longnor brass band in 1867.[79] A Sheen band was mentioned in 1871, and it played at the Sheen celebrations for Queen Victoria's jubilee of 1887.[80]

A Sheen football club was formed in 1907.[81] In 1954 £10 15s. was given to church funds on the winding up of a Hulme End football club.[82] A Women's Institute was formed in 1967.[83]

MANOR AND OTHER ESTATES. Wulfric Spot's endowment of Burton abbey c. 1003 included 1 hide at SHEEN.[84] In 1066, however, Sheen was held by Alward and in 1086 by the king.[85] By the later 12th century the manor had passed to Bertram de Verdun (d. 1192).[86] The overlordship then descended in the Verdun family, passing later to the Furnivalle family and finally to the Talbots, earls of Shrewsbury. Lord Shrewsbury was still described as lord of the manor in 1892.[87]

Bertram de Verdun granted the manor to Hugh of Okeover at a rent of 36s. 8d. Bertram's younger son Nicholas, who had succeeded his elder brother by 1200, confirmed the grant and added exemption from payment of scutage.[88] By 1220 Hugh of Okeover had been suceeded by his son Robert, who was followed by his son Hugh in 1235 or 1236. Hugh's son Robert had succeeded by 1269.[89] By 1272 Robert had granted half the manor to his brother, Richard, though retaining the mesne lordship.[90]

By 1315 that half had evidently passed to Richard's son Robert, who by 1327 had been succeeded by another Richard of Okeover, still alive in 1345.[91] By a settlement of 1335 the reversion after his death was granted to his

63 V.C.H. Staffs. ii. 278–9 (based on W.S.L., D. 1798/617/76; D. 1798/618/15).
64 V.C.H. Staffs. ii. 279; Dodd, Peakland Roads, 122–3; Sheen par. accts. 1720–1803, headborough's accts. 1770, 1779, 1790–1; 1800–38, headborough's accts. 1833–4.
65 Annals of Dioc. of Lichfield (1859), 27.
66 Sheen par. accts. 1720–1803, pp. 10, 45, 53; 1800–38, headborough's accts. 1836–7; J. P. Sheldon, Through Staffs. Stiles and Derb. Dales (Derby, Leicester, and Nottingham, 1894), 4–5. For a view of Brund mill bridge see above, plate 64.
67 P.O. Dir. Staffs. (1868); Kelly's Dir. Staffs. (1908); P.R.O., RG 10/2885; RG 11/2742.
68 Kelly's Dir. Staffs. (1932; 1940); inf. from Mrs. K. Bates of Ridge End Farm.
69 Kelly's Dir. Staffs. (1940); S.R.O., D. 3522/2, p. 98.
70 Inscription on building; inf. from Mr. Nicoll.
71 Alstonfield Deanery Mag. (Sept. 1906).
72 Ibid. (Dec. 1904); S.R.O., D. 3522/1, pp. 11 sqq.
73 Inf. from Mr. Nicoll.
74 Law, Beresford Hopes, 190; Annals of Dioc. of Lichfield (1859), 64; Nicoll, Sheen, 79–80; P.R.O., ED 7/109/272.

75 Alstonfield Deanery Mag. (Dec. 1905).
76 Ibid. xxiii (1).
77 Kelly's Dir. Staffs. (1912); Alstonfield Deanery Mag. lxii (11); inf. from the vicar.
78 Handbill, loose in Sheen par. accts. 1720–1803 (reproduced in Nicoll, Sheen, facing p. 31).
79 Staffs. Advertiser, 30 June 1860, p. 4; 26 Oct. 1867, p. 7.
80 S.R.O., D. 121/A/PZ/2, f. 10; W.S.L. 491/34, p. 56.
81 Alstonfield Deanery Mag. xi (12), 12.
82 Ibid. lvii (2).
83 Inf. from Staffs. Federation of Women's Institutes.
84 V.C.H. Staffs. iii. 199, 201.   85 Ibid. iv. 41.
86 Below (next para.).
87 S.H.C. 1911, 160; 1913, 17–18, 32; White, Dir. Staffs. (1851), 765; Annals of Dioc. of Lichfield (1859), 26; Kelly's Dir. Staffs. (1880).
88 S.H.C. ii (1), 96, 100; ibid. N.S. vii. 135–7.
89 Ibid. N.S. vii. 15–16, 18; p. 15 is corrected by Bk. of Fees, ii. 529.
90 S.H.C. iv (1), 200, 254–5; S.H.C. 1911, 159.
91 S.H.C. ix (1), 51–2, 93; vii (1), 222; xii (1), 40.

grandson John de la Pole, son of Richard's daughter Joan and Richard de la Pole of Hartington (Derb.).[92] The half of the manor which had remained with Robert of Okeover had passed out of the Okeover family by 1316. That year Hugh de Prestwold was found to have been unjustly disseised of half of Sheen by Richard, son of William of Bentley, and others.[93] It was probably the same Richard of Bentley, however, who held the half in 1327, while the Richard of Bentley who held it in 1351 was probably his younger son. That year Richard and his wife Gillian conveyed the reversion after their deaths to John de la Pole.[94] In 1357 John's son John, in whose possession the two parts of the manor were reunited, sued Gillian and her second husband, Robert de Hyde, for causing waste in the estate.[95]

The younger John was dead by 1397 with his son, another John and a minor, as his heir. That John was of age by 1406.[96] A John Pole was living at Sheen in 1450.[97] In 1476 Sir John Pole and his wife Alice sold the manor to the king.[98] By 1506 it was administered as part of the duchy of Lancaster,[99] and it was still held by the duchy in 1698.[1] It had passed to the Sleighs of Broadmeadow Hall by 1709, when Gervase Sleigh sold it to John Hayne of Ashbourne. John's son and heir Henry conveyed it to Hugh Bateman of Derby in 1724.[2] Hugh was succeeded in 1731 by his son Hugh and he in 1777 by his grandson Hugh Bateman, who was created a baronet in 1806 and died in 1824. Sheen passed to his nephew Richard Thomas Bateman.[3] In 1825 the manor was offered for sale with Broadmeadow Hall.[4] By the later 1890s the resident farmers claimed the lordship of the manor.[5]

The seat of the Pole family was at Pool Hall (later Moat Hall) on the Derbyshire side of the Dove in Hartington, and that was still the manor house of Sheen in the early 17th century.[6] Broadmeadow Hall became the manor house when the Sleigh family secured the manor. The family, formerly of Pilsbury Grange in Hartington, had acquired a house at Broadmeadow by 1573 by marriage into the Riley family.[7] Ralph Sleigh was assessed for tax on six hearths there in 1666.[8] The present Broadmeadow Hall, of coursed rubble stone with ashlar dressings, dates from about that time and is an L-shaped two-storeyed building with attics. It was restored in the 19th century, and a central doorway on the entrance front then replaced the original doorway on the extreme left. There was further restoration in the earlier 1990s after the house had stood empty for some years.[9]

The *BERESFORD* estate, which lay mainly in Alstonefield, extended into Sheen, where Lord Beresford owned 94 a. in 1845.[10]

The *TITHES* of Sheen were confirmed to Burton abbey with Sheen chapel in 1185 and descended with the ownership of the chapel until the 18th century.[11] By 1830 the tithes from all but three farms had been sold, evidently to the owners of the property from which they were due.[12] In 1849 an award assigned tithe-rent charges totalling £83 1s. 4d. to 85 tithe owners.[13]

In the early 1480s the Crown as lord of the manor paid a rent of 22s. to the Knights Hospitallers from a tenement called Whitlehege.[14]

ECONOMIC HISTORY. AGRICULTURE. In 1086 Sheen, described as waste, had land for 1 ploughteam.[15] In 1677 there was an open field north of the village called Sheen field and in 1682 one called the Mean field.[16] Exchange of pieces of common waste on Sheen moor took place in 1669,[17] and two closes at Newfield east of Townend were described in 1677 as lately inclosed from the waste.[18] In 1681 Upper Boothlow farm included 38 a. of common on Sheen moor.[19] Much of the waste, however, appears to have been inclosed by then, since responsibility for the churchyard fence was divided that year according to 'the number of acres of common which everyone had in the division thereof'.[20] The main crop in 1801 was oats, which accounted for 286 a. of the 291 a. recorded.[21] By 1849 there were 2,562 a. of meadow and pasture as against 256 a. of arable.[22] The main areas of cultivation were then along the Manifold and the Dove, where there was also good pasture. Scarcity of timber, a source of complaint in 1611, was still a problem in the mid 19th century. By then most of the land had long been in the hands of resident freeholders, but estates had become heavily mortgaged and changed hands frequently.[23] Of the 1,036.5 ha. returned for the civil parish in 1988, grassland covered 873.2 ha. and there were 134.8 ha. of rough grazing. The farming was dairy and sheep, with 1,944 head of cattle and 1,732 sheep and lambs. There were also 725 pigs and 807 hens, with one farm devoted to pigs and poultry. Of the 33 farms returned, 23 were under 40 ha. in size, 7 were between 40 and 49 ha., and 3 were between 50 and 99 ha. Woodland covered 22.9 ha.[24]

MILLS. The Okeovers had a mill at Sheen by the later 13th century,[25] and Sheen mill was

92 Ibid. xi. 139–40, 184.   93 Ibid. ix (1), 61.
94 Ibid. xi. 141, 165.   95 Ibid. xii (1), 151; xvi. 56.
96 Ibid. xv. 83; xvi. 56.   97 Ibid. N.S. iii. 191.
98 *S.H.C.* xi. 251–2; *Cal. Close*, 1476–85, p. 139.
99 *Duchy of Lancaster's Estates in Derb. 1485–1540* (Derb. Arch Soc. rec. ser. iii), 75.   1 W.S.L. 63/16/42.
2 P.R.O., CP 25(2)/966/7 Anne Hil. no. 23; CP 25(2)/1089/10 Geo. I Hil. no. 2; S.R.O., D. 3596/1/1, p. 85.
3 Burke, *Commoners*, iii (1836), 350–1; P.R.O., CP 43/965, m. 366.   4 *Staffs. Advertiser*, 9 July 1825.
5 *Kelly's Dir. Staffs.* (1896; 1940).
6 *Annals of Dioc. of Lichfield* (1859), 26; Nicoll, *Sheen*, 12, 14.
7 A. F. C. Sleigh, *Sleighs of Derb. and Beyond* (Bedhampton, priv. print., intro. dated 1991), i. 6; ii, chart 4; P.R.O., DL 30/51/631, m. 2d.   8 *S.H.C.* 1925, 203.

9 Above, plate 32. Mr. and Mrs. J. W. Critchlow, the owners, are thanked for their help.
10 Above, Alstonefield: Alstonefield, manors.
11 Below, church.
12 *S.H.C.* 4th ser. x. 98; White, *Dir. Staffs.* (1834), 760.
13 L.J.R.O., B/A/5/Sheen.   14 P.R.O., SC 6/825/6.
15 *V.C.H. Staffs.* iv. 41.
16 W.S.L. 63/15/42; L.J.R.O., B/V/6/Sheen, 1682.
17 B.R.L., Keen 368, deeds of 3 Apr. 1669, 1 Apr. 1670.
18 S.R.O., D. 4952/3.   19 D.R.O. 395Z/Z33.
20 S.R.O., D. 3596/1/1, p. 86.
21 *S.H.C.* 1950–1, table facing p. 242.
22 L.J.R.O., B/A/15/Sheen.
23 *Annals of Dioc. of Lichfield* (1859), 24. For 1611 see P.R.O., DL 30/53/657.   24 P.R.O., MAF 68/6128/73.
25 D.R.O., D. 231M/T327; *S.H.C.* xi. 139–40.

mentioned in 1735.[26] By then at least it may be identifiable with Brund mill on the Manifold, which was described as a new mill in 1602.[27] Still a corn mill in 1748,[28] Brund mill was used as spinning mill from 1790 when three members of the Cantrell family began a calico business there. They were declared bankrupt in 1793.[29] Around 1800 the mill was worked by a partnership of cotton manufacturers.[30] John Beardmore worked it as a flax mill in 1834 and 1844 and as a rope mill in 1851.[31] It was advertised for letting as a flax mill in 1859 and as a corn mill in 1861.[32] It was not in use in 1871, and although it appears to have been operating as a corn mill in 1878, it was again out of use by 1881.[33] Part of the three-storeyed stone building had collapsed by the later 1960s, but work began on its conversion into a house in 1975 and was complete by 1984.[34]

A mill in Sheen manor described in 1625 as recently built may have been on the Dove in the south-east of the parish.[35]

FAIR. A fair was held at Sheen in 1771.[36]

TRADE AND INDUSTRY. It was stated in the 1850s that building stone had been quarried on the summit of Sheen Hill and its southern slope for centuries.[37] Stone from Sheen Hill was used for rebuilding the parish church in the late 1820s.[38] In addition Stonepit Hill west of Sheen Hill and Pitts Top west of the main road at Townend, both so named by the 1730s, were presumably then areas of quarrying, as they were in the 19th century.[39] There were quarries and masons throughout the parish in the mid and late 19th century, the number of masons having risen to 14 by 1891.[40] The Pitts Top quarry was owned by John Lomas by 1834, and under his ownership in the 1850s John Mason was producing quantities of scythe stones, which had a wide sale nationally.[41] In the mid 1860s the quarry passed to Edward Wilson, who employed nine men and two boys there in 1871; three of his four sons were then stonemasons.[42] Two of the sons, Thomas and John Edward, took over the business in the earlier 1880s, and the latter ran it on his own in the early 20th century.[43]

About 1950 the disused quarry became the

headquarters of a bus company run by Douglas Blackhurst. In 1958 he began making machine tools there, and in 1960 he switched to concrete mixers. He formed Belle Engineering (Sheen) Ltd. in 1961. The factory was extended in 1989, and in 1990 the production of loaders was added to mixers, with generators also from 1992. The number of employees in 1993 was 120.[44]

There was a furnace in Sheen parish in 1722, evidently at Brund.[45] By 1834 John Kidd was producing tinplate in Sheen village. He was described as a tin man and brazier in 1841 and was still working as such in 1876.[46] By 1880 the business had been taken over by his wife.[47] The corn mill at Brund was used as a textile mill from 1790 but was converted back into a corn mill c. 1860. Wooden button moulds were produced by John Berrisford of Brund in 1834.[48] Thomas Gilman was working as a cheese factor in the parish in 1818. William Gilman of Newfield was a farmer and cheese factor at least between 1851 and the mid 1870s.[49]

LOCAL GOVERNMENT. Sheen was subject to its overlord's court at Alton and still owed suit and service there in 1823.[50] In 1859 it was stated that suit and service had been discontinued a few years before, although a chief rent was still paid.[51] Sheen had two headboroughs in 1600.[52] By 1725 there was only one, normally styled a constable from 1817, and he was still sworn at the Alton court in 1837. He paid head silver at Alton each year, 1s. 7d. for most of the 18th century and sums varying normally from 2s. 1d. to 2s. 6d. between 1797 and 1837.[53] When Bertram de Verdun granted Sheen to Hugh of Okeover in the late 12th century, he reserved 'wart penny' and 'Peter's penny' besides a chief rent.[54] The Okeovers had their own court at Sheen in the later 13th century.[55] By 1506 Sheen, having passed to the Crown in 1476, was administered as part of the duchy of Lancaster.[56] By 1509 and until 1525 or later a Sheen jury presented at the twice-yearly view of frankpledge and great court of the duchy manor of Hartington (Derb.). Matters relating to Sheen were also included in the proceedings of the

[26] D.R.O., D. 231M/T771–2.
[27] Ibid. D. 2375M/57/1, 27 May 44 Eliz. I.
[28] S.R.O., D. 569/M/8.
[29] Sheffield City Archives, Bagshawe C. 3277.
[30] S.R.O., D. 3359/misc. deeds, deeds of 1798 and 1801.
[31] White, Dir. Staffs. (1834), 761; S.R.O., Q/SB, E. 1844, no. 79; P.R.O., HO 107/2008.
[32] Staffs. Advertiser, 19 Mar. 1859, p. 4; 27 Apr. 1861, p. 8.
[33] P.R.O., RG 10/2885; RG 11/2742; O.S. Map 6", Staffs. V. SW. (1887, 1900 edns.).
[34] Sherlock, Ind. Arch. Staffs. 22, 187–8; Leek Libr., newspaper cuttings 1984 (1), pp. 26–7.
[35] P.R.O., C 66/2349.
[36] Sheen par. accts. 1720–1803, overseer's accts. 1771–2.
[37] Annals of Dioc. of Lichfield (1859), 23.
[38] Below, church (note 44: Sheen par. accts. 1800–38).
[39] S.R.O., D. 3596/1/1, p. 60; O.S. Map 6", Staffs. V. SW. (1900 edn.).
[40] P.R.O., HO 107/1007; H.O. 107/2008; ibid. RG 9/1949; RG 10/2885; RG 11/2742; RG 12/2188; O.S. Map 6", Staffs. V. NW. (1884, 1900 edns.); NE. (1899 edn.); SE. (1884, 1899 edns.).

[41] White, Dir. Staffs. (1834), 761; (1851), 787; P.O. Dir. Staffs. (1860; 1864); Nicoll, Sheen, 74; Annals of Dioc. of Lichfield (1859), 23; P.R.O., HO 107/2008.
[42] P.O. Dir. Staffs. (1868); P.R.O., RG 10/2885.
[43] Kelly's Dir. Staffs. (1884 and later edns. to 1916); Nicoll, Sheen, 74; P.R.O., RG 11/2742; RG 12/2188.
[44] Nicoll, Sheen, 90; inf. from Belle Engineering (Sheen) Ltd.
[45] P.R.O., CP 25(2)/1062/8 Geo. I Trin. no. 21.
[46] White, Dir. Staffs. (1834), 761; P.O. Dir. Staffs. (1876); P.R.O., HO 107/1007.   [47] Kelly's Dir. Staffs. (1880).
[48] White, Dir. Staffs. (1834), 761.
[49] Parson and Bradshaw, Staffs. Dir. (1818), villages section, p. 17; White, Dir. Staffs. (1851), 787; P.O. Dir. Staffs. (1876).
[50] S.H.C. iv (1), 254–5; S.H.C. 1913, 32; S.R.O., D. 240/E(A)1/347.
[51] Annals of Dioc. of Lichfield (1859), 26.
[52] Cal. of Shrewsbury and Talbot Papers, ii (Derb. Arch. Soc. rec. ser. iv), 320.
[53] Sheen par. accts. 1720–1803; 1800–38.
[54] S.H.C. N.S. vii. 135.   [55] D.R.O., D. 231M/T327.
[56] Above, manor.

Hartington small court. Two reeves were appointed for Sheen by 1515, and two were still appointed in 1521.[57] By 1529 a separate great court for Sheen was held at Hartington on the same day as the Hartington court; there was a separate small court by 1532, also on the same day as the Hartington small court.[58] A single reeve was appointed by 1542.[59] In 1571 Sheen manor was farmed to the earl of Shrewsbury, and the courts were transferred to Sheen; they continued there when Henry Cavendish became farmer in 1574.[60] When the duchy resumed control in the later 1580s, the courts remained at Sheen and were still held there in 1625.[61] In 1600 the earl of Shrewsbury was high steward of the manor.[62]

By the early 15th century the Whitle area of Sheen lay within Alstonefield manor, and it was still part of that manor in 1680.[63]

There were two churchwardens in 1553 and 1625 but only one by 1635.[64] By 1683 the office was served on a 32-year cycle.[65] The parish clerk was paid 10s. a year by 1742, £1 1s. from 1763, £1 11s. 6d. from 1815, and £2 12s. from 1820. He was appointed by the curate in the earlier 19th century. The office was often combined with that of sexton, who was paid 5s. a year by 1767 and 7s. 6d. from 1786.[66]

There was a single overseer of the poor by 1683, with that office too served on a 32-year cycle.[67] The overseer's expenditure increased sharply in the late 18th century, from just under £50 in 1781–2 to over £96 in 1782–3. Though it fell after that, it rose steadily in the 1790s to a peak of £190 in 1794–5 and reached a new peak of over £266 in 1819–20.[68] There were evidently two poorhouses by the later 18th century. Four Lane Ends House north of Brund seems to have been in use as such by 1751,[69] and in 1769–70 the parish bought property at Stonepit Hill to the south for the overseer's use.[70] Poorhouses outside the parish were also used. Payments were made for Hurdlow poorhouse in Hartington monthly between May 1765 and January 1766, Ipstones poorhouse in the earlier 1780s, and the poorhouse at Earl Sterndale in Hartington in 1791.[71] Four Lane Ends House remained parish property until 1879 and was probably one of the two poorhouses in use in 1837.[72]

By the earlier 18th century there were four surveyors of the highways, supervised by the headborough. Their areas of responsibility were named in 1735 as Upper Quarter, Town Quarter, Water Quarter, and Lower Quarter, still the highway divisions in the late 19th century.[73]

The headborough was responsible for the pinfold in the 18th and early 19th century. It was a stone structure and was rebuilt in 1815. A pinner was sworn at the Alton court in the earlier 1820s, and the headborough accounted for his expenses. The headborough also maintained the stocks in the earlier 18th century.[74]

In the 1790s a molecatcher was paid £1 11s. 6d. a year by the overseer of the poor. Small payments were also made to a Henry Fogg 'upon the account of the moles'.[75]

Sheen was included in Leek poor-law union on its formation in 1837.[76] With the rest of Leek rural district it became part of the new Staffordshire Moorlands district in 1974.

CHURCH. There was a chapel at Sheen by 1185 when it was among the possessions of Burton abbey confirmed by the pope. In 1255 it was described as a dependent chapel of Ilam church, itself a possession of Burton abbey by 1185.[77] Sheen continued as a chapel of Ilam until the 16th century. Meanwhile in 1529 the abbey leased it with its glebe, tithes, and offerings to the curate of Sheen, Henry Longworth, and his brother Thomas for their lives.[78] Henry was granted a 30-year lease in 1536 with responsibility for repairs and providing a priest; he was dead by 1541.[79] Burton abbey was dissolved in 1539, but in 1541 it was reconstituted as a college, which was itself dissolved in 1545.[80] In 1546 the Crown granted most of its possessions, including Sheen chapel, to Sir William Paget.[81]

Later in 1546 Paget was licensed to sell the chapel and its property to Ralph Crane of Middleton, in Wirksworth (Derb.).[82] It was probably then that the chapel ceased to be part of Ilam parish.[83] Crane was succeeded by his daughter Elizabeth and her husband John Wigley evidently in or shortly before 1567.[84] John continued to hold the chapel after Elizabeth's death, and he was succeeded by their son Henry in 1579.[85] On Henry's death in 1610 the chapel and its property passed to his son Thomas, who in 1612 granted what was described as the free chapel of Sheen and the tithes belonging to it to Thomas Hall for 80 years. In 1618 Hall was succeeded by his son Charles, aged 14, who secured possession of the chapel and its property in 1626.[86] By 1638 what was described as the

57 P.R.O., DL 30/49/588, 592–7; DL 30/50/600.
58 Ibid. DL 30/41/431; DL 30/50/603.
59 Ibid. DL 30/50/609, m. 9d.; DL 30/50/611–12.
60 Ibid. DL 30/51/631.
61 Ibid. DL 30/52/643–51; DL 30/53/652–60, 662.
62 Cal. of Shrewsbury and Talbot Papers, ii. 320.
63 D.R.O., D. 2375M/1/1, cts. of 2 and 3 Hen. V, 12 Hen. VII; D. 2375M/63/53, p. 185; D. 2375M/189/14, deed of 25 Sept. 1680.
64 S.H.C. 1915, 230; L.J.R.O., B/V/1/47; B/V/1/55, p. 93. 65 S.R.O., D. 3596/1/1, p. 84.
66 Sheen par. accts. 1720–1803; 1800–38.
67 S.R.O., D. 3596/1/1, p. 84.
68 Sheen par. accts. 1720–1803; 1800–38.
69 Ibid. 1720–1803, p. 100, and overseer's accts. 1765–6, 1767–8, 1773–4.
70 Ibid. overseer's accts. 1769–70, 1778–9.
71 Ibid. 1765–6, 1783–4, 1784–5, 1790–1.

72 Nicoll, Sheen, 51; S.R.O., D. 699/1/1/1, p. 5.
73 Sheen par. accts. 1720–1803, pp. 10, 33, 49; S.R.O., D. 121/A/PS1–3. 6–12.
74 Sheen par. accts. 1720–1803; 1800–38; S.R.O., D. 240/E(A) 1/340–1, 344.
75 Sheen par. accts. 1720–1803, overseer's accts. 1791–2 sqq. to 1796–7. 76 S.R.O., D. 699/1/1/1, p. 1.
77 S.H.C. v (1), 15, 73.
78 S.H.C. 1937, 184; S.H.C. 4th ser. viii. 41.
79 S.R.O., D. (W.) 1734/2/3/112B; L.J.R.O., B/C/11, John Beynett (1541). 80 V.C.H. Staffs. iii. 210, 297–8.
81 S.H.C. 1937, 188.
82 Ibid. 1915, 230–1; L. & P. Hen. VIII, xxi (2), p. 247; S.R.O., D. (W.) 1734/2/3/112B. 83 S.H.C. 1915, 131, 230.
84 S.H.C. xiii. 262; P.R.O., C 60/384, m. 20.
85 P.R.O., C 60/397, m. 9.
86 Ibid. C 60/505, mm. 1–3; C 142/321, no. 95; S.H.C. N.S. iv. 16.

rectory of Sheen was held by Gabriel Armstrong, who was succeeded that year by his son Gilbert.[87] In 1658 another Gabriel Armstrong and his wife Margaret conveyed the chapel and its tithes to Gilbert's daughter, Elizabeth Armstrong.[88] By 1671 she had sold them to Ralph Sleigh of Broadmeadow Hall and Thomas Ward, also of Sheen.[89] Ralph died in 1687, and in 1693 his widow Elizabeth and Thomas Ward were described as the impropriators.[90] By 1705 they had been succeeded by Ralph's son Gervase and John Ward.[91] Gervase sold his share to John Hayne, evidently with the manor in 1709: in 1711 Hayne and Ward were the impropriators.[92]

As a result of a grant from Queen Anne's Bounty in 1743 the curacy became a perpetual curacy. The presentation of the next incumbent in 1749 was exercised by the Crown through lapse, but the patronage was held in 1760 by Hugh Bateman, the lord of the manor, and Thomas Ward, who exercised it jointly that year. In 1785 the patrons were Hugh's grandson Hugh Bateman (later Sir Hugh Bateman, Bt.) and Thomas Gould of Sheen, who again nominated jointly. The right was later exercised alternately, Sir Hugh nominating in 1816 and John Gould of Scaldersitch in 1848.[93] Soon afterwards A. J. B. Hope bought Gould's share and by 1850 had secured the other.[94] The patronage then descended with the Beresford estate, in Alstonefield and Sheen, until 1928, when F. W. Green transferred it to the bishop of Lichfield.[95] The benefice, which was styled a vicarage from 1868,[96] was held by the vicar of Alstonefield from 1976 and by the vicar of Longnor from 1980, each as priest-in-charge.[97] It was united in 1985 with the benefices of Longnor and Quarnford, although the parishes remain distinct. The bishop became a joint patron with the vicar of Alstonefield and the trustees of the Harpur-Crewe estate. Longnor was made the incumbent's place of residence.[98]

The curate was paid £5 in 1635.[99] By 1679 he had £1 a year for preaching four sermons, an endowment given by Gervase Hall of Wolverhampton.[1] By 1693 he also received a stipend of £4 13s. 4d. which was originally intended for the support of a reader and was charged on a house in Sheen called the Mease Place.[2] The house had been part of the property let by Burton abbey to

the Longworths in 1529 and was probably then the curate's house; it remained part of the rectorial estate until the early 18th century.[3] By will of 1711 John Hayne, one of the two lay rectors, left his share of the Mease Place, of land called the Parsonage Piece, and of the tithes of Under Whitle farm to his son Henry in trust in order to augment the minister's income; if a Presbyterian 'or other sectary' ever became minister, the proceeds were to be paid to the poor until an Anglican minister was appointed.[4] By 1722 John Ward, the other lay rector, had left his share of the Mease Place to the curate, who by 1726 received £7 rent from the whole instead of the earlier payments; he also had rent of £2 10s. from the Parsonage Piece, out of which he had to repair the chancel. By 1744 he received 2s. 2½d. as his half share of the Under Whitle tithes.[5] Four grants of £200 were made from Queen Anne's Bounty in 1743, 1765, 1786, and 1802, three of which were used to buy land.[6] In 1836 the curate's income was £68 5s., consisting of £66 8s. rent from glebe, 2s. 6d. tithe modus from Under Whitle, and fees of £1 14s. 6d.; responsibility for the repair of the chancel had passed to the parish by 1830.[7] The curate was assigned a rent charge of £7 9s. 6d. in respect of tithes from three farms under an award of 1849.[8] A. J. B. Hope's mother, Lady Beresford (d. 1851), left £5,000 to augment the curacy,[9] and by will proved 1887 her son left a further augmentation of £255 a year.[10] There was glebe of 66 a. in 1887, with an estimated rental of £94 0s. 7d.[11]

When John Malbon came to Sheen as curate in 1683, he was allowed to live in the Mease Place.[12] In the mid 18th century the incumbent, Robert Robinson, lived on his estate in Waterfall.[13] Matthew Beetham, incumbent 1816–48, had by 1830 rebuilt an existing house on a larger scale.[14] Although about then the house was described as a glebe house,[15] Beetham's successor was living at Bank Top in 1850 and the next incumbent lived in rented premises pending the completion of a new house.[16] That house, which was still unfinished in July 1853, was built by A. J. B. Hope to the design of William Butterfield.[17] About 1970 the stable block was converted into a vicarage house, and the earlier house was sold. The new house was sold in 1982.[18] Butterfield's house was the last building

87 P.R.O., C 142/485, no. 175.
88 Ibid. CP 25(2)/597/1658 East. no. 20; L.J.R.O., B/V/6/Sheen, 1701.
89 L.J.R.O., B/V/6/Sheen, 1701; P.R.O., CP 25(2)/724/23 Chas. II Trin. no. 3.
90 A. F. C. Sleigh, Sleighs of Derb. and Beyond (Bedhampton, priv. print., intro. dated 1991), i. 7–8; ii, chart 4; L.J.R.O., B/V/6/Sheen, 1693.
91 L.J.R.O., B/V/6/Sheen, 1705.
92 Ibid. 1711; above, manor.
93 L.J.R.O., B/A/3/Sheen; White, Dir. Staffs. (1834), 760. For the sale of the tithes see above, manor (tithes).
94 P.O. Dir. Staffs. (1850); 787; Annals of Dioc. of Lichfield (1859), 28; L.J.R.O., B/C/5/1850, Sheen (faculty).
95 L.J.R.O., B/A/3/Sheen; Lich. Dioc. Regy., Bp.'s Reg. R, p. 28; Lich. Dioc. Ch. Cal. (1901; 1902).
96 Lich. Dioc. Ch. Cal. (1869).
97 Lich. Dioc. Dir. (1977; 1981).
98 Lich. Dioc. Regy., Bp.'s Reg. S (Orders in Council), p. 77.   99 L.J.R.O., B/V/1/55.
1 Ibid. B/V/6, Sheen, 1718; B/V/7/1679, Sheen, terrier at end; S.R.O., D. 3596/1/1, p. 86.

2 L.J.R.O., B/V/6/Sheen, 1693, 1701; below, this section.
3 S.H.C. 1937, 184; P.R.O., C 142/321, no. 95; C 142/364, no. 100; L.J.R.O., B/V/6/Sheen, 1701, 1705, 1708, 1711.   4 S.R.O., D. 3596/1/1, p. 85.
5 W.S.L., S.MS. 467, p. 536; L.J.R.O., B/V/6/Sheen, 1726, 1732, 1744, 1776.
6 Hodgson, Bounty of Queen Anne, 358; L.J.R.O., B/V/6/Sheen, 1751, 1776, 1786, 1800, 1841.
7 L.J.R.O., B/V/6/Sheen, 1836.
8 Ibid. 1849, 1853.
9 H. W. and I. Law, Bk. of the Beresford Hopes, 184.
10 Lich. Dioc. Ch. Cal. (1889), 165; Staffs. Endowed Chars. 111.   11 Return of Glebe Lands, 67.
12 W.S.L., S.MS. 467, p. 536.
13 L.J.R.O., B/V/5/Sheen, 1751.
14 S.H.C. 4th ser. x. 98.
15 Rep. Com. Eccl. Revenues, 497.
16 P.O. Dir. Staffs. (1850); Law, Beresford Hopes, 185.
17 L.J.R.O., B/V/6/Sheen, 1853; Law, Beresford Hopes, 186–8; above, plate 20.
18 Nicoll, Sheen, 58–9; Lich. Dioc. Regy., Bp.'s Reg. W, p. 688.

visited by Sir Nikolaus Pevsner during his final tour in 1970 to complete his *Buildings of England*.[19]

The stipend of £4 13s. 4d. paid to the curate by 1693 was originally intended for the maintenance of a reader.[20] James Hambleton, who received the stipend c. 1603, may have been the curate: he was then described as being no preacher and not having a degree.[21] Gervase Mort was reader in 1607.[22] In 1635 the reader was Thomas Birch, but in 1636 he became curate.[23] John Bonsall was admitted to read prayers in Sheen church in 1663 but was described as curate at his death in 1683.[24]

In 1751 Robert Robinson also served Longnor chapel in Alstonefield, officiating at one place at 10 a.m. and the other at 1.30 p.m. He left catechizing to the schoolmaster except in preparation for confirmation. At certain times he preached on catechismal subjects, a practice which 'in a country congregation I take to be the best way of instructing young and old'. Communion was celebrated four times a year, but only c. 20 people attended on each occasion.[25] In 1830 there was one service on Sunday, in the afternoon, and none on any other day. Communion was celebrated four times a year, and there were six communicants. There was no catechism.[26] There were nine celebrations a year by 1849 but only 15 communicants in all.[27] On Census Sunday 1851 there was a service in the morning and another in the afternoon, with attendances respectively of 30 and 65 besides Sunday school children. It was then stated that there were no pew rents, although many of the pews were appropriated to particular houses.[28]

A. J. B. Hope, having secured the patronage by 1850, set about reorganizing the life of the parish on Tractarian lines. Henry Pritchard, incumbent from 1849, was not in sympathy with Hope's ideas and resigned in 1851.[29] Hope then presented his friend Benjamin Webb, secretary of the Cambridge Camden Society and of its successor the Ecclesiological Society and joint editor with Hope of the *Ecclesiologist*.[30] After Hope's rebuilding of the church, school, and incumbent's house in the earlier 1850s, the *Ecclesiologist* claimed that 'the general effect is that of an ecclesiastical colony in the wilds of Australia'.[31] Weekly celebrations of communion and daily matins and evensong were introduced.[32] A weekly offertory was established in 1852, replacing church rates and also providing payments to the poor of Sheen and to causes

outside the parish.[33] Not all Hope's plans were fulfilled, but in 1856 he challenged Webb's view that Sheen was then 'inferior to the dreams of Sheen we had in 1851. It has taken a different line.'[34] Although a plan for a choir school was not carried out, a choir was established whose success, according to the *Ecclesiologist*, proved 'the suitability of Gregorian tones or melodies for an uneducated congregation and to a choir of mere rude country boys'.[35] In 1856 a parish library and reading room was opened.[36] Webb, who had been reluctant to accept the living because of the remoteness of the area, resigned in 1862. He was succeeded by T. E. Heygate, his assistant curate since 1852.[37]

The present church of *ST. LUKE*, a dedication in use by the 18th century,[38] dates from 1852. Its predecessor was built between 1828 and 1832 and itself replaced a church dating from the Middle Ages or the 16th century. In the 18th century that church consisted of a chancel, a nave with a south porch, and a west tower; there was also a 'quire', perhaps an aisle.[39] The tower at least appears to have been built or rebuilt in the 16th century: the curate Henry Longworth (d. 1540 or 1541) left money for building a tower, to be spent within three years of his death, and in 1559 Ralph Gylmen left money for the same purpose.[40] The church was in a poor condition c. 1570, and the chancel was in need of repair in 1584.[41] By 1720 there was a singers' gallery at the west end.[42] There was a sundial by 1789.[43]

The church was rebuilt apart from much of the north wall between 1828 and 1832. For over a year during the early stages of the work no services were held, but the new building was in use by 1830. It was in 'no regular style of architecture' and consisted of an aisleless nave with a communion table at the east end, a south door, and a west tower. There was a west gallery, and a vestry was formed in the base of the tower. A new pulpit and desk were placed at the east end of the central block of pews. The font stood towards the west end and was apparently new: in 1830 the only font mentioned was an old one in the churchyard.[44]

The church was later described by Benjamin Webb as 'a well meant but wholly unecclesiastical structure',[45] and in 1850 A. J. B. Hope offered to rebuild it at his own expense. He countered local opposition by asserting that, as the church was unconsecrated and unlicensed, all rites, including marriages, were of doubtful

19 *The Guardian*, 10 Oct. 1970, p. 8.
20 L.J.R.O., B/V/6/Sheen, 1693, 1718.
21 *S.H.C.* 1915, 231.   22 *Staffs. Cath. Hist.* iv. 9.
23 L.J.R.O., B/V/1/55, p. 93; B/V/1/57 and 62.
24 Ibid. B/A/4/5, 28 July 1663; S.R.O., D. 3596/1/1, p. 31.
25 L.J.R.O., B/A/3/Sheen, 1749, 1760; B/V/5/1751, Sheen.   26 *S.H.C.* 4th ser. x. 98.
27 Nicoll, *Sheen*, 70.
28 P.R.O., HO 129/372/4/12.
29 Law, *Beresford Hopes*, 184; Lich. Dioc. Regy., Bp.'s Reg. 31, pp. 176, 248.
30 Law, *Beresford Hopes*, 128-31, 145, 184-5; *D.N.B.* s.v. Webb, Benj.; Lich. Dioc. Regy., Bp.'s Reg. 31, pp. 262-3.
31 *Ecclesiologist*, xv. 153-5.
32 *V.C.H. Staffs.* iii. 75 n., 76.
33 *Annals of Dioc. of Lichfield* (1859), 64.
34 Law, *Beresford Hopes*, 190.

35 Ibid. 185, 190; *Ecclesiologist*, xv. 153-5.
36 Above, intro. (social and cultural activities).
37 Law, *Beresford Hopes*, 185, 190; *Annals of Dioc. of Lichfield*, 31.
38 Above, intro. (social and cultural activities).
39 Sheen par. accts. 1720-1803, pp. 1 (reproduced in Nicoll, *Sheen*, pl. facing p. 30), 64, and churchwarden's accts. 1766; *Annals of Dioc. of Lichfield* (1859), 28; Pitt, *Staffs.* 244.
40 L.J.R.O., B/C/11, Hen. Longworth (1541), Ralph Gylmen (1559).
41 Ibid. B/V/1/6; B/V/1/17, detecta.
42 Sheen par. accts. 1720-1803, p. 1.
43 Ibid. 1720-1803, churchwarden's accts. 1788-9, 1794-5.
44 Nicoll, *Sheen*, 43 and pl. facing p. 39 (reproduced from L.J.R.O., B/C/5/1850, Sheen, faculty); *S.H.C.* 4th ser. x. 98; Sheen par. accts. 1800-38, accts. of church rebuilding 1828-32.
45 *Annals of Dioc. of Lichfield* (1859), 27.

validity.[46] The new church was consecrated in 1852. Built of rough ashlar gritstone, it consists of a chancel with a north vestry, an aisleless nave of nearly the same size as its predecessor, a south porch, and a west tower, all in a 14th-century syle.[47] It was designed, like the school, by C. W. Burleigh of Leeds. Hope became dissatisfied with him and on his resignation replaced him with William Butterfield, who designed the vestry, the reredos, and the font.[48] The north wall was again retained. The tower of the former church was remodelled, buttressed, and raised by a belfry stage. A spire was planned, but its building was deferred because the foundations of the tower were feared to be inadequate. A temporary pyramidal cap was replaced in 1864 by a short wooden spire, now covered with copper.[49] Most of the fittings were brought from the chapel in Margaret Street, London, which Hope and Butterfield were also rebuilding.[50] A new chancel screen was given in 1902 by Professor J. P. Sheldon of Brund.[51]

In 1553 the church had a silver chalice with a paten, two great bells, and a handbell; other bells and a chalice had evidently been sold.[52] Bells from Sheen were recast at Rotherham (Yorks. W.R.) in 1740, evidently as a peal of three.[53] In 1830 the rebuilt church had three bells.[54] A peal of six cast by C. and G. Mears at Whitechapel in 1851 was given by Hope to his new church.[55]

Besides the singers for whom a gallery had been built by 1720, there was a salaried viol player in 1780 and another from 1786 to 1803.[56] An organ was installed in 1794.[57] There was no organ in the rebuilt church in 1830,[58] but the previous year there was a society of singers with 10 members and a cello, violin, and clarinet belonging to the church.[59] An organ was one of the fittings brought from the Margaret Street chapel for the new church of 1852 and was placed in the south-east corner of the nave.[60]

The registers date from 1595.[61]

By the late 17th century the parishioners were responsible for the repair of what was described as the churchyard fence. In 1716 individual sections were made the responsibility of holders of particular estates. Mention was then made of the lychgate.[62] Twenty lime trees were planted

in the early 1760s, 19 of which still stood south and west of the church in the late 1850s.[63] New lychgates were given by Professor Sheldon in 1905.[64] The churchyard was extended in 1932.[65]

NONCONFORMITY. In 1585 and 1586 Joan Johnson of Sheen was presented for not attending the parish church, and she was recorded as a recusant for the same reason in 1595 and 1596.[66] Otherwise there is no evidence of non-conformity in Sheen before the early 19th century. There was a Wesleyan Methodist class of eight in 1808, and membership had risen to 10 by 1819.[67] Wesleyan services were held fortnightly in 1829 but had ceased by 1832.[68] About 1815 there was Primitive Methodist preaching at Stonepit Hill north of Brund.[69] The Wesleyan cause revived in 1838,[70] and a chapel designed by a Mr. Wilson of Wetton was opened north of Townend in 1878.[71] A Sunday school extension was opened in 1912.[72] The chapel was closed in 1968,[73] and the building was used as a workshop in 1994.

EDUCATION. John Bonsall, appointed reader in 1663, also had the duty of teaching boys in the parish.[74] By will proved 1682 Richard Ward of Sand Hutton (Yorks. N.R.), a native of Sheen, gave £50 to the parish to produce an income for teaching some of the poorest children to read the Bible.[75] By 1705 a rent of £2 10s. charged on land in Sheen was paid in respect of the bequest and six poor children were taught English.[76] The school was at first held in the church, but a parish meeting resolved that a schoolhouse should be built, the church being 'profaned by the rudeness of the scholars'.[77] One was built in 1721.[78] In 1775 there was a move to build a new schoolhouse,[79] but it is not clear that the scheme was carried out. In the early 19th century the building was probably at Townend, the site of the school in 1845.[80]

In 1779 the rent charge was increased to £4 by Thomas Gould, the owner of the land on which it was charged. In 1816 the rent charge and the proceeds of a subscription launched a few years

46 Nicoll, *Sheen*, 45–6; L.J.R.O., B/C/5/1850, Sheen (faculty).
47 *Staffs. Advertiser*, 7 Aug. 1852, p. 8; above, plate 20.
48 *Annals of Dioc. of Lichfield* (1859), 28; Law, *Beresford Hopes*, 84; L.J.R.O., B/C/5/1850, Sheen (faculty).
49 *Annals of Dioc. of Lichfield* (1859), 28; *Lich. Dioc. Ch. Cal.* (1865), rec. of dioc. p. iii, stating that the spire was covered with lead.   50 *Ecclesiologist*, xv. 153–4.
51 *Alstonfield Deanery Mag.* (Nov. 1902); for Sheldon see Nicoll, *Sheen*, 64.   52 *S.H.C.* 1915, 230–1.
53 Sheen par. accts. 1720–1803, pp. 61, 64, 78, and churchwarden's accts. 1766, 1778, 1782–3.
54 *S.H.C.* 4th ser. x. 98.
55 *Staffs. Advertiser*, 7 Aug. 1852, p. 8; Nicoll, *Sheen*, 58.
56 Sheen par. accts. 1720–1803, churchwarden's accts. 1779, 1785–6 sqq.; 1800–38, churchwarden's accts. 1800–1.
57 Above, intro. (social and cultural activities).
58 *S.H.C.* 4th ser. x. 98.
59 Nicoll, *Sheen*, 32.
60 Ibid. 55; *Ecclesiologist*, xv. 154.
61 Those of burials to 1812, marriages to 1836, and baptisms to 1865 are in S.R.O., D. 3596.
62 S.R.O., D. 3596/1/1, p. 86. The churchyard had a stone wall in 1830: *S.H.C.* 4th ser. x. 98.
63 Sheen par. accts. 1720–1803, churchwardens' accts.

1761, 1764; *Annals of Dioc. of Lichfield* (1859), 27.
64 *Alstonfield Deanery Mag.* (Nov. 1905).
65 Ibid. xxxv (7); Lich. Dioc. Regy., Bp.'s Reg. W, pp. 419, 429.
66 *S.H.C.* 1929, 55, 133; *Cath. Rec. Soc.* lvii. 150.
67 S.R.O., D. 3155/1.
68 Leek Libr., Johnson scrapbk. i (2), D/13/15; S.R.O., D. 3156/1/124.
69 J. Leach, *Methodism in the Moorlands* (Wesley Hist. Soc., Lancs. and Ches. branch, occasional paper no. 5, 1987), 12.   70 Wardle, *Methodist Hist.* 46.
71 *Staffs. Advertiser*, 22 Sept. 1877, p. 4; date on building.
72 Nicoll, *Sheen*, 67; S.R.O., D. 3522/1, pp. 145–6.
73 Leach, *Methodism*, 32, 34.
74 L.J.R.O., B/A/4/5, 28 July 1663.
75 W.S.L., S.MS. 467, p. 537; *P.C.C. Wills*, x (Index Libr. lxxi), 354. The will is wrongly dated 1694 in *13th Rep. Com. Char.* 437, citing a table of benefactions in the church.
76 L.J.R.O., B/V/6/Sheen, 1705.
77 Nicoll, *Sheen*, 32.   78 W.S.L., S.MS. 467, p. 537.
79 Sheen par. accts., churchwarden's accts. 1775.
80 *13th Rep. Com. Char.* 437 (giving the site in 1815 as Sheen Lane); L.J.R.O., B/A/15/Sheen, no. 670A. In the later 19th century Sheen Lane was the road running south from the village: P.R.O., RG 9/1949.

before were vested in trustees. The rent was be paid to a master to teach poor children chosen by the trustees; the proceeds of the subscription were to be invested and the income used to repair the school, any residue being paid to the master. The curriculum was enlarged to include writing and arithmetic as well as reading. Fourteen children were taught *c.* 1820 and 16 in 1830.[81] The school apparently became a National school in 1824 or 1825.[82]

In 1851 A. J. B. Hope built a school with a house attached on glebe land south of the church.[83] He and other benefactors provided an additional endowment of £45 a year, and by will proved 1887 he left a capital sum of £1,200.[84] With a capacity for 120 children, the school was run by a master and a mistress.[85] A County Court order of 1859 fixed the number of poor children to be taught free at 12, although the trustees could reduce it to 10 if they saw fit.[86] The number on the roll reached a peak of 75 in 1909.[87] In 1948 the eight senior pupils were transferred to Leek and the school became a primary school with 21 on the roll.[88] In 1980 St. Luke's Church of England (Controlled) primary school had 11 on the roll, and it was closed that year, most of the children going to Warslow first school.[89] The school building and site and the endowments were amalgamated in 1990 to form the Sheen Educational Charity, the income to be used to promote the education of children and young persons in Sheen parish who needed financial help.[90] In 1994 the school building was used as a community centre and the house was a private residence.

There was a Sunday school by 1830 with 20 to 30 children.[91] A night school for adults was held at the National school in the late 19th century.[92]

CHARITIES FOR THE POOR. By will of 1722 John Ashton gave the poor of Sheen a rent of £1 charged on his estate at Calton Green in Croxden along with payments to other places. The residue of the income from the estate was to be spent on copies of the Bible, the Book of Common Prayer, or the Church Catechism for the poor, and 12 copies of each were distributed in Sheen in 1751. In the earlier 1820s the rent charge was distributed at Christmas in sums of up to 5s. to poor people of Sheen not in receipt of parish relief. Every three or four years a parcel of bibles, testaments, prayer books, spelling books, and catechisms was sent to Sheen.[93]

By will proved 1750 Elizabeth Unett gave a rent charge of 10s. to be distributed to the poor of Sheen on St. Thomas's day (21 December).[94] By will of 1780 William Unett, probably her son, gave 20s. to be distributed in the same way, but the gift appears not to have been effective.[95]

Before the later 1780s Ellen Birch gave £10, the income to be distributed to the poor of Sheen on St. Thomas's day. By 1786 and in the earlier 1820s interest of 8s. was being distributed.[96]

Jane Prince of Brund (d. 1823) left £5, the income to be distributed to five poor widows of Sheen.[97]

By will proved 1861 a Mrs. Wood gave money, the income to be distributed to poor widows of Sheen.[98]

In 1994 the Ashton and Unett charities could not be traced. The income from the Birch, Prince, and Wood charities was being allowed to accumulate.[99]

[81] *13th Rep. Com. Char.* 437–8; *Educ. of Poor Digest,* 866; *S.H.C.* 4th ser. x. 98.
[82] Sheen par. accts. 1800–38, churchwarden's accts. 1824–5.
[83] *Annals of Dioc. of Lichfield* (1859), 28; P.R.O., ED 7/109/272; ibid. HO 129/372/4/12; above, plate 20.
[84] Nicoll, *Sheen,* 61; *Staffs. Endowed Chars.* 111.
[85] Nicoll, *Sheen,* 61; P.R.O., HO 107/2008.
[86] *Staffs. Endowed Chars.* 111.
[87] S.R.O., D. 3522/1, p. 63.
[88] Ibid. D. 3522/2, pp. 204–5.
[89] Ibid. D. 3522/ADD/1, pp. 239, 247, 251.
[90] Char. Com. Scheme 29 May 1990. Mr. R. W. Mitchell

of Sheen, a trustee, is thanked for his help.
[91] *S.H.C.* 4th ser. x. 98.
[92] Nicoll, *Sheen,* 61.
[93] *13th Rep. Com. Char.* 355–6, 438; Sheen par. accts. 1720–1803, p. 6.
[94] *13th Rep. Com. Char.* 439.
[95] L.J.R.O., B/V/6/Sheen, 1849. It is not recorded in *Char. Dons.* or *13th Rep. Com. Char.*
[96] *Char. Dons.* 1156–7; *13th Rep. Com. Char.* 438.
[97] *13th Rep. Com. Char.* 439; L.J.R.O., B/V/6/Sheen, 1849.
[98] S.R.O., Charities Index.
[99] Inf. from Mrs. K. Bates of Ridge End Farm.

INDEX

NOTE. Page numbers in bold-face type are those of the principal reference. A page number in italic denotes an illustration on that page. A page number followed by *n* is a reference only to the footnotes on that page.

INDEX

Nicholls (*cont*):
Wm., 189
Nicholson:
Sir Arthur, 97, 112, 116, 147, 161, 196
Lt. B. L., 97
J. O., 153
Joshua, 94, 96, 111–12, 153, 164
Marianne, w. of Sir Arthur, 97, 196
Nickson:
Dan., 182
Miss M., 162
Niness, Ric., 60
Nixon, B. B., 112
Noel:
Margery (or Margaret), *see* Lestrange
Thos., 171, 212
Norbury (Derb.), 15
North, Edw., 59
North Midland Co-operative Society Ltd., 98, 116
North Staffordshire Lead and Copper Mining Co., 60
North Staffordshire Miners' Welfare Association, 68
North Staffordshire Newspaper Co. Ltd., 153
North Staffordshire Railway Co., 68–9, 100, 217, 220, 225
Northamptonshire, *see* Brackley
Northumberland, *see* Kirknewton
Norton-in-the-Moors, 70, 184
Milton, 100
Nottingham, 23, 99, 136
Frank Wheldon sch., 37
Nottinghamshire, 34; *and see* Gotham; Leake, West; Nottingham
Nunns, Wm., 68, 104
nylon, 114

Oakenclough brook, 27, 32–3
Oakes:
John, 119
Thos., 119
Obolensky, Prince Serge, 242
Oddfellows, 28, 58, 150, 212, 225
Offley:
Hen., 59
John, 59
fam. (later Crewe), 59
Oils Heath, *see* Warslow
Okeover:
Hugh of (fl. 1200), 243, 245
Hugh of (d. by 1269), 243
Joan of, m. Ric. de la Pole, 244
Ric. of (fl. c. 1272), 243
Ric. of (fl. 1345), 243
Rob. of (d. 1235 or 1236), 243
Rob. (fl. 1269), 243–4
Rob. of (d. by 1327), 243
fam., 244–5
Oldbury Britannia Building Society, 121
Oldfield, Geo., 23
Oliver:
Albert, vicar of Warslow, 62
Jas. (fl. 1792), 53
Jas. (fl. 1910), 55
Rob., 49
Thos., 53
Oliver Hill, *see* Quarnford
Olynleye (?Hollinhay, in Longsdon), Thos. s. of Rob. of, 101
Onecote, 64, **210–16**
agric., 174, 213–14
Blakemere Ho. (later Mermaid inn), 212
bridges, 211–12
chars., 175, 216
ch., 175, 215; plate 14
clergy, *see* Johnson; Miles; Richardson; Salt
vicarage ho., 215
farms, 168, 211–15
Ford, 211–12, 216

friendly soc., 212
geol., 211
inc., 214
ind., 214
inns, 211–12
man., *see* Onecote: Mixon
manorial govt., 175, 214
map, *210*
Mermaid inn, *see* Onecote: Blakemere Ho.
mills, 214
Mixon, 166, 211–13
ind., 214
man., 171–2, 212–13
prot. nonconf., 215
Mixon Hay, 213–14, 237
Onecote Old Hall, *see* Grindon
place names, 211
poor relief, 20, 214
pop., 211
post office, 211
prehist. remains, 211
prot. nonconf., 215–16
rds., 212
Rom. Cath., 215
schs., 216
tithe, 213
village hall, 216
Women's Inst., 212
Onecote brook, 211
Orford, Wm., 179, 184
organ makers, *see* Glyn & Parker; Jardine & Co.
Orm, *see* Ralph s. of Orm
Orreby, Phil. de, 101 n
Osborne:
Geo., 16
Marcellus, 16
Osbourne, Jas., vicar of Leek, 134
Oswego (New York State, U.S.A.), 143
Over Hulme, *see* Hulme, Upper
Overfield, Alfred, 119
Overfield & Co., 119
Overton, *see* Biddulph
Owen:
John, 185
Mary, 185
W., 121
Oxford university, 165
Oxfordshire, *see* Headington

packhorse ways, 58, 193, 195, 212, 220, 235, 242–3
Paddy, Fra., curate of Alstonefield and of Longnor, 22, 46, 48
Paget, Sir Wm., 246
pannage (customary payment), 72, 181
Panniers Pool, *see* Quarnford
Pantun:
Norman, 217
Wm., 217
paper making, 190
Park Hall, *see* Caverswall
parker, Richard the, *see* Richard the parker
Parker:
Geo. (d. 1675), 122
Geo., earl of Macclesfield (d. 1764), 183, 188
Geo., earl of Macclesfield (d. 1842), 35, 106, 124, 128, 130, 156
Geo. (fl. 1851), 198
Geo., earl of Macclesfield (d. 1975), 156
Thos., 122
Thos. (?another), 88, 122
Thos., Baron Parker, later earl of Macclesfield (d. 1732), 89, 91, 101, 130, 155, 183, 217
Thos., earl of Macclesfield (d. 1795), 83
Thos., earl of Macclesfield (d. 1896), 116, 128, 133–4
Parkes, Kineton, 145
Parr, Peter, vicar of Alstonefield, 22–3
Parr's Banking Co. Ltd., 121
Partrige (or Partridge), Mary, 25

Parwich, Thos. of, 17
Patrick, Ric., vicar of Leek, 133
Pattingham, 21
Paynsley, *see* Draycott-in-the-Moors
Peak Park joint planning board, 5, 15, 42, 195
Peche, Ric., bp. of Coventry, 21
pedlars, 38, 52–3
Pedley:
Eliz., 184
Jos., 184
Pegge, Strelley, 18
Penkhull (in Stoke-upon-Trent), 172
Penkridge, *see* Stretton
Pennocrucium, *see* Stretton
Pennsylvania (U.S.A.), 143
Philadelphia, 116, 143
Penruddock, Chas., 213
Pentecostalists, 145
Percival, Thos., 226
Percy, Hen., 230
Peri-Lusta Ltd., 114
Perry, Humph., 174
Peshall:
Cath., m. Sir John Blount, 13
Hugh, 13
Humph. (d. by 1388), 13
Humph. (d. 1498), 13
Maud, *see* Swynnerton
Ric. (d. 1450s), 13, 225
Ric. (fl. 1500), 13
Peter the clerk, 51–2
Peter the forester, 6
Peter's penny, 245
Pevsner, Sir Nikolaus, 248
Philadelphia, *see* Pennsylvania
Philips, John, 213
Phillips:
Eliz., 93
Sam., 91, 172
Maj.-Gen. Thos., and his w. Jessey, 172
Wm., 91–2, 172
Phillips and Ford, 107
Pickford, Jabez, 115
Pickfords (carriers), 99
Pidcock, Benj., vicar of St. Luke's, Leek, 137
Pidcocke, Ric., curate of Warslow, 62
Pigot, Editha, 207
Pilsbury Grange, *see* Hartington
Pitt:
Wm., agronomist, 79
Wm., statesman (d. 1806), 4
Plant:
Geo., 115
G. H., & Sons, 115
Jas., 48
John, 194
Ric., 235
Thos., 115
Wm., 187
fam., 235
Platt:
Hen., 69
J. E., 140
Plot, Rob., 11, 19–20, 33, 78, 118
Plummer, Hannah, 77
Plymouth Brethren, 146
Pole:
German, 24, 26
Hen. de la, 15
Joan de la, *see* Okeover
John de la (fl. 1334–5), 15, 244
John de la (d. by 1397), 15, 244
John de la (fl. 1406), 15, 244
John (fl. 1450), 244
Sir John (fl. 1476), and his w. Alice, 244
Ric. de la, father of Hen., 15
Ric. de la (fl. 1342), 15, 244
Polish immigrants, 235–6, 239
pony racing, *see* racing
Pool Hall, *see* Hartington
Poole:
Jos., 42
Ray, 118